The New Handbook of Language and Social Psychology

The New Handbook of Language and Social Psychology

Edited by
W. Peter Robinson
University of Bristol, UK
and
Howard Giles
University of California at Santa Barbara, USA

JOHN WILEY & SONS

Chichester · New York · Weinheim · Brisbane · Singapore · Toronto

Other Wiley Editorial Offices

John Wiley & Sons, Inc., 605 Third Avenue,
New York, NY 10158-0012, USA

WILEY-VCH Verlag GmbH, Pappelallee 3,
D-69469 Weinheim, Germany

John Wiley & Sons Australia, Ltd, 33 Park Road, Milton,
Queensland 4064, Australia

John Wiley & Sons (Asia) Pte Ltd, 2 Clementi Loop #02-01,
Jin Xing Distripark, Singapore 129809

John Wiley & Sons (Canada) Ltd, 22 Worcester Road,
Rexdale, Ontario M9W 1L1, Canada

Library of Congress Cataloging-in-Publication Data

The new handbook of language and social psychology / edited by Howard Giles and W. Peter Robinson.
    p. cm.
    Rev. ed. of: Handbook of language and social psychology, c1990.
    Includes bibliographical references and indexes.
    ISBN 0-471-49096-2 (cased)
    1. Language and languages. 2. Communication. 3. Sociolinguistics. 4. Social psychology. I. Giles, Howard. II. Robinson, W. P. (William Peter) III. Handbook of language and social psychology.
    P106 .N447 2000
    302.2'01'9—dc21

                                  00-043913

British Library Cataloguing in Publication Data

A catalogue record for this book is available from the British Library

ISBN 0-471-49096-2 (cloth)
ISBN 0-471-48554-3 (paper)

Typeset in 10/12pt Times by Dorwyn Ltd, Rowlands Castle, Hants.
Printed and bound in Great Britain by Bookcraft (Bath) Ltd, Midsomer Norton, Somerset
This book is printed on acid-free paper responsibly manufactured from sustainable forestry, in which at least two trees are planted for each one used for paper production.

Contents

About the Editors

W. Peter Robinson is Professor of Social Psychology Emeritus at the University of Bristol, England. He obtained his DPhil at Oxford, and since then a major strand of his research has been associated with language and communication. His latest book is *Deceit, deception and detection* (1996, Sage, CA). He is President of the International Association of Language and Social Psychology and a member of the Research Committee of the International Communication Association.

Howard Giles (PhD, DSc, University of Bristol, England) is a Professor of Communication at UCSB with affiliated appointments in Psychology and Linguistics, and Honorary Professor of Communication, Cardiff University, Wales. Giles is past president of the International Communication Association, a member of numerous journal editorial boards, founding Editor of the *Journal of Language and Social Psychology* and *Journal of Asian Pacific Communication*, and General Editor of over a half a dozen sociopsychological Book Series of language. He has published widely and cross-disciplinarily in many areas of language and intergroup communication, including the inter-ethnic, between-gender and intergenerational spheres and across different cultures around the world.

Contributors

Jess K. Alberts, Department of Communication, Arizona State University, Tempe, AZ, USA

D. Eric Anderson, Department of Psychology, University of Virginia, Charlottesville, VA, USA

Charles R. Berger, Department of Rhetoric and Communication, University of California, Davis, CA, USA

Michael Billig, Department of Social Sciences, University of Loughborough, Loughborough, UK

Richard Y. Bourhis, Département de Psychologie, Université du Québec, Montreal, Canada

James J. Bradac, Department of Communication, University of California, Santa Barbara, CA, USA

Judee K. Burgoon, Department of Communication, University of Arizona, Tucson, AZ, USA

Michael Burgoon, Department of Communication and Department of Family and Community Medicine, University of Arizona, Tucson, AZ, USA

Richard Buttny, Speech Communication Department, Syracuse University, Syracuse, NY, USA

Victor Callan, School of Psychology, University of Queensland, Brisbane, QLD, Australia

Aaron Castelan Cargile, Department of Communication Studies, California State University, Long Beach, CA, USA

Richard Clément, School of Psychology, University of Ottawa, Ottawa, Canada

Linda Coates, Okanagan University College, Kelowna, BC, Canada

Justine Coupland, Centre for Language and Communication Research, Cardiff University, Cardiff, UK

Nikolas Coupland, Centre for Language and Communication Research, Cardiff University, Cardiff, UK

Bella M. DePaulo, Department of Psychology, University of Virginia, Charlottesville, VA, USA

Steve Duck, Communication Studies Department, University of Iowa, Iowa, IA, USA

Derek Edwards, Department of Social Sciences, Loughborough University, Loughborough, UK

Nicholas Emler, Department of Experimental Psychology, University of Oxford, UK

Mary Anne Fitzpatrick, Department of Communication, University of Wisconsin, Madison, WI, USA

Jennifer Fortman, Department of Communication, University of California, Santa Barbara, CA, USA

Lawrence R. Frey, Department of Communication, University of Memphis, Memphis, TN, USA

Cynthia Gallois, School of Psychology, University of Queensland, Brisbane, QLD, Australia

John Gardner, School of Psychology, University of Queensland, Brisbane, QLD, Australia

Robert C. Gardner, Department of Psychology, University of Western Ontario, London, Canada

Howard Giles, Department of Communication, University of California, Santa Barbara, CA, USA

Laura K. Guerrero, Department of Communication, Arizona State University, Tempe, AZ, USA

Jennifer S. Hallett, Department of Communication, University of California, Santa Barbara, CA, USA

Michael Hecht, Department of Speech Communication, Pennsylvania State University, University Park, PA, USA

Brian Heisterkamp, Department of Communication, Arizona State University, Tempe, AZ, USA

Denis J. Hilton, UFR de Psychologie, Université de Toulouse, Toulouse, France

Thomas Holtgraves, Department of Psychological Science, Ball State University, Muncie, IN, USA

Mary Lee Hummert, Communication Studies Department, University of Kansas, Lawrence, KS, USA

Ronald L. Jackson II, Department of Speech Communication, Pennsylvania State University, University Park, PA, USA

Karen E. Johnson, Department of Speech Communication, Pennsylvania State University, University Park, PA, USA

Trudy Johnson, Department of Psychology, University of Victoria, British Columbia, Canada

Rolf O. Kroger, Department of Psychology, University of Toronto, Toronto, Canada

Martin Lea, Department of Psychology, University of Manchester, Manchester, UK

Beth A. Le Poire, Department of Communication, University of California, Santa Barbara, CA, USA

Sheryl Lindsley, Department of Speech Communication, Pennsylvania State University, University Park, PA, USA

Sonia Livingstone, Department of Social Psychology, London School of Economics, London, UK

Peter Lunt, Department of Psychology, University College, London, UK

Clare MacMartin, Department of Psychology, University of Guelph, Guelph, Canada

Peter Monaghan, School of Psychology, University of Queensland, Brisbane, QLD, Australia

G.H. Morris, Department of Communication, California State University, San Marcos, CA, USA

Sik Hung Ng, City University of Hong Kong, Hong Kong

Patricia Noller, School of Psychology, University of Queensland, Brisbane, QLD, Australia

William M. O'Barr, School of Anthropology, Duke University, Durham, NC, USA

Miles L. Patterson, Department of Psychology, University of Missouri, St Louis, MO, USA

Neil Paulsen, School of Psychology, University of Queensland, Brisbane, QLD, Australia

Gaylen D. Paulson, Department of Communication Studies, University of Texas, Austin, TX, USA

Tom Postmes, Department of Social Psychology, University of Amsterdam, Amsterdam, The Netherlands

Jonathan Potter, Department of Social Sciences, Loughborough University, Loughborough, UK

Linda L. Putnam, Department of Speech Communication, University of Texas A&M, College Station, TX, USA

Scott A. Reid, School of Psychology, University of Queensland, Brisbane, QLD, Australia

Nigel Roberts, School of Psychology, University of Queensland, Brisbane, QLD, Australia

W. Peter Robinson, Department of Experimental Psychology, University of Bristol, Bristol, UK

Ellen Bouchard Ryan, Department of Psychiatry and Behavioural Neurosciences, McMaster University, Hamilton, Canada

Itesh Sachdev, Department of Applied Linguistics, Birkbeck College, London, UK

Erin Sahlstein, Department of Rhetoric and Communication Studies, University of Richmond, Richmond, VA, USA

Carolyn A. Shepard, Department of Communication, University of California, Santa Barbara, CA, USA

Ben R. Slugoski, Department of Psychology, James Cook University, QLD, Australia.

Russell Spears, Department of Social Psychology, University of Amsterdam, Amsterdam, The Netherlands

Susan Strauss, Department of Speech Communication, Pennsylvania State University, University Park, PA, USA

Richard L. Street Jr, Department of Speech Communication, University of Texas A&M, College Station, TX, USA

Sunwolf, Department of Communication, Santa Clara University, Santa Clara, CA, USA

Jenny S. Tornqvist, Department of Psychology, University of Virginia, Charlottesville, VA, USA

Anita Vangelisti, Department of Communication Studies, University of Texas, Austin, TX, USA

Steven R. Wilson, Department of Communication Studies, North Western University, Evanston, IL, USA

Linda A. Wood, Department of Psychology, University of Guelph, Guelph, Canada

Prologue

W. Peter Robinson

The Prologue to the original *Handbook of Language and Social Psychology* sought to capture the essential history of the study of the intersect of language and social psychology in somewhat less than two pages. That could not be done now, although the field remains almost universally neglected in standard social psychological texts. The propensity of the texts to ignore language and its use is somewhat akin to a zoologist writing about fish without mentioning the role of water. It is also still rare to find undergraduate or postgraduate courses with titles linking language and social psychology.

This continuing situation might be ascribed to a lack of evangelical zeal among its pioneers and present practitioners, but that would be a serious mistake. (Attribution theory work early noted a disposition for people to blame persons rather than situations.) In contrast, a situational attribution could immediately draw attention to the hazards of our concerns having a dual disciplinary base. A social psychologist who is to work on language use requires a serious familiarity with relevant branches of linguistics (see Table 1 in Chapter 1). Such courses are rarely available formally to budding social psychologists. Even the most seductive ways of introducing the linguistic concepts catalogued in Table 1 are rarely attractive to undergraduates anxious to rush into the study of any of the 31 succeeding chapters in this Handbook. In complementary fashion, although aspirant sociolinguists may well follow programs with co-requisites in anthropology, sociology and social psychology, these latter are unlikely to include systematic experience in the empirical methodologies utilized in these disciplines.

While any estimate of the numbers of colleagues working in the field can certainly be no more than a guestimate, around one thousand could be a figure of the right order of magnitude. Will this increase soon, and if so where? Personal ignorance precludes any detailed comment on the European situation beyond noting that there are centres in The Netherlands, Germany and Scandinavia which promote such studies, and there is one in Wales: the Centre for Language and Communication at Cardiff University. England has Loughborough University, which specializes in a conversational, discursive and argumentational orientation.

Fortunately, and as might be expected, North America is more intelligently adventurous with its serious promotion of Schools and Departments of Communication, many of which have a robust sociopsychological presence. These are the most likely contexts in which the full range of both human and technological communicative vehicles can be studied in programmes that articulate and integrate the component disciplines. Within such a framework it also becomes more difficult to dissociate language from its communicative functions, a phenomenon that can affect both single-discipline trained linguists and social psychologists. Linguistics per se can be narrowed to neglect pragmatics and sociolinguistics or to consign them to optional extras. Social psychologists of language should find it easy to remind themselves that the raison d'être of language is communication, but in practice this has not always been reflected in the teaching.

Given this context, it is to be expected that this new text places greater emphasis than the earlier on the communicative functions of language, focusing on the five "ints" of such acts: intentions and interpretations in interpersonal and intergroup interactions. One consequence is that face-to-face interaction has been given two parts. Another is that the dynamic features of encounters gain prominence over the static features markers of personal and social identity, important as these are both theoretically and socially.

The six-part structure has been preserved, and authors were encouraged to choose what and how they would write within a particular topic. Some have chosen to write general reviews. Others have selected particular perspectives or issues. Some have concentrated on syntheses of how matters stand. Others have explored and speculated about new fields. One danger of giving authors such freedom that emerged was an almost universal bursting of the set word length, with some final draftings remaining in excess of twice the prescribed length. The editorial selection of topics was based on ideas of comparable parity, except for the applied areas, any one of which could have been expanded into one or more texts in its own right.

Part 1 opens with a chapter that was given permission to be of double length, given its brief to provide a global tour of the features and characteristics of language and its uses that are available for human beings to exploit – and that simultaneously constrain them. The explicit emphasis on description and explanation of form/function relationship is neither accidental nor idiosyncratic. Functions can be classified at different levels of generality and abstraction, and within any level categories can be constructed against different sets of criteria, but these are not grounds for denying the usefulness of particular schemes. Without taxonomies there can be no descriptions, and without descriptions there can be no explanations. That utterances (texts) are etically multifunctional and that in particular instances the emic functions are potentially contestable issues for the addresser(s), the addressee(s) and any observer(s) adds to the difficulties and uncertainties. But these facts are challenges and not reasons for despair. Functions can be realized only through "units" and "structures" (combinations of units), i.e. forms. The variety of relationships between the two is horrendously complicated, variable, and negotiable across individuals and groups, across situations and across time, but again the relationships are not chaotic. Chaos entails impossibility of communication.

What has been astonishing historically is that anyone would advance ideas that form/function relationships would be simple. Thousands of languages have evolved over thousands of years, and are continuing to change (see Asher, 1994, for a recent encyclopedia). Each of the billions of infants who have been born have developed an idiolect within one or more dialects within one or more languages in cultures whose environments have been changing and have been changed. Hence it is not surprising that pinning down patterns of covariances of form/function relationships in even limited domains of the language/human experience and behaviour interface can take more than one lifetime – and then quickly become registered in dictionaries or grammar books as "archaic" or "obsolete". The current standard work on English Grammar runs to a full 1779 pages (Quirk et al., 1985). The massive monograph Horn (1989) has written just on negation in English indicates the complexities of a feature that might be construed as a single mental operation. In Chapter 1.1 a skeletal and simplified attempt is made to set out some if the parameters for the academic enterprise of studying the intersect of language and its use with social psychology.

Chapters 1.2, 1.3 and 1.4 provide contemporary profiles and prospects for some of the most fecund theoretical positions, each with a strong past and a vigorous present. Chapter 1.7 updates and integrates work on language attitudes, demonstrating the continuing power of one of the foundation concepts in social psychology. Chapters 1.5 and 1.6 review approaches rather than theories, with Chapter 1.5 charting developments since its predecessor, and Chapter 1.6 meriting its place by opening up a seriously fresh perspective. If the trio of Socrates, Plato and Aristotle can be credited with the enduring establishment of the hypothetico-deductive forms of argument which have subsequently become hallmarks of mathematical and scientific reasoning, then Homer might be advanced as a candidate for the maternity of understandings realized through narrative analysis. As the authors note, civil and criminal proceedings in occidental courts are still settled by appeals to relative plausibility of contesting narratives created within the framework of particular forms of procedural justice. Culture itself has been defined succinctly as the stories groups tell themselves about themselves. Social psychologists may have been slower than anthropologists to see the power of storytelling as explanations and justifications guiding the everyday conduct of people, but we are now on track.

In Part 2, Chapter 2.8 consolidates work on non-verbal communication in an impressive general synthesis. Chapter 2.11 explores a critical approach to some of the long-standing assumptions about facework traceable back to Goffman's pioneering theorizing. Neither miscommunication (Chapter 2.9) nor conversation appeared in the earlier Handbook, the omission of the former being more forgivable than the neglect of the latter. While colleagues have long apprehended miscommunication as an issue extending well beyond breakdowns in relationships and diplomatic misunderstandings, it is only in the last 10 years that it has become a domain for study in its own contrastive right (as predicted on

p. 587 of the earlier Handbook). Similarly, on p. 586, we anticipated that this text would devote more space to work on conversation, inspired in large measure by Grice's (1975) assumptions, maxims and implicatures. The wry comment of the authors about the erstwhile neglect of conversation by social psychology is wholly justified, and herewith some amends are offered.

The selection of five or six special interactive activities from the possible array had to be somewhat arbitrary. It is regretted that the commissioned chapter on social influence did not materialize. Accounting (Chapter 3.15) has clearly been considerably advanced in the last decade. Patronising (Chapter 3.13), deceiving (Chapter 3.14) and negotiation (Chapter 3.16) have each benefited from strongly focused research programmes. In contrast, in Chapters 3.12 and 3.17, the authors offer personal insights and challenges in two areas sorely in need of systematic exploration. How much of conversation is made up of argument and gossip?

In Part 4 also, the earlier Handbook (p. 585) prophecy that critiques, elaborations, and amendments to Brown and Levinson's (1987) model of politeness would provide a firm platform for further research is fulfilled. No handbook could omit chapters on those two fundamental coordinates of social relationships, power in Chapter 4.19 and social distance in Chapter 4.20. Chapter 4.21 may be methodologically salutary for more than the study of marriage, pointing out as it does that the quick, easy and cheap means of collecting data are no substitute for more time-consuming and difficult but ecologically valid methods.

Part 5 covers what are probably the four most frequently researched social categories of the 1990s. Gender may have held top place, and it is timely for a considered social theory to be promulgated and evaluated (Chapter 5.24). Both ethnicity and multilingualism likewise present issues of worldwide significance, where research has moved on beyond the not always wittingly ethnocentric biases that could be detected in some earlier work (Chapters 5.22 and 5.23). The study of age and ageism has been a clear beneficiary of research in which multiple methods and multidisciplinary approaches have been coordinated successfully. Why there is no chapter on social class in Part 5 or on education in Part 6 is taken up later.

Second language mastery is a matured success story both theoretically and empirically, as Chapter 6.26 demonstrates, even though the practice of the principles is still less widespread in education than it could be. The study of language use in the field of health generally (Chapter 6.27) and medical consultations more specifically (Chapter 6.28) have both blossomed, and in spite of the constraints on their timetables both health and medical professionals have changed their practices to enhance efficiency and satisfaction in advice, diagnosis and treatment. Sympathetically sardonic smiles cross my face when I attend for consultations in a general practice which has trained its staff along lines recommended by psychologists, including myself. Perhaps even more surprising, the law courts in England and Wales have been swift to legislate and implement procedures that protect children from the terrifying cruelty of having to testify in open court in the presence of an accused abuser. Legislation is in train that will help to ameliorate the awfulness for women, who could be exposed to vicious and malicious cross-examinations by accused rapists and violators. In Chapter 6.28, such legal issues are treated more generally in the context of power differentials and corrupt impression management. Abuse of power differentials has also been brought to the fore in studies of communicative asymmetries in organizations where practice is also being influenced by the findings of colleagues in respect of job (dis)satisfaction and efficiency (Chapter 6.30).

The 1990s have witnessed a qualitative shift in interpersonal, international and mass communication amenities. Prices of phone calls and faxes have been reduced. Mobile phones have transformed the activities of those who can afford them. More dramatically, the Internet and its facilities, combined with the imminent arrival of miniature multimedia equipment, will produce another qualitative shift. So, just as our appreciation of the workings of TV in our lives reaches a measure of maturity with its abandonment of naive and false effects versus use polarizations (Chapter 6.31), we are confronted by a succession of advances in a world mediated by computers. Chapter 6.32 develops one perspective for moving into these challenges. A final chapter was to have looked at explorations of e-mail, e-commerce, and e-finance.

Unfortunately no typed text materialized in any form, ancient or modern. If it had, its brief would not have extended to one of the most dramatic features of the new multimedia world. In the English-speaking world control of these is now in the hands of those few people who control some ten or so gigantic corporations. Alongside them, public broadcasting is weak, even where it exists. This marks a profound shift in the balance of power between commercial corporations and government, with the participation of the public in the political process being reduced to occasional voting on the basis of information selected and spun to serve the interests of those in control of the media. What are the prospects of media bosses coming to play the role of Big Brother in Orwell's *1984*? Or will it be Internet-based risings of the exploited, as in his *Animal Farm*? Will any of the villains portrayed in James Bond films cease to remain fictional? The facts assembled by McChesney (1999) for the US scenario do not present a Goldilocks view of the future for our societies, and it may not be a coincidence that the two chapters missing here, but present in the earlier Handbook, were concerned with social class and education respectively. In both areas, and especially their intersect, what was a flood of research in the 1960s became a trickle in the 1990s. For the more historically and sociologically minded this may not be a surprise. There have been very considerable shifts in the distribution of both wealth and income in the United States and United Kingdom to the benefit of small elites and to the disadvantage of the already poor. An almost unimaginable proposition to entertain is that the wealth of the three richest men in the world exceeds that of the poorest 600,000,000. In Britain the last twenty years have witnessed the emergence of a sociological underclass (Hutton, 1996, Wilkinson, 1994), but, more generally, all UN countries have small wealthy elites, and all have large numbers trapped in cycles of poverty. In the 1960s adequate educational provision was held to be the most feasible means of rescuing the poor, primarily under the banner of equality of opportunity. Language and language use were seen as pivotal for progress. With the emergence of Reaganomics and Thatcherism, such aspirations and concerns disappeared, and so did the relevant academic and action research. For the present, this trend is set to continue, but how will people come to know what is happening in their societies? How will they find out if they wish to do so? With the mass media being under the control of commercial interests and governments spinning their images to be re-elected, even the reporting of instances of misrepresentation, deceit and delusion is increasingly likely to become part of the deception (Robinson, 1996). We live in interesting times for studies of language and language use in communication. Can there be a more important and challenging field for research?

It is ten years since the original Handbook appeared, and it has been evident from subsequent citations (and sales!) that it served its purpose to encourage research across a wide spectrum of areas with a broad array of methods. In this new text we believe that the authors have generated comparable quality, and we trust that the ideas, interpretations and challenges they present will have even greater impact than before, both in respect of numbers inspired to work in this area, and in the consequences for human societies.

REFERENCES

Asher, R.E. (Ed.) (1994). *The encyclopedia of language and linguistics* (10 vols). Oxford: Pergamon.

Brown, P. & Levinson, S. (1987). *Politeness: Some universals in language use*. Cambridge, UK: Cambridge University Press. (Original publication 1978.)

Grice, H.P. (1975). Logic and conversation. In P. Cole & J.L. Morgan (Eds), *Syntax and semantics* (Vol. 3, pp. 41–58). New York: Academic Press.

Horn, L. (1989). *A natural history of negation*. Chicago: University of Chicago Press.

Hutton, W. (1996). *The state we're in*. London: Vintage.

McChesney, R.W. (1999). *Rich media, poor democracy*. Urbana, IL: University of Illinois Press.

Quirk, R., Greenbaum, S., Leech, G. & Svartvik, J. (1985). *A comprehensive grammar of the English Language*. London: Longmans.

Robinson, W.P. (1996) *Deceit, delusion and detection*. Thousand Oaks, CA: Sage.

Wilkinson, R. (1994) *Unfair shares*. Ilford, UK: Barnados.

Part 1

Theoretical Perspectives

Language in Communication: Frames of Reference

W. Peter Robinson
University of Bristol, UK

INTRODUCTION

With 26 chapters in the first Handbook and 32 in the second, the editors are endeavouring to collate personal reviews of some major topics and issues as these are perceived by cutting-edge researchers. There is no pretension to being comprehensive or even representative. There is an aspiration to promote engagement with the issues and to promote interest and research, and this is the primary aim of the volume. A secondary aim is complementary to this, and that is to encourage disengagement from energy-wasting disputes that are based on false premises.

The introductory chapter is an attempt to combine the two, at a broad and general level. By setting out reminders of what is available for study in language and language use by social psychologists, the immense array of possibilities is indicated. In contrast to the individual chapters, the dual focus adopted here is upon the most general conceptual frameworks rather than macro- or micro-theories and upon methodology rather than empirical evidence relevant to theory. By setting out the polar extremes of some of these dimensions within the frameworks, and showing that the labels for the end points of these are no more than idealized abstractions and therefore that do not locate either excluding or exclusive choices, it may be that more people will come to accept that their personally preferred modi operandi are neither incompatible nor inconsistent with the predilections of others. On the contrary, a diversity of perspectives, interests and methods is both desirable and necessary, provided that arguments

The New Handbook of Language and Social Psychology.
Edited by W. Peter Robinson and Howard Giles.
© 2001 John Wiley & Sons Ltd.

as to their value remain focused on the tasks in hand and that the superordinate goals are to achieve the most rational and defensible resolutions of differences in descriptions and explanations of pertinent phenomena.

The diversity of approaches currently extant originates from both inter-disciplinary and intradisciplinary sources. Issues concerning the study of verbal communication are integral to many disciplines other than social psychology: communication and media studies, electronic and electrical engineering, com-mercial advertising and public relations, social policy and political science, so-ciology, anthropology, history, literary studies. Each of these enterprises and disciplines has commitments to its own objects of study, its particular perspec-tives and levels of analysis, along with its preferred epistemologies, and meth-odologies. Given the strongly institutionalized divisions of labour in higher education and the pressures and rivalries and specializations of modern exis-tence, it is not surprising to find interdisciplinary ignorance and, in line with predictions derivable from Social Identity Theory (Tajfel & Turner, 1979), occa-sional outgroup denigration and ingroup favouritism.

Comparable faultlines have appeared within the social psychology of language itself. Some social psychologists target issues requiring complex painstaking micro-analyses of minutiae; others try to comprehend how TV (Chapter 6.31) or computer-mediated communication (Chapter 6.32) are functioning in society as a whole. Some treat interpersonal greetings as essentially power plays, while others see them primarily as rituals of amiability. Some see speech primarily as a realization of thinking in and about a real world; others see it as a network of social constructions beyond which lies nothing knowable. However, in the case of the last contrast, very few "realists" would now accept the detailed demonol-ogy of medieval Christianity as representing a valid construction of reality, and very few social constructivists treat their social constructions of moving traffic or fires as purely social imaginings. These last two observations illustrate the thrust that will be adopted. It is always appropriate to pose questions about the extent to which claims about either putative objective realities or social constructions are delusions or conspiracies, but there have to be criteria that define what kind of conceptual and empirical evidence will count as being valid in the pursuit of answers to the questions posed. Human history is littered with claims about the nature of reality which are now universally discredited, and contemporary com-mon senses around the world are a mosaic of unwarranted claims and useful advice. Each of us has to assess which of the contemporary claims around are well grounded, and there are many which are not. The intention of these com-ments is not to engender cynicism, but to encourage wariness. We should not be too nihilistic or anarchic, but neither is it sensible to demand unattainable de-grees of certainty before adopting beliefs. Given the array of empirical evidence, which are the most plausible interpretations of the phenomena observed? Plau-sibility and probability have to be the constructive benchmarks for the weighing of empirical evidence and competing explanations. Withholding decisions for beliefs or actions is no escape; to withhold a decision is to make a decision of at least a temporary preference for the status quo. Decisions in conditions of uncertainty may be uncomfortable, but for some of us responsible and rational pragmatism is as inescapable as Pascal's dilemma and its resolution.

And so to the substance. Here the conceptual frameworks for the study of language and social psychology are summarized in one figure and five tables, of which Tables 1, 2 and 4 manage to escape from the format of columns of binary oppositions. Figure 1 portrays an early model of communication and asks where the "real message" resides, if there is one; in the process some basic features of verbal communication can be explicated. Table 1 lists Hockett's (1960) distinguishing features of spoken language; this serves as an introduction to the core common characteristics of languages, which are available for communicative use. Table 2 sets out some systemic details of one language, using English as the example. Table 3 opposes language as system and language as resource, a polarization that contrasts what the constitutive and regulative rules are with means by which these can be exploited, developed or changed. Table 4 offers a manageable menu of psychological functions of language, along with listings of characteristically associated units and structures in British English. Table 5 raises questions of methodology and lists some of the significant oppositions which have been treated as ideological alternatives, but that are better viewed as inevitable tensions within which choices of methods are to be made. The coverage is necessarily superficial and cursory, but should point to the vast range of challenges that confront us and will perhaps encourage us to become more sympathetic to multi-method, multidisciplinary approaches which will begin to reflect the complexities of the phenomena we are studying. And so into a tour of the No Man's Land that lies between the trenches. Wisely, several colleagues demurred from the opportunity to write this general chapter about verbal communication. Foolishly, and by default, someone had to take up the challenge.

THE NATURE OF VERBAL COMMUNICATION

While studies of non-verbal communication in human beings and other creatures have flourished impressively without the emergence of fundamental methodological and philosophical conflicts (Cappella & Palmer, 1990; Patterson, this volume, Chapter 2.8), the study of verbal communication has been and is suffering from pronounced disagreements, some of which are both unproductive and destructive.

Successful communication between human beings, by definition, comprises the encoding, production, transmission, reception and decoding of messages within already shared frames of reference. What is novel in any communicative act can be assimilated or accommodated only when it becomes linked to what is already shared contextually, and this in turn will depend upon the particular situation in which the particular participants are engaged. This innocuous-appearing claim can of course be shown to be covering many contestable issues. To proceed, we shall need to analyse the components of communication and the relationships between them, and at this point I have to choose between the horns of various dilemmas of presentation. The strongest binary contrast in approaches to human communication is between starting with such technical problems as transmitting signals along a telegraph wire or with gaining a purchase on the semiotic systems of whole cultures. Let me hasten to say that for a comprehensive analysis both of these have to be addressed and integrated. However, although I have found that while introductory semiotics is more commonly received as being full of exciting questions and insights, the advantages of these surprises are prone to dissipate quickly as students become overwhelmed by the divergent possibilities of interesting questions. Once switched into the game, observant eyes, ears, noses, tongues or skins connected to active brains can proliferate an infinity of pertinent but uncoordinated questions. It becomes feasible and scientifically defensible to write a research monograph on the meanings and significance of the discernible details and their relationships of one page of a newspaper, one TV news broadcast, one choir singing, five minutes of a psychiatric interview, a handshake, an almost anything. Generating questions to pose is easy; answering many of them and evaluating the value of the answers could be the work of more than a lifetime. How do we select what is worth doing from the array? How do we save our brains and minds from being overwhelmed by what we find out? And how do we prevent our ideas from soaring into wild interpretations and implausible world-views?

The first question is unanswerable. One answer to the second is to start with the smaller and simpler. One answer to the third is to demand empirical evidence to support claims made. Of course, we then have to agree on what will constitute adequate evidence, and we need to require that empirical evidence and descriptive/interpretive accounts of phenomena act as reciprocating constraints on each other. Data need to be evidence relevant to some issue. Ideas need to be anchored in plausible constructions of experience.

By such a route I am retreating to a justification for introducing communication as signals travelling as coded impulses along wires, which is of course what some semioticians expect social psychologists to do. The initial "model" to be presented is skeletal and incomplete, emphasizing as it does a single message travelling in one direction only and focusing on the message rather than its origin and fate. It can be and was expanded to cope with multiple sequential exchanges occurring between real people through real time in real contexts (see Gerbner, 1956), but continues to be set up as a straw man to be knocked down.

Message Transmission

To begin at a beginning . . . Shannon and Weaver (1949) developed a flow diagram of information transmission that has become known as the *Conduit Theory of Communication*. It was not and is not a theory. It simply lists some of the components to be considered in any single communicative act (see Table 1), and does so simplistically. To refer to it as a conduit was intended to give the idea of a pipe or wire down which signals travel, relaying a message that emerges at the other end. Shannon and Weaver were primarily concerned with telecommunication and radio problems and the reduction in loss of information between source and destination. The model also presupposes that the encoder is intending to reduce uncertainty in transmission, and knows how to reduce uncertainty, neither of which need be the case in human communication. Here, the object is to introduce the basic model, and note that its features demand attention; there will not be any evaluation of its virtues and limitations. One of the key concepts, noise, will not even figure in this summary, which is confined to the other five: source, transmitter, channel, receiver and destination, along with the concepts of signal, messages, medium and code.

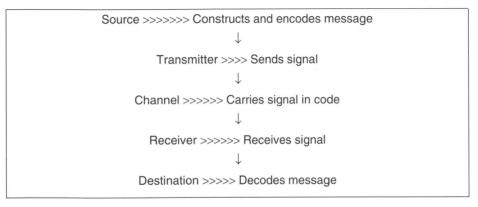

Source >>>>>>> Constructs and encodes message
↓
Transmitter >>>> Sends signal
↓
Channel >>>>>> Carries signal in code
↓
Receiver >>>>>> Receives signal
↓
Destination >>>>> Decodes message

Figure 1   Shannon and Weaver's model of communication

There is nothing contentious in selecting the five features as components to be considered. If we wish, we can pursue any one of these into levels of greater complexity or specificity. We can apply the model from problems of the warning colours of wasps through to human beings negotiating and using private ciphers to mean the opposite of what they say. Here we ask the dangerously idealistic question about the true (real) meaning of any message, because disagreements about the answer to this has proved to be a great stumbling block to progress, and is one of many examples of a false presupposition leading to false oppositions about the nature of both language and communication. Each candidate advanced as having the right to define the "real meaning" of a message can be shown to be unsatisfactory. If we claim that the *speaker's intentions* (the source) have the strongest claim, we may observe that the message itself may not be a culturally correct realization of the intentions, either in construction or delivery – or both, for example. Wrong units (e.g. words) may be selected, either out of ignorance or anxiety. What is intended as a compliment may be delivered insultingly. How can we be sure of what the speaker's intentions were? We cannot be.

If we exclude intention and suggest that the *semantics* of the messages can be defined objectively, then it should be the case that there will be a cultural consensus as to the "real" meaning among proficient users of the language. Disagreements should not arise. If they do, one line of argument would be to invoke the defensible hypothesis of subcultural differences in meanings of the same patterns. But fruitful as such a defence can be initially, it will ultimately fail. The "real meaning" can only be in the message/code if the contextual presuppositions are shared fully. This entails of course that the meaning is *not* in the message/code combination, but in a cultural consensus. Involving abstractions such as the *generalized other* or the *typical member of the culture* will not salvage the situation, because their perceptions are necessarily not objective.

The third possibility of defining the "real meaning" as the *interpretation of the reader* or *hearer* (destination) shares comparable weaknesses with the other two possibilities. Interpreters have no special status as objective judges.

The rejection of all three of these possibilities might be used to advance the idea that the true meanings are not the privilege of any one party, but are simply a matter of negotiation among the participants. If that is so, there is no true meaning, beyond any particular exchange. However, the position of meaning as being negotiated has also been pushed to a *reductio ad absurdum* argument that the transmission model of communication should be abandoned in favour of fuzzy flexible perspectives, that will permit creative constructions by individuals who will be freed from the constraints heretofore imposed upon them. It could be argued that, *in extremis*, this position is self-destructive as well as self-contradictory. Since generally shared conventions are the essence of the systems, particular changes have to be negotiated and cannot be asserted, demanded and enforced by individuals; Humpty Dumpty ends up muttering meaninglessly to himself, or worse.

Since human beings seem to manage to communicate with language, more or less successfully much of the time, perhaps those asking about true meanings have posed inappropriate questions. Information theory was intended to provide ways of analysing reductions (and increases) in uncertainty in transmission and not its elimination. Communication can reduce uncertainty but cannot eliminate it. Such a position copes with what may be defended as the most rational construction of reality without giving rise to a claim that there is an objective reality that can be discovered. In cases where some party claims that communication failure has occurred and where for some reason it is decided to allocate blame for the failure, there will be examples where it would be pragmatically silly not to blame one or other of the participants, but peculiar defences may well be made. In 1998 the President of the USA invoked a legal rather than a commonsense definition of "sexual relations" to justify the claim that he had not lied under oath: no communication failure and no lie. Later he changed his mind.

It is true that the focus on the transmission/reception components led to a relative neglect of the activities of the people, the encoder and decoder, and the terms "source", "transmitter", "receiver" and "destination" are still being attacked as implying passivity, an absence of agency, a neglect of constructive/

interpretive activities, and a lack of interactive extension. This has not been necessary for the 40 years since Gerbner developed, elaborated and humanized these components into a two-person interaction, and thereby rendered further such adverse criticisms as anachronistic. Why critics continue to denigrate a perfectly sensible skeleton of limited purposes for not being more than that is difficult to understand.

Semiotics

Just as the conduit model has been misrepresented by subsequent critics for failing to achieve what it was not intended to achieve, so the semiotic approach has been improperly savaged. Semiotics has been further bedevilled by its multi-discipline origins and continuing variety of practitioners. The philosopher Pierce (1931/1955) introduced an analysis of a relational approach between the signifier and signified, as the basis of the signification linkage to "meaning". The resultant triangle linked "sign", "interprant" and "object" to each other. Part philosophical, part literary critical, Ogden and Richards (1923) introduced a somewhat different triangle in which "reference" as thought was linked to a "referent" on the one hand and a "symbol" on the other, so that the symbol can "stand for" the reference. Both of these similar approaches were attempts to escape from the tangles and muddles that had engulfed philosophers such as Mill, Frege, Wittgenstein and others who had difficulties in distinguishing between sense and reference (Mill, 1873), denotation and connotation (Frege, 1980), semantic and associative meaning, and the relationships between symbolic propositions and what they appear to be about (Wittgenstein, 1951; 1961). The last continues to figure as a central concern (e.g. Davidson, 1984; Putnam, 1988; Rorty, 1991).

Independently, the linguist de Saussure (1959/1925) had been developing his ideas on the distinctions between *langue, parole* and *langage*, which remain of crucial importance, but continue to be neglected by some monolingual English-speaking social scientists. Semioticians cite his observation that "signs" (symbols) gain their "significance" by virtue of contrasts with other signs in the "system". In a sequence of signs, questions of both the sequence selected (syntagmatic) and the choices at each point in the sequence (paradigmatic) are important for meaning. (In non-linguistic systems more general questions of juxtaposition than sequence can arise, and in linguistic systems patterns of collocation [co-occurrence] are also important.)

From these three origins in particular, various systems for classifying signs have been developed, with comments being offered about the ways in which they function in a cultural context. Typically the materials used are referred to as *texts*, a term which can be extended to any cultural artefact(s). If, for example, a page of a newspaper is chosen, then a general question would ask which conventions of the culture are being used to convey what kinds of ideas. Questions can range from the size, shape and quality of the page, through the types of arrangement of language texts, photographs and other graphics, to which items have been selected for reporting and how these have been framed. The Glasgow Media Group (1976) provide classic examples of such ideas in their analyses of news broadcasts. It is not surprising that those who control the media should encourage the adoption of particular points of view through what they present and the way they present issues. It is the task of semioticians to find out how particular "readings" (interpretations) are encouraged and afforded by the devices available. The mention of a media example of presuppositions here should not be seen as exclusive to that domain; the issues are omnipresent in our everyday experience. Analysis of oil paintings through time and across cultures can be subjected to comparable treatment, as can clothes and ornaments worn, literature or any other type of artefact.

Such activities have been very productive in generating ideas that have helped to raise explicit questions about matters previously treated as unproblematic or natural. They have been used to demonstrate how taken-for-granted "facts" should not be taken for granted as facts, and certainly not as immutable ones. In particular they have raised consciousness about the ethical qualities of our cultures and societies, including many of the false beliefs underpinning matters of procedural and distributive justice.

Unfortunately, the field has also generated its own difficulties. Where is the true meaning in an artefact or text? It is probably fair to say that opinions have been polarized between locating the true meaning as either in the text or in the *reader*, with the speaker/writer often being conflated with the text. Either position can be criticized along identical lines to those used against the conduit model. We can never be sure what the intentions of the creator were. We can never be sure that the creator's product instantiates the intention. Which readers are to be credited with the right to decide which reading is correct? If a particular reading is "preferred" by experts, this does not transcend its subjectivity.

If the advocates of the expert approaches were to be criticized for just one characteristic, it would have to be for their predispositions to assume that their own ingenious personal explanations of the richness of texts bear any correspondence either to the intentions of the creators or more importantly perhaps, to the interpretations of or influences upon ordinary readers. Such stories are often advanced and disseminated without any checks on their empirical validity, if they are not so evaluated then they remain as plausible (or implausible) hypotheses awaiting testing. Not all experts make such unsupported claims.

In contrast, if the advocates were to be commended for just one strength, it might be their emphasis on the multiplicity of meanings available in texts (discourse or whatever verbal material is being examined). Eco (1979) introduced a distinction between *closed* and *open* texts. A closed text is one where the reader has in theory only one plausible interpretation, the author having structured the meanings to minimize possibilities of other readings. An open text is not one where interpretations are impossible, but one with multiple possibilities, and in the light of the information provided offers a bundle of options. His illustrations are literary rather than conversational. In stories about crime detection or espionage, for example, the author typically leads the reader along a single track using a variety of literary devices to puzzle, excite, frustrate and otherwise retain the reader's attention on a predestined train of thought. This does not mean that there are no ambiguities or vagueness. It does not mean that the narrative has to follow a linear sequence of real time. The primary focus is on the eventual discovery of who has been deceiving who about what – an exposure of the constructed reality. This kind of story contrasts with those depicted in the film *Rashomon* or Durrell's *Alexandria Quartet*; in both of these, the same events are played out from three different perspectives. As viewers or readers we can appreciate this multiplicity of personal agendas. The use of repetition renders the multiplicity explicit. More commonly the uncertainties are left for individual characters (and readers) to interpret and act upon.

Insofar as many novels are narratives in which biographies of characters are woven together, they bear clear similarities to real life. Films and plays more so, since they add a visual channel. Soap operas go one step further in that their regular and long-term serialization adds a continuity of years or even decades. The audiences they attract on a regular basis can extend to nearly half a country's population. Currently Britain has four indigenous TV soaps: two urban with predominantly working class/lower middle class characters, one rural and one suburban upwardly mobile. As Livingstone (1998) argues and demonstrates, these offer open texts whose characters have entered into the lives of their audiences as "real" people facing comparable difficulties and problems. The episodes provide ideas for ways of overcoming or resolving such difficulties, as well as setting up topics for conversation and characters for evaluation.

The study of ways in which these long-standing narratives mesh psychologically into the everyday lives of real people could help to re-anchor social psychology into the world it is expected to describe and explain. For the present, *narrative analysis* in its various forms is not mainstream (see Chapter 1.6), but just as various forms of conversational analysis have drawn attention to units and structures larger than that of the main clause and its coordinate and subordinate attachments (see Chapter 2.10), so narrative analysis may encourage an elaboration of those social-cognitive and attitudinal approaches which adopt what is essentially a hypothetico-deductive model to single judgements in abstracted situations.

While it is not strange that social psychologists would seek to generate theoretical models that can explain single judgements or actions in terms of general properties of the person in context, such judgements may be no more than task-specific reflective comments and in fact may bear little relation to the mechanisms that typically drive the scripts of the everyday talk and actions of most people most of the time. Schank and Abelson (1977) are normally credited with the introduction of *script theory*, which was an attempt to describe sequences in semi-ritualized contexts. Scripts for speech and writing, for monologues, dialogues and polylogues can also be devised and tested for their descriptive generality. Combinations of narrative analysis and script theory have more than begun to have their status as explanatory models of behaviour recognized

(Abelson & Lalljee, 1988; Antaki, 1988; Cody & McLaughlin, 1990). Conversational analysis is represented in this volume in two chapters especially.

How these various approaches to verbal communication will come to be collated remains to be seen. There are clear kernels of importance, relevance and validity in each. Their diversity in part reflects the frightening breadth of topics embraced by the concept of verbal communication. Some of the possible claims or emphases have already been explored to some limiting *reductio ad absurdum*. Now their individual virtues need to be articulated. But what are the raw materials of language that are used in these communicative activities?

WHAT LANGUAGE IS AND HOW IT FUNCTIONS

Languages function as one type of system of communication. Hockett (1960) generated a list of design characteristic of speech which included functional and structural features but was not expanded to describe language in its full range of manifestations (see Table 1).

Clearly additions have to be made, but here only a few will be noted. The first feature needs to be expanded to include the sensorimotor/visual modes of sign languages and the visual/visual channel of written modes. The second needs to be expanded to include the diverse properties of technological devices. The third likewise should include the revolutions of writings, printings, and information computer technology (ICT). The fifth may be an exaggeration and the sixth also. While the seventh and thirteenth take the step of reminding us that the arbitrary but conventional units and structures are combined to have *meanings*, the crucial further feature of their having *significance for action* is not incorporated. Chomsky (1957) too missed pragmatic significance when he stated that the essence of language was that it linked "patterns of sound to patterns of meaning". The tristratal model that links phonology to semantics via lexico-grammar at least reflects the three levels of coding which apply to all known spoken languages, but the fourth level of *pragmatics* is essential for the study of how language functions in communication. The very incomplete chart in Table 2 provides an indication of the nature and some of the features of English.

A small number of sounds have phonemic significance. One or more of these are combined in accordance with discoverable rules to yield a very large number of morphemes: the smallest units with meaning. One or more of these constitutes a word, of which there are well over a million. The rules of syntax chain words into fewer than 20 types of clause that can be combined to form just four types of self-standing sentences. Economy at the phonological and sentential levels contrast with the great diversity at the lexico-grammatical one. These features characterize language as a system, with its rule-governed sets of units and structure whose articulation both across and within levels is now described in terms that are consistent with claims that permit linguists to be confident that the basic

Table 1 Hockett's (1960) Design features of human spoken language

1. Vocal–auditory channel
   (communication occurs by the producer speaking and the receiver hearing)
2. Broadcast transmission and directional reception
   (a signal travels out in all directions from the speaker but can be localized in space by the hearer)
3. Rapid fading
   (once spoken, the signal rapidly disappears and is no longer available for inspection)
4. Interchangeability
   (adults can be both receivers and transmitters)
5. Complete feedback
   (speakers can access everything about their productions)
6. Specialization
   (the amount of energy in the signal is unimportant; a word means the same whether it is whispered or shouted)
7. Semanticity
   (signals mean something: they relate to the features of the world)
8. Arbitrariness
   (these symbols are abstract; except with a few onomatopoeic exceptions, they do not resemble what they stand for)
9. Discreteness
   (the vocabulary is made out of discrete units)
10. Displacement
    (the communication system can be used to refer to things remote in time and space)
11. Openness
    (the ability to invent new messages)
12. Tradition
    (the language can be taught and learned)
13. Duality of patterning
    (only combinations of otherwise meaningless units are meaningful – this can be seen as applying both at the level of sounds and words, and words and sentences)
14. Prevarication
    (language provides us with the ability to lie and deceive)
15. Reflectiveness
    (we can communicate about the communication system itself, just as this book is doing)
16. Learnability
    (the speaker of one language can learn another)

frameworks and taxonomies of many languages are now describable. This orderliness may endure for a long time.

Semantics focuses on meaning per se, devoid of context and function. Pragmatics poses questions about the significance for actions of the participants, in particular the decoders. What are they to do as a result of messages? A message from a spouse might say "The grass is six inches", which has in context a clear semantic descriptive reference. It could have the pragmatic significance of encouraging the decoder to think in terms of getting out the mower to reduce the height. It may have other interpretations that would need an analysis of Hymes' (1967) SPEAKING variables to disambiguate (see below).

Table 2 Language structure and content

System and resource

	Phonology	Lexico-Grammar	Semantics (meaning: denotation, connotation)	Pragmatics (significance for action)
	Phonetics Phones *Phonemics* Phonemes (45+)	*Morphology* Morphemes[gram.?] [lex, 1000K]	<----------- > Classes: markers of plurality Gender, comparison, case, tense	*Categories of relevance* Setting: where Participants: who Ends: purposes; functions

(air flow)
(shape)
(stop)
	Syllables [1K+]
	
	Feet
		Words : [gram, 150]
		  [lex, 500K + ordy]
		  [lex, 500K + tech]
			Classes? thesauruses
			(a) Elemental features?
			<----------- > (b) Fields, e.g. colour?
				Art: characteristics
				Key: how
				Instrumentality
				    (1) channels
				    (2) code
				Norms
				Genre

Intonation (pitch (pitch change) Tone group [5?] (volume) (duration)		*Syntax* Group [3+] Clause [16+] Sentence [4] (declarative, interrogative, imperative, exclamatory)	<----------- > Nominal, verbal, adverbial <----------- > Free, subordinate, relative etc. Statement, question, command, exclamation	
			Speech act [66+ or α]	
			Propositional content Illocutionary force Perlocutionary force	

Units: One or more units at one level are *combined* sequentially to form a structure which functions as a unit at the next level up (down).

Of the levels, phonology has arrived at definitions and conceptual frameworks that are substantially agreed and offer a strong foundation for its own development and the articulation of phonological phenomena with those from other disciplines. While there remain deep differences in approaches to grammars and the most satisfactory ways of conceptualizing them (Gazdar et al., 1985; Halliday, 1985; Ouhalla, 1994, Quirk et al., 1985), colleagues working in other disciplines have a cornucopia of contesting sets of units and structures rather than an absence of general taxonomic progress. Semantics is perhaps the least well-developed level (Leech, 1983; Levinson, 1983). This is not, however, a result of our not knowing what individual units of morphology, syntax or lexis can mean, but one of not having adequate rationales for grouping these units into sets, except for specific purposes. So we can list ways of achieving plurality, classifications of dogs, or ways of expressing degrees of certainty. Extensive volumes can be written on single concepts, e.g. negation (Horn, 1989). What we cannot do is generate systematic general-purpose hierarchies, as we can with animals in zoology or elements in chemistry (see Lyons, 1995, for a thorough review of the issues).

Likewise with pragmatics. Lists of the functions of language vary from one to infinity. Some older distinctions favoured two (e.g. representational and social) or three (Buhler, 1934), speech act theories more than four but fewer than 10 (Searle 1975). Here Jakobson's (1960) will be selected as the model to be elaborated and expanded to include social and psychological activities. There is nothing wrong with any of the various lists; they are not creating indefensible categories. It becomes a matter of choices being related to purposes, and as with semantics no general-purpose comprehensive model has emerged. Perhaps none will. Typically, such general classificatory schemes in the physical and biological sciences are structural in their foundations, e.g. atomic theory for chemical elements, evolutionary theory for zoological and botanical taxonomies, but of course other schemes are used for special purposes, so that "fit for purpose" becomes a major criterion for evaluation. While there are specifiable relationships between structures and functions, one of the characteristics of living language is of shifting functional/structural relationships. Innovative (rule-breaking) usage grows the language (as this proposition can be expressed now that "grow" has become a transitive verb!). Multiplicity of meanings of individual lexical items is commonplace. Of the possible linkages between the three major sentence structures in English (declarative, interrogative, imperative) and the functions of stating, requesting and commanding, only one seems to be unusable. Declaratives can be adapted to ask questions or make requests, and to give orders. Interrogatives can be exploited to give orders and make statements. Imperatives can be used as interrogatives, but not to make statements whose truth or falsity can be questioned except of course by prior arrangement.

Given the histories of the groupings of our human ancestors, the millions of people involved and the thousands of years over which language developments have taken place, it is not surprising that there has been change. Evolution is an apposite term to apply to the differentiations and consolidations, the additions and the deletions, and the spreads and contractions. Within the multiple varieties of the English language system used by over 500,000,000 people, across and within a host of separate societies, it is the extent of commonality and stability that could be viewed as surprising. On the other hand, some planned changes are notoriously difficult to agree and implement. English speakers are stuck with distinctions that many would like to see eliminated (e.g. gender-free animate singular personal pronouns), and even with the subject matter presently in hand we have to resort to French *langage, langue*, and *parole* to overcome the English ancestral linguistic parsimony with *language*.

Before considering the functions per se, however, yet another set of complications has to be mentioned. Ingeniously but riskily, Hymes (1967) proposed the term SPEAKING as a mnemonic to remind researchers of the host of sociolinguistic and cultural factors affecting the selection of units and structures in context.

1. *Setting.*
2. *Participants.*
3. *Ends as (i) objectives and (ii) outcomes.* Possibly a matter of personal biography or perhaps one of culture, I would have chosen *purpose* instead of *objective* and *function* instead of *outcome*, but in either case the distinction is clear in its contrast between what was intended and what actually transpired.
4. *Art characteristics.* This is an unfortunate label, referring as it does to both the form of the message and to the topic. *Form* is underglossed but appears to refer to a range of distinctions such as poetry versus prose, but also description versus explanation versus narration. *Topics* refers to topics which are infinite in number and possible variety.
5. *Key.* To express key we often use adverbs, such as "sincerely", "humorously", "ironically", to indicate the spirit in which an utterance is intended.
6. *Instrumentalities.* Unfortunately this term is used to refer to two disparate major factors, namely *channel of transmission* and *code* (meaning language and language variety).
7. *Norms of interactions.* Within cultures, subcultures and smaller groupings, there are varied conventions about who is to speak and when, how turns are to be allocated, and how exchanges are to be initiated and terminated.
8. *Genre.* What *genre* is intended to embrace is left unclear, but examples are at the level of prayer versus lecture.

This scheme is still referred to and quoted in its original state. Neither Hymes nor later workers appear to have developed the list. Even as it stands though, it does provide an excellent device for reminding us of the *de facto* complexities of the systems. This does *not* mean that individuals are confronted by the array of choice every time they speak or write. Many of the etic and emic possibilities are only of relevance to researchers trying to comprehend the totality of the system(s). Much of what individuals say may be automated at the phonological, and scripted at other, levels. The kind of reflective planning that is being exercised to generate and evaluate the selection and sequencing of each word, phrase, clause, sentence, paragraph and section of this chapter involves much more complicated information processing than does colloquial conversation. Hymes' list is not then a decision-making menu that has to be gone through for every utterance; it is better viewed as a list of factors which have relevance to the processing and outcomes of communicative acts.

IMPLICATIONS FOR THE STUDY OF LANGUAGE AND SOCIAL PSYCHOLOGY

The summaries of the last few pages have made reference to the form and contents of well-founded beliefs which have been given verbal and more specialized symbolic expression in literally thousands of texts, dating from the early civilizations of China and India and onward. The data on which the descriptions have been based has been the speaking and writing being enacted around the world each day, and in particular those samples of these which have been recorded and stored in archives. The language-related behaviour of each speaking adult reflects a prodigious amount of processing and storage capacity, of which only a small fraction is consciously discussible in metalinguistic terms by most people. These facts are both reassuring and daunting for social psychologists. They are reassuring because some of the general frameworks and many of the details of descriptions of components of language and languages have already been worked upon by others, and hence already available for utilization by social psychologists. They are daunting because there is so much to learn, and this means that any individual researcher can only master and stay abreast of tiny segments of what can be claimed to be known about languages and its workings. They are daunting because one of the implications is that social psychologists increasingly need both to have greater knowledge of linguistics and to enter into collaborative activities with linguists – and other social scientists in cognate disciplines. Finally they are daunting because we are in a moving game where the rules and their realizations change. Groups develop group-speak at the level of youthful gangs, institutional committees and whole societies; appropriate usage of new terminology is a marker of genuine membership and, contrastively, failure to use innovating words and phrases are indicators of outsider status. Social classes and ethnic groups are marked, as is society as a whole. Slang comes and goes. Principles of marking remain; actual markers are changing passwords. The whole movement of "political correctness" is not just about fashionable phrases. It is a power struggle out of which may emerge significant changes in the way we speak and write – and think and live. Certainly the academic journals of various national psychological societies have formalized policies designed to eliminate sexist and racist usage. Progress in implementation of the UNESCO (1948, 1962) guidelines on ethnocentric references in history texts is slower. It is apposite to explore the distinction of language as system and language as resource in a little more depth if not in detail.

LANGUAGE AS SYSTEM AND LANGUAGE AS RESOURCE

Any analysis of the determinants of stability and change in the *langage* of *langue* and *parole* is beyond the current remit, as is an examination of the difficulties of changing basic features of the system, even if most people would endorse the desirability of such changes, for example the already mentioned inauguration of non-sexist human pronouns in English. It is, however, useful to introduce a set of binary contrasts at a fundamental level to point to some of the social factors relevant to stability and change. The set of contrasts is not intended to be exhaustive. It is intended to serve as a basis for thinking about the issues to which it draws attention.

As with other lists of oppositions, it is not a question of either/or, but a set of issues requiring pragmatic resolutions of tensions between idealized impossibilities. Language only developed and continues to develop and change as a system because it is a resource; the developments extend its utility, and changes which are not developments will also have reasons for their occurrence. In complementary manner, language is only viable as a resource because it is a system whose units, structures, and the rules and conventions for their combination and use are known, accepted and followed by a sufficient number of people who are communicating with each other.

Table 3   Language as system and resource

Language as	
System	Resource
Structure	Function
Unity	Diversity
Rule observation	Flexibility
Prescription	Description
Correctness	Effectiveness
Propriety	
"Pure"	"Degenerate"
Knowing "that"	Knowing "how to"
Idealism	Realism
Nominalism	Pragmatism
Stability	Change
Conservative	Progressive
	Anarchic
Educated	Uneducated
Cultivated	Earthy
Elite	Ordinary

Rules are prescriptive, but the rules of language use are not issues of morality; they only need to be followed if people wish to communicate. Hearers and readers can only interpret utterances if the system of communication is shared and the rules are followed. For a networked community of communicators in a stable environment, which is not influenced by outsiders, the language system itself would be stable, with succeeding generations being socialized into community norms. However, such conditions do not obtain indefinitely in the real world. Environments change and are changed. Outsiders impinge. Community members innovate.

There are forces acting for standardization: centralized systems of government, centralized educational systems, centrally controlled media – and linguists. Over the last 1500 years or so English has accumulated massive numbers of units and structures whose conventional rules for use have been codified in written-down grammars, dictionaries, encyclopedias, thesauruses, books of etiquette – and in the *de facto* use made of language in everyday discourse. Once codified and disseminated such texts can become normative: what began as description becomes prescription. Had the descriptions reflected practices universal to the society, they would still have become prescriptive for future generations, but they would not have taken on the excluding and discriminating functions that they have served. The descriptions were of the knowledge and usage of social elites in a strongly stratified society, and have consequently served as aspirant standards for the would-be socially mobile, and as markers of social identity of those whose phonology, grammar, semantics and pragmatics deviate from the codified norms.

On the one hand societies are likely to be more cohesive if they share a core culture, and if all its members can communicate in a *lingua franca and single sociolect*. On the other hand, to prescribe a particular profile of pronunciation as more than one accent among others can be divisive, diminishing and cruel – which may well be the intention, and the latent if not the manifest function.

It is noteworthy that both columns contain terms that can have positive or negative associations. Each also has characteristics which, if eliminated or pushed to excess, are impossible (and undesirable). Optima lie in moderation, where this cannot be defined beyond appeals to the negotiated collective wisdom and practices of the contemporary participants.

Historically and presently, adherence to the concepts on the left-hand side is favoured by members of the power elites, except in those areas of developing technology which have commercial relevance to their interests. As gatekeepers and sponsors of social mobility, they can decide who can be filtered up the social hierarchies to service and perhaps later come to be members of the top strata. Those who are selected for sponsorship face the dilemma of cutting themselves off from their cultural roots and adopting the speech norms of the elites or retaining their own norms and remaining where they are. Teachers in schools are left to resolve this dilemma in their teaching, and to point out the consequences of the decisions for their pupils!

A FUNCTIONAL/STRUCTURAL FRAME OF REFERENCE

Units and structures perform functions, and functions are performed by units and structures. Investigations into how language works in communication can be initiated with either or both, but it is the relationships between the two which are integral for the answering of questions. The exposure of a conceptual dialectic between the two in relation to relevant empirical evidence is the essence of the advancement of useful description and explanation. It is those relationships which determine how to categorize both units and rules governing their combination and which functions should be isolated into a psychologically useful taxonomy. Logical possibilities for classifying either are much more numerous than are the empirically sensible ones, and we have to be careful not to reify the nature of the useful constructions already achieved.

So, for example, the construction of the International Phonetic Alphabet and the manner in which the phonemic structure of English can be mapped into this looks to be a set of discoveries. It is obvious how /b/, /p/ and /d/ are alike and how they differ objectively – at a certain level of analysis, e.g. place and manner of articulation. Unfortunately it is only obvious to those who have studied these matters, and they will be quick to point out that what is recorded by a spectograph is not in one-to-one correspondence with what we hear in context. To English sensitive ears the distinction between /l/ and /r/ is obvious, but it is not so to Japanese ears. To English sensitive ears pitch and duration are not heard as phonemically significant but they are to Bantu or Chinese ears. Once we know and appreciate certain criterial distinctions, we are prone to reify them and forget our previous ignorance and confusion. It has been the dialectic between meaning differences and differences and similarities in sound that has provided the fulcrum for deciding how to classify the sounds. For functions the challenge is more difficult to meet. Phonemes operate at the micro levels of morphemes and lexemes, but for functions the concerns run from those levels up to vast tomes and strings of speeches; what may be useful and defensible categorizations for functions at the most macro levels of analysis may be of lesser or no value at finer levels.

Lists of functions for the social psychological level tend to hover around the level of utterance or exchange, and that would seem to be appropriate for present purposes. While answers to social psychological questions may well need to include reference to sociological, historical and other more macroscopic perspectives, its heartland is interpersonal and intergroup interactions. As Table 2 showed, however, the taxonomies for pragmatics and semantics are less well developed than those for phonology and grammar, and at this point in time some very elementary considerations are still apposite. At the level of an utterance, which may be considered roughly as one or more free clauses (explicit or implied), then the following observations may be made:

1. There are no grounds for assuming or expecting that any utterance will be unifunctional. All utterances have multifunctional potential (etic) and while

only one or a few of these may appear to be dominant in a particular instance (emic), which of those will be realized is not necessarily predictable. A remark intended to display friendship may serve to identify the speaker as a foreign spy. To ask about primary or main functions can be restrictive.

2. In particular instances it may not be possible to diagnose the functions, and in any case diagnoses made will remain no more than probabilistic and contestable. In sequential exchanges, the functions can be explicitly negotiated.

3. Utterances do not always reduce uncertainty; on the contrary, many are constructed to increase uncertainty.

4. Many utterances are intended to obscure or hide "reality" rather than to represent plausible constructions of it.

5. There is no point in expanding taxonomies to levels of detail that become unusable or contracting them to hide important differences. For example, when recording small group discussions in the 1950s, Bales (1951) devised a 12-category system for the observation of half-hour sessions. This exposed much more relatable differentiation over types of groups than did a four-category system and captured what was important better than a 96-category system. This could not have been predicted in advance, and while there were clearly issues missed by the Bales' system for its purposes, it was very useful.

The obvious candidates for a taxonomy of functions arise from philosophy and linguistics. Developmental psychologists had postulated three functions; Halliday (1975) expanded these to seven. Wittgenstein (1951) left the future to cope with an infinite number of functions, while Austin (1962) added five performatives to the constantives (i.e. referential, representational, statements), which had been their earlier prime concern. Searle (1969, 1975) rendered Austin's list more systematic, linking acts to intentions and outcomes, unpacking the rules underpinning the nature of such acts, and reminding us of earlier work that had pointed to variations in the ways that the form of the expression of a request could take (Soskin & John, 1963). He reduced the number to five and included important observations about the direction of fit between world and words. Certainly these ideas have impacted on research in child development and cross-cultural psychology, but less so on social psychology. This is odd because Searle clearly offered claims about relationships between structures and functions, although he made no reference to an earlier categorization by Jakobson (1960) which linked functions to six different aspects of a speech event: addresser, addressee, context, message, contact and code. It is this model which matches most neatly onto some of the categories typically used by social psychologists. Addressers make expressive use of language, but also mark their actual or projected identities. Addressees are subject to social influence by addressers. The phatic function serves the bonhomie of contact with others in social interaction. The poetic function should be a function of the characteristics of the message, while his metalingual function focused on the representation of the code itself. Last but not least, the referential function covers all the statements and questions that can be asked about "context", which in Jakobson's scheme

Table 4 Functions and forms of language

Functions	1. Encounter regulation	2. Expression of affect	3. Regulation of self: (a) behaviour (b) affect	4. Regulation of others: (a) behaviour (b) affect	5. Marking of encoder Emotional state Personality Social identity	6. Role Relationship marking	7. Representation of non-linguistic world involving: discrimination, organization, storage and transmission, in spheres of knowledge: (a) logics (b) sciences (c) ethics (d) metaphysics (e) aesthetics (f) everyday facts	8. Performatives	9. Instruction	10. Inquiry	11. Metalanguage functions
Everyday name of activity or products	Greeting, Leave-taking Turn-taking	Exclamations Swearing	Talking to oneself	Commands Requests Threats, jibes Jokes	–	–	Many: stating, arguing, reporting, remembering, thinking (?). Problem solving: Defining, analysing, processing, synthesizing, evaluation	Promising, betting, etc	Teaching	Questioning	Linguistics Psycholinguistics Sociolinguistics Philosophy English language courses
Prime focus of verbal act	Participant interaction	Encoder	Encoder	Decoder	Encoder	Relationship encoder/ decoder	Correspondence of verbal act to non-verbal world	Non-verbal accomplishments	Mastery by decoder	Acquisition of knowledge for encoder	Language and speech

Essential linguistic forms: description	Finite sets of special words, noises, and phrases Pausing, questions	Vocatives, swear words, Terms of endearment	Abbreviated imperatives?	Imperatives, questions, modal verbs, etc. A finite set of semantically associated verbs and phrases Forms of humour	Para- and extralinguistic features, overt statements Phonology (accent) Grammatical, lexical choices etc.	Rights and duties to use of socially prescribed forms of address, and utterances	Declarative sentence forms	A finite set of semantically associated verbs used in normatively and legally prescribed forms	Various	Interrogatives –
Essential linguistic forms: examples	Hi! Jane! Ciao! What do you think?	Oh my love! xxxx!	Now, one teaspoon mustard Pull yourself together	Jump! Will you . . .? You must . . . If . . . then . . . You creep Joke 42	I, I, I think . . . I'm scared 'otel; Ain't no . . . Lavatory	Sir! Sweetie! Let us pray	The cat is on the mat. If A, then B! Doggie will bite! All gone, Daddy	I name this ship the Bubbly Bosun	–	–
Basis of evaluation	Attention attracted? Contact made? Flow maintained? Ending satisfactory?	Feel better?	Is action facilitated by talking? Is affective state affected?	Obedience obtained? Dissuaded? Humiliated? Made to laugh?	Correct diagnosis made or impression conveyed?	Choice and sequence right for accepted ways of defining roles?	True or false within premisses of universe of discourse? Is argument valid? Are rules of game followed?	Intended act performed?	Did pupil learn?	Are gaps in knowledge filled? Knowledge of how language works increased?

appears to be the sum total of human knowledge and beliefs. The expansion offered by Robinson (1972, 1978) sought to incorporate diagnostic criteria for the identification of functions; it was a framework rather than a challenging theory. A variant of it is repeated here mainly because the functional/structural questions have to be posed and answered about *any* research in the area. We have to hypothesize which functions are being performed, describe *how* they are being performed, and why. Language and the non-verbal systems provide the means by which the (social) psychological functions are realized.

The scheme retains Jakobson's core and its question as to who or what is the *prime focus of the verbal act*. It specifies any *everyday name* for such, if there is one. In relating function to form a serious hazard looms. Having noted the complexities and varieties of structure/function relationships, on what criteria can any fundamental or basic relation be claimed? *Primary* linguistic form cannot be claimed in the absence of historical evidence; *primitive* likewise. *Essential* was chosen in 1978 because to my mind it is simplest to associate statements with declaratives, commands with imperatives, requests with interrogatives, and exclamations to vocatives. Now I prefer *characteristic*, but the label is less important than the purchase the concept provides between simple transparency and opaqueness. The four conjunctions cited for free clauses appear to be the most transparent.

The final column of *basis of evaluation* is, however, an important addition to Jakobson's concerns. It lists the particular questions that have to be seen as relevant and, for successful action to be answered affirmatively, they are the crux of any functional claim. The framework presented here omits some mentioned in 1978 and adds others, but the core and the principles remain identical and appropriate.

Given any utterance, exchange or set of exchanges, questions can be posed about their potential functions and their actual ones. The culture may well have labels for the particular activities: promises, threats, fables, sermons, panegyrics. Such subsystems can then be explored and evaluated. One such which began with forms of request (Soskin & John, 1963) was subsequently expanded greatly by Brown and Levinson (1987). Their model of politeness has been subjected to empirical investigations that have led to constructive developments through linkages of forms and functions, which in turn have been linked into social psychological theory, each component being modified as the triangulated evaluations here proceeded (see Holtgraves, this volume, Chapter 4.18). What has been done with politeness has been pursued with other phenomena and processes (see sections "What language is and how it functions" and "Implications for research"). Just as the Brown and Levinson model might have had its origins in the collection of exemplars fitting into Function Categories 8 and 10, so might the categorization of jokes and the perceived appropriateness of telling them.

More important, the framework can serve as a basis for asking questions about troublesome diagnoses. How can indirect expressions work? How can the correct implicatures of Gricean constructions be inferred? If the manifest function appears to be odd, are there latent functions to be considered, and if so how are possible interpretations to be tested? Critics of Grice (1989) have pointed out that he does not develop his model to indicate how anyone is to work out particular implicatures. The examples he provides are almost certainly culture bound, and some may require the extended experience of Oxbridge Senior Common Room life to interpret. That said, the maxims themselves have stimulated research into conversation (see Chapter 10).

The balance of functions and structures can reach a dynamic equilibrium in a social milieu, but that does not imply that continuing stability is assured. Structures can gain precedence if formal elaboration gains at the expense of substantive purposes. In Merton's (1957) terms, the means can come to overshadow the original ends as in rituals. Historically one of the most dramatic general examples was the development and demise of rhetoric itself. By the sixteenth century in England, the traditions paradoxically inspired in large measure by a functionally minded Aristotle had led to a massive proliferation of structures of pragmatically empty labelled tropes and figures which students had to learn to use in their imitations of classical poems and speeches. Function was overwhelmed by formal exercises. Eventually these elaborate rituals were seen to be pointless and dead, and the teaching of them was abandoned. Rhetoric died, at least for a few centuries.

The complex rules about forms of address and reference to mark the qualities of social relationships have suffered a similar fate in most sectors of most occidental societies, but for different reasons. The fine gradations of pomp and circumstance particularly characteristic for members of the higher-status elites are retained in books of etiquette and for ceremonials, but have shrunk in number, range and significance for those outside such circles with the growth of democratization. As the peculiar rights and privileges functionally associated with each title disappeared, so did the deferential address forms. Archaic and traditional forms remain in legal and religious ceremonies, but as their functional significance fades so the forms change; marrying women no longer have to promise to obey their husbands, and husbands no longer have to endow their wives with all their worldly goods – until such time as they come up against efficient lawyers in the divorce courts. Which structures are likely to be eliminated or changed is indeterminate. Certainly lost wars and civil wars provide occasions for reducing complexities, but vested interests at the head of elites have remarkable capacities for perpetuating their forms. English in England has been building up its stylistics with its relative political stability since 1066: complexities, idiosyncrasies and eccentricities have accumulated over the centuries. However, their proliferation has been tempered over the last 130 years by the existence of a nationally uniform system of education, with successive generations of children and other social groups tending to simplify and streamline what they are told is Standard English. Some newspapers have guidelines that keep their prose at a reading age of 12, which discourages a heavy use of rococo elaborations and subtle implicatures. Telespeak has to match the preference of mass audiences, if it is to retain high audience ratings.

The final kind of complication to be mentioned is the carefully planned use of wordings intended to deceive and thereby control the hearer or reader. With language, the struggles and conflicts are military, economic and political. In times of conflict ever more complex ciphers (codes!) are developed to communicate information among one's own and allied forces while preventing decoding by enemies. Countries pretend not to have cracked ciphers when they have. They misinform and disinform, occasionally misleading their own side as well as their opponents. In the economic world, those selling their wares do not minimize the good qualities of their products and service when advertising and marketing; on the contrary they strive to maximize profit, and it would be odd if they did not; *caveat emptor* is in Latin because the injunction for buyers to be wary is an ancient as well as a modern piece of folk wisdom. In the political sphere, mistrust of governments and ministers was normative in the Soviet Union and its satellites, and is becoming normative rather than exceptional in capitalist regimes. In the United States recent presidents have been taken to task for cover-ups and deception in both their presidential and private conduct. in Britain in the last 20 years, ministerial resignations have been a steady stream, some of which have been associated with carefully worded misleading statements. A profession of *spin-doctors* has emerged on both sides of the Atlantic; their *raison d'être* is to generate appearances that are more positive than plausible constructions of realities warrant. An assurance by UK government ministers that any food is safe is now counter-productive. In recent years a number of cases of denials of risks of food-poisoning from eating contaminated eggs and cheese reached a climax in the case of people dying from CJD, a human form of bovine spongiform encephalitis, after years of ignored warnings about the possible consequences of feeding cattle with diseased sheep brains. What is meant by what is said in the public domain now requires expert interpretation! For many people, evasion and equivocation, along with claims of benefits and advantages, are treated with proper scepticism. Tax cuts are seldom what they appear to be in their initial presentations.

Such activities may be considered relatively trivial compared with the historical and current attempts by rulers and governments to eliminate whole languages and the cultures associated with them. In the Balkans, with its geographical patchwork of ethnic minorities, cultures, dialects and languages, governments continue to write histories that justify singularity of national identities, deny the existence of languages, abolish schools using minority languages, and oblige people to change their names (see Poulton, 1993). The same kinds of oppression have been characteristic of many conquering, colonial powers, and exist today in some measure in some form in all societies. While the existence of communities in which goal-oriented cooperativeness is hegemonic and trust a valued virtue would be a force for the development of genuine transparency in language use, the vested interests of the various elites in all countries extant at present help to ensure that power, wealth and status differentials are preserved or accentuated, with language and its use being a major means for justifying this.

METHODOLOGICAL DIVERSITY

A commentary on the similarities, differences and differential utilities of contrasting approaches to data collection has appeared recently and will not be repeated (Robinson, 1998). The argument was advanced that the oppositions in Table 5 are dimensional and that studies can include the components of either extreme. Which method or position is likely to be most productive as a point of departure will be a function of the contemporary state of well-informed and well-grounded beliefs about the particular issues in hand.

Table 5   Approaches: emphases and contrasts

Quantitative	Qualitative
Imagined speech Elicited speech	Natural speech
Monologue	Dialogue Polylogue
Units and structures	Texts and whole
Behaviour	Accounts
Experiments	Field studies Cases

However, a number of rough generalizations can be made. In the exploratory chases of enquiries, case studies with unobtrusive observation using a maximally open frame of reference will be more advantageous than laboratory-based experiments. The collection of accounts and reflections of involved participants is advisable. It may be that case studies do not yield any ideas and that participants cannot comment plausibly, but not to begin with them both, if feasible, is to risk wasting time and energy. As some understanding develops, and if ethical considerations permit, Garfinkel's (1967) tactic of breaking hypothesized rules is a strong heuristic device whether played out for real or explored in reflective conversational interviews.

The time comes when sufficient apparently significant categories and variables have been identified and sufficient explanatory hypotheses formulated to justify survey-based field studies and/or experiments. These may well help to consolidate both descriptions and explanations, but they are most unlikely to capture all the variance.

Who are these people hidden in the "error variance" term and why are they there? Is it a result of measuring instruments being unreliable and/or invalid or are they genuine exceptions to the hypotheses? If the latter, what has led to their exceptionality? For several centuries in the physical sciences, the exceptional cases have served as the potential stepping-stones for further exploration. They are prime candidates for conjecture and further exploration; they are the springboard for the generation of more differentiated or more comprehensive hypotheses. Then it is back to case studies, and a further cycle.

In sum, the methods typified as qualitative are likely to be most profitably employed at the earliest and latest phases of particular projects, with the so-called quantitative methods manifesting their power for testing the strength of hypotheses within (temporarily) established descriptive and explanatory models.

As Silverman (1993) has pointed out, it is in some forms of so-called qualitative analysis that the exceptions stand out most clearly. While they might figure in graphical displays as outliers in variants of ANOVAs and regression, they are more likely to remain submerged in data sets of numbers, notwithstanding the recent requirements of journals to quote effect sizes. In contrast, in chi-square analyses, there they are, off the diagonal, challenging investigators to come and investigate them. Unfortunately, most fields of enquiry are not followed through the cycles in cumulative series of iterations in which all available and feasible methods and techniques are used and are shown to yield data consistent with precise explanations, which are neither overdetermining or underdetermining (Kuhn, 1991).

It is tempting to insert a sharp polemic on the politico-socio-economic reasons why research is not as efficient as it could be, but that would be out of place. (Colleagues can work out answers as well or better than I can.) Suffice it to say that in an earlier existence as a biologist, I did not experience methodological battles. The means for answering questions depended upon the nature of the questions asked. Progress was prone to follow the sequence outlined, with experiments, where possible, coming at the later phases of a cycle rather than at the beginning. Given current trends in the development of disciplines and their preferred epistemologies, my prediction would have to be that departments of communication and linguistics are more likely to offer supportive environments for the development of social psychology of language than departments of psychology or even social psychology.

SUMMARY AND CONCLUSIONS

So what have been the purposes of this chapter, and have they been achieved? The primary intention has been to reassert that we are embarked upon an important and exciting, but also massive scientific enterprise in a field with peculiar properties. It is scientific, not because we occasionally do experiments and attempt to measure variables, but because we are trying to generate and test systematically precise and concise descriptions and explanations of language phenomena that can be defended as being the most plausible and useful accounts in the light of the full range of empirical evidence contemporaneously available.

It is peculiar, both because of two features of its identity and because of its relationship to the agentive characters of its objects of study. As well being located at the intersect of two disciplines, each with their own topics, levels of

analysis, perspectives and epistemologies, the study of language and social psychology suffers from this dangerous cleavage in the separation of language from
other modes of communication. Useful and necessary for many analytic purposes, language and its use is but one component of communicative activity in
any particular context; its pragmatic significance invariably operates in combination with non-verbal modes, and in a cultural context with its particular SPEAK-
ING conventions. (As Chapter 2 shows, Speech Accommodation Theory had to
become Communication Accommodation Theory.) Always then, we are conscious of the need to be informed about the other systems that may be operating.
To ignore them is to risk posing questions which are misguided or too narrow
and hence failing to find sensible answers. Mid-century examples of this involved
posing issues about ambiguities of meaning in grammatical analyses which were
undertaken independently of the phonological and pragmatic levels. We are still
prone to write out transcripts, or code these objectively (less vocalics, non-
verbals and context) and thereby miss the possible essence of their functioning.
For behavioural and experiential studies, language is a system and resource
within semiotics.

We have also to be informed about two disciplines: linguistics and social
psychology. Unfortunately, most of us are unlikely to have been formally educated in both. Even in sanguine moods, I am concerned about the epistemologies
of both; in melancholic moods I have grave doubts that many practitioners of
either discipline can define clearly and simply what is to count as reasonable
evidence for many of the propositional claims made within each. Unfortunately
our educational systems do not encourage the multidisciplinary and interdisciplinary competencies that might lead to more collaborative ventures within
shared frames of reference. While this Handbook certainly bestrides the cleavage, and exemplifies the use of varied epistemologies, it does not pretend to
explore, explicate and integrate the relevant work of cognate disciplines.

The relationship to its objects of study, viz. human beings, is doubly challenging, presenting us with problems that none of the physical sciences have to
grapple with. Both stem from the agentive character of human beings. In so far
as human beings are self-reflective creatures capable of exercising their will to
shape both their environments and themselves, we have to take into account
that their activities are in states of permanent flux. Phenomena we can describe
and explain today may be of historical interest only in some years' time. For
example, any precocious social scientist in medieval England who set out to
describe the use of "thou", "thee", "ye", "you", and "the" faced a task that
does not exist today. Nowadays the underlying priorities and issues may or may
not be similar to those then: the data would not be. More dramatically, the
current Queen of Britain is unlikely to order our immediate execution if we
make eye contact with her – or if we indulge in any other behaviour that she
chances to deem offensive.

The related feature is that the dissemination of such advances as we make and
publish feed into the implementation of change either real or apparent. For
example, the last few years have witnessed an inflation of occupational titles in

commerce, industry, education and social services. The Environmental Health Officer still has to dispose of rats, cockroaches and other pests. Directors and chief executives may talk only to themselves and family at board meetings. There are university professors who have never conducted any research. The labelling is intended to enhance status. Impression management training relies very heavily on an academic base for its rationale and is now an endemic creature of career development. Character-building courses are less in evidence. In either case language use changes. Most pervasive perhaps has been the shift from male-based descriptors and discourse, an egalitarian practice that has been spread, with the support of legal sanctions.

Discriminatory processes are and have been used to oppress and suppress the use of whole languages, as well as their users. Historically, imperial powers have not only promoted the use of their own languages in their colonies, they were prone to forbid the use and teaching of the indigenous ones. The rationale for the promotion of an imperial language may be the facilitation of communication throughout the empire (or state). When this is combined with parity for the use and teaching of indigenous languages, such claims may be defensible. When people are punished for using their primary language, such arguments become implausible.

Typically social psychologists are less concerned with these grander frames of reference, but there are dangers in neglecting the bigger pictures. The individuals on earth speak one or more varieties of one or more of the 6000 or so languages extant (Crystal, 1997). Languages and their varieties are changing in vitality as well as in character: the number of speakers can be rising, falling or holding steady. Darwinian principles will be relevant. Vitality will be dependent on the language itself and those who use it. Languages (and varieties) promoted by powerful individuals, groups and societies are more likely to flourish, especially if their structures readily afford additions and changes. Among the *nouveau riche* countries, English is in the ascendancy, partly because of the policies of the imperialism of the British in the past, and currently because of the power and status of the United States, with its commanding presence in the new technologies in communication: TV programmes and computers. Chinese has displayed staying power and adaptability. Hittite has disappeared, and the Latin legacy of the Romans has shrunk to its use in the Catholic Church and as a declining component of some school curricula.

The diversity of language and their varieties is correlated with the diversity of cultures and subcultures around the globe. To date social psychologists have worked mainly in Standard Average European and particularly in (American) English. Publications do not typically render this narrowness explicit. One consequence has been a tendency to offer generalizations that will fail to hold in other cultures and other languages. With its extended history, linguistics has typically adopted broader geographical and historical frames of reference, and the study of comparative linguistics has acted as a brake on overzealous generalizations from studies of single languages. In contrast, comparative social psychology hardly exists. Social psychology itself is still in its infancy and, within the discipline's basic texts, language and communication may well not have a chapter; only one on my shelves does. At the present time social psychologists of language are a rare species. It is only in the last three years that we have formed a (small) international society, and there are as yet no national societies. What is therefore surprising is that we have progressed as far as we have in the last few decades. This handbook may help to enlist more volunteers to the cause.

FOOTNOTE

Martin and Nakayama (1999) explicate the dilemmas facing sociologists of communication in their extension of a four-cell combination of two binary oppositions of commitments to metatheoretical paradigms: objective/subjective, emphasis on stability, order, cohesion/emphasis change, conflict, power differentials. They examine forms of interparadigmatic relations of liberal pluralism, interparadigmatic borrowing, multiparadigmatic collaborations and dialectic perspectives. Sociology appears to have more serious difficulties than social psychology at the present time.

REFERENCES

Abelson, R.P. & Lalljee, M. (1988). Knowledge structures and causal explanation. In D. Hilton (Ed.), *Contemporary science and natural explanation* (pp. 175–203). London: Harvester.

Antaki, C. (1988). *Analysing everyday explanation*. London: Sage.

Austin, J.L. (1962). *How to do things with words*. Oxford, UK: Oxford University Press.

Bales, R.F. (1951). *Interaction process analysis*. New York: Academic Press.

Billig, M. (1987). *Arguing and thinking*. Cambridge, UK. Cambridge University Press.

Brown, P. & Levinson, S. (1987). *Universals in language use: Politeness phenomena* Cambridge, UK: Cambridge University Press.

Cappella, J. & Palmer, M.T. (1990). The structure of non-verbal behavior in social interaction. In H. Giles & W.P. Robinson (Eds), *Handbook of language and social psychology* (pp. 141–162). Chichester, UK: Wiley.

Chomsky, N. (1957). *Syntactic structures*. The Hague: Mouton.

Cody, M.J. & McLaughlin, M.L. (1990). Interpersonal accounting. In H. Giles & W.P. Robinson (Eds), *Handbook of language and social psychology* (pp. 227–256). Chichester, UK: Wiley.

Crystal, D. (1997). *The Cambridge encyclopedia of language* (2nd edn). Cambridge, UK: Cambridge University Press.

Davidson, D. (1984). *Inquiries into truth and interpretation*. Oxford, UK: Oxford University Press.

de Saussure, F. (1959). *Course in general linguistics* (W. Baskin, trans.). New York: Philosophical Library. (Original work published 1925.)

Eco, U. (1979). *The role of the reader*. London: Hutchinson.

Frege, G. (1980). On sense and meaning. In P.T. Geach & M. Black (Eds), *Translations from the philosophical works of Gottlob Frege*. Oxford, UK: Oxford University Press.

Gazdar, G., Klein, E., Pullum, G.K. & Sag, I.A. (1985). *Generalized phrase structure grammar*. Oxford, UK: Blackwell.

Glasgow Media Group (1976). *Bad news*. London: Routledge.

Grice, P. (1989). *Studies in the way of words*. Cambridge, MA: Harvard University Press.

Halliday, M.A.K. (1975). *Learning how to mean*. London: Arnold.

Halliday, M.A.K. (1985). *An introduction to functional grammar*. London: Arnold.

Hockett, C.F. (1960). *A course in modern linguistics*. New York: Macmillan.

Hymes, D. (1967). Models of the interaction of language and social setting. *Journal of Social Issues*, **27**(2), 8–28.

Jakobson, R. (1960). Linguistics and poetics. In T.A. Sebeok (Ed.) *Style in language*. New York: Wiley.

Kuhn, D. (1991). *The skills of argument*. Cambridge, UK: Cambridge University Press.

Leech, G. (1983). *Principles of pragmatics*. London: Longman.

Levinson, S. (1983) *Pragmatics*. Cambridge, UK: Cambridge University Press.

Livingstone, S. (1998). *Making sense of television* (2nd edn). London: Routledge.

Lyons, J. (1995). *Linguistic semantics*. Cambridge, UK: Cambridge University Press.

Martin, J.N. & Nakayama, T.K. (1999). Thinking dialectically about culture and communication. *Communication Theory*, **9**(1), 1–25.

Merton, R.K. (1957). *Social theory and social structure*. Glencoe, IL: Free Press.

Mill, J.S. (1873). *A system of logic* (9th edn). London: Longman.

Ogden, C.K. & Richards, I.A. (Eds) (1923). *The meaning of meaning* (10th edn). London: Routledge.

Ouhalla, J. (1994). *Introducing transformational grammar*. London: Arnold.

Pierce, C.S. (1955); *Logic and semiotic*. New York: Dover. (Original work published 1931.)

Poulton, H. (1993). *The Balkans: Minorities and states in conflict*. London: Minority Rights.

Putnam, H. (1988). *Representation and reality*. Cambridge, MA: MIT Press.

Quirk, R., Greenbaum, S. Leech, G. & Svartuik, J. (1985). *A comprehensive grammar of the English language*. London: Longman.

Robinson, W.P. (1972). *Language and social behaviour*. Harmondsworth, UK: Penguin.

Robinson, W.P. (1978). *Language management in education*. Sydney: Allen & Unwin.

Robinson, W.P. (1998). Language and social psychology: An intersect of opportunities and significance. *Journal of Language and Social Psychology*, **17**(3), 276–301.

Rorty, R. (1991). *Objectivity, relativism and truth*. Cambridge, UK: Cambridge University Press.

Schank, R.C. & Abelson, R.P. (1977). *Scripts, plans, goals and understanding*. Hillsdale, NJ: Erlbaum.

Searle, J.R. (1969). *Speech acts*. Cambridge, UK: Cambridge University Press.

Searle, J.R. (1975). A classification of illocutionary acts. *Language in Society*, **5**, 1–23.

Shannon, C.E. & Weaver, W. (1949). *The mathematic theory of communication*. Urbana, IL: University of Illinois Press.

Silverman, D. (1993). *Analysing qualitative data*. London: Sage.

Soskin, W.F. & John, V. (1963). The study of spontaneous talk. In R.G. Barker (Ed.) *The stream of behaviour*. New York: Appleton-Century-Crofts.

Tajfel, H. & Turner, J.W. (1979). An integrative theory of intergroup conflict. In W.G. Austin & S. Warchel (Eds), *The social psychology of intergroup relations* (pp. 33–46). Monterey, CA: Brooks/Cole.

UNESCO (1948). *Handbook for the improvement of textbooks and teaching materials*. Paris: UNESCO.

UNESCO (1962). *Improvement of textbooks*. Goslar seminar, 14–23 May, 1962. Paris: UNESCO.

Wittgenstein, L. (1951). *Philosophical investigations*. Oxford, UK: Blackwell.

Wittgenstein, L. (1961). *Tractatus logico-philosophicus*. London: Routledge. (Original work published 1922.)

Communication Accommodation Theory

Carolyn A. Shepard, Howard Giles *and* **Beth A. Le Poire**
University of California at Santa Barbara, Santa Barbara, USA

The study of language and social interaction has enjoyed a long and industrious cross-disciplinary career in the social sciences, in fields such as social psychology, sociology, sociolinguistics, and communication. Of the frameworks prominent in the study of interaction processes, communication accommodation theory (CAT) is arguably situated as a cornerstone theoretical perspective at the interface of these four areas of research (Bradac, Hopper, & Wiemann, 1989). As a result of its explanatory power and intuitive appeal, formulated (as speech accommodation theory) to explain accent shifts in interactions (Giles, 1973), a considerable amount of research and theorizing has expanded CAT into an "interdisciplinary model of relational and identity processes in communicative interaction" (Coupland & Jaworski, 1997a, pp. 241–242). The scope of the theory now includes several different contexts, communication behaviors of several varieties (i.e. verbal and nonverbal), as well as attitudes and perceptions. CAT's purview encompasses the description, prediction, and explanation of the underlying motivations, communication processes, and consequences of shifts in behavior in interactions (for recent reviews, see Giles & Coupland, 1991; Giles & Noels, 1997; Giles & Wadleigh, 1999).

CAT, originally labeled speech accommodation theory (SAT), was developed as a sociopsychological model to explain modifications in speech style during interactions (Giles, 1973; Giles, Taylor & Bourhis, 1973). In reaction to current theories of the time (e.g., Labov, 1966), which looked to the context to explain communicative behavior in interactions, SAT proposed that social cognitive

The New Handbook of Language and Social Psychology.
Edited by W. Peter Robinson and Howard Giles.
© 2001 John Wiley & Sons Ltd.

processes mediated that relationship and that individual motivation was the driving factor behind choice in speech behaviors. Since that original formulation, CAT has undergone many revisions and advanced from a micro-level theory that explained accent shifts or vocal patterns in conversations into a macro-level theory of communication processes that cuts across situations and contexts.

Nonetheless, the primary focus of the theory has remained upon the importance of language behaviors in interpersonal and intergroup interaction. Language and speech behaviors are important in interactions because they are markers of group membership and individual identity. The language that one uses, or speech behaviors in which one engages, can demarcate ethnic boundaries (Giles, Bourhis & Taylor, 1977), indicate status differentials (e.g., Giles, 1973; Thakerar, Giles, & Cheshire, 1982), define ingroup or outgroup boundaries (e.g. Giles, N. Coupland & J. Coupland, 1991), or enforce role or norm-specific behaviors (Gallois & Callan, 1991).

This theory has been the focus of a quarter of a century of study. In light of the ambitious research agenda which CAT scholars have undertaken, the goal of this chapter is to overview and synthesize research and theorizing about language and accommodation. Toward this end, we first provide a brief overview of the major constructs important to CAT, followed by a history of the development and trajectory of CAT as a theoretical perspective. Next, we compare CAT in relation to two other similar and/or competing theoretical perspectives. We then review the directions in which CAT has branched out. Last, we review the theoretical propositions forwarded by CAT in light of recent empirical support in order to illuminate directions for future research in the area.

THEORETICAL CONCEPTS AND PREMISES

Throughout the evolution of CAT, the theory has undergone several revisions and developments and has been refined through the application of caveats and contextual qualifiers. Nonetheless, the primary thesis of CAT remains that individuals use language to achieve a desired social distance between self and interacting partners (Giles, 1973; Giles et al., 1987). That is, CAT theorists propose that individuals use strategic behaviors to negotiate social distance. These strategies – which are also the focus of the premises upon which CAT is based – are approximation strategies (convergence, divergence, maintenance, and complementary), discourse management, interpretability, and interpersonal control. In this section, we review these constructs in light of the manner in which they inform a general knowledge about the theory. Later in the chapter, we will address how these concepts fit into the central propositions and predictions of the theory. Although seemingly redundant with earlier work (e.g. Giles & Wadleigh, 1999), these definitions are primarily offered for the less familiar reader.

APPROXIMATION STRATEGIES

Convergence

Convergence refers to the strategies by which individuals adapt or modify linguistic, paralinguistic, and non-verbal features to become more similar to their interaction partner (Giles, J. Coupland & N. Coupland, 1991; Giles et al., 1987). Among the many communicative behaviors that may be modified to display convergence are accents, dialects, idioms, and code switching between languages (e.g. Moise & Bourhis, 1994) – characteristics found within language groups, such as idioms, speech rate, pauses, utterance length, phonological variants (e.g., Burt, 1998); and aspects of the interchange itself, like information density and self-disclosure (e.g., Al-Khatib, 1995; Street & Giles, 1982). When individuals converge to one another, their behaviors become more similar or synchronous.

Divergence, Maintenance, and Other Speech Shifts

Divergence consists of strategies that individuals utilize to accentuate differences in speech and non-verbal behaviors between themselves and others. Drawing upon assumptions taken from Tajfel's (1978) social identity theory, CAT theorists propose that when intergroup concerns are primed divergent behaviors may occur in order to emphasize distinctiveness from interlocutors (Gallois et al., 1995). Often in interactions, individuals may opt to continue interacting in their current style of communication. This strategy choice (maintenance) of attempted non-convergence and non-divergence involves continuing one's own original speech style, despite accommodative attempts of the interaction partner. These behaviors are evaluated primarily as psychologically equivalent to divergence, and can signal significant social meanings (Bourhis, 1979; Tong et al., 1999).

Another strategy utilized to diverge from one's interlocutor is speech complementarity (Giles, 1980). This is a speech modification which accentuates valued sociolinguistic differences between interlocutors occupying different roles. One such example may be how, in mixed-gender dyads, men undertake more masculine tones of voice when talking with women than they do with other men, whereas women take on more feminine forms in mixed-sex than in same-sex dyads (Hogg, 1985).

OTHER ACCOMMODATION STRATEGIES

Although the above strategies prevailed as the primary focus of accommodative research for many years, Coupland et al. (1988) pointed out that these strategies focus primarily upon the productive performance of an addressee. Thus, in an effort to recognize that strategies may be utilized for other functions, three other strategies of accommodation were proposed: interpretability, discourse management, and interpersonal control. Interpretability strategies focus upon the receiver's ability to interpret language performance occurring in the interaction. An interactant undertaking such strategies might speak louder or slower so that the conversation partner understands what is being said more clearly. Discourse management strategies focus upon the other person's conversational needs and attune to them, and include conversational moves such as topic selection and sharing, face maintenance and backchanneling, or turn management. Finally, interpersonal control strategies are an attempt to direct the course or nature of the interaction (either explicitly or implicitly) by ways of interruption or forms of address.

MOTIVATIONAL PROCESSES DRIVING ACCOMMODATION

CAT theorists contend that speakers move through their linguistic repertoires for several reasons. The primary motive that has received attention since the theory's genesis revolves around the similarity attraction hypothesis (Byrne, 1971) – that we try to be more like those to whom we are attracted. Thus, convergence is driven by a need to gain approval from an interlocutor (Bourhis & Giles, 1977; Street & Giles, 1982). However, convergence may also arise out of the pragmatic concern of ensuring that the interaction flows more smoothly, which in turn improves the effectiveness of communication (Gallois et al., 1995). Similarity in speech styles between interactants has been associated with enhancing another's predictability (Berger & Bradac, 1982) and his or her intelligibility in the interaction (Triandis, 1960). This allows individuals to engage in clearer or smoother communication.

Divergent behaviors are motivated at two levels, but the purpose is the same: to display distinctiveness from one's interlocutor. At the individual level, divergence may serve to accentuate differences or display disdain for the other. At a group level, divergence may serve to emphasize valued group identity (e.g., Cargile, Giles, & Clément, 1996; Tajfel, 1978; Yaeger- Dror, 1991). To a lesser degree, maintenance strategies and complementarity may be used to distinguish oneself from another individual, or group, as well.

EVALUATION OF ACCOMMODATION STRATEGIES

In general, convergence strategies are evaluated positively (Gregory, Dagan & Webster, 1997; Bourhis, Giles & Lambert, 1975). However, positive evaluations often rely upon the interlocutors' perception of the converger's intent. If the intent is perceived positively, convergence is perceived favorably (Simard,

Taylor & Giles, 1976). For example, convergence in speech behaviors has been found to be positively related to increased competence and social attractiveness (Street, 1984) as well as predictability and supportiveness (Berger & Bradac, 1982). On the other hand, divergence and maintenance are often rated negatively by the target of divergence, especially if the intent is perceived to be dissociative (e.g., signaling dislike or lack of interest/effort in the interaction) (Gallois et al., 1995).

DIRECTION AND DEGREE

The first assumption to be made about accommodation strategies is that they are highly contingent upon the situational context in which the interaction occurs (Giles et al., 1987). Thus, many variables may moderate the situation in determining the final amount or degree of convergence, divergence, or maintenance. One such moderating variable, the power structure of the relationship between the two interactants, can affect whether the accommodation is upward or downward (Street, 1982). Upward movement refers to a shift toward a consensually prestigious variety, whereas downward shifts reflect a move toward more stigmatized or less socially valued forms of communication (Giles, N. Coupland & J. Coupland, 1991). In addition, accommodation can be "partial" (with interactants converging slightly to each other) or accommodation may be "full," where behaviors match exactly (Bourhis, 1991; Bradac, Mulac & House, 1988; Gregory & Webster, 1996; Street, 1982).

Accommodative attempts may occur on only one dimension or behavior, as in the case of unimodal accommodation, or be multimodal, and occur across several behaviors. In addition, accommodation can often be unidirectional (with only one interactant accommodating their behavior) rather than mutual (Giles, Bourhis & Taylor, 1977), and interactions may be symmetrical or asymmetrical (Gallois & Giles, 1998). Symmetrically accommodative interactions result from equal accommodation by both parties whereas asymmetrical accommodation does not. Azuma (1997) found a classic case of asymmetrical accommodation in Japan when Emperor Hirohito would reportedly converge downward to the farmers in Japan. However, his convergence was often met with upward convergence by the farmers toward the level of formality expected of the Emperor such that their respective accommodative behaviors both overaccommodated to each other.

TYPES OF ACCOMMODATION

Accommodation may occur on several dimensions. The most often studied dimension is objective accommodation, or actual communicative behavior measured through direct observations of linguistic interactions. Accommodation is not limited to this level of analysis, however. As Thakerar, Giles and Cheshire (1982) illustrated, the intentions of the speaker, or psychological accommodation, and the perceptions of listeners, or subjective accommodation, can be taken into account as well.

Psychological Accommodation

Often, although the objective behavior may signal convergence or divergence, the speaker's intention may not necessarily be consistent with the behavior. That is, although to an outside observer the behavior signals convergence, due to contextual factors the speaker may intend the behavior to signal divergence. Thakerar et al. (1982) found that although, objectively, individuals in unequal status conditions' behaviors diverged from each other, the speakers themselves were completely unaware of the actual changes. In addition, outside observers evaluated the intentions of the behaviors as converging toward their interactants.

Perceptual/Subjective

Subjective accommodation focuses upon the perceptions of the listener in an interaction (Thakerar et al. 1982). Similar to psychological accommodation, perceptual accommodation does not necessarily correspond with objective behaviors. Although a speaker's intent, or even actual behavior, may signal one meaning, the listener's interpretation of the speaker's act may not be consistent with the speaker's intent. The listener may not detect the behavior or may misinterpret the speaker's meaning.

LEVEL OF ACCOMMODATION

Given that intent, behavior, and perception result in differing evaluations of behavior, this suggests that an optimal level of accommodation may be expected (Giles & Smith, 1979). That is, when engaging in interactions, people have beliefs about what is appropriate and acceptable behavior. The same principle appears to be true for accommodation. For example, convergence on several dimensions may be evaluated positively; however, convergence on all dimensions may be perceived as insincere or over-facilitative, resulting in misinterpretation of intent and miscommunication, and can therefore be evaluated negatively.

Consider the issue of "overaccommodation." Overaccommodation is a category of miscommunication in which a participant perceives a speaker to exceed the sociolinguistic behaviors deemed necessary for synchronized interaction.

Conversely, underaccommodation is a category of miscommunication in which a speaker is perceived to insufficiently utilize the sociolinguistic behaviors necessary for synchronized interaction (Coupland et al., 1988; Williams & Giles, 1996; Williams et al., 1990). This is akin to perceived maintenance (or even divergence) behaviors where one views his or her interactant as not interested in the conversation, or not exerting effort purposely to distinguish oneself from the interaction. What drives perceptions of optimal levels of interactional involvement, are societally and contextually determined expectations for appropriate behavior.

EXPECTATIONS

Stereotypes

In any society or culture, stereotypes are recognized universally. Although the specific stereotype may differ according to the situation, stereotypes nonetheless permeate every society. Often, stereotypes about characteristics of out-group members are used to create expectations about how individuals may respond in a social encounter (Giles & Noels, 1997). Research has found that people even approximate their behavior to accommodate toward a stereotype they have about the other person; that is, not move toward their actual behavior, but rather converge toward (or diverge from) the more (or less) prestigious image they believe their interlocutor portrays (Azuma, 1997; Coupland et al., 1988; Levin & Lin, 1988).

Another form that accommodating toward stereotypes may take is hypercorrection, or "a 'misfire' attempt at prestige pronunciation" or "linguistic overcompensation" as non-standard speakers provide too much linguistic information attempting to speak a second dialect (Giles & Williams, 1992, p. 343). This behavior has also recently been conceptualized as patronizing talk in interability encounters (Fox & Giles, 1996a) and baby talk in intergenerational interactions (Coupland et al., 1988).

Norms

Another factor that may guide the amount of convergence or divergence one engages in with out-group members are norms regarding language use. Norms are socially shared ideas about what constitutes appropriate or inappropriate behavior in any given situation (Argyle, Furnham & Graham, 1981). DeRidder, Schruijer and Tripathi (1992) contend that when two groups coexist in a society for a long period of time, they establish norms for how members from the two groups should interact with each other. In interpersonal encounters, these norms are often situational. For example, in interpersonal encounters situational norms may drive the amount of convergence or divergence that may occur. However, when the situation is defined as "intergroup," often the norm is for the minority group to converge toward the dominant outgroup (see Amiot & Bourhis, 1999; Moise & Bourhis, 1994).

HISTORICAL MILESTONES IN THE DEVELOPMENT OF CAT

Cross-Disciplinary Influences

Since the original conception of CAT, the theory has enjoyed a vibrant career as a heuristic model for the advancement of research in the discipline of socio-linguistics. Two special journal editions devoted to the theory serve as landmarks in its growth. In the early 1980s, a special issue of the *International Journal of the Sociology of Language* was devoted to the key features of SAT (Giles, 1984). In 1987, Giles et al. expanded SAT to include a wider range of communicative contexts, motives, strategies, and behaviors, and thus proposed that the name of the theory be changed to Communication Accommodation Theory in order to better represent its breadth. In part as a result of this move, in 1988, a special edition of *Language and Communication* focused upon the theoretical move proposed by Giles et al. (1987) from SAT to CAT by identifying recent developments in accommodation research that further elaborated the growth of accommodation theory into a generalized model of situated communicative interaction from its original roots in speech style modification (Coupland & Giles, 1988). In addition, chapters devoted to different facets of language and communication (e.g., Gallois et al., 1995; Giles & Noels, 1997; Giles & Wadleigh, 1999) have also been indicators of the heuristic value and research-rich orientation of the CAT perspective. More recently, renewed interest in the theory has been evidenced by an edited reprint of a portion of the book by Giles and Powesland (1975) on accommodation which appears more than 20 years later in a *Sociolinguistics* reader (see Coupland & Jaworski, 1997b). Further, inclusion of the theory in the *Handbook of Pragmatics* (Coupland, 1995) and the *Handbook of Language Contact* (Niedzielski & Giles, 1996) is additional evidence of accommodation's power and appeal as an explanation for behavior across disciplines.

Theoretical Development

Through research and reconceptualization efforts by CAT theorists, the development of the theory itself has undergone several revisions. In 1982, the move toward a propositional format was introduced (Thakerar et al., 1982; Street & Giles, 1982) and later formalized (Giles et al., 1987). In an effort to present complex and detailed propositions more formally, efforts were also made at predictive models (e.g., Coupland & Giles, 1988; Gallois et al., 1988, 1995). In 1982, Thakerar et al. (as above) pointed to the necessity of considering the "subjective" nature of accommodation, or the idea that what is perceived to be occurring in an interaction is of more importance often than what actually occurs. Further, Coupland et al. (1988) renamed "accommodation strategies" as "approximation strategies," arguing that they were but one subset of attuning behaviors. This move turned the focus of some of the theoretical explanation away from the speakers' perceptions of the addressees' performance patterns toward more of an addressee focus in the field of discourse and health care, specifically intergenerational communication (Williams et al., 1990).

Extensions of CAT

One direction in which CAT has flourished is through the formalization of specific context-driven theories using basic CAT propositions. The tradition in CAT research has been to use the general theory to explain phenomena in a wide range of contexts, such as media (Bell, 1984, 1991), asynchronous communication (Buzzanell et al., 1996), organizational and business contexts (Baker, 1991; Bourhis, 1991; Sparks & Callan, 1992), gender interactions (Boggs & Giles, 1999; Fitzpatrick, Mulac & Dindia, 1995; Hannah & Murachver, 1999), variation within specific cultures (e.g., Azuma, 1997; Jones, 1997; Lawson-Sako & Sachdev, 1996; Ross & Shortreed, 1990), in the courtroom (Aronsson, Jonsson & Linell, 1987; Linell, 1991), and second language research (e.g., Burt, 1994; Zuengler, 1991). The edited volume by Giles, J. Coupland and N. Coupland (1991) focusing upon the "contexts of accommodation" provided the first forum for the accumulation of works that applied CAT to different institutional settings. Since that work, applications of CAT into other areas of research and study have provided innovative extensions of this sociopsychological model of language use.

However, a new direction in which CAT researchers are heading appears to be in specific application and focused upon larger contexts. For example, this type of CAT research has emerged in the areas of intercultural encounters (e.g., Gallois et al., 1995), intergenerational contact (e.g., Fox & Giles, 1993; Ryan, Hummert & Boich, 1995), interability interactions (Fox & Giles, 1996b), ethnolinguistic identity theory (e.g., Giles & Johnson, 1981), the intergroup model of second language learning (e.g., Giles & Byrne, 1982), and nonverbal communication (Giles & Wadleigh, 1999). Thus, instead of utilizing CAT within a context to explain interactions, researchers are now formulating predictive models of CAT focused upon specific areas. In doing so, CAT as a theoretical perspective has expanded beyond its focus upon socially significant dialect, accent, and speech shifts within cultural contexts toward increasingly cross-contextual universal interaction processes as well as new concepts and accommodative (or approximative) strategies. As such, CAT is breaking new theoretical ground once again and must distinguish itself from other prominent theoretical perspectives attempting to explain similar processes.

A COMPARISON OF CAT WITH OTHER THEORIES OF INTERPERSONAL ADAPTATION

Accommodation processes as laid out by CAT (including convergence, divergence, non-accommodation, and maintenance) may be subsumed under the larger rubric of approach–avoidance tendencies or interaction adaptation processes. More specifically, there are many theoretical perspectives examining the processes of reciprocity and compensation – concepts which have frequently been equated with the CAT concepts of convergence and divergence. As such, the theories have much to gain from informing one another about the specific processes operating within interpersonal and intergroup adaptation. Important to any theory is its relation to other theories within the same domain. Often, investigation of the theoretical overlap and distinctiveness between theories explaining similar phenomena may illuminate important theoretical and empirical issues that may otherwise be overlooked. In this manner, we will be able to provide a template by which we may illustrate how CAT provides a complementary perspective to other important explanatory frameworks in the area of adaptation in social interactions. In light of recent developments in CAT, we will briefly review theories that historically precede and exist simultaneously with CAT to illuminate interpersonal adaptation processes. While Guerrero, Alberts and Heisterkamp (this volume, Chapter 3) delve in great detail into the mechanisms of these theories, this review will highlight similarities and differences among the theories; for greater detail, please see the aforementioned chapter.

Theoretical History of Interaction Adaptation

Affiliative conflict theory, or equilibrium theory (Arglye & Dean, 1965) was one of the first theoretical treatments of the processes of interpersonal adaptation. This theory is predicated on the assumption that interactants will attempt to maintain the status quo of an intimacy level that has been established in any relationship. Thus, if verbal or non-verbal expressions of closeness are too high or too low, compensation for that change will occur, in that communicators will make moves to adjust the communication level back to the established baseline for the relationship. Many theoretical perspectives have been developed in response to the claim that compensatory behavior is primary. Further theories make the claim that reciprocity of intimacy behavior is just as likely, if not more likely, during ongoing interactions.

Nonverbal expectancy violation theory (NEVT; Burgoon & Jones, 1976) makes the claim that expectancies, violations of expectancies, arousal, reward valance of the communicator, and behavioral valence all combine to create compensatory or reciprocal responses. Thus, reciprocity would be predicted to occur in response to a positively valenced highly intimate behavior that was above and beyond expectations enacted by a high-reward communicator. Similarly, but much less cognitive in its explanatory calculus, discrepancy arousal theory (DAT; Cappella & Greene, 1984) would claim that the very large change in involvement behavior would be perceived as a large discrepancy and would lead to a very large change in arousal, which would necessarily be aversive and lead to a compensatory response of decreased intimacy behaviors. However, had the discrepancy from what was expected been perceived as only moderate, it would have been predicted to be moderately arousing, leading to pleasant emotional experiences, and reciprocity of increases in intimacy behavior.

Like equilibrium theory, cognitive valence theory (CVT) assumes that there is a level of intimacy displayed between interactants that is comfortable and expected, which results in stable arousal levels (Andersen, 1999). Like NEVT and DAT, increases in intimacy levels lead to arousal, and large arousal changes may lead to automatic responses that bypass cognitive processing. Depending upon the type of arousal change, cognitive valencing of the behavior may occur. Andersen posits six valencers, or cognitive schemata, upon which valencing is dependent: (1) cultural schemata (social norms), (2) relational schemata (relational history), (3) interpersonal schemata (reward potential), (4) situational schemata (environmental context), (5) state schemata (situational personal well-being factors), and, finally, (6) individual schemata (personality traits).

In response to an overwhelming amount of research elucidating reciprocity as the overarching tendency of interactants, regardless of expectancies and other cognitive factors, interaction adaptation theory (IAT) explains interaction behaviors in terms of required, expected and desired levels (Burgoon, Stern & Dillman, 1995). Required behaviors are grounded in basic human needs and drives and translate into what an individual deems is necessary at the time. Expectations refer to anticipated behaviors based on social norms or individuated knowledge of the other's behavior. Desired behaviors are highly personal, and include one's goals, likes, and dislikes. These three needs and behaviors interact to form one's interactional position which represents the "net assessment of what is needed, anticipated, or preferred, as the dyadic interaction pattern in a situation" (Burgoon et al., 1995, p. 266). Further considered in this model is the partner's actual behavior. Thus, the theory predicts reciprocal and compensatory (convergent and divergent) behavior based upon one's interactional position and the partner's actual behavior such that if one is desiring more personal interaction, and the partner provides such interaction, the original interactant will converge toward the partner even more.

Although all of the interaction adaptation theories attempt to explain how and why people create or decrease social distance during ongoing interactions, the explanatory calculi and the scope of the theories are more complementary than overlapping. Expectancy violation theories and interaction adaptation theory all attempt to explain what happens when behavior deviates from a baseline of normality across a wide variety of interpersonal relationships, contexts, and situations. Communication accommodation theory, on the other hand, is primarily interested in social integration across varying groups through the expressions of divergence or convergence. Thus, it might be noted that changes in behavior are more of a causal variable in the expectancy approaches and more of an outcome variable in CAT. In other words, these approaches might inform each other in that CAT might best be used to explain why interactants might violate expectancies (diverge or overaccommodate as the case may be), while the expectancy violation or interaction adaptation approaches might best inform predictions concerning the outcomes associated with the divergence or convergence moves enacted by those in intergroup situations.

One further distinguishing feature of these approaches is that IAT approaches rely on the concepts of reciprocity and compensation, while CAT relies on convergence and divergence (which have been equated conceptually and operationally across a wide variety of studies; Burgoon et al., 1995). Thus, while all of these approaches concern functional communication moves toward or away from one's interactant partner, CAT also incorporates the central and important concepts of non-approximation, non-accommodation, and overaccommodation. Whereas most adaptation approaches rely on assumptions of directedness, behavioral contingency, mutual or unidirectional influence, change versus maintenance, and magnitude versus direction of behavioral change (Burgoon, Dillman & Stern, 1993) to conceptualize and measure convergence or divergence, CAT allows for the additional possibilities that interactants simply come into the interaction with a predisposition to behave and are not adapting to their partner in an attempt to maintain social distance (non-approximation and non-accommodation), and for the possibility that interactants may not be adopting to the actual behavior of their interactant partner, but may be accommodating to cognitive stereotypical assumptions of behavior expected to be exhibited by the outgroup member. Thus doctors of non-Hispanic origins might use higher expressions of immediacy with patients of Hispanic cultures because they expect that Hispanics utilize higher expressions of closeness (e.g., Manusov, 1999). This example illustrates one further linking factor between the interaction adaptation theories and CAT. In situations where individuals are accommodating to expected behavior, they are communicating expectancies and thus the models are also similar with regard to consideration of the effect of cognitive expectancies on interaction adaptation processes.

Nonetheless, the final clear distinction between CAT and other adaptation theories is that the expectancy- and arousal-based theories do not focus upon intergroup processes. Thus, CAT represents a much needed bridge between intergroup and interpersonal considerations. Further, while CAT focuses less specifically on interactional behavior (as originally was the focus of the SAT formulation), it focuses more heavily on issues of distinction and differentiation of social groups, which allows a unique boundary-expansive focus on intergroup processes (see, for example, Tong et al., 1999).

EMPIRICAL SUPPORT

CAT is central to an extensive line of research and theorizing about the antecedents, consequences, and behaviors associated with the movements that individuals undergo to create, maintain, or decrease social distance. As contended above, the state of the theory as it stands now spans several disciplines, contexts, and populations. Although this points to the theory's heuristic appeal and explanatory power, little work has been done to accumulate the research in an organized fashion and to establish the empirical validation of CAT's propositions. Predictive models, such as that in Figure 1, have been forwarded in order to better organize and summarize thinking about CAT (see Coupland et al., 1988; Giles, J. Coupland & N. Coupland, 1991; Gallois et al., 1995) over and above propositions forwarded in previous works (e.g., Giles et al., 1987). In light of these efforts, we attempt to draw together some recent CAT research in language behaviors to coherently synthesize the findings around the predictions set down as models and propositions in previous works (Coupland et al., 1988; Gallois et al., 1995; Giles et al., 1987; Street & Giles, 1982; Thakerar et al., 1982).

SOCIOHISTORICAL CONTEXT

All interactions take place within a context. Of special import to the study of accommodation is the use of language within certain contexts to convey particular social meanings. In fact, the effect of sociohistorical context upon interaction is partly the origin from which CAT began (Giles, 1973, Giles et al., 1977). This portion of the theory posits that the sociohistorical context will predict one's accommodative orientation to interact in a situation, and CAT research overwhelmingly supports the notion that sociostructural relations will affect the degree to which people are predisposed to, or actually will, accommodate to one another (Bourhis, 1983, 1984; Lawson-Sako & Sachdev, 1996). The sociohistorical context is the factor that defines who the dominant (and usually more powerful) group is, to whom one should converge, and from whom one should diverge. In order to evaluate the findings of many CAT studies, knowledge of the sociohistorical context in which the interaction occurred is imperative. Giles (1973) found that the cultural tensions between English and Welsh predicted individuals' likelihood to converge or diverge from the outgroup. In Tunisia, although only 2% of the population speak French as a first language, French is perceived to be a "status" language due to the institutional support afforded to French institutions, so much so that individuals often code-switch between Tunisian Arabic (ingroup language) and French (outgroup) in an effort to simultaneously communicate solidarity and status (Lawson-Sako & Sachdev, 1996). The sociohistorical context has also been found to explain language outcomes in Brunei (Jones, 1997), Canada (e.g., Amiot & Bourhis, 1999; Giles et al., 1973), Vanuatu (Meyerhoff, 1998), Hong Kong (Tong et al., 1999), Catalonia (Woolard, 1989),

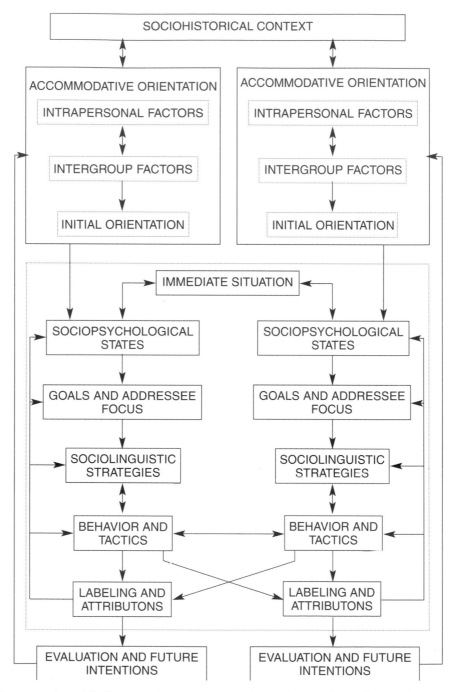

Figure 1 A model of communication accommodation theory (after Gallois et al., 1995)

and Belgium (Bourhis et al., 1979), to name but a few. Thus, an extensive amount of empirical support exists for the prediction that the sociohistorical context influences accommodation attempts and their outcomes.

ACCOMMODATIVE ORIENTATION

The next component in the predictive chain deals with an "individual's ongoing tendency to perceive encounters in either intergroup or interpersonal terms, or both, as well as to converge or diverge psychologically" (Gallois et al., 1995, p. 137). That is, this tendency is predicted by the sociohistorical context and also predicts one's sociopsychological state when entering the interaction. An accommodative orientation itself encompasses intrapersonal, interpersonal, and intergroup factors. Intrapersonal factors deal with relevant social and personal identity issues, and can affect interaction outcomes. For example, Willemyns et al. (1997) found that male job applicants' identification with accent ingroups predicted divergence from outgroup interviewers' accents due to high social identity with their ingroup language. In addition, this area of the theoretical framework may include intergroup factors, such as orientation toward the outgroup. Williams and Giles (1996) reported that conversations perceived by interactants as more indicative of intergroup than interpersonal interaction were also reported as being unsuccessful or personally dissatisfying intergenerational encounters. Also, the element of "accommodative orientation" includes one's interpersonal orientation toward interacting in general. The best established link from interpersonal orientation to accommodative orientation is social desirability. That is, individuals reporting high concern with social desirability are highly likely to converge to their interacting partner on any number of behaviors (e.g., duration of switching pauses) (Natalé, 1975).

SOCIOPSYCHOLOGICAL STATES

Sociopsychological state describes speakers' immediate orientation and short-term motivation in the interaction at hand, and is posited to be predicted by accommodative orientation as well as other factors occurring within the interaction itself. Often, stereotypes and expectations may affect this. For example, young people reportedly hold many negative expectations about interacting with older individuals that affect their likelihood of seeking out such interactions in the future and enjoying them when they occur (Williams & Giles, 1996). Similarly, Boves, van Hout and Vieregge (1990) found that perceived status of the interacting partner affected speech behaviors such that subjects' ratings of their partner were based more on stereotypes held about the relations between status and speech than the actual speech itself. Another study found that perceived status affected the amount of accommodation that occurred. The host of a popular American talk show, Larry King, changed the pitch of his voice as a function of his guests' status (e.g., he converged more toward President Clinton than toward former Vice-President Dan Quayle) whereas guests of lower status would accommodate more to Larry King than he would to them (Gregory & Webster, 1996).

IMMEDIATE SITUATION

This concept captures situational variables that are likely to occur in any encounter and are posited to be related to individuals' sociopsychological states in the interaction. Situational variables include norms and roles that prescribe behavior in any given context. Often, the norms prescribed by the situation override any ability to accommodate at all. Genesee and Bourhis (1988) found that norms appropriate for work roles influenced code choice in interactions between salesmen and customers. Status and solidarity norms were found to guide interpretations of student–lecturer encounters. Behaviors that were over- or under-accommodating behavior were found to be neither typical nor appropriate for either students or lecturers, suggesting that there were limits for acceptable behavior in these situations (Jones et al., 1994).

GOALS AND ADDRESSEE FOCUS: SOCIOLINGUISTIC STRATEGIES

This area of focus includes the short-term motivations to accommodate in social interaction mentioned above: gaining approval, identification with the other, differentiation from interlocutor, and efficient communication. Very few studies actually ask people to report their interactional goals when interacting with others. Rather, this motivation is often inferred by outside observers. Thus, very little direct empirical support has been found for this conceptual link in CAT research.

In addition, this area of research forwarded by the study of accommodation in intergenerational encounters (Coupland et al., 1988) includes focus upon the other's conversational needs, such as attending to productive performance, conversational competence, conversational needs, role relations, and emotional/relational needs. Jones et al. (1994) found that when interacting with academic staff overaccommodating students were rated as utilizing interpersonal control strategies in that they were perceived to be "trying to take the lecturer's power, treating the lecturer as an equal, talking down to the lecturer, and not trying to find common ground with the lecturer" (p. 168). Younger adults strategically varied their speech style when interacting with older adults. That is, younger adults spoke more slowly, used more words and utterances but shorter sentences, and used fewer propositions in response to the conversational needs of their older interaction partners, which were behaviors not used with their younger counterparts (Kemper et al., 1995). In another study of topic management in native–non-native English-speaking dyads, American students relied upon topics of conversation that revolved around the situation at hand in mixed dyads (native–non-native English speaker) more than when interacting with another native English speaker in an attempt to accommodate the Asian international student's lack of familiarity with many implicitly understood "American" topics (Chen & Cegala, 1994).

BEHAVIOR AND TACTICS

The behaviors exhibited in interactions are, by far, the focus of the greatest amount of CAT research to date. The strategies undertaken during interaction affect the behaviors that are displayed in the interaction, which in turn affect the attributions made about each interactant. Research in the area of communicative tactics focuses upon a variety of verbal and nonverbal behaviors studied in an effort to identify objective accommodation strategies. Traditional CAT researchers have focused on convergence and divergence in speech behaviors, such as topic choice and management (Chen & Cegala, 1994), language intensity (Aune & Kikuchi, 1993), interruptions (Hannah & Murachver, 1999), response latency and speech rate (Street, 1984), turn duration (Putnam & Street, 1984), code/language choice (Burt, 1994; Ross & Shortreed, 1990), speaking time (Willemyns et al., 1997), accent mobility (Giles, 1973), and, most recently, patronizing talk (e.g., Fox & Giles, 1996b). In an interesting study on student convergence to professors' answering-machine messages that were either novel or normal, Buzzanell et al. (1996) found that, under this power differential, students converged on some language variables across conditions, such as temporal markers, spatial markers, and denotative specificity, but not on use of qualifiers.

LABELING AND ATTRIBUTIONS

Often, the labels attributed to one's behavior are the driving forces behind the trajectory of an interaction. If intent is labeled positively, convergence may occur (Simard et al., 1976) whereas labeling of behaviors as insincere or patronizing may result in negative evaluation of behavior (e.g., Fox & Giles, 1996a). Several studies have found this to be true. For instance, in the intergenerational realm, in dissatisfying communication encounters between young and older interactants, the older interactants' behaviors were rated by the younger interlocutors as underaccommodative and negatively expressive (Williams & Giles, 1996). Aune and Kikuchi (1993) found that as convergence in language intensity (or deviation from neutrality about a topic) increased, so did perceived source credibility. Actual similarity related positively to perceptions of extroversion and sociability, while perceived similarity corre-lated with perceptions of competence, sociability, and character. Lawson-Sako and Sachdev (1996) found that, in Jordan, individuals who switched codes (indicating greatest convergence) were rated more internationally minded and highly educated as well as cooperative. Competence and social attractiveness have also been associated with greater response latency similarity, speech rate, and response latency convergence (Street, 1984).

Also of growing interest in CAT research are the concepts of over- and under-accommodation (as noted above). That is, individuals take in another's be-haviors and label them as appropriate or inappropriate (over- or underaccommodating) for the situation (Coupland et al., 1988). In a direct test of the effect of over- and underaccommodation upon the evaluation of individuals' behaviors, Jones et al. (1994) found that solidarity ratings were highest for individuals engaging in accommodative behaviors, whereas ratings of status and power were highest for rule-violating over- or underaccommodative behaviors. Edwards and Noller (1993) found evidence that potential miscommunication may occur in intergenerational caregiving interactions due to differing percep-tions of what constitutes patronizing versus respectful talk. Elderly participants rated several vignettes of patient and caregiver interaction as much less patroniz-ing and more respectful than did the nursing and psychology students, who rated the behaviors as overaccommadative or patronizing.

EVALUATION AND FUTURE INTENTIONS

Once two individuals interact, each interlocutor makes evaluations about the other. Based upon these evaluations, decisions about whether future interactions may be possible or desirable are constructed. This may be very important in situations where stereotypes are likely to be formed or expectations for future interaction may be negatively affected. For example, in comparing Anglo-Australians, Chinese nationals, and Chinese Australians, ethnicity influenced individuals' stated future intentions of interacting again, with Anglo-Australians (ingroup members) being rated as the most attractive targets for future interac-tion (Hornsey & Gallois, 1998). Conversely, young individuals who rated inter-generational interactions positively were less likely to stereotype the elderly person with which they interacted and expressed more positive expectations for future interactions than young people who experienced dissatisfying interactions (Williams & Giles, 1996).

CONCLUDING REMARKS

Communication accommodation theory is clearly one of the major theoretical paradigms in the study of language and social interaction. As such, its heuristic appeal has made the perspective a largely interdisciplinary conglomerate of predictions and propositions cutting across contexts, situations, and populations. The purpose of this chapter has been to examine the major concepts and re search history of the perspective, illustrating several critical growth points in the theoretical development. Further, relations to similar theories of approach– avoidance were explored in an attempt to illustrate similarities, as well as distinctiveness. Finally, by identifying a significant amount of empirical validation for CAT's main theoretical propositions (as well as its socially meaningful extensions into the intergroup arena), we hope to have captured readers' imaginations for multiple applications in a wider variety of contexts and its further development and refinement in them.

REFERENCES

Al-Khatib, M. (1995). The impact of interlocutor sex on linguistic accommodation: A case study of Jordan radio phone-in programs. *Multilingua*, **14**, 133–150.

Amiot, C. & Bourhis, R. Y. (1999). *Ethnicity and French–English communication in Montreal*. Paper presented at the 60th Convention of the Canadian Psychological Association, Halifax, NS, May 1999.

Andersen, P. (1999). Creating close relationships through nonverbal communication: A cognitive valence approach. In L.K. Guerrero, J.A. DeVito & M.L. Hecht (Eds), *The nonverbal communication reader: Classic and contemporary readings* (pp. 453–461). Prospect Heights, IL: Waveland Press.

Argyle, M. & Dean, J. (1965). Eye contact, distance, and affiliations. *Sociometry*, **28**, 289–304.

Argyle, M., Furnham, A. & Graham, J.A. (1981). *Social situations*. Cambridge, UK: Cambridge University Press.

Aronsson, K., Jonsson, L. & Linell, P. (1987). The courtroom hearing as a middle ground: Speech accommodation by lawyers and defendants. *Journal of Language and Social Psychology*, **6**, 99–115.

Atkinson, K. & Coupland, N. (1988). Accommodation as ideology. *Language and Communication*, **8**, 821–828.

Aune, R.K. & Kikuchi, T. (1993). Effects of language intensity similarity on perceptions of credibility, relational attributions, and persuasion. *Journal of Language and Social Psychology*, **12**, 224–237.

Azuma, S. (1997). Speech accommodation and Japanese Emperor Hirohito. *Discourse and Society*, **8**, 189–202.

Baker, M.A. (1991). Reciprocal accommodation: A model for reducing gender bias in managerial communication. *Journal of Business Communication*, **28**, 113–130.

Bell, A. (1984). Language style as audience design. *Language in Society*, **13**, 145–204.

Bell, A. (1991) Audience accommodation in the mass media. In H. Giles, J. Coupland & N. Coupland (Eds), *Contexts of accommodation: Developments in applied sociolinguistics* (pp. 69–102). Cambridge, UK: Cambridge University Press.

Berger, C.R. & Bradac, J.J. (1982). *Language and social knowledge*. London: Edward Arnold.

Boggs, C. & Giles, H. (1999). "The canary in the cage": The nonaccommodation cycle in the gendered workplace. *International Journal of Applied Linguistics*, **22**, 223–245.

Bourhis, R.Y. (1979). Language in ethnic interaction: A social psychological approach. In H. Giles & B. Saint Jacques (Eds), *Language and ethnic relations* (pp. 117–141). Oxford: Pergamon.

Bourhis, R.Y. (1983). Language attitudes and self-reports of French–English usage in Quebec. *Journal of Multilingual and Multicultural Development*, **4**, 163–179.

Bourhis, R.Y. (1984). Cross-cultural communication in Montreal: Two field studies since Bill 101. *International Journal of the Sociology of Language*, **46**, 33–47.

Bourhis, R.Y. (1991). Organizational communication and accommodation: Toward some conceptual and empirical links. In H. Giles, J. Coupland & N. Coupland (Eds), *Contexts of accommodation: Developments in applied sociolinguistics* (pp. 270–304). Cambridge, UK: Cambridge University Press.

Bourhis, R.Y. & Giles, H. (1977). The language of intergroup distinctiveness. In H. Giles (Ed.), Language, ethnicity and intergroup relations (pp. 119–135). London: Academic Press.

Bourhis, R.Y., Giles, H. & Lambert, W.E. (1975). Social consequences of accommodating one's style of speech: A cross national investigation. *International Journal of the Sociology of Language*, **6**, 55–72.

Bourhis, R.Y., Giles, H., Leyens, J.P., & Tajfel, H. (1979). Psycholinguistic distinctiveness: Language divergence in Belgium. In H. Giles & R.N. St Clair (Eds), *Language and social psychology* (pp. 158–185). Oxford: Basil Blackwell.

Boves, T., van Hout, R. & Vieregge, W.H. (1990). *Accommodation in cooperative and competitive conversations.* Paper presented to the International Congress of Dialectologists. The Netherlands, July–August.

Bradac, J.J., Mulac, A. & House, A. (1988). Lexical diversity and magnitude of convergent versus divergent style shifting: Perceptual and evaluative consequences. *Languages and Communication*, **8**, 213–228.

Bradac, J.J., Hopper, R. & Wiemann, J.M. (1989). Message effects: Retrospect and prospect. In J.J. Bradac (Ed.), *Message effects in communication science* (pp. 294–317). Newbury Park, CA: Sage.

Burgoon, J.K. & Jones, S.B. (1976). Toward a theory of personal space expectations and their violations. *Human Communication Research*, **2**, 131–146.

Burgoon, J.K., Dillman, L. & Stern, L. (1993). Adaptation in dyadic interaction: Defining and operationalizing patterns of reciprocity and compensation. *Communication Theory*, **3**, 295–316.

Burgoon, J.K., Stern, L.A. & Dillman, L. (1995). *Interpersonal adaptation: Dyadic interaction patterns.* Cambridge, UK: Cambridge University Press.

Burt, S.M. (1994). Code choice in intercultural conversation: Speech accommodation theory and pragmatics. *Pragmatics*, **4**, 535–559.

Burt, S.M. (1998). Monolingual children in a bilingual situation: Protest, accommodation, and linguistic creativity. *Multilingua*, **17**, 361–378.

Buzzanell, P.M., Burrell, N.A., Stafford, R.S. & Berkowitz, S. (1996). When I call you up and you're not there: Application of Communication Accommodation Theory to telephone answering machine messages. *Western Journal of Communication*, **60**, 310–336.

Byrne, D. (1971). *The attraction paradigm.* New York: Academic Press.

Cappella, J.N. & Greene, J.O. (1984). The effects of distance and individual differences in arousability on nonverbal involvement: A test of discrepancy–arousal theory. *Journal of Nonverbal Behavior*, **8**, 259–285.

Cargile, A., Giles, H. & Clément, R. (1996). The role of language in ethnic conflict. In J. Gittler (Ed.), *Conflict knowledge and conflict resolution* (pp. 189–208). Greenwich, CT: JAI Press.

Chen, L. & Cegala, D.J. (1994). Topic management, shared knowledge, and accommodation: A study of communication adaptability. *Research on Language and Social Interaction*, **27**, 389–417.

Coupland, N. (1995). Accommodation theory. In J. Verschueren, J.-O. Ostman & J. Blommaert (Eds), *Handbook of Pragmatics* (pp. 21–26). Amsterdam: John Benjamins.

Coupland, N. & Giles, H. (Eds) (1988). Communication accommodation: Recent developments. *Language and Communication*, **8**, 175–327.

Coupland, N. & Jaworski, A. (1997a). Relevance, accommodation, and conversation: Modeling the social dimension of communication. *Multilingua*, **16**, 235–258.

Coupland, N. & Jaworski, A. (Eds) (1997b). *A Sociolinguistics Reader*. Basingstoke, UK: Macmillan.

Coupland, N., Coupland, J., Giles, H. & Henwood, K. (1988). Accommodating the elderly: Invoking and extending a theory. *Language in Society*, **17**, 1–41.

DeRidder, R., Schruijer, S.G.L. & Tripathi, R.C. (1992). Norm violation as a precipiating factor of negative intergroup relations. In R. DeRidder & R.C. Tripathi (Eds), *Norm violation and intergroup relations* (pp. 3–38). Oxford: Clarendon Press.

Edwards, H. & Noller, P. (1993). Perceptions of overaccommodation used by nurses in communication with the elderly. *Journal of Language and Social Psychology*, **12**, 207–223.

Fitzpatrick, M.A., Mulac, A. & Dindia, K. (1995). Gender-preferential language use in spouse and stranger interaction. *Journal of Language and Social Psychology*, **14**, 18–39.

Fox, S. & Giles, H. (1993). Accommodating intergenerational contact: A critique and theoretical model. *Journal of Aging Studies*, **7**, 423–451.

Fox, S. & Giles, H. (1996a). "Let the wheelchair through!": An intergroup approach to interability communication. In W.P. Robinson (Ed.), *Social groups and identities: Developing legacy of Henri Tajfel* (pp. 215–248). Heinemann: Oxford.

Fox, S.A. & Giles, H. (1996b). Interability communication: Evaluating patronizing encounters. *Journal of Language and Social Psychology*, **15**, 265–290.

Gallois, C. & Callan, V.J. (1991). Interethnic accommodation: The role of norms. In H. Giles, J. Coupland & N. Coupland (Eds), *Contexts of accommodation: Developments in applied sociolinguistics* (pp. 245–269). Cambridge, UK: Cambridge University Press.

Gallois, C., & Giles, H. (1998). Accommodating mutual influence. In M. Palmer (Ed.), *Mutual influence in interpersonal communication: Theory and research in cognition, affect, and behavior* (pp. 135–162). New York: Ablex.

Gallois, C., Franklyn-Stokes, A., Giles, H. & Coupland, N. (1988). Communication accommodation in intercultural encounters. In Y.Y. Kim & W.B. Gudykunst (Eds). *Theories in intercultural communication* (pp. 157–183). Newbury Park, CA: Sage.

Gallois, C., Giles, H., Jones, E., Cargile, A.C. & Ota, H. (1995). Accommodating intercultural encounters: Elaborations and extensions. In R. Wiseman (Ed.), *Intercultural communication theory* (pp. 115–147). Thousand Oaks, CA: Sage.

Genesee, F. & Bourhis, R.Y. (1988). Evaluative reactions to language choice strategies: The role of sociostructural factors. *Language and Communication*, **8**, 229–250.

Giles, H. (1973). Accent mobility: A model and some data. *Anthropological Linguistics*, **15**, 87–109.

Giles, H. (1980). Accommodation theory: Some new directions. *York Papers in Linguistics*, **9**, 105–136.

Giles, H. (Ed.) (1984). The dynamics of speech accommodation. *International Journal of the Sociology of Language*, **46**, 1–155.

Giles, H. & Byrne, J.L. (1982). An intergroup theory of second language acquisition. *Journal of Multilingual and Multicultural Development*, **3**, 17–40.

Giles, H. & Coupland, N. (1991). *Language: Contexts and consequences*. Pacific Grove, CA: Brooks/Cole.

Giles, H. & Johnson, P. (1981). The role of language in ethnic group relations. In J.C. Turner & H. Giles (Eds), *Intergroup behavior* (pp. 199–243). Oxford: Blackwell.

Giles, H. & Noels, K. (1997). Communication accommodation in intercultural encounters. In J. Martin, T. Nakayama & L. Flores (Eds), *Readings in cultural contexts* (pp. 139–149). Mountain View, CA: Mayfield.

Giles, H. & Powesland, P.F. (1975). *Speech style and social evaluation*. London: Academic Press.

Giles, H. & Smith, P.M. (1979). Accommodation theory: Optimal level of convergence. In H. Giles & R. St. Clair (Eds), *Language and social psychology* (pp. 45–65). Oxford: Blackwell.

Giles, H. & Wadleigh, P.M. (1999). Accommodating nonverbally. In L.K. Guerrero, J.A., Devito & M.L. Hecht (Eds), The nonverbal communication reader: Classic and contemporary readings (2nd edn, pp. 425–436). Prospect Heights, IL: Waveland.

Giles, H. & Williams, A. (1992). Accommodating hypercorrection: A communication model. Language and Communication, 12, 343–356.

Giles, H., Taylor, D.M. & Bourhis, R.Y. (1973). Toward a theory of interpersonal accommodation through language: Some Canadian data. Language in Society, 2, 177–192.

Giles, H., Bourhis, R.Y. & Taylor, D.M. (1977). Toward a theory of language in ethnic group relations. In H. Giles (Ed.), Language, ethnicity, and intergroup relations (pp. 307–348). London: Academic Press.

Giles, H., Mulac, A., Bradac, J.J. & Johnson, P. (1987). Speech accommodation theory: The next decade and beyond. In M. McLaughlin (Ed.), Communication yearbook (pp. 13–48). Newbury Park, CA: Sage.

Giles, H. Coupland, J. & Coupland, N. (Eds) (1991). Contexts of accommodation: Developments in applied sociolinguistics. Cambridge, UK: Cambridge University Press.

Giles, H., Coupland, N. & Coupland, J. (1991). Accommodation theory: Communication, context, and consequence. In H. Giles, J. Coupland & N. Coupland (Eds), Contexts of accommodation: Developments in applied sociolinguistics (pp. 1–68). Cambridge, UK: Cambridge University Press.

Gregory, S.W. & Webster, S. (1996). A nonverbal signal in voices of interview partners effectively predicts communication accommodation and social status predictions. Journal of Personality and Social Psychology, 70, 1231–1240.

Gregory, S.W., Dagan, K. & Webster, S. (1997). Evaluating the relation of vocal accommodation in conversation partners' fundamental frequencies to perceptions of communication quality. Journal of Nonverbal Behavior, 21, 23–43.

Hannah, A. & Murachver, T. (1999). Gender and conversational style as predictors of conversational behavior. Journal of Language and Social Psychology, 18, 153–174.

Hogg, M. (1985). Masculine and feminine speech in dyads and groups: A study of speech style and gender salience. Journal of Language and Social Psychology, 4, 99–112.

Hornsey, M. & Gallois, C. (1998). The impact of interpersonal and intergroup communication accommodation on perceptions of Chinese students in Australia. Journal of Language and Social Psychology, 17, 323–347.

Jones, G.M. (1997). Language planning in Brunei Darussalam: The role of accommodation and acculturation. Multilingua, 16, 217–231.

Jones, E., Gallois, C., Barker, M. & Callan, V. (1994). Evaluations of interactions between students and academic staff: Influence of communication accommodation, ethnic group, and status. Journal of Language and Social Psychology, 13, 158–191.

Jones, E., Gallois, C. Barker, M. & Callan, V. (1999). Strategies of accommodation: Development of a coding system for conversational interaction. Journal of Language and Social Psychology, 18, 123–152.

Kemper, S., Vandeputte, D., Rice, K., Cheung, H. & Gubarchuk, J. (1995). Speech adjustments to aging during a referential communication task. Journal of Language and Social Psychology, 14, 40–59.

Labov, W. (1966). The social stratification of English in New York City. Washington, DC: Center for Applied Linguistics.

Lawson-Sako, S. & Sachdev, I. (1996). Ethnolinguistic communication in Tunisian streets: Convergence and divergence. In Y. Suleiman (Ed.) Language and identity in the Middle East and North Africa (pp. 61–79). Richmond, VA: Curzon Press.

Levin, H. & Lin, T. (1988). An accommodating witness. Language and Communication, 8, 195–199.

Linell, P. (1991). Accommodation on trial: Processes of communicative accommodation in courtroom interaction. In H. Giles, J. Coupland & N. Coupland (Eds), Contexts of accommodation: Developments in applied sociolinguistics (pp. 103–130). Cambridge, UK: Cambridge University Press.

Manusov, V. (1999). Stereotypes and nonverbal cues: Showing how we feel about others during cross-cultural interactions. In L.K. Guerrero, J.A. DeVito & M.L. Hecht (Eds), *The nonverbal communication reader: Classic and contemporary readings* (pp. 388–394). Prospect Heights, IL: Waveland Press.

Meyerhoff, M. (1998). Accommodating your data: The use and misuse of accommodation theory in sociolinguistics. *Language and Communication*, **18**, 205–225.

Moise, L.C. & Bourhis, R.Y. (1994). Language et ethnicité: Communication inter-culturelle à Montreal, 1977–1991. *Canadian Ethnic Studies*, **26**, 87–101.

Natalé, M. (1975). Convergence of mean vocal intensity in dyadic communication as a function of social desirability. *Journal of Personality and Social Psychology*, **32**, 790–804.

Niedzielski, N. & Giles, H. (1996). Linguistic accommodation. In H. Goebl, P.H. Nelde, Z. Stary & W. Wolck (Eds), *Contact linguistics: An international handbook of contemporary research* (pp. 332–342). Berlin: Walter de Gruyter.

Putnam, W. & Street, R.L., Jr. (1984). The conception and perception of noncontent speech performance: Implications for speech accommodation theory. *International Journal of the Sociology of Language*, **46**, 97–114.

Ross, S. & Shortreed, I.M. (1990). Japanese foreigner talk: Convergence or divergence? *Journal of Asian Pacific Communication*, **1**, 135–145.

Ryan, E.G., Hummert, M.L. & Boich, L.H. (1995). Communication predicaments of aging: Patronizing behavior toward older adults. *Journal of Language and Social Psychology*, **14**, 144–166.

Simard, L., Taylor, D.M. & Giles, H. (1976). Attribution processes and interpersonal accommodation in a bilingual setting. *Language and Speech*, **19**, 374–387.

Sparks, B. & Callan, V.J. (1992). Communication and the service encounter: The value of convergence. *International Journal of Hospitality Management,* **11**, 213–224.

Street, R.L., Jr. (1982). Evaluation of noncontent speech accommodation. *Language and Communication*, **2**, 13–31.

Street, R.L., Jr (1984). Speech convergence and speech evaluation in fact-finding interviews. *Human Communication Research*, **11**, 139–169.

Street, R.L., Jr & Giles, H. (1982). Speech accommodation theory: A social cognitive approach to language and speech behavior. In M. Roloff & C.R. berger (Eds), *Social cognition and communication* (pp. 193–226). Beverly Hills, CA: Sage.

Tajfel, H. (Ed.) (1978). *Differentiation between social groups*. London: Academic Press.

Thakerar, J., Giles, H. & Cheshire, J. (1982). Psychological and linguistic parameters of speech accommodation theory. In C. Fraser & K.R. Scherer (Eds), *Advances in the social psychology of language* (pp. 205–255). Cambridge, UK: Cambridge University Press.

Tong, Y.-Y., Hong, Y.-Y., Lee, S.-L. & Chiu, C.-Y. (1999). Language use as a carrier of social identity. *International Journal of Intercultural Relations*, **23**, 281–296.

Triandis, H.C. (1960). Cognitive similarity and communication in a dyad. *Human Relations*, **13**, 175–183.

Willemyns, M., Gallois, C., Callan, V.J. & Pittam, J. (1997). Accent accommodation in the job interview: Impact of interviewer accent and gender. *Journal of Language and Social Psychology*, **16**, 3–22.

Williams, A. (1996). Young people's evaluations of intergenerational versus peer under-accommodation: Sometimes older is better? *Journal of Language and Social Psychology*, **15**, 291–311.

Williams, A. & Giles, H. (1996). Intergenerational conversations: Young adults' retrospective accounts. *Human Communication Research*, **23**, 220–250.

Williams, A., Giles, H., Coupland, N., Dalby, M. & Manasse, H. (1990). The communicative contexts of elderly social support and health: A theoretical model. *Health Communication*, **2**, 123–143.

Woolard, K.A. (1989). *Double talk: Bilingualism and the politics of ethnicity in Catalonia*. Stanford, CA: Stanford University Press.

Yaeger-Dror, M. (1991). Linguistic evidence for social psychological attitudes: Hypercorrection or [r] 1 by singers from a Mizrahi background. *Language and Communication*, **11**, 309–331.

Zuengler, J. (1991). Accommodation in native–non-native interactions: Going beyond the "what" to the "why" in second-language research. In H. Giles, J. Coupland & N. Coupland (Eds), *Contexts of accommodation: Developments in applied sociolinguistics* (pp. 223–244). Cambridge, UK: Cambridge University Press.

Discrepancy Arousal Theory and Cognitive Valence Theory

Laura K. Guerrero, Jess K. Alberts *and* **Brian Heisterkamp**
Arizona State University, Tempe, USA

The process of mutual influence has captured the imagination of theorists study-ing social interaction for decades. Conversational partners engage in a series of moves and countermoves, with the verbal and non-verbal behaviors of one individual influencing the behavior of the other individual, and vice versa. These patterns of behavioral adaptation cause messages between two or more people to become more or less similar over time. This chapter focuses on explaining, comparing, and critiquing two popular communication theories that predict such dyadic patterns of mutual influence: Cappella and Greene's (1982) discrepancy arousal theory (DAT) and Andersen's (1985, 1998) cognitive valence theory (CVT).

Although several theories of behavioral adaptation exist, we chose to focus on DAT and CVT because they both cast arousal change as a central player in the adaptation process. In other theories of mutual influence, such as communica-tion accommodation theory (Giles et al., 1987; Street & Giles, 1982) expectancy violations theory (Burgoon, 1978; Burgoon & Hale, 1988), and the sequential–functional model (Patterson, 1983, 1991), arousal change plays a less substantial role. (For more information on these theories, see Chapters 1.1, 1.2, and 1.7). Specifically, DAT and CVT predict that the *level* of arousal change (i.e., high versus moderate change) predicts how one person adapts to another person's behavior. While DAT and CVT share similarities such as this, the two theories differ in several important ways, making it especially fruitful to compare the two. In addition, because both DAT and CVT focus on arousal change, these two theories may be particularly helpful in explaining patterns of adaptation in

The New Handbook of Language and Social Psychology.
Edited by W. Peter Robinson and Howard Giles.
© 2001 John Wiley & Sons Ltd.

arousal-fueled contexts, such as those involving conflict. Thus, this chapter looks at DAT and CVT through three different lenses. First, we explain the theories. Second, the theories are compared and contrasted. Third, we examine the evidence that supports and refutes each theory and propose new research that could lead to theoretical modifications.

DEFINING ADAPTATION AND RELATED TERMS

Before discussing DAT and CVT, it is important to define various terms related to adaptation. Like Burgoon, Stern and Dillman (1995b), we define adaptation as the process whereby people's verbal and non-verbal behaviors are mutually influenced by one another, leading to increased similarity or dissimilarity. Although the term *adaptation* encompasses several different interactional patterns, this chapter focuses on reciprocity and compensation, which are the predicted outcome variables in both DAT and CVT. *Reciprocity* occurs when an individual "responds, in a similar direction, to a partner's behavior" by engaging in behavior that sends a similar (or comparable) message (Burgoon et al., 1995b, p. 129). For reciprocity to take place, one person's response must be *contingent* on the other person's behavior. Also, the enacted response must be functionally comparable to the message triggering the response (e.g., a dominant statement such as "Take out the trash" is met with another dominant statement, such as "Do it yourself"). *Compensation* takes place when one person "responds with behaviors of comparable functional value but in the opposite direction" (Burgoon et al., 1995b, p. 129). For example, if a teenager is upset about having a curfew and says "I hate you" to her mother, the mother might respond by smiling and saying, "I love you anyway" (a compensatory response).

Many theories of adaptation, including DAT and CVT, also include the terms approach and avoidance. *Approach* behaviors are immediacy or involvement cues that increase psychological and physical closeness, signal availability for communication, and express warmth (Andersen, 1985). Examples of approach behaviors include self-disclosure, informal language, close proxemic distancing, touch, forward lean, and non-verbal expressiveness. *Avoidance* behaviors, in contrast, decrease psychological and physical closeness, signal unavailability, and express coldness. Behaviors such as topic avoidance, formal language, far distancing, backward lean, and non-verbal inexpressiveness are typically classified as avoidant.

When the concepts of reciprocity versus compensation, and approach versus avoidance, are considered together, four possible outcomes emerge (see Figure 1), as illustrated by Emily and Fred, a fictional married couple we use as an example throughout this chapter. Imagine that Emily and Fred are at home watching a movie together. The atmosphere is casually intimate. At one point during the movie, Emily tries to increase the level of intimacy by smiling and leaning in extra close to Fred. Fred could respond by engaging in similar

Person B (Fred) reacts by engaging in more:

Person A (Emily):   **Approach Behavior   Avoidant Behavior**

	Approach Behavior	Avoidant Behavior
Increases Approach Behavior	*Reciprocity* (cell 1)	*Compensation* (cell 2)
Increases Avoidant Behavior	*Compensation* (cell 3)	*Reciprocity* (cell 4)

Figure 1   Patterns of reciprocity and compensation

approach behaviors, such as snuggling up to Emily, which would lead to re-ciprocity (cell 1). Or Fred could respond by engaging in avoidance (i.e., pulling away and reaching for the popcorn bowl), which would constitute compensation (cell 2). Now imagine that at a different point during the movie Emily decreases intimacy by ignoring Fred as he comments about the movie. Fred might respond with approach behaviors to try and restore the previous level of interactional intimacy. For example, he might move closer to Emily, ask her "What's wrong?" and try to make her laugh. In this case, compensation would occur (cell 3). However, Fred could instead respond with avoidance behaviors, such as getting off the couch they were sharing and sitting alone on a chair. In this case, re-ciprocity has occurred (cell 4). Although DAT and CVT use somewhat different terminology, both theories examine cells 1 and 2 shown in Figure 1. DAT also examines cells 3 and 4. These two theories are described in more detail next.

DISCREPANCY AROUSAL THEORY

By the early 1980s research had established that mutual influence existed across a variety of expressive behaviors, but no comprehensive theory existed to ex-plain and predict the presence, absence, and extent of mutual influence in ex-pressive behavior. Consequently, Cappella and Greene (1982) developed DAT. Their theory arose out of three pre-existing theories of interspeaker influence: Argyle and Dean's (1965) equilibrium theory, Patterson's (1976) arousal-labeling theory, and Stern's (1974) discrepancy arousal theory. According to equilibrium theory, when one person's affiliation behavior is either greater or less than the level of affiliation desired by a second party, the second party will respond by decreasing or increasing affiliative behavior to establish an equilibrium. Thus, this theory explained compensation, but not reciprocity. In arousal-labeling theory, Patterson (1976) accounted for both compensation and recipocity – positively labeled changes were theorized to be reciprocated, while negatively labeled ones were theorized to be compensated. Cappella and

Greene, however, believed that Patterson overstated the role that labeling played, and that arousal change was more significant in predicting responses. They also believed that the theory's emphasis on cognition was not consistent with actual interaction. That is, since social interaction occurs sequentially in time with speaker switches taking about 0.1 to 0.2 seconds, Patterson's theory could not account for the very brief, almost automatic reactions of respondents to the expressive overtures of others.

Cappella and Greene (1982) argued that Stern's discrepancy arousal theory provided the best platform for developing a comprehensive theory. Stern's theory was similar to Patterson's in that it too was arousal-based, but it differed in that arousal was believed to be a function of the discrepancy between one person's cognitive schema (in this theory, an infant's) and another's behavior (the mother's). Thus, Stern's theory posited that physiological excitation mediated cognitive and affective responses. However, Stern developed his theory only to explain the cycling of involvement in infant–adult interactions. Cappella and Greene believed the theory could be generalized to other expressive behaviors, so they developed DAT.

DAT makes predictions for both non-verbal and verbal communication. In DAT, the term *discrepancy* refers to the difference between expected and actual behavior. Based on situational characteristics, social norms, individual preferences, and past experiences, people expect their partners to engage in a certain "range" of behaviors that fall within an acceptance region. For example, if Emily tells Fred that she received an important promotion at work, she might expect him to display verbal and non-verbal behaviors that indicate support, pride, and/or happiness. A range of behaviors (such as a hug, a compliment, and a high-five) might all fall within this acceptance region.

To the extent that actual behavior differs from expected behavior, discrepancy is experienced. When discrepancies are moderate, Cappella and Greene (1982) theorized that moderate levels of arousal change are also experienced. These moderate discrepancies typically occur *within* the acceptance region. For example, if Fred jumps up, kisses Emily, and then takes her out to dinner, Fred's actual behavior differs somewhat from the expected behavior (i.e., it is more positive and enthusiastic than Emily expected), but it is still probably within the acceptance region. In contrast, Cappella and Greene theorized that high levels of discrepancy, which typically occur when behavior falls *outside* the acceptance region, lead to a correspondingly high increase in arousal. So, if completely contrary to expectations, Fred says "Oh, that's nice, honey" in an apathetic voice and then continues to watch television intently, his behavior is likely to fall outside of Emily's acceptance range and she is likely to feel highly aroused.

According to DAT, there is a direct relationship between the degree of arousal change and the type of affective response (positive versus negative) that people experience. Moderate increases in arousal are theorized to be inherently pleasant, leading to positive emotion. High increases in arousal, in contrast, are theorized to be inherently unpleasant, leading to negative emotion. Thus, people are likely to feel positive affect in response to behaviors that fall within the

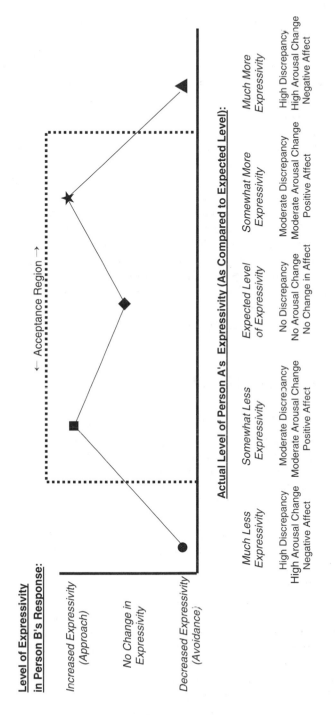

Figure 2 Predictions from Discrepancy-Arousal Theory

acceptance region (and are therefore moderately arousing), and negative affect in response to behaviors that fall outside the acceptance region (and are therefore highly arousing).

In DAT, these affective reactions are then linked to behavioral responses of approach and avoidance. When discrepancy and arousal change are moderate, positive affect is experienced and the individual is likely to engage in approach behaviors. On the other hand, when discrepancy and arousal change are high, negative affect is experienced, and the individual is likely to engage in avoidance (see Figure 2). So, if Emily experiences high levels of arousal and aversion when Fred acts apathetic about her promotion, Cappella and Greene would predict that she would engage in a reciprocal pattern of avoidance (e.g., she might pointedly ignore him). In response to more expected behavior, such as a hug and invitation to dinner, Emily is likely to experience positive affect and to reciprocate by returning Fred's display of non-verbal affection and accepting his invitation to dinner. Imagine, however, that Fred reacts in a way that Emily perceives to be *overly* expressive and affectionate. Perhaps she tells him the news during a business meeting where Emily feels that a strong public display of affection is inappropriate. In this case, Fred's highly affectionate response is likely to fall outside of Emily's region of acceptance even though his behavior is immediate and expressive. As a result, Emily may feel highly aroused and compensate for Fred's behavior by moving away and frowning.

COGNITIVE VALENCE THEORY

Like DAT, CVT, which was originally called arousal valence theory, was grounded in a wealth of empirical research and previous theorizing, most notably Patterson's (1976) arousal-labeling theory and Cappella and Greene's (1982) DAT. Although Andersen (1985) borrowed some principles from these theories, he believed that a complete account of the immediacy exchange process must also include the cognitive factors that help people evaluate immediacy change as positive or negative. Specifically, based on past research, Andersen (1985) argued that: (a) increased immediacy, when perceived, heightens arousal, (b) high levels of arousal change lead to automatic fight or flight responses, whereas moderate levels of arousal change lead to more variable responses, and (c) the six relational valencers impact people's decision to reciprocate or compensate under conditions of moderate arousal change.

As depicted in Figure 3, Andersen's (1985) model starts with the principle that one person must perceive an increase in the partner's level of immediacy if adaptation is to occur. If an individual fails to perceive an increase in immediacy, or if the arousal change connected to the perception of the immediacy increase is low, the interaction proceeds as before and neither reciprocity nor compensation occurs. If an individual perceives an increase in immediacy, and as a result experiences high arousal, CVT predicts that compensation and negative relational outcomes will *always* occur. In contrast, when individuals perceive increases in immediacy and the accompanying arousal change is moderate, Andersen theorizes that *either* reciprocity or compensation can occur based on how the following six cognitive valencers are evaluated: culture, the situation, the relationship, personality, temporary states, and the interpersonal valence of the partner.

Imagine, for example, that Emily discloses something highly personal to Fred in front of a co-worker. According to CVT, this increase in immediacy will be evaluated differently depending on the cognitive valencers. For instance, if the information is highly private, it might not be culturally or situationally appropriate to share in front of a co-worker. The relationship between Emily and Fred may also make a difference. Because they are married, Fred might be more receptive to hearing personal information from Emily than from a stranger. Personality factors, such as how introverted and private Fred is, may also play a role, as might temporary states, such as whether Fred is tired and in a bad mood from having to entertain his co-worker all day. Finally, the interpersonal valence of the partner can be used to help evaluate the increase in immediacy. Interpersonal valence refers to how "rewarding" the person who increases immediacy is (Andersen, 1985, 1998). People who are attractive, credible, and powerful have more leeway to increase immediacy than less rewarding individuals. These cognitive valencers act as a filter or screen for evaluating increases in immediacy. As Andersen has contended, the expectations and cognitive schemata associated with these valencers are already in operation before the immediacy increase occurs. Thus, once the immediacy increase is perceived, individuals usually apply the cognitive valencers very rapidly. When *all* six of these valencers are evaluated positively, Andersen (1992, 1998) predicted that reciprocity will occur (i.e., immediacy will beget more immediacy). The flip side is that when even *one* of the valencers is evaluated negatively, Andersen contended that compensation will occur (i.e., immediacy will beget avoidance). So in the example above CVT would predict compensation rather than reciprocity.

COMPARING AND CONTRASTING THE THEORIES

CVT and DAT share a number of similarities. They both attempt to explain and predict how dyadic partners influence one another verbally and non-verbally during ongoing interaction. Each theory features arousal change as a central factor in this process, and each predicts that high arousal change will automatically lead to aversion, defensiveness, and avoidance. Furthermore, they both include affect and expectancies as components of their theories, although these variables operate differently within the models.

Despite these similarities, CVT and DAT are quite different. DAT, for example, is broader in scope. It includes responses to increases *and* decreases in immediacy behavior, while CVT focuses solely on increases in immediacy. In

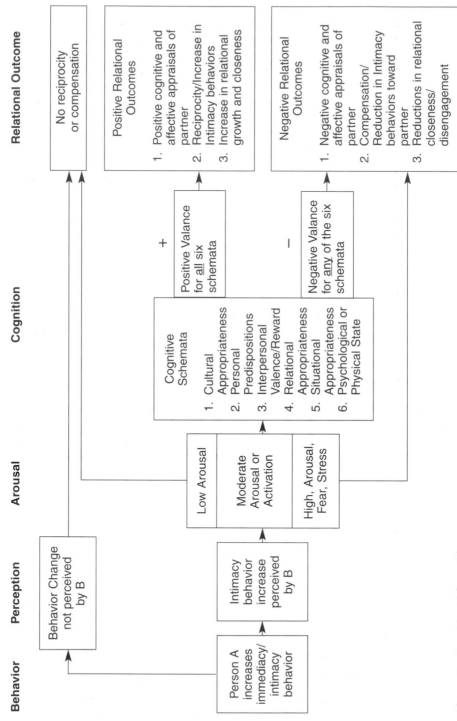

Figure 3   Cognitive Valance Theory

addition, cognition plays a larger and more important role in CVT than in DAT. In DAT, cognition operates in the early stages of the adaptation process. Specifically, it permits individuals to form expectations and to recognize discrepancies. Cognitive processes likely also serve to indicate where a behavior falls within the acceptance/rejection region. Once these activities transpire, however, if arousal occurs, it is arousal that influences an individual's response. Overall, then, cognition appears to play a smaller role than arousal in DAT. In fact, DAT was developed partially in response to models that Cappella and Greene felt were overly cognitive. The quick affective and behavioral responses connected to arousal change were believed to be better able to account for automatic, rapid responses.

In CVT, cognition plays a more central role than does arousal under most circumstances. Highly arousing situations are always aversive; therefore, cognition does not play an active role in individuals' responses in these cases. However, Andersen (1985) argued that *most* immediacy changes produce only moderate arousal. Therefore, because how people respond to moderate arousal is determined by cognitive valencers, cognition is usually a central player in the immediacy exchange process. Of course, as mentioned previously, Andersen believes that cognitive valencers act as an anticipatory frame through which changes in immediacy are viewed. Thus, in most cases, it does not take long to respond to even moderate immediacy changes.

DAT and CVT also differ with regard to the role that affect plays. Affect is a central variable in DAT. The level of arousal change determines whether the resulting affect is positive or negative, and the affect experienced determines whether the individual engages in approach or avoidance behavior. In contrast, in CVT affect is an outcome rather than a predictor variable. Reciprocity is accompanied by positive affect, while compensation is accompanied by negative affect.

Once again, our beleaguered couple, Emily and Fred, can help explain the differences in DAT and CVT. At the end of a long day for Emily, she arrives home to discover that Fred has forgotten to set out the garbage can – again! She is angry and frustrated, because the can is now so full there will be no room for next week's refuse. Fred, on the other hand, left work early to go home and watch his favorite baseball team in the deciding game for the Pennant. Just as Emily enters the house, Fred's team wins the game. He is so excited that as she enters the den he throws his arms around her, gives her a big kiss, and says "We're in the World Series!", which is quite unlike his usual greeting of a peck on the cheek. How will Emily respond?

Assuming that Fred's behavior is moderately arousing and falls within a range of acceptance for the marriage, DAT predicts that Emily will feel increased positive affect (despite her previous bad mood) and respond warmly with approach behavior, perhaps by kissing Fred back. CVT, however, predicts that cognitive valencing would determine whether Emily experiences a positive or negative response. Because at least *one* cognitive valencer is negative (in this case, Emily's temporary state), CVT predicts that Emily would engage in compensatory behavior, such as withdrawing from Fred or complaining about the trash. Thus, the two theories predict different outcomes from the same interaction.

EVALUATING THE THEORIES: EMPIRICAL SUPPORT, CRITICISMS, AND NEW CHALLENGES

Next, our attention turns to evaluating the theories. We begin by discussing two general aspects of DAT and CVT: (1) the arousal–immediacy link, and (2) the inability (so far) to account for mixed reciprocal and compensatory responses. We then discuss some specific issues related to both DAT and CVT.

The Arousal Link

DAT and CVT predict that when one person increases immediacy the partner experiences heightened arousal. DAT also predicts that significant decreases in immediacy lead to arousal change. Numerous studies support this immediacy–arousal link. For example, increases in gaze (Mazur et al., 1980), close distancing and direct body orientation (McBride, King & James, 1965), smiling (Martin & Gardner, 1979), and general non-verbal involvement (Andersen, et al., 1998; Le Poire & Burgoon, 1994) have all been shown to produce arousal change.

Despite these encouraging findings, several issues related to arousal remain unresolved. For instance, it is still unclear how *degree* of arousal change affects both emotional and behavioral outcomes. Both DAT and CVT predict that high levels of arousal change lead to aversive emotional reactions and avoidant responses. This reasoning is based on an inverted U-shaped model of the association between arousal and affective response (see Figure 4). According to this model, there is a curvilinear relationship between arousal and affect, such that low and high levels of arousal lead to negative emotional outcomes, whereas moderate levels of arousal lead to positive emotional outcomes. So far, however, the theories have not been specific regarding where the threshold for high arousal lies, so it is difficult to determine a priori when arousal will be high enough to induce automatic aversion and avoidance. Although proponents of DAT may respond that this occurs once behavior has fallen outside the region of acceptance, a practical way to determine when this region has been violated still needs to be devised.

Some studies (e.g., Andersen et al., 1998; Guerrero, Jones, & Burgoon, 2000; Le Poire & Burgoon, 1994) have induced different levels of immediacy change to determine if high versus moderate levels of arousal change do indeed lead to aversion and compensatory responses. The results of these studies have been mixed. Le Poire and Burgoon, in a study utilizing interviews between strangers wherein the interviewer (who was a confederate) posed as a medical student,

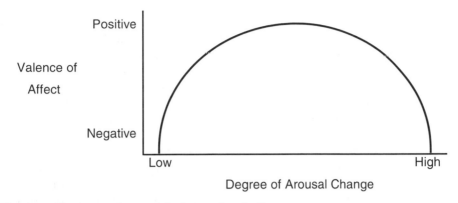

Figure 4 The inverted-U model of arousal and affect

found that immediacy change was not monotonically related to arousal change as DAT and CVT would predict. In fact, more arousal change occurred in a moderately low immediacy condition than a very high or very low immediacy condition, which is contrary to DAT. Guerrero et al.'s study examined reactions to different levels of immediacy within romantic dyads. Reciprocal responses were strongest in a very low immediacy condition. The very low immediacy condition also produced significantly more avoidant responses than a moderately low immediacy condition, as DAT would predict. Andersen et al.'s study utilized interviews between cross-sex friends. Some of the friends (unbeknown to their partners) were instructed to increase immediacy substantially, while others were instructed to increase immediacy moderately. The most arousal change was found in response to high increases in immediacy, as predicted by both DAT and CVT. In addition, moderate increases in immediacy produced purely reciprocal responses, whereas high increases in immediacy produced a mix of reciprocal and compensatory reactions. Taken together, these studies suggest that the most avoidant responses may occur in reaction to very low levels of non-verbal immediacy, and that mixed responses may sometimes surface in the face of very high levels of immediacy.

The question, however, still remains: When is arousal change high enough to lead to automatic aversion and avoidance? In studies manipulating immediacy changes as moderate versus high, when the high condition fails to produce the expected avoidant reaction, the researchers are left wondering, "Was the manipulation strong enough? Was arousal change significantly high?" This lack of specificity in determining a threshold at which arousal change becomes too high makes it difficult to falsify DAT and CVT's prediction that very high levels of arousal automatically produce fight or flight responses.

There may also be different *types* of arousal. Le Poire (1991; Le Poire & Burgoon, 1996) distinguished defensive arousal from an orientation response. A defensive response is based in fear and anxiety, and often produces physiological changes such as rapid heartbeat, constriction of blood vessels, and increases in skin temperature, which all lead to less pulse volume (Le Poire, 1991; Lynn,

1966; Sokolov, 1960). An orientation response, on the other hand, is based on increased attention and vigilance, with orienting individuals scanning their environments to gain more information about the situation and to evaluate their partner and their partner's behavior (Le Poire, 1991; Le Poire & Burgoon, 1996). The orientation response is often accompanied by mild excitement, along with physiological changes such as decreases in heart rate and skin temperature, and increases in pulse volume (Barry, 1982; Le Poire & Burgoon, 1996; Siddle & Packer, 1987; Sokolov, 1960; Spinks, Blowers & Shek, 1985).

The distinction between arousal that is defensive versus orienting adds a new dimension to DAT and CVT. Both theories appear to predict that very high levels of arousal are always defensive, thereby leading to fight or flight responses (Andersen et al., 1998). Other theories, such as expectancy violations theory (Burgoon & Hale, 1988; see also Chapter 1.2) predict that very high levels of arousal can be orienting rather than defensive. Thus, in DAT and CVT, unexpected increases in immediacy that lead to very high levels of arousal change *always* produce defensiveness and avoidance. In theories such as EVT, very high levels of arousal change can also lead to an orienting response, which causes a person to evaluate the situation and the partner, and can ultimately lead to either approach or avoidance. Of course, it would be consistent with DAT and CVT if an orienting response followed moderate changes in immediacy. In many situations, however, people may experience both types of arousal during a given interaction (Andersen et al., 1998; Le Poire & Burgoon, 1994, 1996). People might "orient" to their environments before labeling a behavior as threatening and becoming defensive. Or they might automatically become defensive, scan the environment for more information, and then either relax or become even more defensive.

To complicate matters even further, it is difficult to obtain a valid measure of physiological arousal. Although some studies have shown that certain nonverbal behavior is sometimes correlated with indices of physiological arousal (e.g., Buller et al., 1995; Burgoon et al., 1989), these correlations are not consistent across studies. Moreover, measures of physiological arousal, such as increases in heart beat, blood pressure, and skin temperature, often fail to produce significant intercorrelations (see Buller et al., 1995). Thus, another challenge for researchers studying DAT and CVT involves finding ways to accurately measure arousal.

Some researchers also question whether the inverted U-shaped model of the arousal/affect relationship really holds true, despite the empirical support it has received. According to this model (see Figure 4), it is impossible to be both very highly aroused *and* to experience positive affect, because high levels of arousal interfere with a person's ability to enjoy a particular stimulus. Other researchers, however, have suggested that arousal and affect are independent factors, and that highly unexpected, arousing behavior can sometimes be positive. In the emotion research, it is common to describe a given emotion based on its placement on two orthogonal dimensions of arousal (active versus passive) and affect (positive versus negative). For example, in Russell's (1980) circumplex model, emotions such as fear and anger are defined by high arousal and negative affect, while emotions such as joy and exhilaration are defined by high arousal and positive affect. According to this model, it is possible for people to experience high levels of arousal and *either* positive or negative emotion simultaneously, which runs counter to the logic behind both DAT and CVT.

An example might illustrate this point even further. Imagine the many different experiences a married couple such as Fred and Emily have over the course of their relationship. They are likely to have exhilarating highs and excruciating lows. Telling one another "I love you" for the first time, having sex, and seeing their child born are likely to be arousing, positive experiences. Of course, like most couples, Fred and Emily are likely to go through their rough spots, such as their first big fight, being separated from one another, and experiencing periods of boredom or uncertainty. The question becomes, are these negative experiences inherently more arousing than positive experiences? If they are, then the inverted U-shaped relationship between affect and arousal makes sense. But if events eliciting positive emotion can be just as arousing and powerful as those eliciting negative emotion, then affect and arousal are more likely to be independent factors. Future research is needed to determine which of these models (inverted U-shaped versus independent) best describes the affect–arousal relationship. If the independent model is the better description, DAT and CVT may need to be revised.

Accounting for Mixed Responses

DAT and CVT both predict that *either* compensation or reciprocity occurs in response to changes in immediacy. However, some studies have shown that a mixed pattern of compensation and reciprocity sometimes emerges. Hale and Burgoon (1984), for example, concluded that although their data showed overwhelming evidence for reciprocity in terms of affect and involvement, there were also some compensatory reactions that functioned to maintain equilibrium so that sensory stimulation did not escalate or de-escalate too rapidly. A data set analyzed in Burgoon et al.'s (1995b) book, as well as a study by Guerrero and Burgoon (1996), found consistent patterns of reciprocation for immediacy increases but a mix of reciprocity and compensation for immediacy decreases. These two studies suggest that decreases in immediacy may be met with less positive affect and expressiveness (reciprocity), but more kinesic activity and attention (compensation).

In some cases, a mix of compensation and reciprocity may emerge in response to *very high increases* in immediacy. For instance, Burgoon, Le Poire, and Rosenthal (1995a) found that individuals in high involvement conditions sometimes compensated if they were uncomfortable. They also found that there was an "emotional contagion" effect, with vocal unpleasantness increasing over time when one encountered an unpleasant partner. Andersen et al. (1998) found

reciprocity to prevail in response to moderate increases in non-verbal immediacy. However, both reciprocity and compensation followed high increases in
immediacy. Specifically, observers reported that negative arousal, adaptors, and
blocking behaviors (such as putting a hand in front one's face or body) all
peaked right after the partner increased immediacy, which showed evidence for
compensation. Nonetheless, increases in positive arousal, overall involvement,
and positive affect also followed the increase in immediacy, indicating that reciprocity occurred as well.

Given that studies have produced mixed patterns of reciprocity and compensation, DAT and CVT should be modified to include such a prediction. The
mechanisms for making such a prediction may already be embedded within these
theories. In DAT, the placement of a given behavior within or outside the region
of acceptance may help explain when mixed responses are most likely to occur.
Behaviors falling well within the region of acceptance may be most likely to
produce strictly approach responses, while behaviors falling well outside of the
region of acceptance may be most likely to produce strictly avoidant responses.
Those responses that are closer to the edge of the region of acceptance may
produce more ambivalent, mixed responses. In CVT, the weighting of the different valencers may be key to predicting the likelihood of mixed responses. In
some cases, all six of the cognitive valencers might be relevant to the situation at
hand, whereas in other cases only a subset may be applicable. If all of the
relevant cognitive valencers are evaluated positively, then approach behavior
would appear to be highly likely. If all relevant valencers are evaluated negatively, then avoidant behavior seems to be the most likely outcome. However, if
the relevant valencers are evaluated differently (e.g., some are evaluated
positively and others negatively), a mixed response may occur.

Specific Issues Related to DAT

Various attempts have been made to support DAT's claims. One such attempt
sought to determine the acceptance region width, that is, the size of individuals'
positive versus negative affect regions. In this study, Cappella and Greene (1984)
tested the hypothesis that high-sensation seekers would have wider acceptance
regions compared to low sensation seekers. A wider acceptance region was
thought to cause high sensation seekers to react less negatively to proximal inva-
sions and, consequently, to have a weaker compensatory reaction. In the study,
confederate interviewers sat at a near or normal distance from participants who
had completed a measure of sensation seeking. Initial results did not support the
hypothesis. However, subsidiary analysis using a combined state–trait sensation-
seeking scale did find that those who evaluated the proximity violations more
positively compensated less on eye gaze, lean, and directness of body orientation.
Thus, the researchers found limited support for the notion that personality disposition, in this case sensation seeking, causes differences in reactions to arousal.

Le Poire and Burgoon's (1994) study, which was described earlier, called into question some of the linkages in DAT. In this study, participants' responses to changes in involvement (either very low, low, high, or very high involvement changes) were evaluated along three dimensions: physiological arousal, affective state, and involvement behavior. According to DAT, the very high and very low involvement conditions should have produced the largest arousal changes, followed by the low and high conditions. Instead, low involvement was met with the largest changes in arousal, while very low involvement was met with the smallest changes. The expected arousal to emotional linkages were not supported either. Moderate changes in arousal should have led to positive responses, while large changes should have led to negative responses. Thus, the high involvement and low involvement conditions should have generated the highest positive responses. Although the high involvement condition did lead to the highest positive responses, the low involvement condition did not. Finally, the linkages from emotional experience to behavioral response did not follow DAT predictions. Based on DAT, the low and high conditions should have elicited approach behavior and the two extreme conditions should have elicited avoidance behavior. These patterns did not occur.

However, Le Poire and Burgoon (1994) also found that if arousal was dropped as a mediator then the size of involvement change directly affected emotional experience in a fashion consistent with DAT. They discovered that emotional positivity decreased as discrepancy increased. Therefore, they suggested that DAT could "increase parsimony and predictive validity by removing the troublesome variable of arousal" (p. 587). Thus, discrepancy arousal theory would become discrepancy theory, a theory in which the size of the discrepancy predicts both emotional experience and approach or avoidance responses, but not in a monotonic manner.

Andersen et al.'s (1998) study (described earlier) found mixed support for DAT as well. Results indicated that, as DAT predicts, the highest levels of arousal were found in response to high (as opposed to moderate) increases in immediacy, whether using self-reports, observer reports, or physiological indices. In addition, moderate increases in immediacy produced purely reciprocal responses as DAT predicts, but high increases in immediacy produced a mix of reciprocal and compensatory reactions rather than only the compensatory responses predicted by DAT.

In addition to refining the linkages between discrepancies, arousal, affect, and behavior, DAT may be improved by incorporating a clearer operationalization of the acceptance/rejection region. The notion of an acceptance region is one of the most elegant features in DAT, yet the theory is unclear in terms of the factors that contribute to the establishment of the acceptance region. Perhaps some of the cognitive valencers in CVT, such as the nature of the relationship, the situation, and personality variables, play a role in defining what behavior is deemed acceptable versus unacceptable. Thus, a challenge for researchers testing DAT is to establish a priori what behaviors are likely to be acceptable or unacceptable for a given dyad within a given interactional setting.

Taken together, these findings suggest that work remains to be done before DAT will possess as much predictive ability as its creators had hoped for. The role of arousal, if any, needs to be clarified, and some objective way of determining individuals' acceptance regions must be determined.

Specific Issues Related to CVT

Despite the rich theoretical base that Andersen drew upon, little empirical research has been conducted to directly test CVT. One study testing CVT utilized an account analysis to determine how people react to excessive intimacy (Andersen, 1992). This study found that the relationship was the key valencer predicting responses to very high levels of immediacy. This suggests that the valencers may not all be weighted equally. Indeed, in situations between acquainted interpersonal partners, the relationship factor may be the most critical. In another study, Andersen et al. (1998) tested two hypotheses that were highly relevant to CVT. First, they manipulated immediacy change so that some people received a high level of immediacy change whereas other people received a moderate immediacy change. Consistent with the basic ideas underlying CVT, people showed more negative arousal and defensiveness in the high versus moderate immediacy change conditions. However, as mentioned before, the high immediacy condition also produced some reciprocity, which is inconsistent with CVT. Second, Andersen et al. tested to see whether the moderate immediacy condition would produce greater variability in affective and behavioral responses. The logic here was that if high immediacy changes produce automatic compensatory responses, while moderate immediacy changes produce a wide range of responses based on the composition of the cognitive valencers, then moderate increases in immediacy would be met with more variable responses. However, Andersen et al.'s study failed to support this hypothesis.

Clearly, much more work needs to be done to determine if the principles underlying CVT hold up under empirical scrutiny. Besides inducing moderate versus high immediacy change, scholars should manipulate and measure the various cognitive valencers. For example, researchers could induce positive or negative moods in subjects before subjecting them to immediacy change (e.g., perhaps by showing them "happy" or "sad" video clips before they interact), to see if temporary state influences their reactions. Researchers could also see what relational characteristics (e.g., trust, closeness, attraction) affect how people react to changes in verbal and non-verbal immediacy. In any case, it is essential that future research examine how the cognitive valencers work if CVT is to advance.

Future work should also address some of the criticisms that have been offered regarding CVT. Specifically, Burgoon et al. (1995b) noted that CVT, like DAT, is "at odds with literature showing that high positive arousal can lead to approach and reciprocity; that is, not all large arousal changes are negatively valenced and not all of them result in compensation" (p. 109). Burgoon et al. also criticized CVT for focusing only on increased immediacy, rather than trying to explain reactions to both increased and decreased immediacy, as theories such as DAT and expectancy violations theory do. Because of this narrower focus, CVT is disadvantaged when it comes to theoretical scope.

Perhaps the key criticism of CVT, however, revolves around the prediction that *all* six cognitive valencers must be evaluated positively if reciprocity is to occur. This prediction is at odds with both everyday experience and empirical evidence. Take Emily and Fred as an example. Imagine it is Fred's 40th birthday. He comes home in a bad mood after working all day and just wants to relax alone with his family. Emily, however, planned a small surprise party for him. When Fred walks through the door, a group of a dozen or so family and friends yells "Surprise!" and Emily walks over and kisses him. Even though Fred wishes he could plop down on the couch and say "Thanks everyone, but I'd rather not," he returns Emily's kiss and smiles at everyone. In a case such as this, the one negatively valenced behavior (being in a bad mood) would probably not be enough to cause an avoidant reaction. Instead, Fred put more weight on other factors, such as his relationship with Emily (e.g., he probably didn't want to hurt her feelings) and his public image (e.g., he probably didn't want to seem ungrateful).

In addition, if the contention that all six valencers needed to be positive was carried to its logical conclusion, a considerable amount of compensation would occur since it is unlikely that all six valencers would be positive most of the time. Yet the preponderance of literature suggests that reciprocity or matching is more prevalent than compensation (see Burgoon et al., 1995b). For example, studies have shown that romantic partners tend to match touch behavior (Guerrero & Andersen, 1994) and that smiling tends to be reciprocated in a variety of social situations (e.g., Kendon, 1967). Similarly, studies examining multiple immediacy cues have found stronger patterns of reciprocity than compensation across a variety of situations and relationships (Andersen et al., 1998; Guerrero & Burgoon, 1996; Guerrero et al., 1998; Le Poire & Burgoon, 1994; Manusov, 1995). Thus, the empirical evidence suggests that CVT's prediction that all six cognitive valencers need to be evaluated positively for reciprocity to occur needs to be revisited.

CONCLUSION

As this chapter has illustrated, DAT and CVT both provide useful frameworks for explaining interpersonal processes related to reciprocity and compensation. Both theories would also benefit from further research. Specifically, we have suggested the following four lines of inquiry: (1) determining if and when high arousal change leads to negative affective and behavioral responses; (2) ascertaining the conditions under which mixed reciprocal and compensatory reactions occur, perhaps by employing the region of acceptance from DAT, and/or the cognitive valencers in CVT; (3) devising ways to determine where exactly behaviors falls within or outside the region of acceptance in DAT; and (4) determining how the cognitive valencers work together, including whether some valencers are more important than others, and whether all six really need to be positively valenced for reciprocity to occur.

In addition to this call for tests of specific theoretical principles, we believe that the research on DAT and CVT should be expanded to include more of a focus on language as well as a focus on arousal-charged contexts, such as those involving conflict, relational disengagement, possessiveness, stalking, and sexual harassment. In terms of language, little research has investigated how verbal and non-verbal immediacy work together. In fact, studies testing DAT and CVT, as well as many other theories of adaptation, have typically looked at non-verbal reactions to non-verbal immediacy changes. Yet immediacy includes verbal behaviors such as self-disclosure, using "we" statements instead of "I" statements, and using informal as opposed to formal language (Andersen, 1985). It is easy to think of practical examples of reciprocity and compensation involving verbal communication. For example, if Emily starts acting cold and distant to Fred, he might try to compensate by asking "What's wrong, honey? Did I do something again?" or by telling her a funny story or joke to try to relieve the tension. Indeed, these types of verbal and non-verbal sequences were common in Guerrero's (1994) data. In fact, observers often gave more weight to verbal statements than non-verbal behaviors when judging whether reciprocity or compensation took place (see also Guerrero et al., 2000).

DAT and CVT also seem particularly suited for examining emotionally charged interactions. Andersen (1992; Wertin & Andersen, 1996) has started to do this with his work using CVT to explain reactions to excessive intimacy and sexual harassment. Similarly, work on interpersonal conflict might benefit from an application of DAT, particularly since some of the most consistent findings related to the reciprocity of negativity are found in the research on conflict. This research shows that people often have a hard time initiating positive, compensatory actions when their partners are behaving negatively (Rusbult, Drigotas & Verette, 1994), but a sound theoretical explanation for these negative cycles of behavior has yet to be forwarded. Perhaps DAT can help – once conflict behaviors fall outside the region of acceptance, they may engender so much arousal that they automatically lead to negative affective and behavioral reactions. If this is the case, it would be important for couples (like our friends Emily and Fred) to learn what behaviors fall outside of one another's acceptance regions, and to refrain from using these behaviors in the first place. A DAT explanation also fits with the common practical advice people are given – to take a break and cool down once conflict starts to escalate.

Interpersonal conflict is but one of many examples we could have used to illustrate the far-reaching power that theories such as DAT and CVT could have if applied to different behaviors and contexts. Adaptation is a universal human process that shapes human interaction. Theories such as DAT and CVT take us one step closer to understanding this complex, intricate process. If DAT and CVT are refined further and extended to different behaviors and contexts, we believe the steps they take will be even bigger and bolder.

REFERENCES

Andersen, P.A. (1985). Nonverbal immediacy in interpersonal communication. In A.W. Siegman & S. Feldstein (Eds), *Multichannel integrations of nonverbal behavior* (pp. 1–36). Hillsdale, NJ: Erlbaum.

Andersen, P.A. (1992). *Excessive intimacy: An account analysis of behaviors, cognitive schemata, affect, and relational outcomes.* Paper presented at the 6th International Conference on Personal Relationships, Orono, ME, July 1992.

Andersen, P.A. (1998). The cognitive valence theory of intimate communication. In M. Palmer & G.A. Barnett (Eds), *Progress in communication sciences, Vol 14: Mutual influence in interpersonal communication theory and research in cognition, affect, and behavior* (pp. 39–72). Norwood, NJ: Ablex.

Andersen, P.A., Guerrero, L.K., Buller, D.B., & Jorgensen, P.F. (1998). An empirical comparison of three theories of nonverbal immediacy exchange. *Human Communication Research*, **24**, 501–535.

Argyle, M. & Dean, J. (1965). Eye contact, distance, and affiliation. *Sociometry*, **28**, 289–304.

Barry, R.J. (1982). Novelty and significance effects in the fractionation of phasic OR measures: A synthesis with traditional OR theory. *Psychophysiology*, **19**, 28–35.

Buller, D.B., Jorgensen, P.F., Andersen, P.A. & Guerrero, L.K. (1995). *Correspondence among physiological, nonverbal, and perceptual measures of arousal.* Paper presented at the annual meeting of the International Network on Personal Relationships, Williamsburg, VA, June 1995.

Burgoon, J.K. (1978). A communication model of personal space violations: Explication and an initial test. *Human Communication Research*, **4**, 129–142.

Burgoon, J.K., & Hale, J.L. (1988). Nonverbal expectancy violations. Model elaboration and application to immediacy behaviors. *Communication Monographs*, **55**, 58–79.

Burgoon, J.K., Kelley, D.L., Newton, D.A. & Keeley-Dyreson, M.P. (1989). The nature of arousal and nonverbal indices. *Human Communication Research*, **16**, 217–255.

Burgoon, J.K., & Le Poire, B.A. & Rosenthal, R. (1995a). Effects of preinteraction expectancies and target communication on perceiver reciprocity and compensation in dyadic interaction. *Journal of Experimental Social Psychology*, **31**, 287–321.

Burgoon, J.K., Stern, L.A. & Dillman, L. (1995b). *Interpersonal adaptation: Dyadic Interaction patterns.* Cambridge, UK: Cambridge University Press.

Cappella, J.N. & Greene, J.O. (1982). A discrepancy-arousal explanation of mutual influence in expressive behavior for adult and infant-adult interaction. *Communication Monographs*, **49**, 89–114.

Cappella, J.N. & Greene, J.O. (1984). The effects of distance and individual differences in arousability on nonverbal involvement: A test of discrepancy-arousal theory. *Journal of Nonverbal Behavior*, **8**, 259–286.

Giles, H., Mulac, A., Bradac, J.J. & Johnson, P. (1987). Speech accommodation theory: The next decade and beyond. In M. McLaughlin (Ed.), *Communication yearbook 10* (pp. 13–48). Newbury Park, CA: Sage.

Guerrero, L.K. (1994). *An application of attachment theory to relational messages and nonverbal behaviors in romantic relationships.* Unpublished PhD dissertation, University of Arizona, Tucson.

Guerrero, L.K. & Andersen, P.A. (1994). Patterns of matching and initiation: Touch behavior and touch avoidance across relational stages. *Journal of Nonverbal Behavior*, **18**, 137–154.

Guerrero, L.K. & Burgoon, J.K. (1996). Attachment styles and reactions to nonverbal involvement change in romantic dyads: Patterns of reciprocity and compensation. *Human Communication Research*, **22**, 335–370.

Guerrero, L.K., Jones, S.M. & Burgoon, J.K. (2000). Responses to nonverbal intimacy change in romantic dyads: Effects of behavioral valence, degree of behavioral change on nonverbal and verbal reactions. *Communication Monographs*, **67**, 325–346.

Hale, J.L. & Burgoon, J.K. (1984). Models of reactions to changes in nonverbal immediacy. *Journal of Nonverbal Behavior*, **8**, 287–314.

Kendon, A. (1967). Some functions of gaze direction in social interaction. *Acta Psychologica*, **26**, 22–63.

Le Poire, B.A. (1991). Orientation and defensive reactions as alternatives to arousal in theories of nonverbal reactions to changes in immediacy. *Southern Communication Journal*, **56**, 138–146.

Le Poire, B.A. & Burgoon, J.K. (1994). Two contrasting explanations of involvement violations: Expectancy violations theory versus discrepancy arousal theory. *Human Communication Research*, **20**, 560–591.

Le Poire, B.A. & Burgoon, J.K. (1996). Usefulness of differentiating arousal responses within communication theories: Orienting response or defensive arousal within nonverbal theories of expectancy violation? *Communication Monographs*, **63**, 208–230.

Lynn, R. (1966). *Attention, arousal, and the orientation reaction.* Oxford, UK: Pergamon.

Manusov, V. (1995). Reacting to changes in nonverbal behaviors: Relational satisfaction and adaptation patterns in romantic dyads. *Human Communication Research*, **21**, 456–477.

Martin, W.W. & Gardner, S.N. (1979). The relative effects of eye-gaze and smiling on arousal in asocial situations. *Journal of Psychology*, **102**, 253–259.

Mazur, A., Rosa, E., Faupel, M., Heller, J., Leen, R. & Thurman, B. (1980). Physiological aspects of communication via natural gaze. *American Journal of Sociology*, **86**, 50–74.

McBride, G., King, M.G. & James, J.W. (1965). Social proximity effects of galvanic skin responses in adult humans. *Journal of Psychology*, **61**, 153–157.

Patterson, M.L. (1976). An arousal model of interpersonal intimacy. *Psychological Review*, **83**, 235–245.

Patterson, M.L. (1983). *Nonverbal behavior: A functional perspective.* New York: Springer.

Patterson, M.L. (1991). A functional approach to nonverbal exchange. In R. Feldman & B. Rimé (Eds), *Fundamentals of nonverbal behaviour* (pp. 458–495). Cambridge: Cambridge University Press.

Rusbult, C.E., Drigotas, S.M. & Verette, J. (1994). The investment model: An interdependence analysis of commitment processes and relationship maintenance phenomena. In D.J. Canary & L. Stafford (Eds), *Communication and relational maintenance* (pp. 115–139). San Diego, CA: Academic Press.

Russell, J.A. (1980). A circumplex model of affect. *Journal of Personality and Social Psychology*, **36**, 1152–1168.

Siddle, D.A.T. & Packer, J.S. (1987). Stimulus omission and dishabituation of the electrodermal orienting response: The allocation of processing resources. *Psychophysiology*, **24**, 181–190.

Sokolov, E.N. (1960). Neuronal models and the orienting reflex. In M.A. Brazier (Ed.), *The central nervous system and behavior* (pp. 1–24). New York: Macy.

Spinks, J.A., Blowers, G.H., & Shek, D.T.L. (1985). The role of the orienting response in anticipation of information: A skin conductance response study. *Psychophysiology*, **22**, 385–394.

Stern, D.N. (1974). Mother and infant at play: The dyadic interaction involving facial, vocal, and gaze behavior. In M. Lewis & L.A. Rosenblum (Eds), *The effect of the infant on its caregiver* (pp. 187–213). New York: Wiley.

Street, R.L. & Giles, H. (1982). Speech accommodation theory: A social cognitive approach to language and speech behavior. In M. Roloff & C.R. Berger (Eds), *Social cognition and communication* (pp. 198–226). Beverly Hills, CA: Sage.

Wertin, L. & Andersen, P.A. (1996). *Cognitive schemata and perceptions of sexual harassment.* Paper presented at the annual meeting of the Western States Communication Association, Pasadena, CA.

1.4

Expectancy Theories

Judee K. Burgoon *and* **Michael Burgoon**
University of Arizona, Tucson, USA

The ubiquity of expectancies in guiding human conduct is so widely conceded that it is perhaps unsurprising that expectancy-related concepts populate, under one guise or another, so many theories of human communication and psychology. If we were to cast our net widely enough to encompass all the concepts that are kin to expectancies (e.g., schemata, scripts, frames, norms, anticipatory responses, advance organizers, predictions) or that parade under an expectancy banner (e.g., expectancy value theory, expectancy or behavioral confirmation, the theory of reasoned action, social cognition theory), few theories would escape our ken. Impracticalities of such breadth aside, our own span of expertise, space limitations, and our interest in *social* phenomena have led us to draw the net more narrowly to highlight three theories that pertain to *social interaction*. That is, we focus on instances where Person A's expectations regarding Person(s) B's behavior affect Person A's attitudes, values, and behaviors. Thus, excluded are intra-individual theories such as Mitchell's (1982) expectancy value theory and Fishbein and Ajzen's (1975) theory of reasoned action, which represent instances of Person A's expectations regarding consequences of one's own actions influencing self behavior. The current compilation covers M. Burgoon's language expectancy theory, J. Berger and colleagues' expectation states theory, and J. Burgoon's expectancy violations theory. In addition to having generated a substantial body of research, these theories represent a good sampling of perspectives on expectancies and their violations emanating from the fields and foci of social psychology, sociology, and communication. Throughout, we attempt to highlight similarities and differences among these theories.

The New Handbook of Language and Social Psychology.
Edited by W. Peter Robinson and Howard Giles.
© 2001 John Wiley & Sons Ltd.

DEFINING EXPECTANCIES AND VIOLATIONS

The terms "expectancy" and "expectation" are used here interchangeably to refer to "the act, action, or state of expecting" (Webster's, 1985, p. 292). This definition in itself is not particularly informative. Burgoon and Walther (1990) offer a more precise definition as pertains to social behavior, in this case, communication. They define expectations as enduring cognitions about the anticipated verbal and non-verbal communication of others. Expectations may range from the general – based on contemporaneous roles, rules, norms, and practices that apply to a given culture, community, or context – to the particular – person-specific knowledge related to another's typical communication practices. Expectancy-related theories pitched at the macroscopic (sociological) level draw upon that which is typical, modal, or commonplace for a class of individuals or acts. Theories pitched at the microscopic (interpersonal or psychological) level base predictions for a given individual, message, or transaction on a combination of generic expectancies and any individuating knowledge of how the actor's behavior deviates from those general patterns. The expectation that fear appeals motivate a desire to avoid or escape unpleasant forms of arousal is a macro-level expectation, as is the expectation that physicians as a group will use directives as their primary means of communicating with patients. The expectation that a familiar male friend will avoid nonverbal intimacies is a micro-level expectation that incorporates knowledge of how males and friends typically behave but also adjusts it for one's personal experience with the individual. (Parenthetically, it should be noted that the definition of expectancies adopted here differs from Fishbein & Ajzen's, 1975, theory of reasoned action and other expectancy value theories in which the term "expectations" is reserved for personality-based anticipations of consequences and is distinguished from social norms as alternative guides to behavior. Here, the rubric of expectancy incorporates both.) If the three theories to be reviewed were arrayed on a macroscopic to microscopic continuum, language expectancy theory would qualify as the most molar by virtue of relying entirely on social norms as the basis for expectancies; expectation states would fall in the middle ranges; and expectancy violations theory would be the most particularized because it includes both diffuse and context- or person-specific expectancies.

A further pivotal distinction that needs to be made regarding expectancies is whether they are regarded as predictive or prescriptive. Predictive expectancies pertain only to the typicality of behavior, to its central tendency or regularity of occurrence (as might be measured by the mean, median or mode). Prescriptive expectancies pertain to idealized standards for conduct. They capture evaluative connotations of behavior such as appropriateness and desirability; i.e., they carry an associated *valence* ranging from negative to positive. To say that a guest is expected to arrive at 8 p.m. may mean either that this is the anticipated time of arrival (predictive expectancy) or that this is the appropriate time of arrival (prescriptive expectancy). Recent work (e.g., Burgoon & White, 1997; Floyd & Burgoon, 1999) has attempted to create a crisper distinction by reserving the term "expected" for the predictive variety and using the term "desired" for that which is valenced, but this does not entirely escape the conundrum of social norms, which are both typical and positively valenced, differing from what the individual prefers from another. It may be predictively and prescriptively expected to avoid public displays of affection, for instance, yet a newly engaged couple may desire such behavior from their partner. Though these definitional distinctions have yet to be fully ironed out, the larger point is that many theories employing expectancy concepts lack comparability because they are not operating on the same conceptual plane.

Expectations usually apply to a range or "bandwidth" of typical or accepted behavior rather than to a precise point. It follows, then, that expectancy violations are acts which fall outside that range; that is, they deviate sufficiently from the typical or customary pattern to be regarded as deviant or unexpected. Afifi and Burgoon (2000), among others, note that a violative act need not penetrate conscious awareness to qualify as a violation. It need only surpass some subliminal threshold of recognition and response to qualify (see also Burgoon, 1978). Although much literature regards all expectancy violations as invariably negative (see, for example, Argyle & Dean, 1965; Cappella & Greene, 1984; Cupach & Spitzberg, 1994; Kellermann & Reynolds, 1990; Tedeschi & Norman, 1985), we shall see that violations may also be positively valenced, a possibility that has implications for all expectancy-related theories.

LANGUAGE EXPECTANCY THEORY

In 1985, M. Burgoon and G.R. Miller offered the first complete explication of their theory on the relationship between language and persuasion, which they opened with the following introduction:

> Our language affects our lives powerfully. Others make attributions about social and professional status, background and education, and even the intent of communication by evaluating our language choices. Those intrigued with social influence, whether classical scholars or media image-makers, have long pondered the influence of such language choices on the success or failure of persuasive attempts. The decision to appeal to people's logic or emotional side is manifest in the language used in persuasive messages: persuaders try to mollify, justify, terrify, or crucify by altering the language in their appeals. (pp. 52–53)

Their theory, language expectancy theory (LET; M. Burgoon, 1989, 1990, 1995; M. Burgoon, Jones & Stewart, 1975; M. Burgoon & G.R. Miller, 1985) has undergone a number of iterations, refinements, and extensions over the past 25 years. Compared to the other theoretical positions to be introduced in this chapter, LET was originally *more restrictive* in scope in terms of the situations to which it might be applied. For example, LET specifically excluded interpersonal, relational, and other forms of communication in which altering attitudes and/or behaviors was not the primary or sole goal of the actor. However, while restrictive in this sense, LET was actually *more expansive* than existing models or theories within the social influence literature in that it included not just persuasion (passive paradigm of attitude/behavior change) but also self-persuasion (active participation and forced compliance paradigms), and, importantly, resistance to persuasion, which until that time had been treated as an entirely separate and distinct line of inquiry. LET forged new ground by providing a unified view which incorporates all three areas of research inquiry under one theoretical umbrella.

LET begins with the assumption that language is a rule-governed system and people develop macro-sociological expectations and preferences concerning the language or message strategies employed by others in persuasive attempts. These expectations are primarily a function of (1) cultural norms, and (2) sociological norms. Preferences, according to this sociological perspective, are usually a function of cultural values and societal standards or ideals for what is competent communication performance.

Associated with LET is a detailed propositional logic. The formative explanatory calculus, first outlined by M. Burgoon and G.R. Miller (1985) and later refined substantially by M. Burgoon (1989, 1990; M. Burgoon & J.K. Burgoon, 1990), with the most detailed exposition of the revision appeared in the earlier edition of this handbook (Giles & Robinson, 1990). For purposes of a brief summary, Table 1 from that volume presents the basic tenets of LET.

Table 1   Summary of expectancy theory predictions about message strategies and attitude/behavior change

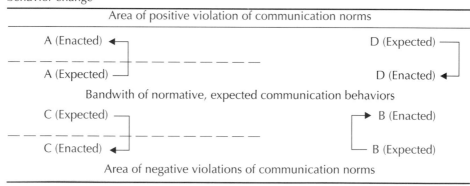

| Area of positive violation of communication norms |
| A (Enacted) ← | D (Expected) |
| A (Expected) | D (Enacted) ← |
| Bandwith of normative, expected communication behaviors |
| C (Expected) | → B (Enacted) |
| C (Enacted) ← | B (Expected) |
| Area of negative violations of communication norms |

Case A.   Positive violation of expectations by performing unexpected, positively valued behaviors. Enacted behavior outside the expected, normative bandwidth in positive direction. Attitude/behavior change in the direction advocated by the source.

Case B.   Positive violation of expectations by negatively evaluated source conforming more closely to norms of communication behavior. Enacted behavior within the expected normative bandwidth. Attitude/behavior change prediction in direction advocated by the source.

Case C.   Negative violation of expectations by performing unexpected, negatively valued behaviors. Enacted behavior outside the expected normative bandwidth in negative direction. No attitude/behavior change or actual changes in opposite direction advocated by the source.

Case D.   Negative violation of expectations by positively evaluated source conforming more closely to norms of communication behavior. Enacted behavior within the normative bandwidth. No attitude/behavior change or actual changes in opposite direction advocated by the source (Burgoon, Birk, & Hall, 1991, p. 183).

Briefly, changes in the direction desired by an actor occur when positive violations of expectations occur. Positive violations obtain in two ways: (1) when the enacted behavior is better or more preferred than that which was expected in the situation, or (2) when negatively evaluated sources conform more closely than expected to cultural values, societal norms, or situational exigencies. Change occurs in the first case because enacted behavior is outside the normative bandwidth in a positive direction and such behavior prompts attitude and or behavioral changes. In the second condition, a person who is expected to behave incompetently or inappropriately conforms to cultural norms and/or expected social roles, which results in an overly positive evaluation of the source and, subsequently, change advocated by that actor. Negative violations of expectations result from language choices or the selection of message strategies that lie outside the bandwidth of socially acceptable behavior in a negative direction. The result is no attitude and/or behavioral changes, or changes in the opposite direction intended by the actor.

The etiology of LET, detailed by M. Burgoon (1995) in a *festschrift* for his collaborator, the late Gerry Miller, warrants some abbreviated retelling in this chapter because of its serendipitous and seminal role in bridging disparate lines of inquiry. At the time of these empirical efforts, there was no real sub-area in the social sciences that combined language and social psychology. Rather, scholars worked in relative isolation around the world and the thought of a handbook, let alone a second edition, exploring the intersection of language interests and "mainstream social psychology" was simply not imaginable. In the last part of the 1960s, the predominant paradigm for studying attitude change was distinctly cognitive in nature and primarily concerned with intrapsychic processes that facilitated or inhibited the reception of and subsequent acceptance of variously structured suasory messages (cf. Festinger, 1957; McGuire, 1969). Less, albeit some, research was focused on processual variables that moderated the impact of specific persuasive messages. However, some research, such as that related to source credibility and prestige suggestion, concerned situations in which attitudes induced by one event influenced attitudes toward another event. For example, simply linking a message with different names could alter people's responses to that message (e.g., Hovland & Weiss, 1952). While no one now would claim this as novel, this led to efforts by social psychologists and communication scientists to examine those instances in which the message and source are somehow directly linked. Other, wholly separate research being conducted by mass media scholars (Pool & Shulman, 1959) attempted to identify situations in which events preceding the reception of a given message influence the communication process. Pool and Shulman (1959) posited that such events create attitudinal response sets which alter the performance of professional encoders. For example, reporters thinking about liked people or pleasant events prior to receiving a writing assignment were better able to write a "good" news story than one containing "bad" news; conversely, reporters thinking about disliked people or events excelled at writing about bad news. M. Burgoon (1970a) hypothesized that the same phenomenon exists in the reception of messages and tested this in a series of experiments. Yet other research showed that so-called differential attitudinal response sets dramatically affected interpretation and acceptance of messages of social import. All of this research was variable-analytic in nature, guided by little more than devising clever manipulations of response sets that might bias subsequent persuasive attempts.

Brooks (1970) followed a bit of a different track in looking at "reversals of previously held attitudes" and specifically at stereotypes. He concluded his brief research report with an insightful comment that sparked the formal development of LET:

> . . . the possibility of contrast effects should be considered. This principle assumes that we carry stereotypes into such social situations as the public speech. There, the speaker's behavior may be discrepant with stereotyped expectations. If the discrepant stimuli cannot be assimilated or ignored, they are likely to be exaggerated in a listener's perception. . . . One explanation . . . is this: unfavorable (or favorable) speakers may be perceived more (or less) favorably not because their behavior is intrinsically persuasive (or dissuasive) but because it contrasts with stereotyped expectations which audiences hold. . . . (p. 154)

These comments prompted questions about the nature of what Brooks called stereotypes, and what determines what would later be labeled as expectations. First, to what degree could the individual as a unit of analysis be jettisoned in favor of a more aggregate look at shared expectations of groups and even societies? Second, would it not be fruitful to pursue research to determine if there are indeed cultural and sociological forces that shape our patterns of ordinary language and determine normative and non-normative usage? There was ample evidence to assume that as communicators mature, they not only learn the mechanics of language, but also what to say and when to say it. Finally, the question of whether such normative expectations were limited to notorious (or popular) public figures, as used in previous research, or applied to all communicators of a given type, group, class, or even all societal members was intriguing. The previously discussed research (Brooks, 1970; M. Burgoon, 1970a) demonstrated that receivers do have shared expectations about the behaviors a communicator *should* exhibit. When these expectations are violated, receivers overreact to the behaviors *actually* exhibited. If an actor is initially perceived negatively, then demonstrates more positive behavior than anticipated, receivers overestimate the positiveness of the unanticipated behaviors (McPeek & Edwards, 1975). The reverse also holds: when an initially positively valenced communicator exhibits unexpectedly negative communication behaviors, receivers exaggerate their negative evaluation of the communicator and/or the message.

While much of the research on expectancy violations involved situations where persuasive actors took unexpected positions or advanced unexpected arguments, another line of research, co-occurring in time (M. Burgoon, 1970b; M. Burgoon & G.R. Miller, 1971), but not resident in any coordinated intellectual plan, was investigating the persuasive impacts of linguistic variations in advocacy attempts. This research, which later proved quite valuable in developing LET, was originally little more than a garden variety variable-analytic program focusing on the effects of persuasive messages varying in language intensity (i.e., the degree to which an actor makes language choices that deviate from neutrality). Burgoon and Chase (1973), working in the resistance to persuasion (inoculation) paradigm, found that refutational pretreatment messages, varying in the use of intense language, created linguistic expectations in subsequent attack messages. When those expectations were met, maximal resistance to persuasion obtained; when linguistic expectations were violated in attack messages, resistance to persuasion was not induced. Later, M.D. Miller and M. Burgoon (1979) further extended knowledge about the relationship between linguistic violations of expectations and the induction of resistance to persuasion by employing a simple expectancy model not requiring inoculation strategies (i.e., refutational pretreatment messages).

In a series of empirical studies, M. Burgoon and associates (M. Burgoon & Stewart, 1975; Jones & M. Burgoon, 1975; M. Burgoon, 1975) provided experimental tests of the combined effects of the previously separate work on communicator-focused and structural linguistic expectations. They identified types of individuals (e.g., females and low credible communicators) who were presumed to be expected to use less aggressive language choices in their persuasive messages. Such people using more instrumental verbal aggression (a term coined much, much later) were seen as negatively violating expectations and, thus, attitude change was inhibited. Further it was revealed that males and high-credible sources could use either aggressive or unaggressive verbal strategies and be persuasive. However, it seemed that more aggressive behavior was the expected and/or preferred mode of argument only for highly credible male advocates. The results of these empirical tests of expectancy-based predictions were accompanied by a discussion of what was then called a message-centered theory of persuasion. What was actually presented was a kernel, perhaps more aptly called a skeletal, formulation of what would later be developed as LET. Arguments were advanced that were markedly different from prevailing theories of social influence of the day.

First, the focus was distinctly macro-social in orientation. It was argued that entire social categories (e.g., females, members of different ethnic groups) were bound by relatively rigid normative expectations of what was "appropriate" or expected communication behavior. Such expectations were not unique to specific communicators, but to aggregates of like individuals in this society. Second, the concept of normative bandwidths (see Table 1), of differential size, for expected language behaviors was empirically demonstrated. People of high credibility and male speakers in general appeared to have linguistic freedom (wide bandwidths) and could select from a number of persuasive strategies without violating pre-set expectations. On the other hand, large numbers of the population had constricted bandwidths of expected communication behaviors, and concomitantly very constrained choices in how they could argue if they wished to be successful at persuasion. Finally, this elementary theoretical formulation provided a plausible explanation for "boomerang" effects, change opposite to the position advocated by the communicator, that had proven enigmatic to persuasion researchers at the time: people negatively violating expectations produce such a contrast effect that people move to opposing attitudinal positions in order to distance themselves from the advocacy of such communicators.

As previously noted, M. Burgoon and G.R. Miller (1985) first attempted to explicate LET as an umbrella for understanding a wealth of diverse, often confusing and contradictory findings in three different persuasive paradigms. Several studies within the traditional passive message reception paradigm (G.R. Miller & M. Burgoon, 1973) investigated situations in which communicators create messages designed to change the attitudes/behaviors of message receivers. A second research effort investigated a radically different persuasive context labeled the active participation paradigm. Most of these studies required the target persuadee to engage in counterattitudinal advocacy, taking positions that they themselves did not hold. The third area was the resistance to persuasion paradigm, where inhibition of persuasive attempts was the paramount concern.

This attempt at theory construction was distinctly not variable-analytic in nature, nor guided by inductive inference making. The purpose in developing the original framework of deductively embedded propositions was to explain extant empirical regularities (and seeming irregularities) in the general body of published social influence research. Burgoon and Miller (1985) carefully articulated the nature of the body of knowledge that their resultant propositional framework would incorporate. They claimed that although their research (and that of many others) could be grouped under the above three broad headings, numerous other questions were also addressed in their examination of the research evidence. They listed the major issues dealt with at various stages as they formulated their original attempt to articulate LET:

1. The research selected language variables commonly used in persuasive appeals.
2. Considerable attention was devoted to determining the relationship between specific communicator attributes (e.g., credibility and gender) and language choices as a determinant of persuasive success or failure.
3. Some attention was given to investigating selected receiver attributes.

Although much has been written about the propositional framework that constitutes LET, it is useful to restate the original propositions and present refinements and extensions since the theory was first published in 1985. The first three below undergird what has already been previewed in some detail.

Proposition 1. People develop cultural and sociological expectations about language behaviors which subsequently affect their acceptance or rejection of persuasive messages.

Proposition 2. Use of language that negatively violates societal expectations about appropriate persuasive communication behavior inhibits persuasive behavior and either results in no attitude change or changes in position opposite to that advocated by the communicator.

Proposition 3. Use of language that positively violates societal expectations about appropriate persuasive communication behavior facilitates persuasive effectiveness.

Detailed reviews of the fear appeals literature, research on opinionatedness, and language intensity are readily available in the social influence literature. M. Burgoon (1989) extended that review to include a number of micro-level message variables as special cases of what has been called a type of instrumental verbal aggression (which includes, but is not limited, to fear appeals, opinionated language, language intensity, and aggressive compliance-gaining strategies). In a chapter published in the earlier edition of this Handbook shortly after that review and extension of LET, M. Burgoon (1990) also explained the results of more macro-level persuasion strategies (e.g., sequential message strategies such as foot-in-the-door (Dillard, Hunter & Burgoon, 1984) and door-in-the face (Cann, Sherman & Elkes, 1975) techniques, as well as the compliance-gaining message strategy research (cf. Marwell & Schmitt, 1967a, 1967b; Miller et al., 1977, 1987) from an expectancy theory perspective. From those efforts, summaries of the contributions made by such an extending beyond just language intensity predictions (Burgoon & Miller, 1985) can be economically stated in the next set of expanded and refined propositions:

Proposition 4. People in this society have normative expectations about the level of fear-arousing appeals, opinionated language, language intensity, sequential message techniques, and compliance-gaining attempts varying in instrumental verbal aggression appropriate to persuasive discourse.

Proposition 5. Highly credible communicators have the freedom (wide bandwidth) to select varied language strategies and compliance-gaining techniques in developing persuasive messages, while low credible communicators must conform to more limited language options and compliance-gaining messages if they wish to be effective.

Proposition 6. Because of normative impacts of source credibility, high credible sources can use low intensity appeals and more aggressive compliance-gaining messages than low credible communicators using either strong or mild language or more pro-social compliance-gaining strategies.

Proposition 7. Communicators perceived as low credible or those unsure of their perceived credibility will usually be more persuasive if they employ appeals low in instrumental verbal aggression or elect to use more pro-social compliance-gaining message strategies.

Proposition 8. People in this society have normative expectations about appropriate persuasive communication behavior which are gender specific such that (a) males are usually more persuasive using highly intense persuasive appeals and compliance-gaining message attempts, while (b) females are usually more persuasive using low intensity appeals and unaggressive compliance-gaining messages.

Proposition 9. Fear arousal that is irrelevant to the content of the message outlining the harmful consequences of failure to comply with the advocated position mediates receptivity to different levels of language intensity and compliance-gaining strategies varying in instrumental verbal aggression such that (a) receivers aroused by the induction of irrelevant fear or suffering from specific anxiety are most receptive to persuasive messages using low intensity and verbally unaggressive compliance-gaining attempts but unreceptive to intense appeals or verbally aggressive suasory strategies.

One criticism that might be lodged against LET research is the possibility that it is teleological in nature (M. Burgoon, 1995). Since normative sociological or ex-pected communication behaviors have not been specified on an a priori basis, it is difficult, if not impossible in many situations, to determine when a positive or negative violation of expectations obtained. Some investigators have concluded that when attitude/behavior change occurs, a positive violation of expectations must have occurred. Similarly, when no attitude/behavior change occurs or there is a boomerang effect, the conclusions drawn are that a negative violation must have occurred. Such interpretations of the empirical data make the theoretical model unfalsifiable. While such a criticism should be directed more at the way science is sometimes conducted than at the theoretical model per se, a priori specification of expectations in experimental situations makes for much stronger scientific claims.

M. Burgoon (1995) claims that the next step is to make the theoretical model less dependent on experimental research of the social psychological type and to present evidence of generalizability beyond laboratory situations that rely pri-marily on convenience samples of undergraduate students. While such criticisms apply to much, or even most empirical work in communication, tests of the theory in applied contexts, using samples more representative of the population at large, have now provided robust and useful tests of the utility of the theoreti-cal formulations.

LET has not been well supported with data illuminating how expectations develop between the same persuader and persuadee over time, or how they impact sequential message acceptance and/or eventual compliance with pos-itions advocated. In an attempt to begin to address such issues, Klingle and Burgoon (1995) undertook an ambitious extension of earlier work that studied adult patients in a number of health care settings where a physician interacted with the same patient in six sequential clinical visits. Expectations for the final scenario were manipulated by varying the amount of verbal aggression (positive or negative kinds of reinforcing messages) over time. Some subjects viewed only patients receiving negative feedback and aggressive communication; others saw patients receiving positive regard and feedback for all six sessions. Still other subjects evaluated different combinations of aggressive and non-aggressive physician communication behavior over time. Gender of the physician was also a predictor of the impacts of different kinds of communication in this clinical context. The resultant reinforcement expectancy theory interpretation extended knowledge of how expectations develop in sequential interactions between the same people and in a very real situation demonstrated the potency of expectancy violations on attitudes/behaviors.

Fortunately, the potential for LET in disease prevention and control efforts has been recognized by a variety of funding agencies. Such extramural support[1] has allowed for tests of this theoretical formulation with family practice patients (Burgoon, Birk & Hall, 1991), with pediatricians and school participants using mediated communication in sun safety campaigns (Buller, Borland & Burgoon, 1998); and with children and adolescents using interactive computer technology in anti-smoking campaigns (Grandpre et al., 1999). In addition to providing evidence of the ecological validity of the propositions of LET, this program of research has also demonstrated that the effect sizes attributable to expectancy violation manipulations in such situations are non-trivial and match, or in most cases, exceed the effect sizes published in earlier laboratory research. Thus, the robust explanatory power of the theory in important social situations continues to accrue impressive support.

Whether the effects of expectancy violations, or any other experimental manipulations in the attitude/behavior literature, are transitory or enduring is difficult to answer without the resources to do longitudinal research. Buller et al. (2000) provide compelling evidence of the long-term effects of predicted language intensity violations on both attitudes toward sun safety and actual behaviors of parents to protect children from sun risks. Current research efforts include testing a number of LET predictions over a three-year period in a 3200+ employee teaching hospital. This effort is aimed at the reduction of tobacco use and the increase of health and wellness in a diverse workforce.[2] Another multi-year longitudinal research design is examining the effects of expectancy violations in mass media campaigns intended to reduce inhalant and marijuana use by adolescents.[3] Obviously, the ability to put a single theoretical formulation to rigorous test in important social situations is a rare opportunity to advance science and also gratifying to one who has spent much of a career attempting to develop LET.

EXPECTATION STATES THEORY

In contrast to the social psychological grounding from which LET evolved, this theory (EST) and its progeny trace their origins to sociological theorizing about task-related encounters. Its domain is therefore group behavior and group performance. As is common in sociological theories, issues of roles, power, and status play a central role.

---

[1] Funding has been provided to the second author for research testing the effects of expectancies in a number of disease prevention and control projects (National Cancer Institute CA62968; National Institutes of Child Health and Development HD31360; Arizona Disease Control Research Commission 9804).
[2] This research is supported by a program project from the Arizona Disease Control Research Commission 9905, Michael Burgoon, Principal Investigator.
[3] Support for the drug prevention research is provided to the second author by the National Institutes of Drug Abuse DA12578. In all cases, the opinions and conclusions of the second author are not necessarily those of the various funding agencies.

Specifically, EST revolves around expectations that establish a *power and prestige order* in groups and thus influence group performance (Berger, Conner & Fisek, 1974; Berger et al., 1977; Ridgeway & Berger, 1986; Ridgeway & Walker, 1995; Shelly, 1998). In face-to-face interactions involving a task focus, individuals develop *performance expectations*: "group members" expectations about the value of their own and other's contributions to group activities' (Ridgeway & Walker, 1995, p. 288). These performance expectations may be general or specific. General expectations arise out of diffuse status characteristics such as gender, age, socio-economic status, occupation, intelligence, or physical attractiveness. These kinds of general status characteristics create general expectations of valued or devalued contributions to group processes and outcomes. Specific expectations are linked to individuals' potential to perform in a clearly defined situation. For example, reputation as a "legal eagle" would create expectations of expertise in a task involving legal ramifications. Specific status characteristics are thought to exert more influence than diffuse ones.

The aggregate of these expectations creates an *order of performance expectations* among group members; i.e., it creates an array from highest to lowest degree of anticipated power and prestige, and establishes each actor's *expectation advantage or disadvantage* relative to other actors in the group. Performance expectations are regarded as implicit, often unconscious views about others' likelihood of contributing favorably to successful task completion. They are thus viewed as a hypothetical construct that mediates observable practices. Specifically, they are theorized to affect how group members behave toward one another and how much influence they exert on group outcomes. Those who possess status-valued external characteristics "are more likely (1) to have chances to perform, (2) to initiate problem-solving performances, (3) to have their performances positively evaluated, and (4) are less likely to be influenced when there are disagreements" (Berger, et al., 1998, p. 381) than those lacking such characteristics or possessing negatively valued characteristics. In this way, expectations translate into actual influence on group problem solving.

Related to performance expectations are *reward expectations*: expectations that valued characteristics are differentially associated with different reward levels drawn from sociocultural beliefs about what characteristics are more or less likely to create benefits for individual actors or the group (Berger et al., 1985). This is the *theory of reward expectations*. Three classes of reward structures have been posited: categorical, ability, and outcome (Ridgeway & Berger, 1986). *Categorical structures* are related to diffuse social status characteristics such as race or gender. In psychological terms, they might be classified as fixed, dispositional, or trait attributes. In the language of source credibility or ethos, these attributes would confer initial, or pre-interactional, credibility. *Ability structures* are associated with the specific task to be performed. So, for example, relevant knowledge or experience would fit this category. In psychological terms, these reward structures may be more situational or state-like because they are context-dependent. In credibility terms, they might constitute another form of initial credibility if they are known or inferred prior to the task commencing, or they could qualify as derived credibility if they emerge during the group encounter. Finally, there are outcome structures that are associated with actual accomplishments during the group task. In psychological terms, these structures are clearly situationally determined. In credibility terms, these structures form terminal credibility, i.e., post-interactional judgments that affect future power and prestige.

These reward structures are intimately linked to status-based expectations in that occupants of valued status positions take on reward value through referential beliefs about their sociodemographic characteristics (e.g., male), their abilities (e.g., intelligent), or their past achievements at relevant tasks (e.g., successful leadership in reaching closure on an issue). Thus, status reinforces reward expectations and vice versa. The interrelatedness of the power and prestige order and reward expectations implies that, relative to their lesser valued counterparts, not only will those with high expectation advantages take more initiative and be more participative but they will also be accorded more deferential treatment by others and will have more of their recommendations acknowledged and accepted. They may also reinforce their initial expectation advantage by exhibiting verbal and non-verbal status and potency cues, referred to as *task performance cues*, which further enable advantaged individuals to make more, and more influential, contributions to the group's communication (Ridgeway, Berger & Smith, 1985) and in the process to legitimate their power and prestige.

That said, even minority group members and those possessing fewer expectation advantages based on categorical attributes can also exert influence on the group by engaging in those behaviors that have become associated with competence and expertise. Rapid response latencies and high degrees of initial eye contact, for example, may signify dominance, power, and/or status (see Burgoon, 1994) and thus elevate an actor's perceived ability during the course of interaction, leading to that person making more contributions to the task outcome.

Although EST focuses primarily on expectations rather than their violations, some research has examined this latter issue by examining non-conformity. Two studies found that high-reward group members were actually more influential when they violated rather than conformed to group norms, whereas non-conformity undermined influence by incompetent, low-status members (Ridgeway, 1981; Ridgeway & Jacobson, 1977), a finding that mirrors predictions from expectancy violations theory. In explaining why violations might be beneficial, the authors speculated that violations both draw attention to actors' reward and status characteristics and can be construed as assertive acts that reinforce their perceived competence, which enhances their ability to influence task outcomes. However, Ridgeway and Berger (1986) contended that actors may have less license to violate performance expectations that are markers of status and affirm the legitimacy of the status position (e.g., participating more, using direct eye contact, speaking firmly and with confidence). This is one point of departure between this theory and expectancy violations theory, discussed next. Other differences are noted below.

EXPECTANCY VIOLATIONS THEORY

Expectancy violations theory (EVT) originated as a theory of proxemic violations (Burgoon, 1978) but was rapidly expanded to encompass a wide range of
nonverbal expectancy violations (Burgoon, 1992, 1993, 1995; Burgoon & Hale,
1988) and is readily applicable to verbal behavior as well. It shares in common
with the preceding theories the belief that actors have extensive expectations
about the likely behaviors of others and that these guide actors' responses to
others. The focus of EVT is exclusively on communication expectations, as
defined earlier. In this theory, expectations are posited to be a combination of
both socially derived and idiosyncratic anticipations for others' actions during
interpersonal encounters. In the case of zero-history groups and encounters
between strangers, expectations are grounded largely in social norms; in the case
of ongoing social and personal relationships, those expectancies become adjusted to take into account knowledge of, and experiences with, the idiosyncratic
behaviors of others.

Three classes of characteristics are thought to shape expectancies: those related to the *actors*, those related to the *relationship* between actors, and those
related to the *communication context*. The first class of characteristics refers to
individual differences such as sex, race, age, personality, ability, and reputation
based on past achievements. Thus, it incorporates all three classes of reward
structures from EST, and, like that theory, assumes that these characteristics
have valences (positive to negative evaluations associated with them). The second class of characteristics refers to all those variables that are defined by the
relationship itself, such as degree of familiarity, degree of liking and attraction,
and status and power differentials. These kinds of expectations, which may
derive from prior interactions, may match the outcomes posited by expectation
states processes. So, for example, power and prestige orders create expectations
about another's behavior for subsequent interactions. But other expectations
may be present at the outset or emerge during the process of interaction. Interactants may expect women and physically attractive others to be gregarious; they
may come to expect playful individuals to laugh and joke. Finally, the communication context itself – its setting, purposes, and content – may set expectations
for behavior. Task-related interaction, for example, and task environments will
shape and constrain everything from where people sit to who talks to whom, to
what topics occupy the majority of floor time, to what behavioral routines are
regarded as appropriate. Whereas EST covers task interaction in groups, expectancy violations theory applies more broadly to social as well as task, and dyadic
as well as group, interaction.

Like EST, the concept of reward is featured prominently in the theory. *Communicator reward valence*, or more simply, communicator valence, refers to the
degree of positive or negative regard that a perceiver has for a given actor. The
degree of rewardingness that a communicator possesses is a function of the same
kinds of attributes identified in EST and the classes of variables associated with

expectancies – e.g., physical attractiveness, intelligence, expertise, personality, status, familiarity, or similarity. Unifying these innumerable variables is their net reward valence – "whether, on balance, a communicator is deemed rewarding or not and by extension, whether an interaction with that person is expected to be pleasurable or not" (Burgoon, 1995, p. 201). All else being equal, more rewarding actors tend to have more successful interactions and to produce more desired interaction outcomes, which may encompass not just task outcomes (e.g., more influence, better decision quality, more productivity, or better knowledge acquisition) but also interpersonal and social outcomes such as higher credibility, more harmonious interpersonal relationships, more liking, trust, and more relational satisfaction and commitment. The concept of reward, then, functions in EVT in much the same fashion as it does in reinforcement models of learning and in social exchange and attraction theories.

Relying just on the principles of expectancies and communicator reward valence, EVT could be utilized to derive a wide range of hypotheses about interpersonal interactions and their consequences. However, the main focus of the theory has been on what happens when expectations are violated. Just as communicators have valences associated with them, so do communicative acts, both those that are expected, i.e., *expectancy confirmations*, and those that are unexpected, i.e., *expectancy violations*. EVT makes the counterintuitive prediction that positive violations produce more favorable interaction patterns and outcomes than confirming expectations, whereas negative violations produce more undesirable results than confirming expectations. In arriving at these predictions, the theory's explanatory calculus relies on violations producing attentional shifts, activating finer-grained information processing, and instigating a two-part appraisal process, with communicator valence often playing a moderating role.

The process begins with an actor engaging in a violation, such as intruding on another's personal space, engaging in an intimate touch, or reducing conversational involvement to a detached, remote level. Violations, like all manner of novel and unexpected stimuli, are thought to be attention-gaining and, in many cases, physiologically arousing. The heightened activation resulting from a violation is posited to create an orienting response – a "stop, look and listen" sort of reaction – that brings features of the actor and the act into central focus (Le Poire & Burgoon, 1994). Communicator reward valence becomes especially salient, information processing deepens, and the perceiver is motivated to make sense of the violation. This assessment process may actually occur rapidly and outside of conscious awareness, due to being an overlearned response, but in more extreme cases may move to "front and center" in one's attentional field.

Because the behaviors under consideration here are part of the communication process, EVT posits that actors will attempt to interpret the violation act itself and/or its relational implicature. Causal and responsibility attributions may be made. Is the act, for example, inadvertent or intentional? controllable or uncontrollable? due to external or internal causes? The possible implicit meanings of the behavior will be assessed. Does prolonged gaze signify attentiveness, interest, surveillance, or threat? And the implications for the relationship definition may be considered. Does the act convey friendliness or hostility? liking or superiority? a desire for affiliation or a desire to control? All of these kinds of questions are part of the interpretation process.

Where meanings are polysemous and ambiguous, communicator valence may play a role in selecting among alternative meanings. For example, a pat on the shoulder from a highly esteemed colleague may be interpreted as a show of solidarity or congratulations, while the same pat from a disliked co-worker may be interpreted as patronizing or domineering. Highly regarded actors may have their behaviors judged more leniently and favorably than poorly regarded actors.

Separate from the interpretations and attributions associated with the act is its evaluation. Some messages, such as non-verbal shows of kindness, may have universally positive appeal; others, such as harsh criticism or extreme intimacy from strangers, may carry universal disapprobation. But many others depend on the "who" committing them to determine if they are evaluated positively or negatively. A friendly overture from a well-liked other may be judged as desirable; the same overture from a disliked other may be objectionable. An attempt to exert influence by a legitimate authority may be viewed as a positive sign of leadership; the same attempt by a minority group member may be viewed as an illegitimate bid for control. Thus, communicator valence may also moderate the evaluation process.

The end result of this interpretation–evaluation appraisal process is to assign a valence to the violation as either positive or negative. In cases where the interpretation and evaluation are both positive, the violation will have a positive valence; the opposite is true of cases where both the interpretation and evaluation are negative. Where the two are incongruent – such as a poorly regarded actor engaging in an unexpected act of kindness – all three elements of interpretation, evaluation, and communicator valence will be weighted to determine whether the act qualifies as a negative or positive violation. (It could be a positive violation if viewed as a genuine gesture but as a negative violation if viewed as manipulative and ingratiating.)

EVT's pivotal proposition is that positive violations produce more favorable interaction patterns and outcomes than behavioral confirmations, whereas negative violations produce (1) less favorable interaction patterns and (2) interaction outcomes rather than behavioral confirmations. Interaction patterns might include such things as how involved, and synchronized, and smooth-flowing the conversation is. Outcomes might include such things as how credible and attractive the actor is judged to be, how much influence the actor is able to exert, how productive groups are, and how much understanding is achieved among participants. To illustrate: suppose an actor displays high degrees of non-verbal immediacy (close proximity, frequent gaze, forward body lean, direct body orientation and use of touch). If the actor is an intimate friend (i.e., a communicator with positive reward valence), this complex of cues is likely to be deemed a positive violation because (1) it may be interpreted as signaling affection and interest and (2) such messages are desired from significant others. This same set of behaviors may be deemed a negative violation if enacted by a disliked other (someone with negative reward valence) because (1) it may be interpreted as overly pushy and domineering and (2) even if interpreted as a mere show of interest, may be unwelcome from someone who is disliked. The theory predicts that the violation by the intimate friend will actually elicit more reciprocal shows of involvement and be judged as more attractive by committing the positive violation of increased immediacy than if the friend had conformed to normal levels of immediacy. Conversely, the same violation by the disliked other, because it is a negative violation, should elicit a compensatory behavior pattern of reduced involvement and should result in the actor being judged as less attractive than if the actor had conformed to the norms.

EVT has been tested in a wide range of laboratory and field experiments and has been used to explain such diverse phenomena as salespeople's reactions to shoppers, decision making about the guilt or innocence of a defendant, problem-solving tasks, patient judgments of physicians and other health care workers, recruiter assessments of job interviewees, social interactions between friends and strangers, marital satisfaction, intercultural interactions, family and friends' responses to sojourners returning to their homeland, and judgments of sexual harassment. Research to date has supported, though not uniformly, the conclusions (see, for example, Burgoon, 1983, 1995; Burgoon & Hale, 1988; Burgoon & Le Poire, 1993; Burgoon, Le Poire & Rosenthal, 1995; Burgoon et al., 1989; Kelley & Burgoon, 1991; Le Poire & Burgoon, 1994; Le Poire & Yoshimura, 1999) that follow:

1. Expectancies do guide behavior and have persistent effects on interaction.
2. Communicator reward valence exerts both main and interaction effects on communication patterns and outcomes such that
   (a) highly regarded communicators (e.g., those having higher socio-economic status, reputed intelligence and expertise, purchasing power, physical attractiveness, similarity to partner, or giving positive feedback) elicit more involved and pleasant communication from interaction partners and receive more favorable post-interaction evaluations (e.g., on credibility, attractiveness, and persuasiveness) than those who are poorly regarded; and
   (b) actors with higher reward valence have more favorable meanings ascribed to their nonverbal behavior than those with lower reward valence.
3. Some violations, such as deviations from normative conversational distances and use of touch, are ambiguous or polysemous and susceptible to reward valence moderating their effects; other violations, such as gaze aversion and substantial increases or decreases in conversational distance, have fairly consensual social meanings that directly affect their status as positive or negative violations.
4. Nonverbal violations heighten attention and create orienting responses.
5. Nonverbal violations often (though not always) alter responses relative to confirmations such that positive violations produce more desirable communication patterns and outcomes, and negative violations produce less desirable ones, than behavioral confirmations.

Recent research has also demonstrated that the aversiveness of uncertainty may play a role in responses to violations (Afifi & Burgoon, 2000) but that even negative violations may confer some added benefit relative to confirmations, once the valence of the violation itself is accounted for, if paired with positive qualities of the communicator (Burgoon & Le Poire, 1993). In this case, the uncertainty may actually permit holding onto initially positive views of the actor.

As is so often true with theories whose domain is expanded, EVT has undergone numerous modifications and its extension into interaction and deception realms has spawned two other theories that incorporate many of the same variables and explanatory mechanisms as EVT. One theory is interaction adaptation theory (IAT; Burgoon, Stern & Dillman, 1995). The other is interpersonal deception theory (IDT; Buller & Burgoon, 1996).[4] IAT is expressly designed to predict and explain when people engaged in dyadic interactions will adapt or not adapt to one another's communication style. In advancing its predictions, the theory includes the concept of *expected* behavioral patterns but also adds to the equation *desired* and *required* behaviors. The former capture what is preferred from another and thus resemble prescriptive expectancies; the latter represent the fact that some forms of adaptation are designed to satisfy basic needs such as safety and sensory stimulation. The theory combines these three elements – requirements, expectations, and desires – to predict both what communication patterns an actor is likely to exhibit initially in an interaction and whether the actor is likely to reciprocate, compensate, or be non-responsive to communication changes enacted by the partner. As with EVT, partner's enacted behavior is thus compared to the actor's own strivings or anticipations but IAT is intended to offer more precision regarding the dynamics of interaction patterns themselves.

IDT is more comprehensive yet in attempting to predict and explain how pre-interaction factors affect ongoing interaction patterns and how those dynamic patterns affect post-interaction outcomes, but it is more narrow in that it focuses expressly on interpersonal deception. The role of expectancies and violations play one, but only one, part of that total dynamic process. EVT is thus subsumed within IDT.

Finally, recent work has attempted to compare and contrast, theoretically and empirically, EVT with the class of expectancy confirmation theories. These theories, which are variously referred to as expectancy signaling, behavioral confirmation, or self-fulfilling prophecy theories (see, e.g., Darley & Fazio, 1980; Jones, 1986; Jussim, 1990; Neuberg, 1996; Rosenthal, 1976, 1985; Snyder, 1984; Snyder & Swann, 1978), concern the ways in which actors' expectancies for a target person elicit the expected behavior from the target, leading to self-fulfilling prophecies and behavioral confirmation (i.e., confirming through their behavior what the actor had expected from them). From a communication standpoint, issues of interest are what verbal and nonverbal behaviors by an actor

[4] Portions of this research were supported by funding to the first author from the US Army Research Institute (Contracts #MDA903–90-K-0113 and #DASW01–98-K-009) and the US Army Research Office (Grant #30235- RT-AAS). The views, opinions, and/or findings in this report are those of the authors and should not be construed as an official Department of the Army position, policy, or decision.

exert this subtle, usually inadvertent influence on targets and the conditions under which targets confirm, disconfirm, or are responsive to these expectancies through their own behavior. Burgoon, Le Poire and Rosenthal (1995) confirmed that although targets reciprocate positive expectancies, they may engage in strategic compensatory responses when the expectancies are negative, responding, for example, to negative expectancies with higher levels of involvement and pleasantness than those who did not have such expectancies. Thus, targets do not inevitably conform to what actors expect of them but instead may employ communication to influence actor behavior.

CONCLUSIONS

The various programs of research that we have discussed under a conceptual umbrella of expectancy theories represent cumulative, progressive efforts on the part of many people to formalize explanatory and predictive propositional frameworks. Hopefully, such attempts will be recognized by those calling for social scientists to be more rigorous in the development of theories of human communication. In the last three decades, there has also been a substantial body of empirical evidence generated to test hypotheses with manifest nomothetic–deductive force. These data are simply not capable of interpretation and/or explanation without reference to the various expectancy theories.

Obviously, these expectancy interpretations have fared very well with the kind of normal social scientific scrutiny that is normative in the discipline. The extension of tests of these theoretical formulations to determine the ecological validity of many of the previously published findings and conclusions in a variety of non-laboratory research endeavors has been made possible by the securing of substantial amounts of extramural funds. Such concern for the ecological validity of our claims is obviously a required step in formal theory development. However, it has been the norm to attract the interest of such funding agencies to allow such refinement and extension of social science theories. Hopefully, the persistence in developing a set of ideas, as discussed in this chapter, from initial interest and speculation, to formalized theoretical models, to tests in both the laboratory and socially important situations, will not only be seen as important scholarship but also have practical applications and policy implications. At least, we can close with that hope proffered.

REFERENCES

Afifi, W.A. & Burgoon, J.K. (2000). The impact of violations on uncertainty and consequences for attractiveness. *Human Communication Research*, **26**, 203–233.

Argyle, M. & Dean, J. (1965). Eye-contact, distance, and affiliation. *Sociometry*, **28**, 289–304.

Berger, J., Conner, T.L. & Fisek, M.H. (1974). *Expectation states theory: A theoretical research program*. Cambridge, MA: Winthrop.

Berger, J., Fisek, M.H., Norman, R.Z. & Zelditch, M., Jr (1977). *Status characteristics in social interaction: An expectation states approach.* New York: Elsevier.

Berger, J., Fisek, M.H., Norman, R.Z. & Wagner, D.G. (1985). The formation of reward expectations in status situations. In J. Berger & M. Zelditch Jr (Eds), *Status, rewards, and influence: How expectations organize behavior* (pp. 215–261). San Francisco, CA: Jossey-Bass.

Berger, J., Ridgeway, C.L., Fisek, M.H. & Norman, R.Z. (1998). The legitimation and delegitimation of power and prestige orders. *American Sociological Review,* **63**, 379–405.

Buller, D.B. & Burgoon, J.K. (1996). Interpersonal deception theory. *Communication Theory,* **6**, 203–242.

Buller, D.B., Borland, R. & Burgoon M. (1998). Impact of behavioral intention on effective of message features: Evidence from the family sun safety project. *Human Communication Research,* **24**, 433–452.

Buller, D.B., Burgoon, M., Hall, J.R., Levine, N. Beach, B., Buller, M.K. & Melcher, C. (2000). Long-term effects of language intensity in preventive messages on planned family solar protection. *Health Communication.*

Brooks, R.D. (1970). The generalizability of early reversals of attitudes toward communication sources. *Speech Monographs,* **37**, 152–155.

Burgoon, J.K. (1978). A communication model of personal space violations: Explication and an initial test. *Human Communication Research,* **4**, 129–142.

Burgoon, J.K. (1983). Nonverbal violations of expectations. In J.M. Wiemann & R.P. Harrison (Eds), *Nonverbal interaction* (pp. 77–112). Beverly Hills, CA: Sage.

Burgoon, J.K. (1992). Applying a comparative approach to nonverbal expectancy violations theory. In J. Blumler, K.E. McLeod & J.M. McLeod (Eds), *Comparatively speaking: Communication and culture across space and time* (pp. 53–69). Newbury Park, CA: Sage.

Burgoon, J.K. (1993). Interpersonal expectations, expectancy violations, and emotional communication. *Journal of Language and Social Psychology,* **12**, 13–21.

Burgoon, J.K. (1994). Nonverbal signals. In M.L. Knapp & G.R. Miller (Eds), *Handbook of interpersonal communication* (2nd ed, pp. 344–390). Beverly Hills, CA: Sage.

Burgoon, J.K. (1995). Cross-cultural and intercultural applications of expectancy violations theory. In R.L. Wiseman (Ed.), *Intercultural communication theory (International and intercultural communication annual* (Vol. 19, pp. 194–214). Thousand Oaks, CA: Sage.

Burgoon, J.K. & Hale, J.L. (1988). Nonverbal expectancy violations: Model elaboration and application to immediacy behaviors. *Communication Monographs,* **55**, 58–79.

Burgoon, J.K. & Le Poire, B.A. (1993). Effects of communication expectancies, actual communication, and expectancy disconfirmation on evaluations of communicators and their communication behavior. *Human Communication Research,* **20**, 75–107.

Burgoon, J.K. & Walther, J.B. (1990). Nonverbal expectancies and the consequences of violations. *Human Communication Research,* **17**, 232–265.

Burgoon, J.K. & White, C.A. (1997). Researching nonverbal message production: A view from interaction adaptation theory. In J.O. Greene (Ed.), *Message production: Advances in communication theory* (pp. 279–312). Mahwah, NJ: Erlbaum.

Burgoon, J.K., Newton, D.A., Walther, J.B. & Baesler, E.J. (1989). Nonverbal expectancy violations and conversational involvement. *Journal of Nonverbal Behavior,* **13**, 97–120.

Burgoon, J.K., Le Poire, B.A. & Rosenthal, R. (1995). Effects of preinteraction expectancies and target communication on perceiver reciprocity and compensation in dyadic interaction. *Journal of Experimental Social Psychology,* **31**, 287–321.

Burgoon, J.K., Stern, L.A. & Dillman, L. (1995). *Dyadic adaptation: Dyadic interactional pattern.* New York: Cambridge University Press.

Burgoon, M. (1970a). The effects of response set and race on message interpretation. *Speech Monographs,* **37**, 264–268.

Burgoon, M. (1970b). Prior attitude and language intensity as predictors of message style and attitude change following counterattitudinal communication behavior. Unpublished doctoral dissertation, Michigan State University.

Burgoon, M. (1975). Toward a message-centered theory of persuasion: Empirical investigations of language intensity III. The effects of source credibility and language intensity on attitude change and person perception. *Human Communication Research*, **1**, 251–256.

Burgoon, M. (1989). The effects of message variables on opinion and attitude change. In J. Bradac (Ed.), *Messages in communication sciences: Contemporary approaches to the study of effects* (pp. 129–164). Newbury Park, CA: Sage.

Burgoon, M. (1990). Social psychological concepts and language: Social influence. In H. Giles & P. Robinson (Eds), *Handbook of social psychology and language* (pp. 51–72). London: Wiley.

Burgoon, M. (1995). Language expectancy theory: Elaboration, explication, and extension. In C.R. Berger & M. Burgoon (Eds), *Communication and social influence processes* (pp. 33–58). East Lansing, MI: Michigan State University Press.

Burgoon, M.H., & Burgoon, J.K. (1990). Compliance-gaining and health care. In J.P. Dillard (Ed.), *Seeking compliance: The production of interpersonal influence messages* (pp. 161–188). Scottsdale, AZ: Gorsuch Scarisbrick.

Burgoon, M. & Chase, L.C. (1973). The effects of differential linguistic patterns in messages attempting to induce resistance to persuasion. *Speech Monographs*, **40**, 1–7.

Burgoon, M. & Miller, G.R. (1971). Prior attitude and language intensity as predictors of message style and attitude change following counter-attitudinal advocacy. *Journal of Personality and Social Psychology*, **20**, 240–253.

Burgoon, M. & Miller, G.R. (1985). An expectancy interpretation of language and persuasion. In H. Giles & R. St Clair (Eds), *The social and psychological contexts of language* (pp. 199–229). London: Erlbaum.

Burgoon, M. & Stewart, D. (1975). Toward a message-centered theory of persuasion: Empirical investigations of language intensity I. The effects of sex of source, receiver, and language intensity on attitude change. *Human Communication Research*, **1**, 241–248.

Burgoon, M., Jones & Stewart (1975). Toward a message-centered theory of persuasion: Three empirical investigations of language intensity. *Human Communication Research*, **1**, 240–256.

Burgoon, M., Birk, T. & Hall, J. (1991). Compliance and satisfaction with physician–patient communication: An expectancy theory interpretation of gender differences. *Human Communication Research*, **18**, 177–208.

Cann, A., Sherman, S.J. & Elkes, R. (1975). Effects of initial request size and timing of the second request on compliance: The foot-in-the-door and door-in-the-face. *Journal of Personality and Social Psychology*, **39**, 752–766.

Cappella, J.N. & Greene, J.O. (1984). The effects of distance and individual differences in arousability on nonverbal involvement: A test of discrepancy-arousal theory. *Journal of Nonverbal Behavior*, **8**, 259–285.

Cupach, W.R., Spitzberg, B.H. (Eds) (1994). *The dark side of interpersonal communication*. Hillsdale, NJ: Erlbaum.

Darley, J.M., & Fazio, R.H. (1980). Expectancy confirmation processes arising in the social interaction sequence. *American Psychologist*, **35**, 867–881.

Dillard, J.P., Hunter, J.E. & Burgoon, M. (1984). A meta-analysis of two sequential request strategies for gaining compliance: Foot-in-the-door and door-in-the-face. *Human Communication Research*, **10**, 461–488.

Festinger, L. (1957). *A theory of cognitive dissonance*. Evanston, IL: Row, Peterson.

Fishbein, M. & Ajzen, I. (1975). *Belief, attitude, intention, and behavior: An introduction to theory and research*. Reading, MA: Addison-Wesley.

Floyd, K. & Burgoon, J.K. (1999). Reacting to nonverbal expressions of liking: A test of interaction adaptation theory. *Communication Monographs*, **66**, 219–239.

Giles, H. & Robinson P. (Eds) (1990). *Handbook of social psychology and language.* London: Wiley.

Grandpre, J.R., Miller, C.H., Alvaro, E.M., Hall, J.R. & Burgoon, M. (1999). *Adolescent reactance and anti-smoking campaigns: A theoretical approach.* Paper present at the National Communication Association annual meeting, Chicago, IL, November.

Hovland, C.I. & Weiss, W. (1952). The influence of source credibility on communication effectiveness. *Public Opinion Quarterly,* **15**, 635–650.

Jones, E.E. (1986). Interpreting interpersonal behavior: The effects of expectancies. *Science,* **234**, 41–46.

Jones, S.B. & Burgoon, M. (1975). Toward a message-centered theory of persuasion: Empirical investigations of language intensity II. The effects of irrelevant fear and language intensity of attitude change. *Human Communication Research,* **1**, 248–251.

Jussim, L. (1990). Social reality and social problems: The role of expectancies. *Journal of Social Issues,* **46**, 9–34.

Kellermann, K. & Reynolds, R. (1990). When ignorance is bliss: The role of motivation to reduce uncertainty in uncertainty reduction theory. *Human Communication Research,* **17**, 5–75.

Kelley, D.L. & Burgoon, J.K. (1991). Understanding marital satisfaction and couple type as functions of relational expectations. *Human Communication Research,* **18**, 40–69.

Klingle, R.S. & Burgoon, M. (1995). Patient compliance and satisfaction with physician influence attempts: A reinforcement expectancy approach to compliance-gaining over time. *Communication Research,* **22**, 148–187.

Le Poire, B.A. & Burgoon, J.K. (1994). Two contrasting explanations of involvement violations: Expectancy violations theory and discrepancy arousal theory. *Human Communication Research,* **20**, 560–591.

Le Poire, B.A. & Yoshimura, S.M. (1999). The effects of expectancies and actual communication on nonverbal adaptation and communication outcomes: A test of interaction adaptation theory. *Communication Monographs,* **66**, 1–30.

Marwell, G. & Schmitt, D.R. (1967a). Compliance-gaining behavior: A synthesis and model. *Sociological Quarterly,* **8**, 317–328.

Marwell, G. & Schmitt, D.R. (1967b). Dimensions of compliance-gaining behavior: An empirical analysis. *Sociometry,* **30**, 350–364.

McGuire, W.J. (1969). The nature of attitudes and attitude change. In G. Lindzey & E. Aronson (Eds), *The handbook of social psychology* (Vol. 3, pp. 136–314). Reading, MA: Addison-Wesley.

McPeek, R.W. & Edwards, J.D. (1975). Expectancy disconfirmation and attitude change. *Journal of Social Psychology,* **96**, 193–208.

Miller, G.R. & Burgoon, M. (1973). *New techniques of persuasion.* New York: Harper & Row.

Miller, G.R., Boster, F., Roloff, M. & Seibold, D. (1977). Compliance-gaining message strategies: A typology and some findings concerning effects of situational differences. *Communication Monographs,* **44**, 37–51.

Miller, G.R., Boster, F., Roloff, M. & Seibold, D. (1987). MBRS rekindled: Some thoughts on compliance gaining in interpersonal settings. In M.E. Roloff & G.R. Miller (Eds), *Interpersonal processes: New directions in communication research* (pp. 89–116). Newbury Park, CA: Sage.

Miller, M.D. & Burgoon, M. (1979). The relationship between violations of expectations and the induction of resistance to persuasion. *Human Communication Research,* **5**, 301–313.

Mitchell, T.R. (1982). Expectancy-value models in organizational behavior. In N.T. Feather (Ed.), *Expectations and actions: Expectancy value models in psychology* (pp. 293–312). Hillsdale, NJ: Erlbaum.

Neuberg, S.L. (1996). Expectancy influences in social interaction. In P.M. Gollwitzer & J.A. Bargh (Eds), *The psychology of action* (pp. 529–554). New York: Guilford Press.

Pool, I. & Shulman, I. (1959). Newsmen's fantasies, audiences, and newswriting. *Public Opinion Quarterly*, **23**, 145–158.

Ridgeway, C.L. (1981). Nonconformity, competence, and influence in groups: A test of two theories. *American Sociological Review*, **46**, 333–347.

Ridgeway, C.L. & Berger, J. (1986). Expectations, legitimation, and dominance behavior in task groups. *American Sociological Review*, **62**, 218–235.

Ridgeway, C.L. & Jacobson, C.K. (1977). Sources of status and influence in all female and mixed-sex groups. *Sociological Quarterly*, **18**, 413–425.

Ridgeway, C.L. & Walker, H.A. (1995). Status structures. In K.S. Cook, G.A. Fine & J.S. House (Eds), *Sociological perspectives on social psychology* (pp. 281–310). Boston, MA: Allyn & Bacon.

Ridgeway, C.L., Berger, J. & Smith, L. (1985). Nonverbal cues and status: An expectation states approach. *American Journal of Psychology*, **90**, 955–978.

Rosenthal, R. (1976). *Experimenter expectancy effects in behavioral research* (enlarged edn). New York: Irvington.

Rosenthal, R. (1985). Nonverbal cues in the mediation of interpersonal expectancy effects. In A.W. Siegman & S. Feldstein (Eds), *Multichannel integrations of nonverbal behavior* (pp. 105–128). Hillsdale, NJ: Erlbaum.

Shelly, R.K. (1998). Some developments in expectation states theory: Graduated expectations? In E.J. Lawler, J. Skvoretz & J. Szmatka (Eds), *Advances in group processes* (pp. 41–57). Stamford, CT: JAI Press.

Snyder, M. (1984). When belief creates reality. In L. Berkowitz (Ed.), *Advances in experimental social psychology* (Vol. 18, pp. 247–305). New York: Academic Press.

Snyder, M. & Swann, W.B., Jr (1978). Behavioral confirmation in social interaction: From social perception to social reality. *Journal of Experimental Social Psychology*, **14**, 148–162.

Tedeschi, J.T. & Norman, N. (1985). Social power, self-presentation, and the self. In B.R. Schlenker (Ed.), *The self and social life* (pp. 293–322). New York: McGraw-Hill.

Webster's Seventh New Collegiate Dictionary (1985). Springfield, MA: Merriam.

Discursive Social Psychology

Jonathan Potter *and* **Derek Edwards**
Loughborough University, UK

Discursive social psychology is the application of ideas from discourse analysis to central topics in social psychology. It is not a social psychology *of* language. Instead, it is an approach to psychology that takes the action-oriented and reality-constructing features of discourse as fundamental. Whereas the dominant social cognition paradigm gives a story of behaviour produced on the basis of information processing done on perceptual input (e.g., Fiske & Taylor, 1991), discursive social psychology's narrative revolves around activities done through discourse as parts of situated practices (Edwards & Potter, 1992). While theory and method in social cognition presume an out-there reality that provides input to cognitive operations, discursive social psychology focuses on the way both "reality" and "mind" are constructed by people conceptually, in language, in the course of their execution of various practical tasks (Edwards, 1997; Potter, 1996a; Potter, Edwards & Wetherell, 1993). Discursive social psychology is a perspective that rejects experiments, surveys and most interview work in favour of rigorous empirical analysis of records of natural interaction.

In this chapter we briefly review the basic theoretical and methodological principles of discursive social psychology (henceforth, DSP). We illustrate its difference from cognitive social psychology using two examples that also focus on language – causal attribution and social representations – and we flesh out its nature by considering two further topics: counselling and racism.

The New Handbook of Language and Social Psychology.
Edited by W. Peter Robinson and Howard Giles.
© 2001 John Wiley & Sons Ltd.

WHAT IS DISCURSIVE PSYCHOLOGY?

Discursive psychology has a complex theoretical lineage drawing on ideas from discourse analysis, rhetoric, sociology of science, ethnomethodology, conversation analysis, and post-structuralism. In DSP discourse is defined as talk and texts, studied as social practices. This definition combines the sense of discourse as an object and as a practice. For theoretical, methodological and empirical reasons DSP takes discourse to be central to social life. For example, most social activity involves or is directly conducted through discourse. Furthermore, even where activity is "non-verbal" (embodiment, physical actions and their settings, etc.), its sense is often best understood through participants' discourse. Discourse is the prime currency of interaction, and if we are studying persons embedded in practices then discourse will be central to that study. Further justifications for giving discourse this pre-eminent position will be developed in the course of this chapter.

The view of social psychology in DSP can be introduced most simply by considering three theoretical features of discourse: it is *situated*, *action-oriented*, and *constructed*. Let us take them in turn.

1. Discourse is situated

DSP focuses on discourse, which it regards as situated in two ways. First, it is *occasioned* in the conversation analytic sense of this term (see Hutchby & Wooffitt, 1998). That is, talk and texts are embedded in some kind of sequence of interaction and in some kind of context. This is not a mechanical contextual determinism; talk is *oriented to*, but not *determined by*, its sequential position. Thus, a "question", say, sets up the normative relevance of an "answer", but an answer is not forced or necessary, and things do not break down if it is not provided. Answers may be deferred or withheld altogether (Heritage, 1984). Likewise, the fact that talk appears in a school or a doctor's surgery does not mean that it must thereby be pedagogic or medical. Rather than being noted, formulated and made omni-relevant by the analyst, institutional activities and identities are made relevant by participants themselves, by being invoked and oriented to, or indeed subverted and ignored (Schegloff, 1997).

Second, DSP conceptualizes discourse as pervasively *rhetorical* (Billig, 1987, 1991). Claims and descriptions that are offered in talk are often designed to *counter* potential alternative versions and resist attempts (perhaps actual, perhaps potential) to disqualify them as false, partial or interested (Edwards & Potter, 1992). That is, they can have both a defensive and an offensive rhetoric (Potter, 1996a). Billig (1991; see also this volume, Chapter 3.12) argues that when people offer evaluations of something they are typically countering some other evaluation.

In DSP analysis has to take into account both the occasioned and rhetorical nature of discourse.

2. Discourse is action-oriented

DSP focuses on how discourse performs actions or practices of various kinds – blamings, invitations, displays of neutrality, and so on. "Action" or "practice" (the precise term is not meant to carry weight here) invokes the vast range of practical, technical and interpersonal tasks that people perform while doing their jobs, living their relationships, and participating in heterogeneous cultural domains. It is central to people's lives, and therefore central to understanding those lives. Following the convention in conversation analysis, DSP uses the notion of *action orientation* to emphasize that actions are pervasively being done even in ostensibly factual, descriptive discourse, and to distance itself from a "speech act" approach that assumes that some discrete set of words correspond to a discrete act.

The corollary of DSP's focus on discourse is its respecification of cognition. Instead of cognitive entities and processes being the principal *analytic* resource, as they are in social cognition research, they are approached empirically as participants' *ways of talking*. The focus is on the way cognitions are constructed in talk, and how their implications are oriented. For example, rather than treating attitudes as inner entities that drive behaviour, in DSP attitudes are evaluations that are studied as part of discourse practices (Potter, 1998a). Such an approach might consider the way evaluations are organized interactionally, as in Pomerantz's (1978) study of compliments; it might consider how attitudes are interactionally produced through social psychological methods (Myers, 1998; Puchta & Potter, in press); or it might consider the way negative evaluations of minority group members are turned from potentially accountable personally held attitudes into more "safely sayable" factual descriptions (e.g., Edwards, in press; Potter & Wetherell, 1988; Wetherell & Potter, 1992).

This non-cognitivist reformulation of attitudes avoids the circularity of many social cognition studies, where evaluative *discourse* (in response scales) is turned into underlying *cognitive* entities (attitudes), which are in turn used to explain *actions* (involving more discourse). It avoids the uncomfortable blurring of everyday and technical notions in the attitude and belief domain, by taking peoples' evaluative terminology (attitude, belief, opinion, position, view, etc.) as *topic* rather than as a competing but rather less adequate theory of behaviour (cf. Edwards, 1997, on psychology and common sense in general). It makes sense of the troubling variability in peoples' evaluative talk, which stems from the fact that people produce evaluations as parts of various discourse practices, rather than expressing pre-formed, all-purpose mental entities when asked to do so by a researcher. It focuses attention on life as a practical realm where evaluations are part of getting things done, rather than existing as disembedded assessments waiting to be produced in moments of reflection.

3. Discourse is constructed

DSP is constructionist in two senses. First, it studies the way discourse itself is constructed. Words, metaphors, idioms, rhetorical devices, descriptions, accounts, stories and so on are drawn on, and built, in the course of interaction and in the performance of particular actions. For example, DSP research might ask how descriptions are assembled in ways that present some piece of conduct as orderly and required by the circumstances, as just what anybody would have done, or else as unusual, specially motivated and implicative of the actor's particular psychology (Edwards, 1994, 1997). Second, it studies the way discourse constructs versions of the world. That is, it studies how versions of inner life, of local circumstances, of history and broader social groups and structures are produced to do particular things in interaction. In DSP, then, discourse is both constructed and constructive.

Although DSP is a constructionist approach, its emphasis on the construction of *versions in discourse* distinguishes it from cognitive constructionisms ranging from Neisser (1967), to Moscovici (1984), to Berger and Luckmann (1966). Construction is studied in DSP as the process of assembling and stablizing versions to make them factual and independent of their producer. Whereas cognitive constructionism tends to guide the researcher away from considering people's practices, DSP's emphasis on the construction of specific versions encourages the researcher to consider the practices that those versions are part of, and the particular work that they are performing.

At the centre of DSP there is an inversion that, initially, appears counterintuitive. In traditional social cognition there is *reality* on the one hand, that is the setting – the "stimulus conditions" that enclose actors – and there is *cognition* on the other, conceived as something existing and quietly computing inside the actors. Activity is treated as something secondary, the output of this system. DSP inverts this. Activity is treated as primary, and reality and cognition are secondary. That is, DSP focuses on what people are doing, and how, in the course of their discourse practices, they produce versions of external reality and psychological states. It asks how people categorize and formulate the world, establishing certain particulars as relevant, characterizing its moral flavour, and it asks how people at the same time formulate a relevant inner world of beliefs, values, emotions and dispositions, that make their actions accountable.

These theoretical principles of DSP lead to a range of analytic principles. We will highlight seven themes in DSP which relate to the issues of empirical analysis, factors and outcomes, detail, hypothetico-deductivism, natural materials, analytic procedures and validation.

1. Empirical analysis

DSP is strongly empirical. It takes the analysis of materials to be central to making claims and developing theory. It is not attempting to replace research with theory, conceptual analysis, intuition or politics. Nevertheless, an awareness of the philosophy and sociology of scientific knowledge (Chalmers, 1992; Woolgar, 1988) leads to caution about the independence of data from theory or method, and the analytic approaches taken in DSP are very different from those commonplace in mainstream social cognition work.

2. Factors and outcomes

DSP decisively rejects the factors-and-outcomes model that underlies much social cognition research. Social life is not viewed as the consequence of an interplay of factors which have more or less regular patterns and determinate outcomes. Instead, DSP treats social life as being organized and produced in a radically different way, as basically normative and rhetorical, and this entails differences in data, theory and method. The norms of social life do not work as templates that govern interaction, but rather, they are participants' resources for action and understanding, for making life accountable (describable and sanctionable: Garfinkel, 1967). Thus, failure to return a greeting is not an occasion to abandon the norm but, rather, the basis for a potential range of inferences about the person and context: are they rude, hard of hearing, sulking, shy or whatever (Heritage, 1988)? In a similar way, rhetoric in DSP is not treated as guaranteeing persuasion; rather it is oriented to persuasion. Any rhetorical device can have a range of counters. Categorization, say, can be countered by particularization (Billig, 1985).

3. Materials

The rejection of the factors-and-outcomes model is one reason for rejecting efforts at experimentally controlling variables using invented materials. DSP prefers to analyse "naturalistic" rather than "got-up" materials. This is not a commitment to an unsustainable philosophy of a natural world free of observer influence. Rather, it is a preference, grounded in DSP's conception of how discourse works, for examining records of people living their lives, telling what happened, arguing about relationships, answering parliamentary questions, and so on, instead of answering researcher's questions, cooperating with experimenters' requirements, and responding to researcher's textual vignettes. The focus on naturalistic materials starts to become inevitable once the importance is fully recognized of discourse being occasioned, action-oriented and constructed. It is also a reflection of what has become technically and analytically possible. Given that such rich materials are increasingly tractable, and can be successfully recorded, digitized, scanned, transcribed and rigorously studied in the wake of several decades of research, why do anything else?

4. Detail

DSP requires an attention to the detail of interaction. Harvey Sacks (1992) suggested that none of the detail of interaction, whether it be pauses and repairs, the selection of particular words, or the placement of interruption and overlaps, should be assumed a priori to be irrelevant to interaction. Sometimes a sniff is just a sniff, the consequence of having a runny nose; yet a sniff, in the right place, with the right kind of in-breath, could also do something else such as displaying indirect disagreement (Roffe, 1996).

5. Analysis

Analysis works with some combination of audio and video tape, transcript and/
or text. Different kinds of studies involve different procedures, sometimes working intensively with a single transcript, other times drawing on a large corpus.
Analysis is a craft that can be developed with different degrees of skill. It can be
thought of as the development of a sensitivity to the occasioned and action-
oriented nature of discourse. This often involves attention to a range of features
of discourse. As well as the *detail* of hesitations, repairs, word choice and so on,
there is *variability* in and between different texts and stretches of talk which can
be an important clue about action orientation, the rhetorical organization of
discourse (how it is put together to counter alternatives) and its accountability.

6. Hypothetico-deductivism

The style of analysis in DSP does not lend itself to the hypothetico-deductivism
that is commonplace in factors-and-outcomes work in social cognition. It has
often been productive to collect and explore a set of materials without being
constrained by a specific hypothesis. Close attention to a recording and transcript, or a collection of documents, often reveals phenomena that were both
previously unnoticed and unexpected. *Starting* with the materials, rather than a
prior hypothesis, is a way of allowing such phenomena into the analysis. Nevertheless, once interesting phenomena or patterns have been identified, the analysis is developed by searching a corpus for further relevant examples and
counter-examples.

7. Validation

The notion of validity in DSP is different from that in much social cognition
research. In DSP it is built more obviously into basic research design – the choice
and presentation of naturalistic materials in something close to their raw form,
for instance – rather than arising as a worry about extending claims and findings
from a research domain into relevant arenas of everyday life. In DSP analysis is
made accountable to the detail of empirical materials, and these are presented in
a form that allows *readers to make their own checks* and judgements. This form
of validation contrasts with much traditional experimental and content analytic
work where it is rare for anything close to "raw data" to be included, or for more
than one or two illustrative codings to be provided. It also permits an accumulation of empirical data and analytic studies against which new findings can be
compared for their *coherence*. For example, work on fact construction builds on
the insights about accountability from earlier studies, and its success provides a
further confirmation of the validity of those studies (Edwards & Potter, 1993).
   Two specific principles of conversation analysis are useful in validating
analytic claims: *deviant case analysis* (checking claims against potential counter
cases) and the *proof procedure* (basing the analysis of a turn at talk on how the

participants themselves treat it, in next turns – see Heritage, 1995; Schegloff, 1992). Both principles are illustrated in studies of television and radio news interviews, where participants routinely avoid treating interviewers as accountable for views expressed in questions. That normative pattern is supported rather than refuted by studying deviant cases in which interviewees treat their interviewer as expressing personal views, whereupon considerable interactional trouble ensues in subsequent turns (Heritage & Greatbatch, 1991; Potter, 1996a).

These points highlight some of what is distinctive about DSP. For more detailed accounts of methods and analysis in this area see Billig (1997), Coyle (1995), Gill (1996), Potter (1996b, 1997, 1998b), Potter & Wetherell (1987, 1994, 1995), Wetherell & Potter (1992), Widdicombe & Wooffitt (1995) and Wooffitt (1990, 1993).

RESPECIFYING SOCIAL PSYCHOLOGY THEORY

Let us further explicate the nature of DSP by comparing and contrasting it to two current alternative approaches that also focus on language: the linguistic category model of causal attribution (Brown & Fish, 1983; Semin & Fiedler, 1989) and the theory of social representations (Moscovici, 1984).

Attribution and the Linguistic Category Model

The linguistic category model (henceforth LCM) of attribution considers the way that causality is semantically presupposed by various categories of verbs. For example, when given a vignette item "John telephones Mary" people will answer the question "Why?" by specifying something about John; but when faced with a vignette item "John thanks Mary", people will answer the question "Why?" by specifying something about Mary. Such studies purport to explain many of the basic phenomena of attribution as a consequence of verb semantics.

Let us emphasize areas of agreement. Both DSP and LCM treat words and descriptions as fundamental to understanding causal attribution. That is, the use of grammatical categories is treated as an active, creative part of causal explanation, rather than being a mere reflection of the organization of events, or a consequence of some kind of non-linguistic cognitive processing.

There are also important areas of disagreement. To clarify this it is useful to distinguish between three kinds of causal responsibility:

1. Responsibility presupposed by verb semantics.
2. Responsibility assigned in a broader description of some interaction.
3. Responsibility of the current speaker in constructing a description to assign responsibility in a particular way.

So in the case of "John thanks Mary", we can distinguish between: (1) the presupposition that Mary must have done something to be "thanked" for; (2) how these words might be part of a description which assigns responsibility to *either* Mary or John or someone or something else; (3) the responsibility of the producer of the description, in assigning responsibility to Mary or John.

In DSP the recognition that discourse is situated, action-oriented and constructed highlights the need to look at all three kinds of responsibility if we are going to understand attribution in natural discourse. People use words to build their accounts, so the various semantic presuppositions that LCM identifies are an important part of understanding what particular words might be used to achieve (type 1 responsibility). However, DSP emphasizes that the sense of discourse is occasioned. The semantics do not govern what is going on; rather they are modified or even inverted as language is brought out of the pages of the dictionary or grammar book (as if that was where it began!) and made to live in practical settings (type 2 responsibility). Moreover, one of the major features of DSP is its emphasis on the way descriptions, as parts of interaction, are *themselves* performing actions, including handling the speaker's stake or interest in what is going on (type 3 responsibility). For extended analytic examples highlighting the limits of the LCM and other kinds of language-based attribution theory, in comparison to DSP, see Edwards and Potter (1993, 1999).

Descriptions and Social Representations

Social representations theory (SRT) has provided an innovative account of the nature of everyday social understanding (Moscovici, 1984). In SRT new information is assimilated to existing representations through the twin processes of anchoring and objectification. Representations circulate through conversation and via the mass media, and develop as they do so. Representations are not simply devices for perceiving social worlds – they construct the nature and value of those worlds.

Let us again emphasize important areas of agreement. DSP and SRT are both constructionist perspectives. They both emphasize the importance of representation, including the central importance of discourse in social life. DSP thus has much more in common with SRT than with many other social cognitive perspectives.

There are also important divergences. First, construction is differently understood. Whereas in SRT it is primarily a perceptual–cognitive process involving the schematic mechanisms of anchoring and objectification, in DSP construction is done in talk and texts as specific versions of the world are developed and rhetorically undermined. There are various advantages of DSP's view of construction, one of which is to make it more analytically tractable. The building, establishment and undermining of representations can be studied using recordings of interaction, and the refined tools of conversation analysis and discourse analysis.

Second, representation is conceptualized differently. In SRT representations are primarily cognitive phenomena which enable people to make sense of the world. The collective nature of this sense-making is taken to enable intra-group communication and to provide a technical definition of the boundaries of social groups. In contrast, DSP's representations are discursive objects that people construct in talk and texts. DSP focuses on how representations are *constructed as* solid and factual, and on how they are specifically fitted to, and selected for, the *occasion* of their use, for their role in *activities*. Understanding discursive actions is therefore the key to understanding representations.

Third, although both SRT and DSP emphasize discourse, SRT draws heavily on traditional metaphors of communication in which "messages" are "transferred" from speaker to speaker. This meshes with SRT's emphasis on cognitive sense-making. So, even though SRT treats conversation as *theoretically* fundamental for the generation and refinement of representations, it is a topic that has received virtually no *methodological* or analytic attention. Indeed, where SRT researchers have used qualitative approaches such as interviews and ethnography they have tended to treat these as pathways to underlying representations rather than realms of conversational interaction in their own right (see Potter, 1996a on Jodelet, 1991).

What we have briefly highlighted, then, is that SRT does not fully recognize the importance of how discourse is occasioned, action-oriented and constructed. For recent discussions of the relation between SRT and DSP see Potter and Edwards (1999), and Potter and Wetherell (1998).

DISCURSIVE SOCIAL PSYCHOLOGY IN ACTION

There is now a wide and varied literature in discursive social psychology. This has reworked traditional topics such as causal attribution (Antaki, 1994; Edwards & Potter, 1992, 1993), prejudice (Edwards, in press; Gill, 1993; Speer & Potter, 2000; Wetherell & Potter, 1992), identity (Antaki, 1998; Edwards, 1998; Widdicombe & Wooffitt, 1995), script theory (Edwards, 1994, 1997), and violence and aggression (Auburn, Lea & Drake, 1999; McKinlay & Dunnett, 1998; Hepburn, 2000); and it has brought to the fore new topics such as the relation between interaction and institutions (Edwards, 1995a; te Molder, 1999) and the construction and establishment of factual accounts (MacMillan & Edwards, 1999; Potter, 1996a; Wooffitt, 1992). Rather than attempt to review this and other related work, we offer two brief illustrations of these strands of DSP.

DSP and Prejudice

We have noted that people construct versions of the world that attend to their factual status, to the psychology of participants in reported events, and to the current interaction in which versions are offered. These moves are often done simultaneously (Edwards & Potter, 1992). For example, a mental state (belief, certainty, fear, doubt) may be produced as determined by the external world, itself known through repeated experiences (Edwards, 1994). Another way of grounding factual claims is to offer them as reluctantly arrived at, or as counter to one's presumptions and biases (Edwards, in press; Potter, 1996a). These (and other) *ways of talking* counter the possibility that you believe what it suits you to believe, or what you believed before you looked, that your beliefs are a function of mental predisposition rather than external reality – that is, they attend rhetorically to a possible dismissal as prejudgement, or prejudice.

Extract 1 is taken from an interview from the early 1980s ("I" is the interviewer, "R" the interviewee) in New Zealand concerning a controversial South African rugby tour, prior to that country's abandonment of apartheid (see Edwards, in press, for an extended discussion of this and other examples).

> **Extract 1**
> → **R:** Uhm (1.2) I would li:ke to see apartheid done away with (1.0) but can
>   anybody come up with a- [a (.)
> **I:**   [Mm mhm
> **R:** positive way of saying "This is how it can be done"
> **I:** Mm mhm
> **R:** It's all very well to turn round and say "Give 'em a vote"
> **I:** Yes
> **R:** I mean the majority of them (1.0) don't know what a vote is
> **I:** Mm mhm

R's argument for apartheid occurs in the context (not reproduced here) of justifying his support of the controversial rugby tour. He offers his position as one that is forced by practical realities. The notion that the speaker might be talking out of some kind of preference or liking for apartheid – that is, because of psychological disposition (prejudice) rather than worldly reality – is further countered by locating his preferences as precisely the opposite. He would *like* it done away with, if only that were realistically possible. This counter-dispositional construction is a feature of talk about sensitive and controversial issues, but it draws on a very general device in factual discourse, which is making a version or conclusion factually robust by formulating it as reluctantly arrived at. The same device is used in Extract 2.

> **Extract 2**
> **I:** (. . .) d'you think there should be res- (.) restrictions on immigration?
>   (.)
> **I:** How do you [feel about
> → **R:**   [Oh yes.= There's got to be.
> **I:** Ye[:h
> → **R:** [Unfortunately,
> **I:** my[e:h
> → **R:** [I would love to see the whole wor:ld y'know,
>   jus' where you: (.) go where you like,

R appeals to necessity in contrast to personal preference or desire, a disposition formulated as an emphatic ("would love", "whole world") counter-preference for a world where people can "go where you like". Note the symmetric appeal to both sides of the psychological equation, to an external known world ("there's got to be") that constrains a reluctant belief or opinion ("unfortunately", "would love"). R's reluctance is not a free-floating indication of his attitude, but deals with the interviewer's specific framing of the questions (both "do you think . . ." and "how do you feel . . ."), and to the possibly unwelcome inferences about him that would be available were he simply to support apartheid.

It is important to emphasize that this kind of analysis entails no commitment to the genuineness or falsity of R's reluctance, preferences, nor any other mental state that might be conceptualized, managed by, or at issue in, the talk. DSP analyses it all as ways of talking that can be unravelled through a detailed analysis of how specific descriptions are constructed in ways that perform discursive actions within sequential, rhetorical sequences of talk.

DSP, Institutions and Interaction

One of the features of social psychology for much of the twentieth century has been its attempt to generate social-cognitive explanations that link underlying variables to outcomes. This has directed attention away from the specific structural organizations that make up any culture, such as factory production lines, doctors' surgeries, family meal times, and so on. In emphasizing the occasioned, action-oriented and constructed nature of discourse, DSP is required to pay attention to such specifics. In this emphasis on talk-at-work it picks up from the success of conversation analysis in productively explicating relations between discourse and social organization (Drew & Heritage, 1992).

Extract 3 indicates some potentially intricate relations between lexical selection and the situated activities that are being done. It comes from early in a couple's first relationship counselling session, and starts with the counsellor asking about their first separation (see also Edwards, 1997; Potter, 1996a). C is the counsellor, W the wife, and H the husband.

> **Extract 3**
> **C:** Was that the time that you left?=
> **W:** =He left the:n that was- [nearl]y two years ago.
> **C:**   [°Yeh.°]
> **W:** He walked out then.
>   (.)
>   Just (.) literally walked out.
>   (0.8)
> **C:** ↑Oka↓y. So, (0.5) for me list↓enin:g, (.) you've
> →   got (0.5) rich an:d, (.) complicated lives,
>   I nee:d to get some his[tory to put-]
> **W:**   [Yyeh. Mmmm,]
> **H:** [Mmmm. (.) Ye:h. (.) Oh ye:h.]
> **H:** [Yeh. (.) That's (.) exactly wha]t ih °um°

Let us focus on the counsellor's *formulation* of what W and H have been saying about themselves, that they have "rich and complicated lives". A number of analysts have observed that "formulations" play an important role in counselling talk (Buttny & Jensen, 1995; Davis, 1986). Indeed they seem to index counselling talk in much the way that initiation–response–evaluation sequences suggest classroom interaction (Mehan, 1979). So, what might such formulations be *doing* in counselling talk? Let us open up some lines of investigation to illustrate DSP's approach.

First, "rich and complicated" converts a rather painful account of trouble and conflict into something positive, or at the very least interesting. In this it may contrast with critical or anxious responses that the couple may have had from friends or relatives. The counsellor presents himself via this formulation as neither judging nor made anxious by talk about difficult relationship problems. Quite the reverse, "rich and complicated" looks forward to the exploration of these complexities.

Second, it is an impartial formulation, neither criticizing nor supporting either party. This, of course, is an issue for relationship counselling where trust might easily be broken if the counsellor is seen as aligning with one party against the other. In its particular sequential placing, following the wife's criticisms of her husband, this turn neither disagrees nor agrees with the criticisms. They are left on the table, as it were, for possible later discussion. The interactional outcome of this can be seen in the couple's simultaneous and emphasized agreement with the formulation (last two lines).

Third, and less obviously perhaps, this avoidance of taking sides, and the treatment of the events as neither bad or worrying, can be *part of* a broader emphasis on how the couple can constructively work toward repairing their relationship. One step will be to become more relaxed about discussing their problems and less fearful of its consequences. Moreover, "complicated" is a descriptive term that sets up relationship problems as a kind of puzzle that can be unravelled via counselling. That is, it provides for the counselling which is to come, as a sensible option where the technical skills will be put to enthusiastic work sorting out complications. These latter orientations of the formulation "rich and complicated lives", and of its specific location in the talk, are rather speculative on their own, and with regard to just this one extract, but could be part of a larger analysis of how the nature and business of counselling, as a discursive activity, are produced and oriented to in various ways.

In Lawrence Wieder's (1974) ethnomethodological terms, such characterizations are multiformulative and multiconsequential; they formulate the world and the identities of the participants in a range of different ways, and they have a range of practical upshots. The general point here is to show the value of treating discourse as *occasioned* (in this sequence, in counselling talk), as *action-oriented* (addressing a range of practical counselling tasks), and as both construct*ed* (from particular terms) and construct*ing* (of the clients' problems in ways that prepares them for counselling work).

THE FUTURE OF DISCURSIVE SOCIAL PSYCHOLOGY

DSP is a relatively new perspective in the area of language and social psychology. Nevertheless it is growing fast and providing challenging new analyses of traditional social psychological topics, as well as opening up new subjects for study. In the next decade we expect to see a number of developments. There will be further productive articulation of the relation between DSP and conversation analysis (Edwards, 1995b, 1998; Frith & Kitzinger, 1998). There will be further theoretical clarification of the relation between DSP and more Foucaultian thinking in discourse analysis (Wetherell & Potter, 1992; Widdicombe & Wooffitt, 1995). There will be less reliance on interview methods and research will become increasingly focused on naturalistic materials, exploiting the technological possibilities of supplementing audio with video records (e.g., Goodwin & Goodwin, 1996). There will be further debate about the role of cognitivism in social psychology and language, and the possibility of taking cognitive notions as topic without at the same time resorting to cognitivist explanations (see, for example, Edwards, 1997, 1999; Potter, 1998c).

ACKNOWLEDGEMENTS

We would like to thank Charles Antaki, Alexa Hepburn, Celia Kitzinger, Claudia Puchta and Sue Speer for making helpful comments on an earlier draft of this chapter.

REFERENCES

Antaki, C. (1994). *Explaining and arguing: The social organization of accounts*. London: Sage.

Antaki, C. (1998). Identity ascriptions in their time and place: "Fagin" and "The Terminally Dim". In C. Antaki & S. Widdicombe (Eds), *Identities in talk* (pp. 71–86). London: Sage.

Auburn, T., Lea, S. & Drake, S. (1999). "It's your opportunity to be truthful": Disbelief, mundane reasoning and the investigation of crime. In. C. Willig (Ed.), *Applied discourse analysis: Social and psychological investigations* (pp. 44–65). Buckingham, UK: Open University Press.

Berger, P.L. & Luckmann, T. (1966). *The social construction of reality*. Garden City: Doubleday.

Billig, M. (1985). Prejudice, categorization and particularization: From a perceptual to a rhetorical approach. *European Journal of Social Psychology*, **15**, 79–103.

Billig, M. (1987). *Arguing and thinking: A rhetorical approach to social psychology*. Cambridge, UK: Cambridge University Press.

Billig, M. (1991). *Ideologies and beliefs*. London: Sage.

Billig, M. (1997) Rhetorical and discursive analysis: How families talk about the royal family. In N. Hayes (Ed.), *Doing qualitative analysis in psychology*. London: Psychology Press.

Brown, R.W. & Fish, D. (1983). The psychological causality implicit in language. *Cognition*, **14**, 237–273.

Buttny, R. & Jensen, A.D. (1995) Telling problems in an initial family therapy session: The hierarchical organization of problem-talk. In G.H. Morris & R.J. Chenail (Eds), *The Talk of the clinic: Explorations in the analysis of medical and therapeutic discourse* (pp. 19–47). Hillsdale, NJ: Erlbaum.

Chalmers, A. (1992). *What is this thing called science? An assessment of the nature and status of science and its methods* (2nd edn). Milton Keynes, UK: Open University Press.

Coyle, A. (1995). Discourse analysis. In G.M. Breakwell, S. Hammond & C. Fife-Schaw (Eds), *Research methods in psychology* (pp. 243–258). London: Sage.

Davis, C. (1986). The process of problem (re)formulation in psychotherapy. *Sociology of Health and Illness*, **8**, 44–74.

Drew, P. & Heritage, J.C. (Eds) (1992). *Talk at work: Interaction in institutional settings.* Cambridge, UK: University of Cambridge Press.

Edwards, D. (1994). Script formulations: A study of event descriptions in conversation. *Journal of Language and Social Psychology*, **13**, 211–247.

Edwards, D. (1995a). Two to tango: Script formulations, dispositions, and rhetorical symmetry in relationship troubles talk. *Research on Language and Social Interaction*, **28**, 319–350.

Edwards, D. (1995b). Sacks and psychology, *Theory and Psychology*, **5**, 579–596.

Edwards, D. (1997). *Discourse and cognition.* London: Sage.

Edwards, D. (1998). The relevant thing about her: Social identity categories in use. In C. Antaki & S. Widdicombe (Eds), *Identities in talk* (pp. 15–33). London: Sage.

Edwards, D. (1999). Shared knowledge as a performative and rhetorical category. In J. Verschueren (Ed.), *Pragmatics in 1998: Selected papers from the 6th International Pragmatics Conference* (Vol. 2, pp. 130–141). Antwerp: International Pragmatics Association.

Edwards, D. (in press). Analysing racial discourse: A view from discursive psychology. In H. van den Berg, H. Houtcoup-Steenstra & M. Wetherell (Eds), *Analyzing interviews on racial issues: Multidisciplinary approaches to interview discourse.* Cambridge, UK: Cambridge University Press.

Edwards, D. & Potter, J. (1992). *Discursive psychology.* London: Sage.

Edwards, D. & Potter, J. (1993). Language and causation: A discursive action model of description and attribution. *Psychological Review*, **100**, 23–41.

Edwards, D. & Potter, J. (1999). Language and causal attribution: A rejoinder to Schmid and Fiedler. *Theory & Psychology*, **9**, 849–863.

Fiske, S.T. & Taylor, S.E. (1991) *Social cognition* (2nd edn). New York: McGraw-Hill.

Frith, H. & Kitzinger, C (1998). "Emotion work" as a participant resource: A feminist analysis of young women's talk-in-interaction. *Sociology*, **32**, 299–320.

Garfinkel, H. (1967). *Studies in ethnomethodology.* Englewood Cliffs, NJ: Prentice-Hall.

Gill, R. (1993). Justifying injustice: Broadcasters' accounts on inequality in radio. In E. Burman & I. Parker (Eds), *Discourse analytic research: Repertoires and readings of texts in action* (pp. 75–93). London: Routledge.

Gill, R. (1996). Discourse analysis: Methodological aspects. In J.E. Richardson (Ed.), *Handbook of qualitative research methods for psychology and the social sciences* (pp. 141–156). Leicester: British Psychological Society.

Goodwin, C. & Goodwin, M.H. (1996). Seeing as situated activity: Formulating planes. In Y. Engeström & D. Middleton (Eds), *Cognition and communication at work* (pp. 61–95). Cambridge, UK: Cambridge University Press.

Hepburn, A. (2000). Power lines: Derrida, discursive psychology and the management of accusations of school bullying, *British Journal of Social Psychology*, **39**, 605–628.

Heritage, J.C. (1984). *Garfinkel and ethnomethodology.* Cambridge, UK: Polity.

Heritage, J.C. (1988). Explanations as accounts: A conversation analytic perspective. In C. Antaki (Ed.), *Analysing everyday explanation: A casebook of methods* (pp. 127–144). London: Sage.

Heritage, J.C. (1995). Conversation analysis: Methodological aspects. In U. Quasthoff (Ed.), *Aspects of oral communication* (pp. 391–418). Berlin: De Gruyter.

Heritage, J.C. & Greatbatch, D.L. (1991). On the institutional character of institutional talk: The case of news interviews. In D. Boden & D.H. Zimmerman (Eds), *Talk and social structure: Studies in ethnomethodology and conversation analysis* (pp. 93–137). Oxford: Polity.

Hutchby, I. & Wooffitt, R. (1998). *Conversation analysis: Principles, practices and applications*. Cambridge, UK: Polity.

Jodelet, D. (1991). *Madness and social representations*. London: Harvester/Wheatsheaf.

MacMillan, K. & Edwards, D. (1999). Who killed the princess? Description and blame in the British press. *Discourse Studies*, **1**, 151–174.

McKinlay, A. & Dunnett, A. (1998). How gun-owners accomplish being deadly average. In C. Antaki & S. Widdicombe (Eds), *Identities in talk* (pp. 34–51). London: Sage.

Mehan, H. (1979). *Learning lessons: Social organization in the classroom*. Cambridge, MA: Harvard University Press.

Moscovici, S. (1984). The phenomenon of social representations. In R.M. Farr & S. Moscovici (Eds), *Social representations* (pp. 3–70). Cambridge, UK: Cambridge University Press.

Myers, G. (1998). Displaying opinions: Topics and disagreement in focus groups. *Language in Society*, **27**, 85–111.

Neisser, U. (1967). *Cognitive psychology*. New York: Appleton-Century-Crofts.

Pomerantz, A.M. (1978). Compliment responses: Notes on the co-operation of multiple constraints. In J. Schenkein (Ed.), *Studies in the organization of conversational interaction* (pp. 79–98). London: Academic Press.

Potter, J. (1996a). *Representing reality: Discourse, rhetoric and social construction*. London: Sage.

Potter, J. (1996b). Discourse anaysis and constructionist approaches: Theoretical background. In J.E. Richardson (Ed.), *Handbook of qualitative research methods for psychology and the social sciences* (pp. 125–140). Leicester: British Psychological Society.

Potter, J. (1997). Discourse analysis as a way of analysing naturally occurring talk. In D. Silverman (Ed.), *Qualitative analysis: Issues of theory and method*. London: Sage.

Potter, J. (1998a). Discursive social psychology: From attitudes to evaluations. *European Review of Social Psychology*, **9**, 233–266.

Potter, J. (1998b). Qualitative and discourse analysis. In A.S.Bellack & M. Hersen (Eds), *Comprehensive clinical psychology* (Vol. 3, pp. 117–144): Oxford: Pergamon.

Potter, J. (1998c). Beyond cognitivism. *Research on Language and Social Interaction*, **32**, 119–128.

Potter, J. & Edwards, D. (1999). Social representations and discursive psychology. *Culture & Psychology*, **5**, 445–456.

Potter, J. & Wetherell, M. (1987). *Discourse and social psychology: Beyond attitudes and behaviour*. London: Sage.

Potter, J. & Wetherell, M. (1988). Accomplishing attitudes: Fact and evaluation in racist discourse. *Text*, **8**, 51–68.

Potter, J. & Wetherell, M. (1994). Analyzing discourse. In A. Bryman and B. Burgess (Eds), *Analyzing qualitative data* (pp. 47–56). London: Routledge.

Potter, J. & Wetherell, M. (1995). Discourse analysis. In J. Smith, R. Harré & L. van Langenhove (Eds), *Rethinking methods in psychology* (pp. 80–92). London: Sage.

Potter, J. & Wetherell, M. (1998). Social representations, discourse analysis and racism. In U. Flick (Ed.), *The psychology of the social* (pp. 138–55). Cambridge, UK: Cambridge University Press.

Potter, J., Edwards, D. & Wetherell, M. (1993). A model of discourse in action. *American Behavioural Scientist*, **36**, 383–401.

Puchta, C. & Potter, J. (in press). Manufacturing individual opinions: Market research focus groups and the discursive psychology of attitudes. *British Journal of Social Psychology*.

Roffe, M. (1996). The social organisation of social work. PhD dissertation, Loughborough University.

Sacks, H. (1992). *Lectures on conversation* (Vols. I & II) edited by G. Jefferson. Oxford: Basil Blackwell.

Schegloff, E.A. (1992). Repair after next turn: The last structurally provided defence of intersubjectivity in conversation. *American Journal of Sociology*, **97**, 1295–1345.

Schegloff, E.A. (1997). Whose text? Whose context? *Discourse and Society*, **8**, 165–187.

Semin, G. & Fiedler, K. (1989). Relocating attributional phenomena within a language–cognition interface: The case of actors' and observers' perspectives. *European Journal of Social Psychology*, **19**, 491–508.

Speer, S. & Potter, J. (2000). The management of heterosexist talk: Conversational resources and prejudiced claims. *Discourse and Society*, **11**, 543–572.

te Molder, H. (1999). Discourse of dilemmas: An analysis of communication planners' accounts. *British Journal of Social Psychology*, **38**, 245–263.

Wetherell, M. & Potter, J. (1992). *Mapping the language of racism: Discourse and the legitimation of exploitation*. London: Harvester/New York: Columbia University Press.

Widdicombe, S. & Wooffitt, R. (1995). *The language of youth subcultures: Social identity in action*. Hemel Hempstead, UK: Harvester/Wheatsheaf.

Wieder, D.L. (1974). Telling the code. In R. Turner (Ed.), *Ethnomethnodology* (pp. 144–172). Harmondsworth, UK: Penguin.

Wooffitt, R.C. (1990). On the analysis of interaction: An introduction to conversation analysis. In P. Luff, D. Frohlich & G.N. Gilbert (Eds), *Computers and conversation* (pp. 7–38). New York: Academic Press.

Wooffitt, R. (1992). *Telling tales of the unexpected: The organization of factual discourse*. London: Harvester/Wheatsheaf.

Wooffitt, R. (1993). Analysing accounts. In N. Gilbert (Ed.), *Researching social life* (pp. 287–305). Beverly Hills, CA: Sage.

Woolgar, S. (1988). *Science: The very idea*. Chichester: Ellis Horwood/London: Tavistock.

Storytelling: The Power of Narrative Communication and Interpretation

Sunwolf
Santa Clara University, USA
Lawrence R. Frey
University of Memphis, USA

story (stor•e), *n.* 1. a narrative, either true or fictitious. 2. a way of knowing and remembering information; a shape or pattern into which information can be arranged and experiences preserved. 3. an ancient, natural order of the mind. 4. isolated and disconnected scraps of human experience, bound into a meaningful whole.
Adapted, from *Webster's Tenth New Collegiate Dictionary* (1993)

People continually experience life through story structure, as narrative offers both a way of knowing and remembering experiences, as well as providing a powerful structure for binding together in a meaningful way seemingly isolated events. Human beings think, perceive, imagine, and make moral choices according to narrative structures (Sarbin, 1986). The study of narrative is itself a dynamic story, offered to diverse audiences and told or retold from multiple perspectives. The plans we make, our rememberings, even our loving and hating, are all guided by narrative plots; survival in a world of meaning would be problematic in the absence of skill to make up and to interpret stories about interweaving lives (Sarbin, 1998). From the conceptual terrain of communication theory to the ethical domain of moral philosophy, from preferred research procedures in anthropology, sociology, and linguistics to particular pragmatic practices in health, education, and jurisprudence, narrative is, at once, a world-view, a field of study, a methodology, and an embodied way of being in the world.

The New Handbook of Language and Social Psychology.
Edited by W. Peter Robinson and Howard Giles.
© 2001 John Wiley & Sons Ltd.

In this chapter, we seek to describe some of the ebbs and flows of narrative scholarship, from the macro-level of narrative forms to the middle ground of narrative methodology to the micro-level of some illustrative examples of narrative research. Further, we suggest a functional approach to understanding the value of narrative research, arguing that the telling of stories serves both cognitive and communicative functions, specifically: (1) relational (ways of connecting people), (2) explanatory (ways of knowing), (3) creative (ways of creating reality), (4) historical (ways of remembering), and (5) forecasting (ways of visioning the future). Finally, we offer new narrative typology pairings for the study of story format (personal/other, shared/never-told, fictional/historical, negotiated/fixed, spontaneous/strategized, and stock/unique). In doing so, we fully recognize that any attempt to build a container that describes the study of narrative is but one story among many others that could be told.

ONCE UPON A TIME: WHAT IS NARRATIVE?

Narrative has been described as a "blurred genre" (Langellier, 1989) and has been argued to be an organizing principle for human behavior (e.g., Bruner, 1986; Cronon, 1992; Fisher, 1987, 1997; Rosaldo, 1989; Sarbin, 1986; Schafer, 1981). Once primarily the province of textual analysis, there has been a narrative turn in the social sciences, invoked more recently by historians (e.g., Cronon, 1992; White, 1981a, 1981b), anthropologists and folklorists (i.e., Rosaldo, 1989), psychologists (e.g., Bruner, 1986, 1996; Polkinghorne, 1988; Sarbin, 1986), social psychologists (e.g., Marsh, Rosser & Harré, 1978), sociologists (e.g., Boje, 1991), sociolinguists (e.g., Gee, 1985; Labov, 1982; Polanyi, 1989), educators (e.g., McEwan & Egan, 1995; Zeller, 1995), and communication scholars (e.g., Adelman & Frey, 1997; Fisher, 1997; Sunwolf, 1999b). Berger (1997) points to many different forms that narrative can take (e.g., speeches, films, comic strips), suggesting that in the simplest sense narratives are stories that take place through time. The word "narrative" comes from the Indo-European root "gna" meaning both "to know" and "to tell" (White, 1987). One issue of the *Journal of Communication* (1985) was devoted to *Homo narrans* – a root metaphor that Fisher (1987) proposed to represent the essential nature of human beings as narrative beings. From such a perspective, people are seen as using stories both to give order to human experience and to share experience with others.

While examples of narrative include personal histories, myths, fairy tales, novels, and conversational stories, scholars disagree about the precise definition of narrative. Polkinghorne (1988) limits narrative to the kind of organizational scheme expressed in story form, including both the cognitive process of making a story and the resulting narrative product. Polanyi (1989) suggests that story is a particular type of narrative in which a teller describes events that took place in one specific past time world in order to make a point about the world which teller and story recipients share. Polkinghorne (1988) describes narratives as joining two separate events ("the father died" and "the son cried") into a single episode ("the son cried when his father died"), which increases understanding of both events. As we use the term here, "narrative" is equivalent to "story", referring to a communication structure in which a teller describes events that took place in the past (factual), might have taken place (speculative), or might yet take place (predictive), for the purpose of creating shared meaning between audience and teller.

What is different about *narrative analysis*, compared, for example, to textual analysis or the study of ethnographic accounts? A large body of research involves discourse or text comprehension, in which the search for structure is the primary goal. Much of the work in narrative studies has focused on spoken narratives, which remain a strong emphasis (Mishler, 1991). Narrative studies are distinguished from textual analyses (e.g., semiotics, hermeneutics, conversational analysis, discourse analysis, and document analysis) by an interpretive thrust (Riessman, 1993); narratives, in fact, invite listener interpretation. The study of accounts, for example, in discourse and social psychology has effectively employed narrative tools (e.g., Marsh et al., 1978, study of the social world of British soccer fans, starting with a body of accounts of fans' behavior on the soccer terraces, finding exaggerated storytelling and a rich vocabulary for constructing stories after the matches). Story-talk is the object for narrative study, either oral, written, or visual, and either researcher-generated or naturally occurring. Scholars using narrative methodology ask questions about: (1) the content and language of story (form), (2) motivation for telling (why), (3) methods of telling (how), and (4) the impact of telling (effects). For example, such questions include how a story is put together by a teller (form), what function a story fulfills for the teller (why), what ways were used to tell a particular story (how), and how a tale persuades or affects listeners (effects). Here we will focus on two of these: function and effects.

CONNECTIONS BETWEEN STORY, SELF, OTHERS, AND EXPERIENCE: *WHY* DO WE TELL STORIES?

> Man is the storytelling animal. Wherever he goes he wants to leave behind not a chaotic wake, not an empty space, but the comforting marker-buoys and trail-signs of stories. He has to go on telling stories. He has to keep on making them up. As long as there's a story, it's all right. Swift (1983, p. 53)

The telling of stories may function as providing a way of connecting people, a way of knowing about the world, a way of creating reality, a way of remembering, and a way of visioning the future.

Bridges: A Way of Connecting (Relational Narrating)

Construction of Self Through Storytelling: Who am I?

Stories are ways of self-making. The psychoanalyst Schafer (1981) claims people are forever telling stories about themselves. One of the first structures of discourse acquired by children, personal narratives, are told throughout the lifespan (Lan-gellier, 1989; see Sutton-Smith, 1986, on problems connected with children's ac-quisition of story making). Constructing personal narratives is, thus, a critical factor in the formation of one's identity. Bruner (1987) argues an important aspect of narrative analysis is to reveal constructed autobiography. The *self*-telling of life narratives is as important a basis for study as *other*-telling. Frank's (1995) research finds that self is being formed in what is told. Scheibe (1986) points out that for some people the stories they have constructed for their lives come to an end *before* their biological lives do. Self-stories that answer "Who am I?", in effect, are open-ended, unfinished, always open to editing and revision.

Weaving Community Through Storytelling: Who are We?

We may be educated by *rationality*, but we are socialized by *narrativity* (Fisher, 1984). *Storytelling* is a tool for the construction of shared identities and commu-nities. Oral tales, told by families, teachers, leaders, are used by many cultures to shape each listener's concept of self, of choice, of relationship to community, and of individual power. Culture, consequently, "speaks itself" through an individ-ual's story (Riessman, 1993). People tell folktales commending people to be-come honest, determined, or generous – attributes cultural communities need from their members (Sunwolf, 1999a). Bormann's (1985) symbolic convergence theory accounts for this property of human narrative communication by ex-plaining the appearance of a *group* consciousness, with its implied shared emo-tions, motives, and meanings in terms of socially shared narrations, rather than individual scripts. Witherell, Tran and Othus (1995) suggest that oral storytelling allows the audience to engage in a leap of empathy, binding them into wider relationships that provide bridges across cultures.

Stories as Theories: A Way of Knowing (Explanatory Narrating)

There is a logic of knowing that derives from story; Fisher (1985, 1987) proposes that all forms of communication are most usefully interpreted from a narrational perspective, since people inherently pursue a *narrative* logic. The narrative para-digm postulates that people are acutely aware of narrative probability in making sense of the world; that is, they are aware of whether a story told by another "rings true" with what they know from their own lives (Fisher, 1985). Explana-tory narrating, as discussed below, promotes knowledge by: (1) ordering experi-ences, (2) representing reality, (3) making sense of lived events, (4) sharing knowledge, and (5) influencing values, beliefs, and actions.

Ordering Experiences

Narratives are recipes for structuring experience (Bruner, 1987). Narrative order-ing makes individual events comprehensible by identifying the whole to which they contribute (Polkinghorne, 1988). Among many African tribes, the oral narrative tradition is simultaneously ancient and contemporary, with images from the past and present intermingled (Scheub, 1998). African tribal tales may be products of long reflections about the relations among humans, between humans and the animal world, responses to the challenges of the unknown, and to the universal need to create order and reason out of chaos and accident (Courlander, 1975). Wanner (1994) argues that the process of sharing oral narratives values a particular logic of knowing; while written language may present deductive or inductive reasoning – spoken language presents a more dynamic view.

Representing "Reality"

People use narratives as organizing schemas (Mandler & Johnson, 1977) as well as interpretive tools (Bennett, 1978). Gee (1985) sees all children as making sense of reality (and doing so in a masterful way) through narrativizing and narrative competence seems to appear early, at about the age of three (Polkinghorne, 1988). As children develop, they use narrative to make sense of the realities they encounter, even apart from non-narrative styles of their teachers. Gee's linguistic analysis of a seven-year-old black child's "sharing time" narrative in school show-and-tell periods argues that a child may make sense of her experience through an oral style that does not share her teacher's literate style of speech.

Making Sense of Lived Events

The role of stories in offering social explanations has been analyzed by Bennett (1992). Narrative has been described as a scheme by means of which humans give meaning to their experience of temporality as well as personal actions (Polkinghorne, 1988). Stories answer both why and why-not questions, allowing people to make sense of lived experiences.

Sharing Knowledge (Pedagogical)

Stories may be pedagogical. Kirkwood (1983) defines "teaching stories" as brief, oral narratives told primarily to instruct, guide, or influence listeners, rather than to entertain. Kaufmann (1996) offers a comprehensive anthropological analysis of *wisdom* literature, including fables, apologues, parables, religious tales, anecdotes, moral tales, jokes, and proverbs; these stories come from a genre which is structured with a double communicative purpose, referred to in Spanish as *instruir deleitando*: stories that entertain, but at the same time teach.

Influencing Values, Beliefs, and Actions (Persuasive)

Story often functions as a type of argument, but differs from traditional formal argument of claim and evidence (usually presented in deductive order). Story avoids the predictable conclusion of argument, providing surprises, coincidences, and encounters that hold the receiver's attention throughout (Polkinghorne, 1988), and Berger (1997) points out that narrative often relies on metaphors and metonyms. Stories are themselves often commentaries on the narratives a community finds valid and compelling, and constitute a form of persuasive argument (Kirkwood, 1985). Past research suggests that one form of argument that occurs in groups specifically involves the production of stories or narratives (Hall & Langellier, 1988; Polanyi, 1981; Robinson, 1981), particularly in dealing with complex decision-making tasks (Pennington & Hastie, 1986). Communication researchers have compared the persuasiveness of using statistical versus narrative evidence (i.e., Allen and Preiss, 1997, reporting that a persuader is slightly more effective with a message that uses a statistical proof as opposed to examples or narratives, but pointing out the unanswered issue as to whether a combination of proofs would be more effective than a single proof; Kopfman, et al., 1998, finding statistical evidence used in health messages produced greater results in terms of cognitive reactions, while narratives produced greater results for affective reactions).

The rhetorical function of stories relies upon persuasive power (Lucaites & Condit, 1985), that is, the intent of narrators to persuade others of their point of view or of the value or legitimacy of their claims. The role played by storytelling in Native North America included the belief that a well-told tale would be remembered longer rather than saying either "You should!" or "You should not!" (Bruchac, 1996a, 1996b). Sufi wisdom tales recognize the power of stories to make points without marshaling the mental resistance that more sharply reasoned rational appeals raise (Friedlander, 1992). The African dilemma tale exercises the puzzle and debate talents of the listeners, and consequently functions as an integral part of moral and ethical training in many African societies, ending with a question to be settled by the listeners (Bascom, 1975). These and other examples suggest that the persuasive effects of narratives may derive from: (a) an audience's self-generated thoughts, (b) active cognitive participation of the audience, (c) modeling of behaviors and values, or (d) provoking conscious deliberation (Sunwolf, 1999b).

Twisted Tales: A Way of Creating Reality (Creative Narrating)

Our daydreams are storied. Telling stories may also be a creative act, whereby the teller uses language to construct and experience fictional events. Narratives can function as recipes for thinking and behaving: creating attitudes, beliefs, values, and actions. Frey (1987) argues that words are generative; in many cultures they are believed to bring about phenomena. In particular, narrative provides a useful structure for *re-creating* past events. Some Native American people view their stories as tools of communication that operate by re-enacting powerful happenings, as well as creating new events. Native people of the southwest have said that telling Coyote stories, for example, at the wrong time is an invitation for the trickster to visit the teller, bringing unwanted trouble (Bruchac, 1996a). Sarbin (1998) argues that "as if" narratives can be used not only to organize experience, but also to create socially significant believed-in imaginings.

Flashbacks: A Way of Remembering (Historical Narrating)

Narrative structures carry culturally significant events from one generation to the next, and, thereby, help community members remember their past. Cultures pass stories from generation to generation; the tales belong to that community, not a particular author. The tales have paradoxical functions: giving continuity and stability to a culture, yet modifying themselves (as all language modifies itself) to adapt to current conditions (Wanner, 1994). Both literature and myth are forms of historical narrative, distilling the historical experiences of a people or culture. Further, narrative *memory* facilitates individual retention and recall. Narratives, however, are important information and interpretations, not merely information storage devices; they act to organize memory (Riessman, 1993).

Schank's (1990) research links narrating to memory, as the process of creating a story also creates the memory structure that will contain the gist of the story throughout a person's life. Memory is, in effect, created by the telling of stories.

Foreflashes: A Way of Visioning the Future (Forecasting)

Narrative structures facilitate the imagining of future possibilities as well as the contemplation of hypotheticals. Wanner (1994) argues that narrative structure allows adolescents, in particular, to look back and make sense of their experiences, while providing a much-needed forum in which to speculate about the future. The unfinished nature of self-stories provokes the contemplation of more than one ending, as new choice paths are imagined in story form (Polkinghorne, 1988). Narratives provide temporal bridges, allowing tellers and receivers to reframe past events and reconsider future possibilities (e.g., conversational production of what-if narratives by deliberating jurors in group argument; Sunwolf, 1999a).

THE TELLING AND THE TOLD: NARRATIVE STRUCTURES

People perceive, imagine, and make moral choices, in part, according to narrative structures (Sarbin, 1986). Narratives depend on certain structures to hold them together, though they may be assembled in diverse ways. Narratives are frameworks that imbue the story with parts, grammar, and voice. Labov's (1972) structural approach, for example, takes a "parts" approach, arguing from a sociolinguistic perspective that fully formed stories include an abstract, orientation, complicating action, evaluation, resolution, and return to present perspective. Burke's (1945) dramatism describes the grammatical resources on which tellers rely. Gee (1985, 1986) examines how a story is told (e.g., pitch, pauses, poetic units, and stanzas).

Significant cultural differences exist in what are considered to be acceptable story structures. Collins (1985) points out that the number of times oppositions, encounters, and sub-parts of a narrative are typically repeated vary (e.g., Western European folktales favor cycles of three, such as three wishes or three tasks, while Canadian and Alaskan Athabaskans more commonly utilize cycles of four, and the Chinook of the Northwest Coast employ cyclic repetitions in groups of five). Interestingly, culturally conditioned expectations about narrative structure carry over from one language to another (see Scollon & Scollon's, 1981, study of Athabaskan children favoring four-part cyclic structures when telling stories in English). Furthermore, cultures differ in enacted structures delineating the role of audience; ethnographic studies of narrative events among African American, Hawaiian American, and American Indian groups show that narrative emerges in an interactive context where the audience's response influences or controls the unfolding of a story, giving narrative performances a strongly dialogic quality (see Collins, 1985; Sunwolf, 1999b).

NARRATIVE METHODOLOGY

While it is not our intent to undertake a particularized review of the variety of narrative methodologies reported to date, it is nonetheless useful to point out some of the methods (such as survey, ethnography, and experimentation), tools (such as interviews and questionnaires), and report forms (such as film and written text) that such research takes. Narrative study gathers storied representations of experience, confronting issues of how to collect appropriate stories, transcribe tellings, and analyze those narratives. The assumptions reflected in different ways of re-presenting gathered narrative need to be illuminated (Mishler, 1991). Conquergood (1985), for example, who has examined narrative performances of the Hmong in refugee camps in Thailand, usefully questions his own bias, foregrounding the ethical tensions and ambiguities surrounding ethnographic praxis.

Narrative method is further challenged by the generalizability (frequently making the case for $N = 1$). This raises questions about how validity, significance, and reliability are measured in narrative study. An argument may be considered strong when it has the capacity to resist challenge, although new information may convince scholars that another conclusion is more likely. Findings are "significant" when they are viewed as meaningful or able to increase understanding of human behavior, and when data demonstrates dependability.

DOING NARRATIVE WORK: ILLUSTRATIVE STUDIES IN APPLIED CONTEXTS

We now turn to applied examples of narrative studies, examining narrative research in contexts of health, law, education, and therapy.

Health/Illness

> I will tell you something about stories.
> They are all we have, you see,
> all we have to fight off
> illness and death. Silko (1977)

Storytelling may function to create the possibility of being *successfully ill*. Frank (1995), a sociologist at the University of Calgary, argues that illness is a call for stories. Becoming ill, in fact, may function to promote narratives by repairing the damage illness does to a person's sense of self and task of redrawing self-maps in light of changed circumstances. *Illness tales* are collective narrative interpretations that ease the stigma of deviant behavior and unusual symptoms by conversion to the absurd (Adelman and Frey, 1997, collecting successful illness tales told and retold which helped create and sustain a unified rhetorical vision of one community, Bonaventure House, where people live, not die, with AIDS).

Hawkins (1993) studied *pathographies*: autobiographical and biographical narratives about illness, treatment, and death. In that sense, illness and death challenge our existential being to construct meanings that make sense of life and create a coherent narrative for what appears to be inexplicable. Clark (1998) has examined childhood imaginative narratives in the face of chronic illnesses. One five-year-old boy shared a narrative he had constructed that used a favorite toy car given magical qualities that took him to other places, in reframing his reality. Fear of death was a universal concern shared during Clark's interviews with asthmatic children; a lack of breath always carried a concurrent sense of life-threatening consequences. Clark reports one child had sheets on his bed depicting Teenage Mutant Ninja Turtles, which provided a basis for the child's imagined what-if stories that, should a nighttime emergency with his breathing occur, one of the Turtles would fly off the sheets and go to get the doctor, which calmed him during attacks.

Adelman and Frey (1997), using a dialectical, longitudinal, ethnographic approach over several years, collected entry experience stories (joining community), as well as exit experience stories (coping with loss and anticipated loss of community members) in a residential setting for people living with AIDS. One resident reported:

> The first week I didn't allow them to make me feel no kind of way. I isolated myself in my room basically till I got used to being there. I had to get used to the place in order to make it my home . . . and then I slowly started to come out and talk with

other people. I would speak and when they asked certain questions, I would say it in such a cold way that they would stand far away from me and be careful with what they say. I kept it like that for a while. (p. 42)

Some of the collected narratives provide examples of the stress of residents' coping with finishing their own life stories, as well as the unfinished stories of others:

Since I've been sick with this disease, I don't allow myself to become emotionally attached anymore, because in this business you have to let go constantly and you get used to letting go. That's important right now, because a lot of people go through depression when someone leaves and they really get sick. And I choose not to, and I hope that doesn't sound cold, but I choose not to, and I am pretty much happier and healthier that way. And all the people that have passed away the last few weeks, man, it's good that I have. When they tell me that someone passed, I'll say, "Now they're resting in peace," and I go on. No more thought, no more nothing. I go on. (p. 77)

Law

Legal systems consist largely of rational argument forms, but storytelling pervades this context. Verdicts in criminal trials may be driven by the most compelling story told by competing advocates (Bennett, 1997). Further, storytelling has been found to function in powerful ways for deliberating jurors: (1) testing validity, (2) communicating interpretations, (3) dueling perspectives, (4) providing immediacy for distant events, (5) reconstructing reality, (6) filling in missing pieces, (7) providing structures for comparisons, (8) capturing attention, (9) stimulating collaborative reasoning, (10) providing economic vehicles for communicating argument, (11) acting as convenient cross-references, and (12) providing alternative points of view (Sunwolf, 1999a). Some jurors tell fictionalized narratives in deliberative argument that inserted themselves into trial events. At other times, jurors offered non-fictional narratives, importing into deliberations events from their past. Beyond sharing narratives, however, jurors invited narrative thinking on the part of other jurors, asking other jurors to speculate on what they might have done under the circumstances (Sunwolf, 1999a).

Bennett and Feldman (1981) have long argued that trials are organized around storytelling in both England and the United States, demonstrating from their research that in order to understand, take part in, and communicate about criminal trials, people transform the evidence introduced in trials into stories about the alleged criminal activities. They argue that the structural features of stories make it possible to perform the complex legal tests for evaluating evidence.

Education

It has been argued that all teachers worthy of the name are storytellers (Wanner, 1994). Bruner (1986) has helped popularize within educational research a conception of the mind that gives renewed prominence to the role of story. Stories perform both an epistemological function (passing on specific knowledge to students), and a transformative function (suggesting new ways of thinking or behaving), and, thus, constitute important pedagogical tools in contemporary education (Sunwolf, 1999b). Storytelling activities in the classroom have been used to construct a cooperative learning experience (Stotter, 1994).

Kirkwood and Gold (1983) offer an application of research on the use of teaching stories to explore philosophical themes in the classroom. Egan (1995) demonstrates how the narrative nature of mind might affect ideas about the learning principles used to guide teaching practice and curriculum structure. Cargile and Sunwolf (1998) offer specific activities for using tales to teach various constructs in an intercultural communication course. Collins (1985) reports how classroom research reveals the manner in which mismatches in general expectations about narrative structure and voice resulted in disharmonious student–teacher exchanges. Wanner (1994) has investigated the use of narrative in high school classrooms, arguing how and why narrative is an extremely rich learning medium for adolescents.

Therapy

Psychotherapy deals both with and *in* stories. Individuals often have typical plots they use to order their own life events (e.g., tragedy, comedy), and yet they may reframe stories and change the meaning of life events; psychotherapists have used this property of narrative in their notion of *life scripts* (Polkinghorne, 1988). Psychotherapeutic work with clients is often centered in narrative discourse, extending back to Freud. Some researchers have begun to acknowledge the analyst's role as a collaborator in the client's narrative (see Polkinghorne, 1988; Victor, 1998). Researchers (de Rivera, 1998; Victor, 1998) have used narrative analysis to examine "false memory syndrome", theorizing that a person who is predisposed to accept certain possibilities will also accept narrative suggestions from therapists who reframe puzzling personal experiences for them (e.g., the belief that one was abducted by an alien or that one was sexually assaulted by a close family member). As de Rivera (1998) points out, therapists and clients often extend the seeds of the offered narrative.

Spence (1986) describes the phenomenon of "narrative smoothing" in therapeutic settings, which involves problematizing the telling of patient stories by psychiatrists. Narrative smoothing occurs when there is an attempt to bring a clinical story into conformity with a public standard or stereotype (i.e., Freud's Wolf Man), although smoothing may occur at another level in the consulting room in the form of a leading suggestion that triggers imagined narratives "Could you have been jealous of your brother when he came home from the hospital?".

HAPPILY-EVER-AFTERING: FUTURE DIRECTIONS

Examining both existing gaps and under-researched aspects of narrative communication and interpretation, we offer new narrative typology pairings for the study of story format. We further suggest four directions for future development of the story of narrative studies, including a focus on: (1) narratives as ways of doing togetherness, (2) narratives as ways of bridging disciplines, (3) narratives structured and affected by scholarly audiences, and (4) unfinished stories.

Narrative Typologies

A central question for narrative scholars is the format enacted narratives take. New narrative taxonomies are useful in suggesting new questions that need to be asked and methodological designs that can help answer them. At this point, we suggest six narrative typology pairings that may prove fruitful: (1) personal versus other, (2) shared versus never-told, (3) fictional versus historical, (4) negotiated versus fixed, (5) spontaneous versus strategized, and (6) stock versus unique. Personal tales include the teller, while other-oriented tales do not; shared tales are those told to one or more receivers, whereas never-told tales are narratives that have been thought about but not communicated; fictional tales do not purport to be reflective of reality, whereas historical tales report past events; negotiated narratives are co-constructed between individuals or among group members, and may vary with each telling, whereas fixed narratives are passed on unchanged; spontaneous narratives occur unrehearsed, in impromptu fashion, compared to strategized narratives, which are premeditated; and stock narratives rely on generic plot structures, or archetypical characters, whereas unique narratives appear unfamiliar and individualized.

Interactive Storybuilding: Narratives as Ways of Performing Togetherness

Stories expand the human capacity to become what we are not (Kirkwood, 1992). The focus of narrative analyses has been on the story and the teller. More attention needs to be paid to the role of the story *receiver* in creating narrative meaning: to what degree, and in what ways, is story as "product" a collaborative effort between teller and receiver, and what is the interactive process that occurs between tale teller and audience/reader?

Narratives as Ways of Bridging Disciplines

New attempts at bridging interdisciplinary territories have emerged. For example, the Narrative Study Group, which began meeting in 1987 as an informal, multidisciplinary, and multi-university collective of scholars sharing interest in narratives (Mishler, 1991), now sponsors the New England Symposia on Narrative Studies in the Social Sciences. Narrative data, collected by one discipline, is a rich resource waiting to be interpreted by another, using new theories and asking novel questions.

Whose Stories are Told? Whose Stories are Heard?

Scientific reports are forms of narrative argument located within the contested terrain of theories and practices within their disciplines (Mishler, 1991). There may be conflicts between the goals of respondents and researchers, with result-ant differences in the narratives they construct, as, for example, the critical story Brodkey and Fine (1988) tell about participants' efforts to suppress and disavow their personal experiences of sexual harassment. Scholars vary in how they are positioned and aligned within the contexts they investigate, which impacts in complex ways the narrativizing of story data. Our pre-commitments, as re-searchers, regarding the nature of narrative is itself a story that functions as a narrative lens through which we view data. Language usages and their connota-tions are contentious and culture-bound and, thus, the potential for interpreta-tive bias must be realized in deconstructing stories.

Unfinished Stories: Living in the Middle of Story

> Some poems don't rhyme, and
> some stories don't have
> a clear beginning,
> middle and
> end
>
> *Comedian Gilda Radner*

An examination of narratives must also acknowledge those stories that best fulfill the desires of both tellers and audience by never ending. Leitch (1986) examines the ideal television soap opera that outlasts plot twists, cast changes, and set furniture, denying the possibility of closure. Narratives are situated within larger contexts. This embeddedness, and the dynamic interchanges and boundary penetrations that occur as a result, has been understudied. We need to know how narratives differ when they are elicited by different questions in different contexts, or when they appear in naturally occurring conversations as opposed to research-generated interviews. The research practice division also needs to be bridged more completely in terms of understanding. How do real-world practitioners (e.g., educators, therapists, health care professionals, or law-yers) work with narrative knowledge?

The seductive paradox of the study of narrative communication is that any completed study is nonetheless never *done*. Not only is it difficult to point to a finished narrative, but narratives may be more *lived* than *observable* (Polkinghorne, 1988). Narratives are notably, wonderfully unstable, which makes them highly susceptible to cultural, interpersonal, and linguistic influences. But there can be little doubt that a focus on narrative ways of knowing suggests a realm for understanding human communication that may make our various research tales more audience-connected and relevant, though the study of narrative remains a never-ending story being recreated and retold. As Frank (1995) suggests, narrative analyses await not only further research, but further *living*, and the subsequent telling of those lives.

> Take the *tale* in your teeth, then, and bite till the blood runs, hoping it's not poison; and we will all come to the end together, and even to the beginning: living, as we do, in the middle. Le Guin (1981)

REFERENCES

Adelman, M.B. & Frey, L.R. (1997). *The fragile community: Living together with AIDS.* Mahwah, NJ: Erlbaum.

Allen, M. & Preiss, R.W. (1997). Comparing the persuasiveness of narrative and statistical evidence using meta-analysis. *Communication Research Reports*, **14**, 125–133.

Bascom, W.R. (1975). *African dilemma tales.* Paris: Mouton.

Bennett, W.L. (1978). Storytelling in criminal trials: A model of social judgment. *Quarterly Journal of Speech*, **64**, 1–22.

Bennett, W.L. (1992). Legal fictions: Telling stories and doing justice. In M.L. McLaughlin, M.J. Cody & S.J. Read (Eds), *Explaining one's self to others: Reasongiving in a social context* (pp. 149–165). Hillsdale, NJ: Erlbaum.

Bennett, W.L. (1997). Storytelling in criminal trials: A model of social judgment. In L.P. Hinchman & S.K. Hinchman (Eds), *Memory, identity, community: The idea of narrative in the human sciences* (pp. 72–103). Albany, NY: State University of New York Press.

Bennett, W.L. & Edelman, M. (1985). Toward a new political narrative. *Journal of Communication*, **35**, 156–171.

Bennett, W.L. & Feldman, M.S. (1981). *Reconstructing reality in the courtroom: Justice and judgment in American culture.* New Brunswick, NJ: Rutgers University Press.

Berger, A.A. (1997). *Narratives in popular culture, media, and everyday life.* Thousand Oaks, CA: Sage.

Boje, D.M. (1991). The storytelling organization: A study of story performance in an office-supply firm. *Administrative Science Quarterly*, **36**, 106–126.

Bormann, E.G. (1985). Symbolic convergence theory: A communication formulation. *Journal of Communication*, **35**(4), 123–138.

Brodkey, L. & Fine, M. (1988). Presence of mind in the absence of body. *Journal of Education*, **170**, 84–99.

Bruchac, J. (1996a). *Roots of survival: Native American storytelling and the sacred.* Golden, CO: Fulcrum.

Bruchac, J. (1996b). The continuing circle: Native American storytelling past and present. In C.L. Birch & M.A. Heckler (Eds), *Who says? Essays on pivotal issues in contemporary storytelling* (pp. 91–106). Little Rock, AR: August House.

Bruner, J. (1986). *Actual minds, possible words.* Cambridge, MA: Harvard University Press.

Bruner, J. (1987). Life as narrative. *Social Research*, **54**, 11–32.

Bruner, J. (1996). *The culture of education.* Cambridge, MA: Harvard University Press.

Burke, K. (1945). *A grammar of motives.* New York: Prentice-Hall.

Cargile, A.C. & Sunwolf (1998). Does the squeaky wheel get the grease? Understanding direct and indirect communication. In T. Singelis (Ed.), *Teaching about race, culture and diversity* (pp. 221–229). Thousand Oaks, CA: Sage.

Clark, C.D. (1998). Childhood imagination in the face of chronic illness. In J. de Rivera & T.R. Sarbin (Eds), *Believed-in imaginings: The narrative construction of reality* (pp. 87–100). Washington, DC: American Psychological Association.

Collins, J. (1985). Some problems and purposes of narrative analysis in educational research. *Journal of Education*, **167**, 57–70.

Conquergood, D. (1985). Performing as a moral act: Ethical dimensions of the ethnography of performance. *Literature in Performance*, **5**, 1–13.

Courlander, H. (1975). *A treasury of African folklore: The oral literature, traditions, myths, legends, epics, tales, recollections, wisdom, sayings, and humor of Africa.* New York: Crown.

Cronon, W. (1992). A place for stories: Nature, history, and narrative. *Journal of American History*, **78**, 1347–1376.

de Rivera, J. (1998). Relinquishing believed-in imaginings: Narratives of people who have repudiated false accusations. In J. de Rivera & T.R. Sarbin (Eds), *Believed-in imaginings: The narrative construction of reality* (pp. 15–30). Washington, DC: American Psychological Association.

Egan, K. (1995). Narrative and learning: A voyage of implications. In H. McEwan & K. Egan (Eds), *Narrative in teaching, learning, and research* (pp. 116–124). New York: Teachers College Press.

Fisher, B.A. (1984). Narration as a human communication paradigm: The case of public moral argument. *Communication Monographs*, **51**, 1–22.

Fisher, W.R. (1985). The narrative paradigm: In the beginning. *Journal of Communication*, **35**, 74–89.

Fisher, W.R. (1987). *Human communication as narration: Toward a philosophy of reason, value, and action.* Columbia, SC: University of South Carolina Press.

Fisher, W.R. (1997). Narration, reason, and community. In L.P. Hinchman & S.K. Hinchman (Eds), *Memory, identity, community: The idea of narrative in the human sciences* (pp. 307–327). Albany, NY: State University of New York Press.

Frank, A.W. (1995). *The wounded storyteller: Body, illness, and ethics.* Chicago, IL: University of Chicago Press.

Frey, R. (1987). *The world of the Crow Indians: As driftwood lodges.* Norman, OK: University of Oklahoma Press.

Friedlander, S. (1992). *Talks on Sufism: When you hear hoofbeats think of a zebra.* Costa Mesa, CA: Mazda.

Gee, J.P. (1985). The narrativization of experience in the oral style. *Journal of Education*, **167**, 9–35.

Gee, J.P. (1986). Units in the production of narrative discourse. *Discourse Processes*, **9**, 391–422.

Hall, D. & Langellier, K. (1988). Storytelling strategies in mother–daughter communication. In B. Bate & A. Taylor (Eds), *Women communicating: Studies of women's talk* (pp. 107–126). Norwood, NJ: Ablex.

Hawkins, A.H. (1993). *Reconstructing illness: Studies in pathography.* West Lafayette, IN: Purdue University Press.

Kaufmann, W.O. (1996). *The anthropology of wisdom literature.* Westport, CT: Bergin & Garvey.

Kirkwood, W.G. (1983). Storytelling and self-confrontation: Parables as communication strategies. *Quarterly Journal of Speech*, **69**, 58–74.

Kirkwood, W.G. (1985). Parables as metaphors and examples. *Quarterly Journal of Speech*, **71**, 422–440.

Kirkwood, W.G. (1992). Narrative and the rhetoric of possibility. *Communication Monographs*, **59**, 30–47.

Kirkwood, W.G. & Gold, J.B. (1983). Using teaching stories to explore philosophical themes in the classroom. *Metaphilosophy*, **14**, 341–352.

Kopfman, J.E., Smith, S.W., Ah Yun, J.K. & Hodges, A. (1998). Affective and cognitive reactions to narrative versus statistical evidence organ donation messages. *Journal of Applied Communication Research*, **26**, 279–300.

Labov, W. (1972). The transformation of experience in narrative syntax. In W. Labov (Ed.), *Language in the inner city: Studies in the Black English vernacular* (pp. 354–396). Philadelphia, PA: University of Pennsylvania Press.

Labov, W. (1982). Speech actions and reactions in personal narrative. In D. Tannen (Ed.), *Analyzing discourse: Text and talk* (pp. 219–247). Washington, DC: Georgetown University Press.

Langellier, K.M. (1989). Personal narratives: Perspective on theory and research. *Text and Performance Quarterly*, **9**, 243–276.

Le Guin, U.K. (1981). It was a dark and stormy night; or, why are we huddled about the campfire? In W.J.T. Mitchell (Ed.), *On narrative* (pp. 187–196). Chicago, IL: University of Chicago Press.

Leitch, T.M. (1986). *What stories are: Narrative theory and interpretation.* University Park, PA: Pennsylvania State University Press.

Lucaites, J.L. & Condit, C.M. (1985). Re-constructing narrative theory: A functional perspective. *Journal of Communication*, **35**, 90–108.

Mandler, J.M., & Johnson, N.S. (1977). Remembrance of things passed: Story structure and recall. *Cognitive Psychology*, **9**, 111–151.

Marsh, P., Rosser, E. & Harré, R. (1978). *The rules of disorder.* London: Routledge & Kegan Paul.

McEwan, H. & Egan, K. (Eds) (1995). *Narrative in teaching, learning, and research.* New York: Teachers College Press.

McGee, M.C. & Nelson, J.S. (1985). Narrative reason in the public argument. *Journal of Communication*, **35**, 139–155.

Mishler, E.G. (1991). "Once upon a time . . .". *Journal of Narrative and Life History*, **1**, 101–108.

Pennington, N. & Hastie, R. (1986). Evidence evaluation in complex decision making. *Journal of Personality and Social Psychology*, **51**, 242–256.

Polanyi, L. (1981). What stories can tell us about their teller's world. *Poetics Today*, **2**, 96–112.

Polanyi, L. (1989). *Telling the American story: A structural and cultural analysis of conversational storytelling.* Cambridge, MA: Massachusetts Institute of Technology Press.

Polkinghorne, D.E. (1988). *Narrative knowing and the human sciences.* Albany, NY: State University of New York Press.

Riessman, C.K. (1993). *Narrative analysis.* Newbury Park, CA: Sage.

Robinson, J.Λ. (1981). Personal narratives reconsidered. *Journal of American Folklore*, **94**, 59–85.

Rosaldo, R. (1989). *Culture and truth: The remaking of social analysis.* Boston, MA: Beacon.

Sarbin, T.R. (1986). *Narrative psychology: The storied nature of human conduct.* New York: Praeger.

Sarbin, T.R. (1998). Believed-in imaginings: A narrative approach. In J. de Rivera & T.R. Sarbin (Eds), *Believed-in imaginings: The narrative construction of reality* (pp. 15–30). Washington, DC: American Psychological Association.

Schafer, R. (1981). Narration in the psychoanalytic dialogue. In W.J.T. Mitchell (Ed.), *On narrative* (pp. 25–50). Chicago, IL: University of Chicago Press.

Schank, R.C. (1990). *Tell me a story: A new look at real and artificial memory.* New York: Charles Scribner's Sons.

Scheibe, K.E. (1986). Self-narratives and adventure. In T.R. Sarbin (Ed.), *Narrative psychology: The storied nature of human conduct* (pp. 129–151). New York: Praeger.

Scheub, H. (1998). *Story*. Madison, WI: University of Wisconsin Press.

Scollon, R. & Scollon, S. (1981). *Narrative, literacy, and face in interethnic communication*. Norwood, NJ: Ablex.

Silko, L. (1977). *Ceremony*. New York: Viking Press.

Spence, D.P. (1986). Narrative smoothing and clinical wisdom. In T.R. Sarbin (Ed.), *Narrative psychology: The storied nature of human conduct* (pp. 211–232). New York: Praeger.

Stotter, R. (1994). Storytelling as a cooperative learning experience. In R. Stotter (Ed.), *About story: Writings on stories and storytelling 1980–1994* (pp. 91–102). Stinson Beach, CA: Stotter Press.

Sunwolf (1999a). *Telling tales in jury deliberations: Jurors' uses of fictionalized and factually-based storytelling in argument*. Paper presented at the meeting of the National Communication Association, Chicago, IL.

Sunwolf (1999b). The pedagogical and persuasive effects of Native American lesson stories, Sufi wisdom tales, and African dilemma tales. *Howard Journal of Communications*, **10**, 47–71.

Sutton-Smith, B. (1986). Children's fiction making. In T.R. Sarbin (Ed.), *Narrative psychology: The storied nature of human conduct*, (pp. 67–90). Westport, CT: Praeger.

Swift, G. (1983). *Waterland*. New York: Pocketbooks.

Victor, J.S. (1998). Social construction of Satanic ritual abuse and the creation of false memories. In J. de Rivera & T.R. Sarbin (Eds), *Believed-in imaginings: The narrative construction of reality* (pp. 191–216). Washington, DC: American Psychological Association.

Wanner, S.Y. (1994). *On with the story: Adolescents learning through narrative*. Portsmouth, NH: Boynton/Cook.

White, H. (1981a). The narrativization of real events. In W.J.T. Mitchell (Ed.), *On narrative* (pp. 249–254). Chicago, IL: University of Chicago Press.

White, H. (1981b). The value of narrativity in the representation of reality. In W.J.T. Mitchell (Ed.), *On narrative* (pp. 1–24). Chicago, IL: University of Chicago Press.

White, H. (1987). *The content of the form: Narrative discourse and historical representation*. Baltimore, MD: Johns Hopkins University Press.

Witherell, C.S., Tran, H.T., & Othus, J. (1995). Narrative landscapes and the moral imagination: Taking the story to heart. In H. McEwan & K. Egan (Eds), *Narrative in teaching, learning, and research* (pp. 39–49). New York: Teachers College Press.

Zeller, N. (1995). Narrative rationality in educational research. In H. McEwan & K. Egan (Eds), *Narrative in teaching, learning, and research* (pp. 211–225). New York: Teachers College Press.

Language Attitudes: Retrospect, Conspect, and Prospect

James J. Bradac
University of California at Santa Barbara, Santa Barbara, USA
Aaron Castelan Cargile
California State University, Long Beach, USA
Jennifer S. Hallett
University of California at Santa Barbara, Santa Barbara, USA

INTRODUCTION

The fourth word of the title of this chapter does not exist as an item in the English lexicon – or *did* not until we invented it to refer to a survey or view of the present scene, in contrast with views of the past and future. The referential meaning of "conspect" can probably be inferred from its immediate verbal context and its connection with other items in the "mental lexicon" (Aitchison, 1994). More pertinently from the standpoint of this chapter, this novel lexical item may trigger evaluative reactions because it is unfamiliar, perhaps surprising. The implication here is that "familiarity" is one of many language features about which message recipients have attitudes.

One goal of this chapter is to discuss some important variables associated with the likelihood that messages will cause hearers to form or change attitudes toward message sources and their proposals. A great deal of language attitudes research has assumed that linguistic features of messages are sufficient to incite evaluative reactions in hearers, paying scant attention to hearers' cognitive or emotional states that may facilitate or inhibit such reactions. For example, anxiety may make

The New Handbook of Language and Social Psychology.
Edited by W. Peter Robinson and Howard Giles.
© 2001 John Wiley & Sons Ltd.

an otherwise relevant language attitude inaccessible, or hearer behavior may be affected more by situational goals than by language attitudes. Accordingly, a model will be offered that focuses upon psychological states of hearers that affect the degree to which language attitudes color reactions to communicators.

A second goal is to characterize the early research on language attitudes (roughly 1960 to the mid-1970s) and to extract from this a research paradigm that has guided work in this area since its inception. In the language attitudes area (perhaps more than in other areas), certain methodological and substantive assumptions have proven extremely tenacious, and these merit scrutiny. Current research (mid-1970s to the present) will be overviewed also in order to illustrate persistent themes and to show some things that are new.

ORIGINS AND EARLY RESEARCH: THE PARADIGM IS SET

It was not until the mid-twentieth century that the attitudinal effects of language variations were studied programmatically and scientifically, i.e., empirically and particularly experimentally. While there was an enormous variety of language variables that the early researchers could have examined, the early research focused almost exclusively on the attitudinal consequences of communicators' use of different languages and dialects. Concerns about "national character" and cultural superiority or inferiority were pervasive in the early and mid-twentieth century and were likely to have inclined researchers toward comparisons of languages in terms of effectiveness. (These concerns are still apparent, certainly.) Notions of superiority and inferiority are also apparent in comparisons of dialects, where assessments of relative status have always played a large part (Haslett, 1990; Robinson, 1979).

Good examples of some of the tendencies mentioned above are two of the earliest language attitudes studies, by Lambert et al. (1960) and Lambert, Anisfeld and Yeni-Komshian (1965). In the first study, Lambert et al. (1960) compared the evaluative reactions of English and French-speaking respondents who listened to English and French versions of a prose passage audio-recorded by four bilingual speakers. Respondents rated each of the eight recordings on scales reflecting a variety of speaker traits: for example, sociability and intelligence. Results indicated that both types of respondents gave more positive ratings on several traits to the speakers presenting the English versions.

In the second study, Lambert et al. (1965) had bilingual speakers record a prose passage in Arabic and two dialectal variants of Hebrew (Ashkenazic and Yemenite). Respondents were Jewish and Arab high school students who completed rating scales, as in the previous study, after listening to each version. In this case the Jewish respondents rated the Arabic speakers relatively negatively and, conversely, the Arab respondents were relatively negative toward the Hebrew speakers. Additionally, the Jewish students responded to scales directly assessing their general attitudes toward Ashkenazic Jews, Yemenite Jews, and

Arabs. Ratings of the spoken passages and responses to the general attitude measures showed low or zero correlations, which suggested that different *types* of attitudes were assessed by the two types of measures and that attitudes inferred from ratings of languages or dialects might exist with low respondent awareness. Presumably, respondents in this study did not know that their ratings of individual speakers revealed something about their attitudes toward the groups that the speakers represented – attitudes that differed from those inferred from explicit attitudinal measures. Low respondent awareness would make language attitude assessment less subject to implicit researcher demand and respondent self-presentational biases than traditional attitude measurement. The idea that persons may have low awareness of their language attitudes has never had much of an impact on research, possibly because it was viewed initially as a potential methodological advantage in measuring social attitudes rather than as a substantively interesting possibility.

These two studies clearly reflect what remains the dominant paradigm in language attitudes research; indeed, their frequent citation in the early research suggests that they helped to *establish* the paradigm. It is worth noting that:

(1) They were *a*theoretical. Their focus upon evaluative consequences of languages and dialects was motivated by "practical" problems, for example, troubled relations between Arabs and Jews. This "practical" motivation is apparent in recent research; for example, Cargile (1997) refers to competition for employment between Chinese Americans and non-Chinese Americans as one reason for studying evaluative reactions to speakers who use Chinese- and American-accented English. There is an unbroken line of research on attitudes toward persons who speak various languages and dialects from the Lambert et al. studies to the present (e.g., Boberg, 1999; Buck, 1968; Cargile, 1997; Hopper & de la Zerda, 1979; Mulac, 1975; Purnell, Idsardi, & Baugh, 1999; Van Bezooijen, & Gooskens, 1999; Zahn & Hopper, 1985). This "unbroken line" has generated a substantial number of integrative reviews and critiques of research (e.g., Bradac, 1990; Cargile et al., 1994; Giles & Coupland, 1991, pp. 32–59; Giles & Powesland, 1975). Arguably, the mapping of attitudes toward the speakers of dialects and languages has been the main project for language attitudes research (cf. Edwards, 1999).

(2) The Lambert et al. studies used the "matched-guise" technique. This means, essentially, that a single speaker records all versions of a message appearing in a given experimental design, for example, dialects A, B, and C. An important assumption, which to our knowledge has not been tested, is that respondents perceive the speaker to be equally skilled in presenting each version. If this assumption is unknowingly violated, differences in respondents' evaluative reactions to dialect versions, for example, may be falsely attributed to the dialects themselves when in fact they are a product of idiosyncratic differences in speaker fluency. The major strength of this technique is thought to be that all unique speaker vocal characteristics are constant across experimental conditions, which would not be the case if

different speakers presented the different message versions. But this strength may be illusory in some cases because speaker characteristics may *interact* with message versions in unknown ways; for example, a given speaker (A) may raise his/her volume when delivering a message high in language intensity (Bowers, 1963) and reduce volume for a low-intensity message, whereas the opposite may be true for another speaker (B). If speaker A alone were to be used in a given experiment, differences in respondent reactions attributed to language intensity may be in fact attributable to variations in volume or volume plus language intensity.

(3) The Lambert et al. studies used attitude questionnaires (verbal scales; paper-and-pencil measures) to assess attitudes toward language. The use of paper-and-pencil measures has been so pervasive in language attitudes research that a person new to the area might almost infer that this use constitutes a methodological requirement. But it seems likely that the heavy reliance on bipolar scales to measure attitudes toward speakers or their proposals (e.g.,

trustworthy ____:____:____:____:____ untrustworthy; or

agree ____:____:____:____:____ disagree)

represents a convenience more than anything else. There are advantages in the use of paper-and-pencil measures: for example, the possibility of examining attitudinal dimensions or factors through complex statistical analysis and the potentially clear interpretability produced by responses to verbal scales (the meaning of "trustworthy" is relatively unambiguous, at least within Anglophone cultures). But there are disadvantages as well: for example, the fact that respondents are necessarily aware of the measurement process (although, as suggested above, they may have low awareness of *what* is being measured) and that responses made with high awareness may not generalize to the many real-world situations where persons respond to attitude objects with low awareness. This problem of generalizability has been recognized for some time and has motivated the search for unobtrusive measures of attitudes (Webb et al., 1966).

(4) The Lambert et al. studies were experiments. Again, to call experimental methods a methodological mainstay of language attitudes research would be to understate the case drastically. (This is true for many areas in the social psychology of language; cf. Robinson, 1998.) The advantages and disadvantages of experiments in the social sciences are well known. Suffice it to say that a methodological imbalance could be corrected to some extent through the use of qualitative approaches and field studies (cf. Milroy & Preston, 1999). Some intriguing qualitative analyses of perceptions of and attitudes toward English language variation in Wales provide a good example of this type of research (Coupland, Williams & Garrett, 1999; Williams, Garrett & Coupland, 1996).

(5) The Lambert et al. studies were *a*contextual; that is, nothing was said to respondents about the situation in which messages were ostensibly produced. Presenting messages in a contextual vacuum was a strategy designed to increase the generalizability of results. But this strategy ignored the likelihood that respondents would generate common or idiosyncratic inferences

about context. Communicators always have intentions, purposes, and goals (Berger, 1997), and if these are hidden or ignored respondents may "fill them in" in order to more fully comprehend communicators' messages. Common inferences would constitute a variable confounded with message condition, problematic only when unknown and therefore unexamined, and idiosyncratic inferences would constitute error variance. Some recent language attitudes studies have included message context as an independent variable (e.g., Cargile, 1997; Street & Brady, 1982), which indicates that this feature of the paradigm has changed to some extent over the years. This is an important change because context can alter the effects of language variation; for example, Cargile (1997) found that a speaker using Chinese-accented English was evaluated similarly to a speaker using standard American-accented English in an employment interview, but the same Chinese-accented speaker was evaluated as comparatively unattractive in the context of teaching in a college classroom.

EXTENDING THE PARADIGM: NEW VARIABLES

Although the features outlined above represent enduring features of a small scientific paradigm, many things have been added to the paradigm in the last quarter century. Specifically, message recipients' reactions to variables beyond whole languages and dialects have been examined. The newer variables might be characterized as relatively molecular, i.e., focusing on specific language features *within* languages and dialects, and primarily syntactic and semantic as opposed to phonological.

SOME MOLECULAR LANGUAGE VARIABLES

Language Intensity

Communicators signal their departure from attitudinal neutrality through lexical choices (Bowers, 1963); for example, "extremely good" is more positive than "rather good". Several types of linguistic structures are associated with high intensity ratings, for example, sex and death metaphors (Bowers, 1964). This language variable is discussed with the "newer" variables because of its molecular form, but it has been investigated since the time of the Lambert et al. studies. Several studies have assessed language intensity levels of speakers in order to make inferences about the strength of their attitudes or feelings (e.g., Rogan & Hammer, 1995), but other studies have examined the attitudinal *consequences* of language intensity. For example, it has been found that highly credible sources are likely to be relatively persuasive when they use high-intensity language, whereas low intensity enhances persuasiveness for low-credibility sources

(Burgoon, Jones & Stewart, 1975). It has also been found that high-intensity language reduces persuasiveness for female communicators (Burgoon, Birk & Hall, 1991; Burgoon et al., 1975). The two findings may indicate that there is a stereotypical link between perceptions of social power and perceived acceptability of language intensity (cf. Bradac, Bowers & Courtright, 1979).

Lexical Diversity

All language exhibits redundancy; in long utterances typically many words are repeated. There are several reasons for this, including: a limited number of frequently occurring function words (in English "to", "and", "the", etc.), a limited number of synonyms, and the desire to emphasize a point. In the previous two sentences there are 45 words, 34 of which are unique, so the type–token ratio (a measure of diversity) is 34/45 or 0.71. Diversity levels can range between 1.00 and (almost, never reaching) 0. Several studies have shown that low levels of lexical diversity in both spoken and written messages produce message-recipient judgments of low communicator status and competence in a variety of contexts: for example, informal discussions, employment interviews, and lectures (Bradac et al., 1979; Bradac, Mulac, & House, 1988).

Power of Style

While examining communication patterns in court trials, O'Barr and associates uncovered several linguistic features that appeared to be associated with the low social power of some speakers: relatively frequent use of intensifiers ("really nice"), hedges ("sort of nice"), tag questions ("nice, wasn't it?"), hesitations (". . . uh . . . nice"), deictic phrases ("that nice man over there"), and polite forms ("nice, thank you"). Early research indicated that messages containing these features reduced communicator credibility (Erickson et al., 1978), but a later study demonstrated that this effect was produced by hedges, hesitations, and tag questions exclusively (Bradac & Mulac, 1984). Recent research has confirmed the negative relationship between use of the low-power style and communicator credibility (Gibbons, Busch & Bradac, 1991), and two studies have shown a negative relationship between the use of low-power language and attitudes toward proposals offered in persuasive messages (Holtgraves & Lasky, 1999; Sparks, Areni & Cox, 1998).

Politeness

According to Brown and Levinson (1987), politeness refers to phrasing one's remarks so as to minimize face threat to others and self. Because an indirect request such as "It feels cold in here" imposes less on a hearer than does a direct form of the same request, "Shut the window!", it should be considered more polite. In light of the ubiquity of politeness in many societies and social contexts, several studies have investigated the effect of politeness on message recipients' responses. For example, Holtgraves and Yang (1990) found that the less a request form encoded concern for a hearer's face, the greater was the perception of the speaker's power. This was true for both Korean and American respondents. However, contrary to Brown and Levinson's prediction, these same respondents associated less polite requests with an increased psychological distance between the requester and hearer. In another study, Holtgraves (1997a) found that politeness interacted with speaker status to affect message recall: impolite messages from high-status speakers and polite messages from equal-status speakers were recalled most often, perhaps due to violation of respondent expectations. In a more naturalistic study, Holtgraves (1997b) analyzed transcripts of actual conversations and found an inverse relationship between speakers' use of positive politeness and perceptions of speaker dominance, assertiveness, and directiveness. *Determinants* of perceived politeness have also been examined; for example, Dillard et al. (1997) found that message dominance, defined as "the relative power of the source *vis-à-vis* the target as that power is expressed in [a] message" (p. 301), showed a strong negative association with judgments of politeness, whereas explicitness of requests and supportive argument (the extent to which reasons are given for requests) showed weaker, positive associations.

Patronizing Speech

There is a style of talk directed to low-power persons that has been labeled "patronizing speech" or "secondary baby talk" (Caporael, 1981). This style includes "slower speech rates, higher pitch, exaggerated intonation, increased loudness, simplified grammar, and simplified vocabulary" (Giles, Fox & Smith, 1993, p. 130). There is evidence that patronizing speech is evaluated negatively by third parties observing exchanges between caretakers and elderly patients on dimensions such as competence, benevolence, supportiveness, and trustworthiness (Giles et al., 1993; Ryan, Bourhis & Knops, 1991). There are mixed and unclear results regarding the effect of respondent age on evaluations of patronizing speech; for example, results from Giles et al. (1993) point weakly (across a few measures only) to increased negativity with increasing age, whereas results of a study by Edwards and Noller (1993) suggest that older persons may show greater tolerance for some forms of patronization.

Gender-Linked Language

Over the last several decades, research in communication and related fields has identified many consistent differences between men and women in language use (for a summary, see Aries, 1996). Mulac, Bradac and Gibbons (1998) summarized over 30 studies and identified six language features used more often by men, for example, directives, and 10 features used more often by women, for example, questions. Not only are there recognizable differences, there are subtle, hidden differences as well. Mulac and associates have identified an attitudinal effect on message recipients produced by a speaker's use of gender-related language features. This "gender-linked language effect" (Mulac & Lundell, 1982) consists of different ratings for male and female speakers on three attitudinal dimensions: socio-intellectual status, aesthetic quality of speaker, and speaker dynamism. Typically, respondents are asked to rate speakers on the basis of orthographic transcriptions of utterances drawn from contexts such as public speaking and problem-solving discussion. Even though respondents cannot accurately determine the speaker sex of transcribed utterances, they consistently rate female speakers higher on variables like "nice", "sweet", and "educated" and male speakers higher on "strong" and "active". The use of transcripts as a stimulus for ratings (as opposed to audio or video tapes) indicates that the attitudinal differences are produced by semantic and/or syntactic differences between male and female speakers.

Hate Speech and Political Correctness

Although the goals of their users are typically opposed, hate speech and politically correct speech are intertwined in that both linguistic forms entail ways of talking about marginalized social groups. Politically correct speech has been defined as "language that serves to manipulate boundaries between groups in an attempt to gain power and control for (marginalized) groups that is equal to that held by the majority" (Hallett, 1995, p. 2). Hate speech has been defined as a subcategory of verbal aggression, and more specifically as language use that denigrates people on the basis of race, ethnicity, religion, gender, sexual orientation, age, disability, or membership in other social categories (Leets & Giles, 1997; Sedler, 1992).

Hallett (1995) attempted to show that politically correct labels can affect people's perceptions of those who use them. There was indirect support for the claim that use of politically correct self-referent labels ("I am an African American . . .") can enhance evaluations of communicators among outgroup members: outgroup respondents evaluated more favorably a person who used a politically correct self-referent label, but only after initial exposure to a person who used a neutral label. One could argue that the push to use politically correct speech grew out of the rising incidence of hate speech. Leets and Giles (1997) devised a study to establish under what circumstances and to what extent people perceive that hate speech is harmful to its recipients. All respondents reported that the harm inflicted by attacks on one's dignity or derogation of one's ethnicity is difficult to bear. However, perhaps surprisingly, respondents who were members of the group at which hate speech was aimed (who read scenarios of an interpersonal exchange in which derogatory remarks were made) perceived indirect messages to be more harmful than direct messages, whereas outgroup members perceived direct messages to be more harmful. Also, respondents who read scenarios in which hate speech was addressed to the object of enmity were more negative toward that speech than were their counterparts who read scenarios in which hate speech was overheard, probably as a result of perceived intentionality of the communicator in the former case.

A MODEL OF THE LANGUAGE ATTITUDES PROCESS

One feature of the language attitudes research paradigm that has changed recently is the theoretical basis of research. Whereas the early research was largely atheoretical, recent studies are more likely to invoke theory: communication accommodation theory (Giles & Coupland, 1991, pp. 60–93; a representative study is Ball et al., 1984), language expectancy theory (Burgoon, 1990; Burgoon et al., 1991), or information processing theory (Hamilton, 1997, Hamilton, 1998). Also, theories not focusing specifically on language have been extended to language attitudes, creating new theoretical perspectives; for example, uncertainty reduction theory (Berger & Calabrese, 1975; Bradac, Bowers & Courtright, 1980) and intergroup theory (Tajfel, 1974, 1981; Ryan, Hewstone & Giles, 1984) have been extended in this way. The following discussion reinforces this theoretical thrust. As suggested above, it is probably simplistic to conceptualize the language attitudes process as nothing more than some language feature eliciting an evaluative reaction in message recipients. This conception, which reflects a basic stimulus–attitude–response model of behavior, informed much of the early (and some recent) language attitudes research. In the model depicted in Figure 1, we offer a more complex view that might suggest some new avenues to future researchers. Although similar in some respects to a model we developed previously (Cargile et al., 1994), the current version has been elaborated significantly in light of recent theoretical advancements.

1. The Speaker

A speaker's language behavior may reflect any of the variables discussed above (politeness, power, etc.). Given the purpose of our model, this behavior is the main "stimulus" under consideration, but language is not the only stimulus to which hearers respond. They also respond simultaneously to the speaker's non-language behavior and to social and physical attributes such as sex, race, attractiveness, age, or occupational status. Non-language behaviors include anything the speaker does apart from speaking; for example, gestures will be used and these can either mitigate or strengthen attributions made on the basis of

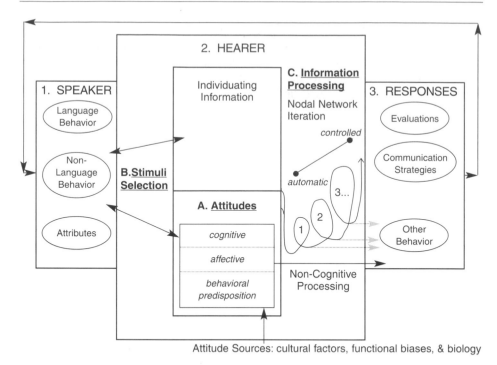

Figure 1   A model of the language–attitudes process

language. Some recent research has examined the additive or interactive effects of language behavior, non-language behavior such as gestures, and speaker attributes such as sex (cf. Mulac, Incontro & James, 1985). When the effects of language are pitted against the effects of the two other types of variables, language often emerges as the most potent influence on hearers' evaluations (Parsons & Liden, 1984; Seligman, Tucker & Lambert, 1972).

2. The Hearer

Compared to the speaker/language interface (the "stimulus" component of the language attitudes process), consideration of the hearer has been seriously neglected. When exposed to language, a hearer is faced with the task of developing some response to the speaker: for example, making an evaluation and/or choosing a communication strategy. Clearly, attitudes toward language are one basis for response, but they are not the only basis – a point that has often been ignored in the language attitudes literature. We will now discuss some potentially important structures and processes intervening in the connection between speaker's utterance and hearer's response.

2A. Attitudes

This construct has been thoroughly explicated and critiqued in the general literature of social psychology, and it has been discussed in the domain of language attitudes, so we will not say much here. We agree that an attitude is "a disposition to react favorably or unfavorably to a class of objects" (Sarnoff, 1970, p. 279) and that it has cognitive, affective, and behavioral components (Edwards, 1982). Typically, cognition (beliefs and stereotypes) and affect (evaluations) have been examined in language attitudes research, but behavioral tendencies have been examined also, as in the study by Kristiansen and Giles (1992), which measured compliance with a request to complete an audience survey.

Apart from the nature of attitudes, it is worth noting that language attitudes arise from (at least) three sources: cultural factors, functional biases, and biology. Some languages, dialects, and styles are valued within a culture, while others are stigmatized, and these preferences are learned at an early age; some linguistic forms are defined as standard and some as high in vitality, while others are non-standard and non-vital (Ryan, Giles & Sebastian, 1982). Also, language attitudes can serve various functions for those who hold them, for example, an explanatory function. As Tajfel (1981) described, individuals use stereotypes to make a complex social world orderly and predictable, particularly to justify and explain intergroup relations. Thus, language attitudes that function to explain a hearer's social world are more likely to endure than are those that serve some lesser function; for example, a negative evaluation of Black English Vernacular made by a committed racist has high survival potential, whereas a positive evaluation of a trendy expression does not. Biological sources of language attitudes are probably less familiar than are cultural factors and functional biases, but they are worth mentioning. It can be argued that evolution has endowed humans with innate tendencies to judge particular vocal qualities, for example, pitch and loudness, favorably or unfavorably. The physics of sound is such that large creatures, which potentially threaten survival and therefore evoke alertness and fear, typically produce deep-pitched vocalizations, whereas small creatures produce vocalizations that are high-pitched (for example, a tiger versus a domestic cat). Accordingly, we would expect that hearers would rate deep-pitched speakers as more powerful, confident, and strong than high-pitched speakers, and this is what one study among American college students found (Tusing & Dillard, 1996). Other results suggest that this type of response may override cultural variation (Montepare & Zebrowitz-McArthur, 1987). Certainly, much of this is speculative and needs to be pinned down further.

2B. Stimuli Selection

A given language behavior rarely occurs in isolation. It co-occurs with other language behaviors and with a host of non-language behaviors and information regarding the speaker's social attributes as well. Because of attentional constraints, a hearer must select some subset of stimuli on which to focus. One way to do this is to employ internally generated, predictive control of attention shifting (Allport, 1989). In this "top-down" mode of attention selection, hearers attend to those stimuli that they think are relevant; perceived relevance may be determined by attitudes accessible to hearers, by their expectancies, and by their goals.

Much research has demonstrated that attitudes exert a great influence on both the perception of and responses to social situations, a fact acknowledged by Fazio's (1986) model of the attitude–behavior relationship, which indicates that the activation of an attitude leads directly to the orienting of attention. Attitudes that are accessible to hearers at a given moment will focus their attention on particular linguistic and contextual stimuli. Expectations are one of several factors that can influence the accessibility of attitudes, thereby indirectly affecting attention. Expectations can also directly influence a hearer's attention by specifying which stimuli are most likely to be useful for responding in a given situation. Cultural conventions can establish expectations, as can individuating information about a speaker possessed by hearers. Goals are a third factor that can orient a hearer to particular stimuli. In fact, Allport (1987) connects the development of attention to the need for goal-directed action. Any such action requires identification of specific features in the environment for its successful execution: in order to catch a baseball, one must distinguish the ball from all other environmental features and maintain focus upon it. Different goals can cause attention to different stimuli: a prison official with the goal of punishing criminals may attend to an inmate's non-standard accent, thus reinforcing the belief that the inmate belongs to a social group whose members are cruel, remorseless, and undeserving of assistance; an official with the goal of re-habilitating offenders may attend to the inmate's slow speech rate and low lexical diversity, allowing an attribution to be made about the inmate's poor educational background.

An attentional system must also be capable of abandoning internal controls when environmental threats (or opportunities) present themselves (Allport, 1989). In other words, attention must also be an externally sensitive, "bottom-up" process. Generally, unexpected stimuli will push the system toward "bottom-up" stimulus selection. Attention to unanticipated speaker features or behaviors can lead to the acquisition of individuating information and/or to the activation of relevant (language) attitudes (as our model illustrates). Conversely, attitudes, individuating information, expectancies, and goals may first direct attention toward particular speaker features; then, once these features are observed, they lead back to the acquisition of individuating information and/or to the activation of attitudes.

An important implication of this "stimuli selection" component of our model is that hearers are *active users* of speakers' language behaviors. Most language attitudes research has assumed that hearers are *passive responders* to linguistic stimuli, in keeping with the implicit stimulus–attitude–response model informing this research.

2C. Information Processing

Impressions of people appear to be based on two kinds of information: stereotypes and individuating information (e.g., Brewer, 1988; Fiske & Neuberg, 1990). Some of our information about others is derived from general and prejudged associations between observed or inferred stimuli (e.g., skin color or speech style) and traits (e.g., intelligence or sociability), whereas other information is person-specific. Hearers must somehow integrate both forms of data as they develop responses to speakers. Kunda and Thagard's (1996) parallel–constraint–satisfaction model (PCSM) provides some useful insights into the dynamics of this process. The model assumes that stereotypes, traits, and behaviors can be represented as interconnected nodes in a network of activation whose spread is constrained by both the positive or negative associations between the nodes and by the relative strength of these associations. Nodes in the network are first activated when either a stereotype or individuating information is made salient. For example, hearers may attend to a speaker's high level of lexical diversity and stereotypically associate it with the trait of "intelligence". Simultaneously, they may also observe that the speaker received poor grades in college. These three nodes (i.e., "lexically diverse", "intelligent", and "poor grades") would be initially and automatically activated. This model assumes that neither stereotypes nor individuating information has special status. Instead of favoring one type of information, hearers in this model holistically interpret the entire activated nodal network containing both types of information when responding to the speaker.

Although Kunda and Thagard (1996) emphasize the quick and automatic integration of information, sometimes hearers process information about speakers in a "controlled" fashion. According to Devine (1989), automatic processes "involve the unintentional or spontaneous activation of some well-learned set of associations", whereas controlled processes "are intentional and require the active attention of the individual" (p. 6). Recent research has shown that perceivers often make two different evaluations of a social actor: one based on automatic information processes and another based on controlled processes (e.g., Banaji & Greenwald, 1995). This implies that information present in the hearer's nodal network that is initially and automatically activated may or may not serve as a basis for responding to the speaker. In our model (see Figure 1), automatic processing occurs if the hearer's activated nodal network "settles" quickly, after few or no iterations. In contrast, controlled processing occurs if the hearer's network spreads (or even migrates) via numerous iterations or elaborations. In the latter case, the spread of the network may be so great that information elements present in the first iteration may have little impact on the hearer's ultimate response. These possibilities are represented in our model as a series of connected and increasingly large loops. Each loop depicts an iteration of the activated nodal network and one is larger than the next because the network presumably spreads in size and complexity over time. With the completion of an iteration, the nodal network may serve as a basis for response, or it may be further elaborated.

The question now becomes: what factors affect the spread of the network? Our model indicates three possibilities, the first two of which are suggested by the elaboration likelihood model (Petty & Cacioppo, 1986b): motivation, ability, and mood. In order for a hearer to elaborate the initial nodal network that is automatically activated in response to accessed language attitudes and speaker-specific information, he or she must possess sufficient motivation to do so. Persons with a high "need for cognition" (a personality variable) will tend to be motivated to go beyond automatic processing. Similarly, perceivers who are involved with the sources, topics, or outcomes of information processing are likely actively to control that processing in some way. In addition to motivation, hearers must possess the *ability* to engage in controlled processing (Petty & Cacioppo, 1986a). In this case, ability consists of available time and cognitive capacity (Devine, 1989). Finally, *mood* may influence both the integration of information in conditions of automatic processing and the direction of network spread in conditions of controlled processing. More specifically, we speculate that both highly positive and highly negative mood states will lead hearers to rely upon automatic processing of speaker-relevant information, whereas less intensely positive and negative moods will facilitate controlled processing; this suggests an "inverted-U" relationship between mood intensity and nodal network elaboration and assumes (perhaps incorrectly; cf. Forgas & Bower, 1987, for example) that mood valence is inconsequential in this case.

In response to the possibility that attitudes may affect hearer responses via means other than the activated nodal network, our model allows for non-cognitive processing to occur. This will be the case when either affective or behavioral predispositions included in an attitude directly shape responses to a speaker.

3. Responses

As has been suggested throughout this chapter, language attitudes are closely related to evaluations of speakers. Giles and Ryan (1982) have argued that the evaluative dimensions of social status and ingroup solidarity are universally important for the understanding of attitudes toward contrasting language varieties. However, the outcomes of language attitudes are not limited to speaker evaluations. Attitudes toward language, in association with the other variables depicted in our model, can also suggest certain communication strategies. For example, Bourhis and Giles (1977) showed that when ingroup members (in this case learners of the Welsh language) were ethnically threatened by an outgroup (English) speaker, they broadened their Welsh accent and even introduced Welsh words and phrases in their responses to this person. It may be the case that these acts of divergence reflected automatic processing, whereas in another situation, perhaps one in which the Welsh speakers anticipated future interaction with the outgroup speaker, processing would have been relatively controlled, which might have resulted in convergent speech or at least non-divergence. This is purely speculative; future studies of communication accommodation might benefit from examining automatic and controlled processing of messages under conditions of similarity and dissimilarity of interactive partners.

CONCLUSION

Our model calls attention to the fact that many variables related to a hearer's psychological state are likely to play a major role in his or her response to a speaker's language behavior. A hearer's attitudes toward language may interact with goals, expectations, and level of processing in the production of responses. As much of the research reviewed in this chapter demonstrates, a concerted emphasis has been placed on speakers, particularly on their many styles and forms of language. This is a prominent feature of the enduring language attitudes paradigm. We believe that a paradigm shift is in order, because in some cases a hearer's evaluations or communication strategies may be influenced as much by factors internal to the hearer as by speaker behaviors. For example, referring back to the paradigm-setting studies of Lambert et al. (1960, 1965), one could study the effects of individuating information and positive mood on status and solidarity ratings of speakers representing ethnolinguistic outgroups (compared to ingroup speakers). Would stereotypically negative ratings be reduced or eliminated as a result of information and mood? Would this effect be enhanced by inducing controlled message processing? At some point it will be useful to ask: under *what conditions* will a hearer's response be affected largely by even subtle variations in a speaker's language behavior, and, on the other hand, when will this response be influenced mainly by psychological state quite apart from what the speaker does? But for now, suffice it to say that more attention should be paid to the *hearer*.

REFERENCES

Aitchison, J. (1994). *Words in the mind: An introduction to the mental lexicon*, (2nd edn). Oxford, UK: Blackwell.

Allport, A. (1987). Selection for action: Some behavioral and neurophysiological considerations of attention and action. In H. Heurer and A.F. Sanders (Eds), *Perspectives on perception and action* (pp. 78–95). Hillsdale, NJ: Erlbaum.

Allport, A. (1989). Visual attention. In M.I. Possner (Ed.), *Foundations of cognitive science* (pp. 631–671). Cambridge, MA: MIT Press.

Aries, E. (1996). *Men and women in interaction*. New York: Oxford University Press.

Ball, P., Giles, H., Byrne, J. & Berechree, P. (1984). Situational constraints on the evaluative significance of speech accommodation: Some Australian data. *International Journal of the Sociology of Language*, **46**, 115–129.

Banaji, M.R. & Greenwald, A.G. (1995). Implicit gender stereotyping in judgments of fame. *Journal of Personality and Social Psychology*, **68**, 181–198.

Berger, C.R. (1997). *Planning strategic interaction*. Mahwah, NJ: Erlbaum.

Berger, C.R. & Calabrese, R.J. (1975). Some explorations in initial interaction and beyond: Toward a developmental theory of interpersonal communication. *Human Communication Research*, **1**, 99–112.

Boberg, C. (1999). The attitudinal component of variation in American English foreign (a) nativization. *Journal of Language and Social Psychology*, **18**, 49–61.

Bourhis, R.Y. & Giles, H. (1977). The language of intergroup distinctiveness. In H. Giles (Ed.), *Language, ethnicity and intergroup relations* (pp. 119–133). London: Academic Press.

Bowers, J.W. (1963). Language intensity, social introversion, and attitude change. *Speech Monographs*, **30**, 345–352.

Bowers, J.W. (1964). Some correlates of language intensity. *Quarterly Journal of Speech*, **50**, 415–420.

Bradac, J.J. (1990). Language and impression formation. In H. Giles & W. P. Robinson (Eds), *Handbook of Language and Social Psychology* (pp. 387–412). Chichester, UK: Wiley.

Bradac, J.J., & Mulac, A. (1984). A molecular view of powerful and powerless speech styles: Attributional consequences of specific language features and communicator intentions. *Communication Monographs*, **51**, 307–319.

Bradac, J.J., Bowers, J.W. & Courtright, J.A. (1979). Three language variables in communication research: Intensity, immediacy, and diversity. *Human Communication Research*, **5**, 257–269.

Bradac, J.J., Bowers, J.W. & Courtright, J.A. (1980). Lexical variations in intensity, immediacy, and diversity: An axiomatic theory and causal model. In R.N. St Clair & H. Giles (Eds). *The social and psychological contexts of language* (pp. 193–223). Hillsdale, NJ: Erlbaum.

Bradac, J.J., Mulac, A. & House, A. (1988). Lexical diversity and magnitude of convergent versus divergent style shifting: Perceptual and evaluative consequences. *Language & Communication*, **8**, 213–228.

Brewer, M.B. (1988). A dual process model of impression formation. In T.K. Srull & R.S. Wyer (Eds), *Advances in social cognition* (pp. 1–36). Hillsdale, NJ: Erlbaum.

Brown, P. & Levinson, S. (1987). *Politeness: Some universals in language usage*. Cambridge, UK: Cambridge University Press.

Buck, J. (1968). The effects of Negro and white dialectal variations upon attitudes of college students. *Speech Monographs*, **35**, 181–186.

Burgoon, M. (1990). Language and social influence. In H. Giles & W.P. Robinson (Eds), *Handbook of language and social psychology* (pp. 51–72). Chichester, UK: Wiley.

Burgoon, M., Jones, S.B. & Stewart, D. (1975). Toward a message-centered theory of persuasion: Three empirical investigations of language intensity. *Human Communication Research*, **1**, 240–256.

Burgoon, M., Birk, T.S. & Hall, J.R. (1991). Compliance and satisfaction with physician–patient communication: An expectancy interpretation of gender differences. *Human Communication Research*, **18**, 177–208.

Caporael, L. (1981). The paralanguage of caregiving: Babytalk to the institutionalized aged. *Journal of Personality and Social Psychology*, **40**, 876–884.

Cargile, A.C. (1997). Attitudes toward Chinese-accented speech: An investigation in two contexts. *Journal of Language and Social Psychology*, **16**, 434–443.

Cargile, A.C., Giles, H., Ryan, E.B. & Bradac, J.J. (1994). Language attitudes as a social process: A conceptual model and new directions. *Language & Communication*, **14**, 211–236.

Coupland, N., Williams, A. & Garrett, P. (1999). "Welshness" and "Englishness" as attitudinal dimensions of English language varieties in Wales. In D. Preston (Ed.), *Handbook of perceptual dialectology* (pp. 333–343). Amsterdam: Benjamins.

Devine, P.G. (1989). Stereotypes and prejudice: Their automatic and controlled components. *Journal of Personality and Social Psychology*, **56**, 5–18.

Dillard, J.P., Wilson, S.R., Tusing, K.J. & Kinney, T.A. (1997). Politeness judgments in personal relationships. *Journal of Language and Social Psychology*, **16**, 297–325.

Edwards, H. & Noller, P. (1993). Perceptions of overaccommodation used by nurses in communication with the elderly. *Journal of Language and Social Psychology*, **12**, 207–223.

Edwards, J.R. (1982). Language attitudes and their implications among English speakers. In E.B. Ryan & H. Giles (Eds), *Attitudes towards language variation: Social and applied contexts* (pp. 20–33). London: Edward Arnold.

Edwards, J.R. (1999). Refining our understanding of language attitudes. *Journal of Language and Social Psychology*, **18**, 101–110.

Erickson, B., Johnson, B.C., Lind, E.A. & O'Barr, W. (1978). Speech style and impression formation in a courtroom setting: The effects of "powerful" and "powerless" speech. *Journal of Experimental Social Psychology*, **14**, 266–279.

Fazio, R.H. (1986). How do attitudes guide behavior? In R.M. Sorrentino & E.T. Higgans (Eds), *The handbook of motivation and cognition: Foundations of social behavior* (pp. 204–243). New York: Guilford.

Fiske, S.T. & Neuberg, S.L. (1990). A continuum of impression formation, from category-based to individuation processes: Influences of information and motivation on attention and interpretation. In M. Zanna (Ed.), *Advances in experimental social psychology* (pp. 1–74). San Diego, CA: Academic Press.

Forgas, J.P. & Bower, G.H. (1987). Mood effects on person perception judgments. *Journal of Personality and Social Psychology*, **53**, 53–60.

Gibbons, P., Busch, J. & Bradac, J.J. (1991). Powerful versus powerless language: Consequences for persuasion, impression formation, and cognitive response. *Journal of Language and Social Psychology*, **10**, 115–133.

Giles, H. & Coupland, N. (1991). *Language: Contexts and consequences*. Buckingham, UK: Open University Press.

Giles, H. & Powesland, P.F. (1975). *Speech style and social evaluation*. London: Academic Press.

Giles, H. & Ryan, E.B. (1982). Prolegomena for developing a social psychological theory of language attitudes. In E.B. Ryan & H. Giles (Eds), *Attitudes towards language variation: Social and applied contexts* (pp. 208–223). London: Edward Arnold.

Giles, H., Fox, S. & Smith, E. (1993). Patronizing the elderly: Intergenerational evaluations. *Research on Language and Social Interaction*, **2**, 129–150.

Hallett, J.S. (1995). Effects of using politically correct speech on attitudes toward marginalized group members. Unpublished master's thesis, University of California, Santa Barbara.

Hamilton, M. (1997). The phase interfaced omnistructure underlying the processing of persuasive messages. In G.A. Barnett & F.J. Boster (Eds), *Advances in communication science* (pp. 1–42). Greenwich, CT: Ablex.

Hamilton, M. (1998). Message variables that mediate and moderate the effect of equivocal language on source credibility. *Journal of Language and Social Psychology*, **17**, 109–143.

Haslett, B. (1990). Social class, social status and communicative behavior. In H. Giles & W.P. Robinson (Eds), *Handbook of Language and Social Psychology* (pp. 329–344). Chichester, UK: Wiley.

Holtgraves, T. (1997a). Politeness and memory for the wording of remarks. *Memory and Cognition*, **25**, 106–116.

Holtgraves, T. (1997b). Yes, but . . .: Positive politeness in conversation arguments. *Journal of Language and Social Psychology*, **16**, 222–239.

Holtgraves, T. & Lasky, B. (1999). Linguistic power and persuasion. *Journal of Language and Social Psychology*, **18**, 196–205.

Holtgraves, T. & Yang, J.N. (1990). Politeness as universal: Cross-cultural perceptions of request strategies and inferences based on their use. *Journal of Personality and Social Psychology*, **59**, 719–729.

Hopper, R. & de la Zerda, N. (1979). Employment interviewers' reactions to Mexican American speech. *Communication Monographs*, **46**, 126–134.

Kristiansen, T. & Giles, H. (1992). Compliance-gaining as a function of accent: Public requests in varieties of Danish. *International Journal of Applied Linguistics*, **2**, 17–35.

Kunda, Z. & Thagard, P. (1996). Forming impressions from stereotypes, traits, and behaviors: A parallel–constraint–satisfaction theory. *Psychological Review*, **103**, 284–308.

Lambert, W.E., Hodgson, R., Gardner, R.C. & Fillenbaum, S. (1960). Evaluational reactions to spoken languages. *Journal of Abnormal and Social Psychology*, **60**, 44–51.

Lambert, W.E., Anisfeld, M. & Yeni-Komshian, G. (1965). Evaluational reactions of Jewish and Arab adolescents to dialect and language variations. *Journal of Personality and Social Psychology*, **2**, 84–90.

Leets, L. & Giles, H. (1997). Words as weapons: When do they wound? Investigations of harmful speech. *Human Communication Research*, **24**, 260–301.

Milroy, L. & Preston, D.R. (1999). Introduction. *Journal of Language and Social Psychology* (Special issue: Attitudes, perception, and linguistic features), **18**, 4–9.

Montepare, J.M. & Zebrowitz-McArthur, L. (1987). Perceptions of adults with childlike voices in two cultures. *Journal of Experimental Social Psychology*, **23**, 331–349.

Mulac, A. (1975). Evaluation of the speech dialect attitudinal scale. *Speech Monographs*, **42**, 182–189.

Mulac, A. & Lundell, T.L. (1982). An empirical test of the gender-linked language effect in a public speaking setting. *Language & Speech*, **25**, 243–256.

Mulac, A., Incontro, C.R. & James, M.R. (1985). A comparison of the gender-linked language effect and sex-role stereotypes. *Journal of Personality and Social Psychology*, **49**, 1099–1110.

Mulac, A., Bradac, J.J. & Gibbons, P. (1998). *Empirical support for the gender-as-culture hypothesis: An intercultural investigation of male/female language differences.* Paper presented at the meeting of the International Communication Association, Jerusalem, July 1998.

Parsons, C.K. & Liden, R.C. (1984). Interviewer perceptions of applicant qualifications: A multivariate field study of demographic characteristics and nonverbal cues. *Journal of Applied Psychology*, **4**, 557–568.

Petty, R.E. & Cacioppo, J.T. (1986a). *Communication and persuasion: Central and peripheral routes to attitude change.* New York: Springer.

Petty, R.E. & Cacioppo, J.T. (1986b). The elaboration likelihood model of persuasion. In L. Berkowitz (Ed.), *Advances in experimental social psychology* (Vol. 19, pp. 123–205). San Diego, CA: Academic Press.

Purnell, T., Idsardi, W. & Baugh, J. (1999). Perceptual and phonetic experiments on American English dialect identification. *Journal of Language and Social Psychology*, **18**, 10–30.

Robinson, W.P. (1979). Speech markers and social class. In K.R. Scherer and H. Giles (Eds), *Social markers in speech* (pp. 211–249). Cambridge: Cambridge University Press.

Robinson, W.P. (1998). Language and social psychology: An intersection of opportunities and significance. *Journal of Language and Social Psychology*, **17**, 276–301.

Rogan, R.G. & Hammer, M.R. (1995). Assessing message affect in crisis negotiations: An exploratory study. *Human Communication Research*, **21**, 553–574.

Ryan, E.B., Giles, H. & Sebastian, R.J. (1982). An integrative perspective for the study of attitudes toward language variation. In E.B. Ryan & H. Giles (Eds), *Attitudes towards language variation: Social and applied contexts* (pp. 1–19). London: Edward Arnold.

Ryan, E.B., Hewstone, M. & Giles, H. (1984). Language and intergroup attitudes. In J.R. Eiser (Ed.), *Attitudinal judgment* (pp. 135–160). New York: Springer.

Ryan, E.B., Bourhis, R. & Knops, U. (1991). Evaluative perceptions of patronizing speech addressed to elders. *Psychology and Aging*, **6**, 442–450.

Sarnoff, I. (1970). Social attitudes and the resolution of motivational conflict. In M. Jahoda (Ed.), *Attitudes* (pp. 279–284). Harmondsworth, UK: Penguin.

Sedler, R. (1992). The unconstitutionality of campus bans on "racist speech": The view from without and within. *Pittsburgh Law Review*, **53**, 631–683.

Seligman, C., Tucker, G.R. & Lambert, W.E. (1972). The effects of speech style and other attributes on teachers' attitudes toward pupils. *Language in Society*, **1**, 131–142.

Sparks, J.R., Areni, C.S. & Cox, K.C. (1998). An investigation of the effects of language style and communication modality on persuasion. *Communication Monographs*, **65**, 108–125.

Street, R.L., Jr & Brady, R.M. (1982). Speech rate acceptance ranges as a function of evaluative domain, listener speech rate, and communication context. *Communication Monographs*, **49**, 290–308.

Tajfel, H. (1974). Social identity and intergroup behaviour. *Social Science Information*, **13**, 65–93.

Tajfel, H. (1981). Social stereotypes and social groups. In J. Turner & H. Giles (Eds), *Intergroup behavior* (pp. 144–165). Oxford: Blackwell.

Tusing, K.J. & Dillard, J.P. (1996). *The sounds of dominance: Vocal precursors of dominance during interpersonal influence*. Paper presented at the annual meeting of the Speech Communication Association, San Diego, CA, November 1996.

Van Bezooijen, R. & Gooskens, C. (1999). Identification of language varieties: The contribution of different linguistic levels. *Journal of Language and Social Psychology*, **18**, 31–48.

Webb, E.J., Campbell, D.T., Schwartz, R.D. & Sechrest, L. (1966). *Unobtrusive measures: Nonreactive research in the social sciences*. Chicago, IL: Rand McNally.

Williams, A., Garrett, P. & Coupland, N. (1996). Perceptual dialectology, folk linguistics, and regional stereotypes: Teachers' perceptions of variation in Welsh English. *Multilingua*, **15**, 171–199.

Zahn, C.J. & Hopper, R. (1985). Measuring language attitudes: The Speech Evaluation Instrument. *Journal of Language and Social Psychology*, **4**, 113–123.

Part 2

Face to Face: Structures and General Functions

Toward a Comprehensive Model of Non-Verbal Communication

Miles L. Patterson
University of Missouri–St Louis, USA

Ten years ago, in the earlier edition of the *Handbook of Language and Social Psychology*, I discussed the role of non-verbal communication in social interaction from a functional perspective. The earlier chapter still provides a representative overview of the importance and utility of non-verbal communication. For example, non-verbal signals (1) communicate specific information about behavioral intentions, emotions, and relationship intimacy; (2) regulate the give-and-take of interactions; (3) provide a vehicle for self-presentation; and (4) operate in the service of interpersonal influence (Patterson, 1990). Although the specific functions discussed in the earlier chapter are well documented, recent developments point to important limitations in the previous theoretical framework. Consequently, the purpose of the present chapter is to discuss and analyze a new and more comprehensive model of non-verbal communication.

The basic question underlying this pursuit is how do we explain the subtle patterns of non-verbal communication between people in social settings? This issue has occupied researchers for more than 35 years and has stimulated a variety of theoretical explanations. In the present chapter, I will focus on a new theory – the parallel process model (Patterson, 1995, 1998) – as a means of integrating the complex dynamics involved in the sending and receiving of non-verbal communication. Of course, the parallel process theory did not develop in a vacuum. Rather, it reflects changing views about communication and the complexity of interdependent processes in the sending and receiving of non-verbal signals. As a participant

The New Handbook of Language and Social Psychology.
Edited by W. Peter Robinson and Howard Giles.
© 2001 John Wiley & Sons Ltd.

for the last 25 years in these attempts to explain interactive patterns of non-verbal communication, it seems beneficial to start by briefly reviewing the theoretical context from which the parallel process emerged.

THEORETICAL BACKGROUND

From 1965 to the early 1980s, explanations of how people made interactive adjustments in their non-verbal behavior were distinctly reactive in nature. For example, how does a person react to a particular change in the partner's behavior? In their equilibrium theory, Argyle and Dean (1965) proposed that people try to maintain a level of involvement consistent with the intimacy level of their relationship. They predicted that compensatory adjustments served to restore non-verbal involvement back to a comfortable or appropriate level. For example, if a too close approach disturbed the intimacy equilibrium, the partner might compensate by turning away or by decreasing both gaze and smiling.

Sometimes, people do the opposite of compensation, that is, they reciprocate a partner's change in non-verbal intimacy. For example, in our everyday interactions, we might respond to a loved one's close approach and touch with a smile and a hug. Later theories, including my intimacy arousal model (Patterson, 1976), Burgoon's (1978) expectancy violations theory, and Cappella and Greene's (1982) discrepancy arousal model all provided explanations for how people might compensate, reciprocate, or make no adjustment at all to a partner's change in non-verbal involvement. It is beyond the scope of this chapter to evaluate the relative merits of these explanations, but extended discussions of these and other interaction theories may be found in a text by Burgoon, Stern and Dillman (1995). It is, however, important to recognize that, besides being reactive in nature, these theories were all affect-driven. That is, the critical determinant in all of these theories is the initial affective response to their partner's behavior. Specifically, if the partner's increased involvement produces positive affect (e.g., liking or love), reciprocation is predicted, but if the increased involvement produces negative affect (e.g., fear or anxiety), then compensation is predicted. This ignores, however, the reality that we often react independently of the feelings we have about others and their behavior. For example, one might feel quite negative about the close approach and smile from the boss as he "asks" you to work overtime. Nevertheless, the diplomatic response is to nod, smile, and reply that, of course, you would be happy to work overtime – reciprocating his initial behavior.

Because the earlier theories were all affect-based and reactive in nature, the functional model (Patterson, 1982, 1983) was developed to address these shortcomings in a still broader theory. Within the functional perspective, people are not simply reactive and constrained by their feelings. That is, as communicators, the pursuit of particular goals requires that we not only react to our partners but, also, initiate behavioral patterns to influence them. Furthermore, the pursuit of specific goals in interaction may require people to behave in a manner that is inconsistent with their underlying affect – contrary to the assumption of the reactive models. For example, in order to create a good impression with the obnoxious personnel manager, an interviewee would try to manage an expressive, pleasant demeanor even though she does not particularly care for this person.

The emphasis in this approach, like that in the early theories, was still on explaining the sending or behavioral side of non-verbal communication. Attention to the receiving or person perception side of non-verbal communication was only episodic. That is, the receiving side was critical only as a means of explaining subsequent behavioral adjustments. But, just as behavior is continuous over the course of an interaction, so too is the processing of information from the social environment. In other words, in social settings we are simultaneously behaving and taking in information. A comprehensive theory of non-verbal communication has to integrate the sending and receiving sides of non-verbal communication into a single framework. The next section discusses the circumstances that facilitated a new approach to conceptualizing non-verbal communication.

TOWARD AN INTEGRATIVE PERSPECTIVE

Social Judgments and Social Behavior

Given the complexity of each side of communication – the sending and the receiving – it is not surprising that most researchers directed their attention to one or the other process in isolation. But it was more than the complexity of the processes that hindered the development of a more integrative perspective. In general, for many years, research and theory on the sending or production side of non-verbal communication was conducted by a mix of social psychologists (like myself) and communication scholars, whereas research and theory on the receiving or person perception side was conducted by an ever-expanding group of social cognition scholars who were part of the "cognitive revolution" in psychology (see, for example, Fiske & Taylor, 1991). For the most part, there was relatively little overlap in the efforts of these two groups.

The landscape began to change, however, in the mid-1980s, sparked in part by Swann's (1984) insightful analysis of the traditional paradigm in person perception. In particular, Swann suggested that the typical approach of concentrating on the processing of social information ignored the active role that perceivers play in forming impressions of others. This "passive perceiver", according to Swann (1984), was a poor approximation of the way that active perceivers operated in the real world. In turn, the common finding of low perceiver accuracy in laboratory experiments was probably the result of requiring passive perceivers to make broad, general judgments of a target (i.e., global accuracy). In contrast, because active perceivers make more limited, practical judgments of a target (i.e., circumscribed accuracy) in everyday life, they are likely to be more accurate in their impressions (Swann, 1984). Furthermore, in the real world, active perceivers choose their partners and the settings in which they interact. This increases the likelihood of greater similarity between interactants and promotes an identity negotiation process that facilitates accuracy in judgments (Swann, 1987).

In a similar fashion, Wright and Dawson (1988) found that, as the utility of the judgment increased, perceivers were more sensitive in judging targets. This theme was reinforced by Fiske's (1992) commentary on the pragmatic link of social cognition to interactive behavior. In fact, Fiske's (1992) message echoed William James's observation from a century earlier that "thinking is for doing" (James, 1983, pp. 959–960). Around the same time, empirical research and theory in person perception began to consider the effects of the additional cognitive demands that perceivers have to balance while they are also making judgments of others. Specifically, Gilbert and his colleagues demonstrated that, because initial judgments of others are virtually automatic, whereas later "corrections" of those judgments engage greater cognitive effort, the accuracy of person perception is dependent on the cognitive demands facing the perceiver (Gilbert & Krull, 1988; Gilbert, Pelham & Krull, 1988).

Just as the receiving, or social judgment, side of non-verbal communication varies from relatively automatic to more cognitively demanding so does the sending, or behavioral, side of non-verbal communication. Although some social behavior is represented in consciousness and is deliberately monitored and managed, a great deal of what we do is relatively automatic in nature (Bargh, 1997; Bargh & Chartrand, 1999). Various kinds of action schemas, such as scripts (Abelson, 1981) and plans (Berger, 1997), provide templates that direct automatic behavioral sequences. In a similar fashion, action identification theory proposes that individuals identify their actions in a variety of ways from low-level descriptions of how the action is performed to high-level descriptions of the purpose of the action (Vallacher & Wegner, 1987). When individuals are skilled in a particular activity, that is, the sequence is highly automatic, performance is maximized with a high-level action identification. In contrast, when individuals are unskilled in an activity, performance is maximized with the low-level action identification that helps them to manage and monitor what they are doing (Vallacher & Wegner, 1987).

In summary, in social settings, communicators are simultaneously sending and receiving non-verbal messages. For the most part, these messages are neither capricious nor arbitrary. That is, they serve specific purposes or goals in relating to our social environments, whether we are aware of it or not. Thus, just as changing our behavior (and often our appearance) to influence others is adaptive, selectively attending to and processing non-verbal information from others is also adaptive. For example, the ecological theory of social perception (McArthur & Baron, 1983) proposes that people are particularly attuned to perceiving social affordances. Although much of the sending and receiving is relatively automatic in nature, not all of it is, and changing circumstances can demand considerable effort in negotiating our social worlds. As a result, the availability of cognitive resources and the effort employed are important determinants of effective communication. Let's take a look at these pragmatic parallel processes in a larger theoretical framework.

OVERVIEW OF THE PARALLEL PROCESS MODEL

The parallel process model frames the encoding and decoding processes of non-verbal communication in a single system, driven by a common set of determinants and mediating processes. In this section, I will discuss the basic structure of the model. Later, more attention will be focused on elaborating the dynamic processes outlined in the model. Figure 1 provides a general illustration of the linkages among variables in the model.

Determinants

The determinants on the left side of the figure identify the most important, though not the only, factors affecting the sending and receiving of non-verbal communication. In effect, the determinants constrain our habitual ways of communicating. That is, the effects of biology, culture, and personality predispose us to communicate in a relatively consistent fashion over time. *Biology* reflects the role of evolutionary pressures in shaping adaptive, hardwired patterns of communicating with others. For example, the positive, nurturant response to the babyface appearance of infants is advantageous to their survival (Zebrowitz, 1997, Chapter 4). Special sensitivity to facial expressions as signals of interpersonal intent may also be the product of natural selection (Fridlund, 1994).

Although natural selection has left us with some common, adaptive patterns of communication, culture and personality both introduce increased variability in communication. For example, even though there is some degree of universality in expressive reactions, differences across *culture* are also evident (Russell, 1994). Since the time of Hall's (1966) early work on culture and proxemics, it is clear that culture affects preferred levels of involvement in social settings. Individual differences in *personality* also contribute to contrasting styles of non-verbal communication. For example, high social anxious individuals show lower levels of involvement with others than do low social anxious individuals (for a review, see Patterson & Ritts, 1997). Thus, the combined effects of the determinants produce both basic communalities and differences in non-verbal communication. Other factors also affect patterns of non-verbal communication, although they may not be as basic or primary as the three mentioned here. For example, gender differences might be seen as the joint product of biology (the hardwired patterns) and culture (societal norms).

Social Environment

The determinants also indirectly affect non-verbal communication through their influence on the social environment in the second stage of the model. It is rare that we find ourselves in a particular setting with a specific partner purely by chance. Just as we select settings, so do settings select us. The combined effect of

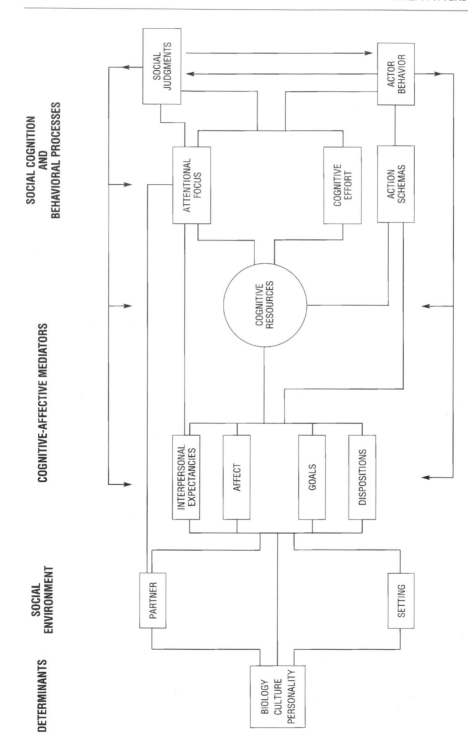

Figure 1 An illustration of the parallel process model of non-verbal communication

self- and setting-selection processes results in greater homogeneity among people in a given setting compared to a random sampling of people across settings (Barker, 1968; Wicker, 1979). In turn, this increased similarity among people in specific settings not only promotes greater accuracy in making social judgments of others (Funder, 1987; Swann, 1984), but also promotes behavioral coordination in interactions.

Cognitive–Affective Mediators

If the determinants and the social environment provide the context for interaction, then the cognitive–affective mediators are the processes that guide the course of communication. First, *dispositions* refer to actor states precipitated in a specific social environment. The more obvious dispositions are related to the actor's personality characteristics, but dispositions may be precipitated by the partner, the setting, or other mediators. Next, *goals* may be the most important of the mediators because they are the cognitive representations of desired states for which people strive (Berger, Knowlton & Abrahams, 1996). Specific goals affect the investment of cognitive resources, as reflected in the type of information noticed and the depth of processing this information.

Affect in interactions is a product of the individual's momentary dispositions and goals, relationship to the partner, and the setting constraints. Affect influences both the formation of social judgments, (e.g., Alloy & Abramson, 1988) and patterns of non-verbal involvement (Burgoon, 1978; Cappella & Greene, 1982; Patterson, 1976). *Interpersonal expectancies* simultaneously affect the social judgment and behavioral processes in non-verbal communication. For example, in the self-fulfilling prophecy, actors' expectancies facilitate the behavior expected of a partner, without the actors' awareness of their role in the process (Rosenthal, 1974). Nevertheless, Jussim (1991) cautions that some effects that look like self-fulfilling prophecies are really accurate perceptions of social reality. Because subtle appearance cues or behavior can signal underlying dispositions (Zebrowitz & Collins, 1997), the perception of such cues represents accuracy in judgment, not a self-fulfilling prophecy.

Finally, *cognitive resources* refers to the total cognitive capacity available for managing our everyday activities. Because the total pool of cognitive resources is limited, the investment of substantial resources to concerns outside of the interaction necessarily means that there is less that can be applied to the sending and receiving of non-verbal messages. Furthermore, whatever resources are committed to the immediate social situation can be variously distributed toward the self, the partner, the setting, or the topic of conversation.

Social Cognition and Behavioral Processes

In the final stage of the model, the social judgment and social behavior tracks are represented. Consistent with the functional approach advocated here, it is assumed that the social judgment and behavioral tracks operate in concert for a common goal, whether this is a friendly exchange with an acquaintance, managing a job interview, or trying to deceive a spouse. Although some social judgments require extensive reflection and some behavioral sequences require considerable monitoring and management, much of the non-verbal system operates relatively automatically. Nevertheless, it is assumed that, at some point in the processes, both the ongoing judgment and behavioral elements are cognitively represented.

In the case of social judgments, it is obvious that some sort of mental representation is required at least for starting the process. Once initiated, the social judgment and behavioral processes often proceed automatically. According to Bargh (1989), the strongest form of automaticity in social judgments is "preconscious automaticity", in which the stimulus event simply has to register in an individual's sensory apparatus. From this point, the judgment process runs to completion without conscious awareness. An example of this type of process would be the activation of a stereotype judgment from simply noticing an out-group person. On the behavioral side, the cognitive representation may simply be a mental recognition of a particular goal that is sufficient to trigger an automatic sequence. For example, I might start an interaction with the purpose of trying to impress another person and this simple goal representation is sufficient to activate a more or less automatic impression management action sequence. My impression management goal not only directs my behavior, but also directs the kinds of judgments made about my partner. That is, in seeking to make a positive impression on my partner, my judgments will be much more focused on what she thinks about me than on what I think about her personality.

This overview described the structure of the parallel process model and identified some basic relationships among the components. In the next section, I shall examine more closely the dynamic relationships among the elements of the parallel process model and suggest how this framework might account for a wide range of phenomena in non-verbal communication.

DYNAMICS OF PARALLEL PROCESSING

As communicators, we are simultaneously engaged in reading our social environments and sending non-verbal messages to the world around us. Just how do we manage this complex and potentially demanding business? This section takes a closer look at this question, with special attention on the role of goals and automatic processes in communication. Then, I shall put the pieces together in describing the dynamic interdependence of the parallel social judgment and behavioral processes.

Goals

A basic assumption underlying the parallel process model, and one consistent with the earlier functional model, is that communication is adaptive and goal oriented. This does not mean, however, that people must be consciously aware of the goals they are pursuing As people strive to attain specific goals, they are typically constrained by broader meta-goals (Berger, 1995). First, a pervasive concern underlying communication is simply attaining a goal in an efficient manner. In their review of the social cognition research, Fiske and Taylor (1991, Chapters 4–9) emphasize efficiency in their description of perceivers as "cognitive misers" who take shortcuts whenever they can in judging other people. Second, on the sending side of communication, we typically try to use socially appropriate means to reach specific goals (Berger, 1995). Of course, the most efficient means of achieving a social goal is not always the most appropriate. Furthermore, those who are in a position of power may be less concerned about social appropriateness than efficiency.

These parallel processes are mediated by mental structures or schemata that can vary from being automatic in nature to cognitively demanding and effortful. In the former case, when actions are well practiced and routine, particular plans or strategies may operate autonomously in pursuit of a goal without any conscious guidance (Bargh, 1997). Nevertheless, the individual still requires information (the receiving side) to keep the goal-directed behavior on course. For example, in an employment interview, a socially skilled applicant may activate an effective "make a good impression" script, but it never plays out exactly the same. In this case, the applicant's sensitivity in reading the interviewer is critical for activating behavioral adjustments that are typically automatic in nature. This example also shows how a single goal simultaneously determines the course of both the sending and receiving operations. Obviously, if the interviewer's reactions are extreme or the applicant is not socially skilled, then behavioral adjustments in the "make a good impression" script may have to be guided by conscious efforts.

In this example, the applicant's social judgments are pragmatic ones that permit appropriate behavioral adjustments in the interview. The utility of social judgments for subsequent actions has received considerable attention in the last decade (e.g., Fiske, 1992; Zebrowitz & Collins, 1997), but the relationship between social judgments and behavior is not a one-way street. Sometimes behavioral strategies may be initiated to test social judgments. Thus, people might manage their behavior toward a partner to precipitate a reaction that supports their initial, preferred judgment (Baumeister & Newman, 1994).

A similar, but less biased, strategy may involve attempts at diagnosing a partner's attitudes or preferences. For example, in dating relationships, one person might escalate behavioral intimacy to determine the partner's readiness for a romantic relationship. A contrasting plan might also be tried to facilitate the same kind of judgment, that is, "playing hard to get" as a means of testing a partner's interest and commitment. In a variety of situations, actors can use a similar tactic of "floating a trial balloon" to get a reading of a partner's sentiment on a particular issue, without making a direct inquiry. Thus, just as social judgments about another person can determine the course of behavioral strategies, behavioral strategies can be used to determine social judgments. A critical factor affecting the efficiency and balance between the parallel processes is the relative automaticity of the social judgment and behavioral tracks.

Automatic and Controlled Processes

The developing empirical and theoretical research on automatic processing has important implications for understanding communication. Whereas verbal communication typically involves some degree of controlled processing, non-verbal communication often happens automatically. Of course, depending on the circumstances, people can also invest a great deal of effort in managing their own behavior and in trying to understand and interpret what others do.

Social Judgments

Evidence from a variety of sources strongly suggests that judgments about others can develop in automatic fashion, outside of conscious awareness (e.g., Bargh, 1994; Brewer, 1988; Smith, 1990). For example, Devine (1989) found that, when the stereotype of African Americans held by whites was activated, later judgments of a stimulus person of unspecified race become more negative. Although some impressions, like those based on race, can be biased, there is considerable empirical evidence that these judgments are not only formed quickly, but also quite accurately (Ambady & Rosenthal, 1992; Zebrowitz & Collins, 1997).

According to the ecological theory of perception (McArthur & Baron, 1983), information from a person's appearance and movement provides the basis for making accurate judgments of people. That is, this approach assumes that judgments are the product of the direct perception of "affordances" (Gibson, 1979). Social affordances are the pragmatic relational information present in the target person's appearance and movements. This information is pragmatic because it suggests what the target person can do for the perceiver or what the perceiver can do to the target person (McArthur & Baron, 1983). For example, the characteristic facial features of an infant – large eyes, small, rounded chin, and a disproportionately large forehead – typically lead to positive, nurturant reactions from adults (Berry & McArthur, 1985, 1986). Presumably, such judgments were biologically selected for their adaptive value in relating to infants who are dependent on the nurturance of others. In general, the ecological approach to social perception suggests that it is much more useful to know who can help us, harm us, be trusted, and benefit from our help than it is to make inferences about a wide range of personality traits (Zebrowitz & Collins, 1997).

Some automatic judgments follow a different developmental course. In particular, impressions can also be the product of specific, conditional rules learned over time (Smith, 1990). That is, with experience in processing social information, we learn that if a particular cue or behavior is present, then a broader inference can be made about a person. Once learned, these conditional "if x, then y" judgments can occur automatically. In other words, as long as "x" is noticed, then the "y" judgment can happen automatically and outside of awareness.

It is not merely a person's physical characteristics and isolated movements that precipitate automatic judgments. Attributions about more elaborate and complex behavioral sequences can also lead to automatic inferences. According to Trope (1986), this may happen quickly in two stages: first, behavior identification and, second, a higher-order process of trait attribution. That is, in the first stage, one immediately identifies the behavior (e.g., friendly) and then quickly proceeds to a characterization or trait attribution (e.g., friendly person). Gilbert and his colleagues added a third, conditional stage in which perceivers might correct trait attributions if there were reason to question them (Gilbert, Pelham & Krull, 1988). Extending the friendly behavior example, one might reflect in the third stage that "It's no wonder this person is being friendly, he's trying to sell me a car."

This three-stage model of trait attribution also suggests some circumstances under which people move from automatic judgments to more controlled, effortful processing (Gilbert et al., 1988). Specifically, people are more likely to initiate controlled processing when they (1) are motivated to consider a different inference about an actor's behavior and (2) have sufficient cognitive resources to weigh an alternative explanation for the behavior. In a similar fashion, other theories of impression formation also recognize that people typically avoid the more demanding, controlled processing if they can (Brewer, 1988) – consistent with the view of perceivers as cognitive misers. Nevertheless, when appearance characteristics are inconsistent or the person's behavior is puzzling, then a motivated perceiver can employ controlled processing.

In summary, much of what happens on the receiving side of non-verbal communication is automatic in nature. Although perceivers typically do not invest much effort in judging others, this is usually not a problem for making relatively accurate judgments. That is, the information present in the appearance and behavior of others is typically sufficient for making pragmatic judgments about people. When the information is inconsistent and people are motivated enough to apply some effort in forming impressions, then more controlled processing is likely – as long as there are cognitive resources available for such an effort.

Social Behavior

The sending side of non-verbal communication, like the receiving side, engages a variety of processes from relatively automatic to more controlled. On the automatic end, our behavioral repertoire encompasses a wide range of basic, hardwired patterns of approach and avoidance that have undoubtedly been selected over the course of evolution. These would include expressive reactions that signal a person's intended course of action (Fridlund, 1994). Automatic patterns of increased involvement (e.g., close approach, gaze, touch) might be activated in response to increased attraction or a need for comforting and supporting another person. In contrast, decreased involvement or behavioral avoidance may be precipitated by dislike, fear, or embarrassment. Representative of these kinds of automatic patterns are the affect-driven adjustments predicted by the reactive models of non-verbal communication, discussed earlier in the chapter. Obviously, with experience, these automatic patterns can be inhibited and replaced by other more pragmatic reactions when the circumstances require it. Consequently, it is possible to substitute a pleasant, friendly reaction for the angry one when the boss makes an unreasonable request.

Besides the hardwired, affect-driven patterns, other patterns become automatic over time as a function of learning. The cognitive representations of these automatic sequences may be described as action schemas. Scripts (Abelson, 1981), plans (Berger, 1997), and high-level action identification (Vallacher & Wegner, 1987) all identify cognitive representations of potentially automatic behavioral sequences. In general, because action schemata provide a template for behavioral sequences, actors are able to anticipate and monitor the sequence of events in an interaction. Thus, the sending side of non-verbal communication can be efficiently managed through the activation of these action schemata and, in the process, cognitive resources are conserved for other, more demanding activities.

Coordinating Judgments and Behavior

The dynamic relationship between the parallel social judgment and behavior processes is constrained by the influence of the determinants (biology, culture, and personality) and the social environment (see Figure 1). Thus, we all come into particular settings with some stable tendencies in social judgments and social behavior. Nevertheless, our specific goals are critical in directing the operation of parallel social judgment and behavioral processes. According to Bargh (1990, 1997), once goals are activated by environmental stimuli, whether consciously or unconsciously, they direct the course of social judgments and social behavior. When this occurs, the entire sequence from the environmental event to the processing of social input and the initiation of behavior can happen unconsciously (Bargh, 1990). On the social judgment side, the unconscious effects of priming in activating stereotypic judgments has long been documented (Brewer, 1988; Devine, 1989). As a result, it is clear that our impressions of others can be formed automatically and outside of awareness.

Automaticity on both the social judgment and behavioral tracks is a great advantage in terms of responding efficiently to our environment. In addition to facilitating a rapid response to changing circumstances, the economy of effort means that cognitive resources may be invested elsewhere. In fact, the availability of cognitive resources and the application of those resources in communication are the final elements in the dynamics of parallel processing. Because (1) automatic processes are not always available and (2) automatic processes may not always work, cognitive effort is sometimes required in making social judgments and in managing social behavior. For example, when automatic judgments do not seem to fit or when it is difficult to categorize people or their behavior, additional cognitive effort may be needed in forming accurate impressions (Gilbert et al., 1988).

The situation is similar on the behavioral side where actions that are not yet well learned or scripted may require considerable monitoring and management. In addition, sometimes the automatic, hardwired action may be inappropriate, unethical, or self-defeating and it is only through reflection and "willpower" that a deliberate and appropriate action may be substituted. One way to conceptualize this is in terms of potentially competing response systems, that is, the automatic versus the controlled options. This kind of approach has been suggested recently in a "hot/cool system analysis" of the conflict involved in the delay of gratification (Metcalfe & Mischel, 1999). Although this theory focused specifically on the dynamics underlying delay of gratification, similar processes may be operating in comparing the relative strength of automatic versus controlled behavioral sequences. Metcalfe and Mischel (1999) assumed that the "hot" response is the automatic approach to immediate gratification that is initially under stimulus control, like Bargh's (1997) automatic actions. In contrast, the "cool" response is a product of self-control. The hot system develops early and is simple, reflexive, and emotional in nature. The cool system develops later and is complex, reflective, and cognitive in nature. The hot system is accentuated by stress, whereas the cool system is attenuated by stress (Metcalfe & Mischel, 1999).

How do coordinated judgment and behavioral processes operate under varying circumstances of interacting with other people? First, the predispositions we bring to social settings for specific judgments and behavior constrain how we manage the pursuit of particular goals. For example, a socially anxious individual who is trying to make a good impression on an important person will be highly sensitive to potentially negative reactions from the other person and have a more difficult time controlling any anxious, avoidant behaviors (hot responses) than would a low anxious person. More generally, as long as the relevant stimulus events register, automatic judgments will occur (e.g., stereotypes) and automatic responses are likely. If these automatic cognitive and behavioral reactions seem to work, that is, they are adaptive, then there is little reason to invest effort in replacing them with more controlled processes.

There are, of course, circumstances where automatic judgments do not fit and automatic behaviors are counterproductive. Nevertheless, if the individual is stressed, cognitive resources are minimal, and controlled judgments and behaviors have low strength, then automatic judgments and behaviors will tend to be dominant. Failure in the pursuit of a goal is likely to feed back and lead to adjustments in expectancies, affect, dispositions, and even the goals themselves (see Figure 1). Unless there are appropriate automatic adjustments at the ready, the subsequent recycling through the parallel processes will typically require additional resources and effort in activating controlled processes in pursuing the previous goal or a revised one. The emphasis here on cognitive resources is, however, a conditional one. If people need to reconsider a faulty judgment, weigh new evidence, or monitor and manage their behavior, then to be effective they have to apply the necessary cognitive resources to those processes. On the other hand, more is not always better in applying cognitive effort to making judgments and managing behavior. Thinking more about automatic judgments can actually decrease accuracy (Patterson & Stockbridge, 1998; Wilson & Schooler, 1991), just as thinking about automatic, high action identification behaviors can decrease the level of performance (Vallacher & Wegner, 1987). The trick is, of course, to know when to leave the automatic reactions alone and when to think about other options.

RESEARCH PROSPECTS

The parallel process model provides a framework for examining a variety of issues in the simultaneous sending and receiving of information in non-verbal communication. In this section, I shall discuss a few options that merit further study. One of the most important concerns is examining the effects of different goals on the interdependent social judgment and behavioral processes. Specifically, different goals in interaction should not only precipitate different patterns of behavior (e.g., Bargh, 1997; Berger, 1997), but also sensitize actors to different types of social judgments (Baumeister & Newman, 1994). For example, a "make a good impression" goal should lead to more smiling and talking than a "get to know the other person" goal. Furthermore, the two goals should focus social judgments on distinctly different aspects of the partner. To facilitate the impression management goal, actors should focus on metaperspective judgments; that is, what does the other person think of me, as a means of evaluating the success of self-presentation. In contrast, if the actor is trying to get to know the partner, direct perspective judgments concerning the partner's personality, attitudes, and interests should be more likely.

Although goals direct the repertoire of behavioral patterns and the content of social judgments, the effectiveness of the behavioral side of non-verbal communication and the accuracy of judgments on the receiving side depend on other factors. The behavioral side should be more effective when the appropriate behavioral routines are well-practiced, scripted patterns than when they are less scripted and more controlled. In addition, the difference between the scripted and non-scripted behavioral patterns should increase under conditions of high cognitive demand. That is, the scripted routines should still play well when the actor is otherwise cognitively engaged. In contrast, the effectiveness of the non-scripted routines decreases when actors do not have the cognitive resources to manage their behavior. In a similar fashion, automatic judgments should be relatively accurate under conditions of high cognitive demand, whereas controlled judgments will suffer under the same kind of high cognitive demand (Patterson & Stockbridge, 1998). Of course, some individuals (e.g., those low on social anxiety) are more socially skilled on the behavioral side and more sensitive in reading the reactions of others and, as a result, they will have an advantage in effectively balancing the demands of these parallel processes (see Patterson & Ritts, 1997).

Finally, it is interesting to consider what the nature and locus of the "traffic controller" for non-verbal communication might be. Recent research suggests that the term *executive function* might be used to characterize a variety of cognitive operations involved in both the planning and execution of behavior and the monitoring, selection, and interpretation of incoming social information (Macrae et al., 1999). Furthermore, although these executive processes are not highly localized in the brain, the frontal lobes seem to be involved in much of this activity (Baddeley, 1996). Thus, it is possible that the developing research in cognitive neuroscience may be particularly relevant for understanding the complexity of communication processes.

CONCLUSION

Because communicators are simultaneously forming judgments and managing their behavior in social settings, it is important to explain how these interdependent operations develop. The parallel process model provides a framework for explaining coordinated social judgments and behavior operating in the service of different goals. Biology, culture, and personality contribute to important communalities and differences in the ways that people process information and behave with others. For example, evolution has helped to shape some hardwired judgments and behaviors that occur more or less automatically. With experience over time, other judgments and behaviors are learned, come under stimulus control, and function automatically. Thus, much of what happens in everyday interactions unfolds in a relatively automatic fashion in the pursuit of various goals, some of which may be activated outside of awareness.

Not all social judgments are simple and straightforward, and sometimes even those that are need correction. In a similar manner, not all behavioral routines are automatic and sometimes those that are still fail to achieve the desired goals. When adjustments are required in social judgments and behavior, then communicators need to apply cognitive effort in making those changes. If adequate cognitive resources are not available or the individual is not sufficiently motivated, then it is unlikely that adjustments will be successful. Because the cognitive resources available at any given time are finite, the manner in which they are applied to either process affects the course of the complementary process. Thus, if someone invests a great deal of effort in managing her behavior, fewer resources are available for making social judgments. Finally, it must be admitted that specific predictions about the outcomes of the parallel process model are necessarily limited and conditional in nature. Nevertheless, compared to previous approaches, the parallel process model better represents interactants as active communicators who efficiently coordinate a complex array of automatic and controlled processes in relating to other people.

AUTHOR NOTE

A version of this chapter was presented at a symposium entitled Nonverbal Communication: Linking Social Behavior and Social Judgments at the annual meeting of the Society of Experimental Social Psychology, October 1999, in St Louis, MO.

REFERENCES

Abelson, R.P. (1981). The psychological status of the script concept. *American Psychologist*, **36**, 715–729.

Alloy, L.B. & Abramson, L.Y. (1988). Depressive realism: Four theoretical perspectives. In L.B. Alloy (Ed.), *Cognitive processes in depression* (pp. 223–265). New York: Guilford Press.

Ambady, N. & Rosenthal, R. (1992). Thin slices of behavior as predictors of interpersonal consequences: A meta-analysis. *Psychological Bulletin*, **111**, 256–274.

Argyle, M. & Dean, J. (1965). Eye-contact, distance and affiliation. *Sociometry*, **28**, 289–304.

Baddeley, A. (1996). Exploring the central executive. *Quarterly Journal of Experimental Psychology*, **49A**, 5–28.

Bargh, J.A. (1989). Conditional automaticity: Varieties of automatic influence in social perception and cognition. In J.S. Uleman & J.A. Bargh (Eds), *Unintended thought* (pp. 3–51). New York: Guilford Press.

Bargh, J.A. (1990). Auto-motives: Preconscious determinants of thought and behavior. In E.T. Higgins & R.M. Sorrentino (Eds), *Handbook of motivation and cognition* (2nd edn., pp. 93–130). New York: Guilford Press.

Bargh, J.A. (1994). The four horsemen of automaticity: Awareness, intention, efficiency, and control in social cognition. In R.S. Wyer & T.K. Srull (Eds), *Handbook of social cognition* (2nd edn., pp. 1–40). Hillsdale, NJ: Erlbaum.

Bargh, J.A. (1997). The automaticity of everyday life. In R.S. Wyer (Ed.), *Advances in social cognition* (pp. 1–61). Mahwah, NJ: Erlbaum.

Bargh, J.A. & Chartrand, T.L. (1999). The unbearable automaticity of being. *American Psychologist*, **54**, 462–479.

Barker, R.G. (1968). *Ecological psychology: Concepts and methods for studying the environment of human behavior*. Stanford, CA: Stanford University Press.

Baumeister, R.F. & Newman, L.S. (1994). Self-regulation of cognitive processes. *Personality and Social Psychology Bulletin*, **20**, 5–19.

Berger, C.R. (1995). A plan-based approach to strategic communication. In D.E. Hewes (Ed.), *The cognitive bases of interpersonal communication* (pp. 141–179). Hillsdale, NJ: Erlbaum.

Berger, C.R. (1997). *Planning strategic interaction*. Mahwah, NJ: Erlbaum.

Berger, C.R., Knowlton, S.W. & Abrahams, M.F. (1996). The hierarchy principle in strategic communication. *Communication Theory*, **6**, 111–142.

Berry, D.S. & McArthur, L.Z. (1985). Some components and consequences of a babyface. *Journal of Personality and Social Psychology*, **48**, 312–323.

Berry, D.S. & McArthur, L.Z. (1986). Perceiving character in faces: The impact of age-related craniofacial changes on social perception. *Psychological Bulletin*, **100**, 3–18.

Brewer, M.B. (1988). A dual process model of impression formation. In T.K. Srull & R.S. Wyer Jr (Eds) *Advances in social cognition* (Vol. 1, pp. 1–36). Hillsdale, NJ: Erlbaum.

Burgoon, J.K. (1978). A communication model of personal space violations: Explication and an initial test. *Human Communication Research*, **4**, 129–142.

Burgoon, J.K., Stern, L.A. & Dillman, L. (1995). *Interpersonal adaptation: Dyadic interaction patterns*. Cambridge, UK: Cambridge University Press.

Cappella, J.N. & Greene, J.O. (1982). A discrepancy-arousal explanation of mutual influence in expressive behavior for adult and infant–adult interaction. *Communication Monographs*, **49**, 89–114.

Devine, P.G. (1989). Stereotypes and prejudice: Their automatic and controlled components. *Journal of Personality and Social Psychology*, **56**, 680–690.

Fiske, S.T. (1992). Thinking is for doing: Portraits of social cognition from daguerreotype to laserphoto. *Journal of Personality and Social Psychology*, **63**, 877–889.

Fiske, S.T. & Taylor, S.E., (1991). *Social cognition*. New York: McGraw-Hill.

Fridlund, A.J. (1994). *Human facial expression: An evolutionary view*. San Diego, CA: Academic Press.

Funder, D.C. (1987). Errors and mistakes: Evaluating the accuracy of social judgment. *Psychological Bulletin*, **101**, 75–90.

Gibson, J.J. (1979). *The ecological approach to visual perception*. Boston, MA: Houghton-Mifflin.

Gilbert, D.T. & Krull, D.S. (1988). Seeing less and knowing more: The benefits of perceptual ignorance. *Journal of Personality and Social Psychology*, **54**, 193–202.

Gilbert, D.T., Pelham, B.W. & Krull, D.S. (1988). On cognitive busyness: When person perceivers meet persons perceived. *Journal of Personality and Social Psychology*, **54**, 733–740.

Hall, E.T. (1966). *The hidden dimension*. New York: Doubleday.

James, W. (1983). *The principles of psychology*. Cambridge, MA: Harvard University Press. (Original work published 1890.)

Jussim, L. (1991). Social perception and social reality: A reflection-construction model. *Psychological Review*, **98**, 54–73.

Macrae, C.N., Bodenhausen, G.V., Schloerscheidt, A.M. & Milne, A.B. (1999). Tales of the unexpected: Executive function and person perception. *Journal of Personality and Social Psychology*, **76**, 200–213.

McArthur, L.Z. & Baron, R.M. (1983). Toward an ecological theory of social perception. *Psychological Review*, **90**, 215–238.

Metcalfe, J. & Mischel, W. (1999). A hot/cool system analysis of delay of gratification: Dynamics of willpower. *Psychological Review*, **106**, 3–19.

Patterson, M.L. (1976). An arousal model of interpersonal intimacy. *Psychological Review*, **83**, 237–252.

Patterson, M.L. (1982). A sequential functional model of nonverbal exchange. *Psychological Review*, **89**, 231–249.

Patterson, M.L. (1983). *Nonverbal behavior: A functional perspective*. New York: Springer.

Patterson, M.L. (1990). Functions of non-verbal behavior in social interaction. In H. Giles & W.P. Robinson (Eds), *Handbook of language and social psychology* (pp. 101–120). Chichester, UK: Wiley.

Patterson, M.L. (1995). A parallel process model of nonverbal communication. *Journal of Nonverbal Behavior*, **19**, 3–29.

Patterson, M.L. (1998). Parallel processes in nonverbal communication. In M.T. Palmer & G.A. Barnett (Eds), *Progress in communicative sciences* (Vol. 14, pp. 1–18). Stamford, CT: Ablex.

Patterson, M.L. & Ritts, V. (1997). Social and communicative anxiety: A review and meta-analysis. In B.R. Burleson (Ed.), *Communication yearbook 20* (pp. 262–303). Thousand Oaks, CA: Sage.

Patterson, M.L. & Stockbridge, E. (1998). Effects of cognitive demand and judgment strategy on person perception accuracy. *Journal of Nonverbal Behavior, 22*, 253–263.

Rosenthal, R. (1974). *On the social psychology of the self-fulfilling prophecy: Further evidence for pygmalion effects and their mediating mechanisms.* New York: MSS Information Corporation.

Russell, J.A. (1994). Is there a universal recognition of emotion from facial expression? A review of the cross-cultural studies. *Psychological Bulletin, 115*, 102–141.

Smith, E.R. (1990). Content and process specificity in the effects of prior experiences. In T.K. Srull & R.S. Wyer Jr (Eds), *Advances in social cognition* (Vol. 3, pp. 1–59). Hillsdale, NJ: Erlbaum.

Swann, W.B., Jr (1984). Quest for accuracy in person perception: A matter of pragmatics. *Psychological Review, 91*, 457–477.

Swann, W.B., Jr (1987). Identity negotiation: Where two roads meet. *Journal of Personality and Social Psychology, 53*, 1038–1051.

Trope, Y. (1986). Identification and inferential processes in dispositional attribution. *Psychological Review, 93*, 239–257.

Vallacher, R.R. & Wegner, D.M. (1987). What do people think they're doing? Action identification and human behavior. *Psychological Review, 94*, 3–15.

Wicker, A.W. (1979). *An introduction to ecological psychology.* Monterey, CA: Brooks/Cole.

Wilson, T.D. & Schooler, J.W. (1991). Thinking too much: Introspection can reduce the quality of preferences and decisions. *Journal of Personality and Social Psychology, 60*, 181–192.

Wright, J.C. & Dawson, V.L. (1988). Person perception and the bounded rationality of social judgment. *Journal of Personality and Social Psychology, 55*, 780–794

Zebrowitz, L.A. (1997). *Reading faces: Window to the soul?* Boulder, CO: Westview Press.

Zebrowitz, L.A. & Collins, M.A. (1997). Accurate social perception at zero acquaintance: The affordances of a Gibsonian approach. *Personality and Social Psychology Review, 1*, 204–223.

Miscommunication and Communication Failure

Charles R. Berger
University of California, Davis, USA

Although the prison chain gang boss and the recalcitrant prisoner Luke in the highly popular 1960s American film *Cool Hand Luke* knew perfectly well what was meant when the chain gang boss said to Luke, "What we've got here is a failure to communicate" (Pearce, 1967), a line that was used to advertise the film, such terms as "communicative breakdown" (Clyne, 1977; Milroy, 1984), "communication failure", "communication mix-up" (Tannen, 1975), "conversation failure" (Ringle & Bruce, 1980), "miscommunication" (Gumperz & Tannen, 1979; Milroy, 1984), and "misunderstanding" (Gumperz & Tannen, 1979) have been used by different researchers to refer to a wide variety of communication-related problems that arise when individuals exchange verbal and non-verbal messages.

Consistent with the notion that concepts like miscommunication and communication failure are at once both interesting and slippery (Coupland, Wiemann & Giles, 1991), Gass and Veronis (1991) have observed that sometimes researchers have used the same term to refer to different problems, while, in other instances, they have used different terms to refer to the same problem. This terminological confusion cannot be sorted out here, but it probably stems from the fact that communication problems giving rise to misunderstanding can be traced to a wide variety of sources ranging from acoustic failure, i.e., failure to hear critical elements of the text; through lexical failures, i.e., hearing but failing to understand specific words; to semantic failures, i.e., failure to understand the meaning of the entire utterance (Reilly, 1987; Ringle & Bruce, 1980). Of course, similar sources of failure may be at work when individuals process written texts

The New Handbook of Language and Social Psychology.
Edited by W. Peter Robinson and Howard Giles.
© 2001 John Wiley & Sons Ltd.

or the non-verbal behaviours of others. Against this somewhat confused terminological background, this chapter will advance a framework, rooted in the
analysis of intentional action, for understanding miscommunication and communication failure in social interaction contexts. This framework will then be
used to analyze communication failures and to illuminate strategies for their
repair. Finally, miscommunication in mass-mediated contexts will be considered.

In addition to the manifold sources of miscommunication and misunderstanding
are the plethora of communication contexts within which such failures may occur.
These range from intercultural encounters that may involve individuals who do
not speak each other's language or who must communicate in a second language
(Gass & Veronis, 1985, 1991; Veronis & Gass, 1985), to intracultural interactions
among individuals who differ with respect to a wide variety of characteristics that
may encourage such problems, for example, interactions between people of different generations or different genders (Boggs & Giles, 1999). Although many
discussions of miscommunication and communication breakdown are predicated
on face-to-face interactions between people, miscommunication is equally possible
when communication between people is mediated (Bell, 1991), or when communication occurs between people and machines (Reilly, 1987, 1991).

The consequences of miscommunication and communication failure can vary
over a wide range, from the inconsequential and potentially humorous to the
highly consequential and deadly serious. The inconsequential end of this continuum are minor misunderstandings that may arise when people who speak
different native languages attempt to engage in small-talk with each other using
a common second language, or when individuals talking in an informal social
setting using their common native language use terms that may have multiple
possible interpretations. These misunderstandings may temporarily impede the
conversation, but once the problem is recognized and repaired the interaction
can continue. By contrast, at the highly consequential end of this continuum are
misunderstandings between air traffic controllers and pilots that are responsible
for mid-air collisions, communication failures among aircraft flight crews that
result in the use of incorrect procedures to fly the plane, thus causing an accident,
or doctor–patient misunderstandings that produce misdiagnosis of a serious illness or failure to take prescribed dosages of medications at proper intervals;
although in the latter case the consequences of communication failure may not
always be so dire. A doctor once told me that in the course of inquiring about the
well-being of a patient for whom he had prescribed a course of treatment involving the use of suppositories, the patient indicated that his condition had shown
marked improvement since beginning the prescribed treatment, but he com-
plained bitterly about the suppository's terrible taste.

In spite of the terminological confusion alluded to previously, there is at least
one sense of terms like "miscommunication" or "misunderstanding" that can be
ruled out of the present discussion. Sometimes individuals use these terms when
they understand each other quite well, but disagree with each other in some way.
For example, in the course of a discussion about a controversial issue, individuals
may remark that those on the opposite side of the issue "do not understand"

their position; that is, the demonstrated lack of assent to their advocated position is attributed to so-called "misunderstanding". However, "misunderstanding" in this context may be more apparent than real. Those on the opposite side of the issue may understand all too well the position being advocated by the opposition and simply choose to disagree with it. Similarly, in the film *Cool Hand Luke*, Luke (Paul Newman) the convict and his chain gang boss (Strother Martin) understood perfectly well what was expected of Luke and his fellow prisoners. Luke simply chose to defy the boss. "Failure to communicate" was not the issue; failure to comply was. We will avoid conflating "misunderstanding", "communication failure", and "miscommunication" with such terms as "disagreement" and "non-compliance", while at the same time recognizing they may be related.

A FRAMEWORK FOR UNDERSTANDING MISCOMMUNICATION

A number of researchers have proposed category schemes for classifying various communication failures (Coupland et al., 1991; Reilly, 1987; Ringle & Bruce, 1980). In their model, Coupland et al. (1991) identified six levels at which miscommunication can take place, ranging from inconsequential episodes to those involving ideological differences. At each level, they considered the degree to which individuals are aware of problems and the degree to which problems can be repaired. While their model presents an inclusive and useful map of the miscommunication terrain, it was not meant to provide a detailed explanation of the dynamics of miscommunication.

In their discussion of conversation failure, Ringle and Bruce (1980) delineated two main failure categories: input failures and model failures. Input failures include perceptual, lexical, and syntactic. Perceptual failures stem from failure to perceive clearly crucial words or phrases, while lexical failures involve either incorrect or no semantic interpretation of words or phrases. Words and phrases are correctly perceived but not correctly interpreted or not interpreted at all. Syntactic failures occur when the speaker's intended meaning is misconstrued, even though words and phrases are perceived and interpreted correctly. Model failures occur when the listener is unable to assimilate inputs into a coherent belief model. These model failures may happen because of incomplete or misleading information arising from input failures or because the listener is unable to place inputs into an appropriate conceptual framework. This latter problem may arise from different thematic emphases of the speaker and listener, the listener's insufficient background knowledge, or failure to make required inferences. Individuals in developing romantic relationships may have significantly divergent interpretations of such utterances as "I really enjoy being alone with you" or "I feel good when I'm close to you", that stem from model failures. More generalized analyses and categorizations of action slips and human errors have been presented by Norman (1981) and Reason (1990).

Although the identification of specific communication failure loci has significant implications for communication theory and praxis, exhaustive taxonomies
of miscommunication sources do not themselves provide a dynamic model of
how failures are diagnosed and repaired once they arise. Notions like miscommunication and communication failure by necessity presuppose a conception of
communication embodying the assumption that message production and comprehension processes are guided by intentions. There must be some kind of
standard by which to adjudicate the notion of "failure", the intention concept
provides one such standard. One intention-based theoretical framework that
may provide considerable purchase for understanding miscommunication is
planning theory. A commonplace assumption underlying theories of natural
language production and comprehension is that persons achieve understandings
of the streams of action and discourse produced by others by making inferences
about the goals they believe others to be pursuing and the plans they believe
others to be using to attain these goals (e.g., Carberry, 1990; Cohen, Morgan &
Pollack, 1990; Schank & Abelson, 1977, 1995).[1] In these treatments of discourse
and text comprehension, goals are viewed as cognitive representations of desired
end states for which individuals strive, while plans are hierarchically organized
cognitive representations of action sequences used to achieve goals. In describing the critical link between plan recognition and discourse understanding,
Green (1989) points out:

> Understanding a speaker's intention in saying what she said the way she said it
> amounts to inferring the speaker's plan, in all of its hierarchical glory, although
> there is room for considerable latitude regarding the details. (p. 14)

Not only are cognitive representations of goals and plans centrally implicated in
discourse comprehension processes, but also they have been viewed as critical
elements in the production of human action in general and discourse in particular (e.g. Berger, 1995, 1997a; Miller, Galanter & Pribram, 1960; Sacerdoti,
1977).[2] It is generally assumed that plans guide rather than energize goal-
directed action (Brand, 1984), although some have suggested that plans may
carry with them commitments to future action (Bratman, 1987, 1990). In the
specific context of speech production, Levelt (1989) has proposed a comprehensive account describing how individuals move from intentions to articulation. He
discusses macroplanning processes that involve the creation of sub-goals to
achieve a main goal, microplanning processes that specify the speech act types
generated during macroplanning, and phonetic plans that are used to transmute
preverbal messages into verbal messages. Butterworth (1980) has proposed similar planning processes in his model of speech production. At the empirical level,

---

[1] There are numerous treatments of plan-based discourse comprehension (Black, Kay & Soloway,
1987; Green, 1989; Hobbs & Evans, 1980; Levison, 1981; Lichtenstein & Brewer, 1980; Litman &
Allen, 1987; Perrault & Allen, 1980; Schmidt, 1976; Wilensky, 1983).
[2] Other theorists have proposed plan-based models of action and discourse production (Alterman,
1988; Butterworth & Goldman-Eisler, 1979; Hobbs & Evans, 1980; Krietler & Krietler, 1987; Pea &
Hawkins, 1987; Srull & Wyer, 1986; Waldron, 1997; Waldron & Applegate, 1994; Wilensky, 1983).

Hjelmquist (1991) and Hjelmquist and Gidlund (1984) have shown how plans are manifested in conversational discourse. In addition, Waldron (1990) has reported that of some 2273 thoughts that subjects reported having during their conversations with others, 44% were concerned with the goals they were pursuing in the conversation and the plans they were using to attain those goals. Because plans influence the production of speech at levels not directly accessible to verbal report (Levelt, 1989), Waldron's data probably underestimate the degree to which goals and plans guide actions on-line, as conversations unfold.

This plan-based approach to discourse comprehension and production has served as a backdrop to discussions of miscommunication (Reilly, 1987; Veronis & Gass, 1985). If communication is viewed as a process by which the goals and plans of participants become mutually known and are altered by exchanges of verbal and non-verbal behaviours, then communication failure emanating from whatever sources and resulting misunderstandings arise when verbal and non-verbal exchanges lead to faulty inferences that may be transmuted into equally faulty acts. These erroneous inferences may involve goals, plans, or both. An important implication that follows from this analysis is that what needs to be fixed when communication fails are these goal–plan inferences.

The idea that communication is about making inferences concerning intentions, as embodied in goals and plans, is compatible with the view that communicative transactions are more akin to problem-solving activity than exercises in information transfer through a conduit, although the language we use to talk about communicative activity may itself encourage the latter view (Reddy, 1979). Producing, comprehending, and interpreting even seemingly mundane messages are communicative activities fraught with uncertainty (Berger, 1995, 1997a, 1997b, 1997c). Because individuals, their relationships with each other and the contexts within which they communicate are dynamic, there is always some measure of uncertainty surrounding the goal–plan inferences that guide message comprehension, interpretation, and production. These uncertainties render "perfect understanding" or "perfect communication" highly transient states at best, and ones that are very rarely attained. Even under optimal communicative conditions, for example, shared languages and cultures, similar educational levels, attitudes and values and so on, some level of semantic slippage is associated with message exchanges. Consequently, communicating under uncertainty forces message producers to hedge against the downside risks of disseminating messages that may produce unanticipated negative consequences (Berger, 1997a, 1997b, 1997c).

WHEN COMMUNICATION FAILS

Having sketched some implications of the planning framework for understanding miscommunication, we now address the question of how this framework accounts for how message producers respond to communication failures. An early study of communication failure found that when communication between individuals over an electronic circuit was systematically interrupted so that the individual giving directions could not be clearly understood by the other, the direction-giver responded by speaking more slowly and increasing the length of their descriptions (Longhurst & Siegel, 1973). These investigators also noted that direction-givers appeared to increase their vocal amplitude in response to not being understood; however, they employed no formal measure of vocal intensity.

A series of experiments designed to test the hierarchy principle has directly assessed the relationships between message plans and responses to communication failure (Berger, 1997a; Berger, Knowlton & Abrahams, 1996). The hierarchy principle is predicated on the notion that message plans are organized in hierarchical fashion with plan elements dealing with message content and structure at the top of the hierarchy and increasing levels of message details at successively lower levels of the hierarchy. The lowest levels of the hierarchy are concerned with such message features as the vocal amplitude and speech rate at which the message is delivered. The hierarchy principle asserts that when message plans fail to bring about desired goals, and the message producer wishes to continue to pursue the desired goals, the initial response is to preserve the most abstract levels of the hierarchy and to alter lower-level hierarchy constituents. The preference for lower-level alterations to the message plan hierarchy is predicated on the assumption that lower-level alterations are less cognitively demanding than are their higher-level counterparts. Merely repeating what one has said previously, but more slowly or in a louder voice, is less demanding than reformulating the content and structure of messages.

Experiments done to assess the plausibility of the hierarchy principle demonstrated that when geographic direction-givers' efforts to provide directions to others were misunderstood, the direction-givers tended to increase their vocal intensity and simply repeat their directions rather than alter the walk routes of their directions when they gave them a second time (Berger, 1997a; Berger & diBattista, 1993). In addition, a series of laboratory and field experiments was conducted to determine whether alterations to progressively higher levels of the message plan hierarchy are indeed more cognitively demanding as postulated by the hierarchy principle. Cognitive load was indexed by determining the amount of time it took individuals to provide the second rendition of their directions after being informed by a confederate that their first directions were not understood. Confederates proffered different reasons for their inability to understand the first rendition of the directions in order to require alterations at different message plan levels.

These experiments demonstrated that when direction-givers were asked to perform a high-level message plan alteration (provide an alternative walk route) in the second rendition of their directions, their speech onset latencies where significantly longer than those of individuals asked to perform the low-level message plan alteration of speaking more slowly while providing their second rendition (Berger, 1997a; Berger et al., 1996). Furthermore, individuals asked to make message plan alterations between these two extremes (providing more landmarks in the second rendition of their directions) showed average speech onset latencies between those of the two extreme groups. The same findings were obtained outside of the laboratory context when naive pedestrians were approach at street corners and asked for directions. These experiments demonstrate that higher-level message plan alterations are indeed more cognitively demanding than lower-level alterations.

This line of inquiry suggests that when the origins of miscommunication are uncertain, individuals are likely to assume that the locus of the failure resides in lower levels of the message plan hierarchy and predicate subsequent message plan adjustments on this assumption. This default diagnosis makes some sense because it requires the least amount of effort to implement; that is, one merely repeats the message, but does so more slowly and in a louder voice. Unfortunately, however, as many English as a Second Language (ESL) teachers are well aware, repeating the same content organized the same way but in a louder voice may completely fail to repair a given communication failure. Interestingly, however, observers of highly experienced ESL teachers report that when English learners fail to understand, some ESL teachers increase their vocal amplitude while trying to repair the failure.

This default option in response to being misunderstood may be related to a more general response to goal failure. Some have argued that goal failure tends to generate negative affect, especially when it happens when one is psychologically close to the goal and when one has pursued the goal for a considerable time period (Srull & Wyer, 1986), although there may be exceptions to this generalization (Berger, 1995, 1997a). Consistent with this general notion, several compliance-gaining studies have found that when individuals learn that their attempts to gain the compliance of others have failed, their subsequent compliance-gaining behaviour tends to become increasingly more coercive (e.g., Berger & Jordan, 1991, 1992; deTurck, 1985, 1987; Hirokawa, Mickey & Miura, 1991).[3]

Increased vocal intensity is a speech attribute that might well potentiate judgments of elevated anger and coerciveness. In the case of being misunderstood, then, it is possible that increased vocal amplitude is born of both the default option that the communication failure is acoustically based, and the negative affect that follows from goal failure. Note too that in the course of pursuing compliance-gaining goals individuals must satisfy the sub-goal of being understood by the targets of their compliance-gaining attempts. Failure to comply with influence attempts may indicate either lack of understanding of what response is being requested, or understanding but defiance. In general, the goals of making oneself understood to others and understanding others are prerequisite to and subserve a wide variety of social goals like affinity seeking, comforting, compliance gaining, informing, and persuading. As noted previously, when these social goals are not attained, one must be careful to distinguish between goal failures induced by miscommunication and misunderstanding and failures caused by other factors.

---

[3] Several social psychologists have reported similar findings (Goodstadt & Kipnis, 1970; Instone, Major & Bunker, 1983; Kipnis & Consentino, 1969).

FIXING "BROKEN" COMMUNICATION

Some theorists have noted that while individuals may miscommunicate during their interactions, they are frequently unaware that any miscommunication has occurred (Milroy, 1984). These instances of miscommunication may be repaired outside of conscious awareness and with little if any disruption to the interaction flow. Obviously, these miscommunication episodes require no consciously guided repair strategies. Even if a problem is sensed, interactants may "let it pass" in the hope that subsequent conversational exchanges will provide clarification (Cicourel, 1972; Garfinkel, 1967; Ragan & Hopper, 1984). In contrast, significant communication failures may be consciously experienced and require equally consciously guided strategies for their amelioration.

Ringle and Bruce (1980) have outlined a number of potential repair strategies conversationalists can employ once they have detected perceptual, lexical, syntactic, and model failures, depending upon the type of failure diagnosed. First, lexical or syntactic failures may prompt the speaker to provide *explicit definition* of the problematic word or phrase. Second, unwarranted inferences may be corrected by *inference explication*. This may be accomplished by drawing out implications of prior discourse. Third, model failures may prompt the speaker to employ *thematic emphasis* to re-emphasize the overall point of the conversation. Fourth, the speaker may find it necessary to expand the listener's knowledge base by providing additional pertinent information (*knowledge base expansion*). Finally, *analogy and examples* may be used to clarify misunderstood concepts. As indicated previously, strategies for overcoming assumed perceptual failures during conversations include increasing vocal intensity or decreasing speech rate.

Although these strategies and others may be used to repair communication failures, other strategies may have to be deployed to repair "collateral damage" created by such failures. Communication failures may potentiate significant threats to face (Brown & Levinson, 1987, 1989; Goffman, 1959). Communication failures that involve lack of ability to speak and comprehend a language or the lack of knowledge in a given content domain may require that considerable work be done to maintain both the face and the line of interactants (Goffman, 1959). Thus, in addition to deploying various repair strategies for mitigating the immediate effects of communication failure, apologies, reassurances, and other face-saving moves may have to be enacted to deal with potential face threats.

Moreover, as observed earlier, communication failure may create considerable negative affect born of the frustrations surrounding goal failure. Consider that during their interactions with others individuals generally pursue primary goals concerned with such desired end states as the acquisition of goods and services, emotional support, and the like. Mutual understanding is an important goal subserving this plethora of possible primary goals, when the pursuit of such goals requires social interaction for their successful achievement. That is, in these cases mutual understanding is an enabling condition that must be met to achieve desired primary goals. Consequently, it is particularly frustrating when progress toward a highly desired focal primary goal or goals is thwarted by misunderstanding. The negative affect growing out of thwarted understanding may have to be strategically managed by interaction participants as they seek the levels of understanding that are prerequisite to attaining desired primary goals.

MASS-MEDIATED COMMUNICATION FAILURE

Most discussions of miscommunication and communication failure are organized around prototypical face-to-face communication situations in which participants are capable of detecting and repairing various communication problems. However, it would be an egregious oversight to assume that communication failures occur only during these interpersonal, unmediated communication episodes. The mass media may disseminate messages that promote erroneous inferences by the audiences that are exposed to them, even when these messages are presented as factual news reports. This general problem may stem from the fact that the goals of media executives, producers and writers, which are to increase audience ratings and associated advertising revenues (McQuail, 1997; Webster & Phelan, 1997), may result in the production of media messages that simultaneously attract audiences but mislead them. Proffering dramatic, compelling, and riveting stories that interest people and arouse their emotions may at the same time encourage them to make invalid inferences about the physical and social world in which they live. Acting on these mistaken inferences might produce outcomes very similar to those encountered in face-to-face communication failures. Granted, these inferences do not involve the goals and plans of interaction partners; nevertheless, faulty inferences about the physical and social world induced by media exposure may have highly significant social consequences. For instance, avoiding travel in a particular section of a city because one erroneously believes those who live in the area are particularly prone to violence is a misunderstanding that could arise as the result of either mediated or face-to-face communication.

Concern about news media's characterizations of a variety of phenomena and how these depictions promote biased and unrealistic judgments among news consumers has been expressed from a variety of quarters (e.g., Baesler, 1991; Brosius, 1993; Zillmann et al., 1994; Zillmann, Perkins & Sundar, 1992). This line of inquiry shares affinities with research subsumed under the cultivation analysis rubric (e.g., Mares, 1996; Shrum & O'Guinn, 1993), and it is also germane to risk communication research (e.g., Dunwoody & Neuwirth, 1991; Fischhoff, Slovic & Lichtenstein, 1981; Tonn et al., 1991).

Cultivation researchers have demonstrated that the world depicted on television is significantly more violent than mundane reality, and that those who watch a large number of hours of television tend to trust others less and to estimate that violent crime is more prevalent in society (Morgan & Signorielli, 1990).

Teenagers who report watching television talk shows every day tend to overestimate the incidences of teenage pregnancy, students in possession of guns at school, and teenagers who run away from home to a greater extent than teenagers who never watch such talk shows (Davis & Mares, 1998). Talk shows frequently address these kinds of issues. These effects presumably occur because vivid instances and anecdotes are highly available in memory and thus exert an inordinate impact on prevalence judgments. This idea is embodied in the concept of the availability heuristic (Nisbett & Ross, 1980; Kahneman, Slovic & Tversky, 1982; Tversky & Kahneman, 1973).

Several studies have directly compared the relative impact of anecdotal information and more diagnostic statistical information on subsequent judgments. Baesler and Burgoon (1994) catalogued some 19 studies that have pitted the two types of information against each other and found that 13 of them produced results that favored the persuasive efficacy of stories and cases over statistical data, while only two of the 19 studies showed the reverse pattern. This pattern is consistent with the base-rate fallacy, which asserts that the availability heuristic privileges the processing of more memorable anecdotes and cases over the processing of more diagnostic but pallid statistical or base-rate information (Bar-Hillel, 1980). Consistent with this notion, additional studies have found that stories and exemplars tend to overwhelm more diagnostic statistical data (Brosius and Bathelt, 1994; Gibson & Zillmann, 1994).

However, even when news reports present potentially more diagnostic base-rate data that are themselves accurate, their mode of presentation may be quite misleading. For example, a Sacramento, California newspaper story about a felony hit-and-run case, introduced by the dramatic headline, "Hit and runs: Sudden impact, lingering anguish", contained a table depicting the number of felony hit-and-run cases each year in Sacramento County from 1989 (706 cases) through 1994 (766 cases). These data served to illustrate this alleged growing problem (Ferris, 1995). The story failed to mention the fact that the county's population increased by some 114,600 people from 1989 to 1994. The 1989 rate of such cases per 100,000 population was 70.24, while the 1994 rate was 68.94. Thus, the rate actually declined slightly during the period.

Unfortunately, this kind of misleading statistical presentation in news reports is not an isolated instance. When trends in threatening phenomena are depicted using quantitative data, inappropriate frequency data are employed significantly more often than are rate data, especially when the trend is a worsening rather than an improving one (Berger, 1998a). Beyond the frequency versus rate data problem, Paulos (1995) has presented an extensive collection of errant presentations and interpretations of quantitative data that have appeared in various newspaper reports, including such common errors as interpreting correlations as evidence for causality and the gambler's fallacy. Misuses of statistical data by the news media probably stem from both a lack of statistical sophistication, although the arithmetic of rates is usually mastered during elementary school years, and the desire to make news stories as dramatic and compelling as possible (Berger, 1998b).

Although it is certainly true that news reports sometimes "get the facts wrong", as Bell (1991) aptly demonstrated in his study of media coverage of ozone depletion and global warming, even when relatively accurate quantitative data are adduced as evidence for a claim in a news story, as we have seen, they may be depicted inappropriately (frequency versus rate) or they may be subject to an erroneous interpretation (correlation implies causality or the gambler's fallacy). Furthermore, the prevalence of anecdotes and cases in news reports promotes further distortion via the availability heuristic. Add to all of these sources of distortion the propensity for various corporations and advocacy groups to present misleading results obtained in self-serving "studies" that they have commissioned (Crossen, 1994), and it is easy to understand why members of the public have a difficult time constructing a reasonably accurate picture of the social reality that surrounds them. For example, people tend to underestimate the risks associated with relatively dangerous activities like swimming; while at the same time, they overestimate the risks associated with the use of nuclear reactors (Slovic, 1987).

CONCLUSION

Although the probability of repairing miscommunication is substantially higher in unmediated communication situations, whether miscommunication occurs within mediated or unmediated contexts it has the potential to interfere with the pursuit of individual and social goals. The coordination necessary for the sake of achieving both individual and group goals requires some measure of mutual understanding. However, this is not to imply that all miscommunication is necessarily dysfunctional; purposeful ambiguity may serve such useful social functions as saving face. And, within the present context, it could be argued that the strategic and successful use of ambiguity to achieve the goal of saving another's face is not an instance of miscommunication at all; after all, intentions were read as intended. In some communication contexts, external criteria may make the assessment of communication accuracy possible, for example, the degree to which an aircraft pilot changes heading consistent with the one given by an air traffic controller. However, when such external criteria are absent, as they are when emotions are at stake, what counts as miscommunication may be considerably more fuzzy, although in these instances intentions may serve as a kind of standard.

Whether individuals use symbols to coordinate actions for accomplishing complex and sometimes risky tasks, for building close personal relationships, or for orienting themselves in an increasingly complex world, it is vital that they recognize the inherent limitations of the symbol systems used to reach these goals and the processing limitations of those who use these systems. Regardless of their disciplinary roots, communication researchers must do more to expose these limitations and to devise strategies for coping with them. In the public's mind, miscommunication is the root cause of many personal and social ills. Perhaps it is time to take this diagnosis more seriously.

REFERENCES

Alterman, R. (1988). Adaptive planning. *Cognitive Science*, **12**, 393–421.

Baesler, E.J. (1991). Message processing of evidence and the long term retention and judgment of beliefs. Unpublished doctoral dissertation, University of Arizona, Tucson.

Baesler, E.J. & Burgoon, J.K. (1994). The temporal effects of story and statistical evidence on belief change. *Communication Research*, **21**, 582–602.

Bar-Hillel, M. (1980). The base-rate fallacy in probability judgments. *Acta Psychologica*, **44**, 211–233.

Bell, A. (1991). Hot air: Media, miscommunication and climate change issue. In N. Coupland, H. Giles & J.M. Wiemann (Eds), '*Miscommunication' and problematic talk* (pp. 259–282). Newbury Park, CA: Sage.

Berger, C.R. (1995). A plan-based approach to strategic communication. In D.E. Hewes (Ed.), *The cognitive bases of interpersonal communication* (pp. 141–179). Hillsdale, NJ: Erlbaum.

Berger, C.R. (1997a). *Planning strategic interaction: Attaining goals through communicative action*. Mahwah, NJ: Erlbaum.

Berger, C.R. (1997b). Producing messages under uncertainty. In J.O. Greene (Ed.), *Message production: Advances in communication theory* (pp. 221–244). Mahwah, NJ: Erlbaum.

Berger, C.R. (1997c). Message production under uncertainty. In G. Phillipsen & T.L. Albrecht (Eds), *Developing communication theories* (pp. 29–57). Albany, NY: SUNY Press.

Berger, C.R. (1998a). *Making it worse than it is: News reports of threatening trends and the scary world of quantitative data*. Paper presented at the annual conference of the International Communication Association, Jerusalem, Israel, July 1998.

Berger, C.R. (1998b). Processing quantitative data about risk and threats in news reports. *Journal of Communication*, **48**, 87–106.

Berger, C.R. & diBattista, P. (1993). Communication failure and plan adaptation: If at first you don't succeed, say it louder and slower. *Communication Monographs*, **60**, 220–238.

Berger, C.R. & Jordan, J.M. (1991). *Iterative planning and social action: Repairing failed plans*. Paper presented at the annual convention of the International Communication Association, Chicago, IL, May 1991.

Berger, C.R. & Jordan, J.M. (1992). Planning sources, planning difficulty, and verbal fluency. *Communication Monographs*, **59**, 130–149.

Berger, C.R., Knowlton, S.W. & Abrahams, M.F. (1996). The hierarchy principle in strategic communication. *Communication Theory*, **6**, 111–142.

Black, J.B., Kay, D.S. & Soloway, E.M. (1987). Goal and plan knowledge representations: From stories to text editors and programs. In J.M. Carroll (Ed.), *Interfacing thought* (pp. 36–60). Cambridge, MA: MIT Press.

Boggs, C. & Giles, H. (1999). "The canary in the coal mine": The nonaccommodation cycle in the gendered workplace. *International Journal of Applied Linguistics*. **22**, 223–245.

Brand, M. (1984) *Intending and acting: Toward a naturalized theory of action*. Cambridge, MA: MIT Press.

Bratman, M.E. (1987). *Intentions, plans, and practical reason*. Cambridge, MA: Harvard University Press.

Bratman, M.E. (1990). What is intention? In P.R. Cohen, J. Morgan & M.E. Pollack (Eds), *Intentions in communication* (pp. 15–31). Cambridge, MA: MIT Press.

Brosius, H.-B. (1993). The effects of emotional pictures in television news. *Communication Research*, **20**, 105–124.

Brosius, H.-B. & Bathelt, A. (1994). The utility of exemplars in persuasive communications. *Communication Research*, **21**, 48–78.

Brown, P. & Levinson, S. (1978). Universals in language usage: Politeness phenomena. In E. Goody (Ed.), *Questions and politeness* (pp. 56–289). Cambridge, UK: Cambridge University Press.

Brown, P. & Levinson, S. (1987). *Politeness: Some universals in language usage*. Cambridge, UK: Cambridge University Press.

Butterworth, B. (1980). Evidence from pauses in speech. In B. Butterworth (Ed.), *Language production. Vol. 1: Speech and Talk* (pp. 155–176). New York: Academic Press.

Butterworth, B. & Goldman-Eisler, F. (1979). Recent studies in cognitive rhythm. In A.W. Siegman & S. Feldstein (Eds), *Of speech and time: Temporal speech patterns in interpersonal contexts* (pp. 211–224). Hillsdale, NJ: Erlbaum.

Carberry, S. (1990). *Plan recognition in natural language dialogue*. Cambridge, MA: MIT Press.

Cicourel, A.V. (1972). Basic and normative rules in the negotiation of status and role. In D. Sudnow (Ed.), *Studies in social interaction* (pp. 229–258). New York: Free Press.

Clyne, M. (1977). Intercultural communication breakdown and communication conflict: Towards a linguistic model and its exemplification. In C. Molony, H. Zobl & W. Stolting (Eds), *Deutsch im kontact mit anderen sprachen* (pp. 129–146). Kronberg, Germany: Scriptor.

Cohen, P.R., Morgan, J. & Pollack, M.E. (Eds) (1990). *Intentions in communication*. Cambridge, MA: MIT Press.

Coupland, N., Wiemann, J.M., & Giles, H. (1991). Talk as "problem" and communication as "miscommunication": An integrative analysis. In N. Coupland, H. Giles & J.M. Wiemann (Eds), *"Miscommunication" and problematic talk* (pp. 1–17). Newbury Park, CA: Sage.

Crossen, C. (1994). *Tainted truth: The manipulation of fact in America*. New York: Simon & Schuster.

Davis, S. & Mares, M.-L. (1998). Effects of talk show viewing on adolescents. *Journal of Communication*, **48**, 69–86.

deTurck, M.A. (1985). A transactional analysis of compliance-gaining behavior: Effects of noncompliance, relational contexts, and actor's gender. *Human Communication Research*, **12**, 54–78.

deTurck, M.A. (1987). When communication fails: Physical aggression as a compliance-gaining strategy. *Communication Monographs*, **54**, 106–112.

Dunwoody, S. & Neuwirth, K. (1991). Coming to terms with the impact of communication on scientific and technological risk judgments. In L. Wilkins & P. Patterson (Eds), *Risky business: Communicating issues of science, risk, and public policy* (pp. 11–30). New York: Greenwood Press.

Ferris, J. (1995). Hit and runs: Sudden impact, lingering anguish. *The Sacramento Bee*, 14 August, B1–B2.

Fischhoff, B., Slovic, P. & Lichtenstein, S. (1981). Lay foibles and expert fables in judgments about risk. *American Statistician*, **36**, 240–255.

Garfinkel, H. (1967). *Studies in ethnomethodology*. Englewood Cliffs, NJ: Prentice-Hall.

Gass, S. & Veronis, E. (1985). Variation in native speaker speech modification to nonnative speakers. *Studies in Second Language Acquisition*, **7**, 37–57.

Gass, S.M. & Veronis, E.M. (1991). Miscommunication in nonnative speaker discourse. In N. Coupland, H. Giles & J.M. Wiemann (Eds), *"Miscommunication" and problematic talk* (pp. 121–145). Newbury Park, CA: Sage.

Gibson, R. & Zillmann, D. (1994). Exaggerated versus representative exemplification in news reports. *Communication Research*, **21**, 603–624.

Goffman, E. (1959). *The presentation of self in everyday life*. Garden City, NY: Doubleday.

Goodstadt, B.E. & Kipnis, D. (1970). Situational influences in the use of power. *Journal of Applied Psychology*, **54**, 201–207.

Green, G.M. (1989). *Pragmatics and natural language understanding*. Hillsdale, NJ: Erlbaum.

Gumperz, J.J. & Tannen, D. (1979). Individual and social differences in language use. In C. Fillmore, D. Kempler & W.S.-Y. Wang (Eds), *Individual differences in language ability and language behavior* (pp. 305–325). New York: Academic Press.

Hirokawa, R.Y., Mickey, J. & Miura, S. (1991). Effects of request legitimacy on the compliance-gaining tactics of male and female managers. *Communication Monographs*, **58**, 421–436.

Hjelmquist, E. (1991). Planning and execution of discourse in conversation. *Communication and Cognition*, **24**, 1–17.

Hjelmquist, E. & Gidlund, A. (1984). Planned ideas versus expressed ideas in conversation. *Journal of Pragmatics*, **8**, 329–343.

Hobbs, J. R. & Evans, D. A. (1980). Conversation as planned behavior. *Cognitive Science*, **4**, 349–377.

Instone, D., Major, B. & Bunker, B.B. (1983). Gender, self-confidence, and social influence strategies: An organizational simulation. *Journal of Personality and Social Psychology*, **44**, 322–333.

Kahneman, D., Slovic, P. & Tversky, A. (1982). *Judgment under uncertainty: Heuristics and biases*. New York: Cambridge University Press.

Kipnis, D. & Consentino, J. (1969). Use of leadership powers in industry. *Journal of Applied Psychology*, **53**, 460–466.

Krietler, S. & Krietler, H. (1987). Plans and planning: Their motivational and cognitive antecedents. In S.L. Friedman, E.K. Skolnick & R.R. Cocking (Eds), *Blueprints for thinking: The role of planning in cognitive development* (pp. 110–178). New York: Cambridge University Press.

Levelt, W.J.M. (1989). *Speaking: From intention to articulation*. Cambridge, MA: MIT Press.

Levinson, S. (1981). Some preobservations on the modelling of dialogue. *Discourse Processes*, **4**, 93–116.

Lichtenstein, E.H. & Brewer, W.F. (1980). Memory for goal directed events. *Cognitive Psychology*, **12**, 412–445.

Litman, D. & Allen, J. (1987). A plan recognition model for subdialogues in conversation. *Cognitive Science*, **11**, 163–200.

Longhurst, T.M., & Siegel, G.M. (1973). Effects of communication failure on speaker and listener behavior. *Journal of Speech and Hearing Research*, **16**, 128–140.

Mares, M.-L. (1996). The role of source confusions in television's cultivation of social reality judgments. *Human Communication Research*, **23**, 278–297.

McQuail, D. (1997). *Audience analysis*. Thousand Oaks, CA: Sage.

Miller, G.A., Galanter, E. & Pribram, K.H. (1960). *Plans and the structure of behavior*. New York: Holt, Rinehart, & Winston.

Milroy, L. (1984). Comprehension and context: Successful communication and communicative breakdown. In P. Trudgill (Ed.), *Applied sociolinguistics* (pp. 7–31). London: Academic Press.

Morgan, M. & Signorielli, N. (1990). Cultivation analysis: Conceptualization and methodology. In N. Signorielli & M. Morgan (Eds), *Cultivation analysis: New directions in media effects research* (pp. 13–34). Newbury Park, CA: Sage.

Nisbett, R.E. & Ross, L. (1980). *Human inference: Strategies and shortcomings of social judgment*. Englewood Cliffs, NJ: Prentice-Hall.

Norman, D.A. (1981). Categorization of action slips. *Psychological Review*, **88**, 1–15.

Paulos, J.A. (1995). *A mathematician reads the newspaper*. New York: Basic Books.

Pea, R.D. & Hawkins, J. (1987). Planning in a chore-scheduling task. In S.L. Friedman, E.K. Skolnick & R.R. Cocking (Eds), *Blueprints for thinking: The role of planning in cognitive development* (pp. 273–302). New York: Cambridge University Press.

Pearce, D. (1967). *Cool hand Luke* [Film]. Hollywood, CA: Warner Brothers.

Perrault, R. & Allen, J. (1980). A plan-based analysis of indirect speech acts. *American Journal of Computational Linguistics*, **6**, 167–182.

Ragan, S.L. & Hopper, R. (1984). Ways to leave your lover: A conversational analysis of literature. *Communication Quarterly*, **32**, 310–317.

Reason, J.T. (1990). *Human error*. New York: Cambridge University Press.

Reddy, M.J. (1979). The conduit metaphor: A case of frame conflict in our language about language. In A. Ortony (Ed.), *Metaphor and thought* (pp. 284–324). London: Cambridge University Press.

Reilly, R.G. (1987). Types of communication failure in dialogue. In R.G. Reilly (Ed.), *Communication failure in dialogue and discourse: Detection and repair processes* (pp. 3–33). Amsterdam: North-Holland.

Reilly, R.G. (1991). Miscommunication at the person–machine interface. In N. Coupland, H. Giles & J.M. Wiemann (Eds), *"Miscommunication" and problematic talk* (pp. 283–300). Newbury Park, CA: Sage.

Ringle, M.H. & Bruce, B.C. (1980). Conversation failure. In W.G. Lehnert & M.H. Ringle (Eds), *Strategies for natural language processing* (pp. 203–221). Hillsdale, NJ: Erlbaum.

Sacerdoti, E. (1977). *A structure for plans and behavior*. Amsterdam: Elsvier.

Schank, R.C. & Abelson, R.P. (1977). *Scripts, plans, goals and understanding*. Hillsdale, NJ: Erlbaum.

Schank, R.C. & Abelson, R.P. (1995). Knowledge and memory: The real story. In R.S. Wyer Jr (Ed.), *Advances in social cognition* (Vol. 8, pp. 1–85). Hillsdale, NJ: Erlbaum.

Schmidt, C.F. (1976). Understanding human action: Recognizing the plans and motives of other persons. In J.S. Carroll & J.W. Payne (Eds), *Cognition and social behavior* (pp. 47–67). Hillsdale, NJ: Erlbaum.

Shrum, L.J. & O'Guinn, T.C. (1993). Process and effects in the construction of social reality: Construct accessibility as an explanatory variable. *Communication Research*, **20**, 436–471.

Slovic, P. (1987). Perception of risk. *Science*, **236**, 280–285.

Srull, T.K. & Wyer, R.S. (1986). The role of chronic and temporary goals in social information processing. In R. Sorrentino & E.T. Higgins (Eds), *Handbook of motivation and cognition* (pp. 503–549). New York: Guilford.

Tannen, D. (1975). Communication mix and mix-up or how linguistics can ruin a marriage. *San Jose State Occasional Papers in Linguistics*, 205–211.

Tonn, B.E., Goeltz, R.T., Travis, C.B. & Phillippi, R.H. (1991). Risk communication and the cognitive representation of uncertainty. In B.J. Garrick & W.C. Gekler (Eds), *The analysis, communication, and perception of risk* (pp. 213–227). New York: Plenum Press.

Tversky, A. & Kahneman, D. (1973). Availability: A heuristic for judging frequency and probability. *Cognitive Psychology*, **5**, 207–232.

Veronis, E.M. & Gass, S.M. (1985). Miscommunication in native/nonnative conversation. *Language in Society*, **14**, 327–343.

Waldron, V.R. (1990). Constrained rationality: Situational influences on information acquisition plans and tactics. *Communication Monographs*, **57**, 184–201.

Waldron, V.R. (1997). Toward a theory of interactive conversational planning. In J.O. Greene (Ed.), *Message production: Advances in communication theory* (pp. 195–220). Mahwah, NJ: Erlbaum.

Waldron, V.R. & Applegate, J.L. (1994). Interpersonal construct differentiation and conversational planning: An examination of two cognitive accounts for the production of competent verbal disagreement tactics. *Human Communication Research*, **21**, 3–35.

Webster, J.G. & Phelan, P.F. (1997). *The mass audience: Rediscovering the dominant model*. Mahwah, NJ: Erlbaum.

Wilensky, R. (1983). *Planning and understanding: A computational approach to human reasoning*. Reading, MA: Addison-Wesley.

Zillmann, D., Perkins, J.W. & Sundar, S.S. (1992). Impression-formation effects of printed news varying in descriptive precision and exemplification. *Medienpsychologie*, **23**, 168–185.

Zillmann, D., Gibson, R., Ordman, V.J. & Aust, C.F. (1994). Effects of human-interest stories in broadcast news. *Journal of Broadcasting and Electronic Media*, **38**, 65–78.

Conversation

Ben R. Slugoski
James Cook University, Townsville, Australia
Denis J. Hilton
Université de Toulouse II, France

This is the first appearance in this Handbook of a chapter devoted to "conversation"; indeed, the word did not even appear in any of the first edition's chapter titles. Since the editors undoubtedly recognized the centrality of conversational structure and processes to human linguistic interaction, we can only speculate that the omission of a dedicated chapter was motivated by a belief that the topic was effectively exhausted by coverage of sub-processes such as face-work, speech accommodation, self-disclosure, paralanguage and prosody, etc., together with its subspecies such as doctor–patient, student–teacher, and husband–wife exchanges. Certainly, the writing of a chapter on conversation *sui generis* runs the risk either of too cursory a treatment of all such variables and processes, or, alternatively, of committing a category mistake, looking for a transcendent but possibly specious framework for *all* modes of conversational activity. This chapter is too short to attempt the former project; consequently, we will risk reifying "conversation" by honing in on two contrasting approaches – the sequential or syntactic and the pragmatic – that purport to characterize resources necessary for engaging in any and all conversations. Our predilection for the latter, pragmatic approach will become evident as we proceed to apply it to two familiar but largely overlooked interactional settings: first, the solicitation and deployment of causal explanations, and second, the "conversations" occurring between psychologists and their research participants in linguistically mediated judgment and decision-making tasks. As will be seen, failure to consider the pragmatic context of such communications brings into doubt the validity of a fair portion of currently popular research into human reasoning and decision making. We

The New Handbook of Language and Social Psychology.
Edited by W. Peter Robinson and Howard Giles.
© 2001 John Wiley & Sons Ltd.

conclude the chapter by providing a set of methodological guidelines, based in pragmatic insights, for distinguishing between "cognitive" and "conversational" accounts of people's tendency to provide ostensibly "irrational" judgments in such studies.

To first delineate our subject, we define "conversation" as an orderly, jointly managed sequence of utterances produced by at least two participants who may or may not share similar goals in the interaction. This serves to differentiate "conversation" from two broader but often confused cognates, "communication" and "discourse," neither of which requires a (contingent) response on the part of the recipient. Our definition allows for the agonistic as well as cooperative exchange of utterances, and by referring to "utterances" rather than "sentences" it recognizes the inherently contextualized nature of all communicative action. Finally, though we recognize the canonical form of conversation to take place within the multidimensional space of face-to-face verbal interaction, the definition allows for reduced forms, such as purely oral (e.g., telephone) or written (e.g., electronic mail) conversations, or those using non-linguistic symbolic devices (e.g., ASL, a hand gesture or period of silence substituting for a verbalization, or even a check-mark or scale rating on a questionnaire). Thus, while we refer generically to "speakers" and "hearers" deploying and receiving "utterances," it is to be understood that the particular code and channel of symbolic transmission employed are relatively unimportant to our conception of conversation.

Central to our definition is the orderly, *jointly managed* sequencing of the speakers' utterances. It is possible to conceive of a full-blown, face-to-face verbal interaction between, say, two schizophrenics, the record of which revealed no contingent responding among their respective utterances; hence, we would not want to admit this as a "real" conversation. We may distinguish such "non-conversations" from "pseudo-conversations," wherein only one of the participants is actually orienting his or her utterances toward those of the other (pseudo-) participant. The following extract of dialogue between a depressed young woman and Weizenbaum's (1976) early natural language understanding program, ELIZA, is illustrative:

Woman: Men are all alike.
ELIZA: In what way?
Woman: They're always bugging us about something or other.
ELIZA: Can you think of a specific example?
Woman: Well, my boyfriend made me come here.
ELIZA: Your boyfriend made you come here.
Woman: He says I'm depressed much of the time.

This extract is remarkable for the illusion of mutual contingency it conveys. In fact, ELIZA's contributions are generated by a rather primitive, "keyword" criterion of response selection, which raises interesting questions about how it is that the woman is able to create sense from the computer's word strings and generally do the "work" of organizing the interaction. Unlike Weizenbaum, who tended to derogate his participants as "naive" and "gullible," or Hewes and Planalp (1987) who attribute the "accomplishment" of mutual responsiveness to ELIZA (or Weizenbaum's ingenuity), we view it primarily as a skilled accomplishment of the woman's (as well as, somewhat reflexively, our own) capacity to go beyond the information given by ELIZA. In any case, given our professed emphasis on the sequential patterning of utterances within conversations, the main questions confronting researchers have to do with (a) how this patterning is to be revealed, and (b) how it is to be explained. We thus begin by considering two approaches to explicating conversation structure; as mentioned, these are the sequential or syntactic and the pragmatic.

SEQUENTIAL/SYNTACTIC APPROACHES

To say that conversations are sequentially organized is to imply that there is a "syntax" or "grammar" of conversation. If so, then it should be possible to identify a set of sequencing rules that will "generate" all and only well-formed conversations. Ideally, this set of rules should characterize all extant conversations, as well as well-formed strings of utterance units (however defined) that have not yet occurred. The approach rests on obvious analogy with linguists' treatment of sentence structure, wherein what is sought is a set of rules for combining morphemes of the language into well-formed sentences. Certainly, across a range of disciplines, there has been no dearth of attempts to uncover the grammar of conversation (see, for example, Clarke, 1983; Gamst, 1982; Goffman, 1976; Labov & Fanshel, 1977; Sinclair & Coulthard, 1975).

Earlier and cruder methods of sequential analysis were essentially inductive exercises aimed at identifying structural regularities in preformed conversations. Research tended to employ common-sense categories for classifying utterances (e.g., Bales', 1950, "agrees," "gives orientation," "asks for opinion," etc.) and relied on constructing matrices of transitional probabilities between the codable events. Dependencies among adjacent utterance types, as well as higher-order dependencies, could thus be investigated and possibly compared to chance expectancies. Somewhat more sophisticated is the Markovian model-testing strategy whereby observed sequences of conversational behaviours could be fitted to any linear stochastic model, the simplest being a Markov chain (i.e., the extent to which each utterance unit is dependent on its immediate precursor). This approach also relies on calculating transitional probabilities between the events, but makes some additional assumptions regarding the process generating the events. Specifically, for a process to be considered Markovian, it must satisfy *order* (that the present event is contingent on the occurrence of the immediately preceding events, with the number of preceding events defining the order of the model), *stationarity* (the magnitudes of the transitional probabilities between events is stable across the sampled sequence), and *homogeneity* (that the transition matrices generated by each dyad or group in the sample are relatively similar). Markov modelling has been used principally to discover recurrent patterns of reactivity (other-dependence) and proactivity (auto-dependence) in conversations, and hence as an aid to inferences regarding the relative power of the speakers, differences between conversation types (e.g., therapeutic or classroom), as well as changes that may occur over time in such episodes (see Russell & Czogalik, 1989, for a review).

It is generally appreciated that sequential analysis and model testing are inadequate to the task of capturing the nuances of actual conversational interaction. The combinatorial explosion in transitional probabilities that results from considering even a modest (10, say) number of categories with only one or two lags can be overwhelming; hence, fitting the utterances to a manageable number of types often is a Procrustean exercise *par excellence*. Further problems associated with identifying non-terminal syntactic elements – typically, speech act types – from observed utterances were explored by Levinson (1981) in a trenchant critique of grammatical models of conversation in general. Rather than the categories being mutually exclusive and jointly exhaustive, as such models must assume, Levinson observes that many utterances perform multiple speech acts (such as a question that also serves as a challenge); utterances are often better described in terms of their perlocutions (intended effects) rather than illocutions (activity types), and since there is a potentially infinite number of the former utterance units cannot easily be paired with act units; finally, due to the pervasive indirectness in language use, Levinson agues that there is no rigorous way of translating particular utterances into particular speech acts. By calling for greater attention to the role of context and speakers' idiosyncrasies in utterance selection, Levinson eschews any possibility of formalistic analysis of conversational activity, preferring instead the idiographic methods of conversational analysis (CA). Goffman (1976) also recognizes the difficulties that indirectness and contextual specification pose for finding general concatenation rules for conversation, but suggests that we keep our eyes on the ball:

> However tortured the connection can become between the last person's talk and current speaker's utterance, that connection must be explored under the auspices of determinism, as though all the degrees of freedom available to whosoever is about to talk can somehow be mapped out, conceptualized, and ordered, somehow neatly grasped and held, somehow made to submit to the patterning out affected by analysis. If contexts can be grouped into categories according to the way in which they render the standard force of an utterance inapplicable and principles thus developed for determining when this meaning will be set aside, then such must be attempted. (p. 72)

Even assuming that problems of unitizing and categorizing utterances ultimately can be overcome – and there is no question but that Austin (1962), Searle (1969) and, indeed, Brown and Levinson (1987) with their theory of politeness, have already laid a robust foundation for such an enterprise – it remains an issue whether sequential models of *any* complexity can deal with the ubiquitous phenomenon of embedding (a.k.a. nesting, side or insertion sequences, etc.) in conversations, of which the following exchange is exemplary:

A1: A Black Russian with little ice, please.
B1: Are you 21?
A2: I thought the law goes into effect January 1!
B2: December 1!
A3: No, I'm 20.
B3: Sorry, I can't help you.
(From Cappella, 1987, p. 192)

Indeed, it is the occurrence of such exchanges, where speakers depart from and later revisit topics, that has motivated the development of proper "syntactical" or rule-based models of conversation. The argument is nicely summarized in Levinson's (1981) *Theorem 1* (which he later goes on to reject):

> The syntax of dialogue is essentially self-embedding and requires an infinity of substitution classes; it cannot therefore be generated by a finite state device and requires a device of at least Type 2, and possibly even more general. And this would be, for such a theory of conversational structure, a significant result, constraining the relevant class of theories about that structure. (p. 95)

This is analogous to Chomsky's (1963) discovery that no linear stochastic process (finite state grammar) is capable of generating the self-embedding sentences, clauses, and phrases observed in natural language. Instead, a set of recursive rewriting rules is postulated to operate on the non-terminal grammatical categories. These rules may be context-free (Chomsky's Type 2), context-sensitive (Type 1), or unrestricted (Type 0), corresponding to increasingly powerful automata. In the case of dialogue structure, the rules apply to speech act categories and hence can generate a potentially infinite number of well-formed "strings" of speech acts.

Grammatical rewriting rules may provide an economical way of describing the output of a conversation-producing system; it is unclear, however, that they elucidate the psychological processes of the humans actually responsible for the output. Sophisticated linear models operating on both the terminal (utterances) and non-terminal (speech acts) elements can, in fact, approximate the output of even the most powerful of the "non-linear" grammars (Cappella, 1987). Another flaw in the analogy with sentence production is, as Clarke (1983) points out, since it takes at least two to converse "it would require one person to start executing terminal elements subtended by a node which had formed in the other person's generative system, but was not as yet represented in its output" (p. 117). In other words, while it makes sense to speak of the top-down processing of a sentence since the processing occurs within a single person's head, it is not at all clear how such processing could be distributed across conversationalists' heads. Also, Levinson (1981) is less than optimistic that a set of grammatical sequencing rules based on abstract structural features is in the cards, since this project encounters the same difficulties of unitizing and classifying the conversational stream as the linear models do, but it also tends to overemphasize the extent to which non-ritualized conversations consist of interlocking sets of adjacency pairs. In

Levinson's view, there are too many degrees of freedom available to interactants to be able to speak of the "well-" or "ill-formedness" of conversations based on some conventional sequencing rules. Rather, he suggests that conversations typically are organized on-line, in terms of Gricean implicatures (which we shall explicate shortly). Thus, the phenomena of embedding, side and insertion sequences, which grammatical models were proposed to account for, can equally be interpreted as responses aimed at the prior speaker's higher-order goals. Viewed this way, even if models that translate utterances into speech acts and apply syntactical rules to those acts are capable of *describing* the structure of mundane conversation, there is little reason to think that this structure is other than an emergent property of other processes including speakers' real-work knowledge together with general expectancies concerning rational and cooperative action.

An alternative suggestion is that conversations gain their structural integrity from speaker/hearers' cognitive schemata (e.g., Ellis, Hamilton & Aho, 1983; Hewes & Planalp, 1987; Hurtig, 1977), an approach that extends ideas developed in textual and narrative analyses to whole conversations. Researchers in this tradition assign a relatively minor role to contiguous relations between utterances and instead view conversational *coherence* (a term they prefer to "well-formedness") to result from a memory component that represents *semantic* relations among topical elements in the dialogue. Speakers employ a variety of *cohesion mechanisms* (de Beaugrande, 1980; Halliday & Hasan, 1976) such as anaphora, cataphora, and paraphrase, to tie semantically related elements of their conversation together, hence providing it with a discernible macrostructure. This structure *may* take the form of a grammar consisting of rewrite rules. Thus, for example, Gamst (1982) tested a hierarchical structural model of conversation in which the macrostructure consisted of encounter + interaction + departure, with encounter rewritten as greeting + inquiry, interaction rewritten as topic identification + topic exchange, and so on. Note that the non-terminal elements are expressed, not as speech acts, but rather in terms of plans, goals, and episodes, in line with typical discourse schemata for representing stories and narratives (e.g., Thorndyke, 1977; Winograd, 1977).

Clarke's "Method of Reconstruction"

Numerous methodologies have been employed empirically to examine structural regularities in conversations, as well as the psychological processes responsible for such regularities. Recall and recognition memory for dialogue, subjective "naturalness" judgments of differently ordered sequences, and computer modelling have all figured prominently in the arsenal of available techniques. However, we have chosen to focus on just one method that has found particular favour with social psychologists interested in factors contributing to orderly conversation.

Kent, Davis and Shapiro (1978) argue that the achievement of mutually understood patterns of communication can be assessed by an experimental technique known as the "method of reconstruction." This technique involves placing individual turns, or floorholdings, of a conversation onto separate index cards, and then presenting these cards in randomized order to participants (or "sorters"), who are asked to reassemble the turns into the order they think the dialogue may have followed. This reconstruction task was pioneered by Pease (1972) and developed into a multifaceted research instrument by Clarke (1975, 1983), who predicted and found that people would be able to reassemble randomized turns in an unfamiliar conversation with greater than chance accuracy. For people to succeed in this task, Clarke assumed that: (1) spontaneous conversation is non-random; each utterance is constrained by characteristics of previous utterances to which it must relate; (2) the native user of a language can use the knowledge of these patterns to make judgements about the speech of others; and (3) a speaker's beliefs about these patterns are largely correct.

Interestingly, sorters' success at the task was not tied to the presence of syntactic cues to turn position in the floorholdings, as Clarke (1983, Experiment 2) found that dialogues made devoid of such cues were, if anything, better reconstructed that those with syntactic cues present. This suggests that turn-by-turn cohesion is largely a result of semantic relations among the floorholdings, and to the extent that speech acts are thought to be syntactically coded (e.g., the "conversational postulates" of Gordon & Lakoff, 1971) suggests that sorters were not making their sequencing decisions based solely on speech acts types. However, Kent et al. (1978) found that a ban on questions significantly reduced reconstructability, but also attesting to the role of semantic information, they demonstrated that shared cultural knowledge was important for reconstruction by showing the superior sorting success of British dialogue by British participants as compared to Canadian participants. Ellis et al. (1983) used the method to test hypotheses concerning specific structural features of dialogue that would aid in detecting inter-utterance contingencies. They found that adjacency pairs occurring within a larger structural unit such as conversational openings (Schegloff, 1968) were particularly easy to sequence, whereas sorters had the greatest difficulty with the embedded sequences. Goldwaithe (1997) found generally poor reconstruction accuracy of her naturally occurring conversation – a hairdressing appointment – which, she notes, contained substantial embedding.

A number of other studies have turned up differences in the reconstructability of dialogue as a function both of speaker and sorter characteristics. Kent, Davis and Shapiro (1981) found that the shared personal knowledge, or common ground, between friends made their conversations less accurately reconstructed by an outsider than were dialogues produced between two strangers, who did not share common knowledge and hence had to be more explicit in their utterances. Another relevant finding on individual differences in the generation of reconstructable speech patterns is that utterances produced by schizophrenic individuals are less accurately sorted than those produced by psychiatrically normal subjects (Rutter, 1979), a difference presumably due to schizophrenics' frequent breaches of the Gricean (1975) maxim of relation; that is, the utterances were not connected in any relevant or meaningful way to one another (see Rochester, Martin & Thurstone, 1977). It turns out, however, that simply telling sorters that the dialogue they are about to reconstruct involves a schizophrenic participant results in significantly poorer reconstruction than among those not so informed (Slugoski & Turnbull, 1987). Apparently, when sorters are unable to assume rationality and cooperative intent among the conversationalists, as their lay theory of schizophrenia would lead them to conclude in this case, they have more difficulty discerning the orderliness latent in the disconnected dialogues.

If we assume with Ellis et al. (1983) that "the act of reconstructing a conversation is not too far removed from what an interactant must do" (p. 280), then the above pattern of results suggests that speakers' pragmatic presuppositions play at least as large a role in creating coherent conversation as do local linguistic mechanisms. We now turn to consider the dominant model outlining people's pragmatic assumptions – Grice's conversational logic – before proceeding to apply his conversational model to two "hot" topics in social cognition research: causal attribution and judgmental heuristics and biases.

GRICEAN LOGIC OF CONVERSATION

Conversational inference is a form of judgment under uncertainty. Hearers have to make hypotheses about the speaker's intended meaning on the basis of what is explicitly said. For example, most hearers routinely go beyond the information given in the utterance "I went to the cinema last night" to infer that the speaker meant to convey that she saw a film last night. The additional information conveyed in this way by the speaker is termed a *conversational implicature* (Grice, 1975). Grice thus argued that to understand a speaker's full meaning, the listener must both understand the meaning of the sentence itself ("what is said") and what it conveys in a given context ("what is implicated").

Conversational inference thus shares some important properties with inductive inference (Levinson, 1983). First, it is *ampliative*, i.e. the conclusion contains more information than the premises. The inference that the speaker went to the cinema and saw a film contains more information than the assertion that she just went to the cinema. Consequently, the conclusions of both conversational and inductive inference are both *defeasible*, i.e. they can be cancelled by the addition of new information. The speaker may cancel the implicature that he or she saw a film at the cinema last night by saying "I went to the cinema last night, but couldn't get in."

Grice's (1975) Cooperative Principle (CP) and its derivative maxims are detailed in Table 1. This scheme describes a form of rational communication in which the maximum amount of valuable information is transmitted with the least amount of encoding and decoding effort. The CP and the subordinate maxims seem to correspond to important psychological dimensions, and the tensions between them produce important logical and linguistic consequences.

Table 1   Grice's (1975) cooperative principle and the maxims of conversation

The cooperative principle
Make your contribution such as is required, at the stage at which it occurs, by the accepted purpose or direction in which you are engaged.

The maxim of quality
Try to make your contribution one that you believe to be true, specifically:
1. Do not say what you believe to be false
2. Do not say that for which you lack adequate evidence

The maxim of quantity
1. Make your contribution as informative as is required for the current purposes of the exchange
2. Do not make your contribution more informative than is required

The maxim of relation
Make your contribution relevant

The maxim of manner
1. Avoid obscurity
2. Avoid ambiguity
3. Be brief
4. Be orderly

Attributional Bases of Conversational Inference

Grice's (1975) assumption of cooperativeness and the corresponding maxims of conversation depend on the hearer making certain default attributions about the speaker. In particular, the assumption of cooperativeness presupposes that utterances are produced by an intentional agent who wishes to cooperate with us, and has the ability to realize this intention. We argue that each set of conversational maxims implies certain kinds of attributions about the speaker (see Table 2).

The *maxim of quality* concerns the likely truth value of an utterance. Thus, if the hearer attributes properties such as sincerity, reliability and knowledgeability to the speaker, then the hearer may well consider the probable truth value of an utterance to be high. If, on the other hand, the hearer considers the speaker to be insincere, unreliable or unknowledgeable, then the hearer may well consider the probable truth of the utterance to be low.

The *maxim of quantity* concerns the perceived informativeness of an utterance. Speakers should not burden hearers with information they are already likely to know. What speakers and hearers take for granted may in part depend on perceptions of class membership. Competent members of Western society do not need to be told why a customer who ate a good meal with good service in a restaurant left a big tip. From their own world knowledge they are able to make the necessary bridging inferences (Clark & Haviland, 1977; Schank & Abelson, 1977). Thus, hearers will often go beyond the information given in making inferences, since they assume that relevant information that they are likely to know has already been omitted.

Table 2 Assumed characteristics of message and speaker implied by Grice's logic of conversation

Assumption/maxim of conversation	Message characteristics	Characteristics attributed to speaker
Cooperativeness (see below)	Observes 4 maxims	Intentional Helpful
Quality	Truth value Probability	Sincerity Honesty Reliability Competence
Quantity	Informativeness	Mutual knowledge Group membership
Relation	Goal relevance	Interactional goals
Manner	Clarity	Knowledge of language Equal or higher status

The *maxim of relation* enjoins speakers to mention information that is relevant to the goals of the interaction. Hearers are entitled to assume that any relevant information which they are not likely to know will have been included. They are also entitled to assume that information which has been included is relevant. Otherwise why mention it? One problem for experimental research is that psychologists routinely violate this assumption by introducing information precisely because it is irrelevant to the judgment task in hand (e.g., Nisbett, Zukier & Lemley, 1981). If hearers (participants) continue to attribute essentially cooperative intentions to speakers (experimenters) then they are liable to be misled by the information given.

The *maxim of manner* enjoins speakers to be brief, orderly, clear and unambiguous. Departures from these sub-maxims are often motivated by considerations of tact or politeness (Brown & Levinson, 1987), and hence may signal status and intimacy differentials between the speaker and recipient (see, for example, Slugoski, 1995; Slugoski & Turnbull, 1988). Adherence to these prescriptions also depends on the speaker's control of the language. Hearers may take this into account in interpreting an utterance. For example, a German tourist in England might conceivably ask a passer-by for directions to "the Townhouse" when she meant "the Town Hall." Rather than direct the tourist to the nearest renovated Georgian residence, a co-operative hearer might attribute the speaker's unclarity to her inexperience in British English and direct her to the Town Hall. Usually such misunderstandings in conversation can be corrected through discussion. However, such opportunities for repair do not exist in experimental and survey research. Consequently, experimenters may not notice ambiguities in their response formats which are systematically reinterpreted by participants, thus leading to systematic biases in the results obtained. This seems to have been the case in much basic attribution research (Hilton, 1991; Turnbull & Slugoski, 1988).

Grice (1975) also noted that there may be *clashes* between two or more of the maxims, such that it may be impossible fully to meet one maxim without breaching the other(s). For example, when required to make judgments under uncertainty, respondents will often find themselves unable both to be completely certain (maxim of quality) as well as maximally informative (maxim of quantity), and will resolve the conflict by finding a principled balance between the two. An example might be the tendency for people to prefer mentioning basic-level categories (Rosch et al., 1976) over their subordinate (informative but unlikely) or superordinate (likely but uninformative) classes in identification tasks (Tversky & Kahneman, 1983). This assumes that cooperative speakers try to be informative, not just truthful.

CONVERSATIONAL PROCESSES AND CAUSAL EXPLANATION

We now address the question of how the conversational approach can illuminate causal attribution and explanation processes, before turning to the hotly debated issue of whether people are rational or irrational decision makers more generally.

We first note that causal explanation is a form of conversation. Explanation is a three-place predicate: someone explains something to someone. This renders causal explanation different from causal attribution and causal induction, with the consequence that causal explanation, being a form of conversation, must follow Grice's (1975) maxims, balancing truth, informativeness, relevance and clarity (Hilton, 1990, 1991; Turnbull, 1986; Turnbull & Slugoski, 1988).

From this it follows that speakers should alter their explanations as a function of what their hearers need to know. Slugoski et al. (1993) demonstrated this in an experiment where participants were asked to explain a young delinquent's behaviour to interlocutors who had varying background knowledge (personal or situational) concerning a juvenile delinquent who had committed a criminal act. Slugoski et al. (1993) hypothesized that participants would try to be informative, and provide their interlocutors with information that they did not already possess, thus satisfying Grice's (1975) maxim of quantity. Their results confirmed this hypothesis: when the interlocutor already had background information about the youth's personality, participants tended to refer to situational factors in order to explain the crime, and vice versa. This finding is striking because it suggests that people are quite aware that events are multidetermined, and can readily shift between internal and external factors in explanation as a function of the conversational context.

Slugoski et al. (1993) note that their results fit in well with the notion of causality as an abnormal condition (Hart & Honoré, 1959), which Hilton and

Slugoski (1986) advanced as an important criterion in common-sense causal ascription. Their results suggest that speakers give explanations that refer to conditions that are unusual or abnormal from the other's point of view. Hilton and Slugoski (1986) suggested that in causal attribution people identify as causes conditions that are abnormal from their own point of view. They showed that participants' prior world knowledge about what was normal affected their causal judgments in the attribution task pioneered by McArthur (1972). They argue that the traditional Kelleyan dimensions of consensus, distinctiveness and consistency can be used to define what is abnormal in a given case.

Hilton and Slugoski's (1986) abnormal conditions focus (ACF) model posits that people tend to identify as a cause the condition that is abnormal in the circumstances. For any given event, there is a plethora of necessary conditions which could all count as causes, yet we typically mention only one or two factors when providing an explanation. Research has shown that people select the condition that is abnormal in the circumstances as the cause. For example, if people learn that a watch smashes after a hammer has hit it, they usually attribute the breaking of the glass to the hammer blow. However, if they then learn that this procedure occurs as part of a routine testing procedure in a watch factory, they tend to prefer the explanation that the watch broke because of a fault in the glass (Einhorn & Hogarth, 1986). Hilton and Erb (1996) showed that this change was not due to any change in the perceived probability of the explanation that the watch broke because the hammer hit it, but due to its decreased informativeness and relevance in the watch factory context. This finding supported the distinction that Hilton and Erb (1996) drew between causal backgrounding, where an explanation is still presupposed to be true but is relegated to the backgrounded "causal field" of necessary conditions (Mackie, 1980), and causal discounting, where the explanation is considered less likely to be true because another, more probable explanation has been offered (cf. Kelley, 1973; Morris & Larrick, 1995). In both cases, additional contextual information may lead to an explanation being discarded, but for quite different reasons (see McClure, 1998, for further discussion).

Verb Effects in Conversational Context: Pragmatic vs. Semantic Aspects of Explanation

Most attribution experiments follow the form: participants are given descriptions of a particular named person performing a behaviour on a specific occasion, and are asked to explain why the behaviour happened. Sometimes no further information is provided (e.g., Brown and Fish, 1983; McArthur, 1972; Semin and Fiedler, 1988). In other cases, further background information is provided, often in the form of covariation information defined by Kelley's (1967) cube (e.g., Cheng & Novick, 1990; Försterling, 1989; Hilton & Slugoski, 1986; McArthur, 1972), and sometimes in a more naturalistic story-like form (e.g., Leddo, Abelson & Gross, 1984; McClure and Hilton, 1998; Slugoski et al., 1993).

However, causal explanation of particular events needs to be distinguished from dispositional attribution (Bassili, 1989; Hamilton, 1988; Hilton, Smith & Kim, 1995), which involves learning about the propensity of an entity to produce a certain kind of effect. Dispositional attributions may be regarded as certain kinds of causal generalizations; thus "Tom is helpful" implies that "Tom helps many people" (Brown and Fish, 1983; Hilton et al., 1995). Dispositional attributions may, of course, be used as causal explanations. Thus we may explain a particular event by saying "Tom gave money to charity because he is generous" (as opposed to "because he was in a good mood that day").

Our perspective predicts some interesting interactions between dispositional attribution and causal explanation. For example, work on "implicit causality" contained in verbs has shown that actions are typically explained with reference to some quality of the actor (Brown and Fish, 1983; Semin and Fiedler, 1988). Thus spontaneous completions of sentences such as "Ted helps Bill because . . ." tend to refer to something about the actor. Participants also are more likely to consider that Ted covaries with the helping behaviour, agreeing that *Ted helps many other people* and *few other people help Paul*, and to attribute the disposition of helpfulness to Ted by rating their agreement on a 7-point rating scale with the statement *Ted helps Paul because he is the kind of person who helps people*. These findings fit in with the idea that causality is determined by covariation (Rudolph & Försterling, 1997). On the other hand, we would note that low consensus, as well as suggesting covariation between the actor and the target event, also throws the actor into focus as abnormal (Hilton & Slugoski, 1986), and therefore that the ACF model would make the same prediction here. However, note that these results have almost all been obtained with contextless sentences involving two named, but otherwise unspecified individuals.

Firstly, consider what happens when the participant is given some relevant prior knowledge about one of the individuals concerned. Slugoski, Hilton and Turnbull (1997) did this by manipulating role expectancies about actors involved in the production of the event. Thus, participants would read a sentence such as *The fireman helps Kevin*. Here, it is part of our world knowledge that firemen help people. When asked to use rating scales, participants judged that it was more likely that the firemen helped Kevin "because he is the kind of person who helps people" than "because Kevin was the kind of person that people help." This presumably reflects the fact that people consider helping behaviour to covary more strongly with the actor when the actor was described as a fireman than simply referred by a male proper name (e.g., Ted).

This finding allowed us to pit the predictions of a simple-minded covariational model of causal explanation directly against those of the conversational model. If participants were just following a simple covariational rule in assigning causality, then spontaneous explanations should refer to something about the fireman. However, an explanation which refers to some quality of the fireman risks being uninformative if it were to refer to culturally presupposed knowledge about what firemen generally do (Grice, 1975). The attribution of a helpful disposition to firemen is just such a culturally shared belief. In line with our prediction, we found that in these cases (e.g., *The firemen helps Kevin*), explanations were significantly more likely to refer to something about the object (Kevin), than when the actor was some unspecified male (as in *Ted helps Paul*). This finding was consistent with our prediction that participants would identify something abnormal about Kevin, that distinguished him, say, from other people that the fireman might have helped. Note that participants follow the abnormality rule even though an unspecified actor is perceived as both covarying less with the target event than the fireman, and as having less of a disposition to help people.

In subsequent experiments, we took the conversational approach further by asking participants to imagine that they had been asked the same questions, but in a "realistic" social context. In line with the conversational model, we reasoned that recipients of causal questions would interpret the intended causal focus of a question differently as a function of their interlocutor's perceived knowledge and interests. Thus, participants were asked to imagine that they were preparing food in the kitchen while their interlocutor was watching television in the next room. If their interlocutor was an adult visitor who had been out of the country for 18 months, and thus could not be expected to be *au fait* about recent developments in television serials, then we reasoned that participants would answer questions of the type *Why did the fireman help Kevin?* as focusing on Kevin, because competent adults would already be assumed to know what firemen do. Our results confirmed this reasoning; participants tended to give explanations that identified characteristics about the individual who might be unfamiliar to the listener (i.e., Kevin).

However, the conversational model will make quite different predictions about perceived question focus if the interlocutor was a four-year-old child or a visitor from outer space. Here, participants cannot presuppose that their interlocutor knows what firemen do. In this case, cooperative participants should focus on aspects of the role-defined figure (i.e., the fireman), whose characteristics would presumably be unknown to this kind of interlocutor. Again in line with the conversational model, our results indicated a very strong tendency for participants to give explanations to children or aliens such as *The firemean helps Kevin because it's his job*.

These examples illustrate the point that although covariation and perceived abnormality often coincide, people seem to follow the abnormality principle where they diverge. This, of course, is not to argue that people attribute causes to factors that do not covary with effects. It is rather to say that where certain covariations are already known about because they are culturally shared, then they are presupposed rather than focused in the communicated explanation (see also McGill, 1989). It is thus the normality principle that determines which covariations get focused on and which are presupposed and hence "back-grounded" in spontaneous explanation. In interpersonal explanation, this normality principle is relativized to what covariations are likely to be already known by the interlocutor, and thus may be treated as mutual knowledge.

Finally, the latter experiment enabled us to assess the attributions made by participants about the speaker posing the question. Recall that the Gricean model presupposes that in normal conversation speakers are fully cooperative and rational, and should have an acceptable reason for posing the question. When the interlocutor was someone who could not be assumed to have relevant world knowledge, such as a four-year-old child or an alien, or an adult who had been out of the country for 18 months, participants could (and did) attribute rationality and cooperativeness to their interlocutors. However, when the questioner was a fellow adult member from the same Western culture who had been following the television serial in previous weeks, questions about normal events (e.g., Why did the con man cheat Bill?) led our respondents to attribute lack of intelligence, irrationality and uncooperativeness to the questioner. This was consistent with our prediction that such questions would be perceived as "unGricean" when posed by a competent adult speaker. Interestingly, these adults were judged to be less cooperative, knowledgeable, reasonable and intelligent than the four-year-old children – a striking finding for any parent!

The Discourse Action Model

Edwards and Potter (1992, 1993) have argued that attribution theory has not paid sufficient attention to the real-life social context in which explanations are furnished. While they see the conversational model outlined above as a step in the right direction, they still consider that it has three major shortcomings: its lack of attention to actual conversation; the lack of recognition of the constructive work of discourse; and the lack of concern with the interestedness of speakers and actors, as displayed in their descriptions and explanations. We will address each of these points in turn, and argue that our approach does allow these issues to be addressed.

Firstly, Edwards and Potter (1993) criticize our approach for its failure to address what they term actual conversation. As an example of the "unreal" conversation, they give Slugoski et al.'s (1993) experiment where participants were required to explain a crime to interlocutors whom they were told had read background case histories on the perpetrator which either emphasized personal or situational factors. Recall that in this experiment participants offered information which complemented their interlocutor's knowledge base, thus verifying the experimental hypothesis that people would follow the given-new contract in causal explanation. We take this as empirical proof that people follow conversational rules in formulating explanations, and would have accepted a null result as disconfirmation of the conversational model, just as we accepted the failure of high self-monitors to be more "Gricean" than low self-monitors to be disconfirmation of the hypothesis that high self-monitors would be more attuned to the given-new contract. We regard it as non-trivial that people follow the same social rules in laboratories as hold in other situations, agreeing with Potter and Wetherell (1987) that the laboratory experiment is just as much a social context as a restaurant or a tutorial.

Secondly, Edwards and Potter criticize our approach for not recognizing the constructive work of discourse "in producing descriptions of the world which are constitutive of an understood reality, rather than reflections of reality as given." As an example, they give a case where the victim of an alleged rape is being cross-examined by defence counsel, who tries to establish that the club in which the incident took place is "where girls and fellas meet, isn't it," in order to invite inferences relevant to establishing the nature of the offence and why it might have happened. This kind of example is in fact quite similar to that given by Turnbull and Slugoski (1988, p. 68) in their discussion of how asking why Mrs Thatcher was "out to smash the miners" constrains the kind of answers that can be given. Indeed, many psychologists would recognize the attempts to influence judgment through choice of leading questions as an instance of priming effects (Loftus & Palmer, 1974). However, it is precisely the pragmatic perspective that helps predict when such description/priming effects are likely to succeed. Thus, Dodd and Bradshaw (1980) found that leading questions did not affect subsequent judgments if the recipient was given a reason to discount them, as when, for example, they were told that the question was posed by a hostile prosecution counsel in a cross-examination (see Hilton, 1995; Schwarz, 1994, for further discussion). Although Edwards and Potter discuss ways in which such contentious descriptions may be challenged, they do not make any predictions about when and why such strategies might be expected to succeed. The kind of pragmatic perspective we advocate clearly does allow such hypotheses to be formulated and tested.

Finally, Edwards and Potter criticize the lack of concern for the interestedness of interactants in the conversational model. While we accept that we have focused on cooperative exchange of information in our model, we would note that Grice's model does allow for other sorts of interest to be at stake. It is precisely because cooperation is such a strong norm in social (including conversational) exchange that Grice (1975) formulated his model of conversation to explain cases where the norms are both respected and flouted. This certainly does not imply that other sorts of interest than efficient exchange of information cannot be at stake in conversation. We would, however, agree with Edwards and Potter that a fuller specification of the kinds of goals that are at stake in conversation and how they influence causal explanation would be useful, and that more could be done here.

JUDGMENTAL BIAS AND THE LOGIC OF CONVERSATION

Bless, Strack and Schwarz (1993) note that in the psychological laboratory setting experimenters and their research participants often enter the interaction with very different communicative goals and assumptions, leading to misinterpretation of the task on the part of participants and the consequent misconstrual of their responses on the part of the experimenter. Although pervasive in psychological research, the potential for such misunderstanding is especially acute in research on social judgment and reasoning because of its reliance on verbally presented stimulus material and response formats. Hilton (1995) has broken down the process of forming judgments from experimenter-provided information into two major stages, both of which require rational choices on the part of respondents. In the first stage, the participant chooses the most *rational interpretation* of the task using the criterion of consistency with higher-order assumptions about conversation and knowledge about the discourse context, and specifically attributions about the speaker. A second stage involves applying a *normative model of reasoning* to the representation thus formed, e.g., by applying Bayes' theorem to a belief-updating problem, Mill's method of difference to a causal attribution problem, *modus tollens* to a conditional reasoning task, etc.

Most research on judgment and reasoning has focused on the second stage of rational inference, wherein anomalous judgments typically have been attributed to inadequate understanding of normative models of inference. This has resulted in a picture of people as cognitively flawed information processors, putatively susceptible to a host of "errors" or "biases" in reasoning (see, for example, Fiske & Taylor, 1991; Kahneman, Slovic & Tversky, 1982; Sherman & Corty, 1984). Such errors and biases are said to be driven by people's reliance on a small number of cognitive "shortcuts," such as the representativeness, availability, and simulation heuristics of Kahneman and Tversky, when faced with a complex decision-making task. However, a large body of research now suggests that many errors and biases are rather due to interpretations formed at the conversational inference stage, and hence that people's judgments may be quite rational given their conversationally licensed representation of the task. Since much of this research has been reviewed elsewhere (see, especially, Bless et al., 1993; Hilton, 1990, 1995; Hilton & Slugoski, 2000; Schwarz, 1994; Strack, 1994; Turnbull & Slugoski, 1988), we shall simply gloss the conversational logic behind four of the most prominent "biases" to illustrate our approach.

There have been a number of errors or biases associated with the *representativeness heuristic* which have been subject to alternative, conversational explanations. Three of these are: *base-rate error*, the tendency to overlook the significance of prior probabilities when making predictions (Kahneman & Tversky, 1973); the *conjunction fallacy*, the tendency to consider the probability of an outcome such as *Linda is a bank teller* to be less probable than the probability of a conjunction which contains the outcome (Tversky & Kahneman, 1983); and the *dilution effect*, the tendency when trying to predict an outcome such a student's exam success to give less weight to a relevant predictor variable when it is embedded in irrelevant information (Zukier, 1982). We will consider each of these in turn.

Kahneman and Tversky (1973) have shown that when participants are given information that is representative of a category (diagnostic or individuating information) they tend to base judgments of category membership on that information to the neglect of accompanying base-rate (prior probability) information, contrary to the dictates of Bayes' theorem. A well-known example is the "lawyers/engineers" problem, wherein participants base decisions about whether a target is likely to be a lawyer/engineer on the basis of the similarity of the target to their stereotype of lawyers/engineers, largely independently of the prior probability of belonging to one of the groups. There is now every reason to believe that pragmatic factors, not faulty reasoning, are in large measure responsible for this "bias." Krosnick, Li and Lehman (1990) demonstrated that presenting base-rate information first increased the likelihood that it would be integrated into judgments, as would be expected if participants believed the experimenter to be cooperatively following Grice's third sub-maxim of manner ("Be orderly"). Ginossar and Trope (1987, Experiment 6) framed the problem as part of a "card game," hence undermining the assumption that the information was produced as part of an intentional communication, and found participants more likely to use base-rate information in this condition. In the most direct test of the conversational account, Schwarz et al. (1991) changed the framing of the problem from that involving psychologists and personality tests, which makes the individuating (personality) information highly relevant, to a *statistics* frame, which would grant relevance to base-rate information. Expectations of cooperative intent were also manipulated by presenting the descriptions to some participants as having been written by a human communicator (who would assumedly strive to be relevant and informative), and informing others that the descriptions were randomly compiled from a pool of data by a computer (to which cooperative intent could not be so unambiguously attributed). They found that the underuse of base-rate information was significantly lessened in the "statistics" condition, as well as in the "computer" condition. Taken together, these studies strongly suggest that participants' pragmatic assumptions play an important role in the interpretation of "relevance" in the experimental setting and hence their likelihood of producing the so-called "base-rate error."

The conjunction "error" (Tversky & Kahneman, 1983) – the tendency to treat the likelihood of a conjunction, P(A&B), as more probable than its least typical constituent – has likewise attracted a range of conversational interpretations, especially as it has been elicited by the famous Bill and Linda problems. In one investigation, Dulany and Hilton (1991) suggested that by virtue of being given both the components *and* the conjunction to rate, it is implicated that, for example, "Bill plays jazz for a hobby and is *not* an accountant." If participants did indeed draw this implicature, their elevated conjunction ratings would not actually be fallacious. Dulany and Hilton (1991) manipulated the possible implicatures by presenting the alternatives in various ways (e.g., "Bill is an accountant *whether or not* he plays jazz for a hobby"), and estimated the occurrence of genuine conjunction error from between 0% and 38%, as opposed to Tversky and Kahneman's claim of 85% to 90%. More recently, Mosconi and Macchi (1996) showed that in a realistic pragmatic context such as the courtroom a person who provides the more inclusive class in response to a question (e.g., "the accused is blond") may be perceived as being evasive or "reticent" relative to the one that provides the included class (e.g., "the accused is blond and has a moustache"), and indeed the latter response was judged to be "more probable" than the former. This undoubtedly reflects the expectation for felicitous responses to be both true *and* informative (see also Fiedler, 1988; Hertwig & Gigerenzer, 1999; Politzer & Noveck, 1991; Wolford, Taylor & Beck, 1991, for related pragmatic interpretations of the conjunction task).

Nisbett et al. (1981) showed that inferences about a person or event become less extreme when diagnostic information is *diluted* with non-diagnostic information. For example, a student's GPA tends to be judged as higher when told *only* that "Michael studies 31 hours/week" (diagnostic of good grades), than if told that "Michael studies 31 hours/week, has two brothers, and went on a blind date once . . ." (irrelevant or non-diagnostic material added). These results make sense if the participant is attempting to incorporate all given material as informative and relevant, as would be expected from a cooperative experimenter. Indeed, Tetlock, Lerner and Boettger (1996) were able significantly to weaken the effect when the conversational norm for relevance was "deactivated" in a manner similar to the Schwarz et al. (1991) manipulation of base-rate information. Again, the conversational explanation calls into question the assumption that a cognitive "bias" is driving the effect.

Of all the means yet devised for demonstrating human irrationality, none has been quite so successful as the Selection Task introduced by Wason in 1966. This task presents subjects with four cards (e.g., "A", "D", "4", "7") together with a rule to be tested ("If there is a vowel on one side, then there is an even number on the other side"). It has consistently been found that participants tend to choose the rule-confirming card ("4") over one of the two potentially rule-falsifying cards ("7") (see Evans, 1989, for a review). Following the earliest accounts of this phenomenon (Wason, 1968; Wason & Johnson-Laird, 1970), social psychologists have typically interpreted participants' performance as evidence for a pervasive "confirmation bias" operative in human inference (see, for example, Higgins & Bargh, 1987; Klayman & Ha, 1987). According to Sperber, Cara and Girotto (1995), participants' typical performance on the Selection Task reflects no more than the standard processes of verbal comprehension. Drawing on Sperber and Wilson's (1986) *Relevance Theory*, they note that it is quite rational for people to attempt to take into account all of the information given by the experimenter on the presumption of its relevance to the performance of the task. Since both "vowel" and "even number" are stated in the rule, the speaker (experimenter) may be assumed by the recipient (participant) to have done so in the expectation that their joint occurrence is relevant to the solution of the task. Otherwise, why would the speaker have made this information salient and hence easily accessed at the time of judgment? In short, participants are rationally justified in choosing the "A" and "4" cards because they are generally correct in using the most easily accessed information from a speaker's utterance as a cue to its relevance for *any* act of utterance interpretation. Sperber et al. (1995) supported their analysis with four experiments showing, across a variety of content domains, that manipulations of accessibility and information yield can result in normatively correct as well as incorrect response patterns.

Conversational Skill and Judgmental Bias

We have argued that human beings can easily be led "up the garden path" into error when socially shared rules of conversation about how information should be communicated are violated. Consistent with this position, we have shown that attention to and respect for socially shared rules of conversation can lead to impressive facilitation of human reasoning performance. This position would seem to imply that people who are skilled at conversational inference should be more susceptible to being "misled" in experiments on judgment and reasoning where the normal rules are exploited by "uncooperative" experimenters.

Consistent with this prediction, Levinson (1995) has argued that Tversky and Kahneman (1974) have identified heuristics such as representativeness which are very adaptive in conversation because they allow inferences to be made about what is presupposed or probably true, and which can easily be corrected if they are mistaken. This is because normal conversation takes place interactively, and we quickly notice and correct a mistaken interpretation by our conversational partner. But in the modern world we often have to deal with decontextualized information where such opportunities for quick repair of misunderstandings do not exist, leading to persistent, and often tragic, errors in the management of complex systems such as nuclear power stations or national economies where there are often long time-lags between an operator's action and the system's response.

If thinking is indeed constrained by processes of conversational inference, then variations in skill at conversational inference should predict propensity to produce biases in reasoning and decision making. Slugoski and Wilson (1998) examined this proposition by constructing measures of conversational skill, and attempting to relate this to the propensity to produce bias on some well-known decision tasks. Their measure of conversational skill was derived using an adaptation of Clarke's (1975) method of reconstruction of conversations described earlier. They had 32 university students divide into pairs and to converse for approximately 10 minutes in a "getting to know you" session. These conversations were tape recorded and each conversational turn was typed on to a file card. Each participant then had to return to the laboratory and try to sort the file cards, which had been randomized, into their original order. This was done for all 15 conversation not involving themselves, and enabled each participant to be scored on (a) how easily her conversation could be reconstructed by others, and (b) how well she could reconstruct others' conversations. These two scores were non-significantly correlated in a negative direction (–0.23), suggesting that the tendency to pursue one's own theme in a conversation differs markedly from the ability to discern patterns in the conversations of others. These scores were combined into an overall measure of conversational skill, termed "pragmatic competence".

The results indicated that pragmatic competence predicted a greater tendency to produce some biases, but also a lesser tendency to produce others. Thus pragmatic competence predicted greater confirmation bias on the Wason selection task (Wason & Johnson-Laird, 1970), greater underuse of consensus information when making attributions about the person (McArthur, 1972) and greater underuse of base-rate information in the engineers-and-lawyers task (Kahneman & Tversky, 1973). However, pragmatically competent individuals exhibited less likelihood of a primacy effect when forming an impression of another person described by a series of traits (Asch, 1946), less likelihood of producing the conjunction effect (Tversky & Kahneman, 1983), and less likelihood of producing the dilution effect (Nisbett et al, 1981). The finding that conversationally adept participants are more prone to certain "biases" and less prone to others has since been broadly replicated and extended on larger samples (McKay & Slugoski, 1997).

Controlling for Conversational Inference: Methodological Implications

The present framework suggests that the interpretation of experimenter-given information should be systematically investigated and controlled for in experimental research. Below are suggested some general methodological procedures that can aid in this task.

First, assumptions about the source of a message can be manipulated or otherwise controlled for. For example, the basic assumption of conversational inference that the source is intentional can be undermined by persuading the participant that the information provided has been randomly generated (e.g., by computer) or has been generated by the participant him or herself (e.g., through their own search efforts).

Second, even where the source is intentional, the participant's perception of the reliability of the source's information may be affected by the perceived cooperativeness or knowledgeability of the source. As argued above (e.g., Dulany & Hilton, 1991), the inference that what is left unsaid did not in fact happen because it would otherwise have been mentioned by a cooperative and knowledgeable speaker rests on attributions about the speaker. These attributions can be measured and manipulated.

Third, key words should be checked for conventional implicatures. Words such as *but* and *although* suggest an adversative relation between items of information and signal the experimenter's expectancies. Likewise quantifiers such as *a few* and *few* and adverbs such as *occasionally* and *seldom* signal the speaker's focus of interest (e.g., on reasons for doing or not doing, respectively). Although different words signalling conventional implicatures are few (Grice, 1968), they are used frequently. Consequently, where their use may signal the experimenter's hypothesis, they should be suppressed, or alternatively, dual versions of the task should be created which signal both the hypothesis and its contrary. For example, Krosnick et al. (1990) made use of this technique in comparing the effects of "but" and "although" on the integration of base-rate and diagnostic information.

Fourth, experimenters need to be fully sensitive to conversational implicatures potentially conveyed in both stimulus and response language. Participants' interpretations of experimenter-given information can be checked by either multiple-choice check methods or analysis of open-ended protocols (e.g., Dulany & Hilton, 1991; Macchi, 1995). Of course, to be effective, the coding of such data needs to be done in terms of categories that can be justified on theoretical grounds. The production of open-ended responses may be controlled by explicitly instructing participants to either maximize the maxim of quality or the maxim of quantity. Such variation in instructions has been shown to affect participants' verbal protocols (Fiedler, Semin & Bolten, 1989), and may be a useful technique in exploring participants' representations of their task.

Fifth, researchers need to test for evidence supporting the implication of any "non-conversational" factors they hypothesize as causing a pattern of judgment. For example, theorists have sometimes made claims about the role of cognitive factors in judgment such as salience (Trope & Ginossar, 1988) or causal relevance (Tversky & Kahneman, 1980) without collecting relevant recall, recognition and belief measures. In future, more studies should include measures that test for the operation of *both* cognitive biases and conversational inference processes.

More generally, data should be sought that distinguishes conversational and cognitive bias explanations. For example, Bar-Hillel and Neter (1993) report an experiment in which monetary incentives failed to remove a "misinterpretation" of a reasoning task (cf. Wolford, Taylor & Beck, 1991). However, it is not clear why increasing the financial stakes in an experiment should cause participants to abandon an interpretation that is pragmatically correct and rational. Recall that Tetlock et al. (1996) manipulated their participants' "conversational" interpretations of the judgment task by undermining the respondents' assumption of intentionality. Participants then rejected or utilized non-diagnostic information on the basis of its perceived conversational relevance. They then found that accountability manipulations, which, like monetary incentives, should accentuate the value of getting a "right" answer, simply amplified the effect of conversational relevance, suggesting that incentives simply made participants adhere more strongly to that answer which seemed conversationally rational. Incentives are *not* going to make participants drop a conversationally rational interpretation in favour of one which is less plausible in the context.

In some cases, investigators have used multiple methods to evaluate claims about biases. For example, in a variant of the "engineer and lawyer" study, Kahneman and Tversky (1973) gave participants personality descriptions and then asked them to estimate the probability that the person described would major in a number of subjects, but also the base-rate of people majoring in that subject. They found that participants underused their own base-rate information, an error that cannot be attributed to conversational inference processes as defined in this chapter. While underuse of base-rate information may well occur in certain conditions, this should not be taken as invalidating the current perspective. Understanding of how the conversational factors reviewed above such as source characteristics, information order and question phrasing influence use of base-rate information will help us better understand when its underuse is truly due to cognitive shortcomings rather than to communicational factors.

CONCLUSION

It is over 15 years since Markus and Zajonc concluded their seminal *Handbook of Social Psychology* chapter on the cognitive perspective in social psychology by portending that "it is likely that in the near future the major new method of studying social cognition and of cognition in general will be the dialogue . . ." (1985, p. 213). While it is difficult to say that this prediction ever came to pass, our chapter has reviewed theory and research that should provide optimism that an understanding of how interactants co-construct a shared social reality through their conversations with others has made significant progress since then. Of course, placing putative cognitive variables and processes within the context of the communicative goals and strategies that people habitually rely on to make "sense" in conversations depends on first having a good understanding of how conversations "work." We began our chapter by reviewing current developments and issues in sequential/structural models of conversation, and concluded, in line with Levinson (1981), that any model that lacks a significant role for interactants' pragmatic presuppositions is likely to be deficient in its predictions. We then presented an attributional interpretation of Grice's logic of conversation, which takes into account the speaker/hearer's social-contextual assumptions when designing and interpreting utterances. Aside from its application to the analysis of everyday conversations, we considered that Grice's model has profound implications for research and theorizing about how people make causal attributions, and how they respond to judgment and decision-making tasks posed in the psychologist's laboratory.

Finally, our approach presents a more optimistic outlook on human rationality than other approaches considered: first, in contrast to mainstream social cognition research, the conversational model allows that many of the so-called "errors" and "biases" previously identified in human inference are the products, not of faulty reasoning processes, but rather of pragmatically skilled behaviour; and second, the approach vindicates the use by researchers of the logic of controlled observation and statistical inference typical of empirically driven science to reveal the inherently social nature of cognitive processes and products (*pace* Edwards & Potter, 1992, 1993).

REFERENCES

Asch, S. (1946). Forming impressions of personality. *Journal of Abnormal and Social Psychology*, **66**, 258–290.

Austin, J.L. (1962). *How to do things with words.* Oxford, UK: Clarendon Press.

Bales, R.F. (1950). *Interaction process analysis: A method for the study of small groups.* Cambridge, MA: Addison-Wesley.

Bar-Hillel, M. & Neter, E. (1993). How alike is it versus how likely is it: A disjunction fallacy in probability judgments. *Journal of Personality and Social Psychology*, **65**, 1119–1131.

Bassili, J.N. (1989). Trait encoding in behavior identification and dispositional inference. *Personality and Social Psychology Bulletin*, **15**, 285–296.

Bless, H., Strack, F. & Schwarz, N. (1993). The informative functions of research procedures: Bias and the logic of conversation. *European Journal of Social Psychology*, **23**, 149–165.

Brown, P. & Levinson, S.C. (1987). *Politeness: Some universals in language usage.* Cambridge, UK: Cambridge University Press.

Brown, R. & Fish, D. (1983). The psychological causality implicit in language. *Cognition*, **14**, 237–273.

Cappella, J.N. (1987). Interpersonal communication: Definitions and fundamental questions. In C.R. Berger & S.H. Chaffee (Eds), *Handbook of communication science* (pp. 148–238). London: Sage.

Cheng, P.W. & Novick, L.R. (1990). A probabilistic contrast model of causal induction. *Journal of Personality and Social Psychology*, **58**, 545–567.

Chomsky, N. (1963). Formal properties of grammars 1. In R. Luce, R. Bush & E. Galanter (Eds), *Handbook of Mathematical Psychology* (Vol. 2, pp. 323–418). Wiley: New York.

Clark, H.H. & Haviland, S.E. (1977). Comprehension and the given-new contract. In R.O. Freedle (Ed.), *Discourse production and comprehension* (pp. 1–40). Norwood, NJ: Ablex.

Clarke, D.D. (1975). The use and recognition of sequential structure in dialogue. *British Journal of Social and Clinical Psychology*, **14**, 333–339.

Clarke, D.D. (1983). *Language and action: A structural model for behaviour.* London: Butterworth-Heinemann.

de Beaugrande, R. (1980). Text and discourse in European research. *Discourse*, **3**, 297–300.

Dodd, D.H. & Bradshaw, J.M. (1980). Leading questions and memory: Pragmatic constraints. *Journal of Verbal Learning and Memory*, **19**, 695–704.

Dulany, D.E. & Hilton, D.J. (1991). Conversational implicature, conscious representation, and the conjunction fallacy. *Social Cognition*, **9**, 67–84.

Edwards, D. & Potter, J. (1992). *Discursive psychology.* London: Sage.

Edwards, D. & Potter, J. (1993). Language and causation: A discursive action model of description and attribution. *Psychological Review*, **100**, 23–41.

Einhorn, H. & Hogarth, R.M. (1986). Judging probable cause. *Psychological Bulletin*, **99**, 1–19.

Ellis, D.G., Hamilton, E.M. & Aho, L. (1983). Some issues in conversational coherence. *Human Communication Research*, **9**, 267–282.

Evans, J. St.B.T. (1989). *Bias in human reasoning: Causes and consequences.* Hillsdale, NJ: Lawrence Erlbaum.

Fiedler, K. (1988). The dependence of the conjunction fallacy on subtle linguistic cues. *Psychological Research*, **5**, 123–125.

Fiedler, K, Semin, G.K., & Bolten, S. (1989). Language use and reification of social information: Top-down and bottom-up processing in person cognition. *European Journal of Social Psychology*, **19**, 271–295.

Fiske, S. & Taylor, S. (1991). *Social cognition* (2nd edn). New York: McGraw-Hill.

Försterling, F. (1989). Models of covariation and attribution: How do they relate to the analysis of variance? *Journal of Personality and Social Psychology*, **57**, 615–625.

Gamst, G. (1982). Memory for conversation: Toward a grammar of dyadic conversation. *Discourse Processes*, **5**, 33–51.

Ginossar, Z. & Trope, Y. (1987). Problem solving in judgment under uncertainty. *Journal of Personality and Social Psychology*, **52**, 464–474.

Goffman, E. (1976). Replies and responses. *Language in Society*, **5**, 257–313.

Goldwaithe, D. (1997). Knowledge of pragmatic conversational structure. *Journal of Psycholinguistic Research*, **26**, 497–508.

Gordon, D. & Lakoff, G. (1971). Conversational postulates. *Papers from the Seventh Regional Meeting of the Chicago Linguistics Society*, **7**, 63–84.

Grice, H.P. (1968). Utterer's meaning, sentence meaning and word meaning. *Foundations of Language*, **4**, 225–242.

Grice, H.P. (1975). Logic and conversation. In P. Cole & J.L. Morgan (Eds), *Syntax and semantics, Vol 3: Speech acts* (pp. 41–58). New York: Academic Press.

Halliday, M.A.K. & Hasan, R. (1976). *Cohesion in English*. London: Longman.

Hamilton, D.L. (1988). Causal attribution viewed from an information-processing perspective. In D. Bar-Tal and A.W. Kruglanski (Eds), *The social psychology of knowledge* (pp. 359–385). Cambridge, UK: Cambridge University Press.

Hart, H.L.A. & Honoré, A.M. (1959). *Causation in the law*. Oxford: Clarendon Press.

Hertwig, R., & Gigerenzer, G. (1999). The conjunction fallacy revisited: How intelligent inferences look like reasoning errors. *Journal of Behavioral Decision Making*, **12**, 275–305.

Hewes, D.E. & Planalp, S. (1987). The individual's place in communication science. In C.R. Berger & S.H. Chaffee (Eds), *Handbook of communication science* (pp. 146–183). London: Sage.

Higgins, E.T. & Bargh, J.A. (1987). Social cognition and social perception. In M.R. Rosenzweig & L.W. Porter (Eds), *Annual Review of Psychology* (Vol. 38, pp. 369–425). Palo Alto, CA: Annual Reviews Inc.

Hilton, D.J. (1990). Conversational processes and causal explanation. *Psychological Bulletin*, **107**, 65–81.

Hilton, D.J. (1991). A conversational model of causal explanation. In W. Stroebe & M. Hewstone (Eds), *European Review of Social Psychology* (Vol. 2, pp. 51–81). Chichester: Wiley.

Hilton, D.J. (1995). The social context of reasoning: Conversationl inference and rational judgment. *Psychological Bulletin*, **118**, 248–271.

Hilton, D.J. & Erb, H.-P. (1996). Mental models and causal explanation: Judgments of probable cause and explanatory relevance. *Thinking and Reasoning*, **2**, 273–308.

Hilton, D.J. & Slugoski, B.R. (1986). Knowledge-based causal attribution: The abnormal conditions focus model. *Psychological Review*, **93**, 75–88.

Hilton, D.J. & Slugoski, B.R. (2000). Judgment and decision-making in social context: Discourse processes and rational inference. In T. Connolly, H.R. Arkes & K. Hammond (Eds), *Judgment and decision-making: An interdisciplinary reader* (2nd edn, pp. 651–676). Cambridge, UK: Cambridge University Press.

Hilton, D.J., Smith, R.H. & Kim, S.-H. (1995). The processes of causal explanation and dispositional attribution. *Journal of Personality and Social Psychology*, **68**, 377–387.

Hurtig, R. (1977). Toward a functional theory of discourse. In R.O. Freedle (Ed.), *Discourse production and comprehension* (pp. 89–106). Norwood, NJ: Ablex.

Kahneman, D. & Tversky, A. (1973). On the psychology of prediction. *Psychological Review*, **80**, 237–251.

Kahneman, D., Slovic, P. & Tversky, A. (Eds) (1982). *Judgment under uncertainty: Heuristics and biases*. Cambridge, UK: Cambridge University Press.

Kelley, H.H. (1967). Attribution in social psychology. *Nebraska Symposium on Motivation*, **5**, 192–238.

Kelley, H.H. (1973). The process of causal attribution. *American Psychologist*, **28**, 103–128.

Kent, G.G., Davis, J.D. & Shapiro, D.A. (1978). Resources required in the construction and reconstruction of conversation. *Journal of Personality and Social Psychology*, **36**, 13–22.

Kent, G.G., Davis, J.D. & Shapiro, D.A. (1981). Effect of mutual acquaintance on the construction of conversation. *Journal of Experimental Social Psychology*, **17**, 197–209.

Klayman, J. & Ha, Y.-W. (1987). Confirmation, disconfirmation, and information in hypothesis-testing. *Psychological Review*, **94**, 211–22.

Krosnick, J.A., Li, F. & Lehman, D.R. (1990). Conversational conventions, order of information acquisition, and the effect of base rates and individuating information on social judgements. *Journal of Personality and Social Psychology*, **59**, 1140–1152.

Labov, W. & Fanshel, D. (1977). *Therapeutic discourse.* New York: Academic Press.

Leddo, J., Abelson, R.P. & Gross, P.H. (1984). Conjunctive explanation: When two explanations are better than one. *Journal of Personality and Social Psychology*, **47**, 933–944.

Levinson, S.C. (1981). Some pre-observations on the modelling of dialogue. *Discourse Processes*, **4**, 93–116.

Levinson, S.C. (1983). *Pragmatics.* Cambridge, UK: Cambridge University Press.

Levinson, S.C. (1995). Interactional biases in human thinking. In E. Goody (Ed.), *Social intelligence and interaction* (pp. 221–246). Cambridge, UK: Cambridge University Press.

Loftus, E.F. & Palmer, J.C. (1974). Reconstruction of automobile destruction. *Journal of Verbal Learning and Verbal Behavior*, **13**, 585–589.

Macchi, L. (1995). Pragmatic aspects of the base-rate fallacy. *Quarterly Journal of Experimental Psychology*, **48**, 188–206.

Mackie, J.L. (1980). *The cement of the universe* (2nd edn). Oxford: Oxford University Press.

Markus, H. & Zajonc, R.B. (1985). The cognitive perspective in social psychology. In G. Lindzey & E.Aronson (Eds), *Handbook of social psychology, Vol. 1: Theory and method* (3rd edn, pp. 137–230). New York: Random House.

McArthur, L.A. (1972). The how and the what of why: Some determinants and consequences of causal attribution. *Journal of Personality and Social Psychology*, **22**, 171–193.

McClure, J.L. (1998). Discounting causes of behavior: Are two reasons better than one? *Journal of Personality and Social Psychology*, **74**, 7–20.

McClure, J.L. & Hilton, D.J. (1998). Are goals or preconditions better explanations? It depends on the question. *European Journal of Social Psychology*, **28**, 897–911.

McGill, A.L. (1989). Context effects in causal judgment. *Journal of Personality and Social Psychology*, **57**, 189–200.

McKay, K. & Slugoski, B.R. (1997). *Pragmatic competence, perspective-taking, and susceptibility to judgmental biases.* Presented at the Sixth International Conference on Language and Social Psychology, Ottawa.

Morris, M.W. & Larrick, R.P. (1995). When one cause casts doubt on another: A normative analysis of discounting in causal attribution. *Psychological Review*, **102**, 331–365.

Mosconi, G. & Macchi, L. (1996). *Pragmatic factors in the conjunction fallacy.* Presented at the Third International Conference on Thinking, London.

Nisbett, R.E., Zukier, H. & Lemley, R.E. (1981). The dilution effect: Non-diagnostic information weakens the implications of diagnostic information. *Cognitive Psychology*, **13**, 248–277.

Pease, K. (1972). Contextual constraints in conversation. *Behavioral Science*, **4**, 217–225.

Politzer, G. & Noveck, I.A. (1991). Are conjunction rule violations the result of conversational rule violations? *Journal of Psycholinguistic Research*, **20**, 83–103.

Potter, J. & Wetherell, M. (1987). *Discourse and social psychology.* London: Sage.

Rochester, S.J., Martin, J.R. & Thurstone, S. (1977). Thought-process disorder in schizophrenia: The listener's task. *Brain and Language*, **4**, 95–113.

Rosch, E., Mervis, C.B., Gray, W.D., Johnson, D.M & Boyes-Braern, P. (1976). Basic objects in natural categories. *Cognitive Psychology*, **8**, 382–439.

Rudolph, U. & Försterling, F. (1997). The psychological causality implicit in verbs: A review. *Psychological Bulletin*, **121**, 192–212.

Russell, R.L. & Czogalik, D. (1989). Strategies for analysing conversations: Frequencies, sequences or rules. *Journal of Social Behavior and Personality*, **4**, 221–236.

Rutter, D.R. (1979). The reconstruction of schizophrenic speech. *British Journal of Psychiatry*, **134**, 356–359.

Schank, R.C. & Abelson, R.P. (1977). *Scripts, plans, goals and understanding: An enquiry into human knowledge structures*. Hillsdale, NJ: Erlbaum.

Schegloff, E. (1968). Sequencing in conversational openings. *American Anthropologist*, **70**, 1075–1095.

Schwarz, N. (1994). Judgment in a social context: Biases, shortcomings, and the logic of conversation. *Advances in Experimental Social Psychology*, **26**, 123–162.

Schwarz, N., Strack, F., Hilton, D.J. & Naderer, G. (1991). Base rates, representativeness, and the logic of conversation: The contextual relevance of "irrelevant" information. *Social Cognition*, **9**, 67–84.

Searle, J.R. (1969). *Speech acts: An essay in the philosophy of language*. Cambridge, UK: Cambridge University Press.

Semin, G.R. & Fiedler, K. (1988). The cognitive functions of linguistic categories in describing persons: Social cognition and language. *Journal of Personality and Social Psychology*, **54**, 558–568.

Semin, G.R. & Fiedler, K. (1991). The Linguistic Category Model: Its bases, applications and range. In W. Stroebe & M. Hewstone (Eds), *European Review of Social Psychology* (Vol. 2, pp. 1–30). Chichester: Wiley.

Sherman, S.J. & Corty, E. (1984). Cognitive heuristics. In R.S. Wyer & T.K. Srull (Eds), *Handbook of social cognition* (Vol. 1, pp. 189–286). Hillsdale, NJ: Erlbaum.

Sinclair, J.M. & Coulthard, R.M. (1975). *Towards an analysis of discourse: The English used by teachers and pupils*. London: Oxford University Press.

Slugoski, B.R. (1995). Mindless processing of requests? Don't ask twice. *British Journal of Social Psychology*, **34**, 335–350.

Slugoski, B.R. & Turnbull, W.M. (1987). *On the psychological status of the Cooperative Principle*. Paper presented at the Second International Pragmatics Conference, Antwerp.

Slugoski, B.R. & Turnbull, W.M. (1988). Cruel to be kind and kind to be cruel: Sarcasm, banter and social relations. *Journal of Language and Social Psychology*, **7**, 101–121.

Slugoski, B.R. & Wilson, A. (1998). Contribution of conversation skills to the production of judgmental errors. *European Journal of Social Psychology*, **28**, 575–601.

Slugoski, B.R., Lalljee, M.G., Lamb, R. & Ginsburg, G.P. (1993). Attribution in conversational context: Effect of mutual knowledge on explanation-giving. *European Journal of Social Psychology*, **23**, 219–238.

Slugoski, B.R., Hilton, D.J. & Turnbull, W.M. (1997). Implicit verb causality: Pragmatic versus semantic contributions. Unpublished manuscript.

Sperber, D. & Wilson, D. (1986). *Relevance: Communication and cognition*. Oxford: Basil Blackwell.

Sperber, D., Cara, F. & Girotto, V. (1995). Relevance theory explains the selection task. *Cognition*, **57**, 31–95.

Strack, F. (1994). Response processes in social judgment. In R.S. Wyer & T. Srull (Eds), *Handbook of social cognition, Vol. 1: Basic Processes* (pp. 287–322). Hillsdale, NJ: Erlbaum.

Tetlock, P.E., Lerner, J. & Boettger, R. (1996). The dilution effect: Judgmental bias or conversational convention or a bit of both? *European Journal of Social Psychology*, **26**, 914–934.

Thorndyke, P.W. (1977). Cognitive structures in comprehension and memory of narrative discourse. *Cognitive Psychology*, **9**, 77–110.

Trope, Y. & Ginossar, Z. (1988). On the use of statistical and non-statistical knowledge: A problem-solving approach. In D. Bar-Tal & A. Kruglanski (Eds), *The social psychology of knowledge* (pp. 143–162). Cambridge, UK: Cambridge University Press.

Turnbull, W. (1986). Everyday explanation: The pragmatics of puzzle resolution. *Journal for the Theory of Social Behaviour*, **16**, 141–160.

Turnbull, W. & Slugoski, B.R. (1988). Conversational and linguistic processes in causal attribution. In D.J. Hilton (Ed.), *Contemporary science and natural explanation: Commonsense conceptions of causality* (pp. 66–93). Brighton: Harvester Press/New York: New York University Press.

Tversky, A. & Kahneman, D.E. (1974). Judgment under uncertainty: Heuristics and biases. *Science*, **185**, 124–1131.

Tversky, A. & Kahneman, D. (1980). Causal schemata in judgments under uncertainty. In M. Fishbein (Ed.), *Progress in social psychology* (pp. 49–72). Hillsdale, NJ: Erlbaum.

Tversky, A. & Kahneman, D. (1983). Extensional versus intuitive reasoning: The conjunction fallacy in probability judgement. *Psychological Review*, **90**, 293–315.

Wason, P.C. (1966). Reasoning. In B. Foss (Ed.), *New horizons in psychology* (pp. 135–151). Harmondsworth, UK: Penuin.

Wason, P.C. (1968). Reasoning about a rule. *Quarterly Journal of Experimental Psychology* **20**, 273–281.

Wason, P.C. & Johnson-Laird, P.N. (1970). A conflict between selecting and evaluation of information in an inferential task. *British Journal of Psychology*, **61**, 509–515.

Weizenbaum, J. (1976). *Computer power and human reason*. San Francisco: Freeman.

Winograd, T. (1977). A framework for understanding discourse. In M. Just & P. Carpenter (Eds), *Cognitive processes in comprehension* (pp. 63–68). Hillsdale, NJ: Erlbaum.

Wolford, G., Taylor, H.A. & Beck, J.R. (1991). The conjunction fallacy? *Memory and Cognition*, **18**, 47–53.

Zukier, H. (1982). The role of the correlation and the dispersion of predictor variables in the use of nondiagnostic information. *Journal of Personality and Social Psychology*, **47**, 1163–1175.

2.11

Facework

Clare MacMartin and Linda A. Wood
University of Guelph, Canada
Rolf O. Kroger
University of Toronto, Canada

. . . that sandy, bandy, polite, lockjawed, French-lettered, i-dotted, Russian t'd, non-committal, B.A.'d, V.D.'d, mock-barmy, smarmy, chance-his-army tick of a piddling crook who lives in his own armpit. (Dylan Thomas, Welsh poet, about a critic and long-time acquaintance)[1]

It is our contention that face and facework are concepts more problematic than has hitherto been acknowledged systematically in the literature. By way of illustration, we begin with the quotation from Dylan Thomas. In the quotation, Thomas is doing aggravation, the opposite and somewhat neglected flip side of the work of politeness. Helped by his poetic gifts, he delivers what appears to be

---

[1] Cited in Tremlett (1991, p. 76). Some of the terms are relatively straightforward: lock-jawed (a symptom of tetanus contracted through association with dirt; mock-barmy (one who feigns eccentricity and is therefore affected); smarmy (one who is oily, sycophantic). We offer our interpretations of the more opaque terms as follows. Sandy = hair colour, neither beautifully blond nor handsomely dark; wishy-washy. Or was it employed by DT as a good rhyme to locate bow-leggedness ("bandy.")? French-lettered = one who would use a condom; not a "real" man, in those by-gone days. B.A.'d = one contaminated with a university degree; foppish. Note that DT regretted that he had not gone to university and felt uncomfortable around academics. V.D.'d = one afflicted with venereal disease, presumably acquired through promiscuous conduct. I-dotted = dots his i's and t's? Compulsively meticulous? Fuss-pot? Russian t'd = touched by Russia? A commie? Allusion to Cambridge defectors? Or the phonetics may provide a clue. The sound "teed" might refer to tea drinking, as an affectation, as opposed to drinking beer. On this one, we throw in the towel. All the adjectives are pejorative to accomplish the aggravation, but "polite"? Used ironically or to mean hoity-toity? Chance-his-army tick = to do with avoiding military service, then compulsory in UK which DT managed to avoid? Chancing your arm is taking a chance, especially if a tick or louse is living in your armpit. (We are indebted to Justine and Nik Coupland, University of Cardiff, for their generous help in interpreting the obscure references in DT's comment. Any mistakes remain our responsibility.)

The New Handbook of Language and Social Psychology.
Edited by W. Peter Robinson and Howard Giles.
© 2001 John Wiley & Sons Ltd.

a face threat of truly epic proportions. His aim is not only to damage the critic's face, it is to bring about its devastation. The critic is said to be a crook, possessed of a string of truly despicable attributes who, in addition, resides in a truly despicable place, ". . . his own armpit". It is a piece of aggravation that in its richness, its density, is rarely equalled and is therefore atypical. Its atypicality, and its illocutionary force, reside in part in the long string of adjectives which upgrade the impact of the central noun, "crook", and in the unexpected coda that follows the central noun. The coda raises the power of the insult by a factor or two. It is the critic's positive face, his self-regard, that suffers the loss. And, somewhat ironically, it is Thomas's own positive face that is enhanced by the same piece of aggravation, at least in the eyes of his friends, one may assume. It shows Thomas in the light in which he wishes to be seen, the poetic genius, the conversationalist who is capable of crafting extemporaneously a memorable putdown.

We ask, does the concept of face add anything to the analysis of the Dylan Thomas quotation or to the analysis of discourse more generally? May its deployment even mislead analysts by precluding disinterested scrutiny of talk as given? It is these and more detailed questions that we take up below.

In everyday parlance, people talk about losing and saving face, about being in someone's face and the like. But such specific usage is not very common. The Oxford Dictionary defines the metaphorical meaning of face as "composure, coolness, effrontery (save one's face, forbear from or evade shaming him or oneself openly)". Face and facework, it appears, are largely social-scientific terms that owe their present currency to the pioneering work of Goffman (1955, 1967), who defined face as "the positive social value a person effectively claims for himself by the line others assume he has taken during a particular contact" (1967, p. 5). Goffman borrowed face terms from the Chinese. Chinese speakers have long been said to be more concerned with matters of face than Western speakers. This may be a matter of nuance rather than of fundamentals. Some time before Goffman, Durkheim (1915) documented the prevalence of face concerns among the pre-industrial Australian aborigines, without using the present terminology. But he did talk about matters of reputation, honour and social relations, not just about matters of survival. Durkheim's work forms the deep background to all the contemporary work on face and politeness, even though this background is rarely acknowledged directly.

There can be little doubt that Brown and Levinson (1978, 1987), whose work the late Roger Brown dubbed "some kind of a masterpiece" (1987, p. 1), occupy the centre of contemporary writing on face. Building on Goffman's earlier writings, Brown and Levinson suggest that face concerns account for the ordinary speaker's deviations from the classical Gricean (1975) maxims of efficient speech, that is, for politeness. "Politeness takes more time and effort but . . . for most of us on most days the work of politeness constitutes a substantial part of the total talking we do" (Brown, 1987, p. 2). Face concerns are of two kinds: positive face (the "want" to be desirable to or solidary with significant others); and negative face (the want that actions be unimpeded by others). Politeness strategies are designed to minimize face-threatening acts (FTAs), moves like requests or complaints that can threaten the face of either the speaker, the hearer, or both. The theory includes a formula whereby the selection of politeness strategies is a function of the degree of imposition of the speech act in the culture, the power of the speaker relative to the hearer, and the degree of social distance between speaker and hearer.

Given the fundamental nature of the questions addressed by Brown and Levinson, it is not surprising that their theory spawned empirical studies in not just one but several disciplines that span a range of epistemological commitments. Nor is it surprising that trenchant conceptual critiques were not long in coming. Criticisms common to a number of traditions include the inadequate specification of positive face; the neglect of speaker-oriented strategies, third parties, and strategies of face aggravation; and the problematic hierarchical relationship between positive and negative face strategies (see, for example, Holtgraves, this volume, Chapter 4.18; Penman, 1990; Ting-Toomey, 1994; Tracy, 1990; Tracy & Baratz, 1994; Wood & Kroger, 1994). In some instances, critiques have been accompanied by the offering of alternative formulations of politeness and facework (e.g., Tracy, 1990).

THE CONTEMPORARY LANDSCAPE

We do not pretend to furnish a complete catalogue, a blow-by-blow inventory of every study ever published on facework. That is neither possible nor desirable. Instead, we attempt to highlight features of the landscape that we hope will advance our understanding. The relevant approaches to facework that we discern can be grouped broadly into two sorts: (1) those in which the emphasis is on the relationship between variables, particularly those between the social-situational factors in the Brown–Levinson formula and particular linguistic features. They involve quantification and prediction and focus upon isolated and decontextualized samples of language use. The interpretation of utterances in terms of specific speech acts or facework is treated as unproblematic; (2) those in which utterances are taken in context, do not involve premature quantification and shun the prediction of language use on the basis of social-situational factors (e.g., see Aronsson & Sätterlund-Larsson, 1987; Tracy & Tracy, 1998).

From our perspective, approaches of the first sort are inherently problematic because of their adoption of a methodology that is unsuited to the questions at hand (Kroger & Wood, 1998). As discourse analysts we favour the second approach, which departs from the comforts of traditional methodologies. But notwithstanding our general commitment to that approach and our own work in that direction (e.g., MacMartin, 1989; Wood & Kroger, 1994), we would like to argue for moving away from the use of face concepts in the actual doing of analysis, at least for the time being. Our preference is for a piecemeal approach to the details of interaction, leaving for later the use of face and facework as organizing principles if warranted by findings in many diverse circumstances.

The issue is not that notions of face should be rejected because they have been tied in the past, especially in the Brown–Levinson model, to the presumed deterministic properties of norms, rules and conventions. The view of norms and rules as prescriptive and regulative in any simple, classical causal sense can be replaced by the notion that norms and rules are invoked by participants to make sense of their conduct (Antaki, 1994; Edwards, 1997; Nofsinger, 1991), that they are a kind of repertoire from which to draw accounts and justifications. Norms and rules come to be resources for both participants and analysts and not only for making intelligible conforming conduct but also its flip side, the work of aggravation and attack, as seen in the Dylan Thomas quotation. In this vein, one could treat the Brown–Levinson model as a description of the norms to which participants orient. Utterances may be characterized as "forward" to mark the failure of a stranger to keep sufficient distance, or as "cheeky", to mark the display of insufficient respect to an older person. But neither of these is an inevitable consequence.

The association of the concept of face with the cognitivist, intentionalist view of language is potentially troublesome. It contains the seeds of an unwonted reductionism that is still widespread, particularly in experimental social psychology (see Holtgraves, this volume, Chapter 4.18). The danger is that the potency of the concept of face will be lost in the morass of an outmoded positivist epistemology. One source of this problem may be that Brown and Levinson's (1978, 1987) formulation of face mixes the North American notion of facework with "linguistic concepts adapted from British speech act theory (notions of verbal propositions, intentionality, implicature, rational conversational principles, maxims, etcetera)" (Janney & Arndt, 1993, p. 13). These sorts of concerns are not restricted to the Brown–Levinson formulation of face. For example, Schegloff (1988) has argued that "putting 'face' at the centre of interaction drives Goffman's account toward the individual and the psychological" (p. 95). We are not against borrowing from disparate theoretical viewpoints. They are often a source of inspiration in the history of science. But we are leery of hybrid systematizations that incorporate cognitive science models (e.g., Schank & Abelson, 1977) that have had an adverse effect, for example, in the field of speech communication (Mandelbaum & Pomerantz, 1991) and that may reinforce the reification of the concept of face as a mentalistic, motivational entity.

Fortunately, it is not necessary to treat face as a cognitive concept. Edwards and Potter (1992, 1993) have successfully reformulated the cognitivist concept of attribution as a participant's resource in talk rather than as a mentalistic construct. The same sort of move can and has been made for other cognitive phenomena, for example, attitudes (Edwards & Potter, 1992), explanations (Antaki, 1994), categories and emotions (Edwards, 1997) and mind (Coulter, 1989). Face as "want" (in the Brown–Levinson treatment) can similarly be formulated as a conversational rather than motivational notion. More generally, issues of politeness, motivation, strategy, intention, rationality, efficiency (and contrasting versions consisting of deviations from these categories) can be reworked as conversational, rather than cognitivist, phenomena. As discursive activities, they may be identified in the sequential flow of talk-in-interaction rather than treated as mentalistic entities in individual (non-discursive) minds (see Coulter, 1992). Contextual categories that have traditionally been viewed as independent variables in politeness theory (e.g., power, social distance) can be investigated as discursive resources. The emphasis is on what linguistic expression does socially for the speaker and for the hearer and for the wider social network in which both are embedded. It is not on what might be going on under the skull. This thrust is a salutary development because it circumvents the bane of the cognitivist position in psychology: the irksome discrepancy between inner states and self-report (see Kroger, 1988).

But the strongest critique of the study of face as done in both the Goffman and Brown–Levinson traditions has come from the ethnomethodologists and conversation analysts (e.g., Schegloff, 1988). They not only argue that we must avoid premature quantification and the deterministic treatment of norms and that we should stick to the analysis of actual talk to reveal reliable patterns (such as preference structures) without jumping into inferences regarding inner states that presumably cause the patterns. Most importantly, their radical anti-positivism also eschews the imposition of the theorist's qualitative categories on participants' actions (see Schegloff, 1992). Our concern here is thus not with face as a normative or cognitive concept, but with its status as a theorist's category. We now consider this issue by taking a closer look at selected examples of research.

Three Examples

Tracy and Tracy (1998) analysed two telephone calls to a 911 emergency centre using Goffman's work on face threats. They define face threats as "communicative attacks perceived by members of a social community (and often intended by speakers) to be purposively offensive" (p. 227). They reported face attacks by call-takers at several levels: (a) increasingly loud speech and controlled enunciation (pausing briefly between each word of a short phrase); (b) selected speech acts, for example, strings of assertion/counter-assertion ("no I'm not"; "yes you are"), reprimands about personhood and metacommunicative directives (e.g., "Do you understand?"); (c) the use of stance indicators, linguistic choices that convey attitudes of disrespect or contempt (e.g., "I *know* what the fuck I'm talking about okay *bitch*"), (d) answering questions in ways that deny the very legitimacy of even asking a question (e.g., "for HOW LONG?"; "As *long* as it takes. As long as it *takes*"). Tracy and Tracy argue that in each of the exchanges a call-taker attacked a caller's face, that is, "conveyed disrespect and/or contempt" (p. 237).

Aronsson and Sätterlund-Larsson (1987) examined doctor–patient communication using Brown and Levinson's theory of politeness. They found that doctors almost invariably used the first-person plural ("we") to describe the actions of a single person (a device identified by Brown and Levinson). They suggest that the doctors' use of "we", as a reference to the doctor and the staff, permits the patient to oppose the doctor without engaging in direct face threats. It diffuses the responsibility of the doctor into the ephemeral presence of her staff and other nether regions of the hospital system. Physicians were also found to use a good deal of indirectness and tentativeness in requests and questions, for example, "You (Tu form) could perhaps undress a little and get on the couch and then we'll examine your (Tu form) thighs while I try to get hold of a report . . .". Aronsson and Sätterlund-Larsson describe this request as a combination of several different sub-strategies in the Brown–Levinson model, both positive (ingroup identity marker, collaborative plural) and negative (conventional indirectness, hedge and minimize imposition). Aronsson and Sätterlund-Larsson report that their data offer numerous politeness strategies, although they do not always invoke a specific face interpretation for the conversational features that they identify. They argue that the use of politeness strategies often serves to render talk, particularly by physicians, so vague and ambiguous that it avoids open disagreement. But it may also lead to misunderstandings. They conclude that politeness constraints can not only affect clarity, but also threaten participation by patients in decision-making.

Finally, we consider an analysis of politeness by Myers (1989) that is unusual in that it involved written texts (scientific articles). He presents a number of examples of pronouns such as "we" that are seen to mitigate face threats such as criticism (by including the writer in the criticism). Other devices, such as the expression of emotions, are interpreted as showing identification with a common goal – the writer wants what others want – and is therefore attending to positive face. The positive politeness strategy of joking appears relatively infrequently, but does crop up in new terms and titles. The giving of gifts appears in the form of giving credit to other researchers, particularly in relation to issues of priority. Myers argues that "Hedging is a politeness strategy when it marks a claim, or any other statement as being provisional, pending acceptance in the literature" (p. 12). He provides examples of various ways of hedging (e.g., via modal verbs such as "would" or "could", modifiers such as "probably" or any device suggesting alternatives). He also points to instances of personalization as methods of hedging one's own claims (e.g., "*We* wish to suggest") or those of others ("he claims"), although the latter works to signal disagreement rather than politeness. Finally, Myers argues that the impersonal constructions identified by Brown and Levinson as a form of negative politeness "do not necessarily reflect the impersonality of science, or the arbitrary dictates of tradition, but rather are rational ways of dealing with interactions, with claims and denials, the necessary FTAs of scientific writing" (p. 17).

Language Use as Facework

These three studies are in many ways exemplary of discourse-oriented work that uses notions of politeness and face in the analysis of particular sorts of discourse. Our descriptions do not do justice to the details of the analyses, nor highlight the contributions of such work to the understanding of practical problems and the dynamic nature of texts. Our concern is with the reading by these analysts of specific instances of language use. Is this kind of talk best conceptualized as facework?

How does one show, for example, that a specific utterance (or sequence of utterances) does face attack or politeness? One could simply handle this problem by definition. For example, one could define the use of obscenities as face attack, or the use of hedges as politeness. This might solve the problem of interpretation, but it is not clear what it would add to analysis – and it would seem to diminish our sense of what is involved in face work. It is not necessarily helpful to see as face attack all instances of the use of bad language (see, for example, Jefferson, Sacks and Schegloff (1987) on obscenities as the display of intimacy) or of teasing (Drew, 1987). The same applies to the interpretation of other features, such as hedges, as unproblematically equivalent to politeness. In addition, the categorization of utterances in terms of face may be differentially problematic for politeness as compared to aggravation.

Most discourse researchers, however, recognize the potential multifunctionality of linguistic strategies in sequences of talk and reject the assumption that discourse markers serve the same, transparent function across all speech situations. Nonetheless, the recognition that particular devices or strategies may or may not be relevant to face and that almost anything could be used to do various and multiple sorts of facework still leaves us with the problem of doing and warranting interpretation. For example, Tracy and Tracy (1998) argue that profanities and yelling are face attacks, but as we have noted above this may not be invariably the case. One could argue that profanities and yelling constitute face attack when uttered by call-takers in the 911 context. But one could also argue that the utterances of callers or call-takers in the Tracy and Tracy study are not necessarily instances of face attack. Loud speech and yelling can have multiple interpretations, particularly under urgent and stressful circumstances. Controlled enunciation can, as Tracy and Tracy themselves suggest, be interpreted either as a speaker trying not to yell or speaking very slowly as if to someone with limited understanding, but we think that in either case it could be taken as a reflection of the limitations surrounding the speaker as a foot-soldier in a bureaucratically complex system with limited resources at least as much as an attack on the face of the recipient. Similarly, the call-taker's utterance "I *know* what the fuck I'm talking about okay *bitch*" immediately follows a statement by the caller that ". . . you don't know what the fuck you're even talking about", in which case it might be interpreted as face defence rather than attack.

There are certainly a number of problematic instances in the two conversations, for example, the argument sequence and the use of "metacommunicative directives" (e.g., "listen to me"). But there are difficulties with the overall characterization of the two calls as face attack. The problem seems to be that the callers just don't "get it"; that is, they do not respond to the multiple indications that their behaviour is confused and seen as unreasonable by the call-taker. Why not characterize the two calls overall as, for example, miscommunication? We are not saying that the call-takers are not discourteous in an abstract, trans-situational sense but that politeness is a kind of civilized luxury that must yield to the Gricean bare-bones in emergencies. We would fault the captain whose ship is about to sink for consulting Ms Manners instead of drawing on his knowledge of seamanship. The point in the 911 exchange is that the utterances are not helpful in solving the problem in hand. As analysts, the best that we can say without further evidence is that the utterances are nasty and unpleasant, a claim that should be grounded in specific lexical features or in something about how the utterances are built.

Similarly, there are other possible interpretations of the discourse features discussed by Aronsson and Sätterlund-Larsson (1987). For example, they argue that the lack of direct requests or questioning by the physicians can "fruitfully be interpreted as negative politeness moves, geared to softening the doctor's face-threatening demands" (p. 11). But if patients do not understand what they are being asked, why not interpret those same features of the doctors' utterances as face-threatening (imposing) rather than softening? Further, those features (e.g., vagueness, ambiguity) that are claimed to save the patient's face by avoiding disagreement could be seen as a form of physician incompetence (or at least, uncertainty) with respect to their diagnosis and recommendations – and function to threaten the physician's own face. The assumption that particular features (e.g., ingroup identity markers, indirectness, hedges) are politeness strategies obscures other functions that such features may serve. For example, "a little" in "you could perhaps undress a little" is interpreted as the negative politeness strategy of minimizing imposition. But could it not just be an instruction to take off only outer clothing rather than getting completely undressed, which nonetheless may confuse the patient already uncertain about bodily exposure, even in the peculiar circumstances of the medical consulting room? To frame misunderstandings as "the joint product of patient and doctor politeness" (p. 25) distracts us from examining utterances more specifically for the ways in which they, for example, omit information and clarity.

Lastly, it seems to us that a number of the usages reported by Myers (1989) could be interpreted without invoking politeness. For example, Myers claims that the phrase "we believe" in relation to one's own work mitigates the potential threat to the face of other members of the field because the authors presumably believe everything they say. But why not treat it as a matter of modalization, that is, a comment on the relative factual status of (or commitment to) the statement that it modifies (see Latour & Woolgar, 1986). Myers suggests that joking may serve to mitigate the face threat of a claim – but it could also serve to make that claim more memorable. Joking may also be interpreted in some cases as ironic, and taken to underscore the importance (and therefore the threat, if any) of the claim. And joking might simply be a recognition that academic discourse is usually in great need of leavening and that it involves the pleasure of playing with words. The giving of gifts in the form of credit for simultaneous, independent claims can be seen as a display of politeness in crediting rival researchers for a discovery while preserving the speaker's own claim for priority. But there may be more (or less) at stake here than facework: in some disciplines at least, the issue of priority has legal and financial implications that go beyond the establishment of cooperation in the scientific community.

In sum, we have some trouble with the interpretations that are offered in these and similar studies of utterances as facework. Myers (1989) argues that theories of face or politeness may sensitize us to particular features, but this is not the only route to noticing such features, nor does it require that we interpret those features in terms of politeness or facework. He also suggests that politeness interpretations are justified because they account for features of discourse that are otherwise unexplained. We are saying that we must be alert to other interpretations before fastening, perhaps prematurely, on those framed in terms of politeness theory. We need to say more than that a feature could be politeness or face attack; we must show that it is a reasonable interpretation in the particular case. Aronsson and Sätterlund-Larsson (1987) treat some requests as unproblematically containing politeness components; Tracy and Tracy say that the call-taker "disparages the caller (*therein* [italics added] engaging in face attack)" (1998, p. 236). Perhaps a pause is in order.

But there is more at stake here than the risk of falling back on some sort of positivist, mechanical coding scheme, rather than engaging in piecemeal analysis. Tracy and Tracy argue that face attack "is best conceived as a social judgment" (1998, p. 242). We agree; more generally, we think that the identification of some utterance in terms of face requires a judgment, that is, it must be recognized as face threat in order to be interpreted as doing face threat. The question is, "Whose judgment?" We think that, in the first instance, the judgment must be that of the participants; that is, we must see that they orient to utterances as matters of face (threat, enhancement, mitigation, damage, attack, etc.). They must display their recognition (see Drew, 1987). If the caller just shrugs off the 911 operator's "I *know* what the fuck I am talking about okay *bitch*" as just another unpleasantness not uncommon in her milieu, said in the heat of the particular moment while her main interest is getting help to her friend, is the analyst justified in calling the operator's utterance a face threat? As analysts we must be sensitive to our middle-class perspective. Unless we can show the relevance of such terms to the participants, "we are back to a 'positivistic' stance, even though the animating concerns may be drawn from quite antipositivistic theoretical sources or commitments" (Schegloff, 1992, p. 109).

Participant's Orientation

The crux of our concern with analyses of facework is the failure of analysts to demonstrate that their reading is the participant's reading. In some cases, the readings of the analysts and of the participants are different . For example, in Tracy and Tracy's (1998) 911 calls, the call-taker at one point says, "like FOR WHATEVER REASON you're calling me, NO, no one can tell you anything over the telephone. Oka:y? Do you understand? To protect the confidentiality of whoever's involved" (p. 245). As we noted above, Tracy and Tracy treat such utterances as face attack in terms of several features (e.g., the vocal delivery, the question about understanding). But the caller merely responds, "Okay well can you dispatch someone else out to this property?" Does her response indicate that she has suffered a face attack? The operator's "I *know* what the fuck I'm talking about okay *bitch*" is not followed by something along the lines of, "How dare you talk to me like that," but by "No you don't" (p. 246). The caller here defines the problem as the operator's incomprehension, not as the use of foul language. In this case, the use of foul language may grate on the civilized ear as a sort of verbal pollution but it does not necessarily work to produce face attack. In the Aronsson and Sätterlund-Larsson study, the possibility that "undress a little" could have multiple meanings for the patient rather than being (simply) a minimization of imposition is supported by the patient's question several turns later, "Shall I take everything off now?" Finally, there is no evidence that the readers of the texts analyzed by Myers (1989) shared his interpretation of utterances as, variously, face threats, mitigation of threat and so on.

A further issue involves differences between facework that is mitigating and facework that is aggravating. There is an asymmetry in that participants seem to orient more to threat or attack than to politeness, as they see it. In contrast, analysts have generally concentrated more on politeness than on aggravation, a reverse asymmetry. Participants may refer to losing or saving face. They may also use the term "polite" to characterize action, as a way of categorizing the action as conventional or expected, perhaps particularly in the context of a challenge to one's actions or in response to someone's failure to display the conventional action. For example, to say that a person was "just trying to be polite" treats the actions as of little moment, as formulaic, not necessarily manipulative or insincere, but as something not to be taken too seriously or literally, that is, as actions that have little or nothing to do with something as important as face. Further participants do not need to use the term "politeness" for us to claim that they are treating something as politeness. Thus, it is appropriate for Kotthof (1993) to claim that concessions that are unelaborated or improperly placed are not treated as concessions but as mere politeness.

The problem here is that the everyday or folk terms are not equivalent to the terms and concepts as used by researchers. There is clearly some overlap between the two usages. Participants may orient to face in ways that are arguably relevant to the notions entertained by analysts. Both talk about honour, reputation, insult, imposition, (in)consideratencss, if in necessarily somewhat different terms. There is overlap but also divergence. For the participant, politeness refers to conventional or normative behaviour. For the analyst, it refers to the intricate matrix of the theory of facework and politeness. How can we reconcile the two?

Face as an Analyst's Resource

Tracy and Tracy state that they "part ways with the conversation analytic position that rejects the use of theoretical concepts as a starting point for analysis of social interaction" (1998, p. 229). An argument could be made that conversation analysts also deploy "theoretical concepts" (even the notion of a "turn" involves an idea about the phenomenon in which one person speaks followed by another). The more critical issue in our view concerns whether those concepts are introduced before or after analysis. Top-down or bottom-up? For example, notions such as order and repair are worked up in terms of what participants themselves are visibly or hearably doing – without recourse to states of mind. The problem may be the tenuous empirical link between conceptions of facework and the assortment of linguistic features drawn upon to ground the enactment of facework in talk. A closer look at some of these conceptions might help us to identify the difficulties in making such linkages.

One important notion is that face is a sequential accomplishment, that it cannot be reduced to any specific linguistic feature. Lerner, for example, talks about the "ongoing and ever-changeable level of regard that accrues to persons engaged in interaction through everything that happens" (1996, p. 303). Brown and Levinson themselves argued that "face-threatening acts need not be realized in sentence-like units" (1987, pp. 10–11) and that "politeness is *implicated* by the semantic structure of the whole utterance, not communicated by 'markers' or 'mitigators' in a simple signaling fashion" (p. 22). For Goffman, face is "something that is diffusely located in the flow of events in the encounter" (1967, p. 7). Perhaps facework practices can be seen as a secondary structure, as Van Langenhove uses this term, that is, something that we can experience only indirectly through its material substrata or conversations linked to it (as "we can, for example, talk with people 'from' the University of Oxford . . . can see some of the buildings which are said to belong to the University, but we cannot experience the University of Oxford as such", 1995, p. 23).

Face is always in some sense a public or interactional notion in contrast to a private, personal characteristic, although the relative emphasis on the former and the way in which these are framed vary across different approaches. For example, as Mao (1994) points out, Goffman's "face is a 'public property' that is only assigned to individuals contingent upon their interactional behaviour", whereas for Brown and Levinson face "belongs to the individual, to the 'self' " (Mao, 1994, p. 454); it is "the public self-image that every member wants to claim for himself" (Brown & Levinson, 1987, p. 61). Our own view is that face is so much an interactional notion that it is constituted not only by but also in the responses of others, somewhat akin to the concept of popularity (Gilbert, 1976). One can only experience face to the extent that one is recognized in particular ways by others and recognizes that one is so recognized. Like reputation (Harré, 1979), face cannot be a property of the individual.

Another issue is the treatment of asymmetry with respect to face mitigation (politeness) and face aggravation. If one assumes minimal mutual regard, face maintenance or politeness is the invisible or unmarked case (Tracy & Tracy, 1998); it is not noticed, and docs not have particular implications. Like housework, it is only noticed when it is not done. We tend to favour this formulation. But not all approaches to facework adopt this view (see Tracy & Tracy);

different treatments involve different assumptions about the usual course of social interaction, that is, whether it is potentially face-threatening or face-supportive. Our position is that interaction is potentially both. In any case, the issue with respect to analysis is not what is potential, but what is realized in the text at hand.

These and other features of facework theory mean that there is a problem when we try to use concepts of face and facework in the actual business of analysis. It is not that face is not relevant to participants; rather, the face that is relevant is not the same as the face that is relevant to analysts. The problem is obscured because of slippage between face as an analyst's resource and face as a participant's resource, a slippage that can occur not only because these overlap in some ways, but also because analysts are also participants – we have made or can imagine making 911 calls; we have interacted with physicians; we have written and read scientific articles. And it is tempting to conduct analysis as if we were the participants, to read in the ways that we might respond. And when we actually are participants – when we read articles, etc. – we may draw on our analyst notions as resources, for example, when we claim that as readers, we find an article to be face-threatening. As Schegloff puts it, "such notions as impoliteness or rudeness need to be recognized as parts of the *vernacular culture* which is the mark of competent membership in the society". They "may work as vernacular accounts of *occasional lapses* in the turn-taking order (and other orders), but do not serve as an account for the existence and character of *the orders themselves*" (1988, p. 98). We therefore run the risk of recycling common-sense categories and at the same time not giving them due attention. More generally, the broad scope and metaphorical nature of concepts of face render them inappropriate as analytical tools. But is there then no place for such rich and powerful notions?

FACE AND FACEWORK IN DISCOURSE ANALYSIS

Our argument is not that we should jettison concepts of face and facework. On the contrary, the large body of literature on these concepts speaks to their importance. And there is work that does not run into the sorts of problems that we have identified. For example, Pomerantz, Ende and Erickson (1995) examined how preceptors (doctors training interns in teaching clinics) correct errors of interns. They found that preceptors minimize explicit exposure of wrong answers by interns in several ways: by providing opportunities for interns to correct their own mistakes, by giving hints to help interns sequentially formulate appropriate assessments, and by treating wrong responses by interns as possible and reasonable. Pomerantz et al. do not invoke notions of face or politeness as part of their analysis, although a number of the preceptors' usages could be treated this way. For example, "I think" used by a preceptor could be interpreted as a hedge that mitigates the threat to the intern's face of the recommendation that it modifies; Pomerantz et al. analyze the phrase simply as an uncertainty marker. Nonetheless, they do refer to face in their discussion section when considering different ways of understanding why preceptors correct the way that they do. They suggest that the practices of gently correcting may be tied to a concern with protecting the other's face. But they also suggest a different, although complementary interpretation, namely that such practices reflect a concern for learning by discovery rather than by direct tutelage.

There are other similar examples of the use of face in conversation analytic work. Kotthof (1993) examined disagreement and concession in disputes in relation to preference structures. The analysis itself does not employ reference to concepts of face, but Kotthof does invoke face threat in explaining her findings, for example, that concessions are often uttered in a hesitant manner. Drew refers to Brown and Levinson (1978) in suggesting that teasing enables people to express conflicts in a way that can "simultaneously express their positive communality" (1987, p. 248), that is, mutual positive face. Thus, the conversation analytic position that rejects the use of concepts such as face in the course of analysis does not prevent their deployment in the interpretation and discussion of analytic findings.

Lerner's (1996) work shows that this approach can be taken to the understanding not only of discourse in specialized contexts or particular conversational actions, but also of basic conversational practices. For example, he connects the concept of face to a number of conversational practices such as turn completion and, particularly, preference structures (e.g., the normative valuing of acceptances of invitations over rejections, of self-repair over other-repair, of agreement over disagreement). We stress that Lerner does not use concepts of face in the analysis of the conversational data that he presents. Rather, he points us to practices that furnish the "possibility and recognizability of both face threat and remediation" (p. 304). That is, he suggests ways in which we can analyze interaction in relation to both its unmarked and marked character without prematurely invoking concepts of face, while at the same time laying a foundation for the understanding of our findings in terms of face.

Thus, in contrast to Tracy and Tracy (1998), we would argue that face can be used as a lens for understanding what is being done rather than for identifying what is being done, as a way of making sense of how participants make sense rather than a way of describing sense-making practices. We agree that considerations of politeness and face can help us to notice important discursive details (Myers, 1989), particularly those details that involve the management of respect and contempt (see Penman, 1990, 1994) and that can be connected to a larger moral order (Tracy & Tracy).

More generally, we agree with Tracy and Tracy (1998) that considerations of face may be important for practical issues, for identifying alternative courses of action. But our concern is that if these are introduced in the first instance we might miss attending sufficiently to the taken-for-granted practices that sustain and protect systemic inequality. If we as social scientists wish to address the moral order, we must be able not only to consider morality in discourse (see

Bergmann & Linell, 1998) but also to challenge the taken-for-granted. There is a sense in which we may wish to make face and facework our topic, even (or perhaps especially) when it is not a topic for participants. Consider, for example, the way in which the taken-for-granted practice of referring to women by their husbands' surnames is taken up, if at all, as a matter of solidarity although it also serves to make women invisible as persons in their own rights.

A major advantage to avoiding face as a resource for analysis is that it permits us to bypass – or at least defer – most of the debates within the literature on politeness and facework. Many of these concern the Brown and Levinson approach (e.g., the on–off record distinction, the concept of imposition, positive and negative aspects), but they also concern other approaches and various sorts of disagreements among them. Many of the challenges come from cross-cultural work, for example, the claim that what counts as facework in some cultures and languages does not do so in others. For example, it has been suggested (e.g., Nwoye, 1992) that the Brown and Levinson view gives insufficient attention to the normative nature of politeness – and that politeness is not necessarily connected to face (see, for example, Ide's, 1989, argument that honorific usage in Japanese is not face-relevant because it is not optional). The abstract nature of politeness theory – which is both its virtue but also its potential bane – makes it perhaps less sensitively attuned to cross-cultural variability than it could be (cf. Tracy & Baratz, 1994). In the meantime, it may not be helpful to substitute one version for another. Lastly, it is worth keeping in mind that debates about face largely revolve around how to conceptualize and analyze it. The debate is not about the importance of the concept itself.

CONCLUSION

The problem of face and politeness in one sense is that everything has to do with face. As Goffman claimed, "almost all acts involving others are modified, prescriptively or proscriptively, by considerations of face" (1967, p. 13). Unfortunately, our recognition of this fundamental concern of social life can lead us to gloss over the details of discourse, over the ways in which politeness and face are made relevant. While we can treat politeness and face as participants' resources, we must be careful not to confuse them with our own analytical resources. The premature imposition of face as a "top-down" analyst's category can decontextualize, abstract, and reify the finely tuned social accomplishments of participants that might be revealed through a more painstaking "bottom-up" exploration. We would like to distinguish between theoretical argument and analytic practice (as Schegloff, 1988, p. 92, does in discussing Goffman's work). Similarly, if we treat face as an explanation for participants' practices, we do not add anything if we use face to describe those practices. The issue is not so much one of losing face from facework, but of watching out for whose (notion of) face is involved (see Widdicombe, 1998, who has raised a similar concern about identity as an analysts' and a participants' resource). Care must be taken not to conflate different approaches, but rather to treat them as running parallel (cf. Watson, 1992, on the possibilities of dialogue between Goffmanian analytic practices and those of conversation analysis/ethnomethodology).

None of these possibilities and concerns would have arisen if we had not had the fundamental contributions of Goffman's theorizing and of Brown and Levinson's efforts to anchor those notions in specific linguistic usage. We must also recognize the work of numerous others to modify and extend these foundational ideas, particularly Tracy, who has drawn our attention to the virtues of case studies and the importance of the moral order.

We have tried to address the question of how these contributions can best be realized in future work. For reasons of space, we have omitted our explorations of the historical background of the contemporary work on face and politeness and have had to set aside the question of how we can manage the delicate balancing of general social theory and the situated understanding of everyday action. Ultimately, we must aim to elucidate the fundamental tensions of social life illuminated by Goffman and by Brown and Levinson through the metaphorical extension of face.

In closing, we return to the quotation from Dylan Thomas. It stands as a challenge to any discourse analyst. Coupland and Coupland (personal communication) have sagaciously suggested that it involves matters of poetics as well as of facework. And they are right in pointing to the richness of the tapestry of discourse which will not easily yield to facile interpretation. But our inquiries into the intricacies of discourse hold the promise of elucidating social life in a way that has been denied to earlier approaches. In this endeavour, the notions of face and facework will occupy a central place.

REFERENCES

Antaki, C. (1994). *Explaining and arguing: The social organization of accounts.* London: Sage.

Aronsson, K. & Sätterlund-Larsson, U. (1987). Politeness strategies and doctor–patient communication: On the social choreography of collaborative thinking. *Journal of Language and Social Psychology*, **6**, 1–27.

Bergmann, J.R. & Linell, P. (Eds) (1998). Morality in discourse (Special issue). *Research on Language and Social Interaction*, **31**(3 & 4).

Brown, P. & Levinson, S.C. (1978). Universals in language usage: Politeness phenomena. In E.N. Goody (Ed.), *Questions and politeness: Strategies in social interaction* (pp. 56–310). Cambridge, UK: Cambridge University Press.

Brown, P. & Levinson, S.C. (1987). *Universals in language usage: Politeness phenomena.* Cambridge, UK: Cambridge University Press.

Brown, R. (1987). *Theory of politeness: An exemplary case.* Invited address to Society of Experimental Social Psychologists, Charlottesville, VA, October 1987.

Coulter, J. (1989). *Mind in action.* Oxford: Polity Press.

Coulter, J. (1992). Bilmes on "Internal States": A critical commentary. *Journal for the Theory of Social Behaviour*, **22**, 239–251.

Drew, P. (1987). Po-faced receipts of teases. *Linguistics*, **25**, 219–253.

Durkheim, E. (1915). *The elementary forms of the religious life.* London: Unwin.

Edwards, D. (1997). *Discourse and cognition.* London: Sage.

Edwards, D. & Potter, J. (1992). *Discursive psychology.* London: Sage.

Edwards, D. & Potter, J. (1993). Language and causation: A discursive action model of description and attribution. *Psychological Review,* **100**, 23–41.

Gilbert, M. (1976). On being categorized in the speech of others. In R. Harré (Ed.), *Life sentences: Aspects of the social role of language* (pp. 10–20). London: Wiley.

Goffman, E. (1955). On facework: An analysis of ritual elements in social interaction. *Psychiatry,* **18**, 213–231.

Goffman, E. (1967). *Interaction ritual: Essays on face-to-face behavior.* Garden City, NJ: Anchor Books.

Grice, H.P. (1975). Logic and conversation. In P. Cole & J.L. Morgan (Eds), *Syntax and semantics, Vol. 3: Speech acts* (pp. 41–58). New York: Academic Press.

Harré, R. (1979). *Social being: A theory for social psychology.* Oxford: Blackwell.

Ide, S. (1989). Formal forms and discernment: Two neglected aspects of universals of linguistic politeness. *Multilingua,* **8**, 223–248.

Janney, R.W. & Arndt, H. (1993). Universality and relativity in cross-cultural politeness research: A historical perspective. *Multilingua,* **12**, 13–50.

Jefferson, G., Sacks, H. & Schegloff, E.A. (1987). Notes on laughter in the pursuit of intimacy. In G. Button & J.R.E. Lee (Eds), *Talk and social organization* (pp. 152–205). Philadelphia: Multilingual Matters.

Kotthof, H. (1993). Disagreement and concession in disputes: On the context sensitivity of preference structures. *Language in Society,* **22**, 193–216.

Kroger, R.O. (1988). The social nature of hypnosis: An ethogenic analysis of hypnotic pain reduction. *New Ideas in Psychology,* **6**, 47–66.

Kroger, R.O. & Wood, L.A. (1998). The turn to discourse in social psychology. *Canadian Psychology,* **39**, 266–279.

Latour, B. & Woolgar, S. (1986). *Laboratory life: The social construction of scientific facts* (2nd edn). Princeton, NJ: Princeton University Press.

Lerner, G.H. (1996). Finding "face" in the preference structures of talk-in-interaction. *Social Psychology Quarterly,* **59**, 303–321.

MacMartin, C. (1989). The politeness of compliments in Miller's "Death of a Salesman". Unpublished master's thesis, University of Toronto, Toronto, Canada.

Mandelbaum, J. & Pomerantz, A. (1991). What drives social action? In K. Tracy (Ed.), *Understanding face-to-face interaction: Issues linking goals and discourse* (pp. 151–166). Hillsdale, NJ: Erlbaum.

Mao, L.R. (1994). Beyond politeness theory: "Face" revisited and renewed. *Journal of Pragmatics,* **21**, 451–486.

Myers, G. (1989). The pragmatics of politeness in scientific articles. *Applied Linguistics,* **10**, 1–35.

Nofsinger, R.E. (1991). *Everyday conversation.* Newbury Park, CA: Sage.

Nwoye, O. (1992). Linguistic politeness and socio-cultural variations of the notion of face. *Journal of Pragmatics,* **18**, 309–328.

Penman, R. (1990). Facework and politeness: Multiple goals in courtroom discourse. *Journal of Language and Social Psychology,* **9**, 15–38.

Penman, R. (1994). Facework in communication: Conceptual and moral challenges. In S. Ting-Toomey (Ed.), *The challenge of facework: Cross-cultural and interpersonal issues* (pp. 15–45). Albany, NY: State University of New York.

Pomerantz, A.M., Ende, J. & Erickson, F. (1995). Precepting conversations in a general medicine clinic. In G.H. Morris & R.J. Chenail (Eds), *The talk of the clinic: Explorations in the analysis of medical and therapeutic discourse* (pp. 151–169). Hillsdale, NJ: Erlbaum.

Schank, R. & Abelson, R. (1977). *Scripts, plans, goals, and understanding.* Hillsdale, NJ: Erlbaum.

Schegloff, E.A. (1988). Goffman and the analysis of conversation. In P. Drew & A. Wootton (Eds), *Erving Goffman: Exploring the interaction order* (pp. 89–135). Boston, MA: Northeastern University Press.

Schegloff, E.A. (1992). On talk and its institutional occasions. In P. Drew & J. Heritage (Eds), *Talk at work: Interaction in institutional settings* (pp. 101–134). Cambridge, UK: Cambridge University Press.

Ting-Toomey, S. (Ed.) (1994). *The challenge of facework: Cross-cultural and interpersonal issues.* Albany, NY: State University of New York Press.

Tracy, K. (1990). The many faces of facework. In H. Giles & W.P. Robinson (Eds), *Handbook of language and social psychology* (1st edn) (pp. 209–226). Chichester, UK: Wiley.

Tracy, K. & Baratz, S. (1994). The case for case studies of facework. In S. Ting-Toomey (Ed.), *The challenge of facework: Cross-cultural and interpersonal issues* (pp. 287–305). Albany, NY: State University of New York Press.

Tracy, K. & Tracy, S.K. (1998). Rudeness at 911: Reconceptualizing face and face attack. *Human Communication Research,* **25**, 225–251.

Tremlett, G. (1991). *Dylan Thomas: In the mercy of his means.* London: Constable.

Van Langenhove, L. (1995). The theoretical foundations of experimental psychology and its alternatives. In J.A. Smith, R. Harré & L. Van Langenhove (Eds), *Rethinking psychology* (pp. 10–23). London: Sage.

Watson, R. (1992). The understanding of language use in everyday life. In G. Watson & R.M. Seiler (Eds), *Text in context: Contributions to ethnomethodology* (pp. 1–19). Newbury Park, CA: Sage.

Widdicombe, S. (1998). Identity as an analysts' and a participants' resource. In C. Antaki & S. Widdicombe (Eds), *Identities in talk* (pp. 191–206). London: Sage.

Wood, L.A. & Kroger, R.O. (1994). The analysis of facework in discourse: Review and proposal. *Journal of Language and Social Psychology,* **13**, 248–277.

Part 3

Face to Face: Special Functions

3.12

Arguing

Michael Billig
Loughborough University, UK

The word "argument" has two basic meanings, both in academic study and in ordinary language. An argument can refer either to a quarrel or to a piece of reasoned discourse (O'Keefe, 1977). At first glance, the simplest tactic would be to separate the two senses of argument, perhaps devoting a separate chapter for each type. For instance, this chapter might concentrate on "arguing as quarrelling" and a later one might discuss "arguing as reasoning". With clear definitions and a good wedge of intervening pages, no confusion should arise. Furthermore, the two types of argument conventionally appear on opposite sides of a moral divide. Argument-as-quarrel seems pre-eminently to be something "bad", that should be avoided. Gage (1996) comments that when we hear the word "argument" most of us react "as if we were remembering the pain of those domestic gut-tearing arguments that, at best, we hope never to relive or, at worst, we feel lucky to have survived" (p. 4). On the other hand, it is a "good thing" to produce "arguments" to support one's views and stances. Indeed, academics such as Gage are professionally engaged in teaching students how to argue reasonably and effectively.

The tactic of separating "bad", quarrelsome argument from "good", wholesome reasoning would soon lead to complications. The two meanings point towards an underlying set of connections, which include both semantic and psychological factors. To engage in argument-as-a-quarrel frequently involves presenting arguments-as-reasoning. Conversely, to present reasoned arguments often involves criticizing other rival positions and, by implication, disagreeing. Disagreement might be thought to belong to the same general type of activity as quarrelling. Thus, as we do the "bad" thing of arguing, so we might be thought to be doing the "good" thing and vice versa.

The New Handbook of Language and Social Psychology.
Edited by W. Peter Robinson and Howard Giles.
© 2001 John Wiley & Sons Ltd.

The present chapter, therefore, will not attempt to keep these two senses of argument totally separate; rather it will examine their interrelations. It will be suggested that putting forward reasoned arguments involves a certain negativity. However, argumentation as disputation, far from being destructive and "gut-wrenching", may be part and parcel of creative thinking. On the other hand, the balance between "good" and "bad" never seems settled in the matter of argumentation. The "good" thing, which enables us to think, also enables us to flee from thought. As such, argumentation, in both senses, provides psychological clues not only for the study of thinking but also for that of repression.

THE ARGUMENT AGAINST ARGUMENT

Rhetoric has a long history of studying argumentation (Billig, 1996; Vickers, 1988). From Aristotle onwards rhetoricians have been concerned with the principles of constructing and presenting well-ordered, persuasive communication. Moreover, ancient rhetoric had a strong competitive, or agonistic, dimension. The sophists used to participate in tournaments, in which speakers would try to overcome their opponents with dazzling displays of competitive rhetoric (Kerferd, 1981). The courtroom, with its conflict between prosecution and defence, preserves this agonistic tradition. Rhetoric in such contexts is a zero-sum game: victory is to be gained by defeating the opponent. As Lakoff and Johnson (1980) point out, the term "argument" conveys military metaphors: positions are "defended" or "attacked", as rhetorical battles are fought (see also Emmel, Resch & Tenney, 1996, for a brief discussion of "the argument-as-war metaphor" in contemporary teaching of rhetoric in US universities).

Recently, Deborah Tannen (1998) has produced a sustained critique on what she calls the "argument culture" of contemporary society. She argues that the media today continually set up argumentative battles, operating on the principle of "no fight, no story" (p. 34). According to Tannen, the metaphors of war frame the reporting of political and social debates, distorting the discussion of issues. Tannen briefly mentions the historical arguments of Walter Ong (1981, 1982), who suggested that in the ancient world, before the spread of alphabetic writing, the enacted winning of debates, and, thus rhetoric as performance, was all-important. As discourses became written, so it became possible to study the form and content of reasoning (see also Olsen, 1994, for a discussion of the psychological consequences of literacy in history). Moreover, with the growth of printing, society became less disputatious. Tannen suggests that in the age of television we are moving back towards an oral culture, where confrontational disputation, with its visible displays of victory and defeat, becomes more important than the development of structures of reasoning. Tannen also suggests that the agonistic style of argumentation is related to gender, with men being both culturally and biologically more confrontational than women, as reflected in the differing speech styles of men and women (Tannen, 1990, 1994). Tannen, however, does not explain why the increase of disputation, which she claims to characterize contemporary Western society, should have coincided with the entry of women into public discourse.

Critiques of argumentation have been also produced by feminist theorists such as Lucie Irigaray (1985) and Julia Kristeva (1986), who see the structure of language itself, with its binary oppositions, as being inherently masculine. Kristeva, unlike Irigaray, is prepared to see rhetorical virtue in negativity. Irigaray, by contrast, suggests that women need to develop a wholly different type of communication, based on signifying agreement and commonality. As has been pointed out, this type of position rests on a paradox: the critique of argumentation is itself an argument framed in language (Billig, 1994). The idea that women are not "naturally" argumentative not only rests on unverified biological assumptions (Kitzinger, 1991); it suggests that feminism, which represents a sustained argument against masculinist theories and practices, is somehow at odds with the "natural" essence of womanhood.

Tannen's argument against argument is more restricted than Irigaray's. Tannen specifically criticizes competitive, aggressive argumentation. In her view, agonism represents a distortion of argumentation, and a destruction of reasoned debate. Tannen does not recommend that we live in a cosy world of total agreement, but that we have "the *real* arguments" (p. 6, emphasis in original). In this regard, her argument against argument is an argument for argumentation in its reasoned sense.

ARGUMENT AS REASONING

Rhetoricians have often posed the question "What makes a good argument?" Historically, two different sorts of answer have been offered: the descriptive and the normative. The descriptive answer has tended to concentrate on social psychological factors, treating good arguments as those that are persuasively effective. Aristotle, having defined rhetoric as the study "of the available means of persuasion" (1909 edn, p. 5), acknowledged that the rhetorician needed to discover what sorts of arguments persuaded different audiences. Because of psychological differences between audiences, he concluded that there were no universal principles of persuasion: the persuasive speaker should tailor content and delivery to the particularities of the auditors. This principle was reiterated through the subsequent history of rhetoric (Billig, 1996; Vickers, 1988). It finds expression in the experimental approach to persuasion, most notably the famous Yale Studies of persuasion (Hovland, Janis & Kelley, 1953; for discussions of the Yale Studies, see Pratkanis & Aronson, 1991; Billig, 1996).

The normative tradition in the study of argumentation does not seek to relate argument type to audiences, but to examine the internal strengths and weaknesses of different types of argumentative reasoning. A link can be made to Aristotelian traditions. Aristotle declared rhetoric to be the "counterpart" to dialectic (or logic) (1909, p. 1). Since formal rules for logical, or syllogistic, reasoning could be produced, the possibility was raised whether analogous rules might be produced for the sorts of arguments used in persuasive discourse, in order to separate "good" argumentative practice from "bad" practice. The normative tradition persists in some notable works which led to a "revival of rhetoric" in the 1950s (see Simons, 1990, and Gaonkar, 1990, for an analysis of rhetoric's revival). For example, Perelman and Olbrechts-Tyteca (1971), in their highly influential book *The New Rhetoric*, stressed the importance of justification and criticism in argumentative discourse. They introduced the notion of a "universal audience", which is the hypothetical audience of all reasonable persons. The "reasonable" justification or criticism was not one which was designed merely to appeal to a particular audience. For example, Hitler's speeches to his Nazi sympathizers may have been pragmatically effective in stirring supporters. However, they were not "reasonable" in a wider sense, for they did not address the imagined "universal audience" of all "reasonable" persons (Bakhtin's, 1986, notion of a super-addressee is similar to that of the "universal audience"; see also Shotter, 1992).

The notion of a "universal audience" has been controversial, and other rhetorical theorists, seeking to construct a normative theory, have tended not to pursue this line of thinking. Toulmin's *The Uses of Argument* (first published in 1958) also attempts to produce a schematic outline of good argumentative practice. Like Perelman, Toulmin was arguing against the influence of classical logic. In everyday reasoning, people do not use syllogistic reasoning, but they make claims and use data to warrant such claims. The warranting is a form of justification, but other persons may seek to rebut either the validity of the warranted data or the warranting that links the data to the claim. As such, claims, or at least the warrants supporting the claims, typically are potentially contestable (for applications of Toulmin's model see, for instance, Fulkerson, 1993, 1996). In this regard, individual justification is related to social argument as contestation.

The pragma-dialectical approach to argumentation also attempts to develop a concept of reasonableness which is not based upon formal logic (van Eemeren & Grootendorst, 1988; van Eemeren et al., 1983). The aim is to produce a normative and universal theory of argumentation, outlining the codes which arguers should follow if there are to be reasonable resolutions of disagreement. Other theorists have concentrated on examining traditional fallacies in argumentation, showing the conditions under which it is reasonable to use supposedly fallacious arguments (Walton, 1992). Similarly, it has been pointed out that philosophical discourse itself does not use logical argument, but rhetorical forms and, thus, philosophy require a normative theory of argumentation (Meyer, 1994).

As Charles Antaki (1994) has pointed out, such normative approaches are typically based on hypothetical examples, rather than on the analysis of actual everyday debates (but see Jackson, 1998). In the main, such approaches have difficulty in stipulating general rules of argument which might be universally accepted, for participants in argumentation themselves often contest the so-called rules (see, for instance, Simons, 1989, and the idea of "going meta"). Part of the problem is that arguments can be, to use Toulmin's terminology, "domain-specific". The sort of argument which might be accepted as being convincing in one context may be unpersuasive in others. For instance, it might be reasonable for the Azande to explain someone's illness in terms of spirits and the anger of the gods; such an explanation would appear unconvincing in the context of a modern Western hospital. The issue is not merely one of cross-cultural differences. It can be a matter of "genres", to use Bakhtin's (1986) term. It might, for instance, be seen to be inappropriate to argue like a lawyer in a domestic, relational dispute.

Once the issue of domain specificity is taken seriously, then the notion of universal audiences or "cross-situational" reasonableness becomes problematic, as does the idea of universal, normative standards of argumentation. Reasoning cannot be considered as something abstract, but has to be considered in its social and historical context, not to mention its specific rhetorical context (Billig, 1996; Hikins, 1995). At this point, the goal of separating argument-as-reasoned discourse entirely from argument-as-quarrel falls into difficulty. As Perelman and Olbrechts-Tyteca stressed, the context of argumentation is one of justification and criticism. An argument-as-discourse is justified in the light of actual or potential criticism (see, for instance, Blair's, 1998, analysis of the differences between "solo" and dialogic arguments). In Toulmin's model, the warranting is a means of defending against rebuttals. Thus, one might say that the business of rhetorical argumentation belongs to the context of disagreement. Where there is total agreement, then beliefs may lack argumentative justifications (as McGuire, 1964, showed experimentally in relation to "cultural truisms"). In this regard, any examination of how people actually go about the business of justification and criticism should return the study of argument to the contexts of disagreement. This seems to lead back to the paradox that the "good" part of argumentation – argument-as-reasoning – is dependent on the "bad" part – namely, argument-as-quarrel.

DEBATE AND ARGUMENTATION

The paradox may be more apparent than actual, for the counterposing of alternative positions, which is involved in the dialogical dialectic of justification and criticism, need not involve the sort of confrontational style that Tannen (1998) criticizes. Tannen's argument against argument is not based on an outright opposition to negativity or criticism. She criticizes a particular style of argumentation, in which opposition and face-threatening actions are maximized (see Brown & Levinson, 1987, for a discussion of face threats). "Real" argument, which she supports, would therefore depend upon a less agonistic form of discussion, in which issues are explored through dialogue. The Socratic dialogue is often held to be the prototype of such discussion (see, for instance, Habermas's, 1976, notion of "unconstrained communication"). It can be pointed out that the

Socratic tradition is not completely male. According to Cicero (see 1959 edn), in *De Inventione*, Aspasia was the true founder of the so-called Socratic method of questioning (I, xxxi, 51–2).

The agonistic zero-sum approach, in fact, threatens debate in the Socratic sense. The agonistic rhetorician seeks a victory that silences the opponent, so that success ends the argument. The debater, by contrast, wishes to keep the argument-as-debate going, in order to continue exploring issues through argumentative discussion (Billig, 1996). If debate requires a certain amount of negativity and disagreement, then this cannot be total. As conversation analytic studies of argument demonstrate, those engaged in argument must, nevertheless, share codes for organizing talk, such as turn-taking or codes for demonstrating disagreement (Antaki, 1994; Goodwin, 1983, 1993; Maynard, 1985).

Argument-as-debate has theoretical significance for understanding the operations of human thinking (Billig, 1996, 1998a). Discursive psychologists have shown how many of the properties of cognition, as traditionally studied by psychologists, can be understood to be constituted in discourse (see, for instance, Antaki, 1994; Edwards, 1997; Edwards & Potter, 1992; Harré & Gillett, 1994; Potter, 1996; Potter & Wetherell, 1987). As Edwards and Potter (1992) stress, people often have a "rhetorical stake" when they use psychological words in ordinary conversation. When partners in therapy give accounts of their emotions, they are typically not giving neutral reports of internal states: they are discussing their relationships in ways that justify themselves and blame the other (Edwards, 1997; Buttny, 1993). More generally, emotional terms – whether in Western or non-Western discourses – convey the morality of relationships as much as they do the claimed internal states (Lutz, 1990; White, 1990; Billig, 1999). Similarly, speakers often have rhetorical stakes when they make memory claims, or when they challenge the memory claims of others (Edwards & Potter, 1992; Edwards, 1997). The memory claims do not replay internal memory traces, but are themselves dialogic actions.

This reinterpretation of the traditional social psychology in terms of rhetoric can be particularly seen in relation to the topic of attitudes. Traditionally, social psychologists have seen "attitudes" as the property of individuals, principally as internal cognitive and affective schemata. The discursive approach to "attitudes" examines how people give their opinions in talk, stressing rhetorical and argumentative dimensions (Billig, 1991; Potter & Wetherell, 1987). Detailed study of the language used by people giving their opinions shows that "attitudes" are rhetorical stances in matters of controversy. The discourse of such argumentation is complex. People rarely just express a personal view, but their expression typically contains a justification of their position. The discourse is ambivalent: the view is presented as subjective – as "their" view – as well as being justified as if objectively to a "universal audience". Both themes can be used as resources in discussion. "Well, that's my view" a speaker might say, in order to dismiss the counter-view and to signal their non-persuadibility. On the other hand, as justifications are given, "my view" will be presented as if it is more justified than the counter-views (Billig, 1991, 1992).

Some discursive psychology explicitly celebrates argument, at least argument-as-debate (see particularly, Billig, 1994, 1996). Partly, this has been a reaction against some forms of micro-sociology, particularly conversation analysis, that have seen disagreement as something that speakers tend to avoid. For instance, some analysts have argued that in speech there is a "preference for agreement", so that disagreement, or refusal to comply, is hedged by mitigations and excuses (Pomerantz, 1984; Bilmes, 1987). There are, however, some cultural contexts where argument, or disagreement, seems not to be hedged, and even, to quote Schiffrin (1984) is a "form of sociability" (see also Horowitz, 1996; Eder, 1990, 1993). The pragma-dialectical approach also implicitly favours agreement, by tending to treat argument, or disagreement, as something to be resolved by rational debate, rather than something whose perpetuation is celebrated (van Eemeren & Grottendorst, 1988).

The celebration of argument is not necessarily a contradiction of Tannen's (1998) critique of the "argument culture", for, as has been suggested, Tannen is referring to a particular confrontational style of conducting a debate. The celebration of argument underlines the creative aspects of discussion. In debate, speakers will formulate utterances, which they have never made before. They will move the talk to new topics – the classic example being the speakers in the fictionalized Socratic debates of Plato. There will be what one analyst has called "topic progression" (Foppa, 1990). Negativity is necessary for this to occur: with complete agreement between speakers, topic progression is unlikely (Billig, 1996).

As speakers move the topic of debate, and as they formulate novel utterances of justification and criticism, so they are engaging in thoughtful activity. One might say that the outward conversational moves are themselves the processes of thought. Utterances can occur too quickly – too spontaneously – to assume that they must be the outward reflection of a prior internal mental state. Instead, analysts, who are studying the details of conversational discussion, may be said to be studying directly processes of thinking (Billig, 1991, 1996).

This provides a clue to the question "How do children learn to think?" If a greater part of human thinking is based in language, then in learning to partake in conversation children are acquiring the resources for thinking. As children partake in conversations, they learn what sorts of justifications and criticisms are to be considered as "reasonable" and convincing (Pontecorvo & Fasulo, 1995; Fasulo & Pontecorvo, 1994). Moreover, the developmental movement is from outward participation in dialogue towards what Vygotsky (1987) called "inner speech". Private individual deliberation about issues, such as the character of friends, what to do tomorrow, morality and so on, involves internal debate. By being incorporated into the sorts of ordinary conversations that saturate the social world, the child acquires the rhetorical skills for internal debate. Consequently, conversational dialogue, in a real sense, provides the resources for thinking. This position takes seriously the remark of the Eleatic Stranger in Plato's dialogue *The Sophist* that "thought and speech are the same; only, the former, which is a silent conversation of the soul with itself, has been given the special name of thought" (Plato, 1948 edn, 263e).

DIALOGIC REPRESSION

Always in the matter of argumentation there is another side to be told: not all is unmitigated celebration. The rhetorical devices of justification and criticism, which enable topics, and thereby thoughts, to be opened up, also permit the closing down of dialogue, and thus the avoidance of thought. This provides clues to the operation of sort of avoidance, which lies at the root of Freud's concept of repression (Billig, 1997a, 1998a, 1999). The ideal explorative, non-agonistic debate by no means always occurs. Not only are there the possibilities of confrontation and quarrel, but also what Kleiner (1998) calls "pseudo-argument". In the pseudo-argument, speakers combine to agree on a point, while using the rhetorical format of argumentation. The participants do not dispute among themselves, as they collectively argue against a non-present, imagined other. In Kleiner's data, white participants were using pseudo-arguments to criticise black others. Because there is combined agreement, counter-arguments were not brought into the debate. Such dialogues provide a clue about Freudian repression. As Billig (1997b) showed, in regard to white English speakers talking about the British Royal Family, a taboo issue, such as that of race, could be collectively avoided. Racial motivations might be discursively projected onto "others"; awkward askable questions might be left unanswered; and the whole topic might be quickly dismissed from the conversation. Consequently, a dialogic repression might be collectively accomplished.

It has been suggested that the child's entry into the world of dialogue necessitates acquiring the skills of repression (Billig, 1997a, 1999). Appropriate talk demands the routine accomplishment and display of politeness. Other speakers cannot be interrupted, indirectness must be appropriately employed etc. Young children typically do not show the practices of adult dialogic politeness, but need to be taught the appropriate codes. However, they often show pleasure in breaking these codes, indulging in the pleasures of rudeness. However, the temptation of rudeness must be resisted and the resistance must become routine (Dunn, 1988). Consequently, one might say that the temptation of rudeness must be repressed, if the child is to develop into a mature speaker. It has been argued that this routine repression contains the clue to understanding the wider Freudian concept of repression (Billig, 1999). In order to repress, one must acquire the skills of repression and these come from acquiring the skills of language, for language is simultaneously both expressive and repressive. Adults in speaking to children, especially when attempting to prevent children from talking about taboo, or socially unacceptable, matters, often use, and thereby teach, children the rhetoric devices of topic-shifting and so on. Consequently, the child grows up learning to repress temptation dialogically and being equipped with the rhetorical means for doing so.

The inner processes of repression can be viewed as the internalization of the outer rhetorics of conversation. Rhetoric not only provides the linguistic devices for opening up debate, but also the means for closing down talk, or shifting dialogue onto other matters (see, for instance, Drew, 1995, on "topic-shifts"). Such devices can be applied to one's own internal debates, shifting the focus of attention from disturbing matters. Repression, far from being a mysterious process of an unseen ego battling against a hidden id, as Freud presupposed, can be outwardly observed in conversation. Freud's classic case histories can be reinterpreted from this perspective, to show how the unconscious is dialogically created (Billig, 1998b, 1999). Little Hans, the young boy whose case Freud claimed to provide direct evidence for the Oedipus complex, can be heard to acquire the subtle rhetoric of repression (Billig, 1998c, 1999). This rhetoric is learnt from the parents, who themselves are routinely practising repression in their patterns of dialogue. From a theoretical perspective, the focus is not merely shifted from inner wordless processes to outer dialogue. It also moves from the Oedipal child to the Oedipal parents.

In conclusion, argument should not be seen as a single phenomenon. There are different types of argument: argument-as-quarrel, as-debate, as-reasoning and so on. The boundary lines between the various forms are hard to draw. Indeed, participants, in everyday life, can debate, or argue, whether they are engaging in debate or argument (Horowitz, 1996). In this regard, all academic research into the topic of argument might be called (or not called) an argument about (perhaps "for" or "against") argument.

REFERENCES

Antaki, C. (1994). *Explaining and arguing*. London: Sage.
Aristotle (1909). *Rhetoric*. Cambridge, UK: Cambridge University Press.
Bakhtin, M.M. (1986). *Speech genres and other late essays*. Austin, TX: University of Texas Press.
Billig, M. (1991). *Ideology and opinions*. London: Sage.
Billig, M. (1992). *Talking of the Royal Family*. London: Routledge.
Billig, M. (1994). Celebrating argument within psychology: Dialogue, negation and feminist critique. *Argumentation*, **8**, 49–61.
Billig, M. (1996). *Arguing and thinking: A rhetorical view of social psychology* (2nd edn). Cambridge, UK: Cambridge University Press.
Billig, M. (1997a). The dialogic unconscious: Psychoanalysis, discursive psychology and the nature of repression. *British Journal of Social Psychology*, **36**, 139–159.
Billig, M. (1997b). Keeping the white queen in play. In M. Fine, L. Weis, L.C. Powell & L.M. Wong (Eds), *Off white* (pp. 149–157). London: Routledge.
Billig, M. (1998a). Rhetoric and the unconscious. *Argumentation*, **12**, 199–219.
Billig, M. (1998b). Freud and Dora: Repressing an oppressed identity. *Theory, Culture and Society*, **14**, 29–55.
Billig, M. (1998c). Dialogic repression and the Oedipus Complex: Reinterpreting the Little Hans case. *Culture and Psychology*, **4**, 11–47.
Billig, M. (1999). *Freudian repression: Conversation creating the unconscious*. Cambridge, UK: Cambridge University Press.
Bilmes, J. (1987). The concept of preference in conversation analysis. *Language in Society*, **17**, 161–187.
Blair, A.J. (1998). The limits of the dialogue model of argument. *Argumentation*, **12**, 325–339.

Brown, P. & Levinson, S.C. (1987). *Politeness: Some universals in language use.* Cambridge, UK: Cambridge University Press.

Buttny, R. (1993). *Social accountability in communication.* London: Sage.

Cicero (1959). *De inventione.* London: Loeb Classical Library.

Drew, P. (1995). Conversation analysis. In J.A. Smith, R. Harré & L. Van Langenhove (Eds), *Rethinking methods in psychology* (pp. 64–79). Oxford: Blackwell.

Dunn, J. (1988). *The beginnings of social understanding.* Oxford: Blackwell.

Eder, D. (1990). Serious and playful disputes: Variations in conflict talk among female adolescents. In A.D. Grimshaw (Ed.), *Conflict talk.* Cambridge, UK: Cambridge University Press.

Eder, D. (1993). "Go get ya a French!" Romantic and sexual teasing among adolescent girls. In D. Tannen (Ed.), *Gender and conversational interaction.* New York: Oxford University Press.

Edwards, D. (1997). *Discourse and cognition.* London: Sage.

Edwards, D. & Potter, J. (1992). *Discursive psychology.* London: Sage.

Emmel, B., Resch, P. & Tenney, D. (1996). Introduction. In B. Emmel, P. Resch & D. Tenney (Eds), *Argument revisited; argument refined* (pp. ix–xxii). Thousand Oaks, CA: Sage.

Fasulo, A. & Pontecorvo, C. (1994). "Si, ma questa volta abbiamo detto la verità". Le strategie argomentative dei bambini nelle dispute familiari. *Rassegna di Psicologia,* **11**, 83–101.

Foppa, K. (1990). Topic progression and intention. In I. Marková & K. Foppa (Eds), *The dynamics of discourse.* Hemel Hempstead, UK: Harvester/Wheatsheaf.

Fulkerson, R. (1993). *Newseek* "My turn" columns and the concepts of rhetorical genre: A preliminary study. In T. Enos & S.C. Brown (Eds), *Defining the new rhetorics* (pp. 227–243). Newbury Park, CA: Sage.

Fulkerson, R. (1996). The Toulmin model of argument and the teaching of composition. In B. Emmel, P. Resch & D. Tenney (Eds), *Argument revisited; argument refined* (pp. 45–72). Thousand Oaks, CA: Sage.

Gage, J.T. (1996). The reasoned thesis: The E-words and argumentative writing as a process of inquiry. In B. Emmel, P. Resch & D. Tenney (Eds), *Argument revisited; argument refined* (pp. 3–18). Thousand Oaks, CA: Sage.

Gaonker, D.P. (1990). Rhetoric and its double: Reflections on the rhetorical turn in the human sciences. In H.W. Simons (Ed.), *The rhetorical turn* (pp. 341–366). Chicago: University of Chicago Press.

Goodwin, M.H. (1983). Aggravated correction and disagreement in children's conversations. *Journal of Pragmatics,* **7**, 657–677.

Goodwin, M.H. (1993). Tactical uses of stories: Participation framework within girls' and boys' disputes. In D. Tannen (Ed.), *Gender and conversational interaction.* New York: Oxford University Press.

Habermas, J. (1976). *The legitimation crisis.* London: Heinemann.

Harré, R. & Gillett, G. (1994). *The discursive mind.* London: Sage.

Hikins, J.W. (1995). The given of achievement and the reluctance to assent: Argument and inquiry in the post-postmodern world. *Argumentation,* **9**, 137–162.

Horowitz, A.D. (1996). "A good old argument": The discursive construction of family and research through argumentation. Unpublished PhD thesis, Loughborough University.

Hovland, C.I., Janis, I.L. & Kelley, H.H. (1953). *Communication and persuasion.* New Haven, CT: Yale University Press.

Irigaray, L. (1985). *This sex which is not one.* Ithaca, NY: Cornell University Press.

Jackson, S. (1998). Disputation by design. *Argumentation,* **12**, 183–198.

Kerferd, G.B. (1981). *The sophistic movement.* Cambridge, UK: Cambridge University Press.

Kitzinger, C. (1991). Feminism, psychology and the paradox of power. *Feminism and Psychology,* **1**, 111–129.

Kleiner, B. (1998). The modern racist ideology and its reproduction in "pseudo-argument". *Discourse and Society*, **9**, 187–215.

Kristeva, J. (1986). *The Kristeva reader*. Oxford: Blackwell.

Lakoff, G. & Johnson, M. (1980). *Metaphors we live by*. Chicago: University of Chicago Press.

Lutz, C. (1990). Morality, domination, and understandings of "justifiable anger" among the Ifaluk. In G.R. Semin & K.J. Gergen (Eds), *Everyday understandings* (pp. 204–221). London: Sage.

Maynard, D.W. (1985). How children start arguments. *Language in Society*, **14**, 1–30.

McGuire, W.J. (1964). Inducing resistance to persuasion: Some contemporary approaches. In L. Berkowitz (Eds), *Advances in experimental social psychology* (Vol. 1). New York: Academic Press.

Meyer, M. (1994). *Rhetoric, language and reason*. University Park, PA: Pennsylvania State University Press.

O'Keefe, D.J. (1977). Two concepts of argument. *Journal of the American Forensic Association*, **13**, 121–128.

Olsen, D.R. (1994). *The world on paper*. Cambridge, UK: Cambridge University Press.

Ong, W.J. (1981). *Fighting for life*. Ithaca, NY: Cornell University Press.

Ong, W.J. (1982). *Orality and literacy*. London: Methuen.

Perelman, C. & Olbrechts-Tyteca, L. (1971). *The new rhetoric*. Indiana, IN: University of Notre Dame Press.

Plato, (1948). *Sophist*. London: Loeb Classical Library.

Pomerantz, A. (1984). Agreeing and disagreeing with assessments: Some features of preferred/dispreferred turn shapes. In J.M. Atkinson & J. Heritage (Eds), *Structures of social action*. Cambridge, UK: Cambridge University Press.

Pontecorvo, C. & Fasulo, A. (1995). Learning to argue in family shared discourse. In L. Resnick, C. Pontecorvo & R. Saljo (Eds), *Discourse, tools and reasoning*. Berlin: Springer.

Potter, J. (1996). *Representing reality*. London: Sage.

Potter, J. & Wetherell, M. (1987). *Discourse and social psychology*. London: Sage.

Pratkanis, A. & Aronson, E. (1991). *The age of propaganda*. New York: Freeman.

Schiffrin, D. (1984). Jewish argument as sociability. *Language in Society*, **13**, 311–335.

Shotter, J. (1992). Bakhtin and Billig: Monological versus dialogical practices. *American Behavioral Scientist*, **36**, 8–21.

Simons, H.W. (1989). "Going meta" in political confrontations. In B. Gronbeck (Ed.), *Spheres of argument*. Annandale, VA: Speech Comunication Association.

Simons, H.W. (1990). The rhetoric of inquiry as an intellectual movement. In H.W. Simons (Ed.), *The rhetorical turn* (pp. 1–31). Chicago: University of Chicago Press.

Tannen, D. (1990). *You just don't understand*. New York: William Morrow.

Tannen, D. (1994). *Gender and discourses*. New York: Oxford University Press.

Tannen, D. (1998). *The argument culture*. London: Virago.

Toulmin, S. (1958). *The uses of argument*. Cambridge, UK: Cambridge University Press.

van Eemeren, F.H., Grootendorst, R., Jackson, S. & Jacobs, S. (1983). *Reconstructing argumentative discourse*. Tuscaloosa, AL: University of Alabama Press.

van Eemeren, F.H. & Grootendorst, R. (1988). Rationale for a pragma-dialectical perspective. *Argumentation*, **2**, 271–291.

Vickers, B. (1988). *In defence of rhetoric*. Oxford: Clarendon Press.

Vygotsky, L. (1987). *Thought and language*. Cambridge, MA: MIT Press.

Walton, D. (1992). *The place of emotion in language*. University Park, PA: Pennsylvania State University Press.

White, G.M. (1990). Moral discourse and the rhetoric of emotions. In C.A. Lutz & L. Abu-Lughod (Eds), *Language and the politics of emotion*. Cambridge, UK: Cambridge University Press.

Patronizing

Mary Lee Hummert
University of Kansas, Lawrence, USA
Ellen Bouchard Ryan
McMaster University, Hamilton, Ontario, Canada

Our interest in patronizing as a function of communication arose from our research programs on communication and aging. Observational studies (Caporael, 1981; Kemper, 1994) and self-reports of older individuals (Hummert & Mazloff, 2001; Seaver, 1994) highlighted communication practices of younger conversants for which "patronizing" seemed the most appropriate label. That is, the younger conversant, e.g., a staff member in a nursing home, addressed the older person in a manner that suggested a low opinion of the older conversant's competence: using loud volume, simple words and sentences, diminutives, inappropriate familiarity, etc. Further, many older informants indicated that they found these practices condescending and insulting. They essentially experienced the practices as a face threat (Brown & Levinson, 1987) to their core identity or value as a person. As a result, each of us has been drawn to the study of patronizing talk as an aspect of communication and aging.

In this chapter we first review the characteristics and consequences of patronizing communication in intergenerational interactions, the domain which has produced the largest body of empirical research. We then move beyond the communication and aging framework to a consideration of patronizing talk as it occurs across multiple types of interpersonal relationships. Second, we consider the role of the recipient of patronizing communication as a co-participant in its enactment and the ways in which this individual may move such exchanges toward more acceptable communication forms. We conclude the chapter with a discussion of the factors that may contribute to the occurrence of patronizing communication – putting some individuals at particular risk – and outline areas for future research.

The New Handbook of Language and Social Psychology.
Edited by W. Peter Robinson and Howard Giles.
© 2001 John Wiley & Sons Ltd.

Before we begin, however, we must acknowledge three dilemmas inherent in labeling any communication *patronizing*. First, patronizing is a highly valenced term. It embodies a negative assessment of one person's contribution to a conversation and implies that the person *intended* the contribution to diminish the other. While some communicators may have patronization as a goal (e.g., Tracy & Tracy, 1998), others may have positive relational goals – e.g., showing care or concern for the other – yet engage in communication practices that are functionally patronizing (Hummert & Ryan, 1996). It is only as a recipient of the communication or as an observer that the patronizing function is perceived. This leads us to the second dilemma in labeling communication patronizing: the label is directional in that it emphasizes the viewpoint of one party to the conversation – the recipient of the "patronizing" talk – when any communication episode is the joint enactment of the two individuals. Compounding this problem is the third dilemma: interpretation of a particular communication practice as patronizing may differ across recipients and observers depending upon their individual orientations to the talk, prior experiences, etc.

One response to these dilemmas would be to choose a less negative and judgmental label for these forms of communication, for example, *problematic talk* (Coupland, Wiemann & Giles, 1991b). We acknowledge these problems and will address the issues of intent, joint enactment of patronization, and ambiguity in interpretation. However, we have chosen to retain *patronizing* as a descriptor for these forms of communication. Despite its limitations, we feel that this label serves as a useful heuristic because, as the literature reviewed in the first section of this chapter will show, it fits people's experience of and emotional responses to these practices.

PATRONIZING COMMUNICATION: CHARACTERISTICS AND CONSEQUENCES

Within the communication and aging literature, patronizing communication has been defined as speech modifications in talk to older persons that are based on age stereotypes of incompetence and dependence (Ryan, Hummert & Boich, 1995). This definition encompasses a set of communication styles used in addressing older persons, ranging from the less extreme – *elderspeak* (Cohen & Faulkner, 1986; Kemper, 1994; Kemper & Harden, 1999) and *dependence-inducing* (Baltes, Neumann & Zank, 1994; Baltes & Wahl, 1996) – to the more extreme – *controlling talk* (Lanceley, 1985; Grainger, 1993) and *secondary baby talk* (Caporael, 1981; Sachweh, 1998). According to Ryan et al. (1995), verbal modifications include a simplified vocabulary, simple grammatical structures, repetitions, brief imperatives, diminutives, and nicknames, among others. Paralinguistic features include high pitch, exaggerated intonation, loud speech, slow rate, and exaggerated enunciation. These may be accompanied by other non-verbal behaviors suggesting inappropriate intimacy (e.g., pat on head), indifference (e.g., low eye contact), feigned deference (e.g., polite words while winking at third person), or irritation (e.g., hands on hips). Discourse level strategies of patronizing may involve ignoring, limited topic selection, or superficiality.

Patronizing communication has been documented in institutional (Caporael, 1981; de Wilde & de Bot, 1989; Gibb & O'Brien, 1990; Grainger, 1993; Sachweh, 1998) and non-institutional settings (Beisecker, 1989; Kemper, 1994; Kemper et al., 1996; Ryan & Cole, 1990). The extreme forms of secondary baby talk and controlling talk are often associated with institutional settings. For instance, Gibb and O'Brien (1990) provided the following excerpt from the talk of a nurse engaged in morning care of an older woman: "That's good. Now I'm going to put your top on before we stand you up. First of all, do a little jump up to release the nightgown. That's a good girl . . ." (p. 1395). This excerpt illustrates secondary baby talk in that it includes several of the characteristics of patronizing communication, including exaggerated praise, inclusive "we", and minimizing words (i.e., little jump). Together these characteristics construct a child-like identity for the resident and place the nurse in the role of a parent.

In non-institutional settings, the modifications may be more subtle. Consider the following exchange reported by Coupland, Coupland and Grainger (1991, p. 200) between May, age 79, and Jenny, age 38. May is describing how she gives her three grandchildren candy and some spending money when they come for Sunday dinner:

May: and the first words the boy says when he come in (.) Gran, sweeties? . . .
    and I give them 20 pence each. I say now that's their pocket money
Jenny: gosh, you manage to do that as well do you!

Considering that May's gift of 20 pence per grandchild sums to 60 pence, Jenny's amazement that May can manage this amount implicitly conveys not admiration, but a low opinion of May's financial position.

CONSEQUENCES OF PATRONIZING

In 1994, an editorial on life in a nursing home appeared in *Newsweek*. The author, Anna Mae Halgrim Seaver, had recently died at age 84. The editorial came from notes her son found after her death. Mrs. Seaver wrote:

> Why do you think the staff insists on talking baby talk when speaking to me? I understand English. I have a degree in music and am a certified teacher. Now I hear a lot of words that end in "y". Is this how my kids felt? My hearing aid works fine. There is little need for anyone to position their face directly in front of mine and raise their voice with those "y" words . . . Am I invisible? Have I lost my right to respect and dignity? . . . I am still a human being. I would like to be treated as one. (p. 11)

While the patronizing function of the modifications that constitute secondary baby talk described by Mrs Seaver and in the Gibb and O'Brien (1990) example may be more obvious than in the J. Coupland et al. (1991) example, both kinds carry potentially negative consequences for older persons. All patronizing talk conveys an assessment that the recipient is less competent than the speaker (Hummert & Ryan, 1996). Sometimes the modifications suggest that the recipient is less intelligent (e.g., simple, almost childish vocabulary), or has poorer memory (e.g., multiple repetitions), or is less capable of independent behavior (e.g., use of inclusive "we" for actions that only affect the recipient), or is physically weaker (e.g., unsolicited assistance), or is less competent on all of these dimensions (i.e., secondary baby talk) than the speaker. Regardless, older persons may accept these negative assessments as valid and incorporate them into their self-concept and subsequent behaviors.

Ryan et al. (1986) described this process in the Communication Predicament of Aging model (see also Coupland, Coupland & Giles, 1991a; Hummert, 1994). The predicament consists of a negative feedback cycle (Rodin & Langer, 1980) in which patronizing communication based on age stereotypes reinforces age stereotypical behaviors in older persons, leading to lower levels of cognitive and physical functioning as well as to lower self-esteem. Baltes and Wahl (1996) provided empirical support for this model, documenting an increase in dependent behaviors of nursing home residents addressed by staff using a dependency-support script. Likewise, J. Coupland et al. (1991) conducted a detailed analysis of the entire conversation between Jenny (age 38) and May (age 79), showing how May's contributions increasingly reflected the diminished view of her situation implicit in our excerpt from that conversation and Jenny's other comments during their meeting. J. Coupland et al. pointed out that this stood in stark contrast to the self-image May projected in a second conversation with another older woman. Finally, Kemper et al. (1996) reported that in a referential communication task older persons who were addressed with the modifications of patronizing communication (elderspeak) had lower assessments of their own communication abilities than older persons who did not experience the patronizing talk.

Other research has shown that there are evaluative consequences for persons who communicate in a patronizing way and for the recipient of the talk. In comparison to a speaker using a neutral speech style, a patronizing speaker is viewed as less warm, less respectful and more dominant (Ryan, Bourhis & Knops, 1991; Ryan, Hamilton & Kwong See, 1994; Ryan, MacLean & Orange, 1994). In comparison to the recipient of the neutral speech style, the recipient of patronizing talk is perceived as less satisfied, more dependent and less competent in both institutional (Ryan, Meredith & Shantz, 1994) and non-institutional settings (Harwood et al., 1997).

PATRONIZING COMMUNICATION IN OTHER INTERPERSONAL RELATIONSHIPS

Behaviors that serve a patronizing function have been reported as critical in other interpersonal interactions, although they have appeared under a variety of labels. These include verbal aggression and hate speech (Leets & Giles, 1997), face attack (Tracy & Tracy, 1998), verbal abuse (Buss, 1989), problematic talk and miscommunication (N. Coupland et al., 1991b; Coleman & DePaulo, 1991), condescending behaviors (Frodi, 1977; Buss, 1989) and neglecting behaviors (Buss, 1989). Consistent with the intergenerational framework, these labels identify patronizing behaviors varying in explicitness, from the blatant (e.g., verbal abuse, face attack) to the subtle (e.g., problematic talk, condescending). As might be expected, the relationships associated with these behaviors often involve individuals who, like older persons, may be stereotyped as incompetent or dependent, i.e., persons with mental illness (Francis, 1985), with developmental disabilities (DePaulo & Coleman, 1986; Markova, 1990), with physical disabilities (Braithwaite, 1990; Coleman & DePaulo, 1991; Emry & Wiseman, 1987; Fox & Giles, 1996; Kleck, 1968, 1969; Kleck, Ono & Hastorf, 1966; Thompson, 1982), of different races or ethnicities (Ben-David & Ben-Ari, 1997; Leets & Giles, 1997; Thackerar, Giles & Cheshire 1982).

For instance, Francis (1985) described the attitude of an emergency room orderly as condescending during her hospitalization for mental illness. He told her that she was going to "a nice department upstairs" (p. 2), which she knew was the psychiatric ward. Further, "the tone of his voice conveyed several messages quite clearly; I was not ill or deserving of sympathy; I was crazy; . . . because I was crazy I could be treated like a child" . . . (p. 2). Francis experienced similar patronizing from nurses and from her doctor, who did not consult with her about her treatment.

Able-bodied persons may also adopt behaviors that serve a patronizing function in communicating with individuals with disabilities. These include using low levels of eye contact (Kleck, 1968) or conversely staring (Braithwaite, 1990), increasing physical distance (Houston & Bull, 1994; Kleck, 1969), modifying opinions on sensitive topics (Kleck et al., 1966), making unsolicited (often unhelpful) offers of assistance (Braithwaite, 1990; Emry & Wiseman, 1987), asking very personal questions (Braithwaite, 1990), etc. An individual with a spinal cord injury reported being ignored by able-bodied persons as a common and patronizing experience: "If I'm with an able-bodied person and I go wheeling in [to the bank] . . . You think that clerk in the bank would talk to me when I'm in there to do business? No, that clerk continuously will talk to the able-bodied person . . . Because somehow, in their minds, hey, I'm not there – I'm a chair" (Braithwaite, 1990, p. 474).

Patronizing communication is not confined, however, to interactions in which obvious differences between the individuals (age, physical ability, race, illness, etc.) make negative stereotypes about the competence of one person salient. It can occur in friendships and marriages (Buss, 1989; Frodi, 1977) and in organizational contexts (Boggs & Giles, 1999; Tracy & Tracy, 1998) as well. In Frodi's (1977) survey of college students, women respondents named condescending behaviors as the most frequent source of anger in their friendships with both men and women, while male respondents named condescending behaviors most often by female friends and physical/verbal aggression by male friends as most likely to provoke anger. Buss (1989) found that condescending behaviors were also sources of anger and upset in romantic relationships and marriages. In both studies, the condescending behaviors fit our definition of patronizing communication. For Frodi (1977), condescending behaviors included "treats me like I'm no good, acts superior, tries to step on me, criticizes my personality, intellect, career" (p. 113), and for Buss (1989), condescending behaviors included "treated me like I was stupid or inferior; . . . tried to act like he/she was better than me" (p. 738). Buss described the condescending factor as involving "belittling the other, placing self on a superior plane, and an element of sexism" (p. 737).

Boggs and Giles (1999) showed how women may be the recipients of patronizing communication in the organizational context. Such patronizing includes labels (e.g., girls, dragon lady) and comments (e.g., on a woman's sexual attractiveness) that trivialize the contributions of women or that mark women as different from their male colleagues. As Boggs and Giles pointed out, such practices carry the implicit message that a woman is less competent, need not be taken as seriously, and is less "adult" than a man.

Tracy and Tracy (1998) provided examples of two 911 emergency calls in which the 911 dispatchers, professionals trained to handle all types of calls calmly and with respect for callers, exhibited apparently purposeful disrespect and contempt. Tracy and Tracy termed these behaviors face attack, but they could as easily be classified as patronizing. For instance, dispatchers used rising volume and controlled enunciation that effectively indicated the incompetence of the caller. In response to a caller's query "How long do I have to wait though"? (p. 235), one dispatcher replied: "Until SOMEBODY GETS (.) THERE. You're *not* listening. I can't *tell* you any better than that" (p. 235). Dispatchers also used reprimands that attacked the personhood of the caller, e.g., "You're getting hysterical for no reason" (p. 232). Their enactment of patronizing ranged from the extreme use of profanity ("I *know* what the fuck I'm talking about, okay *bitch*", p. 233) to more subtle delivery variations ("like FOR WHATEVER REASON you're calling me", p. 245).

Across relationship types, the consequences of patronizing are similar to those we outlined in reference to communication and aging: loss of self-esteem, lower levels of performance, and less satisfaction with the relationship (Boggs & Giles, 1999; Buss, 1989; Coleman & DePaulo, 1991; Emry & Wiseman, 1987; Francis, 1985; Frodi, 1977). The consensus is that these behaviors may be especially harmful to the self-esteem of members of stigmatized groups such as persons with disabilities and those with psychiatric disorders. As Francis (1985) argued, since many psychiatric disorders are accompanied by drops in self-esteem, the patronizing communication of staff may exacerbate this loss and be counterproductive to the recovery process. Theorists also associate patronizing communication with a negative feedback cycle leading to less independent and competent behavior on the part of the recipient of patronizing talk (Coleman & DePaulo, 1991; Emry & Wiseman, 1987). Recipients may display "learned helplessness" (Emry & Wiseman, 1987; Markova, 1990) as they match their behavior to the expectations implicit in patronizing talk.

This literature highlights the emotional and relational consequences for recipients and their partners more than does the intergenerational literature, however. As the work of Frodi (1977) and Buss (1989) shows, patronizing behaviors are a major source of anger in friendships and romantic relationships, and anger is also a response experienced by those with disabilities (Coleman & DePaulo, 1991). As a result of these negative emotions, both parties may find the interaction so uncomfortable that they avoid future contact not only with each other, but also with other similar persons (Coleman & DePaulo, 1991). Patronizing communication can also be quite serious for intimate relationships. In one study, Buss (1989) examined the relationships among sources of anger, marital satisfaction, and sexual satisfaction in 107 newlywed couples. For the wives in the study, condescending behaviors by the partner were negatively related to both marital and sexual satisfaction.

THE RECIPIENT OF PATRONIZING COMMUNICATION

Every communication interaction is the joint accomplishment of (at least) two persons. Yet, as we noted at the beginning of this chapter, a focus on patronizing communication tends to identify one individual as the "perpetrator" of the patronizing act and the other as the "innocent target". Further, it emphasizes the viewpoint of this innocent target in labeling the act *patronizing*. To a certain extent, this problem stems from our lived experience of communication as serial; it may also derive from the powerful emotions elicited by communication that acquires the patronizing label. Here we consider the role of the recipient of patronizing communication in its enactment, and the ways in which the conversational contributions of this individual may reinforce the negative cycle or reverse it for a more positive interaction.

Individuals in stigmatized groups may modify their communication style with those outside their group, just as outsiders do with them (Coleman & DePaulo, 1991; Markova, 1990). For example, Comer and Piliavin (1972) found that disabled participants who interacted with an able-bodied confederate terminated the interview sooner, used less eye contact, and smiled less than did disabled participants who interacted with the same confederate posing as a disabled person. Further, disabled participants reported liking the confederate less and feeling less comfortable with him when he was able-bodied than when he was disabled. This study suggests the possibility that communicative acts of others seen as patronizing by those in stigmatized groups (e.g., low eye contact) may be influenced by and matched to their own behaviors.

This is further complicated by the ambiguity of communication. As Coleman and DePaulo (1991) point out, our interpretations of others' behaviors often fit our expectations. To the extent that able-bodied persons expect those with disabilities to be anxious and reluctant to interact, they may interpret the types of behaviors reported in Comer and Piliavin (1972) as confirming their expectations. As a result, "they might then proceed to act even more in line with those initial (and perhaps erroneous) expectations, thereby exacerbating the cycle of stigma" (Coleman & DePaulo, p. 75).

In other instances, individuals may be forced into positions by a disability, temporary illness, or age which make them dependent on others. A request for assistance by such individuals may be interpreted as evidence of their dependence and result in a patronizing response, when the same request from another person (younger, without the illness or disability) would not (Coleman & De-Paulo, 1991).

Responses to Patronizing Communication

Just as patronizing can occur in many forms, so can responses to patronizing. We consider first two extremes: confrontation and passive acceptance. The tendency for patronizing behaviors to evoke anger in those patronized (Braithwaite, 1990; Buss, 1989; Coleman & DePaulo, 1991; Emry & Wiseman, 1987; Frodi, 1977) may mean that a confrontational response is the first choice of a patronized individual. In some cases, an angry response may be necessary, particularly when the patronizing is purposeful as in Tracy and Tracy's (1998) examples of face attack or when other efforts to change the behavior of the patronizer have failed. However, being patronizing in return may not be the optimal choice as a general rule. Responding in a condescending way may only confirm some negative stereotypes (e.g., bad temper, antisocialism; Hummert & Flora, 1999) and increase the discomfort of both individuals. Recall the disabled person quoted earlier who described being ignored by a bank clerk. That individual described the following tactic for dealing with the situation: ". . . I speak up and say, 'Hey, he or she is not the one here to do business. It's me.' And then they get all embarrassed and flustered and everything" (Braithwaite, 1990, p. 474). This type of response is effective in establishing the independence of the patronized person, but it also attacks the face of the patronizer by calling attention to his or her failings as a communicator, just as the patronizing communication attacked the face of the recipient.

Some individuals, on the other hand, may become comfortable in dependent positions, as "learned helplessness" suggests (Emry & Wiseman, 1987). They may develop a tolerance for what we have labeled patronizing due either to continued exposure or because it is the only type of social interaction available (Baltes & Wahl, 1996; Ryan et al., 1986). Nursing home residents, for example, judged the intonation contours of secondary baby talk less negatively than did community-dwelling seniors (Whitbourne, Culgin & Cassidy, 1996; Ryan & Cole, 1990). Nursing home residents also showed greater tolerance for patronizing communication than staff or community-dwelling seniors (Ryan et al., 2000). Tolerance may not indicate liking for patronizing talk, but a tolerant recipient may be more likely to accept the patronizing without challenge than a less tolerant one. Unfortunately, passive responses to patronizing serve to reinforce staff and others in their use of these strategies (Hummert & Ryan, 1996), making recipients more at risk for the negative consequences of patronizing.

Clearly, confrontational and passive responses to patronizing are not the optimal choices for either participant in an interaction. Patronizing communication seems to emerge most often when one person chooses strategies with reference to stereotypical competencies rather than to actual ones (Coleman & DePaulo, 1991; N. Coupland et al., 1991a; Hummert & Ryan, 1996, Ryan et al., 1986, 1995). That is, one individual sees the other not as a unique person, but as a *type* of person. Confrontational and passive responses reinforce those stereotypes (Hummert & Flora, 1999; Harwood & Giles, 1996). Effective responses to patronizing may be those that move the patronizer to see the recipient as an individual while affirming the identity of the patronizer.

Persons with acquired disabilities told Braithwaite (1990) of several tactics they used to get able-bodied individuals to see them as persons first, and persons with a disability after that or not at all. A statement from one interviewee described an assertive response strategy for personal questions: "If they have asked a direct question I will answer it very directly and then immediately change the subject if it has no bearing on what we're talking about . . . I'd much rather get it out of the way . . . and then just go on with the purpose that for some reason we've been thrown together" (Braithwaite, 1990, p. 477). By using this assertive strategy, the interviewee provides an answer to the other person's question, but at the same time skillfully takes control of the conversation, moving it to a less sensitive topic. Other interviewees identified assertiveness as their preferred means for managing help situations. They emphasized that they would rather request help from able-bodied persons when necessary than let them offer to help. When others did offer assistance first, these interviewees accepted the help willingly only if the helpers followed their directions.

Although assertiveness establishes the independence of a person who has been patronized, it can be perceived negatively from a relational perspective in certain contexts. As one disabled person stated, some people "get very angry if you say, 'Do you mind not holding me round the waist, it makes things a bit difficult' . . . They get rather huffy and say, 'I'm only trying to help, dear,' and stalk off" (Emry & Wiseman, p. 16; originally from Shearer, 1984). In the intergenerational context, an older assertive responder was perceived as more competent (in community settings) and more in control of the conversation than a passive responder, but the assertive responder and patronizer were also rated as less satisfied with the interaction (Harwood et al., 1993, 1997; Ryan et al., 2000). It may be that direct assertive responses carry an implicit threat to the face of the patronizer.

An examination (Hummert & Mazloff, 2001) of older participants' responses to a patronizing message revealed an additional response type labeled *appreciative*. Like the assertive responders, appreciative responders established their autonomy and competence in their responses, but the appreciative responders also indicated that they valued the patronizer's input. These appreciative responses emphasized the face (Brown & Levinson, 1987) of both recipient and patronizer more than did the assertive responses. In a subsequent study (Hummert & Flora, 1999), students and nursing home staff rated appreciative responders as more competent and their conversational partners as more satisfied than assertive, passive, or condescending responders.

Ryan et al. (2000) suggest that a humorous response to patronizing, like an appreciative response, may protect the face of both individuals. Work in clinical settings, for example, shows that humor is a useful coping strategy for older adults, especially women (Thorson & Powell, 1996). Humor can diffuse an otherwise awkward situation by allowing recipients to comment on the patronizing in a socially acceptable way. In addition, recipients can establish their individuality by being funny or witty, and in doing so demonstrate their competence. Use of humor is illustrated in the following refusal of a nursing home resident to a patronizing request to join in yet another craft activity: "I think I'll just pass today. I've made more crafts in my lifetime than an over-achieving Girl Guide group at Christmas" (Ryan et al., 2000, p. 278). Ryan et al. found that listeners evaluated this humorous, indirectly assertive response more positively than a directly assertive response ("I've already planned to watch my favourite TV program, so I won't have time to go today") and a passive response ("I'd rather not, but if you insist, I'll go").

Of the response forms studied to date, appreciative and humorous responses seem to hold the most promise in terms of simultaneously establishing the competence of a person who has been patronized and ensuring a positive interpersonal experience for both parties (Hummert & Flora, 1999; Ryan et al., 2000). Their effectiveness seems to derive from their emphasis on preserving the face of both interactants.

CONCLUSIONS AND FUTURE DIRECTIONS

As the discussion in this chapter has shown, patronizing communication is a robust phenomenon occurring across multiple interpersonal relationships and with potentially serious consequences for the people involved. An assumption underlying this discussion is that there are commonalities in the communication process across these various relationships that constitute certain behaviors as patronizing. We turn now to a consideration of those commonalities.

Although patronizing can occur even in intimate, long-term relationships (Buss, 1989), the literature suggests that it is most likely in interactions between strangers or acquaintances when there are distinct differences in the group identities of the conversants, and the group identity of one conversant is associated with negative stereotypes of incompetence and dependence (age, physical disability, etc.). The relationship of patronizing communication to such stereotypes has been documented in the communication and aging case (Hummert &

Shaner, 1994; Hummert et al., 1998; Ytsma & Giles, 1997). However, communicators do not appear to have the production of patronizing communication as their goal. Rather, the negative age stereotypes encompass beliefs about diminished communication skills of older individuals (Hummert, Garstka & Shaner, 1995; Ryan et al., 1992), and it is in modifying their behavior to fit those beliefs rather than the actual competencies of an older person that they construct patronizing messages. Ironically, those who give patronizing messages may be trying to be effective communicators, a possibility acknowledged in the communication and disability literature as well (Braithwaite, 1990; Coleman & DePaulo, 1991; Emry & Wiseman, 1987).

In a previous work (Hummert & Ryan, 1996), we showed how patronizing talk to older persons could be conceptualized as the relationship between a communicator's enactment of goals (care/relational, control/task) and the face (identity) of the older person. Our argument drew strongly on communication accommodation theory (Giles, Coupland & Coupland, 1991) and politeness theory (Brown & Levinson, 1987). Key aspects of that argument apply, we believe, to the general case of patronizing.

Communication Goals, Social Knowledge, and Patronizing

In most interactions, communicators have multiple goals such as showing care for the other, exerting control over the other, and maintaining positive personal identities (Tracy, 1991). Balancing these sometimes disparate goals – e.g., care and control – creates a challenge for communicators. Communicators draw on their social knowledge, including stereotypes, in order to respond to this challenge and to meet their overarching goal of being effective communicators. In the terms of communication accommodation theory (Giles et al., 1991), communicators use their social knowledge to *accommodate* their talk to a particular person, in a particular context, to accomplish a particular set of goals. Ironically, this reliance on social knowledge may contribute to patronizing communication.

Behavior demanded for effective communication by a stereotype, for example, may create an inherent conflict between simultaneously accomplishing care, control and identity goals. If the stereotype identifies a person as having diminished cognitive ability (as does the age stereotype), it would suggest the need for short, simple phrases or brief imperatives to exert control. However, showing care and protecting the face of the other person would require a longer, more elaborated statement. In this example, structuring talk in reference only to the stereotype may lead to patronizing communication by conveying a low opinion of the other person's competence.

Likewise, social knowledge about contexts and power relationships within contexts may play a role in patronizing. In a physician's office, for example, patients are positioned as less powerful than the doctor. These power differences may be communicated in several ways that the patient experiences as patronizing: the doctor is addressed by title (Dr X), while the patient is addressed by first name or by a role (e.g., "Mom" used by pediatrician to mother of the patient); the doctor controls the turn-taking and length of the visit; the doctor may ignore patient's questions, etc. (Beisecker, 1989; Greene et al., 1994). Social norms for appropriate behavior in such settings may engender patronizing.

This discussion reinforces our earlier statement that patronizing may not be intentional, but may arise from reliance on stereotypes and practices embedded in social contexts. This does not mean, however, that patronizing cannot sometimes be intentional. As Tracy and Tracy (1998) showed, certain strategies are so blatantly face-threatening that they can only be construed as intentional.

Patronizing as Face Threat

Central to the concept of patronizing, as we acknowledged at the beginning of this chapter, is the interpretation by one person that the other's communication constitutes a face threat to his or her core identity, i.e., value as a person. In contrast to Brown and Levinson's (1987) focus on strategies of politeness, the topic of patronizing could be seen as a focus on strategies of impoliteness (Tracy & Tracy, 1998). Because communication is inherently ambiguous, this interpretation is most straightforward when the patronizing is explicit and blatant, such as in face attack or verbal abuse, than when it is implicit and subtle, such as in behavioral norms for a particular context.

Paradoxically, implicit patronizing may carry greater potential for harm than explicit patronizing. With explicit patronizing, the patronizing messages (you are inferior, incompetent, etc.) are laid out clearly for recipients to accept or reject. Recipients may be able to identify explicit patronizing as a problem of the patronizer rather than as evidence of their own deficiencies (Coleman & DePaulo, 1991). In contrast, implicit patronizing may not even be noticed by some recipients or be seen as a normal part of the context. Because implicit patronizing is less obvious, it may be harder to defend against and therefore more damaging to recipients over the long term (Coleman & DePaulo, 1991; Hummert & Ryan, 1996; Levy, 1996).

Future Research

Each of these issues is worthy of attention in future research. The influence of negative stereotypes on use of patronizing strategies has been confirmed only with age stereotypes, and then only in the case of stereotypes about older people. Younger persons also report being patronized by older ones (Giles & Williams, 1994; Williams & Giles, 1996), which could be grounded in negative stereotypes about the competence of young people. The hypothesized ties between stereotypes of incompetence and dependence for other groups (races, ethnicities, those with disabilities, psychiatric disorders, etc.) and patronizing remain to be tested, as do the relationships between context-based social norms and patronizing.

Such research may also reveal which strategies are relationship/context-spanning and which are relationship/context-specific (Tracy & Tracy, 1998). In their discussion of face attack, Tracy and Tracy suggested that explicit strategies may be more likely to be perceived similarly across contexts and relationships, while implicit strategies may be more specific to particular contexts and relationships. The most specific ways of accomplishing patronizing are probably associated with close interpersonal relationships such as friendships and marriages. This type of information would be especially useful in developing training manuals for contexts in which patronizing practices are socially entrenched.

Identifying which patronizing practices are culture/language-specific and which are culture/language-spanning is also a necessary focus for future research. Patronizing communication to older individuals takes similar forms in several Western cultures, including the USA (Caporael, 1981), UK (Grainger, 1993), Canada (Ryan et al., 1991), Australia (Edwards & Noller, 1998), Germany (Sachweh, 1998), and the Netherlands (de Wilde & de Bot, 1989). However, initial research suggests that these forms are not perceived as patronizing when presented in Chinese to residents of Hong Kong (Giles et al., 1998). A complete understanding of patronizing requires a focus on the ways in which it is enacted in non-Western cultures and languages.

Other important areas for future research include outcomes and response strategies. Links between patronizing and outcomes like lower self-esteem and lower functioning (cognitive, physical or social) have been reported in a few studies with older individuals (Baltes & Wahl, 1996; Edwards & Noller, 1998), but that research must be extended to include patronizing in other types of relationships, as well as the dynamics that lead to negative outcomes for some individuals but not for others (e.g., O'Connor & Rigby, 1996). As we have discussed, recipients may respond to patronizing in a number of ways, including passive acceptance. Passive acceptance of patronizing may support the cycle, increasing an individual's vulnerability to negative outcomes. Research attention to effective response strategies for reversing the patronizing cycle is essential. The most promising response forms so far are humorous and appreciative, both of which simultaneously establish the competence of the patronized person and preserve the face of the patronizer. As such, they are representative of an array of possible response strategies fitted to context and participants. We believe that those who have experienced patronizing first hand can help in this process. Support groups, for example, may constitute rich depositories of social knowledge about effective response strategies for particular contexts and participants.

Our discussion in this chapter indicates that patronizing is an accurate description of certain forms of communication across a wide variety of relationships. It is accurate because it captures the essence of individuals' emotional responses to these communication forms: they feel diminished and devalued by the other, whether that person is a stranger in a professional setting (e.g., Francis, 1985) or a spouse (e.g., Buss, 1989). However, our discussion also reveals that the factors which contribute to patronizing – negative stereotypes of incompetence and contextual influences on communication norms – put some individuals at greater risk to experience it. Thus we have poignant examples of patronizing directed toward persons from marginalized groups: older individuals, persons with disabilities, persons with psychiatric disorders, etc. Prolonged exposure to such behaviors may carry serious consequences for all persons; but for those persons whose personal circumstances create implicit challenges to self-esteem, the negative impact of patronizing is magnified. Research of the types outlined here will help us to understand and ameliorate the effects of patronizing behaviors, strategies of impoliteness particularly threatening to identity and well-being.

ACKNOWLEDGEMENTS

Preparation of this chapter was supported by a grant from the US National Institute on Aging/National Institutes of Health and a sabbatical leave provided by the University of Kansas to Dr Hummert, and by a grant from the Social Sciences and Humanities Research Council of Canada to Dr Ryan.

REFERENCES

Baltes, M.M., Neumann, E.-M. & Zank, S. (1994). Maintenance and rehabilitation of independence in old age: An intervention program for staff. *Psychology and Aging*, **9**, 179–188.

Baltes, M.M. & Wahl, H.W. (1996). Patterns of communication in old age: The dependency-support and independence-ignore script. *Health Communication*, **8**, 217–231.

Beisecker, A.E. (1989). The influence of a companion on the doctor–elderly patient interaction. *Health Communication*, **1**, 55–70.

Ben-David, A. & Ben-Ari, A.T. (1997). The experience of being different: Black Jews in Israel. *Journal of Black Studies*, **27**, 510–527.

Boggs, C. & Giles, H. (1999). "The canary in the coalmine": The nonaccommodation cycle in the gendered workplace. *International Journal of Applied Linguistics*, **9**, 223–245.

Braithwaite, D.O. (1990). From majority to minority: An analysis of cultural change from ablebodied to disabled. *International Journal of Intercultural Relations*, **14**, 465–483.

Brown, P. & Levinson, S. (1987). *Politeness: Universals in language usage*. Cambridge, UK: Cambridge University Press.

Buss, D.M. (1989). Conflict between the sexes: Strategic interference and the evocation of anger and upset. *Journal of Personality and Social Psychology*, **56**, 735–747.

Caporael, L.R. (1981). The paralanguage of caregiving: Baby talk to the institutionalized aged. *Journal of Personality and Social Psychology*, **40**, 876–884.

Cohen, G. & Faulkner, D. (1986). Does "elderspeak" work? The effect of intonation and stress on comprehension and recall of spoken discourse in old age. *Language & Communication*, **6**, 91–98.

Coleman, L.M. & DePaulo, B.M. (1991). Uncovering the human spirit: Moving beyond disability and "missed" communication. In N. Coupland, H. Giles & J.M. Wiemann (Eds), *"Miscommunication" and problematic talk* (pp. 61–84). Newbury Park, CA: Sage.

Comer, R.J. & Piliavin, J.A. (1972). The effects of physical deviance upon face-to-face interaction: The other side. *Journal of Personality and Social Psychology*, **23**, 33–39.

Coupland, J., Coupland, N. & Grainger, K. (1991). Intergenerational discourse: Contextual versions of ageing and elderliness. *Ageing and Society*, **11**, 189–208.

Coupland, N., Coupland, J. & Giles, H. (1991a). *Language, society and the elderly*. Oxford: Basil Blackwell.

Coupland, N., Wiemann, J.M. & Giles, H. (1991b). Talk as "problem" and communication as "miscommunication": An integrative analysis. In N. Coupland, H. Giles & J.M. Wiemann (Eds), *"Miscommunication" and problematic talk* (pp. 1–17). Newbury Park, CA: Sage.

DePaulo, B.M. & Coleman, L.M. (1986). Talking to children, foreigners, and retarded adults. *Journal of Personality and Social Psychology*, **51**, 945–959.

de Wilde, I. & de Bot, K. (1989). Taal van verzorgenden tegen ouderen in een psychogeriatrisch verpleeghuis [A simplified register in caregivers' speech to elderly demented patients]. *Tijdschrift voor Gerontologie en Geriatrie*, **20**, 97–100.

Edwards, H. & Noller, P. (1998). Factors influencing caregiver-carereceiver communication and its impact on the well-being of older carereceivers. *Health Communication*, **10**, 317–341.

Emry, R. & Wiseman, R.L. (1987). An intercultural understanding of ablebodied and disabled persons' communication. *International Journal of Intercultural Relations*, **11**, 7–27.

Fox, S. & Giles, H. (1996). Interability communication: Evaluating patronizing encounters. *Journal of Language and Social Psychology*, **15**, 265–290.

Francis, R. (1985). Residual prejudice in the helping profession. *Canada's Mental Health*, September, 2–3.

Frodi, A. (1977). Sex differences in perception of a provocation: A survey. *Perceptual and Motor Skills*, **44**, 113–114.

Gibb, H. & O'Brien, B. (1990). Jokes and reassurances are not enough: Ways in which nurses related through conversation with elderly clients. *Journal of Advanced Nursing*, **15**, 1389–1401.

Giles, H. & Williams, A. (1994). Intergenerational patronizing: Young people's evaluations of older people's patronizing speech. *International Journal of Aging and Human Development*, **39**, 33–53.

Giles, H., Coupland, N. & Coupland, J. (1991). Accommodation theory: Communication, context, and consequence. In H. Giles, J. Coupland & N. Coupland (Eds), *Contexts of accommodation: Developments in applied linguistics* (pp. 1–68). Cambridge, UK: Cambridge University Press.

Giles, H., Harwood, J., Clément, R., Pierson, H. & Fox, S. (1998). Stereotypes of the elderly and evaluations of patronizing speech: A cross-cultural foray. In R.K. Agnihotri & A.L. Khanna (Eds), *Social psychological perspectives on second language learning (Research in applied linguistics series IV)* (pp. 151–186). New Delhi: Sage.

Grainger, K. (1993). "That's a lovely bath dear": Reality construction in the discourse of elderly care. *Journal of Aging Studies*, **7**, 247–262.

Greene, M.G., Adelman, R.D., Rizzo, C. & Friedmann, E. (1994). The patient's presentation of self in an initial medical encounter. In M.L. Hummert, J.M. Wiemann & J.F. Nussbaum (Eds), *Interpersonal Communication in Older Adulthood* (pp. 226–250). Thousand Oaks, CA: Sage.

Harwood, J. & Giles, H. (1996). Reactions to older people being patronized: The roles of response strategies and attributed thoughts. *Journal of Language and Social Psychology*, **15**, 395–421.

Harwood, J., Giles, H., Fox, S., Ryan, E.B. & Williams, A. (1993). Patronizing young and elderly adults: Response strategies in a community setting. *Journal of Applied Communication Research*, **21**, 211–226.

Harwood, J., Ryan, E.B., Giles, H. & Tysoski, S. (1997). Evaluations of patronizing speech and three response styles in a non-service-providing context. *Journal of Applied Communication Research*, **25**, 170–195.

Houston, V. & Bull, R. (1994). Do people avoid sitting next to someone who is facially disfigured? *European Journal of Social Psychology*, **24**, 279–284.

Hummert, M.L. (1994). Stereotypes of the elderly and patronizing speech style. In M.L. Hummert, J.M. Wiemann & J.F. Nussbaum (Eds), *Interpersonal communication in older adulthood: Interdisciplinary theory and research* (pp. 162–185). Newbury Park, CA: Sage.

Hummert, M.L. & Flora, J. (1999). *Responses to patronizing talk: Perceptions of college students and nursing home staff.* Paper submitted to the Fourth International Conference on Communication, Aging, and Health, Brisbane, Australia.

Hummert, M.L. & Mazloff, D. (2001). Older adults' responses to patronizing advice: Balancing politeness and identity in context. *Journal of Language and Social Psychology*, **20**, 168–196.

Hummert, M.L. & Ryan, E.B. (1996). Toward understanding variations in patronizing talk addressed to older adults: Psycholinguistic features of care and control. *International Journal of Psycholinguistics*, **12**, 149–169.

Hummert, M.L. & Shaner, J.L. (1994). Patronizing speech to the elderly as a function of stereotyping. *Communication Studies*, **45**, 145–158.

Hummert, M.L., Garstka, T.A. & Shaner, J.L. (1995). Beliefs about language performance: Adults' perceptions about self and elderly targets. *Journal of Language and Social Psychology*, **14**, 235–259.

Hummert, M.L., Shaner, J.L., Garstka, T.A. & Henry, C. (1998). Communication with older adults: The influence of age stereotypes, context, and communicator age. *Human Communication Research*, **25**, 124–151.

Kemper, S. (1994). "Elderspeak": Speech accommodations to older adults. *Aging and cognition*, **1**, 17–28.

Kemper, S. & Harden, T. (1999). Experimentally disentangling what's beneficial about elderspeak from what's not. *Psychology and Aging*, **14**, 656–670.

Kemper, S., Othick, M., Warren, J., Gubarchuk, J. & Gerhing, H. (1996). Facilitating older adults' performance on a referential communication task through speech accommodations. *Aging, Neuropsychology, and Cognition*, **3**, 37–55.

Kleck, R. (1968). Physical stigma and nonverbal cues emitted in face-to-face interaction. *Human Relations*, **21**, 119–128.

Kleck, R. (1969). Physical stigma and task oriented interactions. *Human Relations*, **22**, 53–60.

Kleck, R., Ono, H. & Hastorf, A.H. (1966). The effects of physical deviance upon face-to-face interaction. *Human Relations*, **19**, 425–436.

Lanceley, A. (1985). Use of controlling language in the rehabilitation of the elderly. *Journal of Advanced Nursing*, **10**, 125–135.

Leets, L. & Giles, H. (1997). Words as weapons – when do they wound? Investigations of harmful speech. *Human Communication Research*, **24**, 260–301.

Levy, B. (1996). Improving memory in old age through implicit self-stereotyping. *Journal of Personality and Social Psychology*, **71**, 1092–1107.

Markova, I. (1990). Language and communication in mental handicap. In H. Giles & W.P. Robinson (Eds), *Handbook of language and social psychology* (pp. 363–380). Chichester, UK: Wiley.

O'Connor, B.P. & Rigby, H. (1996). Perceptions of baby talk, frequency of receiving baby talk and self-esteem among community and nursing home residents. *Psychology and Aging*, **11**, 147–154.

Rodin, J. & Langer, E.J. (1980). Aging labels: The decline of control and the fall of self-esteem. *Journal of Social Issues*, **36**, 12–29.

Ryan, E.B. & Cole, R.L. (1990). Evaluative perceptions of interpersonal communication with elders. In H. Giles, N. Coupland, & J. Wiemann (Eds), *Communication, health and the elderly*, Fulbright Series #8 (pp. 172–190). Manchester: Manchester University Press.

Ryan, E.B., Giles, H., Bartolucci, G. & Henwood, K. (1986). Psycholinguistic and social psychological components of communication by and with the elderly. *Language & Communication*, **6**, 1–24.

Ryan, E.B., Bourhis, R.Y. & Knops, U. (1991). Evaluative perceptions of patronizing speech addressed to elders. *Psychology and Aging*, **6**, 442–450.

Ryan, E.B., Kwong See, S., Meneer, W.B. & Trovato, D. (1992). Age-based perceptions of language performance among younger and older adults. *Communication Research*, **19**, 423–443.

Ryan, E.B., Hamilton, J.M. & Kwong See, S. (1994). How do younger and older adults respond to baby talk in the nursing home? *International Journal of Aging and Human Development*, **39**, 21–32.

Ryan, E.B., MacLean, M. & Orange, J.B. (1994). Inappropriate accommodation in communication to elders: Inferences about nonverbal correlates. *International Journal of Aging and Human Development*, **39**, 273–291.

Ryan, E.B., Meredith, S.D. & Shantz, G.B. (1994). Evaluative perceptions of patronizing speech addressed to institutionalized elders in contrasting conversational contexts. *Canadian Journal on Aging*, **13**, 236–248.

Ryan, E.B., Hummert, M.L. & Boich, L.H. (1995). Communication predicaments of aging: Patronizing behavior toward older adults. *Journal of Language and Social Psychology*, **14**, 144–166.

Ryan, E.B., Kennaley, D.E., Pratt, M.W. & Shumovich, M.A. (2000). Evaluations by staff, residents, and community seniors of patronizing speech in the nursing home: Impact of passive, assertive or humorous responses. *Psychology and Aging*, **15**, 272–285.

Sachweh, S. (1998). Granny darling's nappies: Secondary babytalk in German nursing homes. *Journal of Applied Communication Research*, **26**, 52–65.

Seaver, A.M.H. (1994). My world now: Life in a nursing home, from the inside. *Newsweek*, 27 June, 11.

Thackerar, J.N., Giles, H. & Cheshire, J. (1982). Psychological and linguistic parameters of speech accommodation theory. In C. Fraser & K.R. Scherer (Eds), *Advances in the social psychology of language* (pp. 205–255). Cambridge, UK: Cambridge University Press.

Thompson, T.L. (1982). "You can't play marbles – you have a wooden hand": Communication with the handicapped. *Communication Quarterly*, **30**, 108–115.

Thorson, J.A. & Powell, F.C. (1996). Women, aging, and sense of humor. *Humor: International Journal of Humor Research*, **9**, 169–186.

Tracy, K. (1991). Introduction: Linking communicator goals with discourse. In K. Tracy (Ed.), *Understanding face-to-face interaction: Issues linking goals and discourse* (pp. 1–17). Hillsdale, NJ: Erlbaum.

Tracy, K. & Tracy, S.J. (1998). Rudeness at 911: Reconceptualizing face and face attack. *Human Communication Research*, **25**, 225–251.

Whitbourne, S.K., Culgin, S. & Cassidy, E. (1996). Evaluations of infantalizing intonation and content of speech directed at the aged. *International Journal of Aging and Human Development*, **41**, 109–116.

Williams, A. & Giles, H. (1996). Intergenerational conversations: Young adults' retrospective accounts. *Human Communication Research*, **23**, 220–250.

Ytsma, J. & Giles, H. (1997). Reactions to patronizing talk: Some Dutch data. *Journal of Sociolinguistics*, **1/2**, 259–268.

Deceiving

Jenny S. Tornqvist, D. Eric Anderson and Bella M. DePaulo
University of Virginia, Charlottesville, USA

PERVASIVENESS OF DECEIT

Everyday Lies

Most people would probably like to believe that they are rarely either the perpetrators or the targets of deceit. Yet research suggests otherwise. In a pair of studies, 77 college students and a more demographically diverse group of 70 people from the community kept diaries every day for a week of all of their social interactions and all of the lies they told during those interactions (DePaulo & Kashy, 1998; DePaulo et al., 1996; Kashy & DePaulo, 1996). Participants were told that "a lie occurs any time you intentionally try to mislead someone" (DePaulo et al., 1996, p. 981). Together, the two groups turned in more than 1500 lies. This amounted to an average of two lies a day for the college students – one in every three interactions that lasted 10 minutes or more, and one lie a day for the people from the community – one in every five interactions. The college students lied to 38% of the people they interacted with during the week, and the community members lied to 30% of their interaction partners. Only one of the college students and just a few of the community members claimed not to have told a single lie all week. Clearly, lying is not an extraordinary or unusual social behavior but a fact of everyday life.

The exercise of recording every single lie every day for a week made only a small dent in the self-images of the participants. Although the people from both groups conceded that they had lied more frequently than they expected, they also believed that, on the average, they lied less often than other people in their cohort.

The diary studies of DePaulo and her colleagues are the only studies in the literature in which participants kept track of their opportunities to lie (i.e., their

The New Handbook of Language and Social Psychology.
Edited by W. Peter Robinson and Howard Giles.
© 2001 John Wiley & Sons Ltd.

social interactions) as well as their lies, and they provide the only reports of the everyday deceitfulness of a non-college sample analyzed separately from college students. Despite these differences, the results are consistent with other studies in suggesting the pervasiveness of deceit (e.g., Camden, Motley & Wilson, 1984; Lippard, 1988). In this chapter, we focus primarily on deliberate deceptions, as did the diary studies. If we had extended our discussion to close cousins of deceit, such as equivocations (e.g., Bavelas et al., 1990) and forms of politeness (e.g., Brown & Levinson, 1987), our domain of discourse would have been vast.

The great majority of the lies that participants described in the diary studies were little lies of little consequence. These lies were more often about feelings and opinions than anything else. For example, people claimed to feel more positively about another person or about the plans for the evening than they really did feel, they pretended to agree with others when they really disagreed, and they claimed not to care about a personal rejection when in fact they cared a great deal. They also lied about their small victories and minor defeats (gaining or losing weight, performing disappointingly at school or at work), their actions, plans, and whereabouts, and their reasons for their actions or inactions. Both the college students and the people from the community reported that they usually did not plan their lies very carefully, if at all, they did not regard their lies as very serious, they did not worry much about the possibility of getting caught, they did not feel very badly about their lies before they told them, and they felt only the slightest distress while they were telling them and just afterwards.

For each of the lies that they told, participants described in their own words why they had told the lie. Content analyses revealed that, even by their own admissions, the participants lied primarily for self-serving reasons. These self-serving reasons, however, were not predominantly the crassly materialistic or instrumental motives that might be expected based on cultural stereotypes of liars as cold and exploitative. For example, they rarely lied to attain an illicit financial advantage nor even to get their way at times when their preferences clashed with someone else's. Instead, most self-serving lies were told for psychological reasons, such as to serve the liars' self-presentational goals of appearing kinder or more knowledgeable or more desirable than they really believed themselves to be, or to spare themselves from being embarrassed or having their feelings hurt. One out of every four everyday lies was not self-serving at all but was told with another person in mind. These altruistic lies were told to make someone else look better, or to spare another person from embarrassment or hurt feelings. "What a wonderful dinner", "Your hair looks great", and "Of course you did the right thing" are familiar examples.

Serious Lies

Far less commonplace than the little lies of everyday life are truly serious lies that are often deep betrayals of trust. To learn about these serious lies, DePaulo and her colleagues asked college students and people from the community to describe the most serious lie they had ever told to anyone, and the most serious lie anyone had ever told to them (DePaulo et al., 2001a; see also Metts, 1989). In both groups, the serious lies they described were most often told to hide romantic affairs. Participants also described serious lies that were told to cover misdeeds such as stealing, cheating, and denting a car, and personal facts such as abusive behavior or alcoholism. Tellers of serious lies also made promises and commitments they never intended to honor, and some of them even lied about themselves in ways that were so far reaching and long lasting that they qualified as living a lie. Many of these serious lies were distressing for the liars to tell and saddening, infuriating, and humiliating for the targets to discover. Trust was often lost, especially in the short term, and relationships were sometimes destroyed. Although not all serious lies wreaked such interpersonal havoc, they were far more likely to do so than were the everyday lies described in the diary studies.

The ratio of self-serving lies to altruistic ones in the serious lies research was a dramatic nine to one. Moreover, within the set of self-serving serious lies, far more of them were told for reasons of personal advantage than for the psychological reasons typically given by the everyday lie-tellers. Tellers of serious lies, unlike the tellers of everyday lies, often did fit the stereotypical portrait of liars as cold and exploitative.

LEGIBILITY OF LIES

Direct Deception Detection

More than 100 studies have been reported in which participants try to figure out when other people are lying and when they are telling the truth (DePaulo, Tornqvist & Cooper, 2001c). Typically in these studies, half of the communications are truths and half are lies. That means that if the judges (the people trying to spot the truths and lies) were simply guessing, they would be correct 50% of the time by chance alone. The actual rate of deception detection (percent of truths and lies accurately identified) across the 100+ studies in the literature is 54%. The range of accuracy scores is rather small. About two out of every three studies report mean accuracy levels ranging from 50% to 59%.

The finding that judges guess correctly 54% of the time indicates that people trying to perpetrate lies and truths are caught slightly more often than not. But these are the findings from studies in which judges are asked directly to indicate whether they think another person is lying or telling the truth. It is possible that outside of the experimental context, when attention is not directed explicitly to the issue of deceptiveness, people often do not even think to wonder whether another person might be lying. The results from the diary studies of everyday lying provide suggestive evidence supportive of that possibility. About a week after recording each of their lies, the participants were asked whether the lies had ever been discovered. For less than 20% of their lies did they report that they knew that the lie had been discovered (DePaulo et al., 1996). It is possible, then, that liars are discovered far less often than the 54% figure would suggest. Of course, it is also possible that liars are often oblivious to the discovery of their deceits (DePaulo et al., 2001a).

Indirect Deception Detection

Whereas the diary studies raise the possibility that liars get away with their lies more often than experimental studies suggest, other evidence suggests the alternative possibility that liars are detected more often than it appears from judges' explicit guesses about whether they just heard a truth or a lie. This evidence comes from studies in which judges' perceptions were assessed indirectly rather than directly. The indirect measures consistently show reliable differences in judges' reactions to the truths and lies (DePaulo, 1994). In an early study of this phenomenon (DePaulo et al., 1982), older children showed better direct deception detection accuracy than younger children, but they also showed better indirect deception detection (measured by ratings of the ambivalence of communicators), as well. Further, the participants were able to discriminate truths from lies on the indirect measure at an earlier age than they were able to discriminate truths from lies when explicitly asked about the truthfulness of the communication.

Other research has also found that answers to questions that are not directly about the truthfulness of the story can discriminate truths from lies. These include judges' reports about their confidence in their truthfulness judgments (DePaulo et al., 1997), their responses to open-ended questions about the cues they used to make their deceptiveness judgments (Anderson et al., 1999b), and their reports of their own comfort and suspiciousness (Anderson, 1999; Anderson, DePaulo & Ansfield, 2001).

HOW DO LIARS GET AWAY WITH THEIR LIES?

Although we do not yet know, and perhaps never will know, the actual rate at which liars get away with their lies, it is clear that they do so often enough to merit our attention. In this section, then, we will propose a few of our favorite answers to the question, "How do they do it?"

Perceivers Have a Truth Bias

There is a highly replicable finding in the literature on deception detection: perceivers show a truth bias. In studies in which perceivers are shown equal numbers of truths and lies – sometimes even in studies in which the perceivers are explicitly told that they will observe just as many lies as truths – they reliably judge more of the messages to be truths than lies (DePaulo, Tornqvist & Cooper, 2001c; Levine, Parks & McCornack, 1999). The fact that this bias is abundantly clear even in studies in which perceivers are blatantly warned of the possibility of deceit raises the possibility that the truth bias could be even stronger in naturalistic contexts in which the threat of deception is not made salient. However, there are no naturalistic data on this topic.

Why is it that perceivers are biased to regard other people's communications as truths? One possible reason for a truth "bias" comes from Grice (1975), who states that for language to be effective it must convey the true state of things. If every communication were a lie, it would be very difficult to rely on that communication to navigate the physical and social worlds. For example, if one were to ask the location of a particular campus building, and hear a different, but equally false, answer from each respondent, one is no better off than having received no answer at all. The value of the communication drops to nil. Therefore, at least some reliability is needed in order for language to function as a usable communication tool. Communications need to be truthful most of the time and people need to assume that they are.

Perhaps, then, the truth bias is not really a bias at all. If most communications really are truthful, then a tendency toward saying that any given communication is the truth seems entirely justified. The results of the diary studies do indicate that although lies are plentiful, truths are even more so (DePaulo et al., 1996). Those studies also indicate that the rate of telling the little lies of everyday life is lower in close personal relationships than it is in interactions with strangers. Analogously, in the experimental literature, the truth bias is often stronger when people are judging relationship partners than when they are judging strangers (Anderson, 1999; Anderson, Ansfield & DePaulo, 1999a). It is possible, then, that the truth bias represents an accurate appraisal of the base rate of truthfulness in social interaction.

The truth bias may also be an adaptive response to the pressures of communication. Scrutinizing each proposition from a conversational partner may be quite taxing, and unnecessary if most of the communications one encounters in everyday life are actually true.

The truth bias, like other phenomena of great interest, also has its following of conspiracy theorists. The conspiracy at the heart of the truth bias is to keep individual self-presentations intact and unchallenged. Goffman (1959), in his dramaturgical model of self-presentation, has posited that the world truly is a stage, and the men and women merely players. Behavior enacted "on stage" (in public) serves to convey particular impressions, and "audiences" tend to accept these self-presentations, without question, as accurate representations of the players' real selves. They accept even deceptive self-presentations, as the social norms dictate that these, too, should be taken at face value.

For relational partners, this conspiracy may be enacted both in public, as they do not question each other in front of strangers, and in private interactions, as each partner defers to the other's self-presentation without questioning. Some of these private interactions may be the stereotypical questions for which a lie is the correct answer. For example, if a woman asks her boyfriend if another woman is more attractive than she is, regardless of his actual feelings, the "correct" answer for the question is "No." The boyfriend may be lying in response to this question, but it is unlikely that the woman asking the question will be skeptical about the answer (cf. Anderson, 1999).

Further, there is evidence that belief in a communication is an easier and more automatic process than disbelief. Gilbert (1991), in outlining his Spinozan model of belief, posits a process of comprehension and belief that happen simultaneously, and that the belief process requires neither attention, cognitive resources, nor further processing. Disbelief, on the other hand, requires a person to devote cognitive resources to "unbelieving" the proposition. This requires both effort and motivation to engage in the disbelieving process. Since belief is the default process in this model, truth bias follows directly from it, especially in cases where cognitive resources are constrained.

Relational partners may not be motivated to engage in the extra processing necessary to disbelieve each other's communications. They may instead be satisfied with believing what they hear. Because of the sheer volume of communication between close partners, it may simply be too costly to devote cognitive resources to process every communication to the extent necessary for the disbelief process. Further, there is some evidence to suggest that knowledge of another person may serve as a distraction, depleting cognitive resources and undermining the judge's ability to engage in the process of disbelief (Anderson, 1999; Millar and Millar, 1995). Of course, suspiciousness and distrust can be costly to relationships, and avoided for that reason, too.

WHO GETS AWAY WITH THEIR LIES MOST OFTEN?

People with Honest Demeanors

A number of studies have now documented that there are "demeanor effects" in the communication of deception (e.g., Bond & Atoum, 2000; Zuckerman et al., 1981). Some people consistently look or sound honest, both when they are telling the truth and when they are lying. Conversely, other people consistently come across as dishonest, when they are lying and even when they are telling the truth.

What physical features are characteristic of people who consistently strike others as truthful? This is a question that has not often been addressed in the literature, but there is one answer that has been replicated (Malone et al., 2001). Adults who are baby-faced – that is, who have facial features characteristic of babies, such as big eyes and small noses – are especially likely to be believed by other people (e.g., Zebrowitz, 1997).

There are also reports of the personality characteristics of people who tend to be seen as truthful both when telling the truth and when lying. In those studies, ratings of a communicator's truthfulness are averaged across that person's truths and lies, and that overall truthfulness score is correlated with personality scores. A meta-analytic review has indicated that people who consistently seem truthful arc people who are expressive, warm, extraverted, and enthusiastic. People who seem deceptive, even when they are not lying, tend instead to be people who are anxious and tense (Tornqvist et al., 2001).

Extraverts and High Self-monitors

Success at deceiving has also been measured in a different way that is analogous to the measurement of success at detecting deception. Successful lie detectors are defined as those perceivers who recognize truths as truths and lies as lies. If asked to judge degree of truthfulness, they will rate truths as more truthful than lies. Successful deceivers, on the other hand, are those who can fool their targets. Observers of a skilled liar should have no idea when they are hearing a truth and when they are hearing a lie; in fact, they may even be suckered into believing that the lies are even more truthful than the truths.

There is a growing literature on the personality profile of skilled liars. A meta-analytic review (Tornqvist et al., 2001) concluded that the personality characteristic that most consistently separated the skilled from the unskilled liars was self-monitoring (Snyder, 1987). High self-monitors (people who characteristically try to control and monitor the images of themselves that they convey in social interactions) befuddled their targets more often than low self-monitors in almost every study. Extraverted and expressive people also tended to succeed at their deceits more often than less charismatic people.

People Experienced at Lying?

The intuitively compelling prediction that people who have more experience at lying will be more successful at deceiving others has never been tested rigorously. All we can offer is suggestive evidence from a study of experienced salespeople (DePaulo & DePaulo, 1989). It can be argued that many salespeople will deceive in order to do a better job. Perhaps they do not actually like the product they are selling as much as they claim. Maybe they know of a better price somewhere else, but if their earnings depend on each sale they might not say so. Experienced salespeople whose pay was contingent on the volume of their sales were videotaped as they pitched various products, half of which they actually disliked. When judges subsequently watched the tapes and tried to determine whether the salespeople were lying or not, they were completely unsuccessful. They rated the salespeople as just as honest when they were lying as when they were telling the truth.

Because experience was not manipulated in the salespersons study, it is not possible to know whether the salespersons were so successful at getting away with their lies because they had more practice with sales techniques. Alternatively, it is possible that commission-based sales positions attract naturally skilled deceivers or especially confident performers. Or, perhaps people who are paid to make as many sales as possible feel little guilt about their job-related lies, and it is their moral nonchalance that enables their deceptive success.

ARE LIES MORE SUCCESSFUL WHEN LIARS ARE MORE HIGHLY MOTIVATED AND MORE PREPARED?

The Motivational Impairment Effect

Intuitively, it may seem reasonable to expect that people will be more likely to succeed at getting away with their lies when they are more highly motivated to do so. However, DePaulo and Kirkendol (1989) predicted just the opposite. They suggested that when people care more about telling a successful lie, they will try harder to control their expressive behaviors. However, only those behaviors that are most amenable to willful control – i.e., verbal behaviors – will actually be controlled more successfully. Attempts to control non-verbal behaviors may instead backfire, such that lies will become even more distinguishable from truths whenever perceivers can see or hear any non-verbal cues (such as facial expressions, body movements, or tone of voice cues).

Across a series of studies, DePaulo and her colleagues operationalized motivation to succeed in a variety of ways. For example, in one study, motivated communicators were observed by a panel of their peers and were told that the ability to tell a successful lie was related to personal and professional success (DePaulo, Lanier & Davis, 1983; see also DePaulo et al., 1988; Krauss, 1981). In another, the characteristics of the targets of the communications were manipulated, such that participants believed that they were telling their truths and lies to people who were the same sex as themselves or the opposite sex, and who were unattractive or attractive (DePaulo, Stone & Lassiter, 1985). In still another, people who described themselves as independent and who said that it was very important for them to be seen that way told stories from their lives that did or did not underscore their identities as independent people (DePaulo, LeMay & Epstein, 1991). Almost all of the operationalizations in all of these studies showed the predicted motivational impairment effect: communicators' lies were even more distinguishable from their truths when they were more highly motivated to make them less distinguishable, and this was especially so when perceivers could see or hear any of the communicators' non-verbal cues (i.e., in all conditions except the verbal transcript condition).

DePaulo and her colleagues also predicted and tested a number of moderators of the motivational impairment effect. As hypothesized, they found that high expectations for success can inoculate communicators from the undermining effects of high motivation (DePaulo et al., 1991). They also found that physically attractive people, who have many successes in the interpersonal domain and who are accustomed to being the objects of other people's scrutiny, are relatively impervious to the disruptive effects of high motivation (DePaulo et al., 1988).

A simple motivational hypothesis, that motivation will undermine deceptive success regardless of the particular cues available to perceivers, has been tested even more often than the original motivational impairment hypothesis. There is some support for the simpler hypothesis as well (DePaulo et al., 2001c).

In sum, when the pressure is on, people will often tell lies that are even more obvious than the ones that they tell when they are not as motivated to do well. Typically, under these high motivational conditions, it is their own non-verbal behaviors that betray them.

Effects of Planning

The effects of planning, like the effects of motivation to succeed, seem immediately apparent. Shouldn't the opportunity to plan and rehearse communications result in more successful lies – i.e, lies that are less easily distinguished from truths? Once again, the data were not totally compliant with human intuition. Although some studies reported the expected facilitating effect of planning on deceptive success (e.g., deTurck & Miller, 1990; Littlepage & Pineault, 1985), there have also been contrary reports. For example, DePaulo et al. (1983) found that when communicators had the opportunity to plan their truths and lies, their lies were no less distinguishable from their truths than when they had no planning time at all. However, all of the planned messages – the truthful ones as well as the lies – seemed more deceptive than the unplanned ones. It was obvious to the perceivers that the planned messages had been rehearsed, and perhaps they felt suspicious of rehearsed responses.

Planning does seem to be useful, though, to one particular category of communicators. High self-monitors tell especially successful lies when they have an opportunity to plan their performances (deTurck & Miller, 1990; Miller, deTurck & Kalbfleisch, 1983).

HOW DO LIARS BEHAVE DIFFERENTLY FROM TRUTHTELLERS?

Almost all studies of cues to deception have examined behaviors such as non-verbal cues that might distinguish the truths and lies of any communicators in almost any situation. For example, regardless of the context of the lies, it is theoretically possible that liars will fidget more than truthtellers, or speak less fluently. Perhaps it is unsurprising, then, that behaviors such as fidgeting and fluency have been examined in many different studies.

Less frequently pursued, but perhaps as promising, is the strategy of examining liar behaviors that may be specific to specific contexts. One example of this comes from the literature on polygraph testing. Those who have worked as polygraphers often claim that liars behave differently from truthtellers during the polygraph exam and even before the testing has formally commenced. Guilty people, for instance, are believed to complain about the testing procedure more often than innocent ones. The many specific behaviors believed to distinguish liars from truthtellers in the context of polygraph testing (in addition to physiological ones) were described by Reid (e.g., Reid & Arther, 1953) and tested by Horvath (1973), with some promising results.

Another example is a system for assessing credibility that was originally developed as an investigative tool in cases involving children's reports of sexual abuse. Statement Reality Analysis (Undeutsch, 1989), or Criteria Based Content Analysis (Landry & Brigham, 1992), has now been adapted for use with adults, too, and has been tested in several studies, again with some promising results (Memon, Vrij & Bull, 1998; Yuille, 1989).

In this section, we will first review the cues to deception that are observable in almost all contexts. Then we will describe several context-specific strategies that we have documented in our own work.

Cues to Deception

There are now more than 1200 estimates of the relationship between particular behaviors and whether or not people are lying. A meta-analytic review of that data (DePaulo et al., 2001b) revealed that liars are in many ways less forthcoming than truthtellers. For example, they provide fewer details, they answer questions less directly, and they seem to distance themselves from their answers. In conversations, liars take up less of the talking time than truthtellers do, and interactions with liars are briefer than ones with truthtellers.

Liars' stories are less plausible and less internally consistent than the stories of truthtellers. Liars also sound less involved in the telling of their tales, and they seem more nervous. Specific behavioral indicators also suggest that liars are more aroused than truthtellers; for example, their pitch is higher and their pupils are more dilated. Liars also tend to make a less positive impression than truthtellers do. However, contrary to cultural stereotypes, liars are not any less fluent than truthtellers, nor are they any more fidgety.

Lies in Context: Salespersons and their Customers

The experienced salespersons from the study described above (DePaulo & DePaulo, 1989) used an interesting strategy when trying to pitch products they actually did not like. They did not try to convey as much liking for those products as for the products they really did like, and they even mentioned more unfavorable aspects of their least preferred products than of their most preferred products. It appeared, then, that they were using a strategy documented long ago in the persuasion literature as a successful one (e.g., Hunt, Smith & Kernan, 1984): they were crafting two-sided communications. Perhaps it was their willingness to acknowledge flaws in some of the products that made them seem so credible to observers – so much so, in fact, that the observers thought they were just as honest when they were just pretending to like some of the products as when they were describing products they really did like.

More Lies in Context: Talking to Artists about their Work

In a pair of studies, Bell and DePaulo (1996; DePaulo & Bell, 1996) asked participants to wander through a lab room set up as an art gallery and to choose their favorite and least favorite paintings. They then described in writing what they liked and disliked about each of the paintings they selected. Only then did they learn that they were about to discuss the art work with an artist who (they were told) had created some of the paintings herself. The artist introduced the discussions of one of the participant's favorite paintings, and one of her least favorite ones, by saying, "This is one that I did", and asking the participant what she thought of it. The artist also asked the participant to comment on paintings described as the work of other artists. Of course, the most challenging condition for the participants was the one in which they had to comment on the painting they hated the most to the very person who had created it. One of the strategies they used was a very interesting one: they cleverly implied that they liked the artist's work, without ever saying so directly, by saying very explicitly how much they disliked the work of one of the other artists! When asked explicitly by the artist what they liked or disliked about her own painting (the one they greatly disliked), they tried something else. Of the liked and disliked aspects of the painting that they had recorded previously, the participants mentioned more of the liked aspects than of the disliked ones in their conversations with the artist. The liked aspects that they explicitly mentioned in their conversations were aspects that they truly did like, so they were not lying about them. And they did not exactly lie about the disliked aspects, either. They rarely claimed to like the aspects of the painting they actually detested; instead, they tried not to mention those aspects at all. In a way, their strategy was to find small truths to mask a greater lie. By using truth as a mask, the participants probably felt better about hiding their true feelings than they might have if they told more outright lies, and they may have also felt good about themselves for sparing the feelings of the poor artist.

A LOOK TOWARD THE FUTURE

The study of skill in the communication of deception has more often focused on the detectors of lies than on the perpetrators. For example, there are now enough reports of the possible role of experience in success at detecting lies to support a meta-analytic review (Ansfield et al., 2001), but comparable studies of the role of experience in success at deceiving are virtually non-existent. We think that liars and their lies should more often be the focus of future research.

Underdeveloped both from the deceiver and the detector perspectives is the study of lying in close personal relationships. The first 100 studies of skill at deceiving and detecting deceit were based almost exclusively on communications between strangers (DePaulo et al., 2001c). The study of deception among people who know and care about each other is just beginning to gain momentum (e.g., Anderson et al., 1999a). We hope that trend continues.

REFERENCES

Anderson, D.E. (1999). Cognitive and motivational processes underlying the truth bias. Unpublished doctoral dissertation, University of Virginia.

Anderson, D.E., Ansfield, M.E. & DePaulo, B.M. (1999a). Love's best habit: Deception in the context of relationships. In P. Philippot, R.S. Feldman & E.J. Coats (Eds), *The social context of nonverbal behavior* (pp. 372–409). Cambridge, UK: Cambridge University Press.

Anderson, D.E., DePaulo, B.M., Ansfield, M.E., Tickle, J.J. & Green, E. (1999b). Beliefs about cues to deception: Mindless stereotypes or untapped wisdom? *Journal of Nonverbal Behavior*, **23**, 67–88.

Anderson, D.E., DePaulo, B.M. & Ansfield, M.E. (2001). The development of deception detection skill: A longitudinal study of same sex friends. Manuscript submitted for publication.

Ansfield, M.E., DePaulo, B.M., Adams, R.B. & Cooper, H. (2001). The role of training and experience in success at detecting deception: A meta-analytic review. Manuscript in preparation.

Bavelas, J.B., Black, A., Chovil, N. & Mullett, J. (1990). *Equivocal communication.* Newbury Park, CA: Sage.

Bell, K.L. & DePaulo, B.M. (1996). Liking and lying. *Basic and Applied Social Psychology*, **18**, 243–266.

Bond, C.F., Jr & Atoum, A.O. (2000). International deception. *Personality and Social Psychology Bulletin*, **26**, 385–395.

Brown, P. & Levinson, S.C. (1987). *Politeness: Some universals in language usage.* Cambridge, UK: Cambridge University Press.

Camden, C., Motley, M.T. & Wilson, A. (1984). White lies in interpersonal communication: A taxonomy and preliminary investigation of social motivations. *Western Journal of Speech Communication*, **48**, 309–325.

DePaulo, B.M. (1994). Spotting lies: Can humans learn to do better? *Current Directions in Psychological Science*, **3**, 83–86.

DePaulo, B.M., & Bell, K.L. (1996). Truth and investment: Lies are told to those who care. *Journal of Personality and Social Psychology*, **71**, 703–716.

DePaulo, P.J. & DePaulo, B.M. (1989). Can deception by salespersons and customers be detected through nonverbal behavioral cues? *Journal of Applied Social Psychology*, **19**, 1552–1577.

DePaulo, B.M. & Kashy, D.A. (1998). Everyday lies in close and casual relationships. *Journal of Personality and Social Psychology*, **74**, 63–79.

DePaulo, B.M. & Kirkendol, S.E. (1989). The motivational impairment effect in the communication of deception. In J. Yuille (Ed.), *Credibility assessment* (pp. 51–70). Belgium: Kluwer.

DePaulo, B.M., Jordan, A., Irvine, A. & Laser, P.S. (1982). Age changes in the detection of deception. *Child Development*, **53**, 701–709.

DePaulo, B.M., Lanier, K. & Davis, T. (1983). Detecting the deceit of the motivated liar. *Journal of Personality and Social Psychology*, **45**, 1096–1103.

DePaulo, B.M., Stone, J.I. & Lassiter, G.D. (1985). Telling ingratiating lies: Effects of target sex and target attractiveness on verbal and nonverbal deceptive success. *Journal of Personality and Social Psychology*, **48**, 1191–1203.

DePaulo, B.M., Kirkendol, S.E., Tang, J. & O'Brien, T.P. (1988). The motivational impairment effect in the communication of deception: Replications and extensions. *Journal of Nonverbal Behavior*, **12**, 177–202.

DePaulo, B.M., LeMay, C.S., & Epstein, J.A. (1991). Effects of importance of success and expectations for success on effectiveness at deceiving. *Personality and Social Psychology Bulletin*, **17**, 14–24.

DePaulo, B.M., Kashy, D.A., Kirkendol, S.E., Wyer, M.M. & Epstein, J.A. (1996). Lying in everyday life. *Journal of Personality and Social Psychology*, **70**, 979–995.

DePaulo, B.M., Charlton, K., Cooper, H., Lindsay, J.J. & Muhlenbruck, L. (1997). The accuracy–confidence correlation in the detection of deception. *Personality and Social Psychology Review*, **1**, 346–357.

DePaulo, B.M., Ansfield, M.E., Kirkendol, S.E. & Boden, J.M. (2001a). Serious lies. Manuscript submitted for publication.

DePaulo, B.M., Lindsay, J.J., Malone, B.E., Muhlenbruck, L., Charlton, K. & Cooper, H. (2001b). Cues to deception: A meta-analytic review. Manuscript in preparation.

DePaulo, B.M., Tornqvist, J.S. & Cooper, H. (2001c). Accuracy at detecting deception: A meta-analysis of modality effects. Manuscript in preparation.

deTurck, M.A. & Miller, G.R. (1990). Training observers to detect deception: Effects of self-monitoring and rehearsal. *Human Communication Research*, **16**, 603–620.

Gilbert, D.T. (1991). How mental systems believe. *American Psychologist*, **46**, 107–119.

Goffman, E. (1959). *The presentation of self in everyday life*. Garden City, NY: Doubleday.

Grice, H.P. (1975). Logic and conversation. In P. Cole & J. Morgan (Eds), *Syntax and semantics: Vol. 3. Speech acts* (pp. 41–58). New York: Academic Press.

Horvath, F.S. (1973). Verbal and nonverbal clues to truth and deception during polygraph examinations. *Journal of Police Science and Administration*, **1**, 138–152.

Hunt, J.M., Smith, M.F. & Kernan, J.B. (1984). An attribution theory perspective on using two-sided messages to increase seller credibility. In J. Jacoby & C.S. Craig (Eds), *Personal selling: Theory, research, and practice* (pp. 93–108). Lexington, MA: Lexington Books.

Kashy, D.A. & DePaulo, B.M. (1996). Who lies? *Journal of Personality and Social Psychology*, **70**, 1037–1051.

Krauss, R.M. (1981). Impression formation, impression management, and nonverbal behaviors. In E.T. Higgins, C.P. Herman, & M.P. Zanna (Eds), *Social cognition: The Ontario symposium* (Vol. 1, pp. 323–341). Hillsdale, NJ: Erlbaum.

Landry, K.L. & Brigham, J.C. (1992). The effect of training in Criteria Based Content Analysis on the ability to detect deception in adults. *Law and Human Behavior*, **16**, 663–676.

Levine, T.R., Parks, H.S. & McCornack, S.A. (1999). Accuracy in detecting truth and lies: Documenting the "veracity effect". *Communication Monographs*, **66**, 199–218.

Lippard, P.V. (1988). "Ask me no questions, I'll tell you no lies": Situational exigencies for interpersonal deception. *Western Journal of Speech Communication*, **52**, 91–103.

Littlepage, G.E. & Pineault, M.A. (1985). Detection of deception of planned versus spontaneous communications. *Journal of Social Psychology*, **125**, 195–201.

Malone, B.E., DePaulo, B.M., Adams, R.B. & Cooper, H. (2001). Perceived cues to deception: A meta-analytic review. Manuscript in preparation.

Memon, A., Vrij, A. & Bull, R. (1998). *Psychology and law: Truthfulness, accuracy, and credibility*. London: McGraw-Hill.

Metts, S. (1989). An exploratory investigation of deception in close relationships. *Journal of Social and Personal Relationships*, **6**, 159–179.

Millar, M. & Millar, K. (1995). Detection of deception in familiar and unfamiliar persons: The effects of information restriction. *Journal of Nonverbal Behavior*, **19**, 69–84.

Miller, G.R., deTurck, M.A. & Kalbfleisch, P.J. (1983). Self-monitoring, rehearsal, and deceptive communication. *Human Communication Research*, **10**, 97–117.

Reid, J. & Arther, R. (1953). Behavior symptoms of lie detector subjects. *Journal of Criminal Law, Criminology, and Police Science*, **44**, 104–108.

Snyder, M. (1987). *Public appearances, private realities: The psychology of self-monitoring.* New York: Freeman.

Tornqvist, J.S., DePaulo, B.M., Mahaffey, A., Muhlenbruck, L., Kernahan, C. & Cooper, H. (2001). Sex differences and personality differences in the communication of deception. Manuscript in preparation.

Undeutsch, U. (1989). The development of Statement Reality Analysis. In J.C. Yuille (Ed.), *Credibility assessment* (pp. 101–120). Dordrecht: Kluwer.

Yuille, J.C. (Ed.) (1989) *Credibility assessment.* Dordrecht: Kluwer.

Zebrowitz, L.A. (1997). *Reading faces: Window to the soul?* Boulder, CO: Westview Press.

Zuckerman, M., Larrance, D.T., Spiegel, N.H. & Klorman, R. (1981). Controlling nonverbal displays: Facial expressions and tone of voice. *Journal of Experimental Social Psychology*, **17**, 506–524.

3.15

Accounting

Richard Buttny
Syracuse University, USA
G.H. Morris
California State University, San Marcos, USA

(C)onsider . . . the use of "Why?" . . . (W)hat one does with "Why?" is to propose about some action that it is an "accountable action." That is to say, "Why?" is a way of asking for an account. Accounts are most extraordinary. And the use of accounts and the use of requests for accounts are very highly regulated phenomena. (Sacks, 1992 [1964], pp. 4–5)

This passage illuminates our title. While much of what humans do and say is understood by others in routine, taken-for-granted ways, our actions may not always be self-explanatory. On such occasions, others ask us "Why?" – to grasp our intentions, understandings, or position. The ways of explaining ourselves to others (and to ourselves) constitute the speech activity of accounting.

The above epigram, to our knowledge, represents the first use of "accounts" as a social scientific concept (Scott, 1993). The phenomenon of accounts remains a rich research site today which social scientists from various disciplinary perspectives have been mining for over 30 years. The initial excitement of researching these everyday explanations may have dissipated somewhat, but the concept of accounts has taken its place as an important way of conceiving people's sense-making and remedial practices for maintaining or repairing interactional alignment and telling one's side of things.

To read the accounts literature is to review the panoply of different perspectives and research traditions in the social and human sciences. Different theoretical perspectives have developed the notion of accounts in different directions: accounts as reconfiguring the context of an event, accounts as reality negotiation, accounts as narratives, accounts as an exception to the rule, accounts as a

The New Handbook of Language and Social Psychology.
Edited by W. Peter Robinson and Howard Giles.
© 2001 John Wiley & Sons Ltd.

dispreferred response, and so on. In looking at recent work on accounts, we came across seven reviews of the accounts literature written in the 1990s alone (Cody & McLaughlin, 1990; Nicholas, 1990; Schlenker & Weigold, 1992; Buttny, 1993a; Antaki, 1994; Benoit, 1995, Ch.3; Orbuch, 1997). What is striking from reading these literature reviews is how different authors size up the value and direction of the literature in terms of their own paradigmatic commitments. One broad divergence in these readings of accounts research is reflected by the very title of this Handbook: those who look at the "social psychology" of accounts (i.e., focusing on cognitive components and using primarily quantitative methods) in contrast to those who take accounts as "language" (i.e., as talk-in-interaction – what we will call the language-and-social-interaction paradigm, which uses primarily qualitative methods). These two traditions of accounts research have common roots in the work of Scott and Lyman (1968), but they have diverged due to asking different kinds of questions and using different methodologies and data in trying to answer them (Antaki, 1994). The present authors' background is more steeped in the language-and-social-interaction approach and we suspect that our reading is tilted in that direction, but we attempt to discuss the literatures in the spirit of carrying on a dialogue (Robinson, 1998). We focus on the basic issues of what accounts are, how accounts become necessary, and how accounts are evaluated.[1]

WHAT ARE ACCOUNTS?

The concept "accounts" has been defined in a number of ways. A useful distinction is between (1) accounts *for* actions, in the sense of answering for troublesome conduct and (2) accounts *of* actions in the sense of giving a description or a narrative of events, not necessarily involving troubles. The former sense of accounts involves remedial talk for some problematic or questioned act and the actor's verbal portrayal of it in response. The second notion of accounts looks at the actor's verbal sense-making focusing on events, such as relationships, personal crises, life-course changes, and so on. Both of these approaches share an interest in how people tell their side of the story, that is, interpret and rhetorically reconstruct events through talk.

Scott and Lyman's (1968) well-known article articulates this first sense of accounts, and this conception remains one of the principal views today: accounts are verbal responses offered by individuals to others designed to protect the ongoing social interaction from the disruptive consequences of problematic events. Accounts attempt to explain apparently "untoward" or "unusual" events as understandable, or at least to minimize the actor's responsibility for them. When successful, accounts prevent, or repair, problematic situations and restore social equilibrium between participants. This sense of accounts involves issues of

---

[1] We have omitted the important work on accounts of Potter and Edwards since their chapter on discursive psychology is included in this volume.

practical, moral, or even legal conduct, that is, talk about troubles, agency, intent, blame, responsibility, mitigating circumstances, and the like.

A second sense of accounts is more interested in the content of the account and how we convey our worlds to others. As Garfinkel (1967, p. 1) puts it, "When I speak of accountable . . . I mean observable-and-reportable, i.e., available to members as situated practices of looking-and-telling." On this view, accounts involve how speech, or non-verbal means, are used to render our activities understandable to others, such as by placing our action in a wider framework, as in a part–whole relation (Shotter, 1984). Persons account for their actions such that others can make sense of what they are doing for all practical purposes; accounts are an ongoing feature of social interaction. For example, office workers seated at a desk shuffling papers, jotting notes, making telephone calls, and the like may be seen to account for their activities to co-workers as engaged in what we may gloss as routine work (Watson & Sharrock, 1991). When a person's actions are not accountable by normal typifications or common-sense understandings, then this may be seen as unusual or problematic such that the person may be questioned by others and need to account in Scott and Lyman's (1968) sense for those actions. So the Garfinkel (1967) sense of accounts as ongoing, sense-making procedures is ultimately consistent with the more circumscribed Scott and Lyman (1968) sense of accounts (Heritage, 1984).

A related approach takes accounts as narratives or having a story-like form (Harvey, Orbuch & Weber, 1990). Accounts are conceived as longer and more complex renderings of events than the earlier view of accounts as relatively short and simple statements. Narratives can account by conveying a temporal sequence of events, the cast of characters, and the actor's part to portray events and make actions understandable. The accounts-as-narrative approach captures people's need to explain and make sense of their lives, particularly in times of severe stress or trauma. An early exemplar of this approach is Weiss's (1975) study (cited in Orbuch, 1997) of newly separated people's accounts for what happened to end an intimate relationship. Other studies drawing on the notion of storied accounts have examined interpersonal relationships (Stamp & Sabourin, 1995), life-course changes (Harvey et al., 1990), identity issues (Herzfeld, 1996), and so on. This more in-depth view of accounts as storied seems useful for gaining insight into persons' sense-making and interpretive repertoires.

In related literatures various speech actions have been identified which dovetail with accounts, for instance, confessions, admissions or denials of guilt (Schonbach, 1990), apologies (Owen, 1983), vocabularies of motives (Mills, 1940; Burke, 1969), disclaimers (Hewitt & Stokes, 1975), remedial acts (Goffman, 1971), and aligning actions (Stokes & Hewitt, 1976). Also, the affinity between accounts and attribution theory, which has independently studied such phenomena, has been pointed out (Weiner et al., 1987). Accounts can be seen as self-serving attributions designed to protect one's identity from damaging implications of problematic events (Schlenker & Weigold, 1992). Attributions are the actor's private judgments, while accounts are publicly conveyed to others;

accounts are the communication of "packaged attributions" (Mongeau, Hale & Alles, 1994, p. 330).

Throughout the 1980s and up until around 1990 there was much interest in developing taxonomies or category systems of accounts (Tedeschi & Reiss, 1981; Semin & Manstead, 1983; Schonbach, 1990; Nicholas, 1990). This trend seems to have run its course as researchers have turned from distinguishing types and subtypes of accounts to issues of accounts practices and evaluation. Here we look at just two of the main kinds of accounts: excuses and justifications.

Excuses are considered by some the prototypic form of accounts (Snyder & Higgins, 1990; Weiner, 1992). Excuses account by allowing that the event in question is wrong or in some sense negative, but denying or minimizing the actor's responsibility for it (Austin, 1961). Excuses address circumstances which are designed to alleviate the actor's responsibility for what happened, e.g., it was unintentional, accidental, unforeseen, and so on. The underlying notion of responsibility is central to understanding and evaluating much human action. Indeed, taking responsibility is sometimes synonymous with being accountable.

Accounts have been conceived as having two underlying dimensions: the actor's "linkage" or connection to the undesirable act in question (i.e., responsibility), and the "valence" of that act (i.e., negative evaluation) (Snyder & Higgins, 1990). Accounts which address the actor's linkage to the act can be heard as excuses, while addressing the valence of the act involves justifications – a second main type of account. Accounts which try to change the negative evaluation attempt to justify the act. Justifications challenge the evaluation of the act in question by redescribing events or offering a different label for the act in question, e.g., "I'm not giving you an ultimatum, I want to discuss this" or "I'm just teasing." Justifications and excuses work to account because they each attempt to get recipients to see actions in particular ways (Bilmes, 1994).

Generally accounts may be taken as a kind of reason for action, an explanation for "why" an action was committed (Draper, 1988; see epigram). In the prototypical case, reasons are marked by "because statements", as in "I did X because of Y" (Antaki, 1990). However, in looking at actual cases of accounts in naturalistic contexts, the prototypical "because-statement" accounts are much less common. Instead one finds a variety of other formats which are hearable as accounts, such as descriptions, reports, or versions of events. Atkinson and Drew (1979, pp. 139–140) observe that witnesses in judicial proceedings justify their part in events by descriptions of the scene, for example, "We were under gunfire at the time." Descriptions of scenes, events, relationships, and the like are crucial for recounting what happened, establishing the facts and, ultimately, who is responsible. The larger point here is that accounts are not recognizable by the form of the utterance alone, but rather by their sequential position in context (e.g., responding to a prior question or blame) which makes it hearable as an account. For instance, the statement, "I just don't like to think what would happen," is not obviously identifiable as an account. But when seen in its sequential context (transcript 1, arrow), it can be heard to be an accounting:

Transcript 1 (Buttny, 1993b, p. 58)
  S: Why did you tell me it was a good thing I told you now
      (.) I'm happy you told me?
  W: I don't 'cause eh because Sam it's just (.)
      I don't know
      (4.1)
  W: .hh
      (12.1)
⇒ W: I just don't like to <u>think</u> what would happen.

Examining accounts in context is important; the form of an utterance alone does not tell us what action is being performed.

UNDER WHAT CONDITIONS DO ACCOUNTS OCCUR?

Most of the time people do not account, or call others to account, because social actions are understood in routine, taken-for-granted ways. When a person's actions are seen as "unusual" or "untoward", others may raise questions or call for an account (Scott & Lyman, 1968). Recall Sacks' observation (epigram) that accounts are "highly regulated phenomena". Persons do not account just anywhere, but are responsive to conditions of uncertainty, or practical–moral misalignment with others. The project of specifying these conditions more carefully has been an issue of some importance.

Moral communities need some form of social accountability to control and coordinate the diverse interests and ends of individuals. Members hold each other socially accountable through watching, judging, and sanctioning each other's conduct to certain legitimated standards (Schlenker, Weigold & Doherty, 1991). While being accountable to others works as a constraint on one's actions, this social control aspect involves more than simply matching conduct to social rules. Instead, social control needs to be seen as an emergent feature of interaction which arises from how persons orient and respond to the rules and one another. How rules apply to the individual, with what weight and what authority, are matters which can be interactionally negotiated, especially through accounts. Persons can be seen to follow, circumvent, or even modify the rules to align actions and coordinate conduct (Stokes & Hewitt, 1976). For instance, in a kindergarten setting, teachers invoke rules for social control purposes, but such "rules are continually tested, employed, clarified, and negotiated" by kindergartners and teachers (Much & Shweder, 1978, p. 20).

Starting from the assumption that social actors ordinarily do what they know to be normatively correct, Morris, White and Iltis (1994) view accounts as claims about what was happening in a given case that prevented actors from doing what they ordinarily would. These accounts thus explain divergences and, simultaneously, uphold the rules. Accounts invite recipients to share in the belief that, were it not for the specific troubles that occurred in this situation, the person offering the account would have done what is normal. Accounts are defined as "a description that reports trouble accomplishing what is expected ordinarily and, therefore, is understood or credited by its recipient as an explanation for a divergence from assumptions about what ordinarily will or should happen" (p. 130). The cornerstone of this approach is its concentration on normative assumptions or rules about social interaction and relationships. Speakers treat violations of these as one-time exceptions that are warranted under the circumstances; it is the work of accounts to describe these circumstances and thereby to explain divergence from expectations.

What an actor can be held accountable for, and how the event becomes labeled, reflects local normative standards and vocabulary of motives (Mills, 1940). The magnitude of these failure events ranges from minor (e.g., forgetting an acquaintance's name) to major (e.g., shooting an acquaintance). The more important the failure event, and the stronger the actor's connection to it, the more potentially damaging to the actor, and consequently, the stronger the motive for offering accounts (Schlenker & Weigold, 1992; Higgins & Snyder, 1991). From a social psychological perspective, the initiating force for generating accounts is an actual, or possible, threat to the actor. The failure event has been variously conceived as threatening the actor's self-concept (Snyder & Higgins, 1990), social identity (Schlenker et al., 1991), or face (Gonzales, 1992; Turnbull, 1992). This threat is intensified when there is consensus among audience members as to the actor's failure or when the audience is of high status (Snyder & Higgins, 1990). Such threatening failure events may create severe stress or negative affect for the actor.

The failure event may not only be threatening to the actor, but also may be offensive to the face of another (Gonzales, Manning & Haugen, 1992). Given the emergence of a failure event, an account may be called for in various ways, such as by "blaming", "reproaching", or "finding fault" with the actor. The tactic of directly reproaching the actor is more likely to receive a defensive account in reply. Put in terms of politeness theory, the more aggravating the reproach from another, the more aggravating the account from the actor (Cody & Braaten, 1992). However, contrary to earlier theorizing, a general principle of reciprocity between reproaches and accounts breaks down; mitigating reproaches do not predict mitigating accounts.

Accounts have been conceived of as a way to reassert control and so are important in conflict escalation processes (Schonbach, 1990). The more severe the reproach, the more the recipient experiences a loss of control. Since males have a greater need for control, they are more likely to give defensive accounts (Schonbach, 1990). Consistent with this are the findings that males are more likely to refuse to account, while females are more likely to concede to the failure event (Gonzales et al., 1992; Mongeau et al., 1994). Also, in an organizational setting, female employees reported using more mitigating accounts while males avowed more aggravating accounts (Tata, 1998).

The act of calling for an account from another can itself be face threatening to both interactants. So actors may attempt to protect face in calling for accounts by using "less transactional clarity" (Turnbull, 1992). Accounts may be sought in more indirect ways by use of "priming moves" (Owen, 1983), such as indirect questioning (Atkinson & Drew, 1979), "noticing" some state of affairs about the actor to open up a slot for an account (Antaki, 1994), or proposing an account for the actor so as "to invite corrections" (Sacks, 1992 [1964], pp. 21–22). The greater the perceived threat to face, the less clear the accounts offered (Turnbull, 1992). Accounts may be presented with ambiguous links among the prescription for action, the actor's identity claims, and the event (Sheer & Weigold, 1995). Persons may strategically account in a vague or ambiguous manner for impression management purposes. Sacks (1992 [1964], pp. 23–24) observes that certain responses appear designed to cut off the basis for the search for an account, e.g., "Everyone does it, don't they?" or "They're all like that."

Accounts, of course, may be self-initiated to tell about something unusual or in anticipation of others finding out about a failure event. Manusov (1996) found few direct reproaches from others in an interpersonal accounts study; typically accounts were self-initiated or in response to a question. One way to initiate an account is to avow a state description (e.g., "I'm so:: ti:yid" (line 5)) and immediately add an account to explain it (line 6):

Transcript 2 (Schegloff, 1996, p. 68)
1 Ava: [B't aside fr'm that it's a'right.
2 Bee: [So what-
3   (0.4)
4 Bee: Wha:t?
5 Ava: I'm so:: ti:yid.
6   I j's played ba:skeball t'day since the firs' time since I wz a freshm'n in hi:ghschool.

A variation on this state description plus account format is when one avows a state description, such as a negative emotion, which projects the recipient to ask for an account. Consider, for instance, the three-part sequence, "affect avowal–prompt–account", in the following transcript:

Transcript 3 (Buttny, 1993b, p. 91)
1 S: So I'm a little a:: (2.2) bummed let's just say
2   (3.1)
3 B: Why::?
4 S: Why you know why

Avowals of emotion (line 1) serve as shorthand formulations. They make relevant a question or prompt (line 3) from the recipient to unpack and make understandable the problematic affect with an account (line 4).

Affect or, more broadly, state descriptions may be ascribed of another as a way to prompt an account. Similar to one's avowal of emotion, ascribing emotion to another makes relevant something out of the ordinary which calls for an account (see Mother's ascription below).

Transcript 4 (UTCL: FO1ahard.1, Buttny, 1993b, p. 94)
    Mother: Well you don't sound like you're too excited about it
    Daughter: .h Well no: I think it's fine I just don't want to get my hopes
                 up real high and have it turn out to be some old gu:y that's
                 gonna try to hi:re (0.4) you know for nothin'

Ascribing affect of another commonly results in an agreement or disagreement combined with account. Affect ascriptions are a kind of "noticing" (Antaki, 1994) of something about the other being unusual or deviant in some sense. Given that actors assume a privileged access to their own states or affect, it is not surprising that accounts are used to correct or elaborate on another's ascription.

Relevance is a key factor in accounting. As already seen, accounts become relevant as a response only if the recipient hears the prior as a problematic, reproach, or probe. Secondly, accounts make relevant aspects of the event to tell one's side. What of the event that is made relevant is partial and selective (Goodwin & Goodwin, 1990). In looking again at transcript 4, how the account gets constructed depends on both (a) how the daughter takes the mother's utterance and (b) what the daughter makes relevant about the event at hand to discursively position herself. Regarding (a), the daughter has to hear the mother's comment as noticing something odd about her to warrant the explanatory account. Antaki (1996, p. 420) shows a case of a job applicant missing an implicit criticism from an interviewer as seen in the applicant's agreeing response. The point here from conversation analysis is that a person's response displays how that person understands and orients to the prior utterance (Heritage, 1984). Regarding (b), once an explanation slot gets interactionally opened, as seen in the daughter's response, the account itself makes relevant different aspects of the event – the actors, their motives, actions, and surrounding context – to cohere in one's telling.

Accounts are prototypically conceived of as responses to problematic events, but as the above point about self-initiated accounts suggests, accounts also can work to prevent a problematic from arising. For instance, conversation analysis looks at accounts as a kind of "dispreferred response", which works in refusing a request, declining an offer or invitation, or disagreeing with an assessment (Heritage, 1988). Accounts work, along with other interactional moves, in doing these dispreferred responses. Given the general "preference for agreement" in conversation (Sacks, 1987), when one does not agree or go along with the direction of the initiating utterance, one needs to soften or mitigate the disagreement, lest one be considered rude or self-centered. Notice how B's account, along with other interactional work, declines an invitation.

Transcript 5 (SBL:10:14)
1 A: Uh if you'd care to come over and a little while this morning
2   I'll give you a cup of coffee

3 B: hehh Well that's awfully sweet of you,
4   I don't think I can make it this morning
5   .hh uhm I'm running an ad in the paper and-
6   and uh I have to stay near the phone

B's response displays many of the features of dispreference: the rejection gets delayed by the use of "hehh", "Well", and an appreciation, "that's awfully sweet of you" (line 3). The rejection is pushed back in the turn, is qualified (line 4), and an account is offered to explain (lines 5–6) (Heritage, 1988). The account allows the recipient to withhold agreement with the initial speaker (Beach, 1990/91).

Accounts are also found in other kinds of sequences, such as in making a proposal to another (Houtkoop-Steenstra, 1990). Making proposals can involve a certain delicacy, so accounts can be used before or after the proposal to explain. Accounts which proceed the proposal are taken as more of a problem for the speaker and are oriented to as delicate. For instance, consider transcript 6:

Transcript 6 (Houtkoop-Streenstra, 1990, p. 113)

	L:	U:h I've got a little problem,
Account		I've got to do some washing,
	R:	Ya:h.
	L:	and actually I can't leave the house, because (.) I'm on sick-leave, (.)
		and I think it's risky to (.) be out in the streets.
	R:	Ya:h.
Proposal	L:	So I'd like to ask you if I could do my washing at your place.
Accept	R:	Yeah yeah:. Of course you can.

In response to a failure event, persons engage in what Higgins and Snyder (1991) call "reality negotiation": excuse-making processes designed to maintain positive images and a sense of control. In the process of constructing an account, actors selectively interpret relevant information according to "self-serving attributional biases". Persons have to reconcile the sometimes competing goals of accounts which are beneficial to the actor and accounts which are believable to the audience (Schlenker & Weigold, 1992). Put in reality negotiation terms, persons need to "achieve a biased compromise between what we want to perceive about ourselves and what outside persons will not seriously question" (Snyder & Higgins, 1990, pp. 212–213).

Actors may try out their account first on their own internal audience and accept it if it is consistent with their desired self-concept. Before presenting the account to external audiences, the actor may need to revise the account several times to cohere with "the facts" and others' knowledge. Given the goal of offering an effective account, the actor's cognitive processing works from possible explanations to "the facts". Various pieces of evidence, facts, or fabrication of facts are considered along with what the audience knows of the facts. From this loose array of concepts, the account becomes coherent depending on "how strongly supported it is by other concepts as part of the representation" (Read, 1992, p.12). For example, one may offer an excuse for arriving late due to heavy traffic but this account becomes more coherent if one can cite the cause of the heavy traffic – a multiple car accident.

The constitutive basis of accounts as a remedial practice is that persons need to tell their side of the story. Looked at interactively, an "explanation slot" gets opened by another's reproach or question, or by the actor's initiation, to address some problematic (Antaki, 1996). In other words, a response becomes relevant to convey one's positioning or alignment to the prior utterance. For instance, an account in response to a blame may be conceived as based on "a self-defense rule" (Bilmes, 1988). The self-defense rule prescribes: upon receiving a blame, respond with an account, lest no response be heard by others as an admission to the reproach. An actor may elect not to offer accounts, instead to avoid the situation, to remain silent, or to retreat. But without an account from the actor, others are left to make their own attributions or stories to reconstruct the event. These are likely to be less enhancing of the actor's reputation. It has been claimed that "any account is better than none" (Massey, Freedman & Zelditch, 1997, p. 239).

A canonical model of accounts phases has been proposed (Schonbach, 1990; Cody & McLaughlin, 1990). (1) A "failure event" arises, along the lines described above, for which an actor is seen as responsible. (2) This leads another to "reproach" the actor for the failure event. (3) The actor replies to the reproach by offering an "account". (4) The account is then "evaluated" by the recipient. This model is a useful beginning point for identifying the stages or components of accounts episodes. However, when actual instances of accounts are examined, we will see that problems arise for this model in describing the components, capturing connection between components and variations on the canonical format.

EVALUATIONS OF ACCOUNTS

Just as a blame or question about a problematic event opens up a slot for an account, so an account, in turn, opens up a slot for an evaluation. In the evaluation slot, the account offered may be honored, or not, by the recipient. When the account is honored, the accounts episode comes to an end. If the account is not honored by the recipient, further accounting may be necessary. In some cases, the account may not be addressed at all by the recipient, but oriented to as "incontestable" (Heritage, 1984), so the episode may be terminated without the account ever being accepted (Young, 1997).

Accounts are more likely to be honored by recipients when they are perceived as "adequate" (Bies & Sitkin, 1992), that is, fit the background expectancies and cohere with consensual vocabularies of motive (Massey et al., 1997). There are generally shared assumptions for what counts as a "good excuse". Accounts are more likely to successfully excuse when the causes of the event can be attributed to "external" (rather than internal), "uncontrollable" (rather than controllable), or "unstable" (rather than stable) conditions (Weiner, et al., 1987). This is consistent with findings from conversation analysis on declining invitations or refusing requests in which persons cite "constraints" or "inability" in their account, rather than "an unwillingness" to accept (Heritage, 1988). Gonzales and colleagues (1992) found that accounts are most likely to be accepted when the failure event was accidental, and least likely when intentional. The point is that these conditions are part of our common-sense knowledge and can be drawn on as a resource in constructing accounts to make them more convincing.

Other approaches to evaluation have attempted to determine the most effective type of account. The findings have been mixed. Not surprisingly, apologies and concessions were the most mitigating and favorable (Sheer & Weigold, 1995; Mongeau et al., 1994). Concessions and excuses are deemed more polite than justifications and refusals. Concessions and excuses show more politeness in that they are attentive to other's face by admitting the problematic character of the act in question. Excuses are less polite than concessions since full responsibility is denied. Justifications and refusals are less polite. They support the actor's face, but not other's face, since they challenge the negative evaluation of the act. Schonbach (1990) reports that excuses and justifications are more positively evaluated, while others found justifications as least favored (Sheer & Weigold, 1995).

Recipients interpret accounts by a "response priority" principle (Bilmes, 1993). For instance, denials are the first priority response to reproaches. So if one does not deny a reproach, but offers an excuse or apology, then it can be implicated that conditions for a denial were not available. Also, there is a response priority in the strength of accounts such that strong accounts have first priority. If a weak account is initially offered, it can be implicated that a strong account will not be forthcoming.

The response to an account is often not a straightforward accept or reject evaluation, but rather a question about the account. Given that accounts are commonly partial and selective, one cannot tell "the whole story" in the initial accounts slot. Account-givers may be probed by recipients' questions so that *accounts are incrementally expanded or unpacked*. Questions following accounts may be heard as "challenges" which project further accounts. In a study of a business negotiating setting, the sequence, "accounts–questions–response" works as a problem-defining series to seek out an agreement (Firth, 1995).

Accountings are "collaboratively achieved" among interlocutors. Whether or not the accounts offered are adequate, or require further explanation, is worked out among the participants' themselves. Mandelbaum (1993) shows how the telling of a narrative represents one of the present participants, Shawn, as selfish. Shawn then responds with his own storied account in which the specifics of the event do not change, but missing details are offered. In reconstructing the event, the blameworthiness of the event is altered such that Shawn portrays himself as not fully responsible – he was left no alternative given the circumstances.

An account may not be initially honored by a recipient, but as it is revised or further elaborated upon, it may become seen as adequate. Recipients who did not accept the initial account sometimes helped account-givers form alternative explanatory factors in their revised accounts (Manusov, 1996). That is, in refusing to accept the initial account, recipients offered accounts for the tellers, which the tellers integrated into their subsequent accounts to different audiences about "the same" incident. This process of reality negotiation lends further support for the collaborative, co-constructed character of accounts sequences (Mandelbaum, 1993; Buttny, 1996).

Recipients are positively biased to refrain from negative feedback when the person offering accounts is perceived as similar to them. They may publicly accept, though privately doubt, the veracity of the account, especially when the account-giver has higher status or power (Blumstein et al., 1974). While recipients may be predisposed to honor accounts, there seems to be a limiting factor: the greater the magnitude of the failure event and the actor's connection to it, the less likely are accounts alone to be honored (Snyder & Higgins, 1990; Gonzales et al., 1992). In other words, the more consequential the failure event, the more likely recipients will seek out corroborating evidence for the actor's accounts.

The uses and evaluations of accounts in specialized or institutional contexts have been studied, e.g., in the courtroom (Atkinson & Drew, 1979; Cody & McLaughlin, 1988), in business negotiation (Firth, 1995), among managers (Bies & Sitkin, 1992; Tata, 1998), in medical exams (Fisher & Groce, 1990), and in therapy (Buttny, 1993b, Ch. 5; Buttny, 1996). A theme in this research is how the institutional setting influences accountability and how accounts get evaluated. In medical exams, for instance, there are asymmetries between doctors and patients in terms of accounts and conversational control. Also, in therapy the therapist does not allow clients to detail their problems at great length, but rather attempts to reframe their problems into a formulation which can be addressed through therapy. The importance of knowing how to account in these specialized contexts can have important practical consequences.

There is a growing body of research pointing to the positive psychological health benefits for account-givers. Accounting is correlated with self-esteem, health, performance, positive affect and reduced anxiety and depression (Higgins & Snyder, 1991; Schlenker & Weigold, 1992). Harvey and colleagues (1990) discuss the importance of accounting processes for coping with severe stress. Accounts serve to reduce tension and uncertainty. Developing narrative accounts helps to provide persons with a sense of control and understanding by giving an order to their relational experiences (Orbuch, 1997).

CONCLUSION

By way of conclusion, we offer a more opinionated commentary on some recent developments in accounts research. The literature on remedial accounts appears to overemphasize direct reproaches, accusations, or blame as a condition for accounts. Accounts are not simply responses to failure events; they occur in response to a variety of other conditions besides reproaches. The turn to examining accounts in naturally occurring contexts found that recipients used few direct reproaches; accounts were more often self-initiated (Morris et al., 1994; Manusov, 1996). As we have seen, accounts are used to make sense of the unusual, e.g., one's negative emotional state (Buttny, 1993b) or a delicate proposal (Houtkoop-Steenstra, 1990). Also, accounts occur as part of "dispreferred responses" as a way to prevent face-threatening acts from arising (Heritage, 1988). Reproaches, criticism, or fault finding, of course, do make accounts relevant, but so do these other conditions which need to be part of our accounts models.

Evaluating accounts has been compared to a verdict (Nicholas, 1990), but such a judicial analogue seems overstretched. This becomes most apparent in accounts studies which have subjects evaluate hypothetical vignettes to compare the relative efficacy of different types of accounts. The problem with such research protocols is that they cast the subject as an audience – a detached observer of events merely evaluating another's actions, rather than situated in an interactional context as a co-participant (Shotter, 1984). For some everyday offenses, the recipient of an account is not primarily concerned with the account's truth or falsity as these studies assume (Goffman, 1971). Recipients are frequently more concerned with maintaining interactional alignment and their ongoing relationship, rather than in judging the credibility of the account. As we have seen, recipients commonly accept accounts which privately they may doubt. For interpersonal accounts, this image of the recipient as "audience" or "judge" directs attention to considerations which are often of secondary importance.

Studies that attempt to determine the most effective type of account seem to be asking the wrong question. Doing this assumes that we can take accounts out of their situated context, independent of antecedents and other co-occurring acts, and compare the effectiveness of, for instance, excuses to justifications to concessions and so on. Such procedures (e.g., evaluating hypothetical vignettes of accounts) result in a conception of a "single-shot" account – of a person offering the account, as though accounts are invariably achieved as a single speech act or message. Observations of actual accounts sequences in naturalistic contexts show that accounts are more emergent, open-ended, and modified in response to recipients' questions or assessments.

An important area of convergence in the literature is in attention to how accounts are "interactionally negotiated" or "co-constructed" by participants – also called "reality negotiation". Accounts are made relevant by some exigency – another's question, reproach, noticing, or by a situational contingency. But what the actor's account makes relevant from the event in question is "partial and selective". The initial account offered may be "self-serving according to attributional biases", but its efficacy depends on the uptake and evaluation of the recipient. One cannot tell everything in a single account, so recipients' questions help to "incrementally unpack" (Firth, 1995) the account further. Indeed, recipients may state the point of a storied account (Mandelbaum, 1993) or even help the account-giver revise the account until it is acceptable (Manusov, 1996).

A related development is the attention given to the discursive subtleties of accounting. Given the often delicate or face-threatening character of situations of accountability, interlocutors may use indirection, vagueness, or ambiguity and rely upon recipients to implicate their meanings, e.g., the response priority principle (Bilmes, 1993). Persons may draw on general-purpose resources, e.g., "Everybody does it", to fill the explanation slot so as to attempt to avoid a more careful accounting.

In cognitively constructing an account, one takes into consideration not only one's own wants, but the recipient – what others know about the event and how they are likely to react (Read, 1992). The conditions which make for a "good excuse" (external, uncontrollable, and unstable (Weiner et al., 1987)) are part of our discursive resources, but to draw upon them in forming an account depends on the situational reality constraints and what can be interactionally negotiated. So the emphasis given to the "strategic" character of accounting, e.g., impression management, needs to be seen, not solely as the work of an individual, but as a co-constructed achievement.

In the decade since the first edition of this Handbook, researchers have broadened the scope of activities within which accounts are understood to occur; detailed the variety of ways accounts are occasioned, constructed, and received in naturally occurring social interaction; and established new connections between accounts and other phenomena of interest to students of language and social psychology. This more panoramic, detailed, and relevant view of accounts positions us to launch future accounts research, advance and critique theoretical formulations, and apply knowledge of accounts with greater sophistication, care, and fruitfulness.

REFERENCES

Antaki, C. (1990). Explaining events or explaining oneself? In M.J. Cody & M.L. McLaughlin (Eds), *The psychology of tactical communication* (pp. 268–282). Philadelphia, PA: Multilingual Matters.

Antaki, C. (1994). *Explaining and arguing: The social organization of accounts*. London: Sage.

Antaki, C. (1996). Explanation slots as resources in interaction. *British Journal of Social Psychology*, **35**, 415–432.

Atkinson, J.M. & Drew, P. (1979). *Order in court: The organization of verbal interaction in judicial settings*. Atlantic Highlands, NJ: Humanities Press.

Austin, J.L. (1961). A plea for excuses. In *Philosophical papers* (2nd edn, pp. 175–204). Oxford: Oxford University Press.

Beach, W.A. (1990/91). Avoiding ownership for alleged wrongdoings. *Research on Language and Social Interaction*, **24**, 1–36.

Benoit, W.L. (1995). *Accounts, excuses and apologies: A theory of image restoration strategies*. Albany, NY: State University Press of New York.

Bies, R.J. & Sitkin, S.B. (1992). Explanation as legitimation: Excuse-making in organizations. In M.L.McLaughlin, M.J.Cody & S.J. Read (Eds), *Explaining oneself to others* (pp. 183–198). Hillsdale, NJ: Erlbaum.

Bilmes, J. (1988). The concept of preference in conversation analysis. *Language in Society*, **17**, 161–181.

Bilmes, J. (1993). Ethnomethodology, culture, and implicature: Towards an empirical pragmatics. *Pragmatics*, **3**, 387–409.

Bilmes, J. (1994). Constituting silence: Life in the world of total meaning. *Semiotica*, **98**, 73–87.

Blumstein, P.W., Carsow, K.G., Hall, J., Hawkins, B., Hoffman, R., Ishem, E., Maurer, C.P., Spens, D., Taylor, J. & Zimmerman, D.L. (1974). The honoring of accounts. *American Sociological Review*, **39**, 551–556.

Burke, K. (1969). *A grammar of motives*. Berkeley, CA: University of California Press.

Buttny, R. (1993a). Accounts and the accountability of social action. In B. Dervin & U. Hariharan (Eds), *Progress in communication sciences* (Vol. 11, pp. 45–74). Norwood, NJ: Ablex.

Buttny, R. (1993b). *Social accountability in communication*. London: Sage.

Buttny, R. (1996). Clients' and therapist's joint construction of the clients' problem. *Research on Language and Social Interaction*, **29**, 125–153.

Cody, M.J. & Braaten, D.O. (1992). In M.L. McLaughlin, M.J. Cody & S.J. Read (Eds), *Explaining oneself to others* (pp. 225–244). Hillsdale, NJ: Erlbaum.

Cody, M.J. & McLaughlin, M.L. (1988). Accounts on trial: Oral arguments in traffic court. In C. Antaki (Ed.), *Analysing everyday explanation* (pp. 113–126). London: Sage.

Cody, M.J. & McLaughlin, M.L. (1990). Interpersonal accounting. In H. Giles & W.P. Robinson (Eds), *Handbook of language and social psychology* (pp. 227–255). New York: Wiley.

Draper, S.W. (1988). What's going on in everyday explanation? In C. Antaki (Ed.), *Analysing everyday explanation* (pp. 15–31). London: Sage.

Firth, A. (1995). Talking for a change: Commodity negotiations by telephone. In A.Firth (Ed.), *The discourse of negotiation* (pp. 183–222). New York: Pergamon.

Fisher, S. & Groce, S.B. (1990). Accounting practices in medical interviews. *Language in Society*, **19**, 225–250.

Garfinkel, H. (1967). *Studies in ethnomethodology*. Englewood Cliffs, NJ: Prentice-Hall.

Goffman, E. (1971). *Relations in public: Microstudies of the public order*. New York: Harper & Row.

Goodwin, C. & Goodwin, M.H. (1990). Interstitial argument. In A.D. Grimshw (Ed.), *Conflict talk* (pp. 85–117). New York: Cambridge University Press.

Gonzales, M.H. (1992). A thousand pardons: The effectiveness of verbal remedial tactics during account episodes. *Journal of Language and Social Psychology*, **11**, 133–150.

Gonzales, M.H., Manning, D.J. & Haugen, J.A. (1992). Explaining our sins: Factors influencing offender accounts and anticipated victim responses. *Journal of Personality and Social Psychology*, **62**, 958–971.

Harvey, J.H., Orbuch, T.L. & Weber, A.L. (1990). A social psychological model of account-making: In response to severe stress. *Journal of Language and Social Psychology*, **9**, 191–207.

Heritage, J. (1984). *Garfinkel and ethnomethodology*. Cambridge, UK: Polity.

Heritage, J. (1988). Explanation as accounts: A conversation analytic perspective. In C. Antaki (Ed.), *Analysing everyday explanation* (pp. 127–144). London: Sage.

Herzfeld, M. (1996). Embarrassment as pride: Narrative resourcefulness and strategies of normativity among Cretan animal-thieves. In C.L. Briggs (Ed.), *Disorderly discourse* (pp. 72–94). New York: Oxford University Press.

Hewitt, J.P. & Stokes, R. (1975). Disclaimers. *American Sociological Review*, **40**, 1–11.

Higgins, R.L. & Snyder, C.R. (1991). Reality negotiation and excuse-making. In C.R. Snyder & D.R. Forsyth (Eds), *Handbook of social and clinical psychology* (pp. 769–95). New York: Pergamon.

Houtkoop-Steenstra, H. (1990). Accounting for proposals. *Journal of Pragmatics*, **14**, 111–124.

Mandelbaum, J. (1993). Assigning responsibility in conversational storytelling: The inter-actional construction of reality. *Text*, **13**, 247–266.

Manusov, V. (1996). Changing explanations: The process of account-making over time. *Research on Language and Social Interaction*, **29**, 155–179.

Massey, K., Freedman, S. & Zelditch, M. (1997). Status, power, and accounts. *Social Psychology Quarterly*, **60**, 238–251.

Mills, C.W. (1940). Situated actions and vocabularies of motive. *American Sociological Review*, **5**, 903–913.

Mongeau, P.A., Hale, J.L. & Alles, M. (1994). An experimental investigation of accounts and attributions following sexual infidelity. *Communication Monographs*, **61**, 326–344.

Morris, G.H. (1985). The remedial episode as a negotiation of rules. In R.L. Street & J.N. Cappella (Eds), *Sequence and pattern in communicative behavior* (pp. 70–84). Baltimore, MD: Edward Arnold.

Morris, G.H., White, C.H. & Iltis, R. (1994). "Well, ordinarily I would, but": Reexamining the nature of accounts for problematic events. *Research on Language and Social Interaction*, **27**, 124–144.

Much, N.C. & Shweder, R.A. (1978). Speaking of rules: The analysis of culture in breach. In W. Damon (Ed.), *New directions for child development* (Vol. 2, pp. 19–39). San Francisco, CA: Jossey-Bass.

Nicholas, L. (1990). Reconceptualizing social accounts: An agenda for theory building and empirical research. *Current Perspectives in Social Theory*, **10**, 113–144.

Orbuch, T.L. (1997). People's accounts count: The sociology of accounts. *Annual Review of Sociology*, **23**, 455–478.

Owen, M. (1983). *Apologies and remedial interchanges*. New York: Mouton.

Read, S.J. (1992). Constructing accounts: The role of explanatory coherence. In M.L. McLaughlin, M.J. Cody & S.J. Read (Eds), *Explaining oneself to others* (pp. 3–20). Hillsdale, NJ: Erlbaum.

Robinson, W.P. (1998). Language and social psychology: Opportunities and significance. *Journal of Language and Social Psychology*, **17**, 276–301.

Sacks, H. (1987). On the preference for agreement and contiguity in sequences in conversation. In G. Button & J.R.E. Lee (Eds), *Talk and social organization* (pp. 54–69). Philadelphia, PA: Multilingual Matters.

Sacks, H. (1992 [1964]). *Lectures on conversation*. Gail Jefferson (Ed.). Oxford: Blackwell.

Schegloff, E.A. (1996). Turn organization: One intersection of grammar and interaction. In E. Ochs, E.A. Schegloff & S.A. Thompson (Eds), *Interaction and grammar* (pp. 52–133). New York: Cambridge University Press.

Schlenker, B.R. & Weigold, M.E. (1992). Interpersonal processes involving impression regulation and management. *Annual Review of Psychology*, **43**, 133–168.

Schlenker, B.R., Weigold, M.E. & Doherty, K. (1991). Coping with accountability: Self-identification and evaluative reckonings. In C.R. Snyder & D.R. Forsyth (Eds), *Handbook of social and clinical psychology* (pp. 96–115). New York: Pergamon.

Schonbach, P. (1990). *Account episodes*. New York: Cambridge University Press.

Scott, M.L. (1993). Foreword. In R. Buttny (Ed.), *Social accountability in communication* (pp. ix–x). London: Sage.

Scott, M.L. & Lyman, S.M. (1968). Accounts. *American Sociological Review*, **33**, 46–62.

Semin, G.R. & Manstead, A.S.R. (1983). *The social accountability of conduct*. New York: Academic Press.

Sheer, V.C. & Weigold, M.F. (1995). Managing threats to identity: The accountability triangle and strategic accounting. *Communication Research*, **22**, 592–611.

Shotter, J. (1984). *Social accountability and selfhood*. Oxford: Basil Blackwell.

Snyder, C.R. & Higgins, R.L. (1990). Reality negotiation and excuse-making: President Reagan's 4 March 1987 Iran Arms scandal speech and other literature. In M.J. Cody & M.L. McLaughlin (Eds), *The psychology of tactical communication* (pp. 207–228). Philadelphia, PA: Multilingual Matters.

Stamp, G.H. & Sabourin, T.C. (1995). Accounting for violence: An analysis of male spousal abuse narratives. *Journal of Applied Communication Research*, **23**, 284–307.

Stokes, R. & Hewitt, J.P. (1976). Aligning actions. *American Sociological Review*, **41**, 838–843.

Tata, J. (1998). The influence of gender on the use and effectiveness of managerial accounts. *Group & Organization Management*, **23**, 267–288.

Tedeschi, J.T. & Reiss, M. (1981). Verbal strategies in impression management. In C. Antaki (Ed.), *The psychology of ordinary explanation in social behaviour* (pp. 271–309). New York: Academic Press.

Turnbull, W. (1992). A conversation approach to explanation, with emphasis on politeness and accounting. In M.L. McLaughlin, M.J. Cody & S.J. Read (Eds), *Explaining oneself to others* (pp. 105–130). Hillsdale, NJ: Erlbaum.

Watson, D.R. & Sharrock, W.W. (1991). Something on accounts. *Discourse Analysis Research Group Newsletter*, **7**, 3–11.

Weiner, B. (1992). Excuses in everyday interaction. In M.L. McLaughlin, M.J. Cody & S.J. Read (Eds), *Explaining oneself to others* (pp. 131–146). Hillsdale, NJ: Erlbaum.

Weiner, B., Amirkham, J., Folkes, V.S. & Verette, J.A. (1987). An attributional analysis of excuse giving: Studies of a naive theory of emotion. *Journal of Personality and Social Psychology*, **52**, 316–324.

Young, R.L. (1997). Account sequences. *Symbolic Interactionism*, **20**, 291–305.

3.16

Negotiating

Steven R. Wilson
Northwestern University, Evanston, USA
Gaylen D. Paulson
University of Texas, Austin, USA
Linda L. Putnam
Texas A&M University, College Station, USA

Negotiating is a pervasive activity. Negotiation is central to labor/management and buyer/seller relationships. Corporations and governments negotiate joint ventures and trade agreements. Organizations hire employees and establish budgets via negotiation. Negotiation also occurs within personal relationships, such as when spouses negotiate child care responsibilities.

Negotiating is a process whereby two or more interdependent parties with perceived incompatible goals engage in give-and-take interaction to reach a mutually acceptable outcome (Putnam & Roloff, 1992). The parties discuss issues, defend and refute positions, make offers, and exchange compromises. Both must cooperate to attain a settlement but both also have the ability to interfere with the other's goal attainment. This interdependence contributes to the mixed-motive nature of negotiation.

Language and negotiating are intimately related. Negotiators express arguments, formulate proposals, signal priorities, and portray desired identities via language (Wilson, 1992). Language patterns shape the definition and transformation of issues (Putnam & Holmer, 1992) and reveal how negotiators define their relationship (Donohue & Roberto, 1993). "Understanding the role of language is critical to a complete understanding of negotiation" (Gibbons, Bradac & Busch, 1992, p. 156).

Language itself can be analyzed from various perspectives (see Fisher, 1978). Perspectives offer distinct points of view on phenomena that magnify some elements while distorting or omitting others. Perspectives guide a researcher's

The New Handbook of Language and Social Psychology.
Edited by W. Peter Robinson and Howard Giles.
© 2001 John Wiley & Sons Ltd.

choice of which concepts are relevant and what levels of analysis are fruitful. Because they offer unique viewpoints and highlight distinct questions, perspectives are difficult to compare empirically. Multiple perspectives often are present within a discipline, but individual scholars typically work from one, or at most a few, perspectives.

We do not offer a comprehensive review of research on language and negotiating; rather, we analyze perspectives underlying current work. At least four perspectives can be identified, which we label psychological, interactional, discourse, and symbolic. For each, we identify its general assumptions about language, people, and negotiation, and describe one or more illustrative research programs. Each perspective offers valuable insights about language and negotiating; hence, we clarify what is brought into focus and what may be overlooked from each.

THE PSYCHOLOGICAL PERSPECTIVE

The fundamental premise of this perspective is that language reflects a negotiator's psychological states. From this view, a negotiator's linguistic choices arise from and are driven by his or her psychological states. For example, a negotiator's willingness to move away from opening positions depends, in part, on whether he/she frames proposed concessions as "gains" over the status quo versus "losses" from an ideal settlement point (Neale & Bazerman, 1985). A negotiator's language provides indirect access into how he/she views a negotiation at present. Of course, psychological states change over time as negotiators make sense of the unfolding situation (Wilson & Putnam, 1990).

The psychological perspective assumes that negotiators may engage in integrative or distributive bargaining (Walton & McKersie, 1965). Distributive bargaining occurs when parties perceive that their goals fundamentally conflict and resources are scarce. Agenda items are conceptualized in zero-sum fashion and both attempt to maximize their share of a fixed pie. Integrative bargaining occurs when parties perceive that their goals are not necessarily incompatible. Agenda items are conceptualized in variable-sum fashion; hence, both search for creative solutions to enlarge the pie. The psychological perspective explores how negotiators often miss integrative potential present in situations (Neale & Bazerman, 1991; Pruitt, 1983).

Psychological scholars focuses primarily on the individual negotiator as the unit of analysis. Negotiators are portrayed as goal-oriented, but they often pursue multiple conflicting goals (Wilson & Putnam, 1990) and their decisions are influenced by biases (Neale & Bazerman, 1991). To provide examples of this perspective, we briefly review studies of (a) judgmental errors, and (b) plans/planning.[1]

---

[1] We chose these two research programs to illustrate general features of the psychological perspective. Many other exemplars could have been chosen. Pruitt and his colleagues' Strategic Choice model is one obvious omission from our review of the psychological perspective (see Pruitt, 1983; Pruitt & Carnevale, 1993; for cross-cultural applications, see Graham, Mintu & Rodgers, 1994). Due to space constraints, we are able to discuss only a few exemplars for each perspective.

Psychological scholars assume that individuals attempt to be "rational" (i.e., maximize their own utilities) when considering possible settlements as well as alternatives to negotiating. However, negotiators are hindered by biases, such as: (a) assuming that gain for self must come at the other's expense; (b) relying too much on readily available information while ignoring other relevant data; (c) being overly affected by how concessions are framed; (d) assuming that the other's behavior reflects internal dispositions rather than situational constraints; and (e) being overconfident about alternatives to negotiation (Neale & Bazerman, 1991; Thompson, 1998). Many experiments document the existence of these biases as well as conditions that moderate their effect (e.g., Lim, 1997; Morris, Larrick & Su, 1999; Pinkley, Griffith & Northcraft, 1995; Thompson, Peterson & Brodt, 1996). Participants in these studies, undergraduate and MBA students, typically complete simulations with issues of differential importance that can be logrolled as well as issues where the two sides have incompatible (zero-sum) or compatible (identical) interests. Negotiation processes examined include concession making and information exchange, whereas outcomes include impasse rates, number of transactions completed, individual and joint profits, and settlement equity.

Thompson and Hastie's (1990, Study 1) investigation of the "fixed-pie" myth illustrates this research program. Prior to completing a simulation, most participants assumed that their own and the other party's interests were completely contrary. Participants became more accurate in estimating the other side's priorities after 5 minutes than they had been before negotiating, and more accurate by the end of the simulation than after 5 minutes. Participants were more accurate in estimating the other side's priorities at the end if they had planned to ask for information about the other's priorities, give information about their own priorities, and propose packages among multiple issues. Subsequent research (Thompson, 1991 ; Thompson et al., 1996) shows that negotiators who actually exchange information about priorities hold more accurate perceptions of the other side and reach settlements with higher joint gain compared to negotiators who do not exchange such information.

A second research program reflecting the psychological perspective investigates planning during negotiation. Plans represent a negotiator's knowledge about actions necessary for accomplishing goals. Plans typically include information about one or more goals, potential obstacles to achieving those goals, and actions for overcoming obstacles (Roloff & Jordan, 1992). Planning refers to processes involved as a negotiator recalls, generates, selects, implements, monitors, and modifies plans. Negotiation presents a complex planning environment since the parties often find it difficult to set concrete goals, face conflict between multiple goals, lack information about the other's goals, and alter their goals as new information emerges and issues evolve (Roloff & Jordan, 1992; Wilson & Putnam, 1990). Although pre-negotiation planning is important, negotiators develop and modify mental plans as bargaining unfolds (Thompson & Hastie, 1990). Negotiation teams develop joint plans prior to bargaining and during caucus sessions, and head negotiators may plan collaboratively across the table or in sidebar sessions (Roloff

& Jordan, 1992). Negotiators differ in their planning expertise (Jordan & Roloff, 1997) and benefit from some types of pre-negotiation planning (Weingart et al., 1999). Cultures differ in whether they prioritize long- versus short-term planning (Cai, 1998).

Research on planning has focused on the substance, precursors, and effects of pre-negotiation plans (e.g., Jordan & Roloff, 1997; Roloff & Jordan, 1991; Cai, 1998). For example, Jordan and Roloff explore self-monitoring and pre-negotiation plans. High self-monitors rely primarily on situational norms for appropriate behavior, whereas low self-monitors rely primarily on internal states to guide action. Prior to completing a simulation, undergraduates wrote plans for how they intended to achieve their goals. Written plans were analyzed for examples of: (a) logrolling; (b) impression management; (c) argumentation; (d) distributive tactics; (e) setting limits; and (f) reactivity. High, relative to low, self-monitors rated themselves as more committed to their goals prior to the negotiation; included more "impression management" and "logrolling" elements in their pre-negotiation plans; and included a larger number of distinct elements in their plans. During the subsequent simulation, high self-monitors used impression management and argument strategies more frequently and achieved a larger percentage of their pre-negotiation profit goals.

To summarize, the psychological perspective highlights how negotiators often miss integrative potential. The perspective clarifies how language (i.e., bargaining tactics) mediates effects of psychological states on negotiation outcomes, how negotiators make inferences about other parties' priorities from their language, and how interaction processes can lead negotiators to redefine goals. The perspective offers practical advice for improving negotiating skills (Bazerman & Neale, 1992).

The psychological perspective, like any other, downplays issues highlighted or problematized by other perspectives. Psychological scholars typically employ simulations with predefined issues and outcomes. Critics emphasize that the issues to be negotiated and associated utilities themselves are subject to argument (Gulliver, 1979; Putnam & Holmer, 1992). Psychological scholars pay limited attention to larger social structures (e.g., the institutions of labor and management) in which negotiation occurs (Firth, 1995a; Friedman, 1994). They assume that negotiation language can be classified into macro categories (e.g., threats) that clearly serve integrative or distributive functions. Critics emphasize that integrative and distributive processes are not so easily disentangled (Putnam, 1990) and that the same tactic can promote integrative and/or distributive bargaining depending on its wording, timing, and sequencing (Gibbons et al., 1992). The interactional perspective stresses timing and sequencing.

THE INTERACTIONAL PERSPECTIVE

The interactional perspective's fundamental premise is that language use evolves over the course of a negotiation. These scholars analyze "the interaction patterns of negotiation as they unfold over time" (Weingart et al., 1999, p. 367). Influenced by "systems" thinking, interaction scholars argue that a negotiator's language choices must be understood within the context of preceding and anticipated future actions (Putnam, 1984). Researchers in this perspective take the dyad as their primary unit of analysis, and analyze sequences rather than only frequencies of bargaining tactics.

To illustrate the interactional perspective, we review studies of (a) conflict cycles and (b) bargaining phases. Research on conflict cycles explores how negotiators respond to each other's tactics turn by turn (e.g., Brett, Shapiro & Lytle, 1998; Donohue, 1981; Putnam & Jones, 1982; Weingart et al., 1990, 1999). Participants in these studies, with rare exception, are students completing simulations. Some simulations include predefined issues with associated pay-offs (e.g., Weingart et al., 1999), but others allow participants themselves to define the nature and importance of issues (e.g., Brett et al., 1998). Participants' behaviors are coded using schemes of 10–25 bargaining tactics. Interdependence among bargaining tactics is explored via lag-sequential or Markov chain analysis. Prior to sequential analyses, interaction scholars often conduct factor analyses to group individual tactics into clusters such as "defensive, offensive, and integrative tactics" (Putnam & Jones, 1982). Interactional scholars identify sequential patterns of bargaining tactics and relate these to negotiation outcomes such as: (a) impasse rates (Donohue, 1981; Putnam & Jones, 1982); (b) settlement equity (Brett et al., 1998); and (c) individual and joint profit (Donohue, 1981; Weingart et al., 1990).

This research offers several insights about conflict cycles. First, negotiators reciprocate each other's use of many bargaining tactics at greater than chance levels: multiple-issue offers beget multiple offers, threats beget threats, and statements of concern beget statements of concern (Brett et al., 1998; Weingart et al., 1990, 1999). Distributive tactics as a group follow distributive tactics (Donohue, 1981; Weingart et al., 1999) and the same is true for integrative tactics (Putnam & Jones, 1982; Weingart et al., 1999). Second, negotiators display complementary patterns with some tactics. Asking for information tends to elicit providing information (Weingart et al., 1990, 1999), and offensive tactics by labor are responded to with defensive tactics by management (Putnam & Jones, 1982).

Third, negotiators who rigidly reciprocate each other's distributive tactics often reach undesirable outcomes. Dyads who reach impasse reciprocate each other's attacking or offensive tactics more than agreement dyads, who instead respond to attacking or offensive tactics more often with information-sharing and regressive tactics (Donohue, 1981; Putnam & Jones, 1982). Dyads who reach one-sided settlements also reciprocate each other's contentious tactics more than dyads that achieve equitable settlements (Brett et al., 1998). Dyads who reach higher joint profit reciprocate each other's integrative tactics more than those who miss integrative potential (Weingart et al., 1990). Fourth, the same bargaining tactic can serve distributive or integrative functions depending on its relationship to prior tactics. For example, information sharing covaries with both distributive and integrative tactics (Putnam & Jones, 1982; Weingart et al., 1990), reflecting that negotiators may provide information to defend themselves in response to prior attack (a distributive function) or to address questions about their relative priorities (an integrative function).

Research on negotiation phases investigates more macro-level patterns. A phase is "a coherent period of interaction, characterized by a dominant constellation of communicative acts" (Holmes, 1992, p. 83). Early research built on Douglas's (1962) classic studies, which identified three negotiation phases: establishing the bargaining range, reconnecting the bargaining range, and precipitating the decision-making crisis. Newer research uses techniques such as phase mapping to identify variation in the number, length, and order of bargaining phases (e.g., Donohue & Roberto, 1993; Holmes 1997; Holmes & Sykes, 1993). Holmes compares transcripts of naturalistic and simulated (i.e., training) hostage negotiations provided by law enforcement agencies. Transcripts were divided into 30-second units, and units were categorized for eight activity types derived from Gulliver (1979). A phase was defined as any occurrence of three contiguous acts from the same activity type. Holmes analyzes whether talk enacting the same type of phase (e.g., defining the agenda) occurs at particular points in the negotiations, and whether simulated or naturalistic hostage negotiations contain a more predictable phase structure. In general, simulated hostage negotiations have a more orderly and organized structure. This reflects that authentic hostage negotiations can have: (a) multiple negotiators representing each party; (b) participation by third parties (e.g., families); and (c) participants under the influence of alcohol or drugs.

In sum, the interactional perspectives analyzes negotiations over time to clarify how: parties may reach undesirable outcomes even when they begin with good intentions; language serves multiple functions; and negotiations vary in degree of structure. The perspective provides insight about how participants can modify their own behavior to buffer conflict escalation (Brett et al., 1998).

The interactional perspective downplays issues highlighted by others. Although they identify patterns that lead to impasse or inequitable outcomes, interactional scholars have less to say about why participants enact dysfunctional patterns. Psychological scholars might point to faulty judgments whereas symbolic scholars might implicate long-standing bargaining rituals. Interactional scholars classify negotiation language into gross categories defined by shared content, form, or function. Critics charge that this approach: leads to an unorganized and unwieldy set of categories; imposes a rigid predetermined framework on data; and assumes that meanings are fixed rather than fluid (Firth, 1995a). Discourse scholars address just such concerns.

THE DISCOURSE PERSPECTIVE

The discourse perspective's fundamental premise is that negotiation language is patterned at micro levels. Discourse research reveals regularities in how negotiators: refer to themselves, their constituents, and the other side (Maynard, 1985;

O'Donnell, 1992); formulate the "gist" of the other's talk (Walker, 1995); account for their actions (Firth, 1995b); reformulate their proposals (Boden, 1995); exchange speaking turns (Francis, 1986; O'Donnell, 1992); phrase requests for information (Donohue & Diez, 1985); and return to previous topics (Francis, 1986). Discourse scholars view negotiation talk as interesting in its own right, and not only because it mediates the effects of other factors on outcomes. They focus more on the "how" than the "why" of negotiation (Firth, 1995a). Discourse scholars treat talk and context as reciprocally related. Requests for information, for instance, reflect but at the same time affirm or challenge participants' roles and relational history (Donohue & Diez, 1985).

Work by conversation analysis (CA) and facework/politeness scholars illustrates the discourse perspective. CA scholars view negotiation talk as locally managed, treat units of talk (e.g., adjacency pairs) rather than individuals as their units of analysis, and view negotiation actions as joint accomplishments (Firth, 1995b; Francis. 1986). CA scholars attempt to describe and explain how negotiation is interactionally accomplished without reference to concepts beyond the talk itself. References to intentions, social identities, or other "outside" concepts are resisted unless it can be shown that the participants themselves orient to these concepts in their talk (Bell, 1995, pp. 47–49).

CA scholars typically create detailed transcripts from naturalistic negotiations and warrant claims with examples. As one example, Firth (1995b) analyzes "accounts" in a single negotiation between a Danish cheese manufacturer and a Middle East wholesaler. Initially, the buyer (wholesaler) sends a telex message implicitly rejecting the prices proposed by the seller (manufacturer) in a previous telex. The two parties then engage in a prolonged (over 150 turns) telephone conversation during which: (a) the seller attempts to account for his company's higher prices (e.g., European Community policies) and raises questions about the competitor's offer, whereas (b) the buyer explains the competitor's offer and challenges the seller's account. Firth (1995b) demonstrates that the process of reaching agreement in this case is largely a function of negotiating the validity of accounts.

Research on facework and politeness also illustrates this perspective. Although diverse, this research draws on Goffman (1967) as well as Brown and Levinson (1987). "Face" reflects the value that negotiators attach to their public identities. Negotiators worry about losing face when actions or events potentially discredit a desired identity in the eyes of significant others, such as the other side or their own constituents. Personality, contextual, and cultural factors can magnify a negotiator's concern about face (e.g., Roloff & Campion, 1987). Negotiators rely on facework, or "actions taken by a person to make whatever he [sic] is doing consistent with face" (Goffman, 1967, p. 12). Phrasing demands ambiguously using disclaimers, and hiding disagreement among one's constituents are examples of preventative facework, while distributive behaviors often function as corrective facework (Wilson, 1992).

Discourse studies in this tradition typically analyze negotiation transcripts to explore how language threatens, maintains, and/or restores face. For example,

Wilson, Meischke & Kim (1990) analyze directives, or speech acts aimed to get the other party to perform a desired action (e.g., demands), within a corpus of naturalistic and simulated negotiations. According to Brown and Levinson (1987), directives threaten the other side's desire for autonomy (what they call "negative face"). Wilson et al. (1990) show how directives simultaneously may threaten the other side's and the speaker's own desire to appear competent and trustworthy (what Brown and Levinson call "positive face") under specific conditions (for more detail, see Wilson, Aleman & Leatham, 1998). Such occurrences may disrupt interaction until participants reach a new implicit "working consensus" (Goffman, 1967, P. 11) about situated identities that enables them to discuss agenda issues once again.

To summarize, the discourse perspective highlights how participants actually "do" negotiation through talk, including how they: enact and orient to roles, create and reflect context, and adapt to one another other moment by moment. The perspective clarifies how negotiation talk is similar to and different from talk in other contexts (Francis, 1986).

The discourse perspective also takes for granted issues highlighted by others. Discourse scholars have had little to say about why patterns of talk push negotiations towards integrative or distributive outcomes. People outside the perspective are unlikely to read discourse studies unless linkages with outcomes are drawn. Discourse scholars often downplay sociological concepts such as power (Bell, 1995) and gender (Putnam & Kolb, in press) or psychological concepts such as goals (Wilson & Putnam, 1990) that suggest linkages. Discourse scholars often do not analyze data beyond negotiation interaction itself. Critics argue that field notes and interviews can clarify participants' interpretations (Bell, 1995; Gulliver, 1979). The symbolic perspective places central importance on just such data.

THE SYMBOLIC PERSPECTIVE

The symbolic perspective's fundamental premise is that language is the means by which negotiators create a shared reality. This perspective views negotiation as "an organizational ritual" and thus "a process of constructing social reality" via language (Putnam, Van Hoeven & Bullis, 1991, p. 95).

Symbolic scholars employ analytic concepts such as rites and rituals. Rites are public events that involve careful planning and management, occur at regular time intervals, and serve instrumental and value-expressive functions. Rituals are scripted behaviors performed as part of larger rites (Trice & Beyer, 1984). For example, contract negotiations often are portrayed as a rite of conflict reduction during which labor and management ritualistically present long lists of demands, make angry speeches, signal their real priorities indirectly, and search for solutions in all-night sessions just before an impending deadline (see Friedman, 1994, pp. 4–6; Putnam et al., 1991, p. 90).

Symbolic scholars also employ metaphors of drama and fantasy to analyze negotiation. For example, negotiators often manage mixed motives by enacting distributive behavior "front stage" at the table while searching for integrative solutions "backstage" during sidebar meetings (Friedman, 1994). Units of analysis in symbolic studies include negotiators, teams, sides, and larger audiences.

Rather than developing predictive theories, symbolic scholars develop models that offer new insights about negotiation (see Friedman, 1994, p. 23; Gulliver, 1979, pp. xvi–xvii). Models are developed to help make sense of detailed case studies of naturalistic negotiations. Questions addressed include how a particular set of negotiation practices have evolved over time, how those practices are interpreted by the participants themselves, and why those practices may be resistant to change.

Putnam et al.'s (1991) analysis of teacher–school board negotiations illustrates the symbolic perspective. The authors analyze contract negotiations in two Indiana school districts by taking extensive field notes at all meetings, conducting interviews with negotiators and their bargaining teams, and collecting written offers and final contracts at both sites. They analyze fantasy themes and types as well as bargaining rites and rituals. Fantasy themes refer to the content of a group story such as the plot line, characters, and scenes; fantasy types are stock narratives or similar plotlines told repeatedly by a group.

Putnam et al. (1991) conclude that participants in both school districts preferred to avoid "game playing" while negotiating in isolation from the public, accountants and mediators. Teacher and school board teams in both districts chained out vivid stories about how "outsider" villains had impeded prior negotiations. Rites and rituals, however, were quite different. Negotiators in the larger suburban district reached general agreement on items at the table and then hammered out proposals for exact language within caucus meetings. This negotiation "resembled two vender who were trying to iron out the legal technicalities of a sales contract" (p. 98). Negotiations in the smaller rural district occurred primarily in caucus and sidebar sessions. This negotiation more closely resembled international "shuttle diplomacy".

To summarize, the symbolic perspective highlights how negotiators create a shared reality, and how their actions are interpreted within a larger context that includes institutional roles as well as the prior history of bargaining. The symbolic perspective draws attention to "intraorganizational bargaining" (Walton & McKersie, 1965) or processes of mutual influence between negotiators and their own constituents. Finally, the perspective provides insight about why negotiators frequently resist changes to well-established bargaining rites and rituals (Friedman, 1994).

The symbolic perspective diverts attention away from issues highlighted by others. For example, a negotiation team's interpretation of the other side's actions may reflect not only institutional roles and relational history but also judgmental biases that commonly impede joint problem-solving (Neale & Bazerman, 1991). Although they provide compelling interpretations of particular negotiations, symbolic scholars are less able to draw general conclusions due to limitations of the case-study method. Finally, symbolic scholars present only a limited number of examples from a much larger corpus of data and recount examples only in general terms. Critics charge that this provides insufficient data for readers to evaluate the researcher's claims (Firth, 1995a).

CONCLUSION

Current work on language and negotiation is guided by at least four perspectives, which we label psychological, interactional, discourse, and symbolic. Each is composed of coherent assumptions about language, people, and negotiation, and each offers distinct insights about language use. We close with three general comments about perspectives themselves.

None of the perspectives covered here is static. As one example, psychological scholars are moving from focusing primarily on "cold" cognitions (e.g., judgmental errors) to incorporate affect and emotion as well (e.g., Barry & Oliver, 1996; Kumar, 1997). They are also paying greater attention to the organizational and cultural contexts of negotiation (e.g., Kramer & Messick, 1995). We suspect these developments stem, in part, from attempts by psychological scholars to respond to criticisms leveled from other perspectives while also remaining true to their own commitments.

Our choice of four perspectives is somewhat arbitrary, as others can be identified. Feminist perspectives, for example, emphasize that negotiation concepts and theories (e.g., exchange) reflect gendered assumptions and that alternative ways of envisioning negotiation are possible (Putnam & Kolb, in press). We chose the four perspectives reviewed here based on our judgment about which have been employed most widely in studies of language and negotiation to date. This situation could change.

We encourage tolerance of multiple perspectives. When encountering work from another perspective, our initial reaction is often that the levels of analysis seem wrong, the methods seem artificially complicated, and the answers (nay, even the questions) seem to miss the point. By tolerance we do not mean suspending evaluation; research should be evaluated for the degree to which it accomplishes goals made relevant by its underlying perspective. Like Fisher (1978), however, we mean tolerance "in the sense of understanding what others are doing and thereby understanding what you yourself are doing – and why you are doing it" (p. 323). Seen in this light, understanding multiple perspectives on language and negotiating is well worth the effort.

REFERENCES

Barry, B. & Oliver, R.L. (1996). Affect in dyadic negotiation: A model and propositions. *Organizational Behavior and Human Decision Processes*, **67**, 127–143.

Bazerman, M.H. & Neale, M.A. (1992). *Negotiating rationally*. New York: Free Press.

Bell, D.V.J. (1995). Negotiation in the workplace: The view from a political linguist. In A. Firth (Ed.), The discourse of negotiation: Studies of language in the workplace (pp. 41–60). Oxford, UK: Pergamon.

Boden, D. (1995). Agendas and arrangements: Everyday negotiations in meetings. In A. Firth (Ed.), *The discourse of negotiation: Studies of language in the workplace* (pp. 83–100). Oxford, UK: Pergamon.

Brett, J.M., Shapiro, D.L. & Lytle, A.L. (1998). Breaking the bonds of reciprocity in negotiations. *Academy of Management Journal*, **41**, 410–424.

Brown, P. & Levinson, S.C. (1987). *Politeness: Some universals in language usage.* Cambridge, UK: Cambridge University Press.

Cai, D. (1998). Culture, plans, and the pursuit of negotiation goals. *Journal of Asian Pacific Communication*, **8**, 103–123.

Donohue, W.A. (1981). Development of a model of rule use in negotiation interaction. *Communication Monographs*, **48**, 106–120.

Donohue, W.A. & Diez, M.E. (1985). Directive use in negotiation interaction. *Communication Monographs*, **52**, 305–318.

Donohue, W.A. & Roberto, A.J. (1993). Relational development as negotiated order in hostage negotiation. *Human Communication Research*, **20**, 175–198.

Donohue, W.A., Diez, M.E. & Hamilton, M. (1984). Coding naturalistic negotiation interaction. *Human Communication Research*, **10**, 403–425.

Firth, A. (1995a). Introduction and overview. In A. Firth (Ed.), *The discourse of negotiation: Studies of language in the workplace* (pp. 3–40). Oxford, UK: Pergamon.

Firth, A. (1995b). "Accounts" in negotiation discourse: A single-case analysis. *Journal of Pragmatics*, **23**, 199–226.

Fisher, B.A. (1978). *Perspectives on human communication.* New York: Macmillan.

Francis, D.W. (1986). Some structures of negotiation talk. *Language in Society*, **15**, 53–80.

Friedman, R.A. (1994). *Front stage, backstage: The dramatic structure of labor negotiations.* Cambridge, MA: MIT Press.

Gibbons, P., Bradac, J.J. & Busch, J.D. (1992). The role of language in negotiations: Threats and promises. In L.L. Putnam & M.E. Roloff (Eds), *Communication and negotiation* (pp. 156–175). Newbury Park, CA: Sage.

Goffman, E. (1967). *Interaction ritual: Essays in face-to-face behavior.* Chicago: Aldine.

Graham, J.L., Mintu, A.T. & Rodgers, W. (1994). Explorations of negotiation behaviors in ten foreign cultures using a model developed in the United States. *Management Science*, **40**, 72–95.

Gulliver, P.H. (1979). *Disputes and negotiations: A cross-cultural perspective.* New York: Academic Press.

Holmes, M.E. (1992). Phase structures in negotiation. In L.L. Putnam & M.E. Roloff (Eds), *Communication and negotiation* (pp. 83–108). Newbury Park, CA: Sage.

Holmes, M.E. (1997). Optimal matching analysis of negotiation phase sequences in simulated and authentic hostage negotiations. *Communication Reports*, **10**, 1–8.

Holmes, M.E. & Sykes, R.E. (1993). A test of the fit of Gulliver's phase model to hostage negotiations. *Communication Studies*, **44**, 38–55.

Jordan, J.M. & Roloff, M.E. (1997). Planning skills and negotiator accomplishment: The relationship between self-monitoring and plan generation, plan enactment, and plan consequences. *Communication Research*, **24**, 31–63.

Kramer, R.M. & Messick, D.M. (Eds) (1995). *Negotiation as a social process.* Thousand Oaks, CA: Sage.

Kumar, R. (1997). The role of affect in negotiations: An integrative overview. *Journal of Applied Behavioral Science*, **3**, 84–100.

Lim, R.G. (1997). Overconfidence in negotiation revisited. *International Journal of Conflict Management*, **8**, 52–70.

Maynard, D.W. (1985). The problem of justice in the courts approached by the analysis, of plea bargaining discourse. In T.A. Van Dijk (Ed.), *Handbook of discourse analysis* (Vol. 4, pp. 153–179). London: Academic Press.

Morris, M.W., Larrick, R.P. & Su, S.K. (1999). Misperceiving negotiation counterparts: When situationally determined bargaining behaviors are attributed to personality traits. *Journal of Personality and Social Psychology*, **77**, 52–67.

Neale, M.A. & Bazerman, M.H. (1985). The effects of framing and negotiator overconfi-
dence on bargaining behavior. *Academy of Management Journal*, **28**, 34–49.
Neale, M.A. & Bazerman, M.H. (1991). *Cognition and rationality in negotiation*. New
York: Free Press.
O'Donnell, K. (1990). Difference and dominance: How labor and management talk con-
flict. In A.D. Grimshaw (Ed), *Conflict talk: Sociolinguistic investigations of arguments in
conversation* (pp. 210–240). Cambridge, UK: Cambridge University Press.
Pinkley, R.L., Griffith, T.L. & Northcraft, G.B. (1995). "Fixed pie" à la mode: Informa-
tion availability, information processing, and the negotiation of supoptimal agreements.
Organizational Behavior and Human Decision Processes, **62**, 101–112.
Pruitt, D.G. (1983). Strategic choice in negotiation. *American Behavioral Scientist*, **27**,
167–194.
Pruitt, D.G. & Carnevale, P.J.D. (1993). *Negotiation in social conflict*. Pacific Grove, CA:
Brooks-Cole.
Putnam, L.L. (1984). Bargaining as task and process: Multiple functions of interaction
sequences. In R.L. Street & J.N. Cappella (Eds), *Sequence and pattern in communica-
tive behavior* (pp. 225–242). London: Edward Arnold.
Putnam, L.L. (1990). Reframing integrative and distributive bargaining: A process
perspective. In B.H. Sheppard, M.H. Bazerman & R.J. Lewicki (Eds) *Research on
neotiation in organizations* (Vol. 2, pp. 3–30). Greenwich, CT: JAI Press.
Putnam, L.L. & Holmer, M. (1992). Framing, refraining, and issue development. In L.L.
Putnam & M.E. Roloff (Eds), *Communication and negotiation* (pp. 128–155). Newbury
Park, CA: Sage.
Putnam, L.L. & Jones, T.S. (1982). Reciprocity in negotiations: An analysis of bargaining
interaction. *Communication Monographs*, **49**, 171–191.
Putnam, L.L. & Kolb, D.M. (in press). Rethinking negotiation: Feminist views of com-
munication and exchange. In P.M. Buzzanell (Ed.), *Feminist perspectives on organiza-
tional communication*. Thousand Oaks, CA: Sage.
Putnam, L.L. & Roloff, M.E. (1992). Communication perspectives on negotiation. In L.L.
Putnam & M.E. Roloff (Eds) *Communication and negotiation* (pp. 1–20). Newbury
Park, CA: Sage.
Putnam, L.L., Van Hoeven & Bullis (1991).
Roloff, M.E. & Campion, D.E. (1987). On alleviating the debilitating effects of account-
ability in bargaining: Authority and self-monitoring. *Communication Monographs*, **54**,
145–164.
Roloff, M.E. & Jordan, J.M. (1991). The influence of effort, experience, and persistence
on elements of bargaining plans. *Communication Research*, **18**, 306–332.
Roloff, M.E. & Jordan, J.M. (1992). Achieving negotiation goals: The "fruits and foibles"
of planning ahead. In L.L. Putnam & M.E. Roloff (Eds), *Communication and negotiation* (pp. 21–45). Newbury Park, CA: Sage.
Thompson, L. (1991). Information exchange in negotiation. *Journal of Experimental Social Psychology*, **27**, 161–179.
Thompson, L. (1998). *The mind and heart of the negotiator*. Upper Saddler River, NJ:
Prentice Hall.
Thomson, L. & Hastie, R. (1990). Social perception in negotiation. *Organizational Behavior and Human Decision Processes*, **47**, 98–123.
Thompson, L., Peterson, E. & Brodt, S.E. (1996). Team negotiation: An examination of
integrative and distributive bargaining. *Journal of Personality and Social Psychology*,
70, 66–78.
Trice, H.M. & Beyer, J.M. (1984). Studying organizational cultures through rites and
ceremonials. *Academy of Management Review*, **9**, 653–669.
Walker, E. (1995). Making a bid for change: Formulations in union/management negotiations. In A. Firth (Ed.), *The discourse of negotiation: Studies of language in the workplace* (pp. 101–140). Oxford, UK: Pergamon.

Walton, R.E. & McKersie, R.B. (1965). *A behavioral theory of labor negotiations: An analysis of a social interaction system*. New York: MeGraw-Hill.

Weingart, L.R., Thompson, L.L., Bazerman, M.H. & Carroll, J.S. (1990). Tactical behavior and negotiation outcomes. *International Journal of Conflict Management*, **1**, 7–31.

Weingart, L.R., Hyder, E. & Prietula, M.J. (1996). Knowledge matters: The effect of tactical descriptions on negotiation behavior and outcome. *Journal of Personality and Social Psychology*, **70**, 1205–1217.

Weingart, L.R., Prietula, M.J., Hyder, E.B. & Genovese, C.R. (1999). Knowledge and the sequential processes of negotiation: A Markov chain analysis of response-in-kind. *Journal of Experimental Social Psychology*, **35**, 366–393.

Wilson, S.R. (1992). Face and facework in negotiation. In L.L. Putnam & M.E. Roloff (Eds), *Communication and negotiation* (pp. 176–205). Newbury Park, CA: Sage.

Wilson, S.R., Meischke, H., & Kim, M.S. (1990). A revised analysis of directives and face: Implications for argument and negotiation. In F. van Eemeren, R. Grootendorst, J.Blair & C. Willard (Eds) *Proceedings of the second international conference on argumentation* (pp. 470–480). Amsterdam: SICSAT.

Wilson, S.R., Aleman, C.G. & Leatham, G.B. (1998). Identity implications of influence goals: A revised analysis of face-threatening acts and application to seeking compliance with same-sex friends. *Human Communication Research*, **25**, 64–95.

Wilson, S.R. & Putnam, L.L. (1990). Interaction goals in negotiation. In J.A. Anderson (Ed.), *Communication yearbook* (Vol. 13, pp. 374–406). Newbury Park, CA: Sage

3.17

Gossiping

Nicholas Emler
Oxford University, UK

INTRODUCTION

Opinions differ on the subject of gossiping. On one side are views that it is at best a waste of any intelligent person's time and attention, and at worst so dangerous as to merit the severest punishment. On the other side, its benefits are alleged to be so numerous and certain it should be consumed more regularly than vitamin C, and should be more freely available. Views of the first kind accord more closely with popular opinion across numerous societies and periods of history (Schein, 1994; Spacks, 1985). The second permeates the writings of social scientists (cf. Gambetta, 1994), although it should be said that one of the more striking features of scholarly writing on the topic is that there is so little of it. In this chapter I consider the grounds for these contrasting views, as well as those for a third with which, as the reader will readily detect, I have more sympathy. This is the view that gossiping is the foundation and basis for the social life of humans as distinct from all other social animals so far evolved.

The chapter is organized as follows. The first part briefly reviews the public or popular image of gossip and considers some consequences of this image. The second part provides a brief survey of the writings of anthropologists and sociologists on the subject of gossip. Mindful that this Handbook as a whole is concerned with the social psychology of language, and not with its social history, anthropology or sociology, I confine observations to those most helpful to the construction of a context for a social psychological treatment of gossip. The third part seeks to separate fact from mythology, to establish what and how much we know about the phenomenon, leading finally to a consideration of the possible

The New Handbook of Language and Social Psychology.
Edited by W. Peter Robinson and Howard Giles.
© 2001 John Wiley & Sons Ltd.

significance of gossip – why people do it and with what consequences. But first of all the vexed issue of definition must be confronted.

Although in works of this kind it is the convention to begin discussion of a phenomenon by setting out one's definition, in this particular case this first step is more than usually hazardous. A real hazard is that one will from the outset offend and alienate readers whose favourite conviction about this subject seems thereby excluded. Unfortunately, refuge behind the dictionary definition is not especially helpful. The OED definition – "To talk idly, mostly about other people's affairs; to go about tattling" – merely reveals the difficulty: opinions about gossip are seldom neutral. In popular parlance to describe someone as gossiping is to make a judgment and typically a criticism. However, if we are better to understand the phenomenon, and not merely to reinforce prejudices, it is essential to begin with a behavioural definition that is neutral and non-judgmental. For this reason gossiping will be defined as "informally exchanging information or opinion among two or more persons about named third parties".

For the moment I would point to the following feature of this definition. It makes no stipulations about the kinds of people likely to be involved in such exchanges or their motives, about the truth, validity or value of what is exchanged, or about the consequences of these kinds of exchanges. These all figure prominently in popular images of gossiping, as we shall see in more detail shortly, but I propose they should be treated as questions to be decided empirically rather than features to be assumed a priori.

THE PUBLIC REPUTATION OF GOSSIPING

Among human activities, gossiping has had a dismal reputation. It is true that the degree of opprobrium attached to this particular activity has seen considerable fluctuation over the centuries and that there remain wide cultural variations in the strength of opinion against it. Nonetheless, the same accusations reappear in the literature and folklore of different societies and epochs with considerable consistency (Bergmann, 1993; Schein, 1994; Spacks, 1985). Thus the following are common features in popular images of gossip (cf. Emler, 1994; in preparation):

- participants: people who are intellectually shallow, idle, disloyal, indiscreet; women;
- motivations: prurient interest in others, voyeurism, nosiness (listeners); treachery, malice, spite (tellers);
- content: private matters; trivia;
- truth value: unreliable, inaccurate, error-ridden; untrue (lies);
- effects: invariably negative, potentially damaging, sometimes catastrophically so, to the reputations, livelihoods and lives of others; trust is betrayed; privacy is violated.

This representation of gossip has had two important consequences, one relating to the treatment of those involved, the other the behaviour of those upon whom suspicion of involvement is most likely to fall. In the first case we should expect that if the consensus within social groups holds that gossiping is a damaging activity then there should be sanctions against gossips that bear some relation to the degree of threat they pose. This is indeed the case. Sanctions have ranged from the implied or anticipated disapproval of others to more robust and direct remedies including scolds' bridles, ducking stools, torture, mutilation, and death by burning. In our more enlightend times we are inclined to forget, for example, that gossip was outlawed in medieval England (Oakley, 1972).

As to the chief suspects, they have always been women (Schein, 1994; Aebischer, 1985) and the climate of suspicion has had clear effects on women's behaviour, as a number of anthropological studies show. One well-documented effect is extreme care about whom one is seen talking to (Hutson, 1971), achieved in at least one community by avoidance of social contacts in public places altogether (Naish, 1978). In other words threats of informal and formal sanctions against gossiping have apparently caused those most under suspicion to take evasive action and thus to minimize their overt participation in gossip.

At this point we need to ask about the relationship between gossiping and its reputation. We might first consider the possibility that popular views of gossiping are no more than honest and broadly accurate opinions about a form of language use. This might be called the "naive realism" position. Do the various claims associated with this position fit the facts?

GOSSIPING: VIEWS FROM THE SOCIAL SCIENCES

Many of the theoretical arguments about gossiping seek to account for one or other of the features that form the popular image described above. This section will outline some of the more influential of these together with the idea that gossiping is significant only in a particular kind of society, the pre-industrial. Consider first of all the content of gossip.

The idea has been advanced in both sociology and social anthropology that informal conversations in which others are criticized can serve a social function. The argument that gossiping operates as an important means of informal social control in primary groups has a long history (see, for example, Ross, 1901) but it is most closely associated with the anthropologist Gluckman, who proposed that gossip maintains "the unity, morals and values of social groups". It does this by voicing criticism of specific actions of named individuals within the group, thereby reaffirming the boundaries of acceptable behaviour and reminding potential offenders of the costs of transgression (Gluckman, 1963, 1968; see also Boehm, 1993; Elias & Scotson, 1965; Haviland, 1977; Merry, 1984). A similar thesis has been advanced by social psychologists Sabini and Silver (1982): social norms are sustained, they propose, only by continually circulating and discussing concrete instances of their violation.

According to these views, gossip becomes a positive contribution to collective life rather than a destructive and disruptive activity. Can this be reconciled with another popularly claimed feature of gossip, namely its factual inaccuracy? How could criticism of others provide a useful service if this criticism is regularly mistaken? Two other interpretations of gossip can explain its inaccuracy but would not accord it any particular socially beneficial functions. According to the first of these, gossip will be inaccurate purely as a function of the nature of communication systems. All such systems are subject to a degree of information loss. The more links there are in a communication chain, the more the information will be degraded at each successive transmission. Allport and Postman (1947) adapted Bartlett's (1932) classic demonstration of the fallibility of memory to demonstrate this progressive attenuation, selection and distortion of information as it passes along a chain of human communicators. This assumes, of course, that gossip is directly analogous to the game of Chinese whispers, an assumption I shall reconsider further on.

A different focus of explanation for the unreliability of gossip invokes not the inherent imperfections of communication systems but the motivations of the information transmitter. Barkow (1992), taking the perspective of evolutionary psychology, argues that as genetic competitors we are programmed to disseminate misleading information about sexual rivals. This explanation also makes sense of the negative, indeed slanderous content of gossip. Barkow draws support for his conclusion from research by Buss and Dedden (1990) apparently showing that young adults are strongly disposed to derogate sexual competitors.

As regards the destructive effects of gossip, in so far as theory touches on these at all it does so by implication. Barkow's view, for example, is consistent with the idea that gossip is a form of covert and indirect aggression, a verbal assault on others' reputations. Some of the explanations for women's greater propensity for gossip also emphasize its aggressive nature and purpose. Thus, Scheler (1921) argued that because women are physically weaker than men they are both more vindictive and must use non-physical means to attack others.

Other writers, while equally disposed to accept that there is an association between women and gossip, interpret the link in a more positive light. For Jones (1980) women gossip to sustain solidarity in their identity as women; she does not make it clear, however, why men should not gossip among themselves for the same purpose. Tannen (1990) regards women's gossip as an essential basis for friendship; it allows them to form and sustain relationships with one another that are capable of providing strong mutual support. This argument is based partly on the claim that women are better able than men to chat about nothing in particular, a facility that allows them to keep a relationship going when there is no specific task or problem to discuss. A slightly different kind of explanation starts from the limited power of women and argues that gossip is a weapon of subversion (e.g., Schein, 1994). Thus we are back with the position that gossip is dangerous but how sanguine one feels about this presumably depends on one's degree of sympathy with those who might be endangered.

Finally, a different kind of theme within the social sciences concerns the declining significance of gossip. The argument goes that if it is a mechanism of social control it is best suited to the small-scale face-to-face communities of the pre-industrial age. If an instrument of aggression and competition again it is most likely to be effective in closed communities in which all members are mutually acquainted. And gossip can only threaten reputations so long as individuals inhabit social worlds in which reputations can exist and matter, namely worlds in which they are personally known to most of the other people they encounter and with whom they do business. The kind of society created by the Industrial Revolution supposedly swept away these particular social conditions. According to the authors of a sociology text published in 1950 "In the large community of the modern city, contacts in secondary groups tend to be impersonal and escape into anonymity is possible. Under these circumstances, gossip and ridicule are less effective instruments and their place is taken by the police and the courts" (Ogburn and Nimkoff, 1950, p. 115; see also Locke, 1998).

Thus far we have seen there are theories to explain one or another feature of gossiping but no theory which appears successfully to account for all of them (and there is little if any theorizing about the reasons why gossip should hold a special appeal for those who are intellectually shallow, gullible or idle). A possibility we should now consider, therefore, is that these theories may be at fault because they have misrepresented the phenomenon and too often taken naive realism at face value. Or to put it another way, they have sought to explain properties of gossiping without any strong evidence that it does indeed have these properties. So let us now look at what evidence as distinct from opinion there is about gossip.

SEPARATING FACT FROM THE IMAGE: ISSUES OF METHOD

It would be wrong to suggest that the theories identified above have without exception been completely speculative, unsupported by any empirical observation. At the same time there has been very little systematic hypothesis testing in this area. The reason we have so little secure evidence about the phenomenon of gossiping is not hard to find. The first step in scientific inquiry is, or should be, a sound and objective description of the phenomenon of interest. One needs, in other words, first to establish *what* is happening, before moving on to ask *how* it happens and *why* it happens. Unfortunately, social science's two preferred methods for answering *what* questions, direct observation and self-report, are not ideally suited to this particular phenomenon.

Social anthropology has provided a rich stock of reflections on gossip; indeed this literature has been the principal source of ideas for social scientists interested in the phenomenon. Moreover, most of the material has been derived from direct observation. This is not really so surprising because research methods described technically as "participant observation" or "ethnography" are in practice attempts to participate in the gossip of a community (cf. Malinowski, 1922). However, Bergmann (1993) takes care to point out that as a source of evidence to test hypotheses about gossip these observations have been limited; their primary purpose was not to document and understand gossip as a phenomenon in its own right but to employ gossip as a means of ethnographic inquiry.

Researchers studying gossip in its own right have more often observed without participation. An example is provided by Levin and Arluke's (1985) study of sex differences in gossip (see also Kipers, 1987), which involved eavesdropping on the conversations of students in a residence. An alternative which would seem to offer various obvious advantages is to set up a conversation under laboratory conditions and record it with the full knowledge of the participants (e.g., Leaper and Holliday, 1995). For example, the nature of the relationship between the participants can be determined more accurately, more information can be collected about the content of the conversation and recorded more accurately, and potential ethical problems are avoided. The disadvantages are equally obvious and rather more weighty, such that resemblance to gossip in its natural state may be rather tenuous (cf. Weick, 1985).

But direct if covert observation of spontaneously occurring conversations also has some significant limitations. First, it is expensive and though cost is not an inherent limitation its practical consequences need to be acknowledged; sample sizes for such research have so far been small. Second, it cannot by itself tell us a number of important things about those involved, in particular the relationship between them. Third, direct observation is limited to certain kinds of settings, namely public places in which speech can be overhead by people (the observers) for whom it was not intended. Conversations in such public places are not necessarily representative of conversations in other, less accessible locations. It is entirely possible that people are more guarded about what they will say concerning third parties when they know they can be overheard.

Perhaps for reasons of cost, some researchers have made use of the major alternative to direct observation, self-report. This method has been used so far to answer three questions about gossiping: what kinds of people are most likely to do it (Nevo, Nevo & Derech-Zehavi, 1993a, 1993b, 1994; Jaeger et al., 1994), what kinds of people are most likely to be the targets of gossip (Jaeger et al., 1994; Jeager, Skleder & Rosnow, 1997), and what attitudes people have to gossiping (Wilson et al., 2000).

In so far as self-reports are employed to provide behavioural descriptions – answering the kinds of questions posed in the Nevo et al. and Jaeger et al. studies – we are confronted with some quite severe problems of validity. There are at least two reasons why people's self-reports of their own gossiping behaviour may lack validity. The first is that self-reports may be consciously or unconsciously distorted by self-presentational motives. Thus anyone sensitive to the disreputable image of gossip might not wish to claim they do it very much. For example,

Jaeger et al.'s (1994) finding that people who self-reported gossiping least also had significantly higher scores on a need for social approval measure may have reflected differences in the tendency to distort self-reports in a socially desirable direction.

However real the risk of distortion here, it is probably less serious than a second threat to the validity of such self-reports, the sheer difficulty of giving factually accurate answers about one's own gossiping. Reis and Wheeler (1991) identify three sources of inaccuracy in self-reports. As they note, questionnaires typically require of respondents that they give a global assessment of some activity, for example frequency of interaction with close friends. This requires that the respondent (a) makes an appropriately representative selection of occurrences of the activity in question, (b) accurately recalls the relevant features of these occurrences, and (c) aggregates or combines the recalled events to provide the requested global assessment. Each of these requirements is liable to introduce inaccuracies, all the more so to the extent that the activity in question occurs often, is routine, and is mundane, which is to say unmemorable. There is now ample evidence that self-reports of activities and events with these qualities – such as exercise, diet, television viewing, and mood – can be very inaccurate.

Communicative activity would appear to fall into this category. In a series of studies Bernard, Killworth and Sailer (e.g., Bernard & Killworth, 1977; Bernard, Killworth & Sailer, 1982; Killworth & Bernard, 1977) compared people's recollections, or their predictions, of whom they talked to and how often, with independent records of their communications. There were major inaccuracies of every kind; individuals communicated with were frequently forgotten, others were recalled when they had not been in contact during the specified period, and about half the time respondents were wrong about the person they communicated with most frequently. Bernard et al. (1982) concluded that "what people say about their communications bears no resemblance to their behaviour" (pp. 30–31), a fairly damning judgment on the value of self-reports in this area (but see Freeman, Romney & Freeman, 1987; Kashy & Kenny, 1990). What we do not know is how accurate recall of the *content* of routine conversations is likely to be, and this is crucial to testing hypotheses about gossip.

The limitations of direct observation and self-report have attracted some researchers to a third option: event and experience recording methods in which the actor becomes the observer/recorder. These methods therefore combine some of the features and advantages of both self-report questionnaires and direct, systematic behavioural observation. They also, it should be acknowledged, contain some of the weaknesses of each (Stone, Kessler & Haythornthwaite, 1991). Nonetheless, these methods have become increasingly popular with researchers studying social interaction because they can provide quite large samples at relatively low cost and because they can provide data that would be very difficult to collect by other methods.

In what follows I shall draw upon evidence provided by these newer methods, but recognizing their imperfections I shall not ignore evidence generated from self-reports and direct observation. If quite different research methods give us similar answers to our questions about gossip, we can have some confidence in the answers. If they do not we shall need strong grounds for preferring the answer provided by one of them.

MORE RADICAL STEPS

We now need to consider what questions could usefully be answered if we are better to understand the *what*, *how* and *why* of gossip. My list of such questions includes the following more general parameters: What do humans spend their time doing, and more particularly what proportion of that time is spent in the company of others, interacting with others, and talking to others? In so far as time is spent talking to others, who are these others? Where do these conversations take place, and how do they arise? What are the topics of these conversations? Evidently, only the last of these is directly about gossip. But if the answer to the last question is that a high proportion of the content fits my definition of gossip – information or opinion about named third parties – then answers to the others will have told us a great deal about its nature and significance. To anticipate, I think the best evidence available justifies the following conclusions: most people naturally spend much of their waking time – between 60% and 80% – in the physical presence of others. Where circumstances allow, much of this time is spent in conversation; indeed, conversation is *the* most common form of social interaction. Most conversations occur between people who know one another and most are unscheduled – they occur without prior arrangement. Most occur within private or institutional settings. The most freqent topics of conversations are the doings of named third parties and relationships with and among third parties. These conclusions of course require some significant qualifications and they still leave unanswered the *why* questions about gossip – what is gossip for – but they do give us some powerful clues. To explore these, however, we need first look in more detail at the evidence which leads to these conclusions.

The Place of Talk in Human Time–Energy Budgets

Our scientific knowledge of other species of animals is now likely to include details about the proportions of time they typically spend sleeping or resting, feeding, foraging and procreating. These kinds of details have, for example, supported arguments about the degree to which different species are naturally social or solitary. Thus there is evidence on the proportion of time macaques, as compared to baboons or gibbons, spend feeding, at play, in social observation, etc. Equivalent data about humans is both harder to come by and more difficult to interpret with confidence. A massive cross-national study on the use of time, based on both interviews and self-recording (Szalai, 1972), did reveal something of the characteristic daily pattern for a number of cultures and for different categories of people within these cultures. For example, the data showed that on weekdays adult male Belgians spent an average of 8 hours in sleep, 6.3 hours working, 1.5 hours watching television, 1 hour travelling, 2.9 waking hours alone, and 1 hour reading (the categories here are not all mutually exclusive). Typically, across cultures people spent about 80% of their waking time in the company of others, the daily average ranging from 13-plus hours for the Yugoslav sample to 10 hours for an American sample.

Interpreting these figures is a problem because the societies in the survey do not correspond to any natural pattern. All are products of historical and not merely biological evolution, and the social scientist might have reason to suspect that such conditions as the nature of the economy, level of industrialization, and the diffusion of communication technologies will influence the pattern. If some commentators are to be believed then the slighly less social lifestyles of the Americans in the survey is an accelerating trend to which other nations and cultures will also succumb, if they have not done so already (Locke, 1998). There is some evidence to support this pessimism, at least for the United States. Robinson and Godbey (1997) report a 16% drop in time spent by Americans in social activities over the 20 years to 1985.

It does not follow of course that because or to the extent that people spend a lot of time in one another's presence they are therefore spending this time conversing. Nor does it follow that this is mainly what humans do with their language-using ability. They might, for example, spend more time using this ability to meditate, read, write or pray. But it is still a fair bet that conversation is a more natural and commonplace employment for this ability than the these other four candidates. Reading and writing are very recent innovations in the natural history of the species and the Szalai surveys confirm that they are specialized and occasional activities; the average member of a highly literate society at the time of the surveys was spending little time reading – under one hour a day – and even less writing. Moreover, research in formalized bureaucratic organizations (e.g. Davies, 1953; Mintzberg, 1973; Rogers, 1983) indicates that oral, face-to-face communication has not been displaced by written communication. Language undoubtedly does play an important part in human thinking (cf. Macphail, 1987), and the psychological study of language has placed as much emphasis on its role as a tool of thought as it has upon its manifestation as an aspect of social interaction. But it is not clear how much time is spent in silent reflections or solitary mental calculations associated with language.

If we allow that spoken interaction is a significant form of human social behaviour, just how much of it is there? First it needs to be recognized that people may more often be in the role of listeners than speakers in such interactions. Even if participation is equally distributed it is necessarily the case that in a group of more than two each participant will spend more time listening than talking. We therefore need some indication of the sizes of the groups in which individuals are participants, as well as of their formality and focus. Is it for example the case that "in the company of others" most often means in a work group with no words exchanged beyond those needed for the task at hand, or common-interest groups pursuing their joint interests – amateur dramatics, football games, white-water rafting – or in committees with formal agendas and formalized contributions, or in large meetings addressed by "platform speakers"? It may then be that "the company of others" seldom means or allows informal chat.

Some indication of how much time people devote to conversations has emerged from the use of event recording methods. Wheeler and Nezlek (1977) asked a group of college students to keep a structured record of their own interactions over two separate two-week periods. Their data indicate that from 5 to 6½ hours per day were spent by their sample in social interaction of some form. Seventy per cent of the recorded interaction time was classified as conversation and at least two of the other four categories of interaction involved conversational exchange. For various reasons, the Wheeler and Nezlek results probably underestimate the frequency and cumulative duration of conversational interactions, at least for this population. Their method required participants to record only interactions of at least 10 minutes duration. Data we have collected from student samples (Emler, 1990; Emler & Grady, 1987; Emler & McNamara, 1996), also using event self-recording, indicate they engage in many conversations shorter than 10 minutes.

College students do, of course, form an unusual population and it would be unsafe to generalize from this source alone. We know, for example, that they have more frequent conversational encounters and with more contacts than do similarly aged people who have full-time jobs, are in vocational training or are unemployed (Emler, 2000). College students also inhabit temporary social systems, have few significant responsibilities, and a lot of uncommitted time that could be devoted to socializing. It would be helpful to know more about the conversational activity of other significant groups, such as housewives, blue- and white-collar workers, workers in different occupational sectors, teenagers, retired people and unemployed adults.

The "event-contingent" self-recording methods employed in the studies described above provide information about the frequency of events but are imperfect estimates of the time involved. Better estimates of this are provided by signal-contingent procedures. In response to 42 signals transmitted in normal waking hours at random intervals over seven days, a sample of American teenagers recorded conversation as either the primary or a secondary activity on 41% of occasions (Csikszentmihalyi, Larson & Prescott, 1977). This gives a figure of 6 hours a day involved in conversation. No other category of activity recorded, including TV viewing, games and sports, eating, walking, reading and working, approached this level; the nearest was watching TV, recorded as the primary or secondary activity on 12.5% of occasions.

Let us now return briefly to the question of conversational group size. The Wheeler and Nezlek (1977) study found that the majority of recorded interactions involved only two participants, just as we have found for conversational interactions (e.g., Emler & Grady, 1987). Observations reported by Dunbar, Duncan and Nettle (1995) of informal conversations in a variety of semi-public settings – a college refectory at lunchtime, people waiting outside buildings during fire drills, participants at a reception – also indicate two people as the most common conversational group size (54% of those observed). To conclude therefore, conversations, most often between just two people, constitute a very common form of human social interaction, if not the most common. Moreover, more time may be devoted to this single activity than to any other except sleep.

Who Talks to Whom

As I have suggested elsewhere (Emler, 1994), much hangs on how this question is answered, nothing less than an entire model of social life. The social consequences of the Industrial Revolution was one of the great preoccupations of nineteenth-century social theorists and many of them were convinced that industrialization and the mass urbanization it promoted had initiated a fundamental change in the character of social life (e.g., Tonnies, 1887/1957). The contrast emphasized by Tonnies and later by Durkheim, Weber, Simmel, Parsons and Wirth among others was between the rural community and the city. It was assumed that in the former almost the only people individuals encountered in the course of their daily lives were kin or other acquaintances. In the latter, encounters were typically "impersonal, transitory and segmental" (Wirth, 1938). In other words, the inhabitants of pre-industrial villages interacted exclusively with people they knew whereas the inhabitants of modern cities would be likely to interact not as personal acquaintances but as the impersonal and frequently anonymous occupants of broad social categories or formally defined roles.

The implication of this "community lost" argument (Wellman, 1978) is that the conversations we have with others, unless these others are members of our immediate families, will occur outside any relationship of personal acquaintance. Our transactions with them will be predicated on our organizational roles and not on our respective personal identities or on any established relationship between us as unique individuals. The further implication is that the substance of our talk will relate to the performance of these roles and their associated functions. As shop assistants, teachers, out-patients or building site foremen our talk will relate to the task of discussing a potential purchase, evaluating an essay, describing symptoms or directing work activities.

Although some social scientists argue the trend towards impersonal, depersonalized social relations has merely accelerated since the end of the nineteenth century (cf. the earlier quotation from Ogburn & Nimkoff), others have argued equally strongly and with rather better evidence – namely detailed studies of social life in cities – that the "community lost" model both exaggerates and misrepresents social change in the last 200 years (e.g., Boissevain, 1974; Fischer, 1981; Gans, 1962; Litwak & Szelenyi, 1969; Mitchell, 1969; Wellman, 1978; Young & Willmott, 1957). They assert instead that even those who live in large cities continue "to dwell among friends" (Fischer, 1981), and that most of their interactions occur with people they know personally. Given potential concerns about the validity of self-report evidence, it is reassuring that these conclusions are also consistent with evidence using self-recording methods. For example, we have found over a variety of samples of young people – in higher education or vocational training, in employment or unemployed – that the majority of conversational encounters recorded were with people known to the young person, namely family members, friends or acquaintances (Emler & McNamara, 1996). Among the samples in higher education, 3% of all recorded encounters involved strangers and a similar percentage were classified as purely business or service; the averages in the former category were lower for the non-university samples. Data we have collected from people in middle-level management occupations using this method (Emler, 1990) only superficially suggest managers inhabit the impersonal, anonymous social world imagined by "community lost" theorists. Although they defined their relations with a majority of their contacts as "formal" these were encounters with individuals the managers knew well; on average they had known each contact for two years.

One important finding to emerge from the event recording research concerns sex differences. No differences of this kind have yet been reported either in the frequency of conversational interactions or in the numbers of different people with whom such interactions occur. So, if women really do gossip much more than men, this will reflect the course their conversations take rather than the kinds or numbers of people they talk to or the numbers of conversational encounters they have.

On the other hand, compared to whether one is male or female, differences in institutional status – whether employed or unemployed, in full-time education, or a member of a family household – have far more impact. On the earlier point concerning the likelihood of differences in communicative activity across social groups, our own research on the circumstances of conversational contacts (Emler & McNamara, 1996; Emler, 2000) indicates why group differences should be expected. We examined both where such contacts occurred and how they arose. The most important settings, in terms of numbers of conversational encounters, were homes – one's own and other people's – places of education or training and places of work. In contrast, more public settings such as bars, shops, the street and public transport – the kinds of setting most often sampled in non-participant observational studies of conversation – accounted for a minority of these encounters. In other words, having a formal role in a setting and thus regular legitimate opportunties to be there enables informal social contact. This interpretation is reinforced by evidence on how contacts occur. People seem to rely little on arranging meetings in advance, rather more on knowing others' movements and thus where to find them when wanted, and to a similar degree on chance encounters with acquaintances, but most of all upon their own and others' routines, a strategy supported by the tendency for institutions, both formal and informal, to give a temporal structure to activities.

It is likely therefore that the nature of occupations will influence opportunities for informal conversational contact. Consider, for example, the occupations

Mars (1981) called "donkey" jobs which commit people to a single setting for long periods, and which isolate them physically from others or symbolically through status differentials. But we should also expect an influence of the *variety* of institutional statuses a person has, and thus the settings with their associated routines to which they have legitimate access. We might therefore anticipate that housewives, retired people, the unemployed and the occupants of "total institutions" (cf. Goffman, 1961) will have more limited ranges of conversational contacts than other social categories.

The Content of Conversational Interactions

If it is true that we not only spend a great deal of our waking time in face-to-face, one-to-one conversations but that the people we talk to are people we know personally and perhaps know very well, what are we talking about? Producing a clear answer to this question presents a number of technical difficulties. Conversation may be ubiquitous but it is not easily studied, at least not if one wishes to document with any precision what happens naturally and spontaneously.

Consider first direct observation. A recent example is provided by Bischoping (1993), who attempted to replicate the findings of much earlier studies by Moore (1922) on sex differences in conversational content. Moore had reported that male–male conversations overheard in the street or public bars were mainly about business (50%) whereas the most common topic of female–female conversations was men, followed by clothes and other women. Bischoping found similar but smaller sex differences. Her study also confirms one of the problems of this method of direct observation: sample size. Hers included 27 females but only eight males.

Dunbar, Duncan and Marriott (1997) achieved a slightly larger sample of conversations with this method ($n = 44$), initially attempting to tape the observed conversations. Unobtrusive tape-recording in public and semi-public places proved also to be poor-quality recording and was abandonned in favour of "direct auditory monitoring" (Dunbar et al., 1997, p. 234). In other words, the observers listened, and made a judgment as to the topic, doing this at 30-second intervals, using 14 topic categories. Few significant differences emerged between the sexes. The most prominent of these was a tendency for males to devote more conversation time to intellectual or work-related topics, particularly when females were present. The most striking features of their findings, however, were not these differences but the similarities. In terms of speaking time, the topic to which most attention was given was "personal relationships" in all but one of six groups of subjects observed. Across the six groups the percentage of speaking time for this topic varied from 15.3 to 49.5.

Some problems with purely observational data of this kind have already been noted, among which potentially the most serious concerns representativeness of the conversations that are available for such observation. Evidence based on event self-recording methods indicates that the majority of conversations do not take place in public settings and many occur in places where observers could not enter unnoticed (Emler & McNamara, 1996; Emler, 2000). Gossip, particularly if it involves betrayal of confidences or bad-mouthing acquaintances, both regarded as violations of the informal rules of relationships (Argyle & Henderson, 1984), would surely flourish more readily in private places.

In an attempt to achieve a more representative sample of conversational content we adapted an event-contingent self-recording method (e.g., Emler, 1989). Trial studies with several versions indicated that (a) recorders have difficulty coping with more than a small number of simple categories, and (b) far too much information is exchanged in routine daily conversations for all of it to be recorded in this way with any degree of thoroughness over much more than a single day. However, these trials did indicate that, for a student population, personal topics (about the speakers or people known to them) were far more prevalent than impersonal topics. On the basis of these trials a larger study was undertaken to sample six topics of theoretical interest: own doings, others' doings, own emotional states, others' emotional states, practical information and politics. Participants recorded details of every conversation in which they participated over a seven-day period. However, they were asked to track only one of these six topics and to note whether or not the topic had figured in each conversation. There were approximately 60 participants tracking each topic and for each topic a total of around 22,000 conversations were sampled.

Only two sex differences emerged; males were more likely than females to discuss politics though even in male–male exchanges this topic occurred on only 9% of occasions. The other difference was that females were more likely to discuss the feelings or emotional states of third parties. However, by far the most commonly occurring topic, in more than 40% of conversations, was "others' doings" and there was no difference between males and females in this respect. This contradicts Nevo et al.'s (1994) questionnaire-based evidence in which females report gossiping more (in so far as gossiping is the discussion of others' doings), and Levin and Arluke's (1985) observational data which similarly suggests this sex difference.

The picture of conversational content emerging thus far therefore is that people, or at least those people who are students, frequently discuss the activities of others they know and their relationships with others. It can still be argued that matters may be very different in more task-oriented settings, for example places of work, business, or training. What we know about the conversational topics of people who are not students remains perilously small as a basis for any strong conclusions.

SPECULATIONS ABOUT FUNCTION

An understanding of what motivates gossip – why people do it – needs to be consistent with various observations, particularly that we all seem to do it, that we do it so often and with so many different established partners, that it concerns people we know and that it is information-rich. For this last reason I suspect that the recently promoted hypothesis that the significance of gossip is to perform a social grooming function (cf. Dunbar, 1993, 1996) cannot be the whole story.

I propose the basic reasons why we gossip, why we so regularly exchange observations about other people, are quite straightforward. We are inhabitants of social as well as physical environments. Successful adaptation to the former kind has the same fundamental requirements as adaptation to the latter, namely the achievement of some degree of prediction and influence. If we are to predict the behaviour of our social environment we need to know things about its particular inhabitants, and not just about people in general or in the abstract. Specifically, we need to know what they are like – their personalities, character, abilities – and what their relations are with one another. Other social animals, notably the apes, do this by social observation. Research on attribution indicates how humans might use similar evidence, namely direct observations of others' actions and the effects of their actions, to make inferences about their attitudes, temperament and relationships. But the huge advantage conferred by language is that unlike other apes we are freed from exclusive dependence upon direct observation. Verbal exchange gives us rapid access to a larger sample of the relevant social information than we could ever achieve through our own direct observations. Equally as important as prediction is influence, and gossip is par excellence an instrument for subtle social influence. Gossip, I would submit, is therefore a fundamental tool of social adaptation.

If a goal of gossip is prediction then the quality of the data provided is an issue. We have already seen that gossip has been characterized both popularly and in some scientific treatments as unreliable (in the colloquial rather than the psycho-metric sense). Is this characterization justified? A priori, it would seem odd for people to devote so much time and effort to the collection of tainted evidence. In an interesting study, Wilson et al. (2000) show that when accuracy is important people do pay careful attention to the quality of information obtained through gossiping (see also Harrington & Bielby, 1995), while others have noted that spreading baseless gossip does rebound on the standing of the source (Schein, 1994). This is clearly a matter that deserves more study but it would be reason-able to expect that competent social actors would strive to make accurate judg-ments about their social environments. Psychometrics tells us the basis for valid measurement is aggregation, combining different observations. Thus a sensible strategy is to gossip with several sources about the same matters so as to com-pensate for their different biases (technically, to control for method variance). Is this what is reflected in high rates of conversational interaction involving gossip? This question brings us to two related and important issues: whether multiple sources could *in principle* be used in this way, and whether the validity of verbally transmitted social information is compromised by long communication chains.

By way of introduction, consider the more general goals of adaptation. Suc-cessful adaptation to a social environment involves securing its support for our own aspirations and welfare. Crudely, we want other people to aid us rather than hurt us. Prediction helps us to avoid the fools, scoundrels and carriers of other liabilities and gravitate towards the virtuous and talented. And even scoundrels will want to know the difference. Schumann and Laumann (1994) offer an interesting example of this process: choosing a sexual partner linked to one's social network allows more accurate assessment of the risk of contracting a sexually transmitted disease from that partner. Prediction, then, is important but we can do even better if we can persuade others to act in ways which benefit us.

Biologists have pointed out that the possibility of being exploited or cheated is not just a threat to individual welfare but to the survival of social life altogether. All social species have somehow solved this "prisoners' dilemma": the possibility that the individual member of the group could do better by exploiting the cooperation of others than by supporting it (Axelrod, 1984). However, the solution which Axelrod and others have argued underpins social life, the so-called tit-for-tat behavioural strategy of instant retaliation against cheats, has many imperfections not the least of which is that, as Enquist and Leimar (1993) point out, in large social groups cheats can still do rather well while incurring costs for many of their fellows. But suppose that the normal mechanism of cheater detection, which basically involves learning by being the cheater's victim, was supplemented by gossip – all members of the group talking to each other about the conduct of every other group member. It turns out, at least in a computer simulation – now the preferred method of biologists studying behavioural strategies – that the cheat's effective reign is drastically reduced by gossip (Enquist & Leimar, 1993). Nonetheless, this still seems to involve influence through improved prediction.

A more direct influence mechanism, I would argue, depends upon the actor anticipating such predictions. If I know that you can learn about my treatment of others from others and if furthermore I hope for your cooperation, I would be wise to treat others well, and for similar reasons to treat you well. In other words, influence operates through the concern people have with their reputations and gossip creates a pressure to keep those reputations honest. Gluckman's (1963, 1968) argument for the social control function of gossip has been strongly criticized (Paine, 1967; Bergmann, 1993), partly on the grounds that individuals gossip for their own benefit rather than the common good. But these criticisms lose some of their force if we see social control not as the reason for gossip but as a by-product of individuals pursuing their own interests, namely to be well informed about the conduct of others.

This also relates to the negative tone attributed to gossip by various writers (e.g., Rosnow & Fine, 1976) and indeed assumed in Gluckman's original arguments about its social control function: control is exercised by criticizing others' behaviour. Some researchers have even claimed to identify the predominance of this negative and critical quality in women's if not men's gossip (Eder & Enke, 1991; Leaper & Holliday, 1995). Dunbar et al. (1997), however, found that only a tiny proportion of the conversations observed involved malicious gossip or indeed negative comment of any kind. This may reflect the discretion of speakers in public settings, but the control effect does not require negative or evaluative comment, only factual observations about what a person has or has not done.

Enquist and Leimar's (1993) modelling of the effects of gossiping does assume that information about the same actor can be secured from more than one source. Though this seems a reasonable assumption to make about small-scale and relatively "closed" village communities, is it true of contemporary social conditions? To put it another way, to what extent do the people I talk to also talk to each other? Or are the links of personal acquaintance created through conversational contacts more accurately represented as chains which only ever intersect with each other at one individual? This question is defined by network analysts in terms of the density of an individual's network (cf. Boissevain, 1974; Granovetter, 1973): what percentage of the links (of acquaintance, regular conversational contact, etc.) that could exist among an individual's set of acquaintances do actually exist? Both practically and technically the question is difficult to answer with precision because, for example, there are several options for defining both a link and the set to be analysed. Nonetheless, different methods have produced similar values for samples of adults; among an individual's circle of regular acquaintances, between 30% and 40% of the links that could exist do exist (e.g., Cubbitt, 1973; Emler, 1990; Friedkin, 1980). In other words, when any two acquaintances talk the chances are that they will have a large number of shared acquaintances about whom they *could* talk.

The possibility of this kind of triangulation – I can check your account of your dealings with a mutual friend against his or her account, and indeed against accounts provided by other mutual acquaintances – is, I think, the key to the prediction and influence/control functions of gossip (Emler, 1990, 1994). Coleman's (1988) much discussed argument about social capital provides a complementary analysis. According to Coleman, social capital is a product of a particular structure of social relations, specifically a structure in which A and B not only know one another but both also know C. These conditions, says Coleman, promote the circulation of information, the effective enforcement of social norms, and the creation of trust. I would argue that the most basic of these three is the ready circulation of reliable social information; the other two are derivative features (Emler, 2000; see also Burt & Knez, 1996).

If access to multiple sources of social information supports more accurate judgments about others, is accuracy nonetheless likely to be lost in long communication chains? There is little direct evidence to answer this, but strong reasons to suspect that most gossip chains are actually very short. In one of the studies by Wilson et al. (2000) subjects expected to give less weight to information about another that had been mediated by more than one link. On the basis of his studies of friendship networks, Boissevain (1974) argued that the effective extent of any person's influence seldom reaches beyond the friends of his or her friends, in other words beyond one intermediate link (see also Granovetter; 1973). Combining what we know about interaction rates and the density of social networks, individuals should seldom need to seek information mediated by more than one link from its origin and would anyway have difficulty coping with the volume if they did so on a regular basis; they would simply be exposed to too much information about too many people (Emler, 1990, in preparation).

Finally, the foregoing might seem to imply the happy conclusion that nice guys do finish first (cf. Dawkins, 1989), that the spoils of social life go to those who are cautiously if not enthusiastically virtuous. But this neither accords with the common experience that very unpleasant people can do quite well, nor does it recognize the power of gossip as a subtle instrument of social influence. Part of the reason why gossip provides imperfect protection against ambitious villains is to be found in the operation of top-down mechanisms for the allocation of organizational power. These mechanisms – of selection and promotion – seem to be systematically insensitive to moral flaws (cf. Cook & Emler, 1999). This may in turn be because gossip, which potentially contains the basis for accurate character appraisals, naturally flows less easily along the vertical than the horizotal axes of social organizations, and so less readily reaches decision makers controlling top-down selection. But another part of the reason is surely that both the flow and the content of social information can and will be manipulated by those with sufficient guile, an ability that may be uncorrelated with moral virtue. By careful choice of what one says and does not say and to whom, one can simultaneously promote one's own cause and damage rivals without telling any lies. Gossip is undoubtedly a powerful instrument in the politics of everyday life (Bailey, 1971).

CONCLUSIONS

I have argued that gossip serves functions basic to social life and does so because it provides the inhabitants of human communities with invaluable information about their other members, incidentally a conclusion reached many years ago by the French psychologist Janet (1929). In emphasizing this quality of gossip I would not rule out other significant functions and effects. For example, gossip surely plays an important role in social comparison processes (cf. Suls, 1977). A further use is to manage the boundaries of social groups (Gluckman, 1963; Elias & Scotson, 1965). But the choice of emphasis reflects my judgment that, just as with the enforcement of social norms and trust creation, so these other consequences derive from our dependence on gossip to provide us with social information.

A number of interesting questions have not been addressed here about which much more could be said – why gossip occurs primarily in face-to-face encounters which are also informal, unscheduled, one-to-one and between acquaintances, why an inclination to gossip is unlikely to be associated with intellectual superficiality, or why historically it has been associated with women in public consciousness despite so little evidence that this is the case (see Emler, 1994, in preparation, for further discussion of these issues). But to explore these in the current state of our knowledge would take us even further into the realms of speculation than we have already come. I hope to have made the case for taking gossip much more seriously – seriously enough to give it the research attention already directed to other topics on language, for example the closely linked topic of self-disclosure. In the earlier edition of this Handbook, gossip had no chapter. Should there be a subsequent edition I hope that much more of the speculation will have been replaced by hard evidence and thoroughly tested hypotheses, to the point that gossip will not appear as *an* application of language but one of its principle and most significant applications.

REFERENCES

Aeibischer, V. (1985). *Les femmes et le langage: Representations sociales d'une difference.* Paris: Presses Universitaires de France.

Allport, G. & Postman, L. (1947). *The psychology of rumor.* New York: Holt, Rinehart & Winston.

Argyle, M. & Henderson, M. (1984). The rules of friendship. *Journal of Social and Personal Relationships*, **1**, 211–237.

Axelrod, R. (1984). *The evolution of cooperation.* New York: Basic Books.

Bailey F.G. (Ed.) (1971). *Gifts and poison: The politics of reputation.* Oxford: Blackwell.

Bales, R.F. (1958). Task roles and social roles in problem-solving groups. In E.E. Maccoby, T.M. Newcomb & E.L. Hartley (Eds), *Readings in social psychology* (3rd edn). New York: Holt.

Barkow, J.H. (1992). Beneath new culture is old psychology: Gossip and social stratification. In J.H. Barkow, L. Cosmides & J. Tooby (Eds), *The adapted mind: Evolutionary psychology and the generation of culture* (pp. 627–637). New York: Oxford University Press.

Bartlett, F. (1932). *Remembering.* Cambridge: Cambridge University Press.

Bergmann, J.R. (1993). *Discreet indiscretions: The social organization of gossip.* New York: de Gruyter.

Bernard, H.R. & Kilworth, P.D. (1977). Informant accuracy in social network data II. *Human Communication Research*, **4**, 3–18.

Bernard, H.R., Kilworth, P.D. & Sailer, L. (1982). Informant accuracy in social network data V. An experimental attempt to predict actual communication from recall data. *Social Science Research*, **11**, 30–66.

Bischoping, K. (1993). Gender differences in conversational topics, 1922–1990. *Sex Roles*, **28**, 1–17.

Boehm, C. (1993). Egalitarian society and reverse dominance hierarchy. *Current Anthropology*, **34**, 227–254.

Boissevain, J. (1974). *Friends of friends: Networks, manipulators and coalitions.* Oxford: Blackwell.

Burt, R.S. & Knez, M. (1996). Trust and third party gossip. In R.M. Kramer & T.R. Tyler (Eds), *Trust in organisations: Frontiers of theory and research* (pp. 68–89). Thousand Oaks, CA: Sage.

Buss, D.M. & Dedden, L. (1990). Derogation of competitors. *Journal of Social and Personal Relationships*, **7**, 395–422.

Coleman, J.S. (1988). Social capital in the creation of human capital. *American Journal of Sociology*, **94** (Supplement), 95–120.

Cook, T. & Emler, N. (1999). Bottom-up versus top-down evaluations of managerial potential: An experimental study. *Journal of Occupational and Organizational Psychology*, **72**, 423–439.

Cubbitt, T. (1973). Network density among urban families. In J. Boissevain & J.C. Mitchell (Eds), *Network analysis: Studies in human interaction*. The Hague: Mouton.

Csikszentmihalyi, M., Larson R. & Prescott, S. (1977). The ecology of adolescent activity and experience. *Journal of Youth and Adolescence*, **6**, 281–294.

Davies, K. (1953). Management communication and the grapevine. *Harvard Business Review*, **31**, 43–49.

Dawkins, R. (1989). *The selfish gene* (2nd edn). Oxford: Oxford University Press.

Dunbar, R.I.M. (1993). Coevolution of neocortical size, group size and language in humans. *Behavioral and Brain Sciences*, **16**, 681–735.

Dunbar, R.I.M. (1996). *Grooming, gossip and the evolution of language*. London: Faber & Faber.

Dunbar, R.I.M., Duncan, N.D.C. & Nettle, D. (1995). Size and structure of freely forming conversational groups. *Human Nature*, **6**, 67–78.

Dunbar, R.I.M., Duncan, N.D.C. & Marriott, A. (1997). Human conversational behaviour. *Human Nature*, **8**, 231–246.

Eder, D. & Enke, J.L. (1991). The structure of gossip: Opportunities and constraints on collective expression among adolescents. *American Sociological Review*, **56**, 494–508.

Elias, N. & Scotson, J.L. (1965). *The established and the outsiders*. London: Frank Cass.

Emler, N. (1989). *Social information exchange*. Paper presented at EAESP East–West Meeting, Jablonna, Poland.

Emler, N. (1990). A social psychology of reputation. In W. Stroebe & M. Hewstone (Eds), *European review of social psychology* (Vol. 1, pp. 171–193). Chichester: Wiley.

Emler, N. (1994). Gossip, reputation and social adaptation. In R.F. Goodman & A. Ben-Ze'ev (Eds.). *Good gossip* (pp. 117–138). Lawrence, KS: University Press of Kansas.

Emler, N. (2000). Social structures and individual lives: Effects of participation in the social institutions of family, education and work. In J. Bynner & R.K. Silbereisen (Eds), *Adversity and challenge in life course in the new Germany and in England* (pp. 62–84). London: Macmillan.

Emler, N. (In preparation) *Serpent's tongue: The psychology of gossip*. Oxford: Oxford University Press.

Emler, N. & Grady, K. (1987). *The university as a social environment*. Paper presented at British Psychological Society, Social Psychology Section Annual Conference, Brighton.

Emler, N. & McNamara, S. (1996). The social contact patterns of young people: Effects of participation in the social institutions of family, education and work. In H. Helve & J. Bynner (Eds), *Youth and life management: Research perspectives*. Helsinki: Helsinki University Press.

Enquist, M. & Leimar, O. (1993). The evolution of cooperation in mobile organisms. *Animal Behaviour*, **45**, 747–757.

Fischer, C. (1981). *To dwell among friends: Personal networks in town and city*. Chicago: University of Chicago Press.

Freeman, L.C., Romney, A.K. & Freeman, S.C. (1987). Cognitive structure and informant accuracy. *American Anthropologist*, **89**, 310–325.

Friedkin, N.E. (1980). A test of the structural features of Granovetter's "Strength of Weak Ties" theory. *Social Neworks*, **2**, 411–422.

Gambetta, D. (1994). Godfather's gossip. *Archives Européennes de Sociologie*, **35**, 199–223.

Gans, H.J. (1962). *The urban village*. New York: Free Press.

Gluckman, M. (1963). Gossip and scandal. *Current Anthropology*, **6**, 281–293.

Gluckman, M. (1968). Psychological, sociological and anthropological explanations of witchcraft and gossip: A clarification. *Man*, **3**, 20–34.

Goffman, E. (1961). *Asylums: Essays on the social situation of mental patients and other inmates*. Chicago: Aldine.

Granovetter, M. (1973). The strength of weak ties. *American Journal of Sociology*, **78**, 1360–1380.

Harrington, C.L. & Bielby, D.D. (1995). Where did you hear that? Technology and the social organisation of gossip. *Sociological Quarterly*, **36**, 607–628.

Haviland, J.B. (1977). Gossip as competition in Zinacantan. *Journal of Communication*, **27**, 186–191.

Hutson, S. (1971). Social ranking in a French Alpine community. In F.G. Bailey (Ed.), *Gifts and poison: The politics of reputation* (pp. 41–68). Oxford: Blackwell.

Jaeger, M.E., Skelder, A.A., Rind, B. & Rosnow, R.L. (1994). Gossip, gossipers, gossipees. In R.F. Goodman & A. Ben-Ze'ev (Eds), *Good gossip* (pp. 154–168). Lawrence, KS: University Press of Kansas.

Jaeger, M.E., Skelder, A.A. & Rosnow, R.L. (1997). Who's up on the low down: Gossip in interpersonal relations. In B.H. Spitzberger & W.R. Cupach (Eds), *The dark side of close relationships* (pp. 103–117). Mahwah, NJ: Erlbaum.

Janet, P. (1929). *L'evolution psychologique de la personalité*. Paris: Chahine.

Jones, D. (1980). Gossip: Notes on women's oral culture. *Women's Studies International Quarterly*, **3**, 193–198.

Kashy, D. & Kenny, D. (1990). Do you know whom you were with a week ago Friday? A reanalysis of the Bernard, Kilworth and Sailer studies. *Social Psychology Quarterly*, **53**, 55–61.

Killworth, P.D. & Bernard, H.R. (1976). Informant accuracy in social network data. *Human Organization*, **35**, 269–296.

Kipers, P.S. (1987). Gender and topic. *Language in Society*, **16**, 543–557.

Landis, M.H. & Burtt, H.E. (1924). A study of conversations. *Journal of Comparative Psychology*, **4**, 81–89.

Leaper, C. & Holliday, H. (1995). Gossip in same gender and cross-gender friends' conversations. *Personal Relationships*, **2**, 237–246.

Levin, J. & Arluke, A. (1985). An exploratory analysis of sex differences in gossip. *Sex Roles*, **12**, 281–286.

Litwak, E. & Szelenyi, I. (1969). Primary group structures and their functions. *American Sociological Review*, **35**, 465–481.

Locke, J.L. (1998). *The de-voicing of society: Why we don't talk to each other anymore*. New York: Simon & Schuster.

Macphail, E.M. (1987). The comparative psychology of intelligence. *Behavioral and Brain Sciences*, **10**, 645–696.

Malinowksi, B. (1922). *Argonauts of the Western Pacific*. New York: Dutton.

Mars, G. (1981). *Cheats at work: An anthropology of work-place crime*. London: Unwin.

Merry, S.E. (1984). Rethinking gossip and scandal. In D. Black (Ed.), *Toward a general theory of social control: Fundamentals* (pp. 271–302). Orlando, FL: Academic Press.

Mintzberg, , H. (1973). *The nature of managerial work*. Englewood Cliffs, NJ: Prentice-Hall.

Mitchell, J.C. (1969). *Social networks in urban situations*. Mancheser: Manchester University Press.

Moore, H.T. (1922). Further data concerning sex differences. *Journal of Abnormal and Social Psychology*, **4**, 81–89.

Naish, J. (1978). Desirade: A negative case. In P. Caplan & J.M. Burja (Eds), *Women united, women divided: Cross cultural perspectives on female solidarity* (pp. 238–258). London: Tavistock.

Nevo, O., Nevo, B. & Zahavi, A.D. (1993a). The development of the tendency to gossip questionnaire: Construct and concurrent validation for a sample of Israeli college students. *Education and Psychological Measurement*, **53**, 973–981.

Nevo, O., Nevo, B. & Derech-Zehavi, A. (1993b). Gossip and counselling: The tendency to gossip and its relation to vocational interests. *Counselling Psychology Quarterly*, **6**, 229–238.

Nevo, O., Nevo, B. & Derech-Zehavi, A. (1994). The tendency to gossip as a psychological disposition: Constructing a measure and validating it. In R.F. Goodman & A. Ben Ze'ev (Eds), *Good gossip* (pp. 180–192). Lawrence, KS: University of Kansas Press.

Oakley, A. (1972). *Sex, gender and society.* London: Temple Smith.

Ogburn, W.F. & Nimkoff, M.F. (1950). *Sociology.* Boston: Houghon Mifflin.

Rogers, E.M. (1983). *Diffusion of innovations* (3rd edn). New York: Free Press.

Ross, E.A. (1901). *Social control: A survey of the foundations of order.* New York: Macmillan.

Paine, R. (1967). What is gossip about? An alternative hypothesis. *Man, 2*, 278–285.

Reis, H.T. & Wheeler, L. (1991). Studying social interaction with the Rochester Interaction Record. *Advances in Experimental Social Psychology, 24*, 269–318.

Robinson, J.P. & Godbey, G. (1997). *Time for life: The surprising ways Americans use their time.* University Park, PA: Pennsylvania State University Press.

Sabini, J. & Silver, M. (1982). *Moralities of everyday life.* Oxford: Oxford University Press.

Schein, S. (1994). Used and abused: Gossip in medieval society. In R.F. Goodman & A. Ben Ze'ev (Eds), *Good gossip* (pp. 139–153). Lawrence, KS: University of Kansas Press.

Scheler, M. (1921). *Ressentiment.* New York: Free Press.

Schumann, P.L. & Laumann, E.O. (1994). *The importance of social capital for sexual relations.* Paper presented at International Sociological Association meeting.

Spacks, P.M. (1985). *Gossip.* New York: Knopf.

Stone, A.A., Kessler, R.C. & Haythornthwaite, J.A. (1991). Measuring daily life events and experiences: Decisions for the researcher. *Journal of Personality, 59*, 575–607.

Suls, J. (1977). Gossip and social comparison. *Journal of Communication, 26*, 164–168.

Sultzberger, C.F. (1953). Why it is hard to keep secrets. *Psychoanalysis, 2*, 37–43.

Szalai, A. (1972). *The use of time: Daily activities of urban and suburban populations in twelve countries.* The Hague: Mouton.

Tannen, D. (1990). *You just don't understand: Women and men in conversation.* New York: Ballentine Books.

Tonnies, F. (1957). *Community and society.* New York: Harper (first German edition, 1887).

Weick, K. (1985). Systematic observational methods. In G. Lindzey & E. Aronson (Eds), *The handbook of social psychology* (3rd edn). Vol. 1, pp. 567–634. New York: Random House.

Wellman, B. (1978). The community question: The intimate networks of East Yorkers. *American Journal of Sociology, 84*, 1201–1231.

Wheeler, L. & Nezlek, J. (1977). Sex differences in social participation. *Journal of Personality and Social Psychology, 35*, 742–754.

Wilson, D.S., Wilzynski, C., Wells, A. & Weiser, L. (2000). Gossip and other components of language as group-level adaptations. In C. Heyes & L. Huber (Eds), *The evolution of cognition* (Vienna series in theoretical biology) (pp. 347–365). Cambridge, MA: MIT Press.

Wirth, L. (1938). Urbanism as a way of life. *American Journal of Sociology, 44*, 3–24.

Young, M. & Willmott, P. (1957). *Family and kinship in East London.* Harmondsworth: Penguin.

Part 4

Social Relations

4.18

Politeness

Thomas Holtgraves
Ball State University, Muncie, USA

Politeness has a number of different meanings. For many it calls to mind the advice of Emily Post or Miss Manners, the well-defined protocols for how one is to behave in social settings. But for many language researchers politeness refers to something that is much broader and simultaneously more precise. Politeness in this sense is a technical term, a theoretical construct invoked as a means of explaining linguistic and social behavior, and the relationship between the two. As such, the appeal of politeness theory is quite broad – it offers a perspective for examining and explaining the minute patterning of linguistic behavior in social contexts. And because of this, politeness has been heavily researched by scholars across a variety of disciplines, including communication, philosophy, sociolinguistics, social psychology, cognitive psychology, linguistics, and others.

In this chapter I first briefly discuss various approaches that have been taken with regard to politeness. Then, the majority of the chapter focuses on what is currently the dominant framework – a face management view of politeness. This discussion will center on the motivations for politeness, the manner in which politeness is linguistically realized, and the impact of the social context on politeness. In a final section some recent developments and future directions are noted.

APPROACHES TO POLITENESS

There currently exist a number of different approaches to politeness (see Fraser, 1990). One approach, more popular in the past than in the present, is a social normative view of politeness, a view somewhat akin to lay conceptions of

The New Handbook of Language and Social Psychology.
Edited by W. Peter Robinson and Howard Giles.
© 2001 John Wiley & Sons Ltd.

politeness. In this view, to be polite is to behave in accordance with rules prescribing appropriate behavior in a particular context; violating these rules results in negative evaluations, behaving in accord with them results in positive evaluations. Such rules are culture and situation specific and there is no attempt to specify universal principles of politeness.

A second perspective is best exemplified by the work of Lakoff (1973, 1979) and Leech (1983). For these authors politeness falls within the domain of pragmatics. Hence, their goal is to specify a set of principles regarding pragmatic competence (of which politeness is one component). In general, both authors attempt to supplement Grice's (1975) asocial conversational maxims (relation, quality, quantity, and manner) with various politeness maxims, or principles regarding which linguistic form is to be preferred over another. For Lakoff (1973, 1979) these include: give options, don't impose, and make the other feel good; for Leech (1983) these include maxims of tact, generosity, approbation, and others. Many of the core ideas of Lakoff and Leech are consistent with a face management view of politeness and will be noted below. As a general approach to politeness, however, both of their views share a general weakness in not developing an overarching principle(s) from which the maxims could be derived (politeness maxims could be generated endlessly).

A third approach, and the one that will be the focus of the present chapter, can be termed a face management view of politeness.[1] A face management view of politeness has its clearest expression in the pioneering work of Brown and Levinson. Their theory was originally published as a book chapter (1978), and then reissued whole as a book in 1987 (with an introduction summarizing relevant politeness research). Brown and Levinson's theory has generated a tremendous amount of cross-disciplinary research. Their basic argument is that concerns with face (Goffman, 1967) underlie all politeness, and that politeness is conveyed (implicated) via deviation from Grice's (1975) cooperative principle. Hence, politeness is not the result of linguistic behavior being constrained by maxims, but is instead a means of dealing with a conflict between speaking efficiently (in accord with Grice's maxims) and managing the face of the interactants. A face management view of politeness is clearly a social psychological view of politeness; it focuses on the social context as the primary determinant of face-threat assessment and hence the extent to which one will be polite.

FACE MANAGEMENT VIEW OF POLITENESS

A face management view of politeness begins with the notion of face developed by Goffman (1967). In his view, face is the "positive social value a person effectively claims for himself by the line others assume he has taken during a particular contact" (p. 5). Note that it is not the specific line or identity that a

---

[1] Other approaches to politeness may be identified. However, in most cases these approaches are reactions to the face management view. Several such approaches will be noted in the chapter.

person chooses to convey; rather it is the successful presentation of *any* identity. To fail to have one's identity ratified is to lose face in an encounter, to have one's identity ratified is to have face, to maintain an identity that has been challenged is to save face. And so on. Face is thus a social rather than psychological construct; it resides not within the individual but rather within the encounter itself. Moreover, because face can only be given by others (one might claim a particular identity, but it must be ratified by others) it is in everyone's best interest to maintain each other's face. This is accomplished by engaging in facework, or undertaking behaviors designed to create, support, or challenge a particular line (Goffman, 1971). For example, people generally avoid creating threats to one anothers' face (termed avoidance strategies): they avoid threatening topics, violating another's territory, calling attention to another's faults, and so on. People also engage in approach-based facework (e.g., greetings, compliments, salutations) undertaken as a means of affirming and supporting the social relationship. This is not trivial. In Goffman's view face management is on a par with religious ritual (Durkheim, 1915); it provides a mechanism that constrains the individual desire for self-interest. In effect, the social order is a result of facework.

Brown and Levinson's (1978, 1987) politeness theory is a direct extension of Goffman's analysis of face and facework; politeness is essentially the linguistic means by which facework is accomplished. Their extension took several directions. First, they adopted Durkheim's (1915) concepts of negative and positive rites to divide face into two basic and universal desires: negative face, or the desire to have autonomy of action, and positive face, or the desire for closeness with others. Like Goffman, Brown and Levinson assume face to be quite fragile and subject to continued threat during social interaction. The act of merely addressing a remark to someone imposes on that person at some minimal level by requiring a response (hence negative face – or freedom from imposition – is threatened). Disagreements, criticisms, and refusals all threaten (primarily) the recipient's positive face (the desire for closeness with the other). Importantly, the speaker's own face may be threatened by the performance of certain acts. Promises threaten the speaker's negative face (by restricting subsequent freedom) and apologies threaten the speaker's positive face (via an admission of harming the other). Social interaction thus presents a dilemma for interactants. On the one hand they are motivated to maintain each other's positive and negative face. On the other hand, they are motivated to perform certain acts that threaten those very desires. This conflict is solved (to varying degrees) by engaging in facework, or more precisely by being polite.

Brown and Levinson also extended Goffman's analysis by delineating specific politeness strategies people use as a means of managing face. They developed a typology for classifying these strategies and demonstrated the parallel existence of these forms in three very different languages. Finally, they argued that a speaker's degree of politeness is a result of his or her assessment of three social variables. These two extensions (specific politeness strategies and the role of social variables) plus the status of the concept of face are discussed in detail below.

POLITENESS STRATEGIES

So, how exactly do people convey politeness? In the Brown and Levinson model it is deviation from maximally efficient communication (i.e., communication adhering to Grice's (1975) maxims of relation, quantity, quality, and manner) that communicates a polite attitude. There are, of course, many ways this can be accomplished, and Brown and Levinson (1987) organized politeness into five superstrategies. These superstrategies are assumed to be ordered on a continuum of overall politeness, or extent to which face concerns are encoded in the communication. Consider the act of making a request. The least polite strategy is to perform the act without any politeness. To do so is to perform the act bald-on-record, as for example with an imperative ("Shut the door"). Such a communication is maximally efficient; it is entirely in accord with Grice's maxims.

The most polite strategy is to simply not to perform the act at all. But if the act is performed, then the most polite strategy is to do so with an off-record form. An off-record form can be performed by violating one of Grice's maxims. For example, uttering "It's cold in here" in an obviously cold room violates the quantity maxim (it states the obvious) and hence often functions as a polite request (e.g., to turn up the thermostat). The defining feature of off-record forms is their ambiguity and hence deniability. As a result, this request imposes very little and is very polite; the recipient is given options in responding (Lakoff, 1973).

Falling between these two extremes are on-record acts with redress emphasizing either positive face or negative face. The former, termed positive politeness, functions via an exaggerated emphasis on closeness or solidarity with the hearer. It is an approach-based politeness (Durkheim's, 1915, positive rites). For example, the use of ingroup identity markers (e.g., familiar address forms, slang), jokes, presumptuous optimism ("You'll loan me your car, won't you?") all implicate a view of a relatively close relationship. The latter, termed negative politeness, functions via attention to the recipient's autonomy. It is an avoidance-based politeness (Durkheim's, 1915, negative rites). For example, conventionalized indirect forms (e.g., "Could you shut the door?") symbolically give the recipient an "out" and hence are less imposing than a bald on-record form.

Both positively and negatively polite forms are on-record, meaning that the act performed is relatively clear. Still, these strategies represent deviations from maximum communication efficiency. For example, although the directive force of "Could you shut the door?" is clear, it is performed indirectly rather than with the imperative. The intent of positively polite strategies is even more clear; many times these forms will include the imperative (and hence be very direct), but the imperative will be embedded within verbal markers of closeness, an embedding that is not necessary and hence violates the quantity maxim (do not say more than is necessary).

In Brown and Levinson's (1978) original formulation negative politeness was assumed to be more polite than positive politeness. This was because it avoided the positive politeness presumption of closeness (which may or may not be valid from the recipient's point of view). Moreover, this ordering is consistent with Durkheim's (1915) and Goffman's (1971) ordering of negative rites/avoidance rituals as being more deferential (and hence more polite) than positive rites/ presentation rituals.

Research examining Brown and Levinson's politeness typology has not received unequivocal support. Partial support for the ordering of the super-strategies for performing requests has been reported by Bauman (1988), Blum-Kulka (1987), and Holtgraves and Yang (1990). Additionally, Clark and Schunk (1980) examined the perceived politeness of a set of negatively polite requests, and found perceived politeness to vary (as predicted) with the implied cost (threat) to the hearer. Conceptually similar results have been reported by Hill et al. (1986) with Japanese and North American participants, by Holtgraves and Yang (1990) with North American and Korean participants, and by Fraser and Nolan (1981) with North American and Spanish respondents. These relatively close parallels across languages is consistent with Brown and Levinson's contention that the linguistic manifestation of conventional indirect forms is universal.

Still, Brown and Levinson's politeness scheme has received a fair amount of criticism, and it appears their original formulation will need to be modified in various ways. The two major criticisms of their typology focus on whether utterances can be classified with this scheme, and whether their ordering of politeness strategies is valid. Each of these issues is considered in turn.

A frequent criticism of the classification scheme is that many times an utterance will contain multiple politeness strategies (Baxter, 1984; Craig, Tracy & Spisak, 1986; Tracy, 1990). Thus, positive politeness (e.g., ingroup identity markers) may occur in conjunction with a conventional negatively polite form, thereby making unambiguous classification of the utterance different. No doubt politeness strategies are mixed within a turn. Note, however, that a single utterance can perform multiple speech acts and hence create multiple face threats. For example, a request, which threatens (primarily) negative face, may on occasion function as a criticism, an act threatening positive face. Although all directives threaten the recipient's negative face, there is variability within this speech act category (based on constitutive rules for the act) in terms of whether positive face is also threatened (Wilson, Aleman & Leatham, 1998). Multiple politeness strategies may be oriented to these multiple face threats.

Sometimes the occurrence of multiple politeness strategies may be more apparent than real because markers of politeness can occur for reasons other than politeness. For example, variability in address forms, which may be related to politeness (Wood & Kroger, 1991), can also occur as a function of different social relationships, or be part of an attempt to (re)negotiate a relationship. Compounding the problem is the fact that certain markers of politeness, such as hedges, can function as either positively or negatively polite, depending on the context. The assignment of utterances to politeness categories is not a clear-cut task. It represents the analyst's judgment of the utterance as a whole (not a simple counting of politeness markers) in a particular context. But note an additional difficulty here. Politeness can be conveyed over a series of turns, and this makes judgments of the politeness of single utterances problematic (as Brown & Levinson, 1987, note). For example, a speaker might use an impolite form when making a request and hence appear to threaten the recipient's negative face. But this impolite request may have occurred after a prerequest (e.g., "Are you busy?"), a move that had performed the facework (Levinson, 1983).

The second issue concerns the ordering of politeness strategies. Extant research has not supported this ordering in its entirety. With requests the ordering generally holds, except that off-record forms are usually perceived as less polite than negatively polite forms (Blum-Kulka, 1987; Holtgraves & Yang, 1990). This may be because off-record forms can carry a cost; they may violate an efficiency maxim (Blum-Kulka, 1987; Leech, 1983), or have the appearance of manipulativeness (Lakoff, 1977). This research, then, raises the issue about whether politeness should be equated with indirectness, as many authors have argued (Brown & Levinson, 1987; Lakoff, 1973; Leech, 1983). This is an important issue because it deals with the essence of what politeness is. For requests and other directives, indirectness provides the recipient with options, thereby lessening the imposition and increasing politeness (Lakoff, 1973). But research demonstrating that off-record forms are not the most polite forms clearly contradicts this logic. Moreover, Dillard et al. (1997) found that the perceived politeness of messages was positively correlated with message explicitness (or directness), the exact opposite of the presumed politeness–indirectness link.[2]

Clearly, indirectness can occur for reasons other than politeness, and politeness may be conveyed by means other than indirectness. So, politeness and indirectness are not identical. However, several things need to kept in mind here. First, very indirect remarks (i.e., off-record forms) may not function as truly ambiguous remarks in an experimental context. For example, providing participants with a set of requests to be rated informs them that all of the remarks are requests, and this eliminates the ambiguity of off-record forms, their defining feature. Also, it is very difficult to scale indirectness (other than perceived indirectness); to do so requires an empirical examination of the cognitive processes involved in comprehension, an endeavor that has yet to be undertaken. So, attempts to determine the exact relationship between politeness and indirectness will have to await further research. In the meantime, a weaker ordering might be proposed, whereby indirect remarks are generally perceived as more polite than their direct counterparts, but variations in indirectness may or not correspond to changes in perceived politeness.

A related criticism concerns the proposed ordering of negative and positive politeness. Some researchers have questioned whether negative politeness is always more polite than positive politeness. More specifically, these researchers

---

[2] Note, however, that the message occurred between people in a generally close relationship, and according to Brown and Levinson's (1987) politeness theory, it is in close relationships that more direct/less polite speech is expected. Hence, insults and commands and so on (with the appropriate demeanor) are expected to occur in close relationships (although the theory does not necessarily predict greater directness to be associated with greater politeness).

have argued that these forms are qualitatively different and hence cannot be ordered on a unidimensional continuum (Baxter, 1984; Lim & Bowers, 1991; Scollon & Scollon, 1981; Tracy, 1990). There is some merit to this argument and it seems unlikely that the proposed ordering will be valid across all types of face-threatening acts. For directives (threats to the hearer's negative face) the proposed ordering makes sense both theoretically (negative politeness grants the hearer greater autonomy than positive politeness) and empirically (Holtgraves & Yang, 1990). On the other hand, for acts that primarily threaten the hearer's positive face, positive politeness may be more polite than negative politeness (Lim & Bowers, 1991). One possibility in this regard is that politeness strategies can be ordered on the basis of a specificity principle; a strategy that orients to the specify type of face threatened will be regarded as more polite than a strategy that does not. Thus, negatively polite strategies would be more polite for acts threatening the hearer's negative face, and positively polite strategies would be more polite for acts threatening the hearer's positive face.

THE INTERPERSONAL CONTEXT

The degree of a person's politeness varies over settings. In fact, in a very important way a person's degree of politeness can be taken as an indication of how that person perceives the current setting; it reveals one's social cognitions regarding the interpersonal context. Brown and Levinson (1987) proposed that politeness will vary as a function of the weightiness (or degree of face threat) of the act to be performed (see also Leech, 1983, for a consideration of the effects of similar social variables). Weightiness is contextually determined and is assumed to be an additive weighting of the following three variables: the intrinsic (and culturally bound) degree of imposition of the act itself (e.g., asking for a loan of $5 is less imposing than asking for a loan of $500), the power of the hearer relative to the speaker, and the degree of social distance between the interlocutors. More formally, weightiness can be determined with the following formula:

$$Wx = D(S,H) + P(H,S) + Rx$$

where Wx refers to the weightiness of the act in this particular context, $D(S,H)$ refers to the distance between the speaker and hearer, $P(H,S)$ refers to the hearer's power in relation to the speaker, and Rx refers to the degree of imposition of the act. Thus, increased weightiness (and hence, in general, greater politeness) occurs as a function of increasing imposition, hearer power, and relationship distance.

A fair amount of research has examined the impact of these variables on politeness; this has been the most popular area for empirical tests of Brown and Levinson's model. In general, strong support has been found for the power variable, with most studies demonstrating higher speaker power being associated with less politeness. This result has been found with experimental studies of requests (Holtgraves & Yang, 1990, 1992; Leichty & Applegate, 1991; Lim & Bowers, 1991) as well as with observational studies of actual requests (Blum-Kulka, Danet & Gherson, 1985). The demonstrated impact of speaker power on address forms is also consistent with politeness theory (Brown & Gilman, 1989; Wood & Kroger, 1991). Additionally, power has been found to have the predicted effects on the politeness of messages conveying bad news (Ambady et al., 1996), reminders and complaints (Leitchy & Applegate, 1991), criticisms (Lim & Bowers, 1991), accounts (Gonzales et al., 1990), and questions (Holtgraves, 1986). Cross-cultural studies of the power variable have been rare but supportive (Holtgraves & Yang, 1992; Ambady et al., 1996).

Fairly consistent support has been found for the imposition variable, with increasing imposition associated with increasing politeness. This effect has been found for requests (Brown & Gilman, 1989; Holtgraves & Yang, 1992; Leichty & Applegate, 1991), expressions of gratitude (Okamoto & Robinson, 1997), re-commendations vs. reports (Lambert, 1996), accounts (Gonzales et al., 1990; McLaughlin, Cody & O'Hair, 1983), as well as other speech acts (Brown & Gilman, 1989; Leitchy & Applegate, 1991). Some null findings have been re-ported (Baxter, 1984), but they are in the minority.

The effects of relationship distance have been the most problematic. Consis-tent with the theory, some researchers have reported greater politeness as a function of increasing distance (Holtgraves & Yang, 1992; Wood & Kroger, 1991). Others have reported the exact opposite (Baxter, 1984; Brown & Gilman, 1989), and others (Lambert, 1996) have reported no relationship between dis-tance and politeness. As noted by Slugoski and Turnbull (1988) (see also Brown & Gilman, 1989) a potential problem with the distance variable is that it con-founds distance (i.e., familiarity) and affect (i.e., liking). The meaning of the distance variable needs to be clarified, and additional dimensions such as affect may need to be added.

One consistent finding that has emerged from the empirical research is that the three variables do not have an additive effect. Researchers investigating the impact of these variables have reported Power × Distance interactions (Blum-Kulka et al., 1985; Holtgraves & Yang, 1990; Lim & Bowers, 1991; Wood & Kroger, 1991), Imposition × Power interactions (Gonzales et al., 1990; Holtgraves & Yang, 1992), and Imposition × Distance interactions (Holtgraves & Yang, 1992; Leichty & Applegate, 1991). The meaning of these different interactions is simply this: as one of the three variables becomes quite large, the effects of the other variables on politeness will be reduced. A person making an extremely large request will generally be polite regardless of his or her status. There is also some evidence that power may need to be weighted more heavily than distance, at least for address forms (Wood & Kroger, 1991).

The specification of the impact of social variables on face threat, and hence politeness, is one of the greatest strengths of the face management approach to politeness. The inclusion of power and distance in the model is noteworthy as these two dimensions are clearly two (if not *the* two) major dimensions underly-ing social interaction (Wish, Deutsch & Kaplan, 1976). Now, these variables can obviously interact and may not be weighted equally. Also, other dimensions may need to be considered (Slugoski & Turnbull, 1988), including more situation-specific rights and obligations (Fraser, 1990; Tracy, 1990). Note, however, that power, distance, and imposition are high-level, abstract variables that should subsume more specific variables. Continued work in this area should aid in clarifying these effects. Research should also continue to address the reverse of this relationship. Given that politeness varies as a function of power and distance, perceptions of a speaker on these dimensions should vary as a function of his or her politeness. There is research demonstrating that this is the case for requests (and for both US Americans and South Koreans) (Holtgraves & Yang, 1990), but much more could be done.

STATUS OF FACE CONCEPT

Is face management the fundamental and universal motivation behind politeness? Don't people sometimes attack each other's face via insults and challenges? Isn't there individual and cultural variability in politeness? In other words, are people in all cultures always concerned with the collective management of face? Well, no, they are not. And issues regarding the conceptualization of face and face management as they relate to politeness have received a fair degree of attention. Several specific (and related) issues can be identified in this regard.

First, several theorists have argued that more attention needs to be paid to aggressive facework, that is, verbalizations that directly threaten (rather than support) another's face (Craig et al., 1986; Penman, 1990; Tracy, 1990). Obviously such occurrences need to be explained within a theory of politeness, and the Brown and Levinson model clearly gives short shrift to such occurrences. The lack of politeness (bald-on-record) is not the same as aggressively threatening another's face (Labov & Fanschel, 1977). Hence, following Craig et al. (1986), one might expand the model to include an aggressive facework strategy, a strategy that would be less polite than bald-on-record. It is important to note, however, that aggressive facework (insults and challenges) has its impact in large part because it is assumed that people will be face supportive. It is thus the presumption of politeness that is assumed, not its actual occurrence. So while people may engage in aggressive facework, they succeed in doing so because of the underlying presumption of cooperative facework.

A second and somewhat related criticism is the presumed overemphasis on the management of the hearer's face at the expense of facework directed toward managing one's own face (Craig et al., 1986; Penman, 1990; Ting-Toomey, 1988). These authors suggest that politeness needs to be examined in terms of whether it is directed toward the face of the speaker, the hearer, or both (mutual face for Ting-Toomey, 1988). Note that the self- vs. other-face distinction is included in the Brown and Levinson model, though the politeness strategies they consider are clearly oriented toward the hearer. And this is because face management is assumed to be cooperative; threats to other's face are threats to one's own face. So, by supporting the other's face, one is supporting one's own face. But clearly there are times when there is a tradeoff between protecting one's own face and managing the face of the hearer. This can be seen quite clearly in the case of accounts (Gonzales, Manning & Haugen, 1992; Holtgraves, 1989). Providing an elaborate apology will support the face of the recipient, but will simultaneously humble the speaker's face; conversely, justifying one's actions will support the speaker's face, but at the expense to the face of the hearer.

Finally, one of the most important issues surrounding politeness is its status as a cultural universal. While few would argue the claim that politeness exists in all cultures, the claim that positive and negative face are universal desires motivating the form that politeness takes has been questioned (e.g., Watts, 1992). These arguments take several forms. Some have argued that the Brown and Levinson politeness continuum does not hold in all cultures. Katriel (1986), for example, argues that in Sabra culture in Israel there is a preference for a direct, straightforward style; greater directness (the lack of politeness) is seen as more attuned to the interactants' face than is politeness via indirectness.

A second general critique is that negative face is relevant only in Western cultures, or cultures where there is an emphasis on individual autonomy. For example, Rosaldo (1982), in her analysis of Llongot speech acts, argues that directives in that culture are not particularly face-threatening, referencing as they do group membership and responsibility rather than individual wants and desires (see also Fitch & Sanders, 1994). Hence, directives in that culture will usually not be performed politely. Similarly, Matsumoto (1988) argues that in Japanese culture interactants orient towards their relationships rather than emphasizing individual rights; hence negative face wants are relatively unimportant. As a result, strategies normally viewed as addressing negative politeness may take very different forms in Japan; one can indicate deference by actually attempting to impose on the hearer, by, for example, displaying dependency.

Clearly there is great cultural variability in terms of politeness. The crucial question is whether this variability is a result of differing cultural conceptions of face, or whether these differences can be explained at a lower level of abstraction. Brown and Levinson (1987) assumed face wants to be universal, but that cultures will vary in terms of what threatens face, who has power over whom, how much distance is typically assumed, and so on. In this view politeness can be viewed as a framework for examining cultural differences in interaction. Thus, certain acts are more threatening in some cultures than in other cultures, and hence greater politeness will be expected for those acts in the former than in the latter. So, directives are more threatening in Western cultures than in, say, Ilongot culture, and hence more likely to be performed politely in the former than in the latter. And this framework has been useful in explaining some cultural (Ambady et al., 1996; Holtgraves & Yang, 1992; Scollon & Scollon, 1981) and subcultural (Kleiner, 1996) differences in politeness. For example, cultural differences in politeness can be explained via cultural differences in the weighting of the P, D and R variables (Ambady et al., 1996; Holtgraves & Yang, 1992). Similarly, differences in weighting may explain gender differences in politeness (Holtgraves & Yang, 1992).

Still, the possibility of cultural differences in the concept of face remain. One promising direction in this regard is the linking of face concerns with cultural differences in individualism (emphasis on individual rights) and collectivism (emphasis on group goals) (Triandis, 1994). This would entail a greater emphasis on the self-face vs. other-face distinction. Then, as Ting-Toomey (1988) has argued, one might expect the politeness of people in collectivist cultures to focus more on other-face, and the politeness of people in individualistic cultures to focus more on self-face. But note that these differences are largely a matter of degree rather than being absolute (although group goals predominate in collectivist cultures, individual goals still exist and motivate people). Note also that negative face in collectivist cultures may exist primarily at the ingroup vs. outgroup level, rather than at the level of the individual (Morisaki & Gudykunst, 1994). Relatively stronger ingroup–outgroup distinctions are made in collectivist cultures and this results in greater overall variability in social interaction (Wheeler, Reis & Bond, 1989), including levels of politeness (Holtgraves & Yang, 1992).

RECENT DEVELOPMENTS AND FUTURE DIRECTIONS

One relatively recent development involves the application of politeness theory to the manner in which people interpret indirect remarks, an issue that has received considerable attention from cognitive psychologists (Gibbs, 1994). The major issue is this. Given that much politeness is conveyed via indirectness, how is that a hearer is able to comprehend a speaker's intended meaning? Grice's (1975) theory of conversational implicature is frequently invoked as an explanation for this process. But Grice says nothing about which *specific* implicature (out of a very large number of possible implicatures) a person will make. And it is here that politeness theory provides a partial solution to this problem. A major (though not exclusive) motivation for speaking indirectly is to be polite. Hence, a hearer who encounters a maxim violation is likely to assume that the speaker is engaging in face management, and this realization should serve as a constraint on the interpretation process. Consistent with this logic, Holtgraves (1998) found that participants are very likely to interpret replies that violate the relevance maxim as conveying face-threatening information, and that when face management as a reason for a relevance violation is removed the remarks violating the maxim become very difficult to comprehend. Further investigation of the role of politeness in comprehension is warranted. Given that politeness and face management are general pressures affecting how we talk with one another, it seems likely that politeness will play a role in how we understand one another.

Another relatively recent development in politeness theory involves the empirical examination of non-verbal politeness. This possibility was noted by

Brown and Levinson and emphasized by Goffman (1967), but empirical research has been rare. Recently, Ambady et al. (1996) examined the verbal and non-verbal politeness of South Korean and US American participants who conveyed news (good or bad) to people varying in power. Participants clearly conveyed politeness non-verbally (although the specific mechanisms for doing so were not identified), and their non-verbal politeness was sensitive to the social context. In another recent study, Trees and Manusov (1998) examined the perceived politeness of messages varying in both verbal and non-verbal politeness. Importantly, these authors identified specific non-verbal behaviors assumed to be related to increased politeness (e.g., raised eyebrows, touch, less distance) and those related to impoliteness (e.g., greater distance, lowered eyebrows, lack of touch, loud voice). Perceived politeness was affected by both the manipulated verbal and non-verbal behaviors, as well as the interaction between the two (when impolite non-verbal behaviors were used, linguistic politeness had little effect on overall perceived politeness).

Non-verbal politeness is clearly an important area for future research. There is no doubt that how something is said can be just as important as what was said in determining the overall politeness of an utterance. Also, it appears that non-verbal politeness shows a marked similarity to verbal politeness; it can be classified as positively or negatively polite, and is responsive to the social context in the same manner as verbal politeness (Ambady et al., 1996; Trees & Manusov, 1998). Moreover, non-verbal and verbal behaviors probably interact in complex ways. For example, ambiguous verbal messages (off-record forms) might be partially disambiguated via non-verbal behaviors.

Another development has been the analysis of remarks other than requests, and the attempt to use a face management–politeness framework for the examination of language use in real-world settings. A partial listing of such attempts includes the analysis of political discourse (Bull & Elliot, 1998; Jucker, 1986), tutoring sessions (Person et al., 1995), courtroom discourse (Penman, 1990) negotiation and bargaining (Wilson, 1992), physician communication (Aronsson & Satterlund-Larsson, 1987), self-disclosure (Coupland et al., 1988), and the wording of survey questions (Holtgraves, Eck & Lasky, 1997). This research has provided, and should continue to provide, new insights that will aid in the refinement of politeness theory, and contribute to our understanding of language use in a variety of contexts.

CONCLUSIONS

Politeness is an important construct existing at the interface of linguistic, social and cognitive processes; it is conveyed through language and is a result of a person's cognitive assessment of the social context. Politeness theory, on the other hand, is a tool or framework for examining the interaction of these different phenomena, and as such it provides a rich multilayered approach to language use. Now, a face management view of politeness is pitched at a high level of abstraction; it provides a broad, parsimonious, and universal account of the patterning of linguistic behavior in context. But there are obviously weaknesses with the approach, chief among them being that in many respects it is an overly simplistic view that either overlooks important factors involved in language use, or forces them into an inappropriate framework. Also, as with any broad theoretical enterprise (e.g., Freudian psychoanalytic theory) the approach can begin to border on the non-falsifiable. But the approach has been extremely heuristic and illuminating of some of the very basic features of social life. There is no doubt that our understanding of politeness and its role in social interaction has increased over the past 20 years. There is also no doubt that politeness remains a rich field for future investigation.

REFERENCES

Ambady, N., Koo, J., Lee, F. & Rosenthal, R. (1996). More than words: Linguistic and nonlinguistic politeness in two cultures. *Journal of Personality and Social Psychology*, **70**, 996–1011.

Aronsson, K. & Satterlund-Larsson, U. (1987). Politeness strategies and doctor–patient communication: On the social choreography of collaborative thinking. *Journal of Language and Social Psychology*, **6**, 1–27.

Bauman, I. (1988). *The representational validity of a theory of politeness*. Paper presented at the annual meeting of the International Communication Association Convention, New Orleans, LA.

Baxter, L.A. (1984). An investigation of compliance gaining as politeness. *Human Communication Research*, **10**, 427–456.

Blum-Kulka, S. (1987). Indirectness and politeness in requests: Same or different? *Journal of Pragmatics*, **11**, 131–146.

Blum-Kulka, S., Danet, B. & Gherson, R. (1985). The language of requesting in Israeli society. In J. Forgas (Ed.), *Language in social situations* (pp. 113–139). New York: Springer.

Brown, P. & Levinson, S. (1978). Universals in language usage: Politeness phenomena. In E. Goody, (Ed.), *Questions and politeness* (pp. 56–289). Cambridge, UK: Cambridge University Press.

Brown, P. & Levinson, S. (1987). *Politeness: Some universals in language usage*. Cambridge, UK: Cambridge University Press.

Brown, R. & Gilman, A. (1989). Politeness theory and Shakespeare's four major tragedies. *Language in Society*, **18**, 159–212.

Bull, P. & Elliot, J. (1998). Level of threat: A means of assessing interviewer toughness and neutrality. *Journal of Language and Social Psychology*, **17**, 220–244.

Clark, H.H. & Schunk, D. (1980). Polite responses to polite requests. *Cognition*, **8**, 111–143.

Coupland, J., Coupland, N., Giles, H. & Wiemann, J. (1988). My life is in your hand: Processes of self-disclosure in intergenerational talk. In N. Coupland (Ed.), *Styles of discourse* (pp. 201–253). London: Croom Helm.

Craig, R.T., Tracy, K. & Spisak, F. (1986). The discourse of requests: Assessment of a politeness approach. *Human Communication Research*, **12**, 437–468.

Dillard, J.P., Wilson, S.R., Tusing, K.J. & Kinney, T.A. (1997). Politeness judgments in personal relationships. *Journal of Language and Social Psychology*, **16**, 227–325.

Durkheim, E. (1915). *The elementary forms of religious life*. London: Allen & Unwin.

Fitch, K.L. & Sanders, R.E. (1994). Culture, communication, and preferences for direct-ness in expression of directives. *Communication Theory*, **4**, 219–245.

Fraser, B. (1990). Perspectives on politeness. *Journal of Pragmatics*, **14**, 219–236.

Fraser, B. & Nolan, W. (1981). The association of deference with linguistic form. *International Journal of the Sociology of Language*, **26**, 93–109.

Gibbs, R.W. Jr (1994). Figurative thought and figurative language. In M.A. Gernsbacher (Ed.), *Handbook of psycholinguistics* (pp. 411–446). San Diego: Academic Press.

Goffman, E. (1967). *Interaction ritual: Essays on face to face behavior*. Garden City, NY: Anchor.

Goffman, E. (1971). *Relations in public*. New York: Harper & Row.

Gonzales, M.H., Pederson, J., Manning, D. & Wetter, D.W. (1990). Pardon my gaffe: Effects of sex, status and consequence severity on accounts. *Journal of Personality and Social Psychology*, **58**, 610–621.

Gonzales, M.H., Manning, D.J., & Haugen, J.A. (1992). Explaining our sins: Factors influencing offender accounts and anticipated victim responses. *Journal of Personality and Social Psychology*, **62**, 958–971.

Grice, H.P. (1975). Logic and conversation. In P. Cole & J. Morgan (Eds), *Syntax and semantics 3: Speech acts* (pp. 41–58). New York: Academic Press.

Hill, B., Sachiko, I., Shoko, I., Kawasaki, A. & Ogino, T. (1986). Universals of linguistic politeness. *Journal of Pragmatics*, **10**, 347–371.

Holtgraves, T.M. (1986). Language structure in social interaction: Perceptions of direct and indirect speech acts and interactants who use them. *Journal of Personality and Social Psychology*, **51**, 305–314.

Holtgraves, T.M. (1998). Interpreting indirect replies. *Cognitive Psychology*, **37**, 1–27.

Holtgraves, T. (1989). The form and function of remedial moves: Reported use, psychological reality, and perceived effectiveness. *Journal of Language and Social Psychology*, **8**, 1–16.

Holtgraves, T.M. & Yang, J.N. (1990). Politeness as universal: Cross-cultural perceptions of request strategies and inferences based on their use. *Journal of Personality and Social Psychology*, **59**, 719–729.

Holtgraves, T.M. & Yang, J.N. (1992). The interpersonal underpinnings of request strategies: General principles and differences due to culture and gender. *Journal of Personality and Social Psychology*, **62**, 246–256.

Holtgraves, T.M., Eck, J. & Lasky, B. (1997). Face management, question wording, and social desirability. *Journal of Applied Social Psychology*, **27**, 1650–1672,

Jucker, J. (1986). *News interviews: A pragmalinguistic analysis*. Amsterdam: Gieben.

Katriel, T. (1986). *Talking straight: Durgri speech in Israeli Sabra culture*. London: Cambridge University Press.

Kleiner, B. (1996). Class ethos and politeness. *Journal of Language and Social Psychology*, **15**, 155–175.

Labov, W. & Fanschel, D. (1977). *Therapeutic discourse*. New York: Academic Press.

Lakoff, R. (1973). The logic of politeness: or, minding your p's and q's. In Papers from the Ninth Regional Meeting of the Chicago Linguistic Society, pp. 292–305.

Lakoff, R. (1979). Stylistic strategies within a grammar of style. In J. Orasanu, M. Slater & L. Adler (Eds), *Annals of the New York Academy of Sciences*, **327**, 53–80.

Lambert, B.L. (1996). Face and politeness in pharmacist–physician interaction. *Social Science and Medicine*, **43**, 1189–1199.

Leech, G. (1983). *Principle of pragmatics*. London: Longman.

Leichty, G. & Applegate, J.L. (1991). Social-cognitive and situational influences on the use of face-saving persuasive strategies. *Human Communication Research*, **7**, 451–484.

Lim, T. & Bowers, J. (1991). Face-work, solidarity, approbation, and tact. *Human Communication Research*, **17**, 415–450.

Matsumoto, Y. (1988). Reexamination of the universality of face: Politeness phenomena in Japanese. *Journal of Pragmatics*, **12**, 403–426.

McLaughlin, M.L., Cody, M. & O'Hair, H.D. (1983). The management of failure events: Some contextual determinants of accounting behavior. *Human Communication Research*, **9**, 208–224.

Morisaki, S. & Gudykunst, W.B. (1994). Face in Japan and the United States. In S. Ting-Toomey (Ed.), *The challenge of facework* (pp. 47–94). Albany, NY: State University of New York Press.

Okamoto, S. & Robinson, W.P. (1997). Determinants of gratitude expression in England. *Journal of Language and Social Psychology*, **16**, 411–433.

Penman, R. (1990). Facework and politeness: Multiple goals in courtroom discourse. *Journal of Language and Social Psychology*, **9**, 15–38.

Person, N.K. Kreuz, R.J., Zwaan, R.A. & Graesser, A.C. (1995). Pragmatics and pedagogy: Conversational rules and politeness strategies may inhibit effective tutoring. *Cognition and Instruction*, **13**, 161–188.

Rosaldo, M.Z. (1982). The things we do with words: Ilongot speech acts and speech act theory in philosophy. *Language in Society*, **11**, 203–237.

Scollon, R. & Scollon, S. (1981). *Narrative, literacy and face in interethnic communication*. Norwood, NJ: Ablex.

Slugoski, B. & Turnbull, W. (1988). Cruel to be kind and kind to be cruel: Sarcasm, banter and social relations. *Journal of Language and Social Psychology*, **7**, 101–121.

Ting-Toomey, S. (1988). Intercultural conflict styles. In Y.Y. Kim & W.B. Gudykunst (Eds), *Theories in intercultural communication* (pp. 75–90). Beverly Hills, CA: Sage.

Tracy, K. (1990). The many faces of facework. In H. Giles & P. Robinson (Eds), *Handbook of language and social psychology* (pp. 209–226). London: Wiley.

Trees, A.R. & Manusov, V. (1998). Managing face concerns in criticism: Integrating nonverbal behaviors as a dimension of politeness in female friendship dyads. *Human Communication Research*, **24**, 564–583.

Triandis, H. (1994). *Individualism and collectivism*. Boulder, CO: Westview Press.

Watts, R.J. (1992). Linguistic politeness and politic verbal behavior: Reconsidering claims for universality. In R.J. Watts, S. Ide & K. Ehlich (Eds), *Politeness in language: Studies in its history, theory, and practice* (pp. 43–70). Berlin: Morton de Gruyter.

Wheeler, L., Reis, H.T. & Bond, M.H. (1989). Collectivism–individualism in everyday social life: The middle kingdom and the melting pot. *Journal of Personality and Social Psychology*, **54**, 323–333.

Wilson, S.R., (1992). Face and facework in negotiation. In L.L. Putnam & M.E. Roloff (Eds), *Communication and negotiation* (pp. 176–205). Newbury Park, CA: Sage.

Wilson, S.R., Aleman, C.G. & Leatham, G.B. (1998). A revised analysis of face-threatening acts and application to seeking compliance with same-sex friends. *Human Communication Research*, **25**, 64–96.

Wish, M., Deutsch, M. & Kaplan, S. (1976). Perceived dimensions of interpersonal relations. *Journal of Personality and Social Psychology*, **33**, 409–420.

Wood, L.A. & Kroger, R.O. (1991). Politeness and forms of address. *Journal of Language and Social Psychology*, **10**, 145–168.

4.19

Power

Sik Hung Ng
City University of Hong Kong, Hong Kong
Scott A. Reid
University of Queensland, Australia

We all want to have a good life. For some, the goals may entail no more than to enjoy the simple pleasures of life. Others may want to add honour, riches, authority, and a desire "to make the world a better place". And there are still others who have other goals. Regardless of what the goals are, their realization is, for all practical purposes, socially dependent: none can be achieved independently of other people, and some only at their expense. The pursuit of a good life, constrained by social interdependence, will inevitably lead to the use of power and counter-power. Power, therefore, is intrinsic to social life.

The statement above is a simplified paraphrase of the Hobbesian approach to social power. It is an early example of a psycho-social approach, but it is not alone in reaching the conclusion that power is intrinsic to social life. Nietzsche, for example, made the same point from a philosophical standpoint (the "will" to power), as did numerous political economists and sociologists from a social-structural perspective (see reviews by Ng, 1980; Sidanius & Pratto, 1999). The present chapter will first offer a brief historical overview of the major social psychological approaches to power. This will provide a backdrop to the main discussion of the manifold of power–language links, and the use of language to create social influence. The focus of the discussion will be on the interpersonal exercise of power in small-scale social exchanges, and not on macro-level analysis of power or on the gross oppressions that characterize most of our societies.

The New Handbook of Language and Social Psychology.
Edited by W. Peter Robinson and Howard Giles.
© 2001 John Wiley & Sons Ltd.

POWER AND SOCIAL PSYCHOLOGY

Influence and Power Base

In mainstream social psychology, field theory and social exchange theory have been and continue to be prominent for their explication of the power construct in describing and explaining social behaviour. In field theory, power is the maximum force that the power-wielder can exercise on a target person relative to the latter's maximum resistance. Power becomes influence when force exceeds resistance. From this perspective, power is the potential to influence, and influence is power realized. To understand influence one must, according to field theory, know about the bases of power and their application in relation to any resistance that the application may encounter or evoke.

It is noteworthy that one of the earliest typologies of power bases (French & Raven, 1959; see also Raven, 1992) is grounded in both the agent and the target person. Thus, the agent's ability to mediate positive and negative outcomes for the target person gives rise to power to reward and punish respectively. Referent, legitimate and expert powers are all dependent on the target person's psychological state. That is, they exist only when the target person identifies with the agent (referent power), accepts the agent's position/role as rightful (legitimate power), and respects the agent's credibility (expert power). Informational power, which was added later on, extends the field theoretical analysis to the content of persuasive communication as distinct from perceived expertise. Although the sociological concept of "authority" is not formally used in this typology, it is represented under legitimate and perhaps also referent and expert powers.

Control and Dependence

Social exchange theory has a psychological and a sociological version. Their common starting point is that social interaction can be viewed as an ongoing exchange of mutually reinforcing outcomes between participants. By controlling another's outcomes an agent can alter behaviour. This ability is power; and the greater the range of controllable outcomes, the greater is the power. From this point on, psychological social exchange theorists drop the term power in favour of control, which in turn is analyzed in terms of dependence. The shift from control to dependence is a fundamental refocusing of the analysis of power away from the agent to the target person. Thus agent's fate control over the target person becomes the latter's total dependence on the agent; behaviour control becomes contingency dependence; and contact control becomes relational dependence. The last-named dependence expands the analysis beyond the agent–target dyad to third parties that may provide the target person with an alternative source of relationship. Dependence analysis offers the insight that a power-wielder is only as powerful as the target person's dependence will permit.

It draws attention to factors that entice and keep individuals in a state of emotional and social dependence, and conversely, to mechanisms of power change that are available to the less powerful (see below, especially minority influence).

Historically then, power was wedded to social psychology through field theory and exchange theory as these developed in America. Influence, power bases, control, and dependence are its direct legacies. Beyond these legacies there are various concepts and research topics that are related to power, some more explicitly than others. Examples are: dynamic social impact (Latané, 1981), social dominance (Sidanius & Pratto, 1999), expectancy effects (Snyder, 1984), tactical communication and strategic self-presentation (Cody & McLaughlin, 1990), and control through stereotyping (Fiske, 1993).

Power Distance

In Europe, the resurgence of social psychology during the 1970s coincided with a strong interest in hierarchical social relations, the behaviour of less powerful individuals or groups, and how such behaviour might lead to social change and other large-scale events in history. This interest was clearly evident in the works of Moscovici (1976), Mulder (1977), and Tajfel (1974, 1981a). Of these, Mulder's Power Distance Theory is the most explicitly related to power. The fullest developed part of the theory deals with power distance reduction initiated by less powerful individuals toward more powerful individuals. Its general hypothesis is that the smaller the existing power distance from the more powerful individual, the more subordinates will direct their communication upward and desire to take over the more powerful position when it becomes vacant. The insight here is to view power not as dichotomous categories, but as a variable in terms of power distance. This concept has been assimilated into cross-cultural psychology through Hofstede's (1980) research and further elaborated along bureaucratic (Ng, 1977) and social comparison (Bruins & Wilke, 1992) lines.

Minority Influence

Moscovici's works on minority influence deal with the question of how minorities without numerical strength or material resources can nevertheless influence the majority. This intriguing question, as we have seen, also underlies social exchange theorists' attempt to understand how individuals can overcome their dependence on and influence more powerful others. Moscovici's answer is that minorities can generate influence by creating cognitive conflict and obliging the majority to become responsible for resolving that conflict. To do this, minorities must organize and pattern their collective behaviour in a "synchronically" and "diachronically" consistent style. The underlying theory of socially induced cognitive conflict offers insight into how minorities can exercise influence

without recourse (or access) to the use of power in the limited sense of domination and coercion. In an important development, the theory has been extended
to influence in inter-group situations (Pérez & Mugny, 1998).

Social Identity

Tajfel's seminal work on Social Identity Theory (see also Tajfel & Turner, 1979)
recognizes the importance of ideology (e.g., social myths) and the hierarchical
nature of society (e.g., power), and attempts to define the range of individual and
collective actions that members of lowly placed groups may take to improve
their individual or group position. Power is acknowledged as an important basis
of social structure, and is also inextricably linked to the theory's concept of
cognitive alternatives, as both instability and illegitimacy of the status quo that
define cognitive alternatives are essentially power concepts. But as the theory
unfolds, it is status, not power, that really informs its formulation of the key
concepts of social identity and social comparison (Ng, 1980, 1996). Nonetheless it
has succeeded in making the study of inter-group relations a central topic in
social psychology (Taylor & Moghaddam, 1987; Worchel et al., 1998). In particular, as we shall see later, its descendant Self-Categorization Theory has been
applied to social influence (Turner, 1991).

It should be clear from the brief review above that power is a substantial topic
and has attracted recurrent interest and debate from a wide sector of social
psychology. Below we discuss links between power and language.

POWER AND LANGUAGE USE

From a social psychological perspective, the importance of language to the study of
social behaviour lies in its use. This pragmatic approach to language, with its focus
on the use of language rather than on language comprehension or abstract linguistic
principles (e.g., syntax), was pioneered outside social psychology (e.g., Austin, 1962;
Sacks, Schegloff & Jefferson, 1974). Recognition of its relevance to social psychology
through the early works of Brown, Harré, Robinson, Giles and Powesland (see
Clark, 1985) has set the stage of moving language use from the periphery toward the
core of social psychology. By now, language use has been strongly assimilated into
social psychology under a variety of topics (Krauss & Chiu, 1998). Below we outline
a framework for mapping the power–language links.

Power behind Language and Power of Language: The Big Five

"Look, I gotta loaded gun here, give me the money or I'll shoot!" In terms of
French and Raven's (1959) typology of power bases, the gun is coercive power,
and the wielder is trying to convert it into social influence by uttering a threat.

The example illustrates two pragmatic functions of language use: the wielder uses language to reveal the power base and communicate the intention. As such, language is no more than a passive conduit of power and has no power of its own. In these circumstances, one cannot say the power *of* language, but only the power *behind* language. But let us suppose that the robber's gun is not loaded, or that it is a fake, and yet the bluff is so convincing that the victim succumbs to it. In this case, language is power. There are also, as we shall see shortly, other ways in which language is power.

So, at one level, we may distinguish the power behind language from the power of language. Each category, in turn, has its own facets. The various facets can shade into one other, but for discussion purposes are grouped under five headings: revelation, reflection, influence creation, depoliticization, and routinization (Ng & Bradac, 1993).

Language may reveal or reflect the power that is behind it. The "I gotta loaded gun here" utterance, referred to above, is an example of how speakers use language to reveal their power (assuming that it is not a bluff). In this and other cases of "reveal", the focus of analysis is on the micro-level behaviour of individuals. Parallel to this, but operating at the macro-level, language reflects the collective power of its users. For example, the prestige of a language rises or falls with the ethnolinguistic vitality of the population who use it.

The "power of language" category subsumes three facets: to create influence, to depoliticize an attempt at influence, or to routinize an existing dominance relationship. Language is a symbolic resource that speakers use to influence and control other people, or conversely, to reduce their dependence on others. To the extent that the outcome is successful, language creates the power to influence. (More will be said of this facet later on.) Often, concurrent with the use of language to influence, speakers also cover up their action or make it appear otherwise through lying, obfuscated speech, masked communication, and such like (Robinson, 1996). When this happens, language is said to depoliticize the exercise of power. These two varieties of the "power of language" represent varying degrees of transparency and secrecy, but they all involve a certain degree of intentionality.

The power of language can also function independently of intentionality. When a particular dominance relationship becomes part of everyday discourse, routine participation in the discourse will unwittingly reproduce the relationship. For example, the routine use of a sexist language that is biased against one gender will reproduce the bias in discourse and reinforce the wider unequal gender relationship. Collusion by both genders in the use of a sexist language will, over time, routinize gender dominance (and subordination) by making it appear to be normative, unmarked, and the natural order of things (Crawford, 1995). Similar routinization of a power relationship occurs in patronizing baby-talk addressed to, for example, the aged (Ryan, Hummert & Boich, 1995) or people with disabilities (Fox & Giles, 1996).

In the remainder of this chapter, rather than discuss all five facets in broad terms, we have elected to focus on the "create" facet because of its central relevance to the social psychology of power as reviewed above.

Words, Discourse and Silence: Language Power in Everyday Life

The right words, said in the right way and at the right moment, can make a difference between success and failure in what a person intends to do. Numerous studies on persuasive communication, attitude change, and oratory demonstrate the power of utterances. Below is a brief summary to show the range of what powerful words can achieve in everyday life. Words can influence ("prime") eyewitness testimony. An eyewitness's estimate of a car's speed prior to a crash is higher when the loaded word "smashed" rather than the more neutral phrase "came into contact" is embedded within a question (Loftus & Palmer, 1974). Explicit word meaning can explain this kind of cognitive influence. At a more subtle level, some words also have implicit meanings about causality although these may not be defined in the dictionary. For example, "action verbs" such as "Paul kisses Ann" imply that the sentence subject (Paul) is responsible for the kissing, whereas "state verbs" such as "Fred admires Chris" imply causality in the sentence object (Semin & Fiedler, 1991).

The power of language is not confined to single words or short phrases, but extends to the use of multiple utterances or sentences (discourses). For example, questions can cue answers (Rubini & Kruglanski, 1997). Essentially the same power base can be linguistically reframed from "hard" (e.g., coercion) to "soft" (e.g., information power) power to minimize resistance for optimal influence (Raven, 1997; Raven, Schwarzwald & Koslowsky, 1998). Calls for help that define the situation as a genuine emergency, then single out particular helpers from among bystanders, and finally pinpoint action can turn bystander apathy into effective action that saves lives (Cialdini, 1988). Oratorical devices (e.g., contrast, position-taking, three-part list), carefully timed and coupled with vocalics and non-verbal signals, can generate applause from the audience, move them to tears, and inspire them into action (Heritage & Greatbatch, 1986). Equivocal replies to difficult questions can get the answerer out of a sticky situation (Bavelas et al., 1990). Conversely, reformulation of a question can pin an evasive politician down (Blum-Kulka, 1983). Each of these uses of language (and many more – see Burgoon, 1990) brings forth influence of its own, and collectively they illustrate the pervasive power of language use in everyday life.

The power of language can also be seen, paradoxically, in silence. When talk is expected but not forthcoming, the ensuing silence can serve as a sign of disapproval that is hard to ignore and often strong enough to lead to social ostracism (Williams, 1997). When a government silences oppositions or stops free public communication by introducing martial law or censorship, it imposes silence, on the population to its advantage (Jaworski, 1993). In both cases, it is the absence of talk, and not its active engagement, that gives rise to influence. While acknowledging the power of silence, our prime concern here is with verbal activity and the influence that it may bring.

Speaking Turns and Verbal Content: Powerful Language Behaviour in Small Groups

In small groups where, preceding verbal interaction, the power distance between interlocutors is negligible or not relevant to the matter in hand, a high rate of verbal participation results in influence. The pointeering work of Bales (see below) paved the way for the development of the resource approach to conversational influence (Wilson, Wiemann & Zimmerman, 1984). According to this approach, securing speaking turns and conversational content provide resources for conversational influence.

In a series of studies, Ng and colleagues investigated the role of speaking turns in generating influence within small groups of unacquainted members. To index influence, they asked group members at the end of the group interaction to rank how influential each member had been during the interaction. For most groups, members showed a high degree of concordance in their influence rankings, suggesting that the emergent influence hierarchy was a group property. Brooke and Ng (1986) found that it was numbers of words spoken, and not the avoidance of the so-called "powerless speech", which predicted emergent influence rankings. Further analysis revealed that words spoken were mainly a function of the number of turns, suggesting that the ability to bid successfully for turns was critical to influence. This conclusion, confirmed by other studies (Hollander, 1985; Mullen, Salas & Driskell, 1989; Ng, Bell & Brooke, 1993), supports that part of the resource thesis which emphasizes the role of turns.

Why are turns so important? According to Bales' (1970, pp. 76–77) principle of economy, turns are important because they are a scarce resource:

> To take up time speaking in a small group is to exercise power over the other members for at least the duration of the time taken, regardless of the content . . . Within the small group the time taken by a given member in a given session is practically a direct index of the amount of power he has attempted to exercise in that period. (Emphasis added)

Turns also allow the speaker to influence who will speak next by addressing the end of a turn to a particular listener (Sacks et al., 1974). When next-speaker selection is coupled with the first part of an adjacency pair (e.g., a question in a question–answer pair), the next speaker is more likely to return the speaking turn to the prior speaker than to a third party. In this way, turns can be chained for the development of a floor state (Parker, 1988; Stasser & Taylor, 1991). A floor state, in which the same two speakers alternate speaking over three or more consecutive turns, provides a powerful platform for the formation of conversational cliques. By linking self to these cliques through turn-taking, a speaker becomes the node of the conversational network. From this power base, the speaker forms solidarity with the majority of participants and influences the conversational agenda.

The important roles of turns raise the question of how turns are obtained. Would turns obtained by interrupting other speakers be equally predictive of influence as non-interruptive turns? Stereotypes of an interruptor as a rude loud-mouth suggest (unfairly) that speakers who interrupt frequently would be perceived as impolite and unattractive, and consequently would be unlikely to attract high influence status. Yet turns obtained by interruptions were found to be either as good as (Ng, Brooke & Dunne, 1995), or better than (Ng et al., 1993), non-interruptive turns for predicting emergent influence, suggesting that attractiveness and power are orthogonal group processes. Furthering this work, Ng et al. (1995) found that high-influence speakers were more successful in their interruption attempts, and when being interrupted were better able to maintain the floor than their low-influence counterparts. In another part of this study, two further interesting points about interruptions were revealed. First, not all interruptions were disruptive; on the contrary, many were either constructive in promoting the discussion or altruistic in safeguarding the face of the speaker who had been interrupted. Second, proactive speech acts (dissent, offer, reply) were more strongly associated with the successful enactment of interruptions than were reactive speech acts (consent, request, reaction).

As our review of field theory and social exchange theory has suggested, what the speaker (agent) does is only one side of the power equation that is actually co-determined by target response and perception. Speaking turns are only the first step in the influence process; what happens afterwards depends on whether or not other participants will ratify, accept and develop what the speaker is trying to do (Diamond, 1996). This interactive perspective becomes all the more clear in *inter*-group settings.

Powerful Language Behaviour in Inter-group Settings

The studies reviewed above deal with speaking turns and verbal content in small groups. Do turns and content play similarly important roles in *inter*-group as in intra-group settings? For turns, the answer from an inter-group experiment by Reid and Ng (2000) is positive: speakers who had more turns were rated more influential by ingroup members. Further, they were also rated more influential by outgroup members. With regard to verbal content, and consistent with Self-Categorization Theory (McGarty et al., 1994; Turner ct al., 1987), prototypical utterances (those representing ingroup norms) correlated more strongly with social influence ranking than did non-prototypical utterances. That is, content gathers meaning within a given social context, and it is this contextually grounded meaning that gives it power. Expanding upon this point, the authors found that interruption attempts encoded in prototypical utterances were more successful than unsuccessful in turn bidding, whereas the reverse applied to non-prototypical utterances. It appears that control over turn bidding, while necessarily residing in the conversational behaviour of individual speakers, ultimately derives from the collective perception (by ingroup and outgroup speakers) of the social context. When speakers' utterances are prototypical, thus confirming both ingroup and outgroup members' social identities, speakers are granted speaking rights, and to the extent that speakers' utterances are not identity confirming, speakers are blocked in their attempts to bid for turns.

At this point it is useful to introduce speech style, as distinct from utterance content, to the discussion of prototypicality. Carli (1990) compared the influence of women who used a low- or high-power style. In the cultural context of her study, the low-power style was prototypical of women, and the more assertive high-power style was prototypical of men (see also Carli, LaFleur & Loeber, 1995). Men were found to be influenced more by "feminine" than by "masculine" female speakers, despite perceiving the former as relatively less competent. This finding appears to contradict Self-Categorization Theory's prediction that ingroup-prototypical speakers are more influential than outgroup-prototypical speakers, but may be reconciled by arguing that the finding resulted from the threat to male identity caused by "masculine" female speakers who, despite being ingroup-prototypical on the basis of speech style, remain an outgroup because of their gender. Alternatively, the systemic view of Jost and Banaji (1994) suggests that men are willing to submit so long as this serves to maintain their socio-structural advantage over women. In other words, women can influence men occasionally by making salient their long-term subordinate social position.

Gender issues highlight inter-group settings where traditional power differences between groups are undergoing change. In these dynamic settings, how may language be used to avoid domination and circumvent the power hierarchy? The literature (Taylor & McKirnan, 1984; Worchel, 1998) suggests two critical phases in power change that are inextricably enmeshed in language: first, the definition of a collective identity that is at once distinctive and uniting, and second, the legitimation and mobilization of group actions. In the first phase, linguistic categories can unite hitherto unrelated individuals under a collective identity. This is particularly important in the creation of a new sense of nationhood. Madan (1998) provided evidence for the linguistic delineation of Bangladesh as a state separate from Pakistan. In part this was accomplished with the redefinition of the "Muslims of Bengal" as "Bengali Muslims". The latter served to de-emphasize the significance of religion, which was non-distinct from that of Pakistan, in favour of a definition in terms of territory, which served simultaneously to differentiate Bengalis from Pakistan and also to unite them as the nation of Bangladesh.

In their study of the Rastafarian movement as a self-conscious opposition to Babylon (symbol of Western corruption), Kebede and Knottnerus (1998) showed how Lyaric language was used by Rastafarian followers to preserve and disseminate a sense of Rastafari as a group to enable the movement to spread from Jamaica to other Caribbean islands, the United States, and Britain. This language was based upon word play through the combination of the visual, auditory and semantic features of words to create an ingroup language. For example, "sincerely" which has the sound of sin, was turned into "icerly". "Dedicate", which contains the sound dead, and "appreciate", which contains the sound of hate, became "livicate" and "apprecilove" respectively. These words circumscribe the ingroup while articulating the political/religious spirit of the movement. Importantly "me" and "we" which in Creole English denote sub-missiveness and non-identity were removed from the vernacular and replaced by "I" and "I-and-I" respectively, to recapture a sense of agency and personhood. In sum "The vernacular of the Rastafari serves both as an ingroup language and boundary marker for the group as well as a medium of communication which reflects the ethos of the movement". (Kebede & Knottnerus, 1998, p. 509). This is all the more remarkable since Rastafari have maintained a movement despite no formal hierarchy or bureaucratic organization.

Another phase of inter-group power change in which language plays a critical role is the legitimation and mobilization of group action. Tajfel (1981b) referred to this role in terms of the collective functions of stereotypes, but did not elaborate on the underlying communicative and social constructive processes. A study by Schulz (1998) is instructive. During the Zapatistas uprising in South East Mexico in 1994, Zapatistas faced the daunting task of creating a sense of collective identity both to garner support and legitimate its uprising against the Mexican government.

> [They] present themselves as the latest protagonists in a chain of 500 years of struggle against repression and exploitation from the Spanish conquest of America up to the present PRI-regime. . . . [They] define themselves as the "inheritors" or the "true" nation builders and invoke the constitution for their actions . . . and justify their uprising by appealing to Article 39, which locates the national sovereignty in the people and guarantees them "the inalienable right to alter or modify their form of government." Later communiqués of the EZLN's General Command, usually end with the words "from the mountains of the Mexican Southeast." "Mountains" . . . refers in this context to more than simply a geographical location. The term connotes in Mexico a place outside law and legality, the place where bandits hide, but also the place the constituting forces of revolutionary change came from. . . . A song popular among Zapatista sympathizers affirms that "the voice of change is coming from the mountains". (Schulz, 1998, pp. 595–596)

Thus, the path taken by the Zapatistas was to categorize themselves as a distinct group occupying a specific region of the country, and then to legitimate their political action. The former process served to promote Zapatista solidarity by highlighting an ingroup–outgroup distinction between themselves and govern-ment. The second process served to embed their identity within a superordinate categorization – "national sovereignty in the people". This superordinate categor-ization served to legitimate their action by bringing attention to a shared identity. Popular culture, especially songs in this case, plays a vital role in the process.

CONCLUSIONS

The confluence of power and language makes interesting study. The power of language, in particular, is of considerable theoretical and applied importance (Reid & Ng, 1999). Under this general topic, the power of language to create influence in small groups and in inter-group settings is worth stressing. Speaking turns provide an essential and scarce resource for enacting influence. Other things being equal, the more turns a speaker has the better he or she is resourced to influence others. Turn bidding and the chaining of turns are therefore crucial to the understanding conversational influence. But turns alone are insufficient; verbal content is also needed. Content plays a role in turn-bidding, and also affects how other participants will respond to what the speaker is trying to do. The latter is critical to the study of power in light of what social psychology has said all along about the dynamic nature of power: it takes both the speaker (as influence agent) and the listener (as influence target) to make power and influence. Common group membership with the speaker facilitates speaker influence. Thus, prototypical messages that make the ingroup link salient for the listener are influential; however, prototypicality can backfire if it presents a social identity threat from the outgroup.

Most of the studies reviewed above are experimental simulations of relatively short-lived groups. In life outside the laboratory, as we all know, groups have their own histories and outlive their members. Without exception, groups always develop in the context of outgroups, real or imaginary, with which they often stand in relations of power and status. To illuminate group development and struggle, we have made use of historical studies to sketch a picture of the empowering roles of language in group developments – Bengali Muslims, Rastafaris, and Zapatistas. Other groups, unique in their own histories and in the kinds of outgroups they have to negotiate or contend with, are commonly faced with the challenge of using language, each in its own way, to articulate a collective identity that is distinctive and uniting, and to legitimate and mobilize collective action. Space limit prevents us from discussing a wider range of groups. But in conclusion we highlight the situation of global ageing and the many senior citizens' movements that flow from it. The movements are interesting, *politically* because the number of older adults is rapidly increasing worldwide and inter-generational relations are at risk of being politicized and polarized, and *theoretically* because age, unlike gender, ethnicity, nationality or religion, is a continuous variable that is inherently problematic as a basis of distinctive group identity. We invite readers of all ages to consider these issues when thinking about power and language.

ACKNOWLEDGEMENTS

We wish to thank Bert Raven, Mike Platow, and other colleagues who have read and commented on an earlier draft of the present chapter.

REFERENCES

Austin, J. (1962). *How to do things with words*. Oxford, UK: Oxford University Press.
Bales, R.F. (1970). *Personality and interpersonal behaviour*. New York: Holt, Reinhart, & Winston.

Bavelas, J.B., Black, A., Chovil, N. & Mullett, J. (1990). *Equivocal communication*. Newbury Park, CA: Sage.

Brooke, M.E. & Ng, S.H. (1986). Language and social influence in small conversational groups. *Journal of Language and Social Psychology*, **5**, 201–210.

Bruins, J.J. & Wilke, H.A.M. (1992). Cognitions and behaviour in a hierarchy: Mulder's power theory revisited. *European Journal of Social Psychology*, **22**, 21–39.

Burgoon, M. (1990). Language and social influence. In H. Giles & W.P. Robinson (Eds), *Handbook of language and social psychology* (1st edn, pp. 51–72). Chichester, UK: Wiley.

Carli, L.L. (1990). Gender, language, and influence. *Journal of Personality and Social Psychology*, **59**, 941–951.

Carli, L.L., LaFleur, S.J. & Loeber, C.C. (1995). Nonverbal behavior, gender, and influence. *Journal of Personality and Social Psychology*, **68**, 1030–1041.

Cialdini, R.B. (1988). *Influence: Science and practice* (2nd edn). Glenview, IL: Scott Foresman.

Clark, H.H. (1985). Language use and language users. In G. Lindzey & A. Aronson (Eds), *The handbook of social psychology* (3rd edn, pp. 179–231). New York: Harper & Row.

Cody, M.J. & McLaughlin, M.L. (Eds) (1990). *The psychology of tactical communication*. Clevedon, UK: Multilingual Matters.

Crawford, M. (1995). *Talking difference: On gender and language*. London: Sage.

Diamond, J. (1996). *Status and power in verbal interaction*. Amsterdam: John Benjamins.

Fiske, S.T. (1993). Controlling other people: The impact of power on stereotyping. *American Psychologist*, **48**, 621–628.

Fox, S.A. & Giles, H. (1996). "Let the wheelchair through!" An intergroup approach to interability communication. In W.P. Robinson (Ed.), *Social groups and identities: Developing the legacy of Henri Tajfel* (pp. 215–248). Oxford, UK: Butterworth-Heinemann.

French, J.R.P. & Raven, B.H. (1959). The bases of social power. In D. Cartwright (Ed.), *Studies in social power* (pp. 150–167). Ann Arbor, MI: Institute for Social Research.

Heritage, J. & Greatbach, D. (1986). Generating applause: A study of rhetoric and response at party political conferences. *American Journal of Sociology*, **92**, 110–157.

Hofstede, G. (1980). *Culture's consequences: International differences in work related values*. Beverly Hills, CA: Sage.

Hollander, E.P. (1985). Leadership and power. In G. Lindzey & E. Aronson (Eds), *Handbook of social psychology* (3rd, edn, pp. 485–537). New York: Random House.

Jaworski, A. (1993). *The power of silence: Social and pragmatic perspectives*. Newbury Park, CA: Sage.

Jost, J.T. & Banaji, M.R. (1994). The role of stereotyping in system-justification and the production of false consciousness. *British Journal of Social Psychology*, **33**, 1–27.

Kebede, A. & Knottnerus, J. D. (1998). Beyond the pales of Babylon: The ideational components and social psychological foundations of Rastafari. *Sociological Perspectives*, **41**, 499–517.

Krauss, R.M. & Chiu, C.Y. (1998). Language and social behaviour. In D. Gilbert, S. Fiske & G. Lindzey (Eds), *Handbook of social psychology* (4th edn, pp. 41–88). New York: Guilford.

Latané, B. (1981). The psychology of social impact. *American Psychologist*, **36**, 343–356.

Loftus, E.F. & Palmer, J.C. (1974). Reconstruction of automobile destruction: An example of the interaction between language and memory. *Journal of Verbal Learning and Verbal Behavior*, **13**, 585–589.

Madan, T.N. (1998). Coping with ethnicity in South Asia: Bangladesh, Punjab and Kashmir compared. *Ethnic and Racial Studies*, **21**, 969–989.

McGarty, C., Haslam, S.A., Hutchinson, K.J. & Turner, J.C. (1994). The effects of salient group membership on persuasion. *Small Group Research*, **25**, 267–293.

Moscovici, S. (1976). *Social influence and social change*. London: Academic Press.

Mulder, M. (1977). *The daily power game*. Leiden: Martinus Nijhoff.

Mullen, B., Salas, E. & Driskell, J.E. (1989). Salience, motivation, and artifact as contributions to the relation between participation rate and leadership. *Journal of Experimental Social Psychology*, **25**, 545–559.

Ng, S.H. (1977). Structural and non-structural aspects of power distance reduction tendencies. *European Journal of Social Psychology*, **7**, 317–345.

Ng, S.H. (1980). *The social psychology of power*. London: Academic Press.

Ng, S.H. (1996). Power: An essay in honour of Henri Tajfel. In W.P. Robinson (Ed.), *Social identity: The developing legacy of Henri Tajfel*. (pp. 191–215). Oxford, UK: Butterworth-Heinemann.

Ng, S.H. & Bradac, J.J. (1993). *Power in language: Verbal communication and social influence*. Newbury Park, CA: Sage.

Ng, S.H., Bell, D. & Brooke, M. (1993). Gaining turns and achieving high influence ranking in small conversational groups. *British Journal of Social Psychology*, **32**, 265–275.

Ng, S.H., Brooke, M. & Dunne, M. (1995). Interruption and influence in discussion groups. *Journal of Language and Social Psychology*, **14**, 369–381.

Parker, K.C.H. (1988). Speaking turns in small group interactions: A context-sensitive event sequence model. *Journal of Personality and Social Psychology*, **54**, 965–971.

Pérez, J.A. & Mugny, G. (1998). Categorization and social influence. In S. Worchel, J.F. Morales, D. Páez & J.-C. Deschamps (Eds), *Social identity: International perspectives* (pp. 142–153). London: Sage.

Raven, B.H. (1992). A power/interaction model of interpersonal influence: French and Raven thirty years later. *Journal of Social Behavior and Personality*, **7**, 217–244.

Raven, B.H. (1997). *A power/interaction model of interpersonal influence: Framing influence attempts in confrontations between political figures*. Paper presented at the 20th Annual Meeting of the International Society of Political Psychology, Krakow, Poland, July 1997.

Raven, B.H., Schwarzwald, J. & Koslowsky, M. (1998). Conceptualizing and measuring a power/interaction model of interpersonal influence. *Journal of Applied Social Psychology*, **28**, 307–332.

Reid, S.A. & Ng, S.H. (1999). Language, power and intergroup relations. *Journal of Social Issues*, **55**, 119–139.

Reid, S.A. & Ng, S.H. (2000). Conversation as a resource for influence: Evidence for prototypical arguments and social identification processes. *European Journal of Social Psychology*, **30**, 83–100.

Robinson, W.P. (1996). *Deceit, delusion, and detection*. London: Sage.

Rubini, M. & Kruglanski, A.W (1997). Brief encounters ending in estrangement: Motivated language use and interpersonal rapport in the question–answer paradigm. *Journal of Personality and Social Psychology*, **72**, 1047–1060.

Ryan, E.B., Hummert, M.L. & Boich, L.H. (1995). Communication predicament of aging: Patronizing behaviour toward older adults. *Journal of Language and Social Psychology*, **14**, 144–166.

Sacks, H., Schegloff, E. & Jefferson, G. (1974). A simplest systematics for the organization of turn-taking for conversation. *Language*, **50**, 696–735.

Schulz, M.S. (1998). Collective action across borders: Opportunity structures, network capacities, and communicative praxis in the age of advanced globalization. *Sociological Perspectives*, **41**, 587–616.

Semin, G.R. & Fiedler, K. (1991). The linguistic category model, its bases, applications and range. *European Review of Social Psychology*, **54**, 558–568.

Sidanius, J. & Pratto, F. (1999). *Social dominance: An intergroup theory of social hierarchy and oppression*. New York: Cambridge University Press.

Snyder, M. (1984). When belief creates reality. In L. Berkowitz (Ed.), *Advances in experimental social psychology* (Vol. 18, pp. 248–306). New York: Academic Press.

Stasser, G. & Taylor, L.A. (1991). Speaking turns in face-to-face discussions. *Journal of Personality and Social Psychology*, **60**, 675–684.

Tajfel, H. (1974). Social identity and intergroup behaviour. *Social Science Information*, **13**, 65–93.

Tajfel, H. (1981a). *Human groups and social categories: Studies in social psychology*. Cambridge, UK: Cambridge University Press.

Tajfel, H. (1981b). Social stereotypes and social groups. In J.C. Turner & H. Giles (Eds) *Intergroup behaviour* (pp. 144–167). Oxford, UK: Basil Blackwell.

Tajfel, H. & Turner, J.C. (1979). An integrative theory of intergroup conflict. In W.G. Austin & S. Worchel (Eds), *The social psychology of intergroup relations* (pp. 33–47). Monterey, CA: Brooks/Cole.

Taylor, D.M. & McKirnan, D.J. (1984). A five-stage model of intergroup relations. *British Journal of Social Psychology*, **23**, 291–300.

Taylor, D.M. & Moghaddam, F.M. (1987). *Theories of intergroup relations: International social psychological perspectives*. New York: Praeger.

Turner, J.C. (1991). *Social influence*. Buckingham, UK: Open University Press.

Turner, J.C., Hogg, M.A., Oakes, P.J., Reicher, S.D. & Wetherell. M.S. (1987). *Rediscovering the social group: A self-categorization theory*. Oxford, UK: Basil Blackwell.

Williams, K.D. (1997). Social ostracism. In R.M. Kowalski (Ed.), *Aversive interpersonal behaviors* (pp. 133–170). New York: Plenum.

Wilson, T.P., Wiemann, J.M. & Zimmerman, D.H. (1984). Models of turn taking in conversational interaction. *Journal of Language and Social Psychology*, **3**, 159–183.

Worchel, S. (1998). A developmental view of the search for group identity. In S. Worchel, J.F. Morales, D. Páez & J.-C. Deschamps (Eds), *Social identity: International perspectives* (pp. 53–74). London: Sage.

Worchel, S., Morales, L.F., Páez, D. & Deschamps, J.-C. (Eds) (1998). *Social identity: International perspectives*. London: Sage.

4.20

Interpersonal Relations[1]

Erin Sahlstein
University of Richmond, Richmond, VA, USA
Steve Duck
University of Iowa, Iowa City, USA

We do not have relationships: we *perform* relating. Such performance is conducted through language use and social behaviors that enact actions with other actors and in reference to the knowledge about ways to enact "the personal" and "the cultural". Thus personal relationships are both individual, unique performances but they are also informed by the culture in which they are embedded and therefore can be studied in terms of their common performative acts. Relational performances are also both (re)constituted in their performances and transformed by them. For example, romantic couples who break up have constructed new "states" of relating but also have altered the ways in which they will relate to one another.

In this chapter, we argue that relationships (whether romantic, friendship, familial, or workplace) should be analyzed as performative. Specifically drawing on theories of performance and performativity, we frame personal relationships as unique, historical constructions and at the same time cultural reiterations of more general relational properties. Past research on personal relationships has typically treated partners as simply "in" relationships, has underestimated the requirements of performance, and so has denied the lived, emergent, dynamic – even turbulent and confused – nature of relationships, and so has obscured the *energy and embodiment* that partners need to enact their relationships. Therefore, our discussion will revolve around (1) how performative approaches have been largely ignored in personal relationship research, (2) what a performative

---

[1] This chapter is based on ideas first presented by the first author (Sahlstein 1998) at the annual meetings of the National Communication Association, Chicago, IL, 1997, and the International Network on Personal Relationships, Norman, OK, May 1998.

The New Handbook of Language and Social Psychology.
Edited by W. Peter Robinson and Howard Giles.
© 2001 John Wiley & Sons Ltd.

approach to personal relationships would involve, and (3) how it can inform a reformed view of relational cultures.[2]

THE NATURE OF RELATIONSHIPS

Interpersonal scholars typically think about relationships as the coming together of separate individuals (e.g., Altman & Taylor, 1973; Berscheid, 1986). On this view, individuals are conceptualized and treated as un-evolving bodies enmeshed in a causal frame where certain definitive traits predetermine their action and the outcomes of their interaction. The person is configured as a composite of traits and characteristics who responds to, but does not create, his or her own circumstances. Rather, individuals are conceptualized as products of the world, of exchange matrices, and of cognitive judgmental processes larger than themselves. Emphases are not placed heavily on the performative sociality of relating and how people interacting together (re)construct their relationships and themselves in their performances.

Typical of this style of approach to studying personal relationships has been the study of what goes on inside the heads of individuals in terms of feelings of closeness, liking, intimacy, or love (e.g., Fletcher & Fitness, 1993) and the exploration of the language terms and social cognitions that collect into prototypes to steer people in love (e.g., Fehr, 1993). An alternative or complementary method has been to assess and enumerate amounts of intimate speech passed from one person to another, using a simple sender–receiver model of communication and based on the assumption that the intimacy or disclosiveness of statements can be assessed objectively and uniformly (Davis & Sloan, 1974). On this approach, what is intimate or disclosive for one person in one set of social circumstances can be assumed by a researcher also to be equally intimate and disclosive for another person in another set of social circumstances. Both of these objectivist views have been recently critiqued directly as omitting the contexts and creativity with which individuals carry out social roles (see Dindia, 1994, 1997, for a more complete discussion of these issues) and these critiques are starting points for the remainder of our own review. However, we wish to go beyond these points.

Although the above have seemed to be natural ways to explore emotional connectivity, the objectionable consequence is subtle: relationships are treated as something people *have*, which thereafter are treated as objects about which partners can have opinions or beliefs as entities in their own rights. Rather, we argue for a view that treats a relationship as a process created through the spontaneous and recurrent action and communications of the partners. Of course, once that process has been launched, partners do build some history of

---

[2] We have chosen to use the term "relational culture" in this chapter in order to emphasize the shared rituals, language use, and meanings between relational partners. We acknowledge the large bodies of literature devoted to the study of "culture" and recognize that personal relationships are housed within larger social structures such as national culture.

interactions and feelings that constitute material for reflection, opinion, and further feelings (Duck, 1994), but those ruminations are also part of the relational process and do not attach to something that has independent existence (Baxter & Montgomery, 1996). Yet researchers often ask partners what they think/feel about their relationships as if it were something "out there" in the world, detached and separable from their interactions, language use and social behavior with one another. This view of personal relationships is coming under increased attack by several scholars in the field (Allan, 1998; Baxter & Montgomery, 1996; Duck, 1994; Duck, West & Acitelli, 1997) as researchers focus on the praxis of relationships, the DOING of them through language, discourse and social behavior. A performative approach to relating views the world as a developing, dynamic context that also acknowledges the recognizable, patterned aspects of daily life.

THE NATURE OF PERFORMANCE

A performative approach views personal relationships as processes in action but also as citations of what already exists. To think about personal relationships as performative is to think about the *doing* of relationships (Duck, 1994) and the repeated doing of them as the means of continuing their existence. This perspective sees relating as both performances of uniquely constructed entities but also culturally expected behaviors. Personal relationships can be viewed and analyzed in terms of generalizable concepts such as the state of the relationship (e.g., dating vs. engaged, acquaintances vs. best friends) or the levels of individual satisfaction, but researchers must also recognize relationships as individually unique. Relationships are individually enacted processes, enacted on particular occasions, and these occasions are what we regard as "performances."

There are three key elements to a performative approach to the language use and social behavior of personal relationships. *First*, communication within relationships is not only representative of the relationship but also constructs and performs the relationship. Talk between relational partners can be viewed not only as displaying the type and level of relationship (Planalp, 1993), but talk also constructs the type of relationship partners will have in the future. The communication within relationships is often viewed as representing partner attitudes, feelings, and relational states. However, from a performative perspective, communication also has a constitutive element. *Second*, relationships are emergent processes but are also punctuated by "citational" performances. Relationships emerge and change through the performances of their constituent everyday interactions and hence our experiences of them and our performances during their daily continuance are variable. Performances of relationships are often "citations" of what is expected (e.g., married couples often wear wedding rings). However, relational partners do not always follow the relationship expectations placed upon them; and, although performances are fashioned to be consistent with the context and the social/cultural rules, all performances are not exactly the same. Even though they are guided and patterned after what has already been done and what is expected, performances can be sites of change, thus they add nuances and emanate liveliness and spontaneity. When people interact with one another they need to have some level of intersubjectivity and cultural knowledge in order to relate; however, each time they are relating partners construct a new part of the relationship in the interaction. *Third*, relationships can be studied for both their more celebrated performances and their everyday practices. By this we mean that we cannot look at relationship performances as only the highly public or most memorable instances of the relationship. Much of the research on relational rituals focuses primarily on celebratory performances such as weddings (e.g., Braithwaite & Baxter, 1995) and less on everyday interactions such as dinnertime talks in families (e.g., Aukrust & Snow, 1998; Blum-Kulka, 1997). Relationships are manifested in our everyday routines and interactions with one another (e.g., kiss goodbye) as well as the more celebrated events in life (e.g., a wedding), and the former aspect of relating deserves more attention in the literature (Duck, 1994). *Finally*, a performative approach calls for different theoretical assumptions and methodologies for studying personal relationships. No longer can surveys recording such things as attitudes and contact frequencies be used in isolation as the measure of a relationship's existence or performance. In order to examine communication, emergence, and daily performances, other types of methods, possibly in conjunction with the current predominate practices, should be considered in future research directed towards examining performativity in relating. For example, ethnography is one broad area of inquiry that could be used in order to study relational praxis both as *performance* and as *performative*. Some scholars already have begun to advocate "relational ethnographies" (e.g., Sahlstein, 1997). Ethnographic methods (i.e., in-depth interviewing, observing and/or participating in the "field", conducting auto-ethnographies), which are typically utilized in the study of cultures, may prove useful in an examination of performances of relating.

When above we write about "performance", we intend to go beyond the idea of a public act of artistic presentation (e.g., a play, concert, ballet, etc.), where, from a theoretical vantage point, one might immediately think of Goffman's (1959) dramaturgical model of social behavior. Goffman approaches social life as if it were a staged performance of a play or television show. Individuals have roles to play – several roles – throughout their day and throughout their lives. But what is it about life that moves us from role to role? How do we know what roles to play and when? Are we aware of our role performances in the same way as actors on a stage? Although thinking about life as a highly complex theatrical play can be an informative analogy to individual experience, Goffman and his theatrical metaphor seems to only take us so far in our pursuit of relating as performing. Goffman's perspective of performance emphasizes "front" and "back stages" which at one level implies there is an underlying essence, or self, to every performance and assumes an awareness of the performances. Moreover, the theatrical metaphor for social relations does not focus on how relationships are lived, fluid experiences which can and do change over time. Goffman's ideas do emphasize behaviors and reiterated roles in relational process, but lack a focus on verbal communication.

Speech Act Theory (Austin, 1962) adds attention to language by noting that uttering a word, a phrase, a sentence or an entire speech is an act of performance, because according to this approach speaking is action. Most relevant to our discussion of personal relationship performance is Austin's key distinction between constative and performative utterances. Constatives are speech acts which more or less report something about the world (e.g., "The husband kissed his wife"); whereas performative speech acts call into being that which they state (e.g., "I now declare you husband and wife"). Speech Act Theory emphasizes language and how it can construct and formulate social reality through the utterance of words. It emphasizes the role of everyday talk in relating. Speech Act Theory, however, does not address the history of a relationship and how speech acts, i.e. performances, construct the existence of a relationship between relational partners. The bodies embodying the speech acts and the effects of their repeated performances are also not addressed by this theory. Hence, to strengthen the value of such an approach it is necessary to tie Speech Act Theory to the embodied reiterations, and possibly transformative actions, of relating.

Butler's (1993) theory of gender "performativity" offers a way to stress the open-endedness of performing, which rejects the finality and stability, implied by the term "performance." Butler wants to acknowledge both the materiality of social behavior and the socially constitutive element of language. She sees gender as something (re)constructed in the moment of its embodiment but also does not want to dismiss the power of language to "call out for that which it names" and allow for change. Butler views gender as not wholly socially constructed in discourse but also not something that can be reduced to the origin of the body. Her approach to gender as a series of citations and reiterations informs an approach to personal relationship performativity because of her emphasis on both language use and social (embodied) behavior. However, Butler's ideas are primarily associated with gender performativity. Her ideas as well as theories and approaches of other "performance" scholars need to be further explored in terms of personal relationships (see Desmond, 1997; Taylor & Villegas, 1994; and Case, Brett & Foster, 1995, for recent edited examples of performance theory in theater and cultural studies).

We would thus like to move away from the typical idea of performance as "staged" or inherently in a "public" domain and as behavioral, nor do we want to privilege only the language use(d) in the process of relating. Performances of relating are relational partners improvising within their interactions with one another and in the presence of others while in the face of social and cultural constraints. Partners are constrained (and enabled) both by their relational past/future and the social matrix where they are situated. Moreover, the performativity, or reiteration and emergence of relational practices, should also be studied. A performative approach to personal relationships implies both an examination of both the performances of relationships (i.e., the doing of them) and the performativity of relating (i.e., the reiterative and transformative elements of performances). We need to explore how certain dyads or groupings are recognized as "friends" in their everyday lives as well as how those performances reinforce the relationship as being "friends." For example, Goldsmith and Baxter (1996) examined how different communication events and their frequencies may represent different relational types (e.g., acquaintance vs. parent–child relationships). Their study provides initial evidence for differing relational performances and how people may distinguish relationship types based on communicative performances in everyday life. Future studies could examine how particular performances transform one type of relationship to another "state" (e.g., friends to best friends or friends to lovers). However, much of the current personal relationship literature views relationships more for their stability than their emergence, more as isolated entities than culturally influenced ones, and more similar than different.

In addressing relationships as performative, researchers must face the fact that management of uncertainty is both a personal and a cultural activity. Most research to date is, however, not conducted to analyze relationships at the level of lived, unique performances, but rather extracts the very broadest principles that can describe relationships generally in terms of their simplest common denominator. Relationships are typically lumped all together into one sample, losing their "personal" identities while being examined for predictable patterns across groups. Approaches which privilege both the performances and performativity of relationships in daily life are not emphasized in the personal relationships literature due to the primary focus on psychological attributes and a de-emphasis on context; however, framing relationships as specific "cultures" may be informative to this line of study.

THE NATURE OF RELATIONAL CULTURE

Wood (1982) was one of the first scholars to propose and elaborate on the idea that personal relationships are relational cultures or unique systems of meaning created by the interactions of two individuals. Although Wood's discussion focuses primarily on romantic couples, the notion of a relational culture can be applied across relational genres. Moreover, personal relationship "cultures" may be a useful way of looking at the uniqueness of specific relationships without losing the embedded nature of their performances. Wood (1982) defines relational culture as a

> privately transacted system of understandings that coordinate attitudes, actions, and identities of participants in a relationship. (p. 76)

Similar to the cases we typically think of as "cultures" (e.g., American culture), relationship partners direct or guide perceptions of the world in relation to one another and develop shared constructs, language habits, values and codes of behavior. As relationships develop, the partners create their own unique communication, rules, rituals, and values within the relationship (Wood, 1982). Similar to the ways in which Teamsterville (Philipsen, 1992) and the gangs of Chicago (Conquergood, 1994) have their own unique practices, individual relationships also have their own systems of meaning that are performed in daily life and amount to a relationship culture. Couples often develop their own ways of speaking with one another unique to their relationship (Hopper, Knapp & Scott, 1981) or their own ways of distributing relational "labor." These personal cultures, or at least the idea that they are present, are created, maintained, and dissolved through language use and social behavior – that is to say, through the specific conversations and discourse that the partners have with one another as a part of everyday communication about matters both large and small. Over the course of a relationship, partners renegotiate their rules and values through experiences with one another. Wood states:

> Relational culture is sustained and revised through discourse in which partners correlate definitions of old and new experiences, weaving each amendment into the constantly evolving relational culture that binds them. (1982, p. 77)

Through the perpetual performances of relational cultures, partners both reproduce their relational cultural identities and produce new aspects of their social unit. For example, a family may have dinnertime talk every night which is now a relationship routine for the members and becomes a part of their family culture (Blum-Kulka, 1997). The dinnertime chats are a performance of that relationship and thus help to (re)construct the web of relationships as "this family." However, with every dinner comes new talk. Each dinner has both old and new qualities because the family members' actions retain traces of the previous performance through the dinner act itself but new aspects are constructed for the family as well. Thus the fact that the family has these dinnertime talks is not the most interesting issue: rather the continuous *process* of family identity, power relations, etc. that gets (re)produced and altered from performance to performance. These processes are the focus of a performative approach.

Dinnertime talks as family rituals are one way in which this identity gets constructed, preserved, and transformed over the life of the collective and their performances of "family" (see Wolin & Bennett, 1984). Another example of how relating may get performed is through their relationship narratives or storytelling (see Manndelbaum, 1987). Storytelling often occurs in relational contexts where romantic couples or friends are called on to tell how they met or how they came to be best friends. Relational partners often have origin stories and in the act of jointly telling these narratives they are contributing to the perception of having a relationship. Storytelling may be a place to study the performance of relationships and how couples may " 'do' their relationships in public" (Manndelbaum, 1987) as well as "do" relating as prescribed by societal norms.

Much of the existing research on relational culture has tended to focus on the particular aspects of relationships that function to create and develop relational cultures (e.g., rituals) rather than examining holistically the cultural context and actions of a relationship. Research has shown that relational partners can create and maintain their cultures through specific social behaviors such as rituals (Bruess & Pearson, 1997), idiomatic talk (Hopper, Knapp & Scott, 1981; Oring, 1984; Bell, Buerkel-Rothfuss & Gore, 1987), and cultural artifacts (Baxter, 1987). For instance, Hopper et al. (1981) have looked at couples' idiomatic talk. Relational idioms are words, phrases, or gestures that have specific meaning to the partners in personal relationships. These idioms are created and developed over the history of a relational culture. Similar to larger, societal cultures, relational idioms are the unique communicative acts to a particular *relationship*. Idioms convey messages that relational partners within the relational culture understand. The use of these personal relationship idioms helps solidify and build cohesion within the relationship. These can take the form of nicknames, labels for others, referents to special places and times, greetings and good-byes, and codes of sexual activities (Bell et al., 1987). These idioms of the relationship allow partners to leave implicit the meanings of their words in their conversations and have interactions that only they historically understand. Just as languages and/or slang phrases in a particular culture make it easier for members to communicate with one another, this idiomatic talk/gestures also streamlines communication between relational partners and creates a sense of uniqueness. Nevertheless, the majority of the relational culture research does not look at relating either as performance or through their performance. For example, although research is being done in the area of personal relationship rituals (Bruess & Pearson, 1997; Braithwaite & Baxter, 1995; Berg-Cross, Daniels & Carr, 1992), these studies do not actually look at relational cultures as unique nor do they investigate rituals as "performances" of relationships. In line with mainstream research on personal relationships, rituals have been studied for their general properties across relationships (i.e., frequency, importance, type) and psychological effects versus being studied in situ.

For example, Baxter (1987) conducted a study of relationship cultures by examining the symbols partners create to identify their relationships. Based on the data in this study, Baxter constructed a typology of five relationship symbols types: behavioral actions, prior events/times, physical objects, special places and cultural artifacts. Specific places/times were perceived by the participants to be the most important in terms of defining the relational culture. In general, symbols within a particular relationship are "concrete metacommunicative statements about the abstract qualities of intimacy, caring, solidarity, etc., which the parties equate with their relationship" (Baxter, 1987, p. 263). These symbols help create the unique culture of a couple throughout their relationship with one another; however, how and when these symbols were used in the relationship was not explored in this study. Rather, the properties and types of relational symbols were examined. A future study designed to investigate, possibly ethnographically, how these symbols are used in relating could be informed by and informative of a performative approach to personal relationships.

Personal relationship rituals could be studied for their performative elements by studying how they are accomplished within the context of the relationships examined (e.g., storytelling). As proposed earlier, ethnographic studies of relational rituals may be one option for study for researchers. We believe that attention to the actual performances of these rituals would emphasize the importance of the context, emergence, and constitutive nature of the relational cultures as well as their reinforcement and citation of societal norms and expectations. If researchers were to study rituals from a performative approach they would observe them in naturalistic settings and yet note how more general cultural expectations and rules inform them. Moreover, the researcher would look for resistance to the norms of relating for places where the relational parties enact and construct their own culture. But, Montgomery (1992) proposes an interesting question of "How do couples create and maintain unique identities while still remaining a part of a larger social unit?" And we must reinforce the question of "How are relationships, in a sense, not unique in reference to the cultural scripts and norms prescribed by one's society which are reinforced in relational behaviors?"

Montgomery (1992) wants to reinforce the fact that relationships exist in a larger social order that guides their interaction and development and sets standards for the assessment of the quality of a relationship. Various cultural laws, norms, and traditions guide relating behaviors of their members. She describes a tension between studying interpersonal relationships as "orderly, predictable interactions that are anchored in the institutions and practices of society and seeing them as opportunities for spontaneous, interpersonal expressions that lead to unique experiences" (Montgomery, 1992, p. 476). Montgomery proposes a dialectical tension between couples and culture by stating that couples define their autonomy from the larger culture by creating a "mini-culture" of their own. Couples create their own private message systems that are unique understandings and ways of relating with one another (e.g., idiomatic talk; see Hopper et al, 1981). These private message systems within the larger speech community create the couples' relational culture. Montgomery asserts that the more unique a couple's relational culture, the more autonomous the couple is from the larger social order. Their unique culture sets them apart from other couples and groups; however, it must be noted that the commonalities are sufficient to make the relationship recognizable as a relationship to others. More in situ studies of relating, possibly informed by the performative approach advocated here as well as relational dialectics (Baxter & Montgomery, 1996), may help researchers understand the relationship between particular relationships and the culture in which they are embedded.

Couples' language use and social behaviors are what create the relational culture (Montgomery, 1992). Relational partners create their own stories, idiomatic speech acts, non-verbal acts, etc. which develops a sense of a unique culture and sets it apart from their broader and encompassing "national" culture as well as other relationships' past, present and future. However, relational partners do not create these cultures on their own. They rely on the overarching cultural system to guide them in creating their own unique culture. Cultural artifacts such as television, magazines, music and music videos, newspapers, sculpture, etc. all influence how partners go about "coupling" (Montgomery, 1992). These larger cultural symbols, rules, and norms guide, dictate, and/or facilitate the creation of relational cultures. Social networks also have an impact on how people go about developing their relationships. It is through these relationships that humans reproduce the larger embedding culture and yet also produce new systems of meanings unique to their own particular relational culture. Couples simultaneously react to and reproduce their cultural contexts (Allan, 1979; Milardo & Wellman, 1992). Thus, we feel it is important to recognize and examine how the overall culture has an impact on the "mini-culture" of a particular personal relationship.

Overall, a performative approach to personal relationships and relational culture would be refreshing and supplement the dominant paradigms in personal relationships research. The general tenor of personal relationship research is to focus on the common rather than on the different, on the summary monolith rather than the seething variability, and on the state rather than the process. In short, researchers who have treated relationships as general states rather than as variable management performances have too often overlooked specialty, variability, and difference in relationship partners' minds (Duck, 1994). By looking at relationship cultures as performances and as performative, personal relationship scholars can begin to ask different questions about relating. Future research from this approach could be driven by questions such as: How do relational partners "perform" their relationships? In what ways do relational partners make their relationships "unique" in their everyday interactions? What are the *processes* of constructing uniqueness in a relationship? What do partners perceive to be the unique relational behaviors and language usage in their relationships? How are different types of relationships performed in everyday interactions? Are the performances the defining factor of different relational types?

By framing personal relationships as cultural performances, we can go beyond the idea that our relationships exist outside of *doing* them in our everyday lives. "Relational ethnography" is one logical direction personal relationship scholars could move in order to spotlight performance and performativity in everyday relating. Looking at relationship cultures as performances and as performative, personal relationship scholars can begin to clarify important questions about relating that will refocus the nature of research towards the "doing" of relationships.

REFERENCES

Allan, G. (1979). *A sociology of friendship and kinship*. Boston, MA: Allen & Irwin.
Allan, G.A. (1998). Friendship, sociology and social structure. *Journal of Social and Personal Relationships*, **15**, 685–702.
Altman, I. & Taylor, D. (1973). *Social penetration: The development of interpersonal relationships*. New York: Holt, Reinhart, & Winston.
Aukrust, V.G. & Snow, C.A. (1998). Narratives and explanations during mealtime conversations in Norway and the United States. *Language and Society*, **27**, 221–246.

Austin, J.L. (1962). *How to do things with words*. Cambridge, MA: Harvard University Press.

Baxter, L.A. (1987). Symbols of relationship identity in close relationship cultures. *Journal of Social and Personal Relationships*, **4**, 261–280.

Baxter, L.A. & Montgomery, B. (1996). *Relating: Dialogues and dialectics*. New York: Guilford Press.

Bell, R., Buerkel-Rothfuss, N. & Gore, K. (1987). The idiomatic communication of young lovers. *Human Communication Research*, **14**, 47–67.

Berg-Cross, L., Daniels, C. & Carr, P. (1992). Marital rituals among divorced and married couples. *Journal of Divorce and Marriage*, **18**, 1–30.

Berscheid, E. (1986). Mea culpas and lamentations: Sir Francis, Sir Isaac and the "slow progress of sofl psychology". In R. Gilmour & S.W. Duck (Eds), *The emerging field of personal relationships* (pp. 267–286). Hillsdale, NJ: Erlbaum.

Blum-Kulka, S. (1997). *Dinner talk: Cultural patterns of sociability and socialization in family discourse*. Mawah, NJ: Erlbaum.

Braithwaite, D.O. & Baxter, L.A. (1995). "I do" again: The relational dialectics of renewing marriage vows. *Journal of Social and Personal Relationships*, **12**, 177–198.

Bruess, C. & Pearson, J.C. (1997). Interpersonal rituals in marriage and adult friendship. *Communication Monographs*, **1**, 25–46.

Butler, J. (1993). *Bodies that matter: On the discursive limits of sex*. New York: Routledge.

Case, S.E., Brett, P. & Foster, S.L. (1995). *Cruising the performative: Interventions into the representation of ethnicity, nationality, and sexuality*. Indianapolis, IN: Indiana University Press.

Conquergood, D. (1994). Homeboys and hoods: Gang communication and cultural space. In L. Frey (Ed.), *Group communication in context* (pp. 23–56). Hillsdale, NJ: Erlbaum.

Davis, J.D. & Sloan, M. (1974). The basis of interviewee matching of interviewer self disclosure. *British Journal of Social and Clinical Psychology*, **13**, 359–367.

Desmond, J. (1997). *Meanings in motion: New cultural studies of dance*. Durham, NC: Duke University Press.

Dindia, K. (1994). The intrapersonal–interpersonal dialectical process of self-disclosure. In S.W. Duck (Ed.), *Dynamics of relationships. (Vol. 1: Understanding relationship processes* (pp. 27–57). Newbury Park, CA: Sage.

Dindia, K. (1997). Self-disclosure, self-identity, and relationship development: A transactional/dialectical perspective. In S.W. Duck (Ed.), *Handbook of personal relationships* (2nd edn, pp. 411–425). Chichester, UK: Wiley.

Duck, S.W. (1994). *Meaningful relationships: Talking, sense, and relating*. London: Sage.

Duck, S.W. & Wood, J. (Eds) (1995). *Confronting relationship challenges. Vol. 5: Understanding relationship processes*. Thousand Oaks, CA: Sage.

Duck, S.W., West, L. & Acitelli, L. (1997). Sewing the field: The tapestry of relationship life and research. In S.W. Duck (Ed.), *Handbook of personal relationships* (pp. 1–24). New York: Wiley.

Fehr, B. (1993). How do I love thee? Let me consult my prototype. In S.W. Duck (Ed.), *Individuals in relationships. Vol. 1: Understanding relationships* (pp. 87–120). Newbury Park, CA: Sage.

Fletcher, G.J.O. & Fitness, J. (1993). Knowledge structures and explanations in intimate relationships. In S.W. Duck (Ed.), *Understanding relationship processes. Vol. 1: Individuals in relationships* (pp. 121–143). Newbury Park, CA: Sage.

Goffman, E. (1959). *The presentation of self in everyday life*. New York: Doubleday.

Goldsmith, D.J. & Baxter, L.A. (1996). Constituting relationships in talk: A taxonomy of speech events in social and personal relationships. *Human Communication Research*, **23**, 87–114.

Hopper, R. Knapp, M. & Scott, L. (1981). Couples' personal idioms: Exploring intimate talk. *Journal of Communication*, **31**, 23–33.

Mandelbaum, J. (1987). Couples sharing stories. *Communication Quarterly*, **35**, 144–170.

Milardo, R.M. & Wellman, B. (1992). The personal is social. *Journal of Social and Personal Relationships*, **9**, 339–342.

Montgomery, B.M. (1992) Communication as the interface between couples and culture. In S. Deetz (Ed.), *Communication yearbook 15* (pp. 475–507). Newbury Park, CA: Sage.

Oring, E. (1984). Dyadic traditions. *Journal of Folklore Research*, **21**, 19–28.

Philipsen, (1992). *Speaking culturally*. Albany: State University of New York Press.

Planalp, S. (1993). Friends' and acquaintances' conversations I: Observed differences. *Journal of Social and Personal Relationships*, **9**, 483–506.

Sahlstein, E. (1997). *Personal relationships reframed from a performance perspective*. Paper presented at the annual meeting of the National Communication Association, Chicago.

Sahlstein, E. (1998). *The culture of personal relationships: A performance-centered approach*. Paper presented at the annual meeting of the International Network on Personal Relationships, Norman, OK.

Taylor, D. & Villegas, J. (1994). *Negotiating performance: Gender, sexuality, and theatricality in Latin/o America*. Durham, NC: Duke University Press.

Wolin, S.J. & Bennett, L.A. (1984). Family rituals. *Family Process*, **23**, 401–420.

Wood, J.T. (1982). Communication and relational culture: Bases for the study of human relationships. *Communication Quarterly*, **30**, 75–83.

The Observation of Marital Interaction

Nigel Roberts and Patricia Noller
University of Queensland, Brisbane, Australia

Over the last 25 years, many researchers have used observational techniques to investigate the communication patterns of married couples as they engaged in a variety of activities and tasks. During the 1980s, much of this research took the form of a comparison of the communication patterns of maritally satisfied couples with those of maritally dissatisfied couples. Typically, couples were taken into the laboratory, where they were videotaped interacting in a number of tasks, particularly conflict resolution tasks, generated by having couples first identify, and then discuss, actual topics about which they disagreed (Notarius & Markman, 1989). The videotaped behaviours and emotional displays of couples during these interactions were subsequently coded by trained observers.

Coding systems can be seen as quantifying the significant features of an interaction between the members of a dyad so that researchers can become aware of the types of behaviour occurring, the frequency of those behaviours, and in some cases the sequence in which particular behaviours occur. The couple's interaction is typically divided into discrete units based either on time or events (e.g., 20 seconds or the talk turn), and varying in duration (from a few seconds to entire interactions). Coding these units may entail allocating behaviour to a discrete category (e.g., smile), or making a rating on an appropriate scale (e.g., friendly–unfriendly). A single score represents a data point for subsequent analysis. Thus, typically, the researcher obtains a stream of data for each spouse, consisting of either a sequence of discrete codes or a series of ratings.

The popularity of observational methods is born out of a belief that marital distress results from dysfunctional communication patterns and poor strategies

The New Handbook of Language and Social Psychology.
Edited by W. Peter Robinson and Howard Giles.
© 2001 John Wiley & Sons Ltd.

for dealing with conflict (Markman et al., 1981). Further, because these patterns and strategies may exist outside of the awareness of the spouses themselves, there is a need for more objective methods for identifying these complex patterns of interaction than those provided by self-reports (Weiss & Summers, 1983). Observational measures of conflict behaviour in married couples are less likely to be spuriously correlated with measures of variables like relationship satisfaction, because observations are less susceptible to social desirability biases and, because relationship satisfaction is generally measured by self-report, the two variables are assessed using different methodologies (Miller & Bradbury, 1995).

The assessment of marital interaction using observational techniques is not, however, without its difficulties. Reliability and validity issues include the following: the interaction on which the coding is based usually involves a brief sample of the couple's communication patterns at only one point in time; the behaviours of the interactants may be affected by social desirability factors (e.g., they may work very hard at looking "good"); outsiders are observing the behaviours of people they do not know and may produce, depending on the coding system used, a picture of the couple's interaction that fails to capture its meaning for the couple, or infers inappropriate meaning. In addition, observational coding, particularly of the micro variety, can be both time-consuming and expensive, and researchers have to decide whether the return is likely to be worth the effort involved.

Nevertheless, using a range of different observational systems, a wealth of knowledge has been gained about the interaction patterns of married couples. In particular, much has been learned about the ways in which distressed couples handle conflict in their relationship differently from non-distressed couples. However, it is not our purpose in this chapter to attempt to summarize this wealth of knowledge. For accounts of the differences between happy and unhappy couples, the interested reader can consult a number of already existing reviews (e.g., Gottman, 1994; Noller & Fitzpatrick, 1990; Weiss & Heyman, 1990). Neither is it our purpose to provide a comprehensive summary of the most recent areas of research findings within the field of marital interaction.

It is important, however, to point out that, during the last decade, researchers have increasingly examined more specific questions of interest such as: the association between adult attachment style (both in terms of a general style of functioning and in terms of attachment to the specific partner) and couple communication (Feeney, Noller & Callan, 1994); the effects of marital therapy on couple communication patterns (Greenberg et al., 1993); the associations between depression and couple interaction (McCabe & Gotlib, 1993); the relationship between attributions and couple communication (Bradbury et al., 1996; Noller & Ruzzene, 1991); the psychophysiology of couple interaction (Gottman, 1994; Kiecolt-Glaser et al., 1996); and the construction of couple typologies on the basis of communication patterns (Gottman, 1994; Gottman & Levenson, 1992). Each of these areas of research has its own complexities and controversies, and each is worthy of its own chapter.

Instead, our purpose in this chapter is to provide a discussion of some of the methodological issues and problems that have been raised during some 25 years of research into the observation of couple interaction. There will be some consideration of the implications that the type of coding system has on the research questions that the researcher is able to explore. The distinction between microanalytic and global systems will be highlighted, and their relative advantages and disadvantages discussed.

IMPORTANT PROPERTIES OF CODING SYSTEMS

A number of factors must be considered in assessing the various coding systems that have been developed for studying the interactions of married couples, including reliability and validity issues, the need for greater specificity (particularly with the coding of affect), the importance of the intensity of emotional expression, and the analysis of the sequence in which behaviours occur.

Reliability and Validity Issues in Observational Research

As with any measurement device, issues of reliability and validity are important for observational coding systems (Arkowitz, Lamke & Filsinger, 1981). Although there are a number of different types of reliability (e.g, internal consistency (of scales), and stability over time) the particular aspects of reliability that are important in coding observations concern the level of agreement between coders assessing the same couple interaction, as well as agreement within the same coder who recodes the interaction. Likewise, there are various aspects of validity, but the central issue for researchers using observational measures is whether the codes adequately capture the intended construct (Markman et al., 1981).

Reliability

The specific measures of inter-coder and intra-coder reliability that are most appropriate for an observational system depend, in part, upon the type of analysis intended. If the primary research interest is in the frequencies of behaviours that occur between spouses, it is appropriate to sum codes over the interaction and calculate inter-coder correlations (Gottman, Markman & Notarius, 1977). However, if the interest is in the temporal associations between behaviours, the measure of reliability needs to be tied to specific points in the interaction (Krokoff, 1987). Thus, if behaviours are rated continuously, correlations should be calculated between raters' data streams (Roberts & Krokoff, 1990).

Validity

Although the researcher usually codes at the level of the specific behaviours engaged in by the couples, summary codes involving combining several codes or ratings are also commonly used (the use of summary codes will be discussed in more detail in a later section). Many summary codes have been shown not to reflect adequately the constructs that they are supposed to represent (L'Abate & Bagarozzi, 1992), the central issue in construct validity. For instance, in a recent attempt to formulate an empirically determined system for summarizing individual codes, Heyman et al. (1995a) conducted a factor analysis on an archival data set of 995 couples' conflict interactions coded using the Marital Interaction Coding System (MICS) (Hops et al., 1972; Weiss & Summers, 1983). In this study, only 14 of the 26 items entered into the analysis loaded on any factor and the four factors accounted for only 21% of the variance, thus demonstrating the difficulty involved in trying to form psychometrically sound summary codes. By forming summary codes from codes as disparate as withholding information and seeking information (e.g., Raush et al., 1974), researchers may be seriously jeopardizing the validity of their measures of marital interaction. We will look at this issue again when we discuss the coding of emotional cues.

Another important issue in the validity of observational measures of couple interaction involves the nature of the interaction task itself. Hypothetical scenarios of marital conflict are likely to differ greatly in their salience for different couples, and may therefore fail to result in representative sampling of couples' behaviour (Noller & Guthrie, 1991). To take an example, Raush et al. (1974) had newlywed couples role-play (what they called "improvise") a situation where they had each made different (but secret) plans to celebrate their first anniversary. For couples who would generally discuss the celebration ahead of time and decide together what they would do, this issue would not have been salient, and they may have had difficulty with the role-play. Given this problem, the sample of interaction they provided would be less likely to be typical of their conflict interactions. Consequently, there is a general preference that data collection should involve the observation of real-life situations experienced by married couples (e.g., Notarius & Markman, 1989). It is important to keep in mind, however, that when couples are asked to solve real-life problems, there is likely to be a confound between the intensity of the problems being experienced and couples' relationship satisfaction (Weiss & Heyman, 1997), given that distressed couples may have more serious and more long-standing problems in their relationships than their more satisfied counterparts.

The validity of observational research has also been questioned because of the possibility that married couples may alter their normal behaviours when being observed in the laboratory. Beyond the frequent observation that couples do become highly involved when discussing topics of real disagreement (e.g., Gottman, 1994; Levenson & Gottman, 1983; Weiss & Heyman, 1997), three empirical findings can be cited in support of claims that couples' behaviour, as observed in the laboratory, yield valid data. Firstly, because laboratory-based interactions underestimate the negativity of couples' interaction patterns, any differences obtained between couples as observed in the laboratory are probably underestimates of real differences (Gottman, 1979). Secondly, unhappy married couples have difficulty in "faking good", and happy couples have difficulty in "faking bad" (Vincent et al., 1979). Finally, the interactions generated, by having couples identify an issue of disagreement that is currently a significant issue in their marriage, are rated as typical by the couples themselves (Margolin, John & Gleberman, 1988).

Levels of Inference Required of Observers

The reliability and validity of observational coding systems of couple interaction are heavily dependent upon the level of inference that observers are required to make (Heatherington, 1989). Observational systems differ widely in terms of the level of inference required from observers (Alexander et al., 1995). The more interpretation required by coders in reaching a judgment, the more subjective the observational system. At one level, an observational system may be highly objective in that the observer is simply required to count the number of times a relatively unambiguous behaviour, such as someone touching a partner, occurs. However, if a system requires the observer to assess how much "warmth" is expressed between married partners, much more inference on the part of the observer is required, and consequently, the coding system is more subjective in nature. Nevertheless, even the more subjective systems should still be considered behavioural measures, in that the focus is on what partners do in response to each other, rather than upon individual, underlying traits (Markman et al., 1981).

High-inference observational systems lack the reliability of more elemental or objective observational systems for assessing the interaction of married couples (Weiss & Heyman, 1990). Whenever high levels of inference or abstraction are required of observers, inconsistencies in a rater's judgment across time and inconsistencies across different raters' judgments are likely (Alexander, et al., 1995). Consequently, some have suggested that researchers should reduce interactions to the most elemental of behaviours possible (e.g., Barret, Johnston & Pennypacker, 1986).

In contrast, others have argued that the greater reliability afforded by microanalytic systems does not always translate into greater validity, and that such systems can lead to inconsistent or even misleading findings (Arkowitz et al., 1981; Floyd, 1989). The meaning to married partners of behaviours such as smiling or touching can be very different depending on the context. A smile may well convey warmth, but it may also indicate amusement at the partner's expense or pleasure at winning a point against the partner. A coding system that involves low inference, and thereby ignores context, may fail to fully capture the subtleties of couple interaction (Floyd, 1989; Heatherington, 1989).

As Gottman (1994) has indicated, many codes of microanalytic coding systems, such as "disagrees" or "complains", are not necessarily positive or negative and researchers have differed in how they have summarized these behaviours. The fact that discrepant results have been obtained in studies exploring whether unhappily married couples show more disagreement (e.g.,

Fichten & Wright, 1983) or less disagreement (e.g., Schaap, 1984) than happily married couples may be indicative of the fact that clearer differentiation among behaviours is needed.

The cultural informants' approach

The cultural informants' approach utilizes the fact that people, through the normal processes of socialization, learn the meaning and labelling of social interaction (Smith, Vivian & O'Leary, 1990). This approach is a clearly subjective method of observing couple interaction, which is growing in popularity (Gottman & Levenson, 1986; Weiss, 1989). Rather than identifying specific physical features, observers are required to base their decisions on an integration of all available cues, including the context, and both verbal and non-verbal channels (Roberts & Krokoff, 1990). Coders are expected to apply their socially acquired knowledge to the coding of couple interaction (Weiss, 1989, p. 137). The cultural informants' approach has been adopted in a large number of recently developed systems for coding marital interaction, including the Specific Affect Coding System (Gottman & Krokoff, 1989), the Conflict Rating System (Heavey, Layne & Christensen, 1993), the Marital Interaction Ratings Scales (Roberts & Krokoff, 1990), and the Rapid Couples Interaction Scoring System (Krokoff, Gottman & Hass, 1989).

There are a number of advantages associated with the use of a cultural informants' approach to coding the interactions of married couples. Firstly, the assumed knowledge of observers means that training is used only to fine-tune coders' knowledge, and thereby increase interobserver reliability to acceptable levels (Christensen & Heavey, 1993; Heavey et al., 1993). Thus, although some training is required, much interpretation is left to the observers, who may or may not be professional psychologists (Christensen & Heavey, 1993; Roberts & Krokoff, 1990).

The cultural informants' perspective avoids the problem of having observers code the interactions of married couples to a criterion of unknown validity, because they are coding to an assumed, common set of culturally determined rules (Smith, et al., 1990). For this reason, it is important that the observers be demographically similar to those they will be observing, particularly given the diversity in modern multicultural societies. In addition, the approach can be used in different cultures, provided that the participants and the observers are part of the same cultural group.

Because emotion is often expressed via a number of different channels, an additional advantage of a cultural informants' approach (as opposed to a physical features' approach to observing couple interaction) is that it expressly requires coders to consider the multi-channel nature of couple interaction (Gottman & Levenson, 1986; Notarius, Markman & Gottman, 1983). That is, coders who are focusing on multiple channels are more likely to capture fully the nature and intensity of emotional expression.

However, there are also a number of disadvantages associated with using a cultural informants' approach. Coders are required to combine a large number of diverse cues in order to reach a single label or rating. For this reason, coders are susceptible to the influence of availability heuristics, such as recency and salience effects (Weiss, 1989). Furthermore, all coding systems that require the observer to interpret the interaction between the spouses, rather than simply describe it, are susceptible to observers' biases and observers interpreting more meaning than is warranted (Weiss, 1989). Consequently, as with all subjective systems that require high levels of inference on the part of observers, levels of interobserver agreement in marital studies are only moderate (Weiss & Heyman, 1990). In general, the reliability of such coding systems has not been overly impressive (L'Abate & Bagarozzi, 1992). A further disadvantage is the problem of assuming cultural homogeneity between the coders and the interactions, an issue that has been referred to earlier.

The Use of Summary Categories

Although some observational coding systems, such as the Marital Interaction Coding System (MICS) (Hops et al., 1972; Weiss & Summers, 1983), contain around 30 individual codes, for the purpose of analysis these individual codes are frequently collapsed into broader summary categories. Indeed, sometimes these categories are grouped into as few as two summary categories: positive and negative (Filsinger, 1983).

The procedure of collapsing specific codes into larger summary categories has a number of detrimental effects. First and foremost, there is a loss of information. For instance, collapsing behaviours as different as "put down" and "disagree" together under the broad category of negative verbal behaviours (e.g., Floyd, O'Farrell & Goldberg, 1987) results in the loss of much detail (Gottman, 1994). Furthermore, disagreeing with a partner or making complaints are not necessarily "negative" or "positive" acts in themselves, as their interpretation depends heavily on the context. For example, a husband may disagree with his wife when she assumes that he wants her to do more work around the house. Letting her know that he appreciates what she does and doesn't expect any more may involve disagreeing with her but would be positive in terms of their relationship.

A further problem is that a single statement may contain elements of a number of "summary categories", such as when one partner smiles while criticizing the spouse's behaviour. In addition, the expression of certain "negative" emotions may conceivably have positive influences on a marital relationship, while others may have detrimental effects (Gottman & Krokoff, 1989; Sayers et al., 1991). It is not surprising, therefore, that such summary categories have problems related to their construct validity (e.g., Heyman et al., 1995a). For example, expressing anger that the husband has lost his job would have a very different effect from expressing disappointment or sadness, or even anxiety.

The Separation of Affect

Partly in reaction to the loss of information that results from the use of summary codes, a number of researchers have stressed the need for greater specificity in coding marital interaction. There are two respects in which researchers have called for greater specificity in the coding of the interactions of married couples.

Separation of Affect and Content Categories

Firstly, there has been a call for researchers to distinguish more clearly between behaviour and affect (Markman et al., 1995). Through the use of summary categories, specific affective and behavioural categories are often collapsed into broader categories. For example, Burman, John and Margolin (1993) collapsed the 12 affect scales of the SPAFF (Gottman & Levenson, 1986) and several "withdrawal" codes into four summary categories: anger/contempt, non-hostile negative, neutral and positive affection. Furthermore, researchers have used coding systems that confuse affect and behaviour. The MICS, for example, consists of a mixture of non-verbal affect, behaviours and "affect/behavioural blends" (Weiss & Heyman, 1990).

This procedure of combining behavioural and emotional codes may be problematic. The meaning of the verbal (content) and non-verbal (affect) parts of the same messages are not necessarily the same. For instance, Noller (1985) found that both wives and husbands tended to deliver criticisms of their spouse with a smile (positive affect). Further, the sequential patterning of content and affect variables discriminates differently between distressed and non-distressed married couples (Schaap, 1984). In addition, as Weiss and Heyman (1990) note in their review of marital research in the 1980s, studies that have used both affect and content codes to compare the marital interactions of happy and unhappy couples have found that affect codes prove to be better discriminators than do content codes. Consequently, it may be wise for marital researchers to separate these two components of couple interaction more clearly.

Greater Specificity of Negative Affect

The second way in which greater separation of affect has been called for involves the clearer separation of affect into more specific components than the simple negative–neutral–positive distinction (Haefner, Notarius & Pellegrini, 1991; Sayers et al., 1991). For example, even though the CISS separates behaviour from affect, the CISS only makes the distinction between positive, negative, and neutral affect. Clearly, the procedure of collapsing emotions as different as sadness, anger and anxiety together results in the loss of much information about the couples' interactions.

The importance of separating affect into specific components has been demonstrated empirically. Firstly, Margolin, John and O'Brien (1989) found reciprocity of specific negative affect in the married couples they observed, but no general reciprocity of negative affect. Secondly, Gottman and Krokoff (1989) found different associations between concurrent marital satisfaction and change in satisfaction over time for specific "negative" affect codes such as contempt, anger, and sadness. For example, wife contempt was negatively associated with concurrent satisfaction but positively associated with improvement in satisfaction three years later; on the other hand, wife sadness and wife fear were not associated with concurrent satisfaction but were negatively associated with improvement in satisfaction three years later. It is also interesting to note that although the interactions of depressed couples may be characterized by more depressive behaviours, the interactions of distressed couples seem to be associated with more aggressive behaviours (Schmaling & Jacobson, 1990).

Intensity

Coding schemes that include a combination of frequency and intensity may provide a better picture of couple interaction, by describing a closer approximation to the meaning of a message for the interactants (e.g., Fitzpatrick, 1988). Taking the intensity of displays of negative affect into consideration may be especially important. For instance, the low-intensity expression of negative emotion such as contempt, anger, and disapproval may have positive effects on marital relationships, whereas the expression of these same emotions at high intensity may be detrimental (Sayers & Baucom, 1991). Thus, the consideration of intensity in the analysis of couple interaction may increase our understanding of the complexities of "negativity" in marital interaction.

The Analysis of Sequence

The final factor that needs to be considered in choosing a coding system is its ability to produce data that can be analysed sequentially. The importance of examining sequence when studying the interactions of married couples is paramount, because base rates alone provide no information about the patterning or structuring of interaction (Sayers & Baucom, 1991; Weiss, 1989).

Beyond the wisdom of the maxim that the married couple who kiss after every fight is very different from the couple who fight after every kiss (Hinde, 1979), there is convincing empirical evidence of the importance of analysing sequence. The temporal patterning of behaviours observed during marital interaction adds to the variance accounted for in relationship satisfaction, above that explained by just the frequencies of those behaviours (e.g., Roberts & Krokoff, 1990). The temporal association between variables is logically quite independent of the base rates of those variables (Krokoff et al., 1989). Thus, the frequency of a particular behaviour may not discriminate between happy and unhappy married couples, while the temporal patterning of the behaviour does (e.g., Margolin & Wampold, 1981).

The methods used to analyse the temporal associations between variables can be roughly divided into two groups: either a number of techniques generically known as sequential analysis (including lagged sequential analysis, log-linear models), or a group of techniques known as time-series analysis. Both allow for the investigation of the temporal patterning of communication behaviours within a marital interaction. However, sequential analysis is conducted on categorical data, whereas time-series analysis uses streams of continuous data (Griffin & Gottman, 1990).

Sequential Analysis

A variety of techniques exist for conducting sequential analysis (for reviews, see Bakeman & Gottman, 1986; Griffin & Gottman, 1990; Lichtenberg & Heck, 1986). An important distinction can be drawn between the two main techniques: lag-sequential analysis, which assesses the degree of connectedness within a data stream for each unit of analysis (be it the individual, couple, or family), and log-linear approaches, which assess the degree of connectedness between particular variables using data pooled across subjects (Griffin & Gottman, 1990).

Whether lag-sequential techniques or log-linear techniques are most appropriate is determined by the number of data points. If insufficient data points are present, data should be pooled and log-linear techniques used (Griffin & Gottman, 1990). Log-linear techniques are also necessary if events of interest occur rarely, or if a large number of codes is used. Log-linear techniques are more powerful and flexible than lag-sequential techniques, but collapsing across participants means that certain statistical assumptions need to be met, such as homogeneity and stationarity of the data (Griffin & Gottman, 1990). In contrast, lag-sequential analysis provides, for each unit of analysis (couple), statistics of temporal connection between the behaviours of interest. These statistics can then be used in standard analyses of variance or regression analyses (Griffin & Gottman, 1990).

In conducting sequential analysis on couple interaction data, a number of conditions need to be met – conditions that are affected by the coding system being used. Firstly, the application of sequential analysis requires that coding categories occur frequently, which generally necessitates the use of summary categories if data are generated using a microanalytic system (Sayers et al., 1991). Thus, categories are collapsed or removed before the analysis of sequence. Consequently, categories become less specific and less detailed. Secondly, coding units must be sufficiently small to allow for individual categories to occur with sufficient frequency during a marital interaction (Notarius & Markman, 1989). In addition, categories must follow one another in a sequential pattern, as opposed to occurring concurrently. To deal with these problems, researchers are sometimes required to restructure their data using listener categories (Hooley & Hahlweg, 1989; Weiss & Summers, 1983).

Time-series Analysis

Time-series analysis is an alternative procedure to sequential analysis for assessing the strength of temporal associations between behaviours during the interactions of married couples. In contrast to sequential analysis, time-series analysis requires the use of non-categorical data (Griffin & Gottman, 1990). Like lag-sequential analysis, statistics of temporal connection are calculated for each unit of analysis (couple) and these statistics are then used in standard analyses of variance or regression analyses. In properly determining the degree of temporal connection between two data streams, autocorrelation needs to be controlled (Griffin & Gottman, 1990). Autocorrelation (or autodependence) is the term used for the extent to which a time-series can be predicted from its own past. In contrast, cross-correlation, the statistic of major interest, involves the degree of association between one time-series and another.

It is noted that similar problems with autocorrelation exist when lag-sequential analysis is used to determine the connectedness between behaviours. Nevertheless, according to Heyman, Weiss and Eddy (1995b), to date no study using lag-sequential analysis to investigate the interactions of married couples has controlled for autocorrelation. Despite the hazards of interpreting cross-lag effects without first controlling for autodependence, researchers have done so because controlling for autodependence may lead to conservative results (Heyman et al., 1995b). Fortunately, techniques for statistically controlling autocorrelation are readily available with time-series analysis (e.g., Williams & Gottman, 1981).

Time-series analysis techniques, because they utilize non-categorical data, are more powerful statistically than the various procedures for conducting sequential analysis (Gottman, 1990). Furthermore, the data provided by observational systems in which several categories or ratings are given for each coding unit, rather than a single category, is clearly better handled by time-series techniques. In addition, time-series analysis can be applied to streams of observed behaviour (Roberts & Krokoff, 1990) and streams of physiological data (Levenson & Gottman, 1983). Therefore, time-series analysis can provide a way of determining the linkage, over time, between behaviours observed in couples' interactions and concurrent physiological processes, in a way that is not possible using sequential analysis.

Multimodal Assessment and Psychophysiological Assessment of Couple Interaction

The need for researchers to use multimodal assessment of couple processes during conflict interaction is widely acknowledged (Bradbury & Fincham, 1989; Noller & Guthrie, 1991). Multiple assessment procedures may be particularly important when affective processes are of interest. The measurement of emotion is complicated in that emotion is generally seen as being comprised of a number of distinct processes (Lang, 1995). Observational techniques of couple interaction can only reflect displayed or *expressed* emotion, while emotion as *experienced* can only really be assessed using self-report, or inferred from psychophysiological processes (e.g., Levenson & Gottman, 1983). Further, the success of the few studies that have utilized psychophysiological measures to assess couple interaction has led to repeated calls for the greater use of such measures (e.g., Ney & Gale, 1988; Weiss & Heyman, 1990). Consequently, there may be an increasing need for coding systems that can provide data that complement, and can be directly related to, physiological and self-report measures.

To fully assess the association between observable behaviours and physiological processes during the interactions of married couples, a coding system is required that is capable of linking physiological processes, or self-report measures, to specific behaviours within the interaction (Gottman, 1994; Notarius et al., 1989). In addition, the use of static procedures such as correlation simply cannot capture the sequential nature of the relation (Ney & Gale, 1988; Notarius et al., 1989). Rather, Ney and Gale suggest that techniques such as time-series analysis are required to provide causal modelling over time in order to assess these sorts of relations. Thus, to address these issues, an observational system is required that can provide measures of marital behaviour that can be tied to physiological measures and self-reported affect in a sequential manner, using statistical techniques such as time-series analysis.

THE DISTINCTION BETWEEN MICROANALYTIC AND GLOBAL OBSERVATIONAL SYSTEMS

Having dealt with some of the major properties on which various coding systems differ, it is now appropriate to compare different types of coding systems in terms of these properties.

Coding systems can be seen to vary according to two key characteristics: the size of the unit of measurement, and the complexity of the information being assessed (Floyd, 1989). Unit size refers to the length of a coding unit. Unit size can be defined either in terms of time (fixed time-sampling), or events (event-sampling). With fixed time-sampling, the marital interaction is divided into set intervals of time, and each interval is coded (e.g., Morell & Apple, 1990). In contrast, event-sampling is independent of real time, being defined by naturally occurring events. Examples of event-sampling units include the "talk turn", which is defined as "everything one interactant said before the other spoke" (Roberts & Krokoff, 1990, p. 98), and the thought unit that is constituted by a verbal response that is homogeneous in content, regardless of duration (Hooley & Hahlweg, 1989).

In contrast, unit complexity refers to the variability of the behaviours included within a coding unit. According to Floyd (1989), greater complexity is related to: (a) having to make classifications where many categories exist and definitions for those categories remain open to interpretation; (b) making judgments along a large number and variety of abstract continuous scales; and (c) making judgments where a large number of diverse cues must be combined to reach a single label or rating of the couple's interaction.

Floyd (1989) suggests that unit size ranges from small to large, and unit complexity ranges from elemental to multidimensional. Although units of size and units of complexity are theoretically orthogonal, in practice these two factors are correlated. Consequently, according to Floyd, the majority of marital coding systems have traditionally used units of measurement that are small and elemental, or large and multidimensional. Microanalytic coding systems are characterized by small unit sizes and elemental units of measurement, while global systems are characterized by large unit sizes and multidimensional units of measurement.

Microanalytic Coding Systems

Three microanalytic coding systems have been particularly prominent over the last 25 years in marital research. They are the Marital Interaction Coding System (MICS, Hops et al., 1972; Weiss & Summers, 1983), the Couple Interaction Scoring System (CISS, Gottman, 1979; Gottman et al., 1977; Notarius & Markman, 1981; Notarius et al., 1983), and the Kategoriensystem für Partnerschaftliche Interaktion (KIPS, Hahlweg et al., 1984a; Hahlweg, Revenstorf & Schindler, 1984b; Hooley & Hahlweg, 1989). The complexity of these coding systems lies in the large number of detailed and mutually exclusive categories that they employ. However, these units of measurement remain relatively elemental, in that levels of inference are minimized by requiring observers to adhere to relatively comprehensive and rigid coding instructions (Weiss & Summers, 1983).

The aim of these systems is to provide an exhaustive range of coding categories (Krokoff et al., 1989) which are used to break marital interactions down into a sequence of discrete behavioural categories (Weiss & Heyman, 1990). All three of the major microanalytic systems (KPI, MICS and CISS) use as the unit of analysis the "thought unit". The thought unit is, by definition, the smallest possible segment of classifiable action (Floyd et al., 1987), and is typically a very brief event. As many as six thought units may occur within a 10-second time period (Gottman & Levenson, 1985). There is a belief that, because of the detail and precision these techniques bring to the study of marital interaction, they alone can reveal the subtle but complex patterns of interaction that are otherwise undetectable by outside coders (Notarius & Markman, 1989).

Microanalytic coding systems are capable of providing highly reliable and detailed information about marital interaction (Jacob & Tennenbaum, 1988). These high levels of reliability stem from the fact that the units of measurement are small, and the individual codes are relatively elemental and objectively defined. The objectivity offered by such an approach leads to greater consistency both within and across observers of marital interaction (Floyd, 1989). Furthermore, because unit sizes are small, the data that is produced is able to support the analysis of sequence.

The primary drawback associated with the detail provided by microanalytic coding systems is their high expense. Microanalytic coding systems, as a result of their highly detailed nature, are extremely time-consuming, both in the time taken to train coders and the time taken to code marital interactions (Baucom & Sayers, 1989). For instance, the CISS has been reported to take upwards of 20 hours to code 1 hour of interaction (Krokoff et al., 1989). Because of the consequent expense of such methods, these techniques are not available to most researchers or practitioners (Baucom & Sayers, 1989).

Despite the high reliability of these systems for coding marital interaction, their validity has sometimes been questioned. Firstly, both the MICS and KPI can be criticized in that their summary codes have greater discriminating power than their individual codes (Hahlweg et al., 1984a; Hooley & Hahlweg, 1989). Furthermore, the fact that various researchers have differed in how they have summarized the categories belonging to these systems suggests that researchers disagree as to the fundamental meaning of these categories, or that the meaning of some categories is highly context dependent. The meaning and effect of an "agreement" can vary widely depending on the context. For example, someone agreeing that his or her partner is a fool is very different from someone agreeing with a partner that they should buy a secondhand car. Thus, objectivity may also bring with it a certain starkness or ambiguity, which is further accentuated when categories are collapsed into summary categories for the purposes of sequential analysis or improving reliabilities.

Global Coding Schemes

Largely because of the expense associated with microanalytic coding strategies, researchers have increasingly moved towards using observational systems of a more global nature for assessing marital interaction (Baucom & Sayers, 1989; Weiss & Tolman, 1990). This movement away from microanalytic strategies has also been in response to an awareness of the importance of issues such as intensity (Baucom & Sayers, 1989), and the desire to capture more fully the meaning of partners' behaviours during couple interaction (Floyd, 1989).

There has been a move away from the use of microanalytic coding schemes for assessing marital interaction, towards more global measures, firstly, in terms of using larger coding units, such as the talk turn (e.g., Buehlman, Gottman & Katz, 1992; Krokoff et al., 1989), or even entire interactions (e.g., Heavey et al., 1993). Secondly, coding systems for marital interaction are becoming more global in that they use multidimensional units of measurement, integrating cues across channels, and a number of behavioural events are integrated by the observer to come to a single judgment or coding decision. Therefore, "global" coding systems may contain either large or small coding units. Because they are different, the relative advantages of these two types of global coding systems for coding marital interaction will be considered separately.

Global Systems with Larger Coding Units

Global coding systems with large coding units include the Global Marital Interaction Coding System (MICS-G, Weiss & Tolman, 1990), the Conflict Rating System (CRS, Heavey et al., 1993), and the Interactional Dimensions Coding System (IDCS, Julien, Markman & Lindahl, 1989). Compared with microanalytic coding systems, global systems with large coding units have the potential to give slightly better attention to issues such as the importance of intensity. They also offer a greater opportunity for specificity in the coding of affect, because they utilise a greater number of coding categories. Furthermore, in comparison to microanalytic coding systems, systems with larger coding units are much more economical in terms of the time it takes to code marital interactions.

Nevertheless, there are serious drawbacks associated with treating detail as secondary. The greater the unit size, the less likely it is that coders will attain high levels of interobserver agreement (Floyd, 1989), and the more likely that coders are subject to availability heuristics (Weiss, 1989). Furthermore, and most importantly, if the coding unit is too large, it is not possible to analyse the sequence of marital interaction using sequential analysis (Julien et al., 1989; Weiss, 1989).

Global Systems with Small Coding Units

A number of global coding systems utilize the talk turn as the coding unit, with their coding units being sufficiently small to allow for sequential analysis. For instance, Notarius et al. (1989) used a global coding system in which coders rated each talk turn as positive, neutral, or negative. Analysis of sequence was able to be conducted using log-linear analysis. Other examples of this sort of coding system are the Rapid Couples Interaction Scoring System (RCISS, Krokoff et al., 1989) and the Communication Skills Test (CST, Floyd et al., 1987). Using these coding systems produces data that resembles that generated by microanalytic coding systems, after individual categories have been collapsed into summary categories for the purposes of the sequential analysis of marital interaction.

Consequently, these systems suffer from the same criticisms that can be levelled at those microanalytic systems that use summary categories. Indeed, in general, these three systems are only gauging the positive–negative dimensions of marital interaction. Thus they suffer from problems concerning the loss of information and the inappropriate combination of dissimilar behavioural events. Further, they largely neglect the importance of the intensity of behaviours and emotions that occur during couple interaction. They are more economical than microanalytic measures, however, because the talk turn is generally appreciably longer than the thought unit. In addition, coders have to make more complex judgments, compared with those they make using microanalytic coding systems (Floyd, 1989).

Conclusions on the Comparison of Global and Microanalytic Systems

In terms of validity, Floyd (1989) suggests that there is a lack of evidence to suggest that coding units of one size are better than those of other sizes in their ability to detect differences between the interactions of distressed and non-distressed married couples. Global coding systems have consistently been found to differentiate between distressed and non-distressed couples (e.g., Floyd et al., 1987; Julien et al., 1989; Krokoff et al., 1989; Weiss & Tolman, 1990). Indeed, global coding systems have sometimes been shown to be better able to differentiate between happy and unhappy marriages than microanalytic coding systems (e.g., Weiss & Tolman, 1990). However, if the researcher's intention is to explain the mechanisms underlying marital dysfunction, rather than simply determine whether couples are happy or not, some of the more global observational systems may not be appropriate. Weiss and Tolman (1990) question the utility of an observational measure that may do little more than identify whether a married couple is distressed or not, when self-report measures can do the same with less expense.

The Marital Interaction Rating System

The Marital Interaction Rating System (MIRS, Roberts & Krokoff, 1990) is an observational system that requires special mention, due to its innovative nature. The MIRS utilizes a cultural informants' approach, requiring coders to make ratings on each of three five-point bipolar rating scales: withdrawn–involved, hostile–friendly, and displeasure–pleasure for each coding unit. The use of such an approach still allows for examination of the temporal patterning of marital communication processes using time-series analysis. As a rating is made for each communication process for each coding unit, there is no need to collapse specific codes into a smaller number of broad categories as is often necessary when sequential analysis is used (Sayers & Baucom, 1991). Such rating systems recognize that a single statement may include elements of "negativity" as well as being "problem-focused". Furthermore, this rating system is able to take the intensity of married couples' behaviours into consideration. Rating systems like the MIRS combine some of the depth and complexity of the information provided by global systems with some of the precision associated with microanalytic techniques.

The Couple Conflict Scales

Finally, we would like to briefly mention the observational rating system designed specifically for our research program, which has been labelled the Couple Conflict Scales (CCS). We mention it not as an ideal, but as an example of a coding system that has been developed on the basis of the recommendations of previous researchers, and, more particularly, one that has been designed to address a specific research issue; namely the temporal associations between observable behaviours and ongoing physiological arousal in married couples.

The CCS utilizes a cultural informants' approach, giving the coding system a culturally derived validity (Weiss, 1989). In using the CCS, coders rate each interactant on 12 five-point scales for every 10 seconds of interaction. There are seven content scales (e.g., facilitation, invalidation, and withdrawal) and five negative affect scales (e.g., anxiety, anger, and contempt). Thus, this coding system separates content from affect codes, and distinguishes between various types of negative affect. The relatively brief coding unit (10 seconds) allows for reasonable reliability as well as the generation of sufficient data points for the analysis of sequence using more powerful time-series analysis. Importantly, because coding units are defined by time, it is possible to match segments of behaviour with segments of psychophysiological arousal. Consequently, the investigation of temporal associations between physiological arousal and observational measures of behavioural and affective processes in married couples is possible.

Like the MIRS, the CCS, in using ratings, avoids the necessary use of summary codes. In addition, rating systems are readily able to take into account issues such as intensity and context, and so develop a more meaningful picture of the interaction than that provided by many traditional microanalytic techniques (Floyd, 1989). Furthermore, the CCS does not require the allocation of one and only one affect for each coding unit. Thus, the CCS allows for the occurrence of affective blends, which are far more likely to occur than the expression of "pure" affect during normal interaction (Burgoon & Saine, 1978), and also recognizes that a single behavioural event may communicate several messages, and have multiple functions.

CONCLUSIONS

The observation of couple interaction has provided much information about the communication patterns of married couples. However, the type of information that can be gained from observational techniques is highly dependent upon the particular coding system used. Different marital researchers have utilized different observational systems, and have emphasized different aspects of the couples' interactions, including the importance of sequence, the need for greater specificity (particularly with the coding of affect), the importance of intensity, as well as issues of reliability and validity. However, as Weiss (1989) suggests, different systems are not intrinsically better than one another; rather their appropriateness depends upon the issues and research questions that they were designed to investigate.

REFERENCES

Alexander, J.F., Newell, R.M., Robbins, M.S. & Turner, C.W. (1995). Observational coding in family therapy process research. *Journal of Family Psychology*, **9**, 355–365.

Arkowitz, H., Lamke, L.K. & Filsinger, E.E. (1981). Issues of behavioral assessment: Final reflections. In E.E. Filsinger & R.A. Lewis (Eds), *Assessing marriage: New behavioral approaches* (pp. 287–297). Beverley Hills, CA: Sage.

Bakeman, R. & Gottman, J.M. (1986). *Observing interaction: An introduction to sequential analysis*. New York: Cambridge University Press.

Barret, B.H., Johnston, J.M. & Pennypacker, H.S. (1986). Behavior: Its units, dimensions, and measurements. In R.O. Nelson & S.C. Hayes (Eds), *Conceptual foundations of behavioral assessment* (pp. 156–200). New York: Guilford.

Baucom, D.H. & Sayers, S. (1989). The behavioral observation of couples: Where have we lagged and what is the next step in sequence? *Behavioral Assessment*, **11**, 149–159.

Bradbury, T.N. & Fincham, F.D. (1989). Dimensions of marital and family interaction. In J. Touliatos, B.F. Perlmutter and M.A. Straus (Eds), *Handbook of family measurement techniques* (pp. 37–60). Newbury Park, CA.

Bradbury, T.N., Beach, S.R.H., Fincham, F.D. & Nelson, G.M. (1996). Attributions and behaviour in functional and dysfunctional marriages. *Journal of Consulting and Clinical Psychology*, **64**, 569–576.

Buehlman, K.T., Gottman, J.M. & Katz, L.F. (1992). How a couple views their past predicts their future: Predicting divorce from an oral history interview. *Journal of Family Psychology*, **5**, 295–318.

Burgoon, J.K. & Saine, T. (1978). *The unspoken dialogue: An introduction to nonverbal communication*. Boston, MA: Houghton Mifflin.

Burman, B., John, R.S. & Margolin, G. (1992). Observed patterns of conflict in violent, nonviolent, and nondistressed couples. *Behavioral Assessment*, **14**, 15–37.

Christensen, A. & Heavey, C.L. (1993). Gender differences in marital conflict: The demand/withdraw interaction pattern. In S. Oskamp & M. Costanzo (Eds), *Gender issues in contemporary society* (pp. 113–141). Newbury Park, CA: Sage.

Feeney, J.A., Noller, P. & Callan, V.J. (1994). Attachment style, communication and satisfaction in the early years of marriage. In K. Bartholomew & D. Perlman (Eds), *Advances in personal relationships. Vol. 5: Attachment processes in adulthood* (pp. 269–308). London: Jessica Kingsley.

Fichten, C.S. & Wright, J. (1983). Problem-solving skills in happy and distressed couples: Effects of videotape and verbal feedback. *Journal of Clinical Psychology*, **39**, 340–352.

Filsinger, E.E. (1983). A machine-aided marital observation technique: The Dyadic Interaction Scoring Code. *Journal of Marriage and the Family*, **45**, 623–632.

Fitzpatrick, M.A. (1988). Approaches to marital interaction. In P. Noller & M.A. Fitzpatrick (Eds), *Perspectives on marital interaction* (pp. 1–28). Clevedon, UK: Multilingual Matters.

Floyd, F. (1989). Segmenting interactions: Coding units for assessing marital and family behaviors. *Behavioral Assessment*, **11**, 13–29.

Floyd, F.J., O'Farrell, T.J. & Goldberg, M. (1987). Comparison of marital observational measures: The marital interaction coding system and the communication skills test. *Journal of Consulting and Clinical Psychology*, **55**, 423–429.

Gottman, J.M. (1979). *Marital interaction: Empirical investigations*. New York: Academic Press.

Gottman, J.M. (1990). How marriages change. In G.R. Patterson (Ed.), *Depression and aggression in family interaction* (pp. 75–102), Hillsdale, NJ: Erlbaum.

Gottman, J.M. (1994). *What predicts divorce? The relationship between marital processes and marital outcomes*. Hillsdale, NJ: Erlbaum.

Gottman, J.M., & Krokoff, L.J. (1989). Marital interaction and marital satisfaction: A longitudinal view. *Journal of Consulting and Clinical Psychology*, **57**, 47–52.

Gottman, J.M. & Levenson, R.W. (1985). A valid procedure for obtaining self-report of affect in marital interaction. *Journal of Consulting and Clinical Psychology*, **53**, 151–160.

Gottman, J.M. & Levenson, R.W. (1986). Assessing the role of emotion in marriage. *Behavioral Assessment*, **8**, 31–48.

Gottman, J.M. & Levenson, R.W. (1992). Marital processes predictive of later dissolution: Behavior, physiology, and health. *Journal of Personality and Social Psychology*, **63**, 221–233.

Gottman, J.M., Markman, H. & Notarius, C. (1977). The topography of marital conflict: A sequential analysis of verbal and nonverbal behavior. *Journal of Marriage and the Family*, **39**, 461–477.

Greenberg, L.S., Ford, C.L., Alden, L.S. & Johnson, S.M. (1993). In-session change in emotionally focused therapy. *Journal of Consulting and Clinical Psychology*, **61**, 78–84.

Griffin, W.A. & Gottman, J.M. (1990). Statistical methods for analyzing family interaction. In G.R. Patterson (Ed.), *Depression and aggression in family interaction* (pp. 131–168). Hillsdale, NJ: Erlbaum.

Haefner, P.T., Notarius, C.L. & Pellegrini, D.S. (1991). Determinants of satisfaction with marital discussions: An exploration of husband–wife differences. *Behavioral Assessment*, **13**, 67–82.

Hahlweg, K., Reisner, L., Kohli, G., Vollmer, M., Schindler, L. & Revenstorf, L. (1984a). Development and validity of a new system to analyze interpersonal communication: Kategoriensystem für partnerschaftliche interaktion. In K. Hahlweg & N.S. Jacobson (Eds), *Marital interaction: Analysis and modification* (pp 182–198). New York: Guilford.

Hahlweg, K., Revenstorf, D. & Schindler, L. (1984b). The effects of behavioral marital therapy on couples' communication and problem-solving skills. *Journal of Consulting and Clinical Psychology*, **52**, 553–566.

Heatherington, L. (1989). Toward more meaningful clinical research: Taking context into account in coding psychotherapy interaction. *Psychotherapy*, **26**, 436–447.

Heavey, C.L., Layne, C. & Christensen, A. (1993). Gender and conflict structure in marital interaction: A replication and extension. *Journal of Consulting and Clinical Psychology*, **61**, 16–27.

Heyman, R.E., Eddy, J.M., Weiss, R.L. & Vivian, D. (1995a). Factor analysis of the Marital Interaction Coding System (MICS). *Journal of Family Psychology*, **9**, 209–215.

Heyman, R.E., Weiss, R.L. & Eddy, J.M. (1995b). Marital Interaction Coding System: Revision and empirical evaluation. *Behavior Research and Therapy*, **33**, 737–746.

Hinde, R.A. (1979). *Towards understanding relationships*. London: Academic Press.

Hooley, J.M. & Hahlweg, K. (1989). Marital satisfaction and marital communication in German and English couples. *Behavioral Assessment*, **11**, 119–133.

Hops, H., Wills, T.A., Patterson G.R. & Weiss, R.L. (1972). The marital interaction coding system (MICS). Unpublished manuscript, University of Oregon, Eugene, OR.

Jacob, T. & Tennenbaum, D.L. (1988). *Family assessment: Rationale, methods, and future directions*. New York: Plenum Press.

Julien, D., Markman, H.J. & Lindahl, K.M. (1989). A comparison of a global and micro-analytic coding system: Implications for future trends in studying interactions. *Behavioral Assessment*, **11**, 81–100.

Kiecolt-Glaser, J.K., Newton, T., Cacioppo, J.T., MacCallum, R.C., Glaser, R. & Malarkey, W.B. (1996). Marital conflict and endocrine function: Are men really more physiologically affected than women? *Journal of Consulting and Clinical Psychology*, **64**, 324–332.

Krokoff, L.J. (1987). The correlates of negative affect in marriage: An exploratory study of gender differences. *Journal of Family Issues*, **8**, 111–135.

Krokoff, L.J., Gottman, J.M. & Hass, S.D. (1989). Validation of a global Rapid Couples Interaction Scoring System. *Behavioral Assessment*, **11**, 65–79.

L'Abate, L. & Bagarozzi, D.A. (1992). *Sourcebook of marriage and family evaluation*. New York: Brunner/Mazel.

Lang, P.J. (1995). The emotion probe: Studies of motivation and attention. *American Psychologist*, **50**, 372–385.

Levenson, R.W. & Gottman, J.M. (1983). Marital interaction: Physiological linkage and affective exchange. *Journal of Personality and Social Psychology*, **45**, 587–597.

Lichtenberg, J.W. & Heck, E.J. (1986). Analysis of sequence and pattern in process research. *Journal of Counselling Psychology*, **33**, 170–181.

Margolin, G. & Wampold, B. (1981). Sequential analysis of conflict and accord in distressed and nondistressed marital partners. *Journal of Consulting and Clinical Psychology*, **49**, 554–567.

Margolin, G., John, R.S. & Gleberman, L. (1988). Affective responses to conflictual discussion in violent and nonviolent couples. *Journal of Consulting and Clinical Psychology*, **56**, 24–33.

Margolin, G., John, R.S. & O'Brien, M. (1989). Sequential affective patterns as a function of marital conflict style. *Journal of Social and Clinical Psychology*, **56**, 24–33.

Markman, H.J., Notarius, C.I., Stephen, T. & Smith, R. (1981). Behavioral observation systems for couples: The current status. In E.E. Filsinger & R.A. Lewis (Eds), *Assessing marriage: New behavioral approaches* (pp. 234–262). Beverly Hills, CA: Sage.

Markman, H.J., Leber, B.D., Cordova, A.D. & St Peters, M. (1995). Behavioral observation of family psychology – strange bedfellows or happy marriage? Comment on Alexander et al. (1995). *Journal of Family Psychology*, **9**, 371–379.

McCabe, S.B. & Gotlib, I.H. (1993). Interactions of couples with and without a depressed spouse: Self-report and observations of problem-solving situations. *Journal of Social and Personal Relationships*, **10**, 589–599.

Miller, G.E. & Bradbury, T.N. (1995). Refining the association between attributions and behaviour in marital interaction. *Journal of Family Psychology*, **9**, 196–208.

Morell, M.A. & Apple, R.F. (1990). Affect expression, marital satisfaction, and stress reactivity among premenopausal women during a conflictual marital discussion. *Psychology of Women Quarterly*, **14**, 387–402.

Ney, T. & Gale, A. (1988). A critique of laboratory studies of emotion with particular reference to psychophysiological aspects. In H.L. Wagner (Ed.), *Social psychophysiology and emotion: Theory and clinical applications* (211–229). Chichester, UK: Wiley.

Noller, P. (1985). Video primacy: A further look. *Journal of Nonverbal Behavior*, **9**, 28–47.

Noller, P. & Fitzpatrick, M.A. (1990). Marital communication in the eighties. *Journal of Marriage and the Family*, **52**, 832–843.

Noller, P. & Guthrie, D. (1991). Studying communication in marriage: An integration and critical evaluation. *Advances in Personal Relationships*, **3**, 37–73.

Noller, P. & Ruzzene, M. (1991). The effects of cognition and affect on marital communication. In G. Fletcher & F.D. Fincham (Eds), *Affect and cognition in close relationships* (pp. 203–233). New York: Erlbaum.

Notarius, C.L. & Markman, H.J. (1981). The couples interaction scoring system. In E.E. Filsinger & R.A. Lewis (Eds), *Assessing marriage: New behavioral approaches* (pp. 112–127). Beverley Hills, CA: Sage.

Notarius, C.L. & Markman, H.J. (1989). Coding marital interaction: A sampling and discussion of current issues. *Behavioral Assessment*, **11**, 1–11.

Notarius, C.L., Markman, H.J. & Gottman, J.M. (1983). Couples interaction scoring system: Clinical implications. In E. Filsinger (Ed.), *Marriage and family assessment* (pp. 117–136). San Francisco: Jossey-Bass.

Notarius, C.L., Benson, P.K., Sloane, D., Vanzetti, N. & Hornyak, L.M. (1989). Exploring the interface between perception and behavior: An analysis of marital interaction in distressed and nondistressed couples. *Behavioral Assessment*, **11**, 39–64.

Raush, H.L., Barry, W.A., Hertel, R.K. & Swain, M.A. (1974). *Communication, conflict, and marriage*. San Francisco: Jossey-Bass.

Roberts, L.J. & Krokoff, L.J. (1990). A time-series analysis of withdrawal, hostility, and displeasure in satisfied and dissatisfied marriages. *Journal of Marriage and the Family*, **52**, 95–105.

Sayers, S.L. & Baucom, D.H. (1991). Role of femininity and masculinity in distressed couples' communication. *Journal of Personality and Social Psychology*, **61**, 641–647.

Sayers, S.L., Baucom, D.H., Sher, T.G., Weiss, R.L. & Heyman, R.E. (1991). Constructive engagement, behavioral marital therapy, and changes in marital satisfaction. *Behavioral Assessment*, **13**, 25–49.

Schaap, C. (1984). A comparison of the interaction of distressed and nondistressed married couples in a laboratory situation: Literature survey, methodological issues, and an empirical investigation. In K. Hahlweg & N.S. Jacobson (Eds), *Marital interaction: Analysis and modification* (pp. 133–158). New York: Guilford.

Schmaling, K.B. & Jacobson, N.S. (1990). Marital interaction and depression. *Journal of Abnormal Psychology*, **99**, 229–236.

Smith, D.A., Vivian, D. & O'Leary, K.D. (1990). Longitudinal prediction of marital discord from premarital expressions of affect. *Journal of Consulting and Clinical Psychology*, **58**, 790–798.

Vincent, J.P., Friedman, L.L., Nugent, J. & Messerly, L. (1979). Demand characteristics in observations of marital interaction. *Journal of Consulting and Clinical Psychology*, **47**, 557–566.

Weiss, R.L. (1989). The circle of voyeurs: Observing the observers of marital and family interactions. *Behavioral Assessment*, **11**, 135–147.

Weiss, R.L. & Heyman, R.E. (1990). Observation of marital interaction. In F.D. Fincham & T.N. Bradbury (Eds), *The psychology of marriage* (pp. 87–117). New York: Guilford.

Weiss, R.L. & Heyman, R.E. (1997). A clinical research overview of couples interactions. In W.K. Halford & H.J. Markman (Eds), *Clinical handbook of marriage and couples interventions* (pp. 13–41). Chichester, UK: Wiley.

Weiss, R.L. & Summers, K.J. (1983). Marital Interaction Coding System–III. In E.E. Filsinger (Ed.), *Marriage and family assessment* (pp. 85–115). Beverly Hills, CA: Sage.

Weiss, R.L. & Tolman, A.O. (1990). The Marital Interaction Coding System–Global (MICS-G): A global companion to the MICS. *Behavioral Assessment*, **21**, 271–294.

Williams, E.A. & Gottman, J.M. (1981). *A user's guide to the Gottman-Williams time-series analysis computer programs for social scientists*. New York: Cambridge University Press.

Part 5

Social Categories

Multilingual Communication

Itesh Sachdev
Birkbeck College, University of London, UK
Richard Y. Bourhis
Université du Québec à Montréal, Canada

To be bilingual or multilingual is not the aberration supposed by many (particularly, perhaps, by people in Europe and North America who speak a "big" language); it is, rather, a normal and unremarkable necessity for the majority of the world today. (Edwards, 1994, p. 1)

The vast majority of people in the world speak more than one language yet the scientific literature is currently dominated by analyses of communication in a single language (for exceptions, see Edwards, 1994; Grosjean, 1982; Hamers & Blanc, 2000; Romaine, 1995). Our focus is on bilingual and multilingual communication, moving away from the monolingual bias that is probably rooted in Chomsky's (1965) analysis of the "ideal" speaker–listener. The aim of this chapter is to present an outline model of multilingual communication with a special focus on *code-switching* (CS), regarded by many researchers as the most common form of bilingual and multilingual communication (e.g., Hamers & Blanc, 2000; Romaine, 1995). For the remainder of this chapter, references to "bilingual" are generally subsumed under the more general term of "multilingual", unless specifically indicated. An intergroup perspective is emphasized in this chapter since multilingual communication, where two or more languages (and dialects) are used, generally involves members of different ethnolinguistic groups (Hamers & Blanc, 1982).

Linguistic competence, desires to increase communication accuracy, and the normative demands of situations are important factors governing language choice (Giles & Coupland, 1991). There is a also a substantial body of literature showing that languages and language choices are not just "neutral" means of

The New Handbook of Language and Social Psychology.
Edited by W. Peter Robinson and Howard Giles.
© 2001 John Wiley & Sons Ltd.

communication (Fishman, 1977; Giles & Johnson, 1981; Gumperz & Hymes, 1972; Sachdev & Bourhis, 1990). Which language(s) is(are) used, when, why and by whom, are important questions given the crucial role that language plays as "the recorder of paternity, the expressor of patrimony and the carrier of phenomenology" (Fishman, 1977, p. 25). In accordance with the theme of this Handbook, a social psychological approach is employed to integrate micro-individual aspects with the macro-collective levels of multilingual communication (Bourhis, 1979; Clément & Bourhis, 1996; Giles, Bourhis & Taylor, 1977). This review is necessarily selective, and the rich contributions from other conceptual and empirical orientations including sociolinguistics, the ethnography of speaking, interactional linguistics, linguistic anthropology and the sociology of language are discussed relatively briefly.

The widespread phenomenon of multilingual CS has generated much discussion, with researchers generally agreeing that it involves "the alternate use of two or more languages in the same utterance or conversation" (Grosjean, 1982, p. 145; Gardner-Chloros, 1991; Milroy & Muysken, 1995; Myers-Scotton, 1997). In order to illustrate CS, three short examples are provided. For instance, CS where two languages are employed in the same sentence may be of the type: "Have *agua*, please" (the Spanish word in the middle is translated as "water"; Romaine, 1995, p. 2). Switching languages between sentences may be of the type: "Now it's really time to get up. *Leve-toi*." (The French is translated as "get up"; Grosjean, 1982, p. 114.) CS by speaker turn in a conversation between a father and son in English and Luo is reported in an example by Myers-Scotton (1993, p. 148):

Father: "Where have you been?"
Son: "*Onyango nende adlu aora, baba*" (translated as "I've been to the river, father").

Researchers have investigated a large variety of CS, including switching by turn, tag, single-word, multi-word, inter- and intra-sentential, metaphorical, situational, and so on (e.g., Cheshire & Gardner-Chloros, 1998; Milroy & Muysken, 1995). Linguists and sociolinguists have debated about the phenomena that may be subsumed under the umbrella term of CS (e.g., Blommaert, 1992; Eastman, 1992; Myers-Scotton, 1997; Poplack, 1980, 1997; Romaine, 1995). Issues in question include: whether language borrowing and CS are one or two types of behavior; whether borrowing is a form of CS or vice versa (Poplack, 1997); whether CS and code-mixing are the same or different phenomena (Gibbons, 1987; Hamers & Blanc, 2000); and what distinguishes CS and borrowing from the use of loan words (Eastman, 1992; Milroy & Muysken, 1995). A major enterprise has been to identify the structural aspects of CS with a specific focus on linguistic constraints (see Romaine, 1995; Myers-Scotton, 1997; Hamers & Blanc, 2000). Other research has focused on the developmental aspects of CS. For example, longitudinal studies have examined the appearance and development of CS as a language acquisition strategy in young children (e.g., Grosjean, 1982; Köppe &

Meisel, 1995). Sociolinguists have also looked at CS from the perspective of "languages in contact" and language choice, often analysed within the framework of domain theory (Fishman, 1972; Gardner-Chloros, 1991; Milroy & Muysken, 1995).

Social psychological factors and processes, which are addressed relatively infrequently in much of the linguistic and sociolinguistic literature, are postulated to be mediator variables influencing CS and other aspects of multilingualism in our exploratory model of multilingual communication outlined in Figure 1. According to this model, three classes of variables may be expected to affect multilingual communication: (i) societal intergroup context variables; (ii) sociolinguistic setting variables; and (iii) social psychological variables. Our discussion begins with a consideration of intergroup context variables including the objective "Ethnolinguistic Vitality" of groups (Giles et al., 1977; Harwood, Giles & Bourhis, 1994; Landry & Allard, 1994a; Sachdev & Bourhis, 1993), state language policies (Bourhis, 1984a, 1984b, in press) and the stability, legitimacy and permeability of intergroup stratification (Tajfel & Turner, 1979). The macro-level intergroup context factors greatly affect variables associated with the sociolinguistic setting. Sociolinguistic setting variables, considered next, include normative factors governing language use (Gumperz, 1982; Myers-Scotton, 1993; Scotton, 1983), and the networks of linguistic contacts within and between language groups (e.g., Landry & Allard, 1994b; Milroy, 1980). The next section considers a variety of social psychological processes as mediators, with the individual as the unit of analysis, while also incorporating the influence of the broader intergroup context and the sociolinguistic setting. In this chapter, social psychological processes are discussed with reference to conceptual models that focus on ethnolinguistic identification (Giles & Johnson, 1981; Sachdev & Bourhis, 1990), vitality perception and beliefs (Harwood et al., 1994; Landry & Allard, 1994a; Sachdev & Bourhis, 1993), communication accommodation (Giles et al., 1987; Shepard, Giles & Le Poire, this volume, Chapter 1.2) and acculturation orientations (Bourhis, in press), while aptitude and motivations for learning languages are covered in the chapter by Clement and Gardner (this volume, Chapter 6.26).

In Figure 1, the main classes of outcome (or dependent) variables include language behavior, additive/subtractive multilingualism and multiculturalism, language and cultural maintenance and loss (see Giles & Coupland, 1991, for an overview). In this chapter, our concerns are restricted to aspects of language behavior focusing on CS. The major predictor variables in this model (intergroup context, sociolinguistic setting and social psychological factors) are also expected to affect discourse content and non-verbal communication but this literature is not systematically addressed in this chapter. Language behavior is also expected to contribute to additive–subtractive multilingualism and multiculturalism, which in turn contributes to the longer-term maintenance and loss of languages and cultures. This model is considerably broader than the focus of this chapter and is meant to account for the macro-level language shift across generations, shifts which lead to language loss or "reversing language shift" (Fishman,

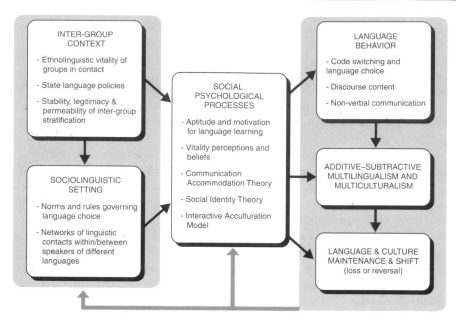

Figure 1   A model of multilingual communication

1991), in which a minority reclaims its language loss through a language shift towards language maintenance and language revival (see Bourhis, 2001, in press). In terms of our focus on CS, new patterns of CS towards first language maintenance rather than convergence to a high-status second language can signal the beginning of a language shift and revival. It is important to note that our model is a dynamic one, with all classes of language outcomes affecting social psychological processes, intergroup context variables and the sociolinguistic setting (as indicated by feedback arrows in Figure 1).

Following a discussion of each class of predictor variables, some future priorities are discussed. Note that in order to permit an unambiguous examination of the social psychological aspects of CS, this chapter does not focus on CS resulting from interlocutors' lack of linguistic competence (referred to as "restricted CS" by Hamers & Blanc, 2000; also see Dabene & Moore, 1995). Additionally, the primary concern here is with CS between languages, though it should be noted that switching between dialects, styles and registers is also common (e.g., Bell, 1984; Coupland, 1984).

INTERGROUP CONTEXT

Multilingual communication cannot be assumed to occur in a sociostructural vacuum as differences in group numbers, power and status characterize most intergroup situations (Giles et al., 1977; Sachdev & Bourhis, 1984, 1987, 1991).

Thus, Singh, Lele and Martohardjono (1988) have been critical of much previous sociolinguistic research which they claim takes a dominant centric approach that fails to acknowledge that multilingual communication usually occurs between speakers who are members of groups of unequal power and status within majority/minority settings. One of the most important developments in social psychology for assessing the impact of sociostructural factors in the social psychology of multilingual communication has been the introduction of the construct of *Ethnolinguistic Vitality* by Giles et al. (1977; see reviews by Bourhis, 2001; Harwood et al., 1994; Sachdev & Bourhis, 1993). Defining the vitality of ethnolinguistic groups as the ability of groups to behave and survive as distinctive and active collective entities in multigroup settings, they examine it using three main sets of variables: demographic strength, group status and institutional support.

Demographic variables relate to the sheer number of ethnolinguistic group members and their distribution throughout urban, regional and national territories. Demographic variables also include the rates of immigration, emigration, endogamy and the birth-rates of groups. Status variables pertain to the sociohistorical prestige, social and economic status of language groups as well as the status of the languages used by speakers locally and internationally. Institutional support variables refer to the representation and control that language groups have in formal and informal institutions in the spheres of education, politics, religion, economy, culture and mass media. Groups' strengths and weaknesses on each of these dimensions gathered from available sociological, economic and demographic information may be combined to provide an overall classification of ethnolinguistic groups as having low, medium or high objective vitality. This could then be linked to patterns of CS and other outcome measures shown in Figure 1. For instance, it might be expected that people would have more positive attitudes about, and use the language(s) of objectively high-vitality groups to a greater extent for CS than the languages of objectively low-vitality groups.

The original formulations of Giles et al. (1977) focused largely on an "objective" analysis of ethnolinguistic vitality. The *Subjective Vitality Questionnaire* (SVQ; Bourhis, Giles & Rosenthal, 1981) was developed to take into account individuals' perceptions of vitality thought to mediate ethnolinguistic attitudes and behavior. Findings of early studies using the SVQ suggest that speakers who perceive own group vitality to be high have more positive attitudes about the use of their own group language in a wider range of public and private settings than speakers who perceive own group vitality to be low (e.g., Bourhis & Sachdev, 1984; Sachdev et al., 1987). Allard and Landry (1986) proposed further development of the vitality construct by arguing that the predictive power of the SVQ is greatly increased if it is considered to be part of a belief system reflecting individual predispositions and orientations about vitality. This reflects the empirically well-supported notion that generalized attitudes and perceptions are not reliable predictors of behavior unless accompanied by specific behavioral intentions (see Ajzen, 1988). In an impressive programme of research, Allard and Landry gathered evidence from several studies confirming that vitality is a better predictor of multilingual attitudes and behavior when *egocentric* (self) and *exocentric* (non-self) beliefs about individual vitality variables are incorporated into a *Beliefs about Ethnolinguistic Vitality Questionnaire* (BEVQ; Allard & Landry, 1986, 1994; Landry & Allard, 1984, 1990, 1991, 1994b; Landry & Bourhis, 1997). Perceptions and beliefs about vitality are social psychological factors in our model of multilingual communication (see Figure 1).

The "objective" vitality of groups is an outcome of the inter-group dynamic between groups of high and low vitality. In his analysis of Western democratic societies, Bourhis (in press) proposes that dominant groups impose state language policies that vary on an ideological continuum ranging from *pluralism* at one pole, through *civic* and *assimilation* in the middle, to *ethnist* at the opposite pole. Groups in society are expected to adopt the *public* values of the dominant groups under all these clusters of ideologies. Public values include founding principles enshrined in constitutions and charters of rights and freedoms as well as basic laws constituting the civil and criminal codes of the state. However, the *private* values of different groups are expected to fare differently under these ideologies. Whereas there may be both official and financial support for minority languages and cultures in states which endorse the pluralism ideology (e.g., Canada), states which endorse the civic ideology avoid outright official support and provide little or no financial support for the maintenance of minority languages and cultures (e.g., the UK until devolution). States which endorse the assimilationist ideology usually impose conformity to the dominant ethnolinguistic group in the name of a unitary founding myth advocating the equality of all citizens regardless of ethnocultural background (e.g., France, United States). States which endorse the ethnist ideology tend to repress linguistic minorities as a way of enforcing assimilation to the dominant language, while they may exclude from citizenship targeted minorities deemed undesirable or "incapable" of ever assimilating to the ethnolinguistic "mainstream" (e.g., Germany, Israel). Contrasting language policies situated along this ideological continuum may be adopted at the national, regional and local levels, and together contribute to the climate of tolerance or intolerance towards minority language maintenance which in turn may affect the use of CS not only in public settings but also in private settings such as the home and friendship networks.

The intergroup stratification of dominant and subordinate language groups may be objectively stable or unstable (e.g., on economic dimensions), legitimate or illegitimate (e.g., on political dimensions), while "passing" from one language group to the other via bilingualism or linguistic assimilation may be easy or difficult (i.e., permeable or impermeable boundaries; see Giles & Johnson, 1981; Tajfel & Turner, 1979). State language policies may be changing from civic to pluralist as a function of demographic changes or, following active minority agitation, the dominant language group may be forced to move from an oppressive assimilationist language policy to a more tolerant civic language policy. Alternatively, as in the rise of right wing lobbies such as the English Only Movement in the United States, language policies and the general social mood may reverse a civic trend back towards a more assimilationist climate (see

Bourhis & Marshall, 1999, for a comparison of US and Canadian language policies). Taken together, the intergroup context variables create communication climates that influence the sociolinguistic setting, social psychological factors and the various outcomes of multilingual communication. For instance, in an unstable intergroup hierarchy under an assimilationist state language policy, CS by low-vitality linguistic minorities from the dominant language to the minority language in public situations may be more marked, giving rise to unfavorable discourse content, dissociative non-verbal communication and divergent language switching by dominant language interlocutors. These dominant group reactions are likely to be mediated by social psychological variables such as those subsumed by Communication Accommodation Theory (Giles et al., 1987; Shepard et al., this volume, Chapter 1.2), and are most likely to be voiced by dominant group members whose acculturation orientations towards linguistic minorities are segregationist and exclusionist (Bourhis, in press). This illustrates how variables of the intergroup context (state-level language policies, intergroup vitality and the stability/legitimacy of intergroup situations) combine with social psychological factors (including acculturation orientations), to predict CS and other types of language behavior. Macro-level factors associated with the intergroup context also affect the normative framework of communication and the networks of linguistic contacts in the sociolinguistic setting (Figure 1).

SOCIOLINGUISTIC SETTING

Traditional theoretical and empirical efforts by sociolinguists focused on developing taxonomics of situational norms affecting communication (e.g., Fishman, 1972; Gumperz & Hymes, 1972; Hymes, 1972; Trudgill, 1974). Their interest in these approaches was on the topic of communication, the social setting in which it occurs, the purpose of the communication and the characteristics of the interlocutors. For example, early research in Israel (Herman, 1961), Tanzania (Beardsley & Eastman, 1971) and Japan (Ervin-Tripp, 1964) showed that bilinguals revert to their native dialect or language when discussing emotional issues or when talking about topics relevant to the cultural contexts in which they live. Similarly, in the Philippines and Paraguay, the use of English and Spanish, respectively, was normative amongst courting couples who, once wedded, would switch to Tagalog and Guarani, respectively (Rubin, 1962; Sechrest, Flores & Arellano, 1968). In all of these and numerous other cultural contexts, the local vernacular is restricted to the role of informal communication in private settings, while the more prestigious cosmopolitan language is considered the voice of intellect and of public formal communication. Similar situational determinants of language choice have been observed in Morocco (Bentahila, 1983), Hong Kong (Gibbons, 1987), Kenya (Myers-Scotton, 1993; Scotton, 1983), India (Pandit, 1979), Singapore (Platt, 1980) and many other settings across the world (see Eastman, 1992; Hamers & Blanc, 2000; Milroy & Muysken, 1995; Romaine, 1995). A variety of multilingual settings mentioned above may be termed diglossic (Ferguson, 1959; Fishman, 1967) or polyglossic (Platt, 1977) in the sense that certain codes are specifically reserved for high-status formal functions, while others serve as modes of communication in private and informal situations. Extensive discussions of the relationships between di-glossia, CS and bilingualism may be found in Fasold (1984), Romaine (1995) and Hamers and Blanc (2000) and cannot be considered here.

Dissatisfaction with traditional analyses of language choice arose from their conceptualization of interlocutors primarily as "situational automatons", and led some researchers to postulate "cooperative" rules guiding discourse such as the Principles of Charity (Davidson, 1974) and Humanity (Grandy, 1973; Grice, 1975). Interactional sociolinguists have subsequently focused on identi-fying discourse strategies relevant in multilingual communication based on the operation of a "cooperativeness principle" (e.g., Gumperz, 1982; Scotton, 1983). Cooperative discourse principles assume that code choices are primarily concerned with communication efficiency and, moreover, serve to maintain the status quo (Scotton, 1983). However, there is considerable evidence that lan-guage switches are not always designed to increase communication efficiency (Brown & Levinson, 1980; Giles, Taylor & Bourhis, 1973) and that code choices often aim to challenge the status quo (e.g., "speech divergence" below, Bourhis & Giles, 1977).

Following Grice's proposal of the "cooperative principle", Scotton (1983) developed her *markedness model* to argue that language choices are determined by the negotiation of rights and obligations between interlocutors. Unmarked codes are chosen when interlocutors identify with their positions in well-defined role relationships, and marked codes are chosen to reject predefined roles. It should be reiterated that a normative framework underlies this markedness model as speakers make judgements of markedness on the basis of prevailing community norms. In a recent version of the model, Myers-Scotton (1993) sys-tematized her approach in terms of three main maxims determining code choices: (a) the *unmarked-choice* maxim; (b) the *marked-choice* maxim; (c) the *exploratory-choice* maxim; (auxiliary maxims such as those of *deference* and *virtuosity* are not discussed here).

First, speakers who follow an unmarked-choice maxim, where code choices affirm established roles, result in CS either as a sequence of unmarked choices or CS itself as the unmarked choice. The former is assumed to be due to a change in situational factors, while the latter is expected to depend on interlocutors' atti-tudes to each other as well as the social connotations of the codes and their alternation. An example of the former might be when a speaker uses a different language to different people in a group as a function of the addressee. An example of CS itself as the unmarked choice may be when fluent bilinguals engage in frequent and continuous CS, often intrasentential and sometimes even within the same word. Second, speakers follow a marked-choice maxim to "ne-gotiate a change in the expected social distance holding between participants, either increasing or decreasing it" (p.132). According to Myers-Scotton (1993) this "single, general motivation for marked choices" (p.132) subsumes diverse sets of reasons ranging from displays of a wide variety of emotions (e.g., anger, affection) to assertions of authority and group identity. A relevant example of this is the type of switching referred to as speech divergence in the discussion of Communication Accommodation Theory below (also see Shepard et al., this volume, Chapter 1.2). Third, speakers who follow the exploratory-choice maxim are unclear about the normative demands of the situation and are likely to use CS as a "neutral" or "safe" code-choice.

Unlike traditional sociolinguists, Scotton's (1983; Myers-Scotton, 1993) approach is interactional and may be seen as complementing social psychological approaches discussed below. However, on a more cautious note, the social psychological status of her maxims is unclear and there is some potential for circularity in attributing code choices to the operation of maxims. This stems from the practice of defining original maxims using examples of code choices and then re-citing those particular instances as empirical evidence of the existence and operation of those maxims. Approaches attributing CS to the operation of multiple and competing situational norms are also likely to have similar drawbacks. Moreover, though CS in multilingual contexts may be attributable to social norms and rules, switching also occurs either in the absence of, or in spite of, a normative framework (Bourhis, 1979; Giles & Coupland, 1991). Even within normatively constrained settings there may be a wide latitude of acceptable language behaviors, and language use may be negotiated creatively to dynamically define and redefine social norms (Myers-Scotton, 1993; Scotton, 1983; cf. Brown & Fraser, 1979).

In Myers-Scotton's (1993) theory, norms do not determine language choices, but language switches take place within a normative framework so that norms determine the relative markedness of linguistic codes. Myers-Scotton further suggests that interlocutors are free to assert their individual motivations as all code choices are open to them with interlocutors weighing up the relative costs and rewards in seeking their goals (cf. social exchange analysis discussed below). However, it is debatable whether a model based largely on "readings of markedness and calculations of the consequences of a given choice" (Myers-Scotton, 1993, p. 110) copes well with the complexity and diversity of motivational factors discussed in social psychological research on multilingual communication (e.g., Giles et al., 1987).

Sociolinguistic research such as Milroy's (1980) study of linguistic variation and social class in Northern Ireland cogently demonstrates the importance of individual social networks in reinforcing norms of communication. Relatedly, though without reference to norms, Landry and Allard (1990, 1994b) propose the notion of *individual networks of linguistic contact* (INLC) as a "bridge between the sociological and psychological levels" (Allard & Landry, 1994, p. 121) in their macroscopic model of bilingual behavior. According to them, the INLC represents the level where the "individual lives the totality of his ethnolinguistic experiences" (Allard & Landry, 1994, p.121). It consists of all occasions in which individuals have the opportunity to use their own languages when interacting with family members, friends, neighbors, school peers, co-workers and others. The INLC also includes occasions to use the ingroup language when consuming services from private and public sector bodies including education, culture, municipal and state governments, shops, businesses, financial establishments, electronic and printed mass media. In bilingual and multilingual environments, the INLC incorporates contact with both ingroup and outgroup language users. High "objective" ethnolinguistic vitality of the ingroup allows wider and stronger ingroup INLC, leading to greater opportunities for speaking the ingroup language (Bourhis, 1991). Conversely, low "objective" ingroup vitality leads to smaller ingroup INLC, and fewer occasions for speaking the ingroup language. The mediating role of INLC between a group's "objective" vitality, perceptions of group vitality, and patterns of language use by individuals, has received good support in a sustained programme of research across Canada (Landry & Allard, 1991, 1994b; Landry & Bourhis, 1997).

Bourhis (1994a) adapted the INLC notion to study English–French communication amongst employees of the Canadian Federal Administration in the officially bilingual province of New Brunswick, where Anglophones constitute a two-thirds majority relative to Francophones. Bilingual civil servants' self-reports of their use of French and English were related to the intensity of Francophone presence experienced by each individual in their respective work environment. As expected, environments with a higher intensity of Francophone presence were associated with greater use of French than those with low intensities of Francophone presence, especially for Francophone respondents. Interestingly, differences between Anglophone and Francophone use of French and English were also observed in that convergence to Francophones by Anglophones (by using French) was significantly lower than convergence to Anglophones by Francophones (by using English). The high status of English as the language of work in such organizational settings was thought to underlie this pattern of results, suggesting that factors other than INLC were also important in explaining patterns of language choice. Even in a non-status stressing setting such as casual encounters between Francophone and Anglophone pedestrians in downtown Montreal, Moïse and Bourhis (1994) found that while 90–100% of Francophones made the effort to converge to English while giving directions to an Anglophone, only 60–70% of Anglophones made the effort to switch to French when giving directions to a Francophone. These results were obtained in studies conducted from 1977 to 1991, representing 15 years of language planning effort designed to increase the status of French relative to English in Quebec (Bourhis, 1994b; 81% of the Quebec population has French as a mother tongue). Such findings confirm the importance of considering the interactive effects of the intergroup context and the sociolinguistic setting in multilingual communication. Additionally, from a social psychological perspective, it is important to consider how individuals' perceptions and beliefs about the inter-group context and the sociolinguistic setting mediate the impact of the "objective" intergroup context and the sociolinguistic setting.

SOCIAL PSYCHOLOGICAL PROCESSES

As seen in Figure 1, we propose that a number of social psychological processes, incorporated by various conceptual models and theories, are important mediators in multilingual communication. Although language aptitude and motivation for language learning are part of the model, such elements cannot be discussed here (see Clement & Gardner, this volume, Chapter 6.26), especially as multilingual CS assumes that language learning has already occurred. Given that vitality perceptions and beliefs have been discussed earlier, this section focuses on social psychological processes underlying CS that have been incorporated into three conceptual models: Communication Accommodation Theory (Giles et al., 1973, 1987), Social Identity Theory (Tajfel & Turner, 1979) and the Interactive Acculturation Model (Bourhis, in press; Bourhis et al., 1997).

Our discussion of Communication Accommodation Theory (CAT) focuses on its role in accounting for CS within multilingual communication, and as such, complements the overview of the theory provided by Shepard ct al. (this volume). As in the case of interactional sociolinguistics, CAT was also developed as a reaction to the normative bias in traditional sociolinguistics, and sought to account for language use in terms of interlocutors' motives, attitudes, perceptions and group loyalties. CAT attempts to explain and predict language use in terms of social psychological processes operating at both the interpersonal level (e.g., similarity-attraction, Byrne, 1969) and at the intergroup level where social categorization processes are of primary importance (Tajfel, 1978). The major focus has been on communication strategies of convergence, divergence and maintenance, although other strategies have also been investigated (see Shepard et al., this volume, Chapter 1.2). Briefly, convergence refers to interlocutors becoming more alike in their communication; maintenance refers to interlocutors maintaining their own manner of communication, while divergence is a dissociative strategy adopted by speakers who accentuate differences in their communicative behavior relative to their interlocutor. These strategies have been found to occur simultaneously on a variety of linguistic levels (language, paralinguistic, content, style, accent, etc.), and speakers are not always aware that they were modifying their communication. Levels of awareness about divergence appear to be higher than for convergence (e.g., Bourhis, 1983; Street, 1982).

Central to CAT is the notion that people adapt their communication in order to satisfy a variety of motivations. An early study in a bilingual context in Canada by Giles et al. (1973) provided empirical support for the notion that desire for social approval underlies language convergence. They found that Anglophone Quebecers (AQ) perceived Francophone Quebecers (FQ) more favorably and showed greater reciprocity in convergence to FQs (by using French) when FQs had converged to English than when they had maintained French. The results of this study and several others suggest that mutual language convergence facilitates interpersonal and intergroup interaction where linguistic dissimilarities may otherwise be a barrier to communication (Bourhis, 1979; Giles & Coupland, 1991; Giles et al., 1987). Convergence may reflect motivations to maximize rewards and minimize costs (Homans, 1961; van den Berg, 1986), and is perceived more favorably if it can be attributed to the converger's intentions rather than to external pressures (Simard, Taylor & Giles, 1976). In addition, linguistic convergence has been thought likely to increase interlocutors' intelligibility (Triandis, 1960), predictability (Berger & Bradac, 1982), and interpersonal involvement (LaFrance, 1979).

Using Tajfel and Turner's (1979) Social Identity Theory (SIT), CAT explains phenomena of language maintenance and divergence in terms of speakers' desires for differentiation from their interlocutors (Giles et al., 1977). Intergroup research using SIT as a conceptual framework has shown that discriminatory behavior enhances ingroup identification and does improve the positive social identity of group members (Gagnon & Bourhis, 1996; Perreault & Bourhis, 1998). Furthermore, dominant and high-status group members have been shown to discriminate more than subordinate and low-status group members (Sachdev & Bourhis, 1987, 1991). In multilingual contexts, language provides an important cue for social categorization and is often considered to be the most important and valued dimension of group identity (see Giles & Johnson, 1981; Sachdev & Bourhis, 1990; cf. Le Page & Tabouret-Keller, 1985; Tabouret-Keller, 1997). When language becomes the most salient dimension of group identity, linguistic divergence can be used to assert ingroup identification, contribute to positive social identity and accentuate intergroup boundaries. Bourhis et al. (1979) obtained perhaps the most dramatic demonstration of linguistic divergence for identity assertion in the multilingual context of Belgium, where English was used as the emotionally "neutral" compromise for communication between the Flemish and Francophone speakers. In response to a culturally threatening message voiced by an outgroup Francophone who had switched to French after previously using English, *all* Flemish participants diverged from their Francophone interlocutor by switching into Flemish and vehemently disagreed with the content of his statements. It is noteworthy that the importance of group identity in determining language switching has also been implicated in studies that have obtained divergence under non-threatening conditions of interethnic contact. For instance, Lawson-Sako and Sachdev (1996) reported that requests (in either Arabic or French) made by an African confederate to Arab pedestrians in Tunisia resulted in greater linguistic divergence (e.g., responding in French to a request in Arabic, and vice versa) than requests made by a European or an Arab confederate (cf. Moïse & Bourhis, 1994). Clearly, ingroup–outgroup identification is an important mediator variable in determining levels of CS behavior.

The focus of much previous research has been on convergent and divergent responses to/from actual language behavior. However, a number of studies have shown that people converge or diverge not to the actual language of their interlocutor, but to what they believe to be the listener's language (or speech style; see Giles & Coupland, 1991; Giles et al., 1987; Hewstone & Giles, 1986). For instance, Beebe (1981) conducted a study amongst ethnically Chinese children, bilingual in Chinese–Thai, being interviewed by a standard Thai speaker who was either ethnically Chinese or Thai. Findings of this study showed that participants consistently code-switched into Chinese phonological variants more with the Chinese than with the Thai interviewer, even though both interviewers actually spoke in standard Thai. These findings suggest that the presence of an ingroup interviewer probably "switched on" the ethnic identity of the ingroup interviewee, leading them to converge to the linguistic stereotype of the ingroup. Sachdev and Bourhis (1990) argue that evidence of convergence to ingroup stereotypes is supportive of Self-Categorization Theory (Turner et al., 1987), though space precludes further discussion of this here. It is similarly not possible to include here the situated identity approach of Clément and Noels (1992), which also models the "switching-on/off" of ethnolinguistic identity in bilingual contexts.

Changes in ethnolinguistic identity, and their impact on language behavior, may be related to the general process of "acculturation". Acculturation is the process of bidirectional transformation that takes place within language groups when they come into contact with one another. The Interactive Acculturation Model (Bourhis, in press; Bourhis et al., 1997) proposes that consensual or discrepant acculturation orientations can be adopted by the dominant language group and by subordinated low-vitality minorities. Dominant language group members who adopt the *integration* orientation value the maintenance of the minority languages, while accepting that such minorities adopt important features of the majority culture and language. The *assimilation* orientation corresponds to the concept of absorption, whereby dominant group members expect linguistic minorities to relinquish their language and culture for the sake of adopting the language of the majority society. Dominant majority *segregationists* do not wish linguistic minorities to adopt or transform the dominant culture, though they tolerate that national minorities and immigrants maintain their language and culture, as long as this is done within the minority enclaves or regions. Dominant group *exclusionists* are not only intolerant of minority language maintenance but also believe that such minorities can never be incorporated culturally as rightful members of the dominant society. By virtue of their strong vitality position, dominant language groups tend to have a stronger impact in shaping the acculturation orientations of low-vitality language minorities than the converse. Low-vitality language minorities who adopt the integration orientation seek to maintain key features of their linguistic and cultural identity while adopting the dominant language and culture. Minorities who adopt the assimilation strategy relinquish their own linguistic and cultural identity for the sake of adopting the dominant language and culture. The *separation* orientation is characterized by the desire to maintain all features of the minority identity including its language while rejecting key aspects of the dominant language and culture. *Marginalization* characterizes minority individuals who reject both their own and the dominant language and culture while feeling rejected by both and experiencing anomie. Present within both the dominant and minority language groups, *individualists* reject group ascriptions per se, and prefer to treat others as individual persons rather than as members of group categories. Since space precludes detailed examination of how such orientations affect multilingual communication generally, and CS behavior specifically, a limited illustration is provided next.

Based on some of our arguments thus far, integrationist individuals from low- and high-vitality groups are likely be additive bilinguals and more likely to code-switch to express their pluralist identities than assimilationist low-vitality individuals, whose bilingualism may be transitional and subtractive (Hamers & Blanc, 2000). Whereas assimilationists are expected to code-switch in line with prevailing language norms and emphasize dominant languages in all aspects of multilingual communication, separatists and segregationists may be expected to diverge in *inter*-group yet converge in *intra*-group communication encounters. Segregationists and exclusionists are expected to diverge in encounters with members of linguistic minorities, be least likely to abide by sociolinguistic norms of intercultural politeness, and unlikely to converge to minority language-greeting or leave-taking expressions. Predictions at a further level of specificity such as type of CS (see Cheshire & Gardner-Chloros, 1998) may also be made. For instance, we may predict that integrationist individuals would use intrasentential CS to a greater extent than those with separatist and segregationist orientations, as intrasentential CS is not as dissociative as outright language divergence, but can emphasize that the ingroup minority language is valued by the integrationist. Perhaps the most difficult predictions to make would be for those with individualist and marginalization orientations. Members of marginalized low-vitality minorities would be expected to be alienated from ingroup and outgroup culture and language (Bourhis, in press), and thus likely to employ unpredictable CS strategies. Individualist orientations, though not leading to alienation, are also expected to lead to unpredictable CS, since individuals with such orientations prefer to interact with others as individuals rather than as members of contrasting social categories. Individualists are likely to be linguistic chameleons, ready to code-switch to suit their own motives, agendas, dictates of sociolinguistic norms and/or the linguistic and psychological needs of their interlocutor.

It is important to note that the acculturation orientations described above are not reductionistic personality differences but rather orientations likely to manifest themselves in person-by-situation circumstances. Thus the basic CAT processes governing language switching are likely to prevail, though acculturation orientations are likely to interact with social psychological processes postulated within CAT. Taken together, social psychological factors are likely to be important mediators of the different outcomes of multilingual communication shown in Figure 1. Language behaviors including CS, discourse content and non-verbal communication are manifest within the immediacy of intercultural encounters at the interpersonal level and affect the climate of multilingual communication. Additive–subtractive multilingualism and multiculturalism are developmental outcomes affected by the combined effects of the predictor (and mediator) variables and language behavior over time, within an individual and across linguistic communities. Perhaps the most distal long-term outcomes of the cumulative effects of all the variables discussed thus far are language maintenance and language shift (loss or reversal). This is measured by examining patterns of knowledge and use of first and second languages across decades in official census data and also in terms of the intergenerational transmission of languages (Bourhis, 2001, in press; Fishman, 1991; Sachdev, 1998).

SOME FUTURE PRIORITIES

Reviews of the literature assessing social psychological approaches to multilingual communication show that previous approaches have yielded invaluable insights and provided useful frameworks for understanding CS phenomena (e.g., Bourhis, 1979; Giles & Coupland, 1991; Hamers & Blanc, 2000). In this chapter, previously neglected variables such as state language policies have been included explicitly as macro-level variables, while mediator variables such as acculturation orientations have been conceptually integrated with other social psychological processes in a broader model of multilingual communication. Our discussion has been restricted mainly to a discussion of CS and needs further conceptual refinement in terms of the multifactorial complexities underlying multilingual communication. Empirical elaboration of several aspects of the model is perhaps even more pressing, especially on factors that have received little attention in the past like state language policies and acculturation orientations. Additionally, although findings in many areas of multilingualism have shown that information about group vitality is important to understand a variety of issues (Harwood et al., 1994; Landry & Allard, 1994b, Sachdev & Bourhis, 1993), few studies have actually investigated the relationship between vitality and CS. This sociostructural gap needs to be addressed, especially in terms of designing field studies from different sociostructural contexts that systematically assess the generalizability of findings of the experimental studies in the social psychology of intergroup relations (e.g., Sachdev & Bourhis, 1991). Research in intergroup relations is likely to benefit from this enterprise as multilingual CS represents an ideal naturally occurring intergroup phenomenon, where language choice is inextricably linked to the expressive and symbolic salience of group identity. Note that an intergroup perspective on CS is particularly important as it focuses on the interaction of ingroup *and* outgroup identities (Fishman, 1989; Giles & Coupland, 1991). Such a perspective is appropriately dynamic in that it focuses on how the vitalities, ideologies, acculturation orientations and other characteristics of dominant groups affect, and are affected by, those of subordinate groups (Bourhis, in press).

The determinants of multilingual CS are not only multifactorial but may also be expected to interact dynamically throughout the course of communication, though few studies have addressed this systematically. For instance, Genesee and Bourhis (1982, 1988) found that whereas normative considerations were important in the evaluations of the language choices of clerks in initial speaker turns, interpersonal accommodation processes were more influential in evaluations of clerks' later code choices. Such findings clearly suggest that future studies need to adopt a sequential analysis of multilingual communication (Bourhis, 1985; Lawson-Sako & Sachdev, 1996). Indeed, at a broader level, it is important that the synchronic perspective of most previous research on CS is balanced by future field and laboratory studies that adopt a diachronic perspective, comparing language behavior over short and long periods of time. For instance, in a follow-up of the Moïse and Bourhis (1994) field study with pedestrians conducted in Montreal, Amiot and Bourhis (1999) found that it was only by 1997 that 100% of Anglophone pedestrians made an effort to converge to French with the Francophone who had made her plea for directions in French. As in the 1977–1991 studies, 95% of Francophone pedestrians made an effort to switch to English when providing directions to the Anglophone whose plea for direction had been made in English. In the earlier studies from 1977 to 1991, private French–English language choices seemed imbued with intergroup connotations related to intergroup differentiation and power differentials favoring the elite Anglophone minority relative to the lower-status Francophone majority in Montreal (Bourhis, 1994b). The 1997 results suggest that, after 20 years of implementation, pro-French laws may have had their intended effects of improving the status and use of French by Quebec Anglophones (Bourhis, 2001). That both Anglophones and Francophones overwhelmingly converged to each other's linguistic needs suggests that such intercultural encounters are being emptied of their implicit intergroup symbolism and may become more neutral and functional, at least as regards language choices in private face-to-face encounters between anonymous French and English interlocutors. Studies such as these attest to the conceptual and public policy value of doing long-term diachronic research on code switching and language behavior in multilingual settings. The remainder of this discussion focuses briefly on other issues that have specific conceptual and methodological relevance to the study of CS in the social psychology of language.

Unlike studies in sociolinguistics (see Myers-Scotton, 1997), most social psychological research has operationalized CS as switching *between* rather than *within* speaker turns. Though awaiting wider empirical generalization, the findings of some studies on CS within speaker turns are consistent with the notion that it is a distinct linguistic and autonomous code having its own special social, psychological and cultural significance in multilingual communication (Bentahila, 1983; Gibbons, 1987; Hamers & Blanc, 2000). For instance, Lawson and Sachdev (2000) obtained findings showing that Tunisian Arabic–French CS may be used for intra-ethnic but not inter-ethnic communication in Tunisia. They also argue that the use of CS with ingroup members probably bridges the sociolinguistic Arabic–French duality of Tunisia in a cooperative, non-conflictual manner by *simultaneously* connoting socio-educational status (via French) and solidarity (via Tunisian Arabic; also see Myers-Scotton, 1993). Clearly, future social psychological studies that focus on CS responses as a distinct code will improve our understanding of multilingual communication and the predictive utility of models in multilingual settings.

In spite of the fact that CS is "a quite normal and widespread form of bilingual interaction" (Muysken, 1995, p.177), attitudinal aspects of CS have rarely been addressed in a systematic manner (see Lawson & Sachdev, 2000; Romaine, 1995). A few studies have reported ambiguous attitudes in that code-switchers may be accused both of not being able to speak either language correctly and of "showing off" (Bentahila, 1983, p.111). Among the Punjabi-speaking community in Britain, Romaine (1995) reports a conflict between the prestige of using English words when speaking Punjabi and "condemnation as foreign elements destroying the purity" of the Punjabi language (p. 292; also see Agnihotri, 1998). In other contexts such as Hong Kong, CS is considered to be a compromise between traditional attitudes represented by the local variety (Cantonese) and Westernization represented by the ex-colonizer's language (English; Gibbons, 1987). Indeed, in this context, Gibbons (1987) suggests that CS may have some form of "covert prestige" associated with it (Trudgill, 1974). Given this ambivalence in attitudes to CS, it is not surprising that previous research suggests a discrepancy between evaluation and behavior. However, these studies provide little actual empirical evidence of the conditions under which CS is likely to be positively evaluated and where the discrepancy between attitudes and behavior is likely to be reduced.

In their recent study in Tunisia, Lawson and Sachdev (2000) report that bilinguals may hold relatively negative attitudes about CS but their levels of actual and self-reported use of CS are much greater than would be expected of a negatively evaluated code or variety. They suggest that the discrepancy between attitudes and actual behavior (cf. Bourhis, 1983, 1984a) may be a function of the status-stressing contexts in which language attitude studies were conducted. They argue that previous studies have normally been conducted in contexts where the emphasis is on the formal aspects of language (e.g., in institutionalized language learning and speaking contexts) and where the use of more than one language in a single utterance is generally devalued (especially when interviewers are teachers or university researchers). Future research designed to obtain attitudes in less status-stressing contexts may reveal more positive attitudes to CS and thus reduce the discrepancy between attitudes and behavior.

CONCLUSION

In this chapter we have attempted to counterbalance the monolingual bias that exists in analyses of communication. We have presented an outline of a model of multilingual communication with a special focus on code-switching. Though this model is tentative, it may serve as a useful heuristic in future empirical research. One of our main concerns has been the importance of bridging the gap between macro-societal phenomena and micro-sociolinguistic and social psychological phenomena. However, analyses like those presented in this chapter remind us that the integration of approaches from the social psychology of language, the ethnography of speaking, interactional sociolinguistics, pragmatics and discourse analysis constitutes an important challenge for the future.

REFERENCES

Agnihotri, R. (1998). Mixed codes and their acceptability. In R.K. Agnihotri, A.L. Khanna & I. Sachdev (Eds), *Social psychological perspectives on second language learning* (pp. 215–230). New Delhi: Sage.

Ajzen, I. (1988). *Attitudes, personality and behavior*. Milton Keynes: Open University Press.

Allard, R. & Landry, R. (1986). Subjective ethnolinguistic vitality viewed as a belief system. *Journal of Multilingual and Multicultural Development, 7*, 1–12.

Allard, R. & Landry, R. (1994). Subjective ethnolinguistic vitality: A comparison of two measures. *International Journal of the Sociology of Language, 108*, 117–144.

Amiot, C. & Bourhis, R.Y. (1999). *Ethnicity and French–English communication in Montréal*. Poster presented at the 60th convention of the Canadian Psychological Association, Halifax, NS, Canada.

Beardsley, R.B. & Eastman, C.M. (1971). Markers, pauses, and code-switching in bilingual Tanzanian speech. *General Linguistics, 11*, 17–27.

Beebe, L. (1981). Social and situational factors affecting the strategy of dialect code-switching. *International Journal of the Sociology of Language, 32*, 139–149.

Bell, A. (1984). Language style as audience design. *Language in Society, 13*, 145–204.

Bentahila, A. (1983). *Language attitudes among Arabic–French bilinguals in Morocco*. Clevedon, UK: Multilingual Matters.

Berger, C.R. & Bradac, J.J. (1982). *Language and social knowledge*. London: Edward Arnold.

Blommaert, J. (1992). Codeswitching and the exclusivity of social identities: Some data from Campus Kiswahili. *Journal of Multilingual and Multicultural Development, 13*, 57–70.

Bourhis, R.Y. (1979). Language in ethnic interaction: A social psychological approach. In H. Giles & B. Saint-Jacques (Eds), *Language and ethnic relations* (pp. 117–142). Oxford: Pergamon Press.

Bourhis, R.Y. (1983). Language attitudes and self-reports of French-English usage in Quebec. *Journal of Multilingual and Multicultural Development, 4*, 163–179.

Bourhis, R.Y. (1984a). Cross-cultural communication in Montreal: Two field studies since Bill 101. *International Journal of the Sociology of Language, 46*, 33–47.

Bourhis, R.Y. (Ed.) (1984b). *Conflict and language planning in Quebec*. Clevedon, UK: Multilingual Matters.

Bourhis, R.Y. (1985). The sequential nature of language choice in cross-cultural communication. In R.L. Street Jr & J.N. Cappella (Eds), *Sequence and pattern in communicative behavior* (pp. 120–141). London: Edward Arnold.

Bourhis, R.Y. (1991). Organizational communication and accommodation: Towards some conceptual and empirical links. In H. Giles, J. Coupland & N. Coupland (Eds), *Contexts of accommodation: Developments in applied sociolinguistics* (pp. 270–303). Cambridge, UK: Cambridge University Press.

Bourhis, R.Y. (1994a). Bilingualism and the language of work: The linguistic work-environment survey. *International Journal of the Sociology of Language, 105–106*, 217–266.

Bourhis, R.Y. (1994b). Ethnic and language attitudes in Quebec. In J. Berry & J. Laponce (Eds), *Ethnicity and culture in Canada: The research landscape* (pp. 322–360). Toronto: Toronto University Press.

Bourhis, R.Y. (2001). Reversing language shift in Quebec. In J. Fishman (Ed.), *Reversing language shift: Can threatened languages be saved?* (in press). Oxford: Blackwell.

Bourhis, R.Y. (in press). Acculturation, language maintenance and language loss. In J. Klatter-Folmer & P. Van Avermaet (Eds), *Language maintenance and language loss*. Tilburg, Netherlands: Tilburg University Press.

Bourhis, R.Y. & Giles, H. (1977). The language of intergroup distinctiveness. In H. Giles (Ed.), *Language, ethnicity and intergroup relations* (pp. 119–135). London: Academic Press.

Bourhis, R.Y. & Marshall, D.E. (1999). The United States and Canada. In J.A. Fishman (Ed.), *Handbook of language and ethnic identity* (pp. 244–264). New York: Oxford University Press.

Bourhis, R.Y., Giles, H., Leyens, J.-P. & Tajfel, H. (1979). Psycholinguistic distinctiveness: Language divergence in Belgium. In H. Giles & R. St Clair (Eds), *Language and social psychology* (pp. 158–185). Oxford: Basil Blackwell.

Bourhis, R.Y., Giles, H. & Rosenthal, D. (1981). Notes on the construction of a "Subjective Vitality Questionnaire" for ethnolinguistic groups. *Journal of Multilingual and Multicultural Development*, **2**, 144–155.

Bourhis, R.Y., Moise, L.C., Perrault, S. & Senecal, S. (1997). Towards an interactive acculturation model: A social psychological approach. *International Journal of Psychology*, **32**, 369–386.

Bourhis, R.Y. & Sachdev, I. (1984). Vitality perceptions and language attitudes: Some Canadian data. *Journal of Language and Social Psychology*, **3**, 97–126.

Brown, P. & Fraser, C. (1979). Speech as a marker of situation. In K.R. Scherer & H. Giles (Eds), *Social markers in speech* (pp. 33–62). Cambridge, UK: Cambridge University Press.

Brown, P. & Levinson, S. (1980). Universals in language usage: Politeness phenomena. In E.N. Goody (Ed.), *Questions and politeness: Strategies and social interaction* (pp. 256–289). Cambridge, UK: Cambridge University Press.

Byrne, D. (1969). Attitudes and attraction. *Advances in Experimental Social Psychology*, **4**, 35–89.

Cheshire, J. & Gardner-Chloros, P. (1998). Code-switching and the sociolinguistic gender pattern. *International Journal of the Sociology of Language*, **129**, 5–34.

Chomsky, N. (1965). *Aspects of the theory of syntax*. Cambridge, MA: MIT Press.

Clément, R. & Bourhis, R.Y. (1996). Bilingualism and intergroup communication. *International Journal of Psycholinguistics*, **12**, 171–191.

Clément, R. & Noels, K. (1992). Towards a situated approach to ethnolinguistic identity: The effects of status on individuals and groups. *Journal of Language and Social Psychology*, **11**, 203–232.

Coupland, N. (1984). Accommodation at work: Some phonological data and their implications. *International Journal of the Sociology of Language*, **46**, 49–70.

Dabene, L. & Moore, D. (1995). Bilingual speech of migrant people. In L. Milroy & P. Muysken (Eds), *One speaker, two languages: Cross-disciplinary perspectives on code-switching* (pp. 17–44). Cambridge, UK: Cambridge University Press.

Davidson, D. (1974). Psychology as philosophy. Reprinted in Davidson. D. (1980). *Essays on actions and events* (pp. 229–244). Oxford: Clarendon Press.

Eastman, C.M. (1992). Codeswitching as an urban language-contact phenomenon. *Journal of Multilingual and Multicultural Development*, **13**, 1–17.

Edwards, J. (1994). *Multilingualism*. London: Routledge.

Ervin-Tripp, S.M. (1964). An analysis of the interaction of language, topic and listener. In J.A. Fishman (Ed.), *Readings in the sociology of language* (pp. 192–211). The Hague: Mouton.

Fasold, R. (1984). *The sociolinguistics of society*. Oxford: Blackwell.

Ferguson, C.A. (1959). Diglossia. *Word*, **15**, 325–340.

Fishman, J. (1967). Bilingualism with and without diglossia; diglossia with and without bilingualism. *Journal of Social Issues*, **32**, 29–38.

Fishman, J.A. (1972). Domains and the relationship between micro- and macro-sociolinguistics. In J.J. Gumperz & D. Hymes (Eds), *Directions in sociolinguistics: The ethnography of communication* (pp. 435–453). New York: Holt, Rinehart & Winston.

Fishman, J.A. (1977). Language and ethnicity. In H. Giles (Ed.), *Language, ethnicity and intergroup relations* (pp. 15–57). London: Academic Press.

Fishman, J. (1989). *Language and ethnicity in minority sociolinguistic perspective*. Clevedon, UK: Multilingual Matters.

Fishman, J. (1991). *Reversing language shift*. Clevedon, UK: Multilingual Matters.

Gagnon, A. & Bourhis, R.Y. (1996). Discrimination in the minimal group paradigm: Social identity or self-interest? *Personality and Social Psychology Bulletin*, **22**, 1289–1301.

Gardner-Chloros, P. (1991). *Language selection and switching in Strasbourg*. Oxford: Clarendon Press.

Genesee, F. & Bourhis. R.Y. (1982). The social psychological significance of code-switching in cross-cultural communication. *Journal of Language and Social Psychology*, **1**, 1–28.

Genesee, F. & Bourhis, R.Y. (1988). Evaluative reactions to language choice strategies: The role of sociostructural factors. *Language and Communication*, **8**, 229–250.

Gibbons, J. (1987). *Code-mixing and code choice: A Hong Kong case study*. Clevedon, UK: Multilingual Matters.

Giles, H., Bourhis, R.Y. & Taylor, D. (1977). Towards a theory of language in ethnic group relations. In H. Giles (Ed.), *Language, ethnicity and intergroup relations* (pp. 307–348). London: Academic Press.

Giles, H. & Coupland, N. (1991). *Language: Contexts and consequences*. Milton Keynes: Open University Press.

Giles, H. & Johnson, P. (1981). The role of language in ethnic group relations. In J.C. Turner & H. Giles (Eds), *Intergroup behaviour* (pp. 199–243). Oxford: Blackwell.

Giles, H., Mulac, A., Bradac, J.J. & Johnson, P. (1987). Speech accommodation theory: The first decade and beyond. In M.L. Mclaughlin (Ed.), *Communication yearbook 10* (pp. 13–48). Beverly Hills, CA: Sage.

Giles, H., Taylor, D. & Bourhis, R. (1973). Toward a theory of interpersonal accommodation through speech: Some Canadian data. *Language in Society*, **2**, 177–192.

Grandy, R. (1973). Reference, meaning and belief. *Journal of Philosophy*, **70**, 439–452.

Grice, H.P. (1975). Logic and conversation. In P. Cole & J.L. Morgan (Eds), *Syntax and semantics. Vol. 3: Speech acts* (pp. 41–58). New York: Academic Press.

Grosjean, F. (1982). *Life with two languages: An introduction to bilingualism*. Cambridge, MA: Harvard University Press.

Gumperz, J.J. (1982). *Discourse strategies*. Cambridge, UK: Cambridge University Press.

Gumperz, J.J. & Hymes, D. (Eds) (1972). *Directions in sociolinguistics*. New York: Holt, Rinehart & Winston.

Hamers, J. & Blanc, M.H.A. (1982). Towards a social-psychological model of bilingual development. *Journal of Language and Social Psychology*, **1**, 29–49.

Hamers, J.F. & Blanc, M.H.A. (2000). *Bilinguality and bilingualism*. Cambridge, UK: Cambridge University Press.

Harwood, J., Giles, H. & Bourhis, R.Y. (1994). The genesis of vitality theory: Historical patterns and discoursal dimensions. *International Journal of the Sociology of Language*, **108**, 167–206.

Herman, S. (1961). Explorations in the social psychology of language choice. *Human Relations*, **14**, 149–164.

Hewstone, M. & Giles, H. (1986). Social groups and social stereotypes in intergroup communication: A review and a model of intergroup communication breakdown. In W. Gudykunst (Ed.), *Intergroup communication* (pp. 10–26). London: Edward Arnold.

Homans, G.C. (1961). *Social behavior*. New York: Harcourt, Brace & World.

Hymes, D. (1972). Models of the interaction of language and social life. In J.J. Gumperz & D. Hymes (Eds), *Directions in sociolinguistics* (pp. 35–71). New York: Holt, Rinehart & Winston.

Köppe, R. & Meisel, J.M. (1995). Code-switching in bilingual first language acquisition. In L. Milroy & P. Muysken (Eds), *One speaker, two languages: Cross-disciplinary perspectives on code-switching* (pp. 276–301). Cambridge, UK: Cambridge University Press.

LaFrance, M. (1979). Nonverbal synchrony and rapport: Analysis by the cross-lag panel technique. *Social Psychology Quarterly*, **42**, 66–70.

Landry, R. & Allard, R. (1984). Bilinguisme additif, bilinguisme soustractif et identité ethnolinguistique. *Recherches Sociologiques*, **15**, 337–358.

Landry, R. & Allard, R. (1990). Contact des langues et développement bilingue: Un modèle macroscopique. *Revue Canadienne des Langues Vivantes/Canadian Modern Language Review*, **46**, 527–553.

Landry, R. & Allard, R. (1991). *Subjective ethnolinguistic vitality and subtractive identity in Canada*. Paper presented at the Fortieth International Communication Association Convention, Chicago.

Landry, R. & Allard, R. (1994a). Ethnolinguistic vitality: A viable construct? *International Journal of the Sociology of Language*, **108**, 5–14.

Landry, R. & Allard, R. (1994b) Diglossia, ethnolinguistic vitality and language behavior. *International Journal of the Sociology of Language*, **108**, 15–42.

Landry, R. & Bourhis, R.Y. (1997). Linguistic landscape and ethnolinguistic vitality: An empirical study. *Journal of Language and Social Psychology*, **16**, 23–49.

Lawson-Sako, S. & Sachdev, I. (1996). Ethnolinguistic communication in Tunisian streets. In Y. Suleiman (Ed.), *Language and ethnic identity in the Middle East and North Africa* (pp. 61–79). Richmond, UK: Curzon Press.

Lawson, S. & Sachdev, I. (2000). Codeswitching in Tunisia: Attitudinal and behavioural dimensions, *Journal of Pragmatics*, **32**, 1343–1361.

Le Page, R.B. & Tabouret-Keller, A. (1985). *Acts of identity: Creole-based approaches in language and ethnicity*. Cambridge, UK: Cambridge University Press.

Moïsc, L.C. & Bourhis, R.Y. (1994). Langage et ethnicité: Communication interculturelle à Montréal, 1977–1991. *Canadian Ethnic Studies*, **26**, 86–107.

Milroy, L. (1980) *Language and social networks*. Oxford: Blackwell.

Milroy, L. & Muysken, P. (1995). Introduction: Code-switching and bilingualism research. In L. Milroy & P. Muysken (Eds), *One speaker, two languages: Cross-disciplinary perspectives on code-switching* (pp. 1–14). Cambridge, UK: Cambridge University Press.

Muysken, P. (1995). Code-switching and grammatical theory. In: L. Milroy & P. Muysken (Eds), *One speaker, two languages: Cross-disciplinary perspectives on code-switching* (pp. 177–198). Cambridge, UK: Cambridge University Press.

Myers-Scotton, C. (1993). *Social motivations for codeswitching: Evidence from Africa*. Oxford: Clarendon Press.

Myers-Scotton, C. (1997). Code-switching. In. F. Coulmas (Ed.), *The handbook of sociolinguistics* (pp. 217–237). Oxford: Blackwell.

Pandit, P.B. (1979). Perspectives on sociolinguistics in India. In W.C. McCormack & S.A. Wurm (Eds), *Language and society* (pp. 171–182). The Hague: Mouton.

Perreault, S. & Bourhis, R.Y. (1998). Social identification, interdependence and discrimination. *Group Processes and Intergroup Relations*, **1**, 49–66.

Platt, J. (1977). A model for polyglossia and multilingualism with special reference to Singapore and Malaysia. *Language in Society*, **6**, 361–378.

Platt, J. (1980). The lingua franca of Singapore: An investigation into strategies of inter-ethnic communication. In H. Giles, W.P. Robinson & P.M. Smith (Eds), *Language: Social Psychological Perspectives* (pp. 171–177). Oxford: Pergamon.

Poplack, S. (1980). "Sometimes I'll start a sentence in Spanish y terminol Espanol": Toward a typology of code-switching. *Linguistics*, **18**, 581–618.

Poplack, S. (1997). *Are there any code-switches in the data? Theory vs. fact in language contact*. Paper presented at the International Symposium on Bilingualism, University of Newcastle upon Tyne, UK.

Romaine, S. (1995). *Bilingualism*. Oxford: Blackwell.

Rubin, J. (1962). Bilingualism in Paraguay. *Anthropological Linguistics*, **4**, 52–58.

Sachdev, I. (1998). Language use and attitudes amongst the Fisher River Cree in Manitoba. *Canadian Journal of Native Education*, **22**, 108–119.

Sachdev, I. & Bourhis, R.Y. (1984). Minimal majorities and minorities. *European Journal of Social Psychology*, **14**, 35–52.

Sachdev, I. & Bourhis, R.Y. (1987). Status differentials and intergroup behaviour. *European Journal of Social Psychology*, **17**, 277–293.

Sachdev, I. & Bourhis R.Y. (1990). Language and social identification. In D. Abrams & M. Hogg (Eds.), *Social identity theory: Constructive and critical advances* (pp. 33–51). Hemel Hempstead, UK: Harvester Wheatsheaf.

Sachdev, I. & Bourhis, R.Y. (1991). Power and status differentials in minority and majority group relations. *European Journal of Social Psychology*, **21**, 1–24.

Sachdev, I. & Bourhis, R.Y. (1993). Ethnolinguistic vitality: Some motivational and cognitive considerations. In M. Hogg & D. Abrams (Eds), *Group motivation: Social psychological perspectives* (pp. 33–51). London: Harvester Wheatsheaf.

Sachdev, I., Bourhis R.Y., Phang, S.-W. & D'Eye, J. (1987). Language attitudes and vitality perceptions: Intergenerational effects amongst Chinese Canadian communities. *Journal of Language and Social Psychology*, **6**, 287–307.

Scotton, C.M. (1983). The negotiation of identities in conversation: A theory of markedness and code-choice. *International Journal of the Sociology of Language*, **44**, 115–136.

Sechrest, L., Flores, L. & Arellano, L. (1968). Language and social interaction in a bilingual culture. *Journal of Social Psychology*, **76**, 155–161.

Simard, L., Taylor, D. & Giles, H. (1976). Attribution processes and interpersonal accommodation in a bilingual setting. *Language and Speech*, **19**, 374–387.

Singh, R., Lele, J. & Martohardjono, G. (1988). Communication in a multilingual society: Some missed opportunities. *Language in Society*, **17**, 43–59.

Street, R.L., Jr (1982). Evaluation of noncontent speech accommodation. *Language and Communication*, **2**, 13–31.

Tabouret-Keller, A. (1997). Language and identity. In. F. Coulmas (Ed.), *The handbook of sociolinguistics* (pp. 315–326). Oxford: Blackwell.

Tajfel, H. (Ed.) (1978) *Differentiation between social groups: Studies in the social psychology of intergroup relations*. London: Academic Press.

Tajfel, H. & Turner, J.C. (1979). An integrative theory of intergroup conflict. In W.G. Austin & S. Worchel (Eds), *The social psychology of intergroup relations* (pp. 33–47). Monterey, CA: Brookes/Cole.

Triandis, H.C. (1960). Cognitive similarity and communication in a dyad. *Human Relations*, **13**, 175–183.

Trudgill, P. (1974). *The social differentiation of English in Norwich*. Cambridge, UK: Cambridge University Press.

Turner, J.C., Hogg, M., Oakes, P., Reicher, S. & Wetherell, M. (1987). *Rediscovering the social group: A self-categorization theory*. Oxford: Basil Blackwell.

van den Berg, M.E. (1986). Language planning and language use in Taiwan: Social identity, language accommodation and language choice behavior. *International Journal of the Sociology of Language*, **59**, 97–115.

A Layered Approach to Ethnicity: Language and Communication

**Michael Hecht, Ronald L. Jackson II, Sheryl Lindsley,
Susan Strauss and Karen E. Johnson**
Pennsylvania State University, University Park, USA

The problem of the twentieth century is the problem of the color line – the relation of the darker to the lighter races of men in Asia and Africa, in America and the islands of the sea. (DuBois, 1903, p. 12)

Dr DuBois' words ring prophetic throughout the century and, if we substitute the broader constructs of "ethnicity" and "intergroup relations" (Giles & Coupland, 1991; Gudykunst, 1986), are particularly salient to the late twentieth century, whose history has been marked by the emergence of extreme forms of "ethnic strife." Thus, an exposition of the relationships among ethnicity, language, and culture is timely in our current historical context.

The observant reader will note the movement in the central terms of the previous paragraph. The quote from DuBois starts us off with the term "race." Then, our discussion moves to terms such as "intergroup relations" and "ethnicity." All are terms denoting group-based identity – that is, a sense of personhood associated with a community or collectivity. "Race" itself denotes biological origin, characteristics and commonalities of social group members. As DuBois' quote implies, race is more of a political rather than physiological construction. Many anthropologists reject the term, claiming that it is an inaccurate construction designed to prove the superiority of white Europeans (Gould, 1981). In response, the term "ethnicity" has come into scientific and common

The New Handbook of Language and Social Psychology.
Edited by W. Peter Robinson and Howard Giles.
© 2001 John Wiley & Sons Ltd.

usage in an attempt to avoid biological assumptions but at the same time call attention to and allow us to talk about these group-based identities. This new category, however, has been critiqued as a surrogate for race – a term that politely means biological race or simply the "other", referring to non-whites (Jackson & Garner, 1998). While acknowledging that "ethnicity" as a social term does, at times, allow people to refer to race in politically correct terms, the turn to ethnicity within the intergroup framework (Giles & Coupland, 1991; Gudykunst, 1986) focuses us on group-based identities that derive from a common sense of group membership. Accordingly, we define ethnicity as a group-based identity based on ancestry/heritage. In this sense, we feel that ethnicity provides a useful way of talking about these group-based identities that are so salient to the everyday experiences of people in a multicultural world. We highlight two aspects that are central to this definition: identity and ancestry/heritage.

Our approach to identity is derived from the Communication Theory of Ethnic Identity (Hecht, 1993) and the Layered Perspective (Baldwin & Hecht, 1995; Hecht & Baldwin, 1998). Typically, social psychological approaches have focused on identity as the characteristic of the individual – how the individual sees him/herself. Sometimes seen as analogous to self-concept or an aspect of self, identity is conceptualized as an individual difference variable. Within linguistics and language-based approaches, this analysis is expanded to include interaction which is seen as an expression or enactment of identity.

The Communication Theory of Identity seeks to integrate and expand these analyses by conceptualizing identity as multilayered. Identity is not only the characteristic of a person expressed in the labels used to define it (e.g., racial terms), but it is also a way of expressing self through language and interaction. Moreover, there are other layers or levels of identity. Briefly, the theory defines four such levels:

- personal identity or an individual's conception of self. Often called self-concept, this level captures who a person thinks that he/she is;
- enacted identity or how an identity is expressed in language and communication;
- relational identity or identities in reference to each other;
- communal identity or identities as defined by collectivities.

The approach, then, expands and broadens our view of identity to examine a wider range of frameworks. In applying this approach to ethnicity, we define ethnic identity as images or conceptualizations of personhood (Carbaugh, 1996) or self held by individuals and communities. These codes of personhood are expressed through interaction and exist in relationship to each other as well as in relationships between and among people and groups. We can profitably understand identity on any of these levels. This allows us to juxtapose the social psychological (individual) with the interactive layers; the individual with the communal; the relational with the communal; and so forth. Here, the approach is in keeping with others derived from Social Identity Theory (Tajfel & Turner, 1992) which link

individual identity to social interaction, and particularly the extensions to Ethnolinguistic Identity Theory (Giles & Coupland, 1991) and other language-based
approaches (Sachdev & Bourhis, 1990) which stress sociostructural factors such as
group power and relative population size. However, for the purposes of this chapter we focus on the enacted and communal levels – enacted in our attention to
ethnic identity as expressed in language and communication, communal in our
focus on ancestry and heritage as the basis for defining ethnicity.

With this as our conceptual framework, we now turn to the central task of
explicating the relationships among ethnicity, language, and communication.
These relationships manifest themselves in many layers of social life. No single
chapter could ever hope to adequately portray all of these layers. We start our
description by looking within particular groups and chose African/African
American, Mexican/Mexican American and Asian/Asian American ethnicities
due to their salience within our own cultural milieu, the United States, and due
to the availability of research which demonstrates these relationships. We then
move on to explore the contexts within which ethnicity operates, choosing to
focus on business organizations and educational settings.

AFRICAN AND AFRICAN AMERICAN COMMUNICATION

No description of a cultural or linguistic system is complete without reference to
the ancestral traditions from which it emanated. Both African American language and communication have their origins in the African diaspora with a
heritage that is over 5300 years old. With well over 2000 different languages and
dialects in continental Africa, the interrelationships between the various language families are quite complex. Nonetheless, the linguistic and communicative
functions and structures of African languages are relatively parallel. Noted African linguist and physicist Diop (1987) explains:

> There is also a common linguistic background. The African languages constitute
> one linguistic family, as homogeneous as that of Indo-European tongues. Nothing is
> easier than to set down the rules that allow transfer from a Zulu Language (Bantu)
> to one of those of West Africa (Serer-Wolof, Peul), or even to ancient Egyptian.
> (p. 7)

As with all languages, the speech community serves to create, expand, preserve,
validate, and perpetuate the language. The language is valuable not only because
it facilitates the expression of ideas, but also because it brings those ideas to life
by denoting and connoting the culturally prescribed meanings of human
phenomena. Within Africological communication studies, this natural process
and divine ability is known as *Nommo, Chi or Ka.*

Within African and African American communication studies, language or
verbal communication is not to be understood as separate from non-verbal

communication, but as a location on the preverbal to postverbal continuum. This is consistent with the African philosophical resistance to fragmentation and embrace of interdependency. One African system of thought that explains the universal nature of being is known as ntuology. German Africologist Jahn asserts, "Ntu is Being itself . . . that force in which Being and Beings coalesce . . . Only if one could call a halt to the whole universe, if life suddenly stood still, would NTU be revealed" (Jahn, 1961, p. 99ff.).

There are common links between African philosophies and ways of life, no matter how diverse they may be. The connectedness between all beings and things in the universe is a vivid characteristic of African cultures and a direct commentary upon existence. Human communication is culture-specific; therefore, it is best understood when examining the particularities of any given culture as revealed in their discourses.

African and African American Communication as Framed Reality

If human communication can be defined as the universe of forms, processes and structures that conveys meaning(s) about how humans relate to the world, then certainly African Americans, as all cultural groups, can be said to communicate distinctively, since there are forms, processes and structures that are culturally specific (Wright, 1998; Wright & Hailu, 1988/89). The studies of African and African American communication are multilayered. Hecht (1993) introduces four interpenetrating layers of communicated identities, which he identifies as frames; however, only the enacted and communal frames are discussed here.

Enacted identities are manifested in many forms; however Ebonics is one exemplary form of the enacted identity frame for African Americans. According to Hecht, "we can only experience identity through communication and one may frame identity in terms of its (behavioral and social) enactments" (Hecht, 1993, p. 79; parenthetic remarks added). Ebonics is the name given by Smith (1974) to the structured linguistic system of African Americans, which has evolved from the Niger–Congo African language family (see Figure 1).

Sociolinguist Smitherman (1998) has commented extensively on Ebonics, which she contends is a primarily West African language derivative. She claims:

> Ebonics reaffirms the interrelatedness of language and culture and links Africans in America with Africans around the globe. What gives Black Language its distinctiveness is the nuanced meanings of these English words, the pronunciations, the ways in which the words are combined to form grammatical statements, and the communicative practices of the US Ebonics-speaking community. (Smitherman, 1998, p. 30)

The flexible development and patternization of Ebonics reflect the dynamism of linguistic identities in the African Diaspora. This is reflected in the emerging area of African American communication studies known as Africology or

- **Tendency to avoid consonant clustering**
  Ernie Smith (1974) contends that Ebonics has retained the syllable structure of (e.g. "fifth" and "with" are pronounced "fif" and "wit") *the Niger–Congo language family which does not typically include "homogeneous consonant clusters."*

- **"Aspectual be"** (e.g. "she be actin' like that all the time.")
  Geneva Smithermann (1998) uses this term to refer to the diachronic "be", which refers to the past, present, and future, and also accents the subsequent verb.

- **Zero copula** (e.g. "She so crazy.")
  It has been argued that "zero copula" is a misnomer, because nothing has been deleted or removed if we are speaking of a truly Niger–Congo linguistic form. However, in Standard American English, the sentence above is said to have omitted the verb to be.

- **Double Negative** (e.g. "I ain't got no mo' ")
  The double negative functions so as to reaffirm the first negation rather than cancel it.

- **Unique lexical forms** (e.g. "I' finna {getting ready to} go to the store.")
  Neologisms are quite common in Ebonics, perhaps because African American culture places a high premium on spontaneity, creativity and uniqueness as found when observing the ritual "playing the dozens."

Figure 1 Five distinguishing characteristics of Ebonics

afrocentric communication inquiry, which is based upon Asante's metatheory of afrocentricity. These works are central to African American communication studies because of their shared systematic approach, which accents rhythm, style, improvisation, harmony, wholism, polycentrism, storytelling, lyrical codes, and repetition as modes of enacted African-centered discourse (Asante, 1987, 1990, 1996; Jackson, 2000).

Although the recent attention given to the Ebonics debate on the western coast of the United States appears to discredit Ebonics as a substantial linguistic system, there is plenty of scientific support which validates Ebonics as a language. The structure and function of Ebonics are indicative of the African cultural world-view from which it emanates.

At the communal level, much of the research concerning African American communication has utilized a collectivist typology to derive meaning from what are thought to be culture-specific discursive behaviors. This is not by mistake. Historically, African Americans have defined themselves first as a community and last as individuals. For members of individualistic cultures such as the United States this might seem illogical, since the self is defined as an independent, self-contained, and self-responsible unit. In a competitive, survival-of-the-fittest environment such as the United States, the individual is considered capable of controlling his or her own destiny. Many white Americans construct personal and cultural identities that are consonant with this ideology and ethos.

By contrast, African Americans are relationally driven. Consequently, an individual's success is not nearly as important as the success of the community. One's destiny is dialectically defined in relationship to others – hence the proverb, "I am because we are, and since we are, I am" (Mbiti, 1970, p. 209). As a frame, communal engagement is critical to identity development, and this maturity of perspective and effect on self-definition is exhibited within everyday communicative episodes.

Whether a reality is framed via enacted discourse(s) or a communal understanding of cultural experiences, it is still clear that language is one of the most important tools for gaining access to others' lives. Moreover, the behaviors that accompany language offer further evidence of how language itself shapes the way we respond to the contexts in which we live.

MEXICAN AND MEXICAN AMERICAN LANGUAGE AND COMMUNICATION

The growing number of Mexican Americans in the United States as well as the increasing international interdependencies between the United States and Mexico create an exigency for enhanced understanding of the ways cultural identities are communicated. Since culture is both historically transmitted and dynamically recreated through symbolic interaction processes, we now compare and contrast Mexican and Mexican American language and communication.

Colonial histories in Mexico and the United States influence the dominant languages spoken in both countries: Castilian Spanish in the former, and American English in the latter. However, numerous factors have contributed to linguistic diversity within each nation. Among Mexicans, indigenous groups including the Nahuatl, Mayan, Zapotecs, and Mixtecs continue to speak a variety of native language dialects (Bernard & Pedraza, 1989). Although Mexican history celebrates indigenous heritage, government policy has promoted Spanish at the expense of native languages (Bernard & Pedraza, 1989) along with the economic and political marginalization of indigenous groups (Collier & Quaratiello, 1994). Therefore, maintenance of indigenous languages serves to reinforce ethnic identity; however, the lower social status of native peoples contributes to the negative evaluation of native speech varieties.

Among most Americans, people of Mexican descent also experience pressure for cultural and linguistic autocolonialization (Arteaga, 1994). European American policies including English-first and English-only legislation have pragmatically and symbolically elevated English to a high-status position while simultaneously relegating Spanish – and Spanish speakers – to lower-status positions (Baron, 1990). The continued prevalence of diverse linguistic dialects among people of Mexican descent reflects heterogeneity in terms of ethnic assimilation, bicultural/multicultural identification, and ethnic separatism. Sociolinguistic studies of Mexican American speech have identified varying typologies of Spanish, English, intermediate codes, and unique Chicano linguistic creations (e.g., pocho, calo) as variable systems of linguistic expressions of identity (Penalosa, 1980). These linguistic varieties serve multiple kinds of functions. For example, Padilla (1997) argues that the ways *Spanglish* speakers often defy rules of standard English and/or Spanish serve to make Spanglish a form of counterhegemonic vernacular speech. In addition to its purpose in critiquing European American dominance, various types of Chicano speech function to affirm cultural identification with Mexican and Aztec heritage and build collective strength for political action (Delgado, 1998).

Although Mexican Americans experience pressure to adopt European American cultural and linguistic systems, resistance to assimilation is facilitated through the preservation of economic, social, familial, and political ties between Mexico and the United States. These transnational ties are reinforced by physical and symbolic border crossings. Such transnational interactions may be viewed as interpenetrating varying levels of experience. For example, business transactions between Mexicans and Mexican Americans may simultaneously reflect and reinforce transnational cultural group identity across other levels of relationships: interpersonal, familial, and organizational (Alvarez, 1991). Therefore, a layered approach is used as a descriptive framework for understanding the ways identity is manifested across multiple levels of relationships (Baldwin & Hecht, 1995).

Mexican and Mexican American Communication Frames

While Mexican and Mexican American communication takes many forms, we will focus on the enacted and communal manifestations of these identities. We begin our discussion by looking at how language and communication express these identities and then move on to discuss communal representations.

Our multilayered framework reveals significant commonalities in symbolic expressions of examining Mexican and Mexican American cultural identities. Communication within both groups reveals identities as linked to important indigenous practices (e.g. linguistic creativity in self-expression), intertwined with Mexican cultural norms for communication style (e.g. simpatia) and bounded by traditional cultural values (e.g., familism and collectivism). In addition to communication practices which affirm a common cultural heritage, research reveals the dynamic nature of identity. Change is apparent in the use of both traditional modes of communication (e.g., storytelling, song, theater) and new kinds of communication technologies (e.g., cartoons, television, news media, electronic mail) to challenge societal structures which reinforce inequalities and to affirm new kinds of multifaceted identities. Finally, innovation is apparent in the ways Mexican Americans create new linguistic codes to communicate multifaceted identities in interaction across relationships and contexts.

At the level of discourse, ethnographic case studies have articulated the multifaceted ways ethnic identity is conceptualized and performed in community settings. These studies reveal important commonalities in Mexican American and Mayan use of linguistic creativity through the use of metaphor, allusions, and humor in public and private discourse (e.g., Briggs, 1988). Although both groups emphasize verbal artistry in expression, competency is manifested through adherence to the respective communal rules and norms of each group.

Other scholars have also examined the importance of rules and norms in communicating ethnic identity (e.g., Collier, 1988; Collier, Ribeau & Hecht, 1986). Scholars have found that both Mexicans and Mexican Americans prefer communication emphasizing affiliation and relational solidarity in both intracultural and intercultural interaction (Lindsley, 1999) and use more cooperative and avoidance strategies than European Americans in conflict situations (Gabrielidis et al., 1997; Kagan, Knight & Romero 1982; Madsen, 1971). The importance of Mexican and Mexican American concerns for relationships can be understood in terms of the ways identity is conceptualized as interconnected to others, undergirded by familistic and collectivistic values. These collectivistic values support strategies linked to identity management which emphasize the positive face of self and the relationship in symbolic interaction (Ting-Toomey, 1988).

At the mass-mediated, communal level of communication, research on multi-channeled and multilingual media – television, electronic web, music, newspapers, periodicals – reveals constraints on freedom of expression created by socio-structural power inequalities in both countries, as well as dynamic changes in power, culture and gender roles. Mexican media have historically been constrained by monopolies and government controls (del Campo & Corella, 1986). Recently, journalists have challenged this control, seeking increased freedom of speech through critiques of government officials and policies (e.g., Korzenny, 1987). These challenges have resulted in decreased state control (Korzenny, 1987; Montgomery, 1984). Mexican mass media also have contested traditional ascribed identities. Whereas popular Mexican comics depict women in submissive roles (Hinds & Tatum, 1985), recently female journalists and popular cultural literature portray the emergence of more egalitarian roles for Mexican women (Carty & Carty, 1987). Finally, Mexican media also have critiqued what they see as US cultural imperialism (Butler, 1984) in order to establish a separate and more positive cultural identity.

In the United States, the dominant culture has controlled portrayals of Mexican American identities (Berg, 1990), often reflecting negative stereotypes (Flores, 1994). Partly in reaction to these portrayals and as a reflection of growing Mexican American commercial class identity, US Latino-controlled media have been increasing in quantity and power (Gutierrez & Schement, 1984), with increased numbers of Spanish and dual-language tracks as a result (Rodriguez & Mackey, 1985). This allowed Mexican Americans to control the communal portrayals of their identities. Latino-controlled media in the United States have challenged European American's negative stereotypes of Mexican Americans with multifaceted, self-avowed, positive identities (e.g., Delgado, 1998). Thus, as in Mexico, more positive identities are being portrayed by seizing control of the images at their source.

ASIAN AND ASIAN AMERICAN LANGUAGE AND COMMUNICATION

In an introductory chapter to a recent intercultural communication reader, Porter and Samovar (1997) propose a scale reflecting a minimum to maximum continuum of sociocultural differences among various groups of people. At the apex of this scale appear the groups "Western/Asian"; these two sociocultural groups are framed here as being maximally different from each other in terms of such cultural factors as "physical appearance, religion, philosophy, economic systems, social attitudes, language, heritage, basic conceptualizations of self and the universe" (Porter & Samovar, 1997, p. 22).

Presumably the groups being referred to in the Porter and Samovar scale are Americans and East Asians, given the examples provided by the authors to illustrate such a dichotomy (i.e., a Chinese, running a small, communal farm near Beijing, and an American running a highly modern automated soybean, corn, and dairy farm in Michigan). And while the original contraposition is an oversimple one, since "Westerners" could span the range of people inhabiting all of the Americas and Europe, and "Asians" could also include South East Asians, Indians, and Asian Pacific Islanders, communication styles and identities as they relate to the broad categories of "Westerners" and "Asians" in this very general sense can indeed be considered quite different from each other.

In terms of communicative style, Westerners are generally viewed as verbal, expressive, and direct, deploying such immediacy behaviors as smiling, physical touch, and vocal animation. Messages communicated in this way tend to be both conveyed and interpreted at the surface level, requiring little if any added inference. In sharp contrast, East Asians appear far more reserved, much less verbally and non-verbally expressive, and extremely indirect, relying at times on inferences to be made by the interlocutor to fill in unsaid portions of messages (Barnlund, 1989; Doi, 1971; Lebra, 1976; Varenne, 1977; Yum, 1988). Much of the literature has attributed these broad distinctions to the antipodean dimensions of individualism and collectivism, with Westerners embodying the former, and East Asians the latter (e.g., Gudykunst, 1998; Hui and Triandis, 1986; Ting-Toomey, 1988).

However, while the sociocultural construct of individualism versus collectivism may well assist us in accounting for what appears to be dichotomous cultural values and radically distinct social behaviors, a more detailed analysis of identity is necessary. Such an analysis complexifies the concept of the individual *vis-à-vis* culture, society, and self, and is expected to shed more light on East Asian society in general and make salient certain distinctions and commonalities between Asia and the West. This heretofore may have been blurred by a simultaneous overemphasis on the differences between the two groups, on the one hand, and an oversimplification of the group referred generally to as East Asians, on the other. Further, this complexified perspective of identity will also shed light on the range of identities of Asian Americans in today's society who share communication styles, cultural values, and identity attributes with both Asians and Westerners.

Asian and Asian American Communication Frames

Before we begin our analysis at the level of enacted and communal identities, it is important to establish one crucial distinction. That is, while East Asians in general may somewhat resemble each other physically, and while specific aspects of their more formal communicative styles may indeed be similar, we must bear in mind that East Asians, in and of themselves, do not comprise a single sociocultural group. East Asia, at the most general level, is comprised of three distinct nations: China, Korea, and Japan, each of which possesses its own history, its own art, its own music, its own social structure, its own language, and its own ways of using language. Communally, however, all three nations share the philosophical underpinnings of Confucianism (McNaughton, 1974; Nakane, 1970; Yum, 1997), the basic tenets of which reveal a perspective on human nature "that defines society as profoundly human, and self as quintessentially social" (Bachnik, 1994, p. 21).

And it is precisely this perspective on human nature and society that sets East Asians quite sharply apart from Westerners, since it is the focus on "social order" that is primary rather than the focus on "self." Confucian cultures value harmony, social relationships, family, education, conformity, and self-effacement, and equally devalue conflict, self-promotion, and individual prominence, hence the common communal elements across East Asian cultures which account for the apparent similarities in overall communicative behaviors.

In moving to enactment identity, one may notice a blur, whereby radical distinctions in communication styles between East and West dissipate, especially in instances where ingroup members address and interact with other ingroup members. In such contexts, communication by East Asians can indeed be, and frequently is, expressive, animated, explicit, and even direct (if not even more so than Westerners) (Maynard, 1997; Spees, 1994); voice volumes rise, facial expressions relax, smiles widen, and eyes dance. When conflicts arise, ingroup members will argue; when they are happy, they will laugh, sing, express their joy; and when they are sad, they will express their sadness in culturally appropriate ways. While the mechanisms motivating this social deixis both within the various cultures and contexts of East Asian society and between East Asia and the West may differ, we certainly do find commonalities in communication styles in all contexts investigated thus far – a point which may tend to be neglected in favor of the search for only pronounced differences.

A deeper look into enactment identity, however, reveals some substantial distinctions among the three East Asian societies. As noted, social order in

Confucian contexts is at once a crucial and complex element, based on such hierarchical rankings as age, social status, profession, and even gender. Cross-cutting the social hierarchy concept, and further complexifying social relationships and interaction, is the ingroup/outgroup distinction that scholars seem to globally associate with so-called "collectivistic" societies (Hofstede & Bond, 1984). That is, when Asians speak to, among, and even about each other, they must perforce orient themselves to both the status hierarchy as well as the group membership affiliation (ingroup versus outgroup) of the person to or about whom the talk is designed. And this social deixis (Wetzel, 1994) is explicitly marked through various arrays of linguistic choices available in the three major languages in question (i.e., Chinese, Japanese, and Korean).

With respect to outgroup communication, social distance is marked linguistically (through the use of honorifics, polite verb forms, indirect expressions), paralinguistically (through decreased volume, silences), and kinesically (withholding of expressiveness or impulsivity, deflected eye gaze). Outgroup members typically include elders, teachers, acquaintances, strangers, and especially foreigners. In the case of the latter, then, it is not inconceivable that many of the early Western scholars, when they observed East Asian communication, witnessed and documented outgroup communicative styles, since they themselves represent the outgroup par excellence.

In looking at the level of communal identities, however, exactly who constitutes an outgroup member and who an ingroup member varies from culture to culture. That is, the boundaries can be more or less fluid or more or less rigid, depending on the particular cultural context. In modern Japanese culture, for example, ingroup or uchi relationships prototypically include family members, friends, and co-workers, while soto or outgroup relationships are typically constituted by strangers, elders, and teachers. In an average Japanese family, a child addressing her parent or grandparent generally does not use honorific language, whereas a Korean child from a similar background may well be expected to. Similarly, a receptionist in a Japanese firm would inform a caller (soto or outgroup member) that her boss is out of town by using the humble form of the existential verb "to be" rather than the honorific one, constituting her relationship with the company and her boss as an uchi (ingroup type) and their collective relationship with the caller as a soto or outgroup type. Yet, in a completely parallel Korean context, the receptionist would be both expected and obliged to employ honorific forms in referring to her boss as a manifestation of respect, as well as in addressing the caller, thus indexing a somewhat different system of social deixis than we observed in the Japanese setting.

Thus, it clearly is not sufficient to analyze Eastern versus Western societies using the global construct of collectivism versus individualism, since communication between members of these various societies varies crucially according to a number of contextual and linguistic factors. Moreover, to simply categorize the entirety of Asians into one group and observe them as a collective whole in opposition with the collective whole of Western society represents a serious oversimplification.

Communication Contexts

The layered perspective focuses us on the *contexts* in which language and communication are used. These contexts or settings are interpenetrated into language and communication use – one cannot separate the usage from the sites of use. In this section, we discuss two of the more salient contexts: the business organization and the educational setting.

Ethnicity, Language, and Communication in Business Organizations

In response to our increasingly pluralistic domestic workforce and our interdependent global economy, we recognize the need for enhanced understanding of the influence of cultural diversity in organizations. Indeed, there is a trend in recent decades to recognize diversity as a significant and vital asset to an organization; accordingly, many executives are learning new ways of "managing diversity." One way to create an organizational environment that supports diversity is to align the company's values with those of its employees. While most organizational cultures in the United States tend to reflect the values of European American males, research on value congruence has shown that the degree of cultural fit between employees and their organization impacts a variety of work outcomes, including organizational commitment, job satisfaction, efficiency in organizational socialization, and employee turnover (Cox, 1994).

Thus, adapting the organizational culture to reflect the diverse values of its employees has become a paramount concern for many business executives who are interested in improving organizational productivity and bottom-line profits. In addition, moral, humanitarian, and legal concerns also influence leaders to adopt a "value-in-diversity" management philosophy in their organizations.

The seminal studies of work-related values in organizations conducted by Hofstede (1980, 1991) have provided important insights into some of the ways cultural values are manifested in organizational settings. This section uses two of Hofstede's dimensions – individualism–collectivism and high–low power distance – as a framework for explaining the research on ethnic/cultural communication in organizations.

The first dimension, individualism–collectivism, refers to the extent to which members of a culture are taught that individuals take precedence over ingroups (individualism) or, in contrast, ingroups take precedence over outgroups (collectivism) (Triandis, 1988). In organizations, individualists' communication patterns reflect the value of asserting oneself as a unique person, relatively independent from others. On the other hand, collectivists' communication patterns emphasize the values of respecting interdependencies and maintaining harmony within the group. While European Americans tend to be more individualistic and African Americans, Latin Americans, and Asian Americans more collectivistic in value orientations, it is important to recognize that "cultures have both individualistic and collectivistic tendencies that influence behavior in different spheres of life" (Gudykunst, 1998, p. 111). For example, Latinos tend to emphasize collectivistic values in terms of prioritizing concerns for relationships at work, emphasizing affective interdependencies with co-workers, and avoiding or compromising in a conflict situation (e.g., Collier, 1988; Lindsley, 1999, Triandis et al., 1984), yet still highly value being respected as individuals. African Americans' communication reflects collectivistic values in terms of emphasizing relationships and highly participative interaction (Foeman & Pressley, 1987; Hecht, Collier & Ribeau, 1993). However, communication patterns also demonstrate individualism in terms of emphasizing self-assertion, emotional expressivity, and forthrightness in interaction, as well as confrontation in conflict situations (Kochman, 1981). Asian Americans' traditional collectivistic values may be manifested in communication which reflects predominant concerns for others in work-relationships, modesty in self-presentation, honor for mutual obligations, and emphasis on high-context communication (Farh, Dobbins & Cheng, 1991; Gao, 1998), but scholars have argued for the need to understand ethnic diversity within Asian American populations (e.g., Wu, 1997) and more research is needed to comprehend the way it is manifested in United States' organizational contexts.

The second dimension of high–low power distance refers to the extent to which cultural groups accept the inequality that exists in societies (Hofstede, 1980). A high-power distance orientation, as found among many people of Latino and Asian descent, is manifested through communication patterns which recognize one's position as existing within a hierarchy of role relationships. In contrast, low-power distance cultures, like dominant US culture, tend to emphasize communication which reflects a minimization of status differences. Respect for power status significantly impacts superior–subordinate organizational relationships, with subordinates showing more obedience to authority, and expecting superiors to be directive.

Not surprisingly, these cultural differences in communication patterns result in process problems in heterogeneous ethnic group interaction (Oetzel, 1998; Watson, Kumar & Michaelson, 1993). For example, in group contexts European Americans tend to engage in more verbal assertiveness than Latino Americans and Asian Americans, whose focus is often on actively listening to and supporting others (Watson et al., 1993), which results in European American domination of floor time (Shen, Sanchez & Huang, 1984). While these communication patterns clearly reflect different value orientations for self and task concerns versus other and relational concerns, unequal participation decreases group cohesiveness and increases intercultural misunderstandings. In spite of these process problems, one study found that ethnically heterogeneous groups produced more feasible and effective ideas than ethnically homogeneous groups (McLeod, Lobel & Cox, 1996). Therefore, there is a need for greater understanding of the ways that heterogeneous groups overcome intercultural barriers to achieve high levels of performance outcomes in working toward organizational goals.

Ethnicity, Language, and Communication in Classrooms

Classrooms are typically characterized as places where teachers teach and students learn. Yet, from a communication perspective, classrooms become a specialized arena of human interaction since they represent routinized social events that contain conventionalized roles and routines based on shared norms and expectations. In fact, social routinization is essential in classrooms in order to ensure a sense of security, to guard against loss of face, and to maximize student learning. The classroom lesson is a sort of social genre; when conformed to it goes largely unnoticed; however, when violated it can result in anything from minor disruptions to major misunderstandings. Moreover, what might be termed the classroom ethic is deeply grounded in the historical, economic, and social traditions of the dominant group within any given society. All of this seems quite inconsequential if teachers and students share the same ethnic, cultural, socio-economic, and linguistic backgrounds and set of expectations about schools and schooling. However, if they do not, what goes on in classrooms can have a devastating impact on diverse students' social, linguistic, and academic achievement.

Before children ever enter classrooms, they possess a highly sophisticated accumulation of culturally acquired knowledge through which they interpret and respond to the world around them. Embedded in this knowledge is their use of language, the medium through which they understand and represent their experiences to themselves and others. Such learned ways of communicating enable children to acquire both their native language and the social rules for how to use that language. Moreover, learned ways of communicating reflect the sociocultural values of a particular group and enable children to use language to successfully participate in that group. If children enter classrooms where the norms and expectations for who talks, when, and in what manner differ, their linguistic behavior and communicative styles are likely to be unappreciated and misunderstood (Ogbu, 1982, 1987).

Such discontinuities can function in more pronounced ways, as when, for example, teachers do not know the native language of their students. While the teaching of bilingual children in North America is wrought with social, political, and economic controversy, teachers, administrators, parents, and even politicians do recognize that differences between the language of the home and the language of the school create impediments to the social, linguistic, and academic development of these children. And, while there is often intense and sometimes hostile disagreement over how to best educate bilingual children, both linguistic and cultural discontinuities are a recognized dimension of the schooling of bilingual children at the federal, state, and local levels of the American educational system (Crawford, 1990; Krashen, 1996).

However, cultural discontinuities can and do exist in much less pronounced ways, almost hidden, as when, for example, teachers and students share the same native language but not the same cultural or ethnic background. It is within this educational context that ethnographic descriptions of the social conditions that govern verbal participation at home and in school have uncovered negative consequences on ethnically diverse students. Heath's (1982) research in a rural Appalachian area of the American South East identified subtle differences in the language socialization patterns in three nearby English-speaking communities. Over a five-year period, Heath examined the literacy event of "book-reading" and its relationship to the development of children's narrative skills in Maintown (an Anglo-American middle-class community), Roadville (an Anglo-American working-class community), and Trackton (an African American working-class community). She found that each community used different ways of talking and interacting in this particular literacy event, the most striking of which were found within the working-class African Americans in Trackton. Trackton parents rarely used questions as a mode of interaction with their children; thus Trackton children were not expected to be information givers or conversational partners, and while their linguistic environments were extremely rich, language was typically not directed at them. When questions were asked, Trackton children were expected to relate an entire incident, but rarely to identify or name its individual parts. Consequently, when Trackton children entered classrooms with Anglo-American teachers, where the asking of known-answer and identification questions dominates classroom talk, they were suddenly expected to respond to questions in ways that were unlike what they had experienced at home. This incongruence caused a great deal of frustration for their teachers, who perceived the African American students' lack of appropriate responses as an unwillingness and/or inability to participate in classroom activities.

Similar differences in communicative styles have also been found between Anglo-American and Mexican American children in Anglo schools. Delgado-Gaitan (1987) observed Mexican American students at home and in their Anglo-American elementary schools and found that the communicative styles learned at home were not recognized at school. At home, Mexican American students were expected to work collectively and cooperatively with others. There was an expected amount of turn-taking, negotiation of shared responsibility, and collaboration in the completion of any task. While Mexican American students were sometimes expected to demonstrate their ability to lead, by assuming a more competitive role, more often than not, they were encouraged to cooperate in collaborative ways with others. At school, Mexican American students were found to resist working individually, and instead seemed to want to share their answers with others. This violated their Anglo-American teachers' belief in the importance of individual work and that any sort of "cheating" was unacceptable.

In addition, other sources of discontinuity were found between the authoritarian roles of Mexican American parents and Anglo-American teachers. Mexican American parents expected their children to obey and respect their authority, but at the same time afforded them the freedom to select how such requests would be accomplished, either with adult assistance, through peer collaboration, or on their own. In contrast, Anglo-American teachers tended to control all aspects of an assigned task, allowing the students little, if any, opportunity to negotiate their role in how the task would be completed. Thus, while these Mexican American students were found to possess competencies in collaboration, cooperation, and independent decision making, their communicative styles were not recognized, and in some cases were even discouraged at school. Delgado-Gaitan (1987) describes the need for Anglo-American teachers to recognize Mexican American students' culturally learned communicative styles and create a wider range of learning structures through which Mexican students can maximize their communicative styles and, therefore, fully participate in and learn from classroom events.

For ethnically diverse students to participate successfully in classroom events it is essential to recognize that differences in communicative styles do exist and, more importantly, that these differences are the result of a process of socialization and do not represent cognitive or social deficiencies. In addition, ethnically diverse students must have opportunities to become aware of the implicit rules for participation that are embedded in classroom events. And finally, teachers must reconceptualize their own notions of classroom participation, allow for greater variability in both the academic and social participation structure of classroom events, and begin not only to recognize but also value multiple forms of participatory learning by all students.

CONCLUSION

Issues of language, communication, and ethnicity are inextricably entwined for people whose identities are invested in ethnic communities. By applying a layered perspective to identity, we have attempted to describe the interpenetrations of the various levels or layers of ethnicity within language and communication. Focusing first on three ethnic groups and then on two contexts of use, this chapter presents an overview of a complicated and diverse body of knowledge. Our analyses point to at least four important implications.

First, language, communication, and ethnicities must be tied to ancestral, cultural, and linguistic roots. Ancestry is manifested in the forms and meanings that constitute language and culture. Without a sense of these roots we cannot fully understand the current manifestations of ethnic identity in language and communication. The time-binding function of language and communication, in turn, sheds light on ethnicity and identity. Following the lead of Ethnolinguistic Identity Theory, it would be informative to begin to develop both communal and individual representations of ancestry salience. Under what conditions do these links become more or less conspicuous? How do the political/historical aspects of ancestry play out in other ethnolinguistic traditions?

Second, these are not unitary ethnic cultures. While we can name them as if they were singular (African, African American, Mexican, Mexican American, Asian, and Asian American), they are diverse linguistic and communication communities. However, by examining the links within these heterogeneous ethnic collectivities we can understand some underlying commonalities and connections. Moreover, the "typicality" of a member as group exemplar seems to play an important role in how that person is treated and the impact of contact with outgroup members (Marsiglia & Hecht, 1998). Indeed, even ingroup members may impose restrictions when people stray to far from the center (e.g., African Americans who "talk white"). Thus, there is often a perceptual construction of the center of the group that has important implications. This is complexified because individuals rarely focus on a single identity during interaction. Instead, multiple identities (ethnic, individual, role) may be enacted that have conflicting norms and which present inconsistent patterns of overlap with others (e.g., a white male accountant talking with a black female accountant share occupational identity only). The multiple patterns of the communal representations are further complexified by multi-ethnic backgrounds. Work is needed to clarify how individuals, dyads, and communities deal with these complexities. Do people simplify at a certain point by focusing on a single identity? Are certain identities superordinate in certain situations? How do people linguistically manage these negotiations?

Third, we need to be careful to avoid binary contrasts between two groups. In the United States, communication and language analyses often center on mainstream American English and provide binary contrasts of individual language forms to this normative standard. Not only does this privilege the mainstream but it also distorts the everyday exigencies of life in the multicultural community where communication between, for example, Korean Americans and African Americans or between Mexican Americans and Japanese Americans are just as important as those involving European Americans. While mainstream culture is implicated in African American, Mexican American, and Asian American cultures, we do not need to highlight or centralize mainstream culture in order to understand the interpenetrations of ethnicity, language, and culture. Moreover, by focusing on the juxtapositions of the various layers we complexify our analyses of any particular group as well as comparisons across groups.

Finally, there are important implications for intergroup relations as well as policy. We need to understand how individuals manage their personal identities, their identity enactments, and their relationships in particular social-cultural systems. How do people negotiate across identity similarity and differences? How can groups relate to each other? How can communities structure public spaces to facilitate positive interaction? Further, we need to understand the implications of policies for all the layers. For example, when the city of Oakland in the United States was considering training its teachers in Ebonics, the focus was on privileging a language system and group on the one hand, and on the collective good associated with having a national language on the other. However, less attention was paid to the need for these particular teachers to be able to communicate with their particular students, many of whose primary language system was Ebonics. Thus, a multilayered analysis of all these issues is needed to fully understand our increasingly diverse and complex world and to develop systems at all levels that support healthy and successful functioning of individuals, conversations, relationships, and communities.

REFERENCES

Alvarez, R., Jr (1991). *Familia: Migration and adaptation in Baja and Alta California.* Berkeley, CA: University of California Press.

Arteaga, A. (Ed.) (1994). *An other tongue: Nation and ethnicity in the linguistic borderlands.* Durham, NC: Duke University Press.

Asante, M.K. (1987). *The Afrocentric idea.* Philadelphia, PA: Temple University Press.

Asante, M.K. (1990). *Kemet, Afrocentricity, and knowledge.* Trenton, NJ: Africa World Press.

Asante, M.K. (1996). The principal issues in afrocentric inquiry. In M.K. Asante & A. Abarry (Eds), *African intellectual heritage* (pp. 256–261). Philadelphia, PA: Temple University Press.

Bachnik, J.M. (1994). Uchi/Soto: Challenging our conceptualizations of self, social order, and language. In J.M. Bachnikand & C.J. Quinn (Eds), *Situated meaning: Inside and outside in Japanese self, society, and language* (pp. 3–37). Princeton, NJ: Princeton University Press.

Baldwin, J.R. & Hecht, M.L. (1995). The layered perspective on cultural (in)tolerance(s): The roots of a multidisciplinary approach to (in)tolerance. In R.L. Wiseman (Ed.), *Intercultural communication theory* (pp. 59–91). Thousand Oaks, CA: Sage.

Barnlund, D.C. (1989). *Communicative styles of Japanese and American.* Belmont, CA: Wadsworth.

Baron, D. (1990). *The English-only question.* New Haven, CT: Yale University Press.

Berg, C.R. (1990). Stereotyping in films in general and the Hispanic in particular. *Howard Journal of Communications,* **2**, 286–300.

Bernard, H.R. & Pedraza, J.S. (1989). *Native ethnography: A Mexican Indian describes his culture.* Newbury Park, CA: Sage.

Briggs, C.L. (1988). *Competence in performance: The creativity of tradition in Mexicano verbal art.* Philadelphia, PA: University of Pennsylvania Press.

Butler, F.C. (1984). Roasting Donald Duck: Alternative comics and photonovelas in Latin America. *Journal of Popular Culture,* **18**, 163–183.

Carbaugh, D. (1996). *Situating selves: The communication of social identities in American scenes.* Albany, NY: State University of New York Press.

Carty, J.W., Jr & Carty, M.T. (1987). Notes on Latin American women in the media: A mid-1980s sample of voices and groups. In H.E. Hinds Jr & C.M. Tatum (Eds), *Studies in Latin American popular culture* (pp. 511–534). Tucson, AZ: University of Arizona.

Collier, G.A. & Quaratiello, E.L. (1994). *Basta! Land and the Zapatista rebellion in Chiapas.* Oakland, CA: Institute for Food and Development Policy.

Collier, M.J. (1988). Competent communication in intercultural unequal status advisement contexts. *Howard Journal of Communications,* **1**, 3–22.

Collier, M.J., Ribeau, S.A. & Hecht, M.L. (1986). Intracultural communication rules and outcomes within three domestic cultures. *International Journal of Intercultural Relations,* **10**, 439–457.

Cox, T. (1994). *Cultural diversity in organizations.* San Francisco, CA: Berrett-Koehler.

Crawford, J. (1990). *Bilingual education: History, politics, theory and practice.* Trenton, NJ: Crane.

del Campo, A.M. & Corella, M.A. (1986). Commercial television as an educational and political institution: A case study of its impact on the students of Telesecundaria. In R. Atwood & E.G. McAnany (Eds), *Communication and Latin American society: Trends in critical research.* (pp. 143–164). Madison, WI: University of Wisconsin Press.

Delgado, F. (1998). Chicano ideology revisited: Rap music and the (re) articulation of Chicanismo. *Western Journal of Communication,* **62**, 95–113.

Delgado-Gaitan, C. (1987). Traditions and transitions in the learning process of Mexican children: An ethnographic view. In G. Spindler & L. Spindler (Eds), *Interpretive ethnography of education: At home and abroad* (pp. 333–359). Hillsdale, NJ: Erlbaum.

Diop, C.A. (1987). *Black Africa: The economic and cultural basis for a federated state.* Trenton, NJ: Africa World Press and Lawrence Hill Books.

Doi, T. (1971). *Amae no koozo* [*The anatomy of dependence*]. Tokyo: Koobundoo.

DuBois, W.E.B. (1903). *Souls of black folks.* Chicago, IL: A.C. McClurg.

Farh, J.L., Dobbins, G.H. & Cheng, B. (1991). Cultural relativity in action: A comparison of self-ratings made by Chinese and U.S. workers. *Personnel Psychology,* **44**, 129–147.

Flores, L. (1994). *Shifting visions: Intersections of rhetorical and Chicana feminist theory in the analysis of mass media.* Unpublished dissertation, University of Georgia.

Foeman, A.K. & Pressley, G. (1987). Ethnic culture and corporate-culture: Using Black styles in organizations. *Communications Quarterly,* **35**, 293–307.

Gabrielidis, C., Stephan, W.G., Ybarra, O., Dos Santos Pearson, V.M. & Villareal, L. (1997). Preferred styles of conflict resolution: Mexico and the United States. *Journal of Cross-Cultural Psychology,* **28**, 661–677.

Gao, G. (1998). "Don't take my word for it": Understanding Chinese speaking practices. *International Journal of Intercultural Relations,* **22**, 163–186.

Giles, H. & Coupland, N. (1991). *Language: Contexts and consequences.* Pacific Grove, CA: Brooks/Cole.

Gould, S. (1981). *The mismeasure of man.* New York: Norton.

Gudykunst, W.B. (Ed.) (1986). *Intergroup communication.* London: Edward Arnold.

Gudykunst, W.B. (1998). Individualistic and collectivistic perspectives on communication: An introduction. *International Journal of Intercultural Relations,* **22**, 163–186.

Gutierrez, F.F. & Schement, J.R. (1984). Spanish international network: The flow of television from Mexico to the United States. *Communication Research,* **11**, 241–258.

Heath, S.B. (1982). Questioning at home and at school: A comparison study. In G. Spindler (Ed.), *Doing the ethnography of schooling: Educational anthropology in action* (pp. 103–131). New York: Holt, Rinehart & Winston.

Hecht, M.L. (1993). 2002: A research odyssey toward the development of a communication theory of identity. *Communication Monographs,* **60**, 76–82.

Hecht, M.L. & Baldwin, J.R. (1998). Layers and holograms: A new look at prejudice. In M.L. Hecht (Ed.), *Communicating prejudice* (pp. 57–86), Newbury Park, CA: Sage.

Hecht, M.L., Collier, M.J. & Ribeau, S.A. (1993). *African American communication.* Newbury Park, CA: Sage.

Hinds, H.E., Jr & Tatum, C.M. (Eds) (1985). *Handbook of Latin American popular culture.* Westport, CT: Greenwood Press.

Hofstede, G. (1980). *Culture's consequences: International differences in work-related values.* Beverly Hills, CA: Sage.

Hofstede, G. (1991). *Cultures and organizations: Software of the mind.* London: McGraw-Hill.

Hofstede, G. & Bond, M. (1984). Hofstede's culture dimensions. *Journal of Cross-Cultural Psychology,* **15**, 417–433.

Hui, C.H. & Triandis, H.C. 1986. Individualism–collectivism: A study of cross-cultural research. *Journal of Cross-Cultural Psychology,* **17**, 225–248.

Jackson, R.L. (2000). Africalogical theory building: Positioning the discourse. In A. Gonzalez (Ed.), *International and intercultural communication annual. Vol. 22: Rhetoric in Intercultural Contexts* (pp. 31–41). Newbury Park, CA: Sage.

Jackson, R.L. & Garner, T. (1998). Tracing the evolution of race, ethnicity, and culture in communication studies. *Howard Journal of Communication,* **9**, 47–56.

Jahn, J. (1961). *Muntu: The new African culture.* New York: Grove.

Kagan, S., Knight, G.P. & Romero, S. M. (1982). Culture and the development of conflict resolution style. *Journal of Cross-Cultural Psychology,* **13**, 43–58.

Kochman, T. (1981). *Black and White styles in conflict.* Chicago: University of Chicago Press.

Korzenny, F. (1987). Mass communication in Mexico: Structure, philosophy, and research. In H.E. Hinds Jr & C.M. Tatum (Eds), *Studies in Latin American popular culture* (pp. 197–216). Westport, CT: Greenwood Press.

Krashen, S.D. (1996). *Under attack: The case against bilingual education.* Culver City, CA: Language Education Associates.

Lebra, T.S. (1976). *Japanese patterns of behavior.* Honolulu, HI: University of Hawaii Press.

Lindsley, S.L. (1999). A layered model of problematic communication in U.S.-owned maquiladoras in Mexico. *Communication Monographs,* **66,** 145–167.

Madsen, M.C. (1971). Developmental and cross-cultural differences in the cooperative and competitive behavior of young children. *Journal of Cross-Cultural Psychology,* **2,** 365–371.

Marsiglia, F.F. & Hecht, M.L. (1998). Personal and Interpersonal Interventions. In M.L. Hecht (Ed.), *Communicating prejudice* (pp. 287–301). Thousand Oaks, CA: Sage.

Maynard, S.K. (1997). *Japanese communication: Language and thought in context.* Honolulu, HI: University of Hawaii Press.

Mbiti, J. (1970). *African religions and philosophy.* (2nd edn). London: Heinemann.

McLeod, P.L., Lobel, S.A. & Cox, T.H. (1996). Ethnic diversity and creativity in small groups. *Small Group Research,* **27,** 248–264.

McNaughton, W. (1974). *The Confucian vision.* Ann Arbor, MI: University of Michigan Press.

Montgomery, L.R. (1984). Stress on government and press criticism of governmental leaders: Mexico, 1951–1980. *Gazette,* **34,** 163–174.

Nakane, C. (1970). *Japanese society.* Berkeley, CA: University of California Press.

Oetzel, J.G. (1998). Culturally homogeneous and heterogeneous groups: Explaining communication processes through individualism–collectivism and self-construal. *International Journal of Intercultural Relations,* **22,** 135–161.

Ogbu, J.U. (1982). Cultural discontinuities and schooling. *Anthropology and Education Quarterly,* **13,** 290–307.

Ogbu, J.U. (1987). Variability in minority responses to schooling: Nonimmigrants vs. immigrants. In G. Spindler & L. Spindler (Eds), *Interpretive ethnography of education: At home and abroad* (pp. 255–278). New York: Erlbaum.

Padilla, F.M. (1997). *The struggle of Latino/Latina university students: In search of a liberating education.* New York: Routledge.

Penalosa, F. (1980). *Chicano sociolinguistics: A brief introduction.* Rowley, MA: Newbury House.

Porter, R.E. & Samovar, L.A. (1997). An introduction to intercultural communication. In L.A. Samovar & R.E. Porter (Eds), *Intercultural communication: A reader* (8th edn, pp. 5–26). San Francisco, CA: Wadsworth.

Rodriguez, R.R. & Mackey, J. (1985). Direct broadcast satellites and their potential impact on North American Hispanics. In A. Valdez (Ed.), *Telecommunications and Latinos: An assessment of issues and opportunities* (pp. 29–39). Stanford, CA: Stanford Center for Chicano Research.

Sachdev, I. & Bourhis, R. (1990). Bilinguality and multilinguality. In H. Giles & W.P. Robinson (Eds), *Handbook of language and social psychology* (293–308). Chichester: Wiley.

Shen, W.W., Sanchez, A.M. & Huang, T.D. (1984). Verbal participation in group therapy: A comparative study on New Mexico ethnic groups. *Hispanic Journal of Behavioral Sciences,* **6,** 277–284.

Smith, E. (1974). The evolution and continuing presence of the African oral tradition in Black America. Unpublished doctoral dissertation, University of California, Irvine.

Smithermann, G. (1998). Black English/Ebonics: What it be like ? In T. Perry & L. Delpit (Eds), *The real Ebonics debate.* Boston, MA: Beacon.

Spees, H. (1994). A cross-cultural study of indirectness. *Issues in Applied Linguistics,* **5,** 231–253.

Tajfel, H. & Turner, C. (1992). The social identity theory of intergroup behavior. In *Readings on communicating with strangers* (pp. 112–118). New York: McGraw-Hill.

Ting-Toomey, S. (1988). Intercultural conflict styles: A face-negotiation theory. In Y.Y. Kim & W.B. Gudykunst (Eds), *Theories in intercultural communication* (pp. 213–238). Newbury Park, CA: Sage.

Triandis, H.C. (1988). Collectivism vs individualism: A reconceptualization of a basic concept in cross-cultural psychology. In G. Verma & C. Bagely (Eds), *Cross-cultural studies of personality, attitudes and cognition* (pp. 60–95). London: Macmillan.

Triandis, H.C., Marin, G., Hui, C.H., Lisansky, J. & Ottati, V. (1984). Role perceptions of Hispanic young adults. *Journal of Cross-Cultural Psychology*, **15**, 297–321.

Varenne, H. (1977). *Americans together: Structured diversity in a Midwestern town*. New York: Teacher College Press.

Watson, W.E., Kumar, K. & Michaelson, L.K. (1993). Cultural diversity's impact on interaction process and performance: Comparing homogeneous and diverse task groups. *Academy of Management Journal*, **36**, 590–602.

Wetzel, P. (1994). A movable self: The linguistic indexing of uchi and soto. In J.M. Bachnik & C.J. Quinn (Eds), *Situated meaning: Inside and outside in Japanese self, society, and language* (pp. 73–88). Princeton, NJ: Princeton University Press.

Wright, R. (1998). Sociolinguistic and ideological dynamics of the ebonics controversy. *Journal of Negro Education*, **67**, 5–15.

Wright, R. & Hailu, H. (1988/89). Conceptualizing language as ideology. *Howard Journal of Communication*, **1**, 174–186.

Wu, D.T.L. (1997). *Asian Pacific Americans in the workplace*. Walnut Creek, CA: Altamira Press.

Yum, J.O. (1997). The impact of Confucianism on interpersonal relationships and communication patterns in East Asia. In L.A. Samovar & R.E. Porter (Eds), *Intercultural communication: A reader* (8th edn, pp. 78–88). San Francisco: Wadsworth.

Yum, J.O. (1988). The impact of Confucianism on interpersonal relationships and communication patterns in East Asia. *Communication Monographs*, **55**, 374–388.

Towards a Social Theory of Gender

Linda Coates and Trudy Johnson
University of Victoria, British Columbia, Canada

INTRODUCTION

Researchers who focus on language and social psychology have the unique opportunity to make advances in gender research. The study of language and gender offers the possibility of moving beyond the mechanical cataloguing of gender differences to the study of social interaction. We begin this chapter by discussing the need for social research, summarizing the gender difference research, and criticizing the "mechanical features" approach to gender and language studies. In the rest of the chapter, we articulate guidelines for conducting research that holds language as primary. That is, rather than viewing language as a reflection of underlying psychological processes, such as attitudes, these guidelines emphasize the reality-making, social-action-performing functions and powers of language. This chapter and the proposed methods of analysis focus on meaning.

THE NEED FOR SOCIAL RESEARCH

In the mid-1980s, another episode occurred in the ongoing crisis in social psychology (see Tajfel, 1972, for an earlier discussion of this crisis). Critics pointed to the individualistic perspective espoused by mainstream social psychologists as impeding truly social research (Danziger, 1990, 1992; Senn, 1989; Solano, 1989; Tolman, 1995). The research done within this individualistic perspective

The New Handbook of Language and Social Psychology.
Edited by W. Peter Robinson and Howard Giles.
© 2001 John Wiley & Sons Ltd.

"isolated the individual from the social context of their existence" (Danziger, 1990, p. 187), and treated social interaction as linear person–object relations or stimulus–response sets (Tolman, 1995). Rigid adherence by many social psychologists to constraining methodologies exacerbated the problem (Jackson, 1988; Potter & Wetherell, 1995). In fact, Danziger (1990) coined the phrase "methodolatry" to refer to the practice of worshipping methods to such a degree that methods determine what is studied.

A consequence of the individualistic perspective and constraining methods adopted by mainstream researchers is that many either neglected language and social interaction as a possible focus of study or regarded such processes as "too messy" to study. The crisis once again brought the need for truly social examinations of the world to the forefront (Danziger, 1990, 1992; Folger, 1987; Schneider, 1991; Senn, 1989; Solano, 1989), and many psychologists called for studies of the previously neglected area of language and social interaction (Clark, 1985; Edwards & Potter, 1992; Potter & Wetherell, 1987; Schneider, 1991; Solano, 1989). In short, researchers have argued, as we do here, that language is "a primary mode of social activity" (Edwards & Potter, 1992, p. 12), and studies of language use will yield a better understanding of our social world.

As a sub-area of social psychology, gender research also suffered from these problems, and a number of reviewers have critically assessed this literature (Ashmore & Del Boca, 1986; Deaux, 1984, 1985; DeFrancisco, 1997; James & Clarke, 1993; James & Drakich, 1993; Kahn & Gaeddart, 1985; Kramarae, 1990; Tannen, 1994; West, Lazar & Kramarae, 1997; West & Zimmerman, 1985). Given the number of excellent reviews available, we will not undertake yet another extensive review of this research literature. Instead, the focus of this chapter will be to discuss the implications for research methodology through the examination of past trends and selected current research. That is, we will attempt to articulate guidelines for conducting truly social gender research. For, as Danziger (1992) recognized, the choice of method is an important one; it "limits the kind of reality that can be represented in the products of scientific investigation" (p. 310). Past gender research constructed severely limited views of men and women. In the next section we will discuss one of the more prevalent approaches to gender and language research: the taxonomy of differences.

GENDER DIFFERENCES: MYTH AND REALITY

Much of the literature in the area of gender and language has focused on developing a catalogue of gender differences, whether real, perceived, or assumed. In general, research looking for gender differences has yielded inconsistent, often conflicting results (Ashmore, Del Boca & Wohlers, 1986; James & Clarke, 1993; James & Drakich, 1993; Tavris, 1992; Wodak, 1997). However, as Tavris (1992) argued:

> Many people persist in believing that men and women differ in important qualities, in spite of innumerable studies that have failed to pin these qualities down and keep them there. (p. 287)

The problem inherent in investigating gender differences in a framework of opposites is that "all polarities of thinking, like all dichotomies of groups, are by nature artificial, misleading, and oversimplified" (Tavris, 1992, p. 288). Many researchers who have studied gender differences have implicitly or explicitly assumed the existence of differences and, having constructed gender differences, attributed oppositional meanings to the behavior of men and the behavior of women. As Tannen (1994) found, these researchers "assume that whatever women do results from or creates their powerlessness and whatever men do results from or creates their dominance" (p. 31). In essence, this research describes all men as if they were the same, all women as if they were the same, and men and women as opposites.

The literature as a whole, however, does not support this notion of men and women as opposites. Even biologically, men and women are anatomically more similar than different. Represented statistically, even when gender differences in language are found, substantially overlapping distributions are far more common than two non-overlapping distributions (Tavris, 1992) because men and women are more similar than they are different. As Hansen and O'Leary (1985, p. 67) concluded:

> Empirical evidence published during the last decade clearly suggests that the behavioral similarities between women and men are substantially greater than the differences. (p. 67)

Therefore, even when the research finds a significant difference on the basis of gender, the finding may not have any predictive value for how an individual (male or female) would use language or behave in social interaction. It is unlikely that one set of traits or one way of using language will fit all men or all women. We must recognize intra-gender differences and inter-gender similarities.

In addition, the tradition in psychology of publishing only statistically significant results may be creating the impression of more gender differences than have actually been found. If gender similarity is operationalized as non-significance, such findings will be systematically under-reported. Wallston and Grady (1985) suggested that all of the gender differences literature may suffer from the tradition of publishing only significant differences.

Unfortunately, the consequences of the gender differences approach go beyond attempts to merely create a taxonomy of differences between men and women. The research frequently casts any differences as a natural consequence of biology (a position which feminists have argued against) or a natural consequence of socialization. The reality that only some men or some women act in these ways in certain situations gets lost. Moreover, what we construct as the cause of gender differences will have direct implications for the possibility of social action with the goal of promoting change. That is, if we accept biological explanations for inequities, then change is virtually impossible; and indeed, many would question the desire to change "natural" conditions of life. If we accept theories that suggest socialization results in inequity, then more possibilities for social action exist, but socialization itself may seem too vast a process for us to exert an influence upon. In contrast, if we reject theories that cast inequities as natural consequence and instead adopt theories that examine gender inequities as socially constructed in, and maintained through, language and social interaction, then we create immediate possibilities for social action and change (Jenkins, 1990).

THE MECHANICAL FEATURES APPROACH

Social psychologists have tended to study de-contextualized, often mechanical features of talk.[1] The literature on interruptions serves as a good example of a mechanical approach to the study of language and interaction. Many of these studies have defined interruption as overlapping speech (see James & Clarke, 1993, and Tannen, 1994, for reviews of this literature). Having done so, the analysts merely count the frequency of overlapping speech in the interaction. While this approach is appealing in terms of the ease of analysis, it fails to consider the *meaning* of the overlapping speech to the interactants. That is, in order to determine whether overlapping speech is an interruption or something else entirely, one must closely examine how it is functioning within the interaction. Consider the following interaction: One person was describing an incident where he and a friend were fishing in the flood zone of a hydro-electric dam when the warning horn blew to indicate that the area was going to be flooded. The narrator (N) had previously indicated to the listener (L) that there were two ways to get out of the flood zone: to go up the road or climb up the cliff. After saying that the horn had gone off, the narrator said:

N: I, like an idiot, decide to climb up the cliff instead of . . .
L: going up the road.
N: taking the easy way out and going up the road.

As the narrator said "taking the easy way out", the listener said "going up the road". Yet, his overlapping speech does not function as an interruption. The interactants were actually *co-telling* the narrative together (Bavelas, Coates & Johnson, 2000). The listener had anticipated the direction of the story, and his utterance ("going up the road") not only indicated he was following closely but also advanced the telling of the narrative. Without hesitation the narrator smoothly incorporated the listener's contribution into the continuing narrative. Studies that mechanically count the frequency of overlapping speech would have counted this splendid act of co-telling as an interruption.

---

[1] A relatively early system of analysing domineering behavior by Rogers and Millar (1977) serves as an example of a non-mechanistic, function-oriented approach.

Given all of these problems with the language research on gender, it is clear that "it is time to break away from the old, literal emphasis on counting differences" (Tavris, 1992, p. 288) and time to build different methods.

IMPLICATIONS FOR GENDER AND LANGUAGE RESEARCH

Meaning as Central

But how do we move beyond the cataloguing of individualized, de-contextualized mechanical features or differences? Developing and using alternative methods will be important in advancing the area of gender and language (DeFrancisco, 1997; Wodak, 1997). Future research in this area must abandon mechanical and atomistic methodology; in its place, we propose that analysts use methods that focus on meaning. Mechanical, physical features are not central to our actions; meaning is central to our actions (Bruner, 1990). Fortunately, those of us who study language and interaction are in a position to study meaning as a central element to our methods of analysis. Meaning is not private and secret, it is public and shared (Bruner, 1990). That is, meaning is socially negotiated and achieved in social interaction and in language use and therefore can be observed directly; through observation, it can be understood. As researchers we must uncover this meaning without forcing a priori expert interpretations onto the interactions, because "it is always necessary to ask what people are *doing* or *trying* to do" (Bruner, 1990, p. 118) within context.

A direct implication of this shift is that the unit of analysis would cease to be the individual. Rather than viewing gender as property inherent to the individual, gender would be viewed as a product of interaction. The minimum unit of analysis would then be the dyad (e.g., female–female, male–female, male–male). Language research could then move away from treating gender as an isolated variable reflected in mechanical features (such as interruptions) to examining the process of constructing gender or the process of constructing inequity in and through discourse.

Context

Research such as we are proposing will necessarily involve the microanalysis of language and communicative behaviour, studied in context and treated as acts of meaning. As many have noted, "language and communication are integrally tied to the context in which they occur" (Gallois & Pittam, 1995, p. 10). Studies that have examined both gender differences and context demonstrate the importance of context. In their review, West and Zimmerman (1985) concluded that gender differences in language use can be more accurately described as gender-preferential than gender-exclusive. That is, males and females are equally capable of using various linguistic strategies and features, but certain strategies or features may be more commonly used by one gender in certain situations. Similarly, in their study of communication styles, Fitzpatrick, Mulac and Dindia (1995) predicted "the communication differences between men and women [would] be subtle, few in number, and gender-preferential rather than sex exclusive" (p. 19). They found that shifts in communication styles were better predicted by the context of the interaction rather than gender.

In another example, Anderson and Leaper (1998) studied emotion talk between same- and mixed-gender dyads.[2] Unlike questionnaire studies, which tend to find gender differences in emotion talk, their study of actual behaviour revealed no significant difference between same and mixed dyads. Instead, what best predicted the occurrence of emotion talk was the topic of conversation. When subjects were asked to talk about a emotionally laden topic, more emotion talk occurred, regardless of gender.

Both of these studies support our position that the context (including task, relationship between interactants, topic, etc.) must be considered in understanding social behavior. That is, if we are to understand and accurately represent the experience and behavior of males and females, we must consider the interactional setting or context that subjects are acting within. While this kind of research is labour intensive, it is far more likely to yield results that will contribute to understanding our social world. In their review, West and Zimmerman (1985) reached the conclusion that

> where researchers have turned their attentions from gender as an isolated variable in sociolinguistic surveys to speech as a kind of action between humans of varying situational identities, we have developed a much richer understanding of the ways in which discourse helps construct the fabric of social life. (p. 119)

Addressing Inequalities

The inclusion of context also permits language and gender researchers to examine the broader social relations that may be of interest, such as inequalities. Many researchers investigate gender because they see unjust differences in our world that have not been ameliorated or even addressed. We argue that language is critical in creating and maintaining these inequities. Many problems with current language use have been documented – for example, the use of "man" instead of the more accurate term, "human" (Lakoff, 1975; Ng, 1990; Penelope, 1990) and the pejorative meanings that are attached to terms for women, such as the word "mistress" (Penelope, 1990; Schulz, 1975; West et al., 1997). Language is also critical in marginalizing violence and discrimination against women. For example,

---

[2] This study is notable for avoiding the common assumption in psychology that emotion talk and experience of emotion are irrevocably linked (i.e., that one cannot speak of emotion without experiencing emotion). Instead, the authors take a communication-based approach which makes room for the fact that emotion talk serves a communicative function which may or may not co-occur with the experience of the corresponding emotion.

governments marginalize discrimination and violence against women by describing them as "women's issues", which are distinct from "human rights issues". While human rights violations receive international attention,

> these rarely include violations of women's rights such as denial of suffrage, wife-beating, genital mutilation, forced prostitution, or sweatshops that run on underpaid female labor. Somehow, these are "women's issues," not "human rights issues". (Tavris, 1992, p. 17)

One practice that promotes inequity is constructing women as "other". The discursive construction of women as other is accomplished by holding male behavior (which, of course, is also socially constructed) as the norm to which women must be compared. In research, this bias frequently takes the form of describing women as different and then interpreting any difference, no matter how small or trivial, as evidence of women's inferiority or their need to be more like men. This discursive practice is widespread:

> The perception of female otherness occurs in every field, as we are learning from critical observers in science, law, medicine, history, economics, social science, literature, and art. (Tavris, 1992, p. 17)

The consequences of these descriptions are serious: women have been encouraged to feel guilty and to regard themselves as deficient and inadequate. Normal female bodily processes (e.g., menstruation, pregnancy, menopause) have been reconstructed as sicknesses or syndromes, and their normal experiences of living have become diseases (Tavris, 1992).

Some people have reacted against the construction of women as inferior by constructing them as superior (Tavris, 1992). This bias is evident in the areas of emotion and love, where women are cast as superior in everything from talking about emotions to maintaining loving relationships. Unfortunately, this approach still discursively constructs men and women as opposites and in fact still compares women to a male norm.

Investigating the creation of meaning in language and social interaction will allow us to identify current discursive practices that create, promote, or maintain inequality. For example, researchers will be able to examine how current theories of gender socially construct males and females. Do current theories construct them as opposites? And, if so, how is this accomplished? Language researchers need to dispel gender myths by deconstructing them and showing the processes by which language can be used to create or maintain inequity.

Power and Status

One developing area of inquiry into inequities is the relationship between gender and power. A focus on language and its reality-making, social-action-performing functions is particularly well suited to the study of power. Where power differences exist, language is likely to be "an important instrument of inequality" (Fowler, 1985, p. 62). These differences are not natural; they are socially constructed, and therefore the construction will be observable in language and social interaction. Rather than simply assuming that men are powerful and women are powerless, research needs to investigate the interrelation between gender and power. As Kahn and Gaeddert (1985) found in their review:

> A swelling list of authors have pointed out that what appear to be sex and gender differences in social behavior may be better described as differences due to status and power. (p. 140)

For example, in our workshops on sexual assault, participants often ask questions that presuppose that women in positions of power will not behave similarly to men. For example, it is frequently assumed that female judges will deliver qualitatively different judgments from male judges, yet we have not seen any evidence of this. Similarly, the media becomes fascinated by women who commit sexual assaults, concentrating on their gender and not the social status of these offenders (i.e., that they tend to be in positions of power).

Thus, while gender and power may be correlated in that men still frequently occupy more powerful positions in many societies, maleness and power are not isomorphic. Further investigation in this area could conduct studies that examine power and gender as distinct independent variables and determine their separate effects on language and interaction.

Finally, we can investigate the exercise of power in areas previously thought to be unrelated or only marginally related to power. For example, because sexual assault is usually committed by men against women, these crimes have been cast as sexual rather than as violent. Men are seen as having voracious sexual drives that compel them to seek release on their reproductive counterparts (Coates & Wade, 1994). This position lends itself to the view that men must strive to control their urges, and women must strive not to arouse them. We, however, take a completely different position in our research programme on sexualized violence[3] (Bavelas & Coates, 2001; Coates, 1997; Coates, Bavelas & Gibson, 1994; Coates & Wade, 1994). We consider these assaults to be crimes of power and propose that the correlation between gender and sexual assault exists because gender is correlated with power. Therefore, we are not interested in the sociobiological make-up of men, but we are interested in the language that supports and maintains these crimes. In our research, we found that the language used in sexual assault trial judgements tended to trivialize sexualized assaults (e.g., Coates et al., 1994), arguably precluding justice for the victim. We examined the characterization of sexual assault, of perpetrators of sexual assault, and of victims of sexual assault, and found that these assaults were most frequently described as if they were erotic, romantic, or affectionate acts that were distinct from violence.

---

[3] We use the term sexualized to emphasize that these assaults are unilateral violent acts and not mutual sexual acts. When referring to a legal charge, we will use the legal term: sexual assault.

These descriptions worked to minimize the seriousness of the assaults by casting them as mutual acts, insufficiently resisted by the victims, and beyond the offenders' control. From this research, we not only identified problematic practices but have also suggested concrete ways to promote equity, justice, and human rights in this area.

Investigating Consequences

Examinations of language also permit researchers to move beyond the immediate research situation to the examination of the real social consequences of discursive constructions, as the following two studies illustrate. Coates (1996, 1997) investigated the consequences of language in sexual assault trial judgements that frequently constructed the perpetrators of these assaults as not responsible for their actions and attributed the assault to a non-violent motivation. These discursive attributions were significantly associated with the offender receiving lower sentences.

Similarly, Henley, Miller and Beazley (1995) found that the media used more phrases constructed in passive voice to describe violence against women than other types of violence. Then, experimentally, they found that passive voice affected the interpretation of these reports in that subjects were more accepting of violence described in passive voice. Male subjects in particular attributed less harm to the victim and less responsibility to the perpetrator. Thus, these two studies taken together demonstrate the important social consequences from using explanations which obscure agency and responsibility. As the authors pointed out, the explanations work to justify the continuation of violence against women.

Finally, a focus on language also permits researchers to examine the consequences of current theories. Theories that construct men and women as opposites (e.g., the "two cultures" theory of language) can lead to excusing male violence against females. For example, several researchers (Shotland & Craig, 1988; Lipton, McDonel & McFall, 1987) have suggested that males cannot understand female refusals of sexual advances, particularly non-verbal refusals. Rape, according to these theories, is simply a matter of miscommunication – not, as Coates (Coates, 1996, 1997; Coates et al., 1994) argues, a unilateral decision to be violent.

Diverse Methods for Diverse Purposes

Given the diverse goals for conducting research, a variety of methods and systems of analysis will be needed to adequately study topics concerned with gender and language. The system of analysis developed or applied should be determined by the purpose of the research (Bavelas, 1987; Coates, 1999). Moreover, researchers may want to use a combination of experimental and non-experimental, qualitative and quantitative analyses to fully investigate the phenomenon of interest. For example, Coates' (1996, 1997) study of causal attributions and sentencing patterns in sexual assault trial judgements used a combination of qualitative and quantitative analyses. The qualitative analysis identified how language functioned to excuse perpetrators' violent actions (e.g., creating them as non-violent or out of the perpetrator's control), and the quantitative analysis demonstrated one consequence of using such explanations (i.e., lower sentence).

Similarly, the research by Henley et al. (1995) combined content analysis and experimental methods in their research. Content analysis of newspaper articles made comparisons across topics and time. Another segment of their study involved attribution-style research that examined the effects on individual perceptions of sexualized violence towards women. In all of this research, limiting the analysis to just one method of analysis (e.g., only experimental or only non-experimental; only qualitative or only quantitative) would not have provided such a broad analysis of the phenomena.

As Bavelas pointed out:

> the differences between various methods of analysis are socially constructed, and to the extent that we insist on maintaining them, we will severely limit the number of approaches we can invent to explore our common interests. (Bavelas, 1995, pp. 50–51)

Such limitations place constraints not only on the methods used to investigate phenomena of interest but also determine what can be studied (Danziger, 1990). For some researchers, if naturally occurring language processes do not fit "standard" methods, they cannot be studied. We must permit diverse methods to study diverse phenomena.

CONCLUSION

We must step outside the framework which creates, permits, reproduces, and supports many of the discriminatory and inequitable conclusions and practices that we have identified. As long as research continues to be limited to the paradigm of establishing which gender is superior and which is inferior, research will not be able to contribute to positive changes in the real world. Constructing a dichotomy between genders oversimplifies human interaction and merely supports the notion of opposition, which in turn supports the continuing existence of inequitable conditions. Instead of constructing men and women as opposites, we must examine gender as socially constructed in, and maintained through, language and social interaction.

We have suggested that the methods used must examine the meaning of language and social behaviours in the context of the situation within which they occur. This research may involve the examination of text or speech, verbal and non-verbal behavior, using qualitative or quantitative analysis, or experimental or non-experimental methods. Critical linguistics, discourse analysis, conversational analysis, or other meaning-based approaches (e.g., West et al., 1997; Wodak, 1997) may be used to analyse the phenomena of interest. Through such examinations, we may demonstrate the consequences of current theories and practices and, in doing so, address inequities and power differences, and recommend action to promote social change.

REFERENCES

Anderson, K.J. & Leaper, C. (1998). Emotion talk between same and mixed gender friends: Form and function. *Journal of Language and Social Psychology*, **17**, 419–445.

Ashmore, R.D. & Del Boca, F.K. (1986). Toward a social psychology of female–male relations. In R.D. Ashmore & F.K. Del Boca (Eds), *The social psychology of female–male relations: A critical analysis of central concepts* (pp. 1–17). Orlando, FL: Academic Press.

Ashmore, R.D., Del Boca, F.K. & Wohlers, A.J. (1986). Gender stereotypes. In R.D. Ashmore & F.K. Del Boca (Eds), *The social psychology of female–male relations: A critical analysis of central concepts* (pp. 69–119). Orlando, FL: Academic Press.

Bavelas, J.B. (1987). Permitting creativity in science. In D.N. Jackson & P. Rushton (Eds), *Scientific excellence* (pp. 307–327). London: Sage.

Bavelas, J.B. & Coates, L. (2001). Is it sex or assault? Erotic vs. violent language in sexual assault trial judgments. *Journal of Social Distress and Homelessness*, **10**(in press).

Bavelas, J.B., Coates, L. & Johnson, T. (2000). Listeners as co-narrators. *Journal of Personality and Social Psychology*, **79**, 941–952.

Bruner, J. (1990). *Acts of meaning*. Cambridge, MA: Harvard University Press.

Clark, H.H. (1985). Language use and language users. In G. Lindsey & E. Aronson (Eds), *Handbook of social psychology* (3rd edn, Vol. 2, pp. 179–231). New York: Random House.

Coates, L. (1996). Discourse analysis of sexual assault trial judgements: Causal attributions and sentencing. Unpublished doctoral dissertation, University of Victoria.

Coates, L. (1997). Causal attributions in sexual assault trial judgements. *Journal of Language and Social Psychology*, **16**, 278–296.

Coates, L. (1999). *Qualitative methods: A guide for developing reliable systems of analysis*. Manuscript submitted for publication.

Coates, L. & Wade, A. (1994). *The use of psychological language in sexual assault trial judgements*. Presented at the Canadian Psychological Association Conference, Penticton, BC.

Coates, L., Bavelas, J.B. & Gibson, J. (1994). Anomalous language in sexual assault trial judgments. *Discourse and Society*, **5**(2), 189–206.

Danziger, K. (1990). *Constructing the subject*. Cambridge, UK: Cambridge University Press.

Danziger, K. (1992). The project of an experimental social psychology: historical perspectives. *Science in Context*, **5**, 309–328.

Deaux, K. (1984). From differences to social categories: Analysis of a decade's research on gender. *American Psychologist*, **39**, 105–116.

Deaux, K. (1985). Sex and gender. *Annual Review of Psychology*, **36**, 49–81.

DeFrancisco, V. (1997). Gender, power and practice: Or, putting your money (and your research) where your mouth is. In R. Wodak (Ed.), *Gender and discourse* (pp. 37–56). London: Sage.

Edwards, D. & Potter, J. (1992). *Discursive psychology*. London: Sage.

Fitzpatrick, M.A., Mulac, A. & Dindia, K. (1995). Gender-preferential language use in spouse and stranger interaction. *Journal of Language and Social Psychology*, **14**, 18–39.

Folger, R. (1987). Theory and method in social science. *Contemporary Social Psychology*, **12**, 51–54.

Fowler, R. (1985). Power. In T.A. Van Dijk (Ed.), *Handbook of discourse analysis* (Vol 4, pp. 61–82). Orlando, FL: Academic Press.

Gallois, C. & Pittam, J. (1995). Social psychological approaches to using natural language texts. *Journal of Language and Social Psychology*, **14**, 5–17.

Hansen, R.D. & O'Leary, V.E. (1985). Sex-determined attributions. In V.E. O'Leary, R.K. Unger & B.S. Wallston (Eds), *Women, gender, and social psychology* (pp. 67–99). Hillsdale, NJ: Erlbaum.

Henley, N.M., Miller, M. & Beazley, J. (1995). Syntax, semantics, and sexual violence: Agency and the passive voice. *Journal of Language and Social Psychology*, **14**, 60–84.

Jackson, J.M. (1988). *Social psychology, past and present: An integrative orientation*. Hillsdale, NJ: Erlbaum.

James, D. & Clarke, S. (1993). Women, men, and interruptions: A critical review. In D. Tannen (Ed.), *Gender and conversational interaction* (pp. 231–280). New York: University Press.

James, D. & Drakich, J. (1993). Understanding gender differences in amount of talk: A critical review of research. In D. Tannen (Ed.), *Gender and conversational interaction* (pp. 281–312). New York: Oxford University Press.

Jenkins, A. (1990). *Invitations to responsibility*. Adelaide: Dulwich Centre Publications.

Kahn, A.S. & Gaeddert, W.P. (1985). From theories of equity to theories of justice: The liberating consequences of studying women. In V.E. O'Leary, R.K. Unger & B.S. Wallston (Eds), *Women, gender, and social psychology* (pp. 129–148). Hillsdale, NJ: Erlbaum.

Kramarae, C. (1990). Changing the complexion of gender in language research. In H. Giles & W.P. Robinson (Eds), *Handbook of language and social psychology* (pp. 345–362). Chichester: Wiley.

Lakoff, R. (1975). *Language and women's place*. New York: Harper & Row.

Lipton, D.N., McDonel, E.C., & McFall, R.M. (1987). Heterosocial perception in rapists. *Journal of Consulting and Clinical Psychology*, **55**, 17–21.

Ng, S.H. (1990). Language and control. In H. Giles & W.P. Robinson (Eds), *Handbook of language and social psychology* (pp. 271–285). Chichester: Wiley.

Penelope, J. (1990). *Speaking freely: Unlearning the lies of the fathers' tongues*. Elmsford, NY: Pergamon Press.

Potter, J. & Wetherell, M. (1987). *Discourse and social psychology: Beyond attitudes and behaviour*. London: Sage.

Potter, J. & Wetherell, M. (1995). Natural order: Why social psychology should study (a constructed view) of natural language, and why they have not done so. *Journal of Language and Social Psychology*, **14**(1), 216–222.

Rogers, F. & Millar, E. (1977). Domineeringness and dominance: A transactional view. Unpublished manuscript, University of Cleveland, Department of Communication.

Schulz, M. (1975). The semantic derogation of women. In B. Thorne & N. Henley (Eds), *Language and sex: Difference and dominance* (pp. 64–75). Rowley, MA: Newbury House.

Schneider, D.J. (1991). Social cognition. *Annual Review of Psychology*, **42**, 527–561.

Senn, D.J. (1989). Myopic social psychology: An overemphasis on individualistic explanations of social behavior. In M.R. Leary (Ed.), *The state of social psychology: Issues, themes, and controversies* (pp. 45–52). Newbury Park, CA: Sage.

Shotland, L. & Craig, J.M. (1988). Can men and women differentiate between friendly and sexually interested behavior? *Social Psychological Quarterly*, **51**, 66–73.

Solano, C.H. (1989). The interactive perspective: getting the social back into social psychology. In M.R. Leary (Ed.), *The state of social psychology: Issues, themes, and controversies* (pp. 35–44). Newbury Park, CA: Sage.

Tajfel, H. (1972). Experiments in a vacuum. In J. Isreal & H. Tajfel (Eds), *The context of social psychology: A critical assessment* (pp. 69–119). London: Academic Press.

Tannen, D. (1994). *Gender and discourse.* New York: Oxford University Press.

Tavris, C. (1992). *The mismeasure of women.* New York: Touchstone.

Tolman, C.W. (1995). Toward a societal conception of the individual in social psychology. In I. Lubek, R. Hezewijk, G. Peterson & C. Tolman (Eds), *Recent trends in theoretical psychology* (Vol. 4, pp. 164–170). New York: Springer.

Wallston, B.S. & Grady, K.E. (1985). Integrating the feminist critique and the crisis in social psychology: Another look at research methods. In V.E. O'Leary, R.K. Unger & B.S. Wallston (Eds), *Women, gender, and social psychology* (pp. 7–33). Hillsdale, NJ: Erlbaum.

West, C., Lazar, M.M. & Kramarae, C. (1997). Gender in discourse. In T.A. van Dijk (Ed.), *Discourse as social interaction. Vol. 2: Discourse studies: A multidisciplinary introduction* (pp. 119–143). London: Sage.

West, C. & Zimmerman, D.H. (1985). Gender, language, and discourse. In T.A. Van Dijk (Ed.), *Handbook of discourse analysis* (Vol. 4, pp. 103–124). Orlando, FL: Academic Press.

Wodak, R. (1997). Introduction: Some important issues in the research of gender and discourse. In R. Wodak (Ed.), *Gender and discourse* (pp. 1–20). London: Sage.

Language, Ageing and Ageism

Nikolas Coupland and Justine Coupland
Cardiff University, Wales, Cardiff, UK

SOCIAL AGEING

The importance of a social perspective on ageing is apparent when we see how resolutely asocial other, dominant perspectives can be. In the context of medical geriatrics, for example, one influential handbook (Hall, Maclennan & Dye, 1993) suggests that "the basic concept of ageing is loss with time of the organism's adaptability to internal and external stress . . . Any [adequate] theory [of human ageing] must satisfy four criteria – the process must be intrinsic, deleterious, progressive and universal to the species" (p. 39). In this formulation, "intrinsic" rules out any interaction between the ageing process and social and environmental factors. "Progressive" implies ineluctable change, and again no susceptibility to social influence. "Deleterious" firmly anchors ageing as a movement towards incapacity and disadvantage. The term "universal" condemns us all, equally and inevitably, to participate in this steady decline. Hall et al. are clearly characterizing biological ageing here. Yet they see it as "the basic concept of ageing", and it is one that permeates lay and academic thinking. Social science in general, and the social psychology of language in particular, have the opportunity and probably the obligation to establish alternative perspectives, grounded in genuinely social models of ageing.

Our view that the biological model dominates even social and linguistic research led us to subtitle our contribution (N. Coupland & J. Coupland, 1990) to the first edition of the *Handbook of Language and Social Psychology* (Giles & Robinson, 1990) "The diachrony and decrement predicament". Our review of research showed that societal beliefs about ageing and social stereotypes of old people were generally prejudicial. If ageing can be defined in influential sources

The New Handbook of Language and Social Psychology.
Edited by W. Peter Robinson and Howard Giles.
© 2001 John Wiley & Sons Ltd.

as universal, progressive decrement, little wonder that people in late life suffer the stigma of being assumed, often, to be incompetent and marginal to the mainstream of social life. Continuing empirical studies into the sociopsychology of ageing show that stereotypes of old people are in fact complex and multidimensional, and by no means uniformly negative (Brewer, Dull & Lui, 1981; Hummert, 1990; Hummert, Shaner & Gartska, 1995). There is, however, a preponderance of negative stereotypes in circulation (Hummert, 1994). Also, ideological pressures linked to so-called "political correctness" (Cameron, 1995) may play an important part in silencing the most prejudicial of representations in research designs, so literatures are very likely to have underestimated age prejudice and-age based discrimination. It is certainly true that public discourses about minoritized groups are required to be positive, or at least hedged (see below), and therefore the reporting contexts in, for example, attitude studies need to be examined with great care. This is also the case with experimental research on "elderspeak" (Kemper, 1994) and the "patronizing speech" tradition of research (e.g. Hummert, 1994; Hummert & Ryan, this volume, Chapter 3.13).

The general challenge for social scientific research is to show how the assumptions of the decremental model of ageing are inappropriate as guiding principles for understanding social ageing; also to show how the decremental model excludes old people from opportunities and positive self-images. Yet the mainstream of social scientific research on ageing is the quest to confirm decrement. In the earlier chapter (N. Coupland & J. Coupland, 1990) we noted that several research programmes in language/communication and ageing look to substantiate claims about declining communicative competence during late life. More recent instances include studies demonstrating age-related decline in the retrieval of proper names (Cohen, 1994), in "off-target verbosity" (Gold, Arbuckle & Andres, 1994), and in syntactic and discourse processing linked to reductions in working memory (Kemper, 1992). While empirical psycholinguistic studies must of course report findings showing "communicative competence decrement" where it exists, that notion should be invoked cautiously. It is not always clear that measurable changes in communicative behaviour (such as reduced syntactic complexity) impact negatively on the quality of verbal interactions involving old people – that is, that they are "socially decremental". The social circumstances of late life are complex and diverse, as changing social circumstances foreground different lifestyles and communicative priorities. The history of sociolinguistics, particularly in respect of language and social class, clearly shows the narrow-sightedness of taking measurable differences in linguistic usage to represent social deficits (Edwards, 1976; Montgomery, 1986). But our main observation on this pattern of research is simply that it is driven by the assumption that what is researchable as communication in late life is decrement, and this is an inherited, asocial model. Social ageing cannot comprehensively be modelled as "declining competence", any more than childhood per se can be characterized as acquisition of the lexicogrammatical system of a native language. Social ageing is far more complex and interesting, and far more theoretically challenging, than that.

We do not set out to update the overview of empirical research we offered in 1990 in the present chapter. Sociolinguistic and communicative research on ageing has certainly built steadily over the last decade, and there are many important programmes which a new overview would have to encompass. Monographs and compilations of studies in the 1990s include N. Coupland, 1993; N. Coupland, J. Coupland & Giles, 1991; N. Coupland & Nussbaum, 1993; Giles, 1998; Giles, N. Coupland & Wiemann, 1990; Hamilton, 1999; Hummert & Nussbaum, in press; Hummert, Wiemann & Nussbaum, 1994; Nussbaum & J. Coupland, 1995; Williams & Nussbaum, 2001; Williams & Ylänne-McEwen, 2000. Much of the newer research reported is explicitly sociopsychological, in the sense that it models age in group terms, investigating attitudes, stereotypes and language use by one age group relative to (and often in conflict with) another. We refer to some parts of this literature below.

But rather than attempt to integrate these and other sources and their findings here, we shall outline a perspective on ageing – a social practice perspective – which we take to be fundamentally social, and which is so by virtue of its theoretical basis in language. It does not represent the mainstream tradition of sociopsychological research on ageing, particularly in that it requires a certain scepticism about age categories and "intergroup relations". It assumes that the social meaning of ageing resides in local contexts of language and interaction, in spoken and written meaning-making practices. Although this approach falls within what is usually referred to as "discourse analysis", we think it is essentially sociopsychological, in its emphasis on the linguistic construction of dominant structures of belief and prejudice about ageing. Its methodological distinctiveness from the main current of sociopsychological research, however, is that it is an inductive orientation, based on analyses of local textual instances – rather than a deductive one, testing pre-existing theory on contrived data. Necessarily, then, we will be examining diverse language texts for what they tell us about the cultural constitution of ageing. We first need to set out our assumptions about the link between language and social categorisation.

AGE: A "RENDERED REALITY"

The phrase "rendered reality" is Green's (1993). Green defends a radical stance on ageing and its academic study, taking "the essential character of gerontology to lie in its determinate organization of thought in writing" (p. xii), seeing it as basically a "literary enterprise" (p. 34). His perspective extends beyond the constitution of gerontology to the constitution of ageing, our main concern in this chapter:

> there is no such extralinguistic thing as aging or the aged (or any other sociological category). They are rendered realities achieved in linguistic practices of naming, describing, classifying, referencing, and the like, both in ordinary language and specialized discourse. (Green, 1993, p. 15)

How should we react to this striking claim?

Popularly, old age is a "bottom line" concern, defining the limits of humanity and viable lives. Old age is usually held to be determinate – it certainly is, in a physical sense – and to be materially evidenced, for example in old people's faces and posture (Featherstone & Hepworth, 1991). Fear of ageing, gerontophobia, and its reflexes in various forms of societal ageism are grounded precisely in the view that old age is a reality that cannot be re-rendered, and a reality that we approach with extreme reluctance. What we recognize as the physical and physiological attributes of old age – grey hair, wrinkles, stooping posture – seem to be the genuine extralinguistic stuff of ageing, to use Green's phrase.

From another perspective, however, these are more icons than physical realities of ageing. It is not possible, or necessary, to deny the probabilistic existence of wrinkles or grey hair – or even of reduced syntactic complexity in some communicative contexts – with advancing old age. But we can ask how intrinsic these features need be to the experience and definition of old age, and how they come to be construed as the "essential" characteristics of old people. Wrinkles are invested with age significance, as age markers, even though they are part of the physiognomy of most ages of human life. They are inscribed in the social formation we call ageing; they are a small part of the routine referential practice that fills out the meaning of ageing, in our own cultural circumstances. Woodward (1991) makes the point that grey hair is, in distributional terms, a feature that we acquire in mid-life rather than in old age, yet its symbolic significance is as an icon of old age. Grey hair presages old age, and so we invest it with symbolic potency, shaping it as a symbol of a life stage we hope not to have reached. In this very particular way, we can see how our social understanding of old age is built semiotically, and this is the basis of Green's general case. A social perspective on ageing needs to deconstruct the semiotic processes that socially constitute old age, rather than have the thrust of its work delimited by the icons and assumptions that particular societies have conventionalized. Language is the most actively constitutive semiotic medium, and is centrally involved in the "rendering" of age. The social practice perspective we are proposing is essentially a critical analysis of the classificatory work done through language and discourse to construct our routine cognitive orientations – our definitions, evaluations and presuppositions – about ageing and old people.

Up to now, research on ageing has not developed a clear metalanguage to distinguish biologically based from sociopsychologically based and ideological categories and perspectives. The terminological distinction between "sex" and "gender" has been important in foregrounding the fact that biological (sex) and social (gender) principles of categorization have very different relevances. In the same way, the "universal" quality of ageing that Hall, Maclennan and Dye point to (see above) disguises a host of socially variable processes and outcomes, which these authors do not recognize. When they write about the sociopsychological attributes of "elderly people", they claim that "as people age there is a tendency for them to become more rigid in their response to life and more set in their ways" (Hall et al., 1993, pp. 53–54). Once again, this shows a willingness to make universalist judgements about ageing, even in the social arena. Social scientific research on gender, on the other hand, has learned to be wary of over-generalizing to "men" and "women" on the basis of biological sex, and of essentializing these categories. Sex may often be a non-salient dimension of social life, and the social experiences of men and women in many domains are more similar then different. Also, since biological sex is binary, a sex perspective implies the need to adopt a "difference" perspective, when a "dominance" perspective is often more relevant socially.

It is no less important to distinguish analyses and observations based on biological/chronological age categories from ones based on social ageing. Rubin and Rubin's (1986) concept of "contextual age" is a useful step towards correcting this trend, although for them contextual age is a quantifiable index of life position and lifestyle more than a general research perspective. At a very practical level, it is therefore important to ask whether research based on categories of chronological age is adequately sensitive to diverse social experiences of ageing (Williams & N. Coupland, 1998, pp. 140–143). After all, people do not exclusively coalesce into communities organized on the lines of chronological age, and the experience of "being sixty-five" can be hugely variable – in terms of health, lifestyles and affluence, and in terms of social networking. Late life can be a period of either affluence or extreme poverty, of insecurity or fulfilment, of power or powerlessness. Lived cultural histories will differ from epoch to epoch and from one social environment to another, creating a complex cultural experience on which individual lifespan experiences and meanings are overlaid. When we write about "the elderly" or "older people" or "elders" or "pensioners" or "the aged", there is an important sense in which we are invoking constructs which, although deceptively familiar categories, represent variable and fuzzy realities. They are familiar because our society naturalizes them according to its dominant ideological assumptions, and these terms therefore come with in-built social biases. The word "pensioners" voices old people's position outside of the economic workforce – a highly politicized assumption; "elders" encodes attributes of respect and sagacity, and so on. These terms tell us far more about speakers' or writers' ideological orientations than about old people's generic characteristics. There are no value-free linguistic labels, although "old people" is perhaps the starkest and least richly ideologized.

From some theoretical standpoints, social collectivities in general exist only in the semiotic acts that represent them (Anderson, 1983; Rampton, in press), for example in how they are routinized through print media (Gal and Woolard, 1995). Whether or not this is an overreaching claim, the symbolic packaging of our social worlds has important implications for social organization and social relations. The study of linguistic representations develops Whorf's perspective on cultural and linguistic relativity (e.g., Whorf, 1956/1997; see also Gumperz & Levinson, 1996; Lee, 1992), seeing language as a means of naturalizing world views which are likely to be relative (to specific cultures) rather than universal. On the other hand, linguistic representations tend to be durable once established within a community's usage or practice. Sacks suggested that "a large amount of the knowledge that Members hold about how a society works [is] . . . 'protected against induction'. What that means is that it isn't automatically modified if events occur which it doesn't characterize" (Sacks, 1995, p. 196). Since linguistic communication requires some form of representation, and since all realities must be represented, it follows that speakers and writers do not have the option of refashioning representations on each instance of their use. There will therefore be patterned representations, which may be uncovered by empirical means.

DISCOURSE AS SOCIAL PRACTICE

Discourse analysis takes many forms (Jaworski & N. Coupland, 1999). But discourse analysis can be distinguished from other forms of language analysis in several ways. It attends to communicative function rather than linguistic form; it attempts to build rich contextualized readings of meaning rather than trusting in distributional overviews of language behaviours or features; it is dialogically based, stressing the co-construction of meaning. While discourse analysis is an empirical project, it bridges the micro–macro gap by building interpretations of local linguistic or textual events in relation to social and cultural norms. Discourse analysis is "critical" (see Fairclough, 1992; Hodge & Kress, 1988) when it sets out to reveal otherwise hidden power structures and their impact on communicators and communicative events. A critical discourse analytic perspective is therefore appropriate for the analysis of how ageing is socially constructed through acts of language, and for the analysis of societal ageism. Discourse analysis is certainly no panacea, and its empirical limitations are readily apparent. But proponents of discourse analysis have generally stressed the limitations of alternative, empiricist research designs (as in Potter & Wetherell, 1987). We cannot summarize and assess this debate here.

The emphasis in discourse analysis is therefore on what language in use achieves, and this includes what it achieves for interest groups in situations of ideological conflict. Ideologies (Blommaert & Verschueren, 1998) are established value systems expressed through specific "discourses" – in the countable use of that term. Individual speakers or language texts can be said to articulate or fill out specific ideologies, although most texts will contain echoes of more than one ideological set. Texts will be "polyphonic" (Bakhtin, 1986) or multi-discursive. Individual texts will derive much of their meaning from pre-existing texts or text types, so discourse analysis needs to be open to exploring inter-textual linkages (Fairclough, 2000). A general rationale for such a perspective, when applied to ageing, is offered in Chappell and Orbach's (1986) Meadian account of social identity (cf. Mead, 1934), emphasizing identity as lived experience and interactionally framed. One important implication of the discourse analytic perspective on ageing is that we should expect to see many different and even contradictory constructions of old age, reflecting the interests of particular groups in particular circumstances.

THE DISCURSIVE "OTHERING" OF OLD PEOPLE

The dominant sense of the term "Other", in a cultural context, is in identifying a group – or an individual held to typify that group – that is considered not only different or distant but also alien or deviant, relative to the norms and expectations of the speaker's own group (Riggins, 1997). "The Other" is therefore an inter-group perception (Tajfel, 1981; Tajfel & Turner, 1979; see also Giles & N. Coupland, 1991). It raises issues about group boundaries, group-based discrimination and inter-group conflict. "The Other" is therefore an entirely familiar concept for social psychologists, except in that it enshrines the social practice perspective – representing a person or a group as "Other" is an active, constitutive process. What we can call "Othering" is the practice of representing an individual or a social group to render them distant, alien or deviant. It is the construction of an outgroup (outgrouping), but usually a process of social exclusion or marginalization. Contemporary theorizing of "The Other" stems most directly from Georg Simmel's concept of "the stranger", developed in the earliest years of the twentieth century (Simmel, 1950; see also Rogers, 1999), and the term is usually used in connection with the minoritization of racial/ethnic groups (Said, 1978) (see N. Coupland, in press, for an overview). Ageism, which is at the core of social scientific concerns with ageing but which is a complex attribution (see below), can usefully be construed in terms of "Othering". Many different patterns of social representation and discursive social practice can be identified which have the effect or rendering old people "alien". As an extreme case, Woodward (1991) comments about the "unwatchability" of "deep" old age, popular revulsion at the aged body and physiognomy. This response is a gerontophobic one, in Woodward's definition of it as "an individual's response of fear and anxiety" towards old age and death (p. 194). As such it can be distinguished from other, more general senses of the term "ageism", which Woodward takes to be a political prejudice (cf. Butler, 1969; Nuessel, 1982). Unwatchability implies reticence to confront old age rather than inter-group conflict or sociostructural bias. It is repression rather than oppression. It is typically a tacit ideology; its expression is silence or avoidance. If death is "the last taboo" (N. Coupland & J. Coupland, 1997, 1999), old age is its close partner (cf. the claim that old people are "invisible" in many genres of print journalism – Kubey, 1980). There are strong echoes of unwatchability in texts which set themselves against the ageing process, and especially those involved in selling so-called "anti-ageing" products. A small-scale survey of skin-care advertisements in the British magazine press during May and June 1999 (J. Coupland, forthcoming) provided data to explore the precise means by which popular media discourses negotiate visible ageing, and we can refer to two of those ads here. In the first instance, an advertisement for Nivea Visage (June 1999) suggests that visible ageing is, or brings, bad luck; that time, and therefore ageing, are our enemies and that without our intervention through using the product they will inevitably defeat us. The unquestioned assumption is that younger-looking skin is "better-looking skin".

Extract 1

If we're lucky, it isn't until our thirties that we really start to notice any fine lines and wrinkles . . . The trouble is, time has a nasty habit of catching up with us in the end . . . (some details are then given about the product and its use). The result is a proven reduction in visible lines and wrinkles, together with improved firmness and elasticity. Or put simply, better-looking skin.

In Extract 2 the processes by which ageing is rendered unwatchable are represented in more detail.

Extract 2

Introducing the latest intervention
In the fight against skin ageing.

Reti C
Pure Retinol and Pure Vitamin C.
A new force in anti-ageing.
Visible results from 15 days.

VICHY laboratoires have perfected the first
three-phase emulsion containing Pure Retinol.
And Pure Vitamin C in their stable and active forms
to correct the signs of ageing.

Reti C combines the rapid radiance renewal
action of Vitamin C with the wrinkle corrective
benefits of Retinol.

Use morning and/or night. Hypo-allergenic.
With VICHY Thermal Spa Water.
Effectiveness tested by dermatologists.

Ask your pharmacist for advice.

NEW
Patent pending

VICHY. SOURCE OF HEALTHY SKIN

Together with the accompanying visual image, which shows a young, line-free model with her face swathed in a bandage, the first two lines are reminiscent of the discourse of medical treatment for illness or disease. This is partly realized through the war metaphor, in "intervention", "fight" and "force" (Sontag, 1991), which renders visible ageing as a pathology requiring treatment at the hands of trained experts. This expertise is referenced in "laboratoires", "dermatologists" and "pharmacist". But alongside this, the text works to frame visible ageing as a mistake, a misdemeanour, a lapse or an aberration, in the terms "correct" and "corrective", and finally, returns to linking visible ageing with degenerating health status by implicitly equating younger-looking skin (the implied goal of the product) with "healthy skin". The designation "A new force in anti-ageing" presupposes that "anti-ageing" endeavours are normal, even universal. The skin-care industry profits to the extent that anti-ageing is a widespread project, so it naturalizes this ideology in its promotional texts.

DISCURSIVE HOMOGENIZATION

It is worth noting that Simmel's "stranger" was by no means a uniformly disadvantaged individual, and by implication that "The Other" need not be a feared or vilified other. In fact Simmel saw definite strengths in the stranger position, including improved perspective, objectivity and a certain form of freedom (from normative constraint), as well as an openness to innovation. As Riggins (1997) suggests, the perception or construction of social distance can equally be associated with admiration, mystique and even envy.

The "Othering" of old people can be based on relatively neutral or even apparently favourable representations, even though demeaning representations of old people are still common, certainly in the UK. (A widely mentioned instance is the imagery of road signs warning drivers that they are approaching a residential home for old people – portraying two bent figures, one male one female, crossing a road.) A more general quality of age "Othering" is, however, to represent old people as a homogeneous group. "Treating people as individuals" is a cornerstone of the ethics of liberal democracies. It is directly linked to political processes such as individual suffrage and the protection of human rights which are held to be invested in individuals. Correspondingly, denying individuals their individuality is illiberal, but also a productive means of outgrouping and minoritization. This is where it is again relevant to ask whether social science research is not itself implicated in reductive homogenizing of "the elderly", by developing paradigms based on social categories defined in age terms (Williams and N. Coupland, 1998). One example is the sociolinguistic tradition of "apparent time" research (e.g., Labov 1994, pp. 43ff.), which uses age-stratified samples to trace dialect change. This approach is of course revealing about language change processes, but it is based on the assumption that old people are "time-bound" repositories of earlier dialect usage.

A social practice perspective principally needs to uncover the routine ways in which old age is discursively fixed. To illustrate, we can consider a fragment from a UK geriatric medical interaction (J. Coupland & N. Coupland, in press). In the corpus of more than 100 consultations we found occasional outgrouping linguistic representations of old people such as the following:

Extract 3

(The Doctor is a male professor, in his sixties. The patient is a woman aged 75, accompanied by her daughter. The doctor has finished taking the patient's medical history.)

Doctor: no (.) right okay fine (.) right would you like to pop onto the couch (.) we'll pull the curtain around you and we'll come and have a little look at you

Daughter: it'll be alright don't worry (.)
                   (to doctor, outside the patient's hearing) if I wasn't here she wouldn't speak at all (laughs slightly)

Doctor: (laughs slightly) yes (.) they do get a bit nervous don't they? (.) strange places
                   [

Daughter: yeah they do ((get a bit))
                   (20 seconds pause, as the doctor goes through case notes)

Daughter: she's a worrier

Doctor: pardon?

Daughter: she is a worrier

Doctor: yes (.) gets a bit anxious does she?
                   (15 seconds pause)

Daughter: she's not quite sure whether she's got angina or no this is what ((could be))
                                                                           [

Doctor: yes well we'll
                   sort all that out (.) yes now (3.0) yes it's difficult when you know (.) when one's not quite certain what is wrong (.) then people get much more anxious about (.) er

Daughter: I think when they do get a bit nervous don't they? you get a bit confused actually
                                                  [   ]

Doctor: yes   yes
(Some seconds later)

Daughter: and this is what I tried to explain but (.) when they get to their age they think well why are they doing it =

Doctor: = yes

The doctor and the patient jointly fashion a representation of the patient as behaving in an age-prototypical way and generalize rather freely about old people as a homogeneous and deficient group. In the utterance "they do get a bit nervous don't they?", and later in the extract, "they" clearly refers to "old people" (cf. "when they get to their age"). Old people are represented as conforming to a predictable pattern of behaviour, which is then held to provide an adequate account of the patient's circumstances in this case. The instance is particularly significant because the outpatients clinic where this interaction was recorded is overtly committed to a firmly anti-ageist ideological stance.

If this "theying" usage seems unexceptional, we should ask whether it would be acceptable with other social group memberships (e.g., "women do get a bit nervous don't they?" or "Adults do get a bit nervous don't they?"). Perhaps only young children would be considered appropriate as a group to be homogenized in this way. The semiotic alignment of old people and children is in fact a productive ageist theme (Hockey & James, 1993). It is the basis of the "inverted-U" model of the life-course, which imputes frailty and incompetence to people at each "end" of life (Coupland et al., 1991).

AGE-NORMATIVE DISCOURSE

Post-colonial theory (Ashcroft, Griffiths & Tiffin, 1998) emphasizes the flexibility of social identities. It argues that contemporary social life, in post- or late modernity, is characterized by hybrid identities, as opposed to the more fixed, predictable and institutionalized pattern of the modern (e.g., industrial) period. Hybridity is the creation or existence of mixed or multiple forms or identities. The concept challenges the orthodox view of social or cultural groups as sealed systems, and people as unique exemplars of cultural types. Hybridity is mainly associated with the theoretical work of Homi Bhabha (e.g., 1994), and his perspective that people inevitably sustain complex, mixed subjectivities and occupy ambiguous cultural spaces in the modern world. There is a close connection between this view and Giddens' theorizing of late modernity as an environment where traditional boundaries of many sorts are loosened and made available for more creative reworking. Giddens (e.g., 1991) writes about the compression and disembedding of time and space, through vastly more sophisticated telecommunication links, rapid international travel and the reflexivity promoted through the mass media. It seems to follow that self-identity, which Giddens insists is an ongoing project rather than a fixed set of allegiances or priorities, will be malleable and relativized.

    There is only sporadic support in the literature for late life being a time of flexible social identification. Featherstone and Hepworth (1990) write about the advent of a "uni-age" society, mentioning how styles of dress in Western societies are more uniform across the ages today than they have traditionally been, and this paradoxically implies a certain flexibility of self-representation, compared with traditional strictures (e.g. that old people should dress conservatively). There does appear to be a wider set of lifestyle options for old people today, e.g. in retirement (Bernard & Phillipson, 1995; Williams & Ylanne-McEwen, 2000). But, in terms of discursive social practice, what is most striking is precisely the converse of a shift to hybridity – how age normativity is continually reasserted, and how age group members are ideologically corralled into predictable patterns of behaviour. Behaviours and attitudes are often subject to an age appropriateness criterion. People often talk about health in age-relative ways – a person is "good for her age" or "not doing too badly for seventy-five" (N. Coupland, J. Coupland & Giles 1989). Children suffer repeated experiences of being "not old enough to" engage in adult-defined practices, and being told to "act their age". But cultural norms dictate that people can, correspondingly, be too old, perhaps most obviously for work. Anti-discrimination legislation may outlaw the specification of preferred ages in job advertisements, but texts of the form "Wanted: enthusiastic young person . . ." are commonplace in the UK.

A pervasive discourse expresses the illegitimacy of old people not behaving to type. Consider the following extract from a newspaper feature on "The dinosaurs of rock".

Extract 4

ROCK DINOSAURS CASHING IN ON NOSTALGIA FIND YEARS OF DRINK AND DRUGS PUNISHING THEM
Life in the fast lane is finally catching up with rock music's dinosaurs, those ageing sixties and seventies performers cashing in on nostalgia tours and the devotion of grey-haired, pot-bellied fans.

These days, it's rock me gently.

Medical problems have recently sidelined such venerable performers as David Crosby of Crosby, Stills and Nash, Glenn Frey of the Eagles, Jerry Garcia of the Grateful Dead and John Mellencamp.

The culprits: aches and pains from growing older, the rigours of the road, and in some cases, the cumulative effect of drug and alcohol abuse. (*Western Mail*, 8 October, 1994)

While the argumentative line is that rock stars' years of self-abuse is punishing them in later life, there is a clear sense in which the text and its author are also punishing the named "venerable performers". They are said to be "cashing in", implying a non-legitimate (see below) extension of their careers beyond some putative norm of legitimate exposure.

Cultural mythology in the West also punishes old people who present themselves as "younger than they really are". The salient metaphor is "mutton dressed as lamb". Woodward (1991) develops the concept of "masquerade" to capture human efforts to self-present as younger:

In a culture which so devalues age, masquerade with respect to the aging body is first and foremost a denial of age, and effort to erase or efface age and to put on youth. Masquerade entails many strategies, among them: the addition of desired body parts (teeth, hair); the removal or covering up of unwanted parts of the body (growths, gray hair, "age spots") the "lifting" of the face and other body parts in an effort to deny the weight of gravity; the moulding of the body's shape (exercise, clothing). (p. 148)

These practices obviously include commercially promoted "anti-ageing" products of the sort we considered above. But the irony is that people who pursue "anti-ageing" strategies lay themselves open to potential vilification. Perceptible traces of the effort to look or act young (imperfect renditions of youthspeak, or hyper-engagement with contemporary music, or a slightly mismanaged attempt at a youthful style of clothing) are laughable. According to dominant ideologies, incompatibilities in age semiosis (wrinkles and a mini-skirt; grey hair and a guitar) trigger judgements of inauthenticity: "past it but doesn't know when to quit" etc. Woodward in fact suggests that the only life-stage acknowledged to be authentic is youth: Old age is figured as a dirty secret that had best remain undetected, latent, not manifest (Woodward, 1991, p. 151).

The ideological force behind these responses is that life-stages are uniquely and normatively linked to identity sets, which we interfere with at our peril. The double-bind of social ageing is of course that remaining within a prescribed identity set confirms the social stereotype for that age, such as being held to be "set in one's ways" as an old person. The tension between acting "within age" versus "out of age" has generated familiar ageing tropes such as "growing old disgracefully", as we sense ourselves or others pressing against the normative boundaries of old age.

OLD AGE: SILENCE, THEN HUMOUR

We are aware that this overview of age construction through language is far from comprehensive, and there are several reasons for this. One is that rather little research has taken this epistemological line (although most studies of inter-generational communication are compatible with it – see Giles et al., 1994, for an overview). Another reason – one that is admittedly difficult to evidence – is that cultural discourse about ageing is not widespread. The instances we have mentioned are when ageing is problematized (to sell skin-care products), or when age is specifically salient for other reasons (e.g., in geriatric medicine) or when age portrayals are commented on critically ("rock dinosaurs", etc.). More gener-ally, ageing as a social process is rather rarely entertained as a theme of public discourse, just as the "invisibility" of old people in print media has been com-mented on (see above). Exceptions would include social policy debates, for example about the financial burden imposed by "a rapidly ageing population". Academics whose research focuses on ageing often comment on the small au-diences they receive for their presentations! Similarly, we have previously ob-served how talk about age-in-years is largely restricted to the young and the old – chronological age "goes underground" in the mid-years of life (Coupland et al., 1989). The concept of ageism is, as we also suggested, not firmly established within the public consciousness, at least in the UK – certainly far less so than sexism or racism.

This implies that one of the most general discursive representations of age-ing is in fact silence. This is consistent with the psychoanalytic line (Becker, 1973; N. Coupland & J. Coupland, 1997) that old age and death are sys-tematically repressed by the non-old, and that silence is a predictable geron-tophobic response. So, how is gerontophobic silence broken? Rather often, it is broken through laughter, and we can demonstrate this at both the micro (inter-actional practice) and macro (cultural practice) levels. In the study of age-telling just mentioned, based on first-acquaintance interactions, we noted that old people's reports of their own age-in-years are often accompanied by slight laughter; for example:

Extract 5

(May is 77 years old, talking to Sue, who is 35.)

```
Sue:     have you got any family?
May:     I have a daughter
Sue:     does she does she live in Cardiff
              [        ⌐              [
May:          she                she's living
         in Pencoed near Bridgend . . . she comes up every
         Tuesday and er (.) we go shopping and have a
         run around you know
Sue:     you haven't got any grandchildren?
                    [        ]
May:             she
         yes I have er (laughs) I have (coughs) two grandchildren
              [              ]
Sue:          (laughs)
May:     and I have four great-grandchildren (laughs)
                              [         ]   [
Sue:                          (gasps)       (laughs)

Sue:     oh! nice yes (.) you don't look that old (laughs)
         ⌐              ]                        [
May:       they're lovely                        (laughs)
         oh dear
Sue:     (quietly) oh dear
May:     well I'm seventy-seven
Sue:     (high pitch) really?
May:     yes (laughs)
              [
Sue:             I thought you were sort of sixty I just assumed
                                            [
May:                                        did you? Oh
         that's nice
Sue:     yeah yeah it's funny most people I know who are seventy-
         seven aren't (gasps) dashing in and out of day centres (.)
         oh that's nice (.) oh
```

The laughter here first accompanies the elderly woman's disclosure that she pre-sides over not just two descending generations but three; both her laughter and the young woman's seems to be marking surprise at being "old enough" to have great-grandchildren. Once that topic has faded, the elderly woman's disclosure of her chronological age (DCA) is responded to again by both as surprising (cf. Sue's "that old" and "it's funny"). This telling of age seems to be, and certainly is responded to as if, claiming credit. The laughter may well also reflect the counter-normativity or marked focus of telling age in the context of age disclosure being suppressed in mid-life; DCA becomes a face-threatening act both to the teller and the recipient, which would again account for the laughter, as a way of releasing embarrassment. That there is a sequencing link between talking old age and laughter supports the claim that silence about old age is the unmarked form.

In broader terms, we can point to the institutionalized jocularity of age-marking, at events like decade birthdays. Many commonplace pejorating representations of racial, age and other groups involve humour. The vast commercial enterprise of producing, selling and mailing greetings cards in Western societies invests heavily in group stereotyping, and in age stereotyping as a large part of this. A dominant genre of UK birthday cards involves humorous age taunts, such as "Still naughty at forty" or "Still nifty at fifty". Humour is a widely used strategy in anti-PC discourse because it can imply that PC itself is humourless. Humour is multifaceted, however, because it obfuscates on-record versus off-record stances. So it allows its users to claim, if challenged, that they are "only kidding". One is open to the charge of "taking age too seriously" if one does not operate within these norms.

Humorous, and sometimes parodic, representations of old people on television are further evidence. The one TV genre where old people have substantial representation (at least in the UK, currently) is humour, and specifically in sitcoms – see Harwood and Giles's (1992) analysis of *The Golden Girls*. Age stereotypes certainly abound in these shows, although the dominant portrayal is of generally likeable, healthy old people (but sometimes irascible, as in the UK-derived sitcom *One Foot in the Grave*, or childishly enthused by trivia, as in *Last of the Summer Wine*, or strong-willed and quirky as in *Waiting for God*). Harwood and Giles conclude that the regular association of humour with the portrayal of difficult life circumstances in old age may trivialize old people's problems. It may also be, however, that the breaking of a rather pervasive silence about old age, through humour, will lead to more open and more differentiated portrayals and debates.

In the other direction, much more pernicious representations can be found. One example is a UK quiz show (*It's Only TV But I Like It*) which plays video-clips of old people talking about characters on television programmes, when guests are required to identify those characters. The implication is that old people's talk is rambling and incoherent, so that the identification task is adequately demanding.

AGEING AND SELF-OTHERING

It is easy to see language and representation, and indeed what we have called "Othering" as processes by which one individual or group influences another.

Many technical and most lay accounts of communication encourage this dyadic perspective. When we frame our research as "intergenerational" research, we are led into this perspective very directly. But there is also a link between self identification and other representation. Our representations of others, and certainly other people's representations of us, are based on social comparisons. In psychoanalytic terms (Elliott, 1996), self-identification involves borrowing aspects of identity from others, or adopting traits and values associated with fictional and even mythical figures, perhaps to cope with threatening circumstances. Riggins (1997, p. 4) says that the experience of self-estrangement can be captured through a concept of the "internal Other". "The Other" is therefore capable of penetrating the self in various ways. In one sense, discursive representations of ageing are inevitably self-representations, since ageing (as the universalist, decremental discourse has it) is a process we can never escape.

It might therefore be appropriate to conclude this essay with an interactive sequence that shows self-negotiation in progress. It is again taken from the corpus of geriatric outpatient consultations mentioned above (see J. Coupland & N. Coupland, in press; N. Coupland & J. Coupland, 1998, for a full account of these and related data).

Extract 6

(The doctor is a male registrar, in his thirties. The patient is a woman aged 81, accompanied by her daughter. The patient has had a stroke which has affected her eyesight. She is depressed and reports that the antidepressants prescribed are not helping.)

Doctor:	how do you think things are going?
Patient:	(sighs) (2.0) well sometimes I feel alright and sometimes (.) I feel (.) er oh it's not what the hell's er living in when you put the <u>news</u> on what do you get? (.) it's all trouble here and (.) everywhere in the world is is <u>misery</u> and trouble <u>(.)</u> you think what the <u>hell's</u> the good of living (.) in a world like this?
Daughter:	you could do with a good <u>laugh</u> couldn't you? (chuckles)
Patient:	(laughs slightly) <u>yes</u> yeah <u>(3.0)</u>
Daughter:	well you went on <u>holiday</u> didn't you had a week's holiday
	[ ]
Patient:	there's nothing to laugh at
	(nearing the end of the consultation)
Doctor:	but er (.) I think things are <u>OK</u> and I think they'll <u>improve</u>
Patient:	mm
Doctor:	OK?
Patient:	well what the hell do I ex<u>pect</u> (.) I must be <u>mad</u>!
Daughter:	(chuckles)
Doctor:	(sounding amused) I don't think you're mad
Patient:	(laughs) I'm just a crabby old=
Daughter:	=a thirty year old er brain inside an eighty year old (laughs)

		[
Doctor:		that's right
	(.) it's frustrating isn't it?	
Patient:	I can't get on	
	[	
Daughter:	oh but she's much better ((than she says))	
Doctor:	she is better?	
Daughter:	yes	
Doctor:	OK	
Patient:	yes (sounding heartfelt) thanks ever so much	
Doctor:	that's alright (2.0) look after yourself . . .	

The doctor and the patient's daughter have constructed a confederation during this consultation, in an effort to "talk up" the patient, who is severely depressed. The daughter, for example, reminds her mother that she had a week's holiday, proposing the implication that therefore her life has its positive moments, in contradiction of the patient's earlier formulation that her life and the world in general is "misery and trouble". Similarly, the doctor's contribution is to emphasize the positive, saying that "things are OK and . . . they'll improve". As the consultation ends, the three participants all contribute to an assessment of the patient's psychosocial state. As part of this process, the patient is doing on-line self-reassessment. She says "what the hell do I expect . . . I must be mad". Her self-representation "I'm just a crabby old . . ." is interrupted by her daughter's contrasting assessment that she is "a thirty year old er brain inside an eighty year old". Both these assessments are made in age-relative terms. The patient's "crabby old" invokes a prejudicial stereotype of the disgruntled old person, to recontextualize her earlier expressions of distress and frustration. She pulls in a familiar representation of "crabby old people", presumably to withdraw from the consultative mode and restore a degree of social equilibrium as the consultation ends. On the other hand, the daughter offers an age-denying alternative, which the doctor endorses. She constructs a vivid image (the young brain in an old body), a version of the "good for your age" disjunction, to de-essentialize old age in her mother's case. Her mother, she suggests, is "old" only in a physical, incorporated sense.

CONCLUSION

The general perspective we are suggesting under the rubric of social practice is one that traces the age-constitutive forces at work in texts and talk. In the last textual instance, above, the patient's age, and how she should accommodate it, were being actively renegotiated. Indeed, in that case, it was a collaborative renegotiation, done through multi-party talk. In that brief exchange, however, participants gave voice to some of the discursive representations we have suggested are pervasive in Western cultural discourses of ageing. Age normativity and an "Othered" old age were invoked, even though participants worked to deny the salience of these constraints in this particular case. Ageist formulations provided the ideological framework for the discussion. The meanings generated were therefore both new and old, both recycled and creative. In such data we can see talk at the micro-level of social interaction animating meanings and values which define ageing, but also putting them to work in the service of local interactional goals. It is in the accumulation of countless individual representational acts of this sort that the ideological values of ageing are socially and culturally constructed and confirmed. As we suggested at the beginning of this chapter, language practices are the social mechanisms through which we build meanings and ideologies of ageing. Those "higher-order" sociopsychological structures cannot, we would suggest, exist independently of the grounded social practices that form our data.

From the point of view of a more empiricist social psychology, the fragments of media text and social interaction we have considered will no doubt seem eclectic and prone to over-interpretation. This would in part be fair comment, but it is also partly a consequence of our wanting to illustrate a wide range of text types for the purposes of this overview chapter. It is certainly necessary to address language data and their social contexts more systematically and extensively, and this is what we have done in relation to geriatric medical discourse, but also "anti-ageing" product advertisements in our own studies (see references above). But we would also argue that the social psychology of language needs to recognize text and talk – and particularly data which routinely represents age and other social categories – as an important primary resource. As others have argued (e.g., Edwards & Potter, 1992), a "discursive psychology" is certainly a coherent complement to more "traditional" quantitative approaches.

Theories which articulate inter-group (e.g., inter-generational) relations may be more elegantly and more cumulatively built around series of controlled, experimental studies which can manipulate "language variables" of various sorts. Important generalizations can be made on the basis of such studies, although their ecological validity will always be open to challenge. The risk inherent in manipulating language experimentally is considerable, when language is dislocated from the communities of practice that sustain it, and that are sustained by it. We have tried to stress the socially embedded nature of the textual instances we have examined, and the fact that we can point to age values as routinely activated in specific sociolinguistic genres – matters of regular practice – is crucial. At the very least, studies of actual practice are necessary to confirm that trends in social cognition (attitudes, prejudices, etc.) have currency outside the laboratory.

But the more fundamental, and epistemological, point has to do with how we theorize the link between language, cognition and society. Our position is that language cannot be seen as an assemblage of forms or styles, which have evaluative and other social attributes independently of their contexts of animation. Social values reside not in language itself but in the interplay between language and social context. If that is so, then we need to locate our research at that intersection – where the intersection routinely exists – and be wary of trying to fabricate new, idealized interfaces where "language" and "social context" might conspire in quite different ways. Our best opportunity to understand social formations such as ageing and ageism is, it would follow, in the detail of everyday events, and language practice needs to assume a more dignified role than it otherwise would in the social psychology of language.

REFERENCES

Anderson, B. (1983). *Imagined communities: Reflections on the origin and spread of nationalism.* London: Verso.

Ashcroft, B., Griffiths, G. & Tiffin, H. (1998). *Key concepts in post-colonial studies.* London: Routledge.

Bakhtin, M. (1986). *Speech genres and other late essays.* Austin: University of Texas Press.

Becker, E. (1973). *The denial of death.* New York: Free Press.

Bernard M. & Phillipson, C. (1995). Retirement and leisure. In J. Nussbaum & J. Coupland (Eds), *Handbook of communication and aging research* (pp. 285–312). Mahwah, NJ: Erlbaum.

Bhabha, H. (1994). *The location of culture.* London: Routledge.

Blommaert, J. & Verschueren, J. (1998). *Debating diversity: Analysing the discourse of tolerance.* London: Routledge.

Brewer, M.B., Dull, V. & Lui, L. (1981). Perceptions of the elderly: Stereotypes as prototypes. *Journal of Personality and Social Psychology*, **41**, 656–670.

Butler, R.N. (1969). Age-ism: Another form of bigotry. *Gerontologist*, **9**, 243–246.

Cameron, D. (1995). *Verbal hygiene.* London: Routledge.

Chappell, N.L. & Orbach, H.L. (1986). Socialization in old age: A Meadian perspective. In V W Marshall (Ed.), *Later life: The social psychology of aging* (pp. 75–106). Beverly Hills, CA: Sage.

Cohen, G. (1994). Age related problems in the use of proper names in communication. In M. Hummert, J.M. Wiemann & J.F. Nussbaum (Eds), *Interpersonal communication in older adulthood: Interdisciplinary theory and research* (pp. 40–57). Thousand Oaks, CA: Sage.

Coupland, J. (forthcoming). "Time has a nasty habit of catching up with us": Discourses of skin care product advertising. In J. Coupland & R. Gwyn (Eds), *Discourses of the body.* Proceedings of the fourth Cardiff Roundtable in Language and Communication.

Coupland, J. & Coupland, N. (in press). Roles, responsibilities and alignments: Multiparty talk in geriatric care. In M.L. Hummert and J. Nussbaum (Eds). *Aging, communication and health: Linking research and practice for successful aging.* Mahwah, NJ: Erlbaum.

Coupland, N. (Ed.) (1993). Discourse, institutions and the elderly. *Journal of Aging Studies*, **7**, 3 (special issue).

Coupland, N. (in press). Other representation. In J. Blommaert & J. Verschueren (Eds), *Handbook of pragmatics.* Amsterdam: Benjamins.

Coupland, N. & Coupland, J. (1990). Language and later life: The diachrony and decrement predicament. In H. Giles & P. Robinson (Eds), *Handbook of language and social psychology* (pp. 451–470). Chichester: Wiley.

Coupland, N. & Coupland, J. (1997). Discourses of the unsayable: Death-implicative talk in geriatric medical consultations. In A. Jaworski (Ed.), *Silence: Interdisciplinary perspectives* (pp. 117–152). Berlin: Mouton de Gruyter.

Coupland, N. & Coupland, J. (1998). Reshaping lives: Constitutive identity work in geriatric medical consultations. *Text*, **18**, 159–189.

Coupland, N. & Coupland, J. (1999). Ageing, ageism and anti-ageism: Moral stance in geriatric medical discourse. In H. Hamilton (Ed.), *Language and communication in old age: Multidisciplinary perspectives* (pp 177–208). New York: Garland.

Coupland, N. & Nussbaum, J. (Eds) (1993). *Discourse and lifespan identity.* Newbury Park, CA: Sage.

Coupland, N., Coupland, J. & Giles, H. (1989) Telling age in later life: Identity and face implications. *Text,* **9**, 129–151.

Coupland, N., Coupland, J. & Giles, H. (1991). *Language, society and the elderly: Discourse, identity and ageing.* Oxford: Blackwell.

Edwards, A.D. (1976). *Language in culture and class.* London: Heinemann.

Edwards, D. & Potter, J. (1992). *Discursive psychology.* London: Sage.

Elliott, A. (1996). Psychoanalysis and social theory. In B.S. Turner (Ed.), *The Blackwell companion to social theory* (pp. 177–193). Oxford: Blackwell.

Fairclough, N. (1992). *Critical language awareness.* London: Longman.

Fairclough, N. (2000). Discourse, social theory and social research: The discourse of welfare reform. *Journal of Sociolinguistics,* **4**, 163–195.

Featherstone, M. & Hepworth, M. (1990). Ageing and old age: Reflections on the postmodern life course. In B. Bytheway, T. Keil, P. Allatt & A. Bryman (Eds), *Becoming and being old: Sociological approaches to later life* (pp. 133–157). London: Sage.

Featherstone, M. & Hepworth, M. (1991). The mask of ageing and the postmodern lifecourse. In M. Featherstone, M. Hepworth and B. Turner (Eds), *The body: Social process and cultural theory* (pp. 371–389). London: Sage.

Gal, S. & Woolard, C. (1995). Constructing languages and publics: Authority and representation. *Pragmatics,* **5**, 129–138.

Giddens, A. (1991). *Modernity and self-identity.* Cambridge UK: Polity Press.

Giles, H. (Ed.) (1998). Applied research in language and intergenerational communication. *Journal of Applied Communication Research,* **26**, 1, (special issue).

Giles, H. & Coupland, N. (1991) *Language: Contexts and consequences.* Milton Keynes: Open University Press and Pacific Grove, CA: Brooks/Cole.

Giles, H. & Robinson, P. (Eds) (1990). *Handbook of language and social psychology.* Chichester: Wiley.

Giles, H., Coupland, N. & Wiemann, J. (Eds) (1990). *Communication, health and the elderly.* Manchester: Manchester University Press.

Giles, H., Fox, S., Harwood, J. & Williams, A. (1994). Talking age and aging talk: Communicating through the lifespan. In M.L. Hummert, J.M. Wiemann & J.F. Nussbaum (Eds), *Interpersonal communication in older adulthood: Interdisciplinary theory and research* (pp. 130–161) Thousand Oaks, CA: Sage.

Gold, D.P., Arbuckle, T.Y. & Andres, D. (1994). Verbosity in older adults. In M.L. Hummert, J.M. Wiemann, & J.F. Nussbaum (Eds), *Interpersonal communication in older adulthood: Interdisciplinary theory and research* (pp 107–129). Thousand Oaks, CA: Sage.

Green, B.S. (1993). *Gerontology and the construction of old age: A study in discourse analysis.* New York: Aldine De Gruyter.

Gumperz, J.J. & Levinson, S.C. (Eds) (1996). *Rethinking linguistic relativity.* Cambridge, UK: Cambridge University Press.

Hall, M.R.P., Maclennan, W.J. & Dye, M.D.W. (1993). *Medical care of the elderly* (3rd edn). Chichester: Wiley

Hamilton, H.E. (Ed.) (1999). *Language and communication in old age: Multi-disciplinary perspectives.* New York: Garland.

Harwood, J. & Giles, H. (1992). "Don't make me laugh": Age representations in a humorous context. *Discourse and Society,* **3**, 403–436.

Hockey, J. & James, A. (1993). *Growing up and growing old: Ageing and dependency in the life course.* London: Sage.

Hodge, R. & Kress, G. (1988). *Social semiotics.* Cambridge, UK: Polity Press in association with Basil Blackwell.

Hummert, M.L. (1990). Multiple stereotypes of elderly and young adults: A comparison of structure and evaluations. *Psychology and Aging*, **5**, 183–193.

Hummert, M.L. (1994). Stereotypes of the elderly and patronising speech. In M.L. Hummert, J.M. Wiemann & J.F. Nussbaum (Eds), *Interpersonal communication in older adulthood: Interdisciplinary theory and research* (pp.162–184). Thousand Oaks, CA: Sage.

Hummert, M.L. & Nussbaum, J.F. (Eds,) (in press). *Aging, communication, and health: Linking research and practice for successful aging*. Mahwal, NJ: Erlbaum.

Hummert, M.L. Shaner, J.L. & Gartska, T.A. (1995). Cognitive processes affecting communication with older adults: The case for stereotypes, attitudes and beliefs about communication. In J. F. Nussbaum & J. Coupland (Eds), *Handbook of communication and aging research* (pp. 105–132). Mahwah, NJ: Erlbaum.

Hummert, M.L., Wiemann, J.M. & Nussbaum, J.F. (Eds) (1994). *Interpersonal communication in older adulthood: Interdisciplinary theory and research*. Thousand Oaks, CA: Sage.

Jaworski, A. & Coupland, N. (Eds) (1999). *The discourse reader*. London: Routledge.

Kemper, S. (1992). Adults' sentence fragments: Who, what, when, where and why? *Communication Research*, **19**, 444–458.

Kemper, S. (1994). Elderspeak: Speech accommodations to older adults. *Aging and Cognition*, **1**, 17–28.

Kubey, R.W. (1980). Television and aging: Past, present and future. *The Gerontologist*, **20**, 16–35.

Labov, W. (1994). *Principles of linguistic change. Vol. 1: Internal factors*. Oxford: Blackwell.

Lee, D. (1992). *Competing discourses: Perspectives and ideology in language*. London: Longman.

Mead, G.H. (1934). *Mind, self and society* (edited by C.W. Morris). Chicago: Chicago University Press.

Montgomery, M. (1986). *An introduction to language and society*. London: Methuen.

Nuessel, F. (1982). The language of ageism. *The Gerontologist*, **22**, 273–276.

Nussbaum, J. & Coupland, J. (Eds) (1995) *Handbook of communication and aging research*. Mahwah, NJ: Erlbaum.

Potter, J. & Wetherell, M. (1987). *Discourse and social psychology*. London: Sage.

Rampton, B. (in press). Speech community. In J. Blommaert & J. Verschueren (Eds), *Handbook of pragmatics*.

Riggins, S.H. (Ed.) (1997). *The language and politics of exclusion: Others in discourse*. Thousand Oaks, CA: Sage.

Rogers, E.M. (1999). Georg Simmel's concept of the stranger and intercultural communication research. *Communication Theory*, **9**, 58–74.

Rubin, A.M. & Rubin, R.B. (1986). Contextual age as a life position index. *International Journal of Aging and Human Development*, **32**, 27–45.

Sacks, H. (1995). *Lectures on conversation*, (Ed. G. Jefferson) Oxford: Blackwell.

Said, E. (1978). *Orientalism*. London: Routledge & Kegan Paul.

Simmel, G. (1950). *The sociology of Georg Simmel* (Transl. K.H. Wolff). NewYork: Free Press.

Sontag, S. (1991). *Illness as metaphor: Aids and its metaphors*. Harmondsworth, UK: Penguin.

Tajfel, H. (1981). Social stereotypes and social groups. In J.C. Turner & H. Giles (Eds), *Intergroup behaviour* (pp. 144–165). Oxford: Blackwell.

Tajfel, H. & Turner, J. (1979). An integrative theory of intergroup conflict. In W.C. Austin & S. Worchel (Eds), *The social psychology of intergroup relations* (pp 33–53). Monterey, CA: Brooks/Cole.

Whorf, B.L. (1956/1997). The relation of habitual thought and behavior to language. In J.B. Carroll (Ed.) *Language, thought and reality: Selected writings of Benjamin Lee*

Whorf (pp. 134–159). Cambridge, MA.: MIT Press. Reprinted in N. Coupland and A. Jaworski (Eds), *Sociolinguistics: A reader and coursebook* (pp. 443–463). London: Macmillan.

Williams, A. & Coupland, N. (1998). Epilogue: The socio-political framing of communication and aging research. *Journal of Applied Communication Research*, **26**, 2139–2154.

Williams, A. & Nussbaum, J. F. (2001). *Intergenerational communication across the lifespan*. Mahwah, NJ: Erlbaum.

Williams, A. & Ylänne-McEwen, V. (Eds) (2000). Lifestyles and the lifecourse. *Journal of Communication* (special issue) **50**, 4–99.

Woodward, K. (1991). *Aging and its discontents: Freud and other fictions*. Bloomington: Indiana University Press.

Part 6

Applied Settings

Second Language Mastery

Richard Clément
University of Ottawa, Canada
Robert C. Gardner
University of Western Ontario, London, Canada

What does it mean to master a second language? An extensive vocabulary? A good grasp of grammar? Oral fluency? An awareness of idioms? When is someone bilingual? In 1952, Lambert proposed that bilingualism could be measured in terms of comparative automaticity in the two languages, thus avoiding the definition of bilingualism in terms of vocabulary and/or grammar knowledge, oral fluency, aural comprehension, accent, and/or writing skills, etc. There are large individual differences in all of these various facets of language proficiency among native speakers of a language, thus it is difficult to define mastery in terms of any or all of them. The present chapter does not attempt to define second language mastery. Instead it discusses research and issues that are concerned with the social psychology of second language learning, and within this context, the focus is often on one or more of the aspects of language proficiency referred to above.

We wrote a chapter for the previous *Handbook of Language and Social Psychology* (Gardner & Clément, 1990) in which we focused on "Social psychological perspectives on second language acquisition". In that chapter we provided an overview of individual differences in second language acquisition, and the contextual aspects that influence and moderate the effects of relevant individual difference variables in the language-learning process. This chapter continues in that same vein, drawing on results and generalizations in the 1990 chapter, and following through with research developments since then. It will be evident that much of the research focus is the same, but that there has been an increase in the number of models proposed to understand the issue of second language mastery.

The New Handbook of Language and Social Psychology.
Edited by W. Peter Robinson and Howard Giles.
© 2001 John Wiley & Sons Ltd.

Also, the contexts have broadened and the focus is much more extensive than it was in the previous version of this chapter. Finally, in this version we have focused explicit attention on a number of issues that have arisen in the last 10 years in this general area of research.

LANGUAGE-LEARNING SCENARIOS

Although it is difficult to state precisely what constitutes bilingualism, it has been noted that bilingualism is the norm in many countries (Tucker, 1981). Second language learning is commonplace, and it is varied. In some countries, many students view the second language largely as a school subject, much like algebra or biology, though, as we will show, this may be a somewhat misguided view. Nonetheless, their own language is that of the majority, and although they study the second language in school, they live in an environment where it is seldom heard or seen, and they rarely, if ever, use it outside the classroom. Other students in the same class may not speak the majority language in the home (or even the second language they are learning in school) but, because of their schooling and their life experiences, use the language of the majority in most other contexts. Like the students described above, they seldom if ever use the second language outside the classroom. Still other students in the class may actually speak the second language in the home (and sometimes even the language of the majority as well), and nonetheless study the second language in the classroom. Unlike the other students discussed, these students might well use the second language outside of class, though if differences exist between the form used at home and that taught in the classroom, they would probably use the home form. Of course, any of the above students may live where the second language is also dominant in the community, and this will change greatly the dynamics involved in learning the second language. The point is that although we often consider a class of students in a language program as relatively uniform, we must realize that they all bring their own personal experiences and situations with them, so that learning a second language is not one simple monolithic phenomenon. This is true whether the classroom context is that of a regular second language class or a bilingual immersion program. A later section of this chapter will discuss research relevant to such contextual differences. First, we will consider issues and research concerned with individual differences and second language acquisition.

SECOND LANGUAGE VERSUS FOREIGN LANGUAGE LEARNING/ACQUISITION

A distinction is sometimes made between second and/or foreign language *learning* versus *acquisition*. Gardner (1958; see also Krashen, 1988) proposed that second language learning should be used to refer to the development of knowledge or skill in the second language, so that an individual has knowledge about elements of the language, and/or can make use of the language where applicable. Second language acquisition, on the other hand, should be used when referring to making the second language part of the individual's very being. That is, second language acquisition involves some degree of identification with the other language community in that the language is a definable part of the individual's identity.

A distinction is also sometimes made (see, for example, Oxford & Shearin, 1994) between *second* vs *foreign* language acquisition (or learning). *Second language acquisition* is generally taken to mean the acquisition of a language other than the native language which is recognized as an official language in the homeland. For example, Canada is officially a bilingual country, so that English would be considered the second language for Francophone Canadians, while French is a second language for Anglophone Canadians. *Foreign language acquisition* is generally seen as referring to the acquisition of a language that is not characteristic of the individual's homeland. Thus, the acquisition of Spanish in Canada would be considered an instance of foreign language learning by both Anglophones and Francophones alike. Although these two definitions are relatively straightforward, it is often further assumed that, as a consequence, second language acquisition takes place in an environment where the individual has ample opportunity to experience both languages, while foreign language acquisition takes place in environments where the learner has little opportunity to practice it outside the classroom environment.

On the surface, this seems like a very useful distinction, and it may very well be, provided the excess meanings apply. But do they always? The answer is, of course not! Canada is officially a bilingual country. French and English are both recognized as official languages. The last census conducted in Canada was in 1996, and at that time the population was given as 28,528,125. Of these, 67.1% reported that they knew only English, 14.3% only French, and 17.0% both English and French. Such statistics certainly justify the identification of Canada as a bilingual country, with 84.1% (i.e., 67.1 + 17.0) reporting that they know English, and 31.3% reporting that they know French.

There are important regional differences, however, that belie the simplicity of this characterization. Consider the provinces of Quebec and Ontario, for example. In Quebec, 5.1% of the population know only English, 56.1% know only French, and 37.8% know French and English, while in Ontario the comparable figures are 85.7% (English), 0.4% (French), and 11.6% (French and English). Thus, comparing the two provinces, it can be said that while 93.9% of the population of Quebec know French, only 12% of the population of Ontario knows French. The corresponding values for knowledge of English are 42.9% (Quebec) and 97.3% (Ontario). From this it can be seen that whereas the language character of Quebec might be described as bilingual, that for Ontario is largely monolingual English. Thus, a student learning French (or English) as a second language in Quebec could certainly be said to be learning in an environment where both French and English are readily available, but the same cannot be said for many students in Ontario.

The United States is officially an English-speaking country. The last census was taken in 1990, where the population is listed as 230,445,777. This census indicates that 7.5% of the population speak Spanish in the home. In some parts of the United States, however, there are relatively large numbers of Spanish-speaking individuals. The percentage of Spanish speakers is 27.9% in New Mexico, 22.1% in Texas, 20% in California, 14.2% in Arizona, 12% in Florida, and 11% in New York. Spanish is considered a foreign language in the United States, though clearly in many of these settings the language environment is comparable to that often used to characterize second language situations. Thus, although one can make a distinction between second and foreign language learning, many of the assumed differences between the two contexts do not exist necessarily.

INDIVIDUAL DIFFERENCES IN SECOND LANGUAGE ACQUISITION

There are a number of individual difference variables that have been investigated as possible correlates or causes of second language achievement. In our chapter in the previous Handbook (Gardner & Clément, 1990), we distinguished between three classes of individual difference variables and discussed the relevant research. One of the classes of variables was referred to as "Cognitive Characteristics", and included language aptitude and language-learning strategies. The second class was "Attitudes and Motivation", which referred to a number of affective measures, which were in turn grouped into three subclasses. These three subclasses were Integrativeness (involving attitudes toward the other language group or other language groups in general), Attitudes toward the Learning Situation (specifically the course and the teacher), and Motivation (defined in terms of desire to learn the language, effort expended to learn the language, and satisfaction with the activity of learning the language). The final class was "Personality Variables". This included a number of personality characteristics such as sociability, extraversion, empathy, field dependence/independence, anxiety, and linguistic self-confidence. All three classes of these variables were seen as factors that influenced how well and/or how quickly an individual could learn another language.

In 1995, researchers at the University of Western Ontario[1] searched three databases (ERIC, Linguistics and Language Behaviour Abstracts, and PsycLit) to identify publications from 1985 to 1994 that involved either of eight different classes of individual difference variables: Attitudes, Field Independence, Intelligence, Language Anxiety, Language Aptitude, Learning Strategies, Motivation, and Self-Confidence. Since many abstracts involve the investigation of more than one class of variables, this resulted in a number of abstracts being

---

[1] This research was conducted by Paul Tremblay, Joy Bergshoeff, and R. C. Gardner, at the University of Western Ontario.

identified in more that one class. In all, 1041 different abstracts were obtained. Figure 1 presents a summary of the number of abstracts each year for the five most frequently investigated variables. As can be seen, the most frequently investigated variables were *Attitudes*, followed by *Learning Strategies* and *Motivation*, then *Language Aptitude* and *Anxiety* (including *Self-Confidence*). It will be noted further that research on Language Aptitude tended to decline over this period, while that for Attitudes increased and the others remained relatively constant. As indicated by this analysis, there is an active research interest in all of these variables, and although there are exceptions and disagreements with respect to interpretation, all these variables have been shown to be implicated in second language acquisition.

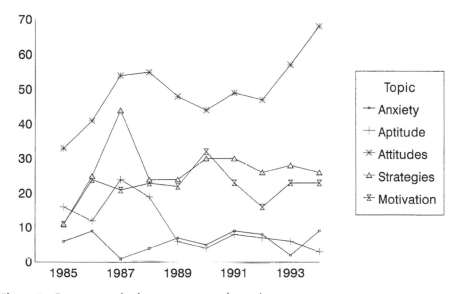

Figure 1   Frequency of references per year by topic

Space does not permit a review of the studies that have been conducted on these variables, though it is necessary to point out their complexity. For example, the concept of Attitudes is a general one, since there are many possible attitude objects, such as the group who speaks the language, the teacher, the course, the act of learning the language, etc. (see, for example, Gardner, 1985). Motivation is broadly conceived, varying from the nature of the motives (or orientations) (i.e., Clément & Kruidenier, 1983), to a complex of effort, desire, and affect in learning the language (Gardner, 1985), to expectancy, attributions, valence, and goal setting (Dörnyei, 1998; Tremblay & Gardner, 1995). Language anxiety can focus on different aspects such as communication apprehension, test anxiety, and fear of evaluation (Horwitz, 1986), it can involve anxiety associated with input, processing, or output (MacIntyre & Gardner, 1994a), it can be identified as either trait or state anxiety (MacIntyre & Gardner, 1994b), or as a component of self-confidence with the second language (Clément, Dörnyei & Noels, 1994).

Language-learning strategies can refer to different techniques as defined by the Strategy Inventory for Language Learning (Oxford, 1990) used by students to learn the language, or by mnemonic devices such as the Key Word technique (Atkinson & Raugh, 1975) recommended by researchers and taught by some teachers. Language aptitude refers to a host of memory, reasoning, and first language skills that students bring with them to the language classroom. The Modern Language Aptitude Test (MLAT) (Carroll & Sapon, 1959) was the first measure of language aptitude developed using factor analytic methods to identify specific abilities associated with learning a second language, and it remains the criterion against which other measures of language aptitude are (or should be) evaluated (see, for example, Carroll, 1990; Skehan, 1991).

One issue that is problematic in this area is that of causation. In the socio-educational model of second language acquisition, Gardner (1985) distinguishes between two classes of outcomes of language study: linguistic outcomes (such as objective and subjective indices of proficiency) and non-linguistic outcomes (such as the behavioural intention to continue language study, favourable attitudes and motivation). As indicated above, there is ample evidence showing relationships between all classes of variables mentioned above and various outcomes of language training, but a particularly problematic issue is the direction of causation. That is, are individual differences in attitudes, learning strategies, motivation, language anxiety, and language aptitude responsible for individual differences in the outcome variables? Are there other variables correlated with these that are responsible? Or does the experience in the classroom lead to differences in these variables? The simple truth is that since the concern here is with the relationship between individual differences, it is impossible to ever state unequivocally what is responsible for what. Gardner (2000) does, however, discuss research strategies that can be used to increase the probability that particular causal interpretations are more likely.

One of the implications of the ambiguity about the causal nature of associations between indices of second language achievement and individual difference variables is the abundance of models that have been proposed to account for individual differences in second language acquisition. Gardner (1985) identified some models that derive from social psychology such as the Social Psychological model (Lambert, 1978), the Acculturational model (Schumann, 1978), the Socio-Educational model (Gardner, 1979), the Social Context model (Clément, 1980), and the Intergroup model (Giles & Byrne, 1982). Since then, there have been others such as the Macroscopic Model (Landry & Allard, 1992), the Willingness to Communicate model (MacIntyre et al., 1998), the Self-Determination model (Noels, Clément & Pelletier, 1999), and at least two extended motivational models (Dörnyei, 1994a; Williams & Burden, 1997). Each of these models offers many insights into the second language-learning situation, but it is the considered opinion of the present authors that no one model is uniformly better or more meaningful than the others. Some of the models centre on the same variables, adding or subtracting others, and often reordering their relative importance; others place more emphasis on slightly different variables. Some have little empirical research associated with them that was done specifically to test the model, others have some research with more forthcoming, and others have a relatively large database supporting the model.

One point that stands out in an examination of these models is that none of them makes predictions that are diametrically opposed to those made by any other model. There have been disagreements in the literature to be sure (see, for example, an interesting exchange between Crookes and Schmidt (1991), Oxford and Shearin (1994), Oxford (1994), Dörnyei (1994a, 1994b) and Gardner and Tremblay (1994, 1995). Although these discussions are interesting, a bit heated on occasions, and sometimes amusing, it is clear by the end that the major differences are in terms of interpretation and not in substance. All of these researchers believe that most or all of the individual difference variables referred to above are implicated in second language acquisition. Their disagreements rest in how the variables are implicated, the relative dominance of the variables, and the processes by which they operate, as well as the context in which the model is most relevant, and the nature of the causal sequences.

CONTEXTUAL ASPECTS

As conceptual and methodological tools, individual differences were the first to be used in social psychological forays into second language acquisition. With variations observed in results obtained in different areas, under different programs and political–ideological orientations, it became evident that contextual factors had to be considered. Even though these had been discussed early in the establishment of the field (e.g., Lambert, 1967), systematic interest in the issue is more recent, and has certainly been at the core of second language acquisition and use research since the first version of this chapter was published, in 1990. According to Giles and Coupland (1991), the role of language in human affairs is to be understood as depending on *and* determining context. The study of contextual effects must, therefore, necessarily proceed from an interactive approach to the relation between language use and the characteristics of the environment in which it takes place. Specifically here, the social psychological perspective on context is proposed to encompass all interpersonal and intergroup phenomena, real or imagined, likely to result from or influence the acquisition of a second language.

That definition remains of course out of proportion with the available evidence. Hopefully the lacunae revealed by this review will point to as many avenues for future research. In what follows, three levels of context will be examined: (a) the pedagogical context; (b) the sociostructural context and (c) the psychological context.

The Pedagogical Context

The learning context has, for a number of years, been an issue at the interface of social psychology and education. The learning environments, including attitudes towards the teacher and the course, were incorporated early in Gardner's (Gardner & Smythe, 1975) socio-educational model. In education, the development of immersion programs aimed at providing the student with a complete range of pedagogical activities in the target language represented a further step in engineering the context of second language acquisition. The results reviewed by Clément (1994) and by Noels and Clément (1998) suggest that students benefit from such programs as regards passive, but not active language skills, as well as attitudes towards the other group and bilingualism (see Genesee, 1987).

The apparent contrast between active language skills and other outcomes could be linked to a number of other contextual factors. Positive attitudes may develop as a result of positive parental and institutional support for sharing cultural knowledge, promoting intercultural harmony and more fruitful interactions with members of the other group. Achieving fluency in the second language, particularly the active skills, however, requires more. From the little we know about what happens in the second language classroom (Allen et al., 1990; Genesee, 1987), the students' use of the second language is mostly reactive and limited in terms of amplitude. Hammerly (1989) also claims that the immersion classroom fosters a pidginized variety of the second language which may not be usable with native speakers. The fundamental problem may, therefore, be very closely related to social interaction patterns taking place in the classroom.

In conjunction with the above, social psychological approaches themselves were evolving towards closer scrutiny of the classroom context (cf. Dörnyei, 1998). Noels et al. (1999) studied teachers' communicative style using self-determination theory to show its effect on student motivation and achievement. Likewise, Liskin-Gasparro (1998) exemplified the complex socio-emotional process of students involved in an intensive total immersion summer session. The programmatic analysis of classroom interaction as group dynamics presented more recently by Ehrman and Dörnyei (1998) confirms the potential usefulness of a perspective presenting classroom activities as responding to the social psychological principles. Optimally, the classroom itself should approximate a microcosm of live interactions with native speakers, with its linguistic and non-linguistic aspects (Firth & Wagner, 1997).

Structural Aspects

The above suggests that the issue of contact with the second language-speaking group in naturalistic contexts is a key issue to understanding second language acquisition. It does appear that aspects of inter-ethnic contact in the context of second language programs serves to develop more positive attitudes and greater self-confidence in the ability to use the second language efficiently (for reviews, see Clément, 1994; Gardner, 1985; Gardner & Clément, 1990). The assumption that such interaction could occur and have consequences that would be independent of the wider structural context in which it occurs is, however, challenged in a number of ways.

A relevant theme here is the idea that positive benefits from language acquisition will only be achieved to the extent that the first language and culture are well established within the individual (Carey, 1991; Clément, 1984; Cummins & Swain, 1986; Hamers & Blanc, 1988; Landry & Allard, 1992). This presupposes a familial, educational, and social context which allows the development and transmission of the first language and culture. Although such conditions may be present for majority group members, they may not characterize the situation of minority group members, immigrants, refugees, and sojourners. The relative status of the first and second language-speaking groups and the linguistic composition of the community are here key determinants of the linguistic and cultural outcomes of second language acquisition.

Under the concepts of additive and subtractive bilingualism, Lambert (1978) proposed that language-learning outcomes could be very different for members of majority and minority groups. Giles, Bourhis and Taylor (1977) subsequently formalized definitions of minority and majority status under the concept of ethnolinguistic vitality which encompasses demographic representation of the communities, their institutional representation and the socio-economic status of their members. These factors were further developed by Prujiner et al. (1984) in terms of the relative demographic, political, economic and cultural capital of the in- and outgroup communities. The results obtained to date show a consistent relation between these structural factors and first language retention and competence (e.g., Landry & Allard, 1992; Landry, Allard & Henry, 1996).

Does this imply the inevitable disappearance of language endowed with less vitality or capital? This question has come to be a key issue for government authorities in a number of countries. Language planning (cf. Haugen, 1959; Maurais, 1987) has been the political and administrative instrument used to promote and protect language according to predetermined societal options (e.g., Martin, 1997). Accordingly, the State may determine the goals of language education, the medium of interaction with government agencies, tribunals and schools, and the relative visibility of different languages in public and commercial signs – the *linguistic landscape* (Landry & Bourhis, 1997). The effectiveness of such measures depends to a large extent on conditions already present in the communities on which it is imposed. Promoting English as the only language among Americans seems to be relatively easy (cf. Frendreis & Tatalovitch, 1997). In fact, the promotion of English outside the United States and England has been referred to as "linguistic imperialism" (Boyle, 1997; Clachar, 1998) and has raised some concerns about the faith of local, demographically dominant languages. The promotion of French as the only official language by the Quebec government has, however, not met with as clear-cut results. Although the degree of French use among Quebec Anglophones seems to have increased, field studies of language preferences (e.g., Moïse & Bourhis, 1994) show a constant preference for English. Thus, the effectiveness of language planning in the protection and promotion of languages is heavily moderated by factors which escape legislation, such as historical aspects and the extra-territorial hegemony of non-native languages such as English. With the exception of tangential evidence, some of which is noted above, little research is available to assess the social psychological impact of language planning. The effects of attempts by States at controlling the vitality of languages still remain to be assessed thoroughly.

The Psychological Context

Understanding the effects of structural aspects requires an array of psychological constructs likely to mediate their influence on individual characteristics and behaviour. A first step towards bridging the structural–psychological gap has been to recast structural factors as subjective perceptions of the individual. Thus, Bourhis, Giles and Rosenthal (1981) defined subjective ethnolinguistic vitality as the perceived counterpart of "objective vitality". Subsequent studies tended to show a stable relation between objective and subjective measures of vitality (e.g., Bourhis & Sachdev, 1984; Landry & Allard, 1992). Although Clément (1980, 1984) hypothesized a relation between individual subjective vitality and motivation to learn the second language as well as proficiency in the second language, these were not confirmed (Clément, 1986; Labrie & Clément, 1986). Subsequent studies (e.g., Cenoz & Valencia, 1993) and a review by Harwood, Giles and Bourhis (1994), however, suggest a number of direct and indirect effects through the influence of vitality on interethnic contact experiences.

Aspects of contact also are the precursors to the development of self-confidence, which is an important determinant of motivation and second language proficiency (Clément & Kruidenier, 1985). In addition, self-confidence in using the second language has been shown to be positively correlated with the degree of identification with the second language group and, in the case of minority group members, negatively correlated with identification to the first language group (Noels & Clément, 1996; Noels, Pon & Clément, 1996). In the latter case, it is likely that competence in and preference for using the second language will entail the loss of the first language and culture (Cameron & Lalonde, 1994; Clément, Gauthier & Noels, 1993). Erosion of original identities among minority groups would, in turn, feed back on both subjective and objective vitalities, frequency of interethnic contact, and their linguistic and affective correlates. The dynamics of this system is further reinforced by the fact that better adjustment and well-being are often correlated with greater self-confidence in using the second language and greater social support from the second language network (Clément, Michaud & Noels, 1998; Noels & Clément, 1996; Noels et al., 1996). Learning a second language may therefore be, at once, a vector of individual psychological adjustment and collective language and culture loss.

The preceding discussion places second language acquisition in the context of an acculturation process involving factors and issues which largely extend beyond the classroom or even the immediate neighbourhood. Acquiring a second language involves certain costs and benefits which are directly related to the relative status of the communities in contact. For majority group members learning a minority language, whether that group is represented or not in the community, benefits in terms of personal enrichment might well outweigh the cost incurred by a momentary culture shock and communication anxiety. It is possible, however, that teaching a second dominant language to help in the adaptation of minority group members entails the disappearance of the minority community as a distinct cultural entity of a nation. This would certainly be counterproductive in political contexts boasting a pluralist approach to ethnic diversity. It is therefore urgent to envisage language planning and pedagogical approaches that would avoid these pitfalls through a better understanding of identity and adaptation patterns.

FUTURE DIRECTIONS

As the preceding indicates, the context can have a profound effect on the dynamics of second language acquisition. Also, as indicated earlier, there are many social psychologically based models of second language acquisition that, in general, are in agreement that a host of individual difference variables promote achievement in the second language. The models differ, however, in the contexts to which they are directed, the variables emphasized or the variables that are presumed to operate directly on achievement, and those that play a more mediating or supportive role.

In the future, it is recommended that the developers of the various models direct attention to conducting research that bears directly on the validity of the processes proposed. Although it will probably be the case that unequivocal support for only one model will never be obtained, tests directed to supporting any given model will aid in understanding the underlying processes. To do such tests, it will probably be necessary to formulate the actual process more precisely than is generally the case with most of the existing models. This will serve to eliminate some of the ambiguity that currently exists, which is evident in discussions of the models by individuals in the different camps (see, for example, the discussions in the articles in the 1994 and 1995 issues of the *Modern Language Journal* by Oxford and Shearin, Oxford, Dörnyei, and Gardner and Tremblay).

One way of increasing the precision of the models is to attempt to formulate hypotheses based on the models that can be tested in a laboratory context. For example, it has long been argued that integrative motivation and instrumental motivation facilitate second language acquisition. This type of hypothesis is difficult to evaluate in a classroom context (except by showing correlations with achievement), but it has been possible to demonstrate it directly in a laboratory analogue study. Thus, Gardner and MacIntyre (1991) demonstrated that the rate of learning French vocabulary over a series of trials was faster for individuals who could be characterized as integratively motivated, as well as for those who could be classified as instrumentally motivated than for those who were low on either type of motivation. The laboratory analogue may be criticized as being somewhat artificial, but what it lacks in real-world authenticity it makes up for with the control that can be exercised over extraneous variables. As indicated above, there has been some research using this approach but most of it has been focused on aspects of the socio-educational model of second language acquisition (Gardner, 1985). It is recommended that more research of this type be directed to elements of the other theoretical models so that some of the implications of these models can be tested more directly.

As indicated earlier, there is also ample evidence that a number of individual difference variables are related to various indices of achievement in the second language such as classroom grades, scores on objective measures of proficiency, a willingness to communicate in the language, an intention to continue language study, performance in the classroom etc. With all the research that has been conducted, it now seems opportune to conduct meta-analyses of the various predictor variables and indices of achievement to obtain reasonable estimates of the strength of the relationships obtained. Such estimates might give us a clearer indication of the relative importance of the various predictor variables, and help us to understand which variables are better thought of as major determinants, which as minor, and which as mediators. Currently many of these decisions seem more dependent on the theoretical orientation of the individual researcher than on a careful analysis of the research that has been done. Moreover, by considering the role of context when performing the meta-analysis, the precise nature of contextual influences could be clarified.

There has been considerable research conducted on the social psychological approach to second language acquisition since the previous chapter was written, as evidenced by the observation that 54% of the entries to the reference list to the present article were published since the previous Handbook chapter was written. It might also be noted that 61% of the articles discussed in the present chapter refer to research conducted in Canada and/or are written by Canadian researchers. Whether this represents a bias by the two authors of this chapter because they work in the Canadian context, or whether it reflects the relative contributions of researchers throughout the world to this area of research, cannot be ascertained. Such a bias was certainly not intended. The previous chapter cited approximately twice as many articles as the present one (we were advised by the editors to reduce the number of citations in this presentation), but in that chapter 56% of the items listed in the references were of Canadian origin. Thus, the Canadian representation is comparable in the two chapters. It is our view that second language acquisition and bilingualism are important issues in Canada, and that consequently the topic is of greater interest here. This is one of the many hypotheses that could be answered, however, by meta-analytic investigations of this research area.

ACKNOWLEDGEMENTS

Production of this chapter was facilitated by Social Sciences and Humanities Research Council of Canada grants no.410–99-1044 and 410–99-0147, respectively, to the first and second author. The authors are grateful to Vicki Galbraith, Gordon Josephson, Ljiljana Mihic and Viviane Ruest for their invaluable help. The authors'names appear in alphabetical order.

REFERENCES

Allen, P., Swain, M., Harley, B. & Cummins, J. (1990). Aspects of classroom treatment: Towards a more comprehensive view of second language education. In B. Harley, P. Allen, J. Cummins & M. Swain (Eds), *The development of second language proficiency* (pp. 57–81). Cambridge, UK: Cambridge University Press.

Atkinson, R.C. & Raugh, M.R. (1975). An application of the mnemonic keyword method to the acquisition of Russian vocabulary. *Journal of Experimental Psychology: Human Learning and Memory*, **140**, 126–133.

Bourhis, R.Y. & Sachdev, I. (1984). Vitality perceptions and language "attitudes": Some Canadian data. *Journal of Language and Social Psychology*, **3**, 97–126.

Bourhis, R.Y. Giles, H. & Rosenthal, D. (1981). Notes on the construction of a "Subjective Vitality Questionnaire" for ethnolinguistic groups. *Journal of Multilingual and Multicultural Development*, **2**, 145–155.

Boyle, J. (1997). Imperialism of the English language in Hong Kong. *Journal of Multilingual and Multicultural Development*, **18**, 169–181.

Cameron, J.E. & Lalonde, R.N. (1994). Self-ethnicity and social group memberships in two generations of Italian Canadians. *Journal of Personality and Social Psychology*, **20**, 514–520.

Carey, S.T. (1991). The culture of literacy in majority and minority language schools. *Canadian Modern Language Review*, **47**, 950–976.

Carroll, J.B. (1990). Cognitive abilities in foreign language aptitude: Then and now. In T.S. Parry & C.W. Stansfield (Eds), *Language aptitude reconsidered* (pp. 11–29). Englewood Cliffs, NJ: Prentice-Hall.

Carroll, J.B. & Sapon, S.M. (1959). *Modern Language Aptitude Test (MLAT)*. New York: Psychological Corporation.

Cenoz, J. & Valencia, J.F. (1993). Ethnolinguistic vitality, social networks and motivation in second language acquisition: Some data from the Basque country. *Language, Culture & Curriculum*, **6**, 113–127.

Clément, R. (1980). Ethnicity, contact and communicative competence in a second language. In H. Giles, W.P. Robinson & P.M. Smith (Eds), *Language: Social psychological perspectives* (pp.147–159). Oxford: Pergamon Press.

Clément, R. (1984). Aspects socio-psychologiques de la communication inter-ethnique et de l'identité culturelle. *Recherches Sociologiques*, **15**, 293–312.

Clément, R. (1986). Second language proficiency and acculturation: An investigation of the effects of language status and individual characteristics. *Journal of Language and Social Psychology*, **5**, 271–290.

Clément, R. (1994). The acquisition of French as a second language in Canada: Towards a research agenda. In J.W. Berry & J.A. Laponce (Eds), *Ethnicity and culture in Canada: The research landscape* (pp. 410–434). Toronto: University of Toronto Press.

Clément, R. & Kruidenier, B.G. (1983). Orientations in second language acquisition: The effects of ethnicity, milieu and target language on their emergence. *Language Learning*, **33**, 273–291.

Clément, R. & Kruidenier, B.G. (1985). Aptitude, attitude and motivation in second language proficiency: A test of Clément's model. *Journal of Language and Social Psychology*, **4**, 21–37.

Clément, R., Gauthier, R. & Noels, K. (1993). Choix langagiers en milieu minoritaire: Attitudes et identité concomitantes. *Revue Canadienne des Sciences du Comportement*, **25**, 149–164.

Clément, R., Dörnyei, Z. & Noels, K.A. (1994). Motivation and the foreign language classroom: A study of Hungarians learning English. *Language Learning*, **44**, 417–448.

Clément, R., Michaud, C. & Noels, K.A. (1998). Effets acculturatifs du support social en situation de contact intergroupe. *Revue Québécoise de Psychologie*, **19**, 189–210.

Clachar, A. (1998). Differential effects of linguistic imperialism on second language learning: Americanisation in Puerto Rico versus Russification in Estonia. *International Journal of Bilingual Education and Bilingualism*, **1**, 100–118.

Crookes, G. & Schmidt, R.W. (1991). Motivation: Reopening the research agenda. *Language Learning*, **41**, 469–512.

Cummins, J. & Swain, M. (1986). *Bilingualism in education*. New York: Longman.

Dörnyei, Z. (1994a). Motivation and motivating in the language foreign language classroom. *Modern Language Journal*, **78**, 273–284.

Dörnyei, Z. (1994b). Understanding L2 motivation: On with the challenge. *Modern Language Journal*, **78**, 515–523.

Dörnyei, Z. (1998). Motivation in second and foreign language learning. *Language Teaching*, **31**, 117–135.

Ehrman, M.E. & Dörnyei, Z. (1998). *Interpersonal dynamics in second language education*. Thousand Oaks, CA: Sage.

Firth, A. & Wagner, J. (1997). On discourse, communication and (some) fundamental concepts in SLA. *Modern Language Journal*, **81**, 285–300.

Frendreis, J. & Tatalovich, R. (1997). Who supports English-only language laws? Evidence from the 1992 national election study. *Social Science Quarterly*, **78**, 334–368.

Gardner, R.C. (1958). Social factors in second-language acquisition. Master's thesis, McGill University.

Gardner, R.C. (1979). Social psychological aspects of second language acquisition. In H. Giles & R. St Clair (Eds), *Language and social psychology* (pp. 132–147). Oxford: Basil Blackwell.

Gardner, R.C. (1985). *Social psychology and second language learning: The role of attitudes and motivation*. London: Edward Arnold.

Gardner, R.C. (2000). Correlation, causation, motivation and second language acquisition. *Canadian Psychology*, **41**, 10–24.

Gardner, R.C. & Clément, R. (1990). Social psychological perspectives on second language acquisition. In H. Giles & P. Robinson (Eds), *The handbook of language and social psychology* (pp. 495–517). Chichester: Wiley.

Gardner, R.C. & MacIntyre, P.D. (1991). An instrumental motivation in language study: Who says it isn't effective? *Studies in Second Language Acquisition*, **13**, 57–72.

Gardner, R.C. & Smythe, P.C. (1975). Second language acquisition: A social psychological approach. *Research Bulletin No. 332*, Department of Psychology, University of Western Ontario, London, Canada.

Gardner, R.C. & Tremblay, P.F. (1994). On motivation, research agendas, and theoretical frameworks. *Modern Language Journal*, **78**, 359–368.

Gardner, R.C. & Tremblay, P.F. (1995). On motivation: Measurement and conceptual considerations. *Modern Language Journal*, **78**, 524–527.

Genesee, F. (1987). *Learning through two languages*. Cambridge, MA: Newbury House.

Giles, H. & Byrne, J.L. (1982). An intergroup approach to second language acquisition. *Journal of Multilingual and Multicultural Development*, **1**, 17–40.

Giles, H. & Coupland, N. (1991). *Language: Contexts and consequences*. Pacific Grove, CA: Brooks/Cole.

Giles, H., Bourhis, R.Y. & Taylor, D.M. (1977). Towards a theory of language in ethnic group relations. In H. Giles (Ed.), *Language, ethnicity and intergroup relations* (pp. 307–348). New York: Academic Press.

Hamers, J.F. & Blanc, M. (1988). *Bilinguality et bilingualism*, Cambridge, UK: Cambridge University Press.

Hammerly, H. (1989). French immersion (Does it work?) and the development of Bilingual Proficiency Report. *Canadian Modern Language Review*, **45**, 567–578.

Harwood, J., Giles, H. & Bourhis, R.Y. (1994). The genesis of vitality theory: Historical patterns and discoursal dimensions. *International Journal of the Sociology of Language*, **108**, 167–206.

Haugen, E. (1959). Language planning in modern Norway. *Anthropological Linguistics*, **1**(3), 8–21.

Horwitz, E.K. (1986). Preliminary evidence for the reliability and validity of a Foreign Language Anxiety Scale. *TESOL Quarterly*, **20**, 559–562.

Krashen, S.D. (1988). *Second language acquisition and second language learning*. London: Prentice-Hall.

Labrie, N. & Clément, R. (1986). Ethnolinguistic vitality, self-confidence and second language proficiency: An investigation. *Journal of Multilingual and Multicultural Development*, **7**, 269–282.

Lambert, W.E. (1952). Measurement of the linguistic dominance of bilinguals. *Journal of Abnormal and Social Psychology*, **50**, 197–200.

Lambert, W.E. (1967). A social psychology of bilingualism. *Journal of Social Issues*, **23**, 91–109.

Lambert, W.E. (1978). Cognitive and socio-cultural consequences of bilingualism. *Canadian Modern Language Review*, **34**, 537–547.

Landry, R. & Allard, R. (1992). Ethnolinguistic vitality and the bilingual development of minority and majority group students. In W. Fase, K. Jaspaert, & S. Kroon (Eds), *Maintenance and loss of minority languages* (pp. 223–251). Amsterdam: John Benjamins.

Landry, R. & Bourhis, R.Y. (1997). Linguistic landscape and ethnolinguistic vitality. *Journal of Language and Social Psychology*, **16**, 23–49

Landry, R., Allard, R. & Henry, J. (1996). French in south Louisiana: Towards language loss. *Journal of Multilingual and Multicultural Development*, **17**, 442–468.

Liskin-Gasparro, J.E. (1998). Linguistic development in an immersion context: How advanced learners of Spanish perceive SLA. *Modern Language Journal*, **82**, 159–175.

MacIntyre, P.D. & Gardner, R.C. (1994a). The subtle effects of language anxiety on cognitive processing in the second language. *Language Learning*, **44**, 283–305.

MacIntyre, P.D. & Gardner, R.C. (1994b). The effects of induced anxiety on three stages of cognitive processing in computerized vocabulary learning. *Studies in Second Language Acquisition*, **16**, 1–17.

MacIntyre, P.D., Clément, R., Dörnyei, Z. & Noels, K.A. (1998) Conceptualizing willingness to communicate in a L2: A situational model of L2 confidence and affiliation. *Modern Language Journal*, **82**, 545–562.

Martin, D. (1997). Towards a new multilingual language policy in education in South Africa: Different approaches to meet different needs. *Educational Review*, **49**, 129–139.

Maurais, J. (Ed.) (1987). *Politique et aménagement linguistiques*. Québec: Conseil de la langue française.

Moïse, L.C. & Bourhis, R.Y. (1994). Langage et ethnicité: Communication interculturelle à Montréal, 1977–1991. *Canadian Ethnic Studies*, **26**, 86–107.

Noels, K.A. & Clément, R. (1996). Communicating across cultures: Social determinants and acculturative consequences. *Canadian Journal of Behavioural Science*, **28**, 214–228

Noels, K.A. & Clément, R. (1998). Language in education: Bridging educational policy and social psychological research. In J. Edwards (Ed.), *Language in Canada*. (pp. 102–124). Cambridge, UK: Cambridge University Press.

Noels, K.A., Pon, G. & Clément, R. (1996) Language, identity and adjustment: The role of linguistic self-confidence in the adjustment process. *Journal of Language and Social Psychology*, **15**, 246–264.

Noels, K.A., Clément, R. & Pelletier, L. (1999). Perceptions of teachers' communicative style and students' intrinsic and extrinsic motivation. *Modern Language Journal*, **83**, 23–34.

Oxford, R.L. (1990). *Language learning strategies: What every teacher should know*. New York: Newbury House.

Oxford, R.L. (1994). Where are we regarding language learning motivation. *Modern Language Journal*, **78**, 512–514.

Oxford, R.L. & Shearin, J. (1994). Language learning motivation: Expanding the theoretical framework. *Modern Language Journal*, **78**, 12–28.

Prujiner, A., Deshaies, D., Hamers, J., Blanc, M., Clément, R. & Landry, R. (1984). *Variation du comportement langagier lorsque deux langues sont en contact*. Québec: International Centre for Research on Language Planning.

Schumann, J.H. (1978). The acculturation model for second language acquisition. In R.C. Gingras (Ed.) *Second language acquisition and foreign language teaching*. (pp. 27–50). Arlington, VA: Center for Applied Linguistics.

Skehan, P. (1991). Individual differences in second language learning. *Studies in Second Language Acquisition*, **13**, 275–298.

Tremblay, P.F. & Gardner, R.C. (1995). Expanding the motivation construct in language learning. *Modern Language Journal*, **79**, 505–518.

Tucker, G.R. (1981). Social policy and second language teaching. In R.C. Gardner & R. Kalin (Eds), *A Canadian social psychology of ethnic relations* (pp. 77–92). Toronto: Methuen.

Williams, M. & Burden, R. (1997). *Psychology for language teachers*. Cambridge, UK: Cambridge University Press.

Communication, Relationships and Health

Mary Anne Fitzpatrick
University of Wisconsin, Madison, USA
Anita Vangelisti
University of Texas, Austin, USA

INTRODUCTION

The underlying premise of this chapter is that social interaction is the fundamental instrument by which various therapeutic relationships are crafted and health goals are pursued (Roter & Hall, 1992). By social interaction, we do not limit ourselves to linguistic communication but consider the full range of non-verbal and symbolic exchanges that can occur between people. To predict and explain health through interpersonal communication processes may seem at first glance either a naive or futile undertaking. Whereas we agree that no amount of talk between care giver and patient will cure end stage Oates cell carcinoma, interpersonal communication may prolong life and certainly can affect the quality of life for the affected individual. And, communication may prompt another individual to give up smoking or comply with a treatment recommendation and thus prevent the disease from occurring.

One of the difficulties of examining the research on health communication is the disease specificity of the work. Although there may, for example, be particular issues with diseases such as HIV (e.g., stigmatization, fear of the victim) that make them "different" in terms of central relationship issues, we have opted in this chapter to be concerned with uncovering common threads that might inform us of the tapestry linking linguistic choice, interpersonal processes and health outcomes. Although we do not doubt that an in-depth understanding of the

The New Handbook of Language and Social Psychology.
Edited by W. Peter Robinson and Howard Giles.
© 2001 John Wiley & Sons Ltd.

nature, duration, and experience of a given disorder is important to conducting socially significant research on a specific health problem, the theories and models can be examined independent of the disease in question. Let us turn to our model that attempts to capture processes associated with social interaction, relationships and health.

SOCIAL INTERACTION, RELATIONSHIPS AND HEALTH

In any model of language, social interaction, relationships and health, a key focus should be on the need to consider communication processes as they unfold between people over time. The time-span ranges from the microscopic moment-to-moment changes that can be mapped in conversation to macroscopic changes that occur in interpersonal systems as they develop and change over the life cycle of the patient, health care organization/setting, or the family. We could consider the time dimension solely in terms of a given disease syndrome over the life-span of the identified patient (e.g., prevention; coping with the diagnosis and the disease; post-trauma). Underlying the process notion is a dynamic of change over time in how both parties adapt to the "objective" reality of the health of an individual.

Within the framework that emphasizes interpersonal processes, social interaction is the main performance variable: verbal and non-verbal messages that *inform*, *disclose*, *persuade*, and *comfort* take center stage. Each of these message types, considered as part of behavioral routines enacted between (and among) conversational partners, exists along a continuum. Informing often involves explaining difficult and often anxiety-provoking concepts (West & Frankel, 1991) and must be tailored to the recipient as individuals from very different backgrounds may have significant gaps in their health knowledge (Alcalay & Bell, 1996; Bell & Alcalay, 1997). Disclosure or the direct expression of facts and feelings to specific others varies as individuals grapple with maintaining boundaries and privacy (Greene & Serovich, 1996). Persuading involves the full range of interpersonal compliance-gaining techniques through linguistic means (Noller & Fitzpatrick, 1993) as well as the management of fear and anxiety (Witte, 1997). The final performance process is comforting or the giving of emotional support (Kunkel & Burleson, 1999).

Kaleidoscope Model of Health Communication

One way to conceptualize the research on interpersonal processes and health is as a kaleidoscope. Researchers twist the scope in order to break off a few manageable fragments of glass to examine how they fit together for a particular context or disease. The kaleidoscope model sees the research on interpersonal processes and health care as bits of beautiful multi-colored glass held loosely at one end of a rotating tube. These bits of glass are shown in continuing changing symmetrical forms – forms that reveal different interconnections across the segments of the optical puzzle. With every spin of the dial, the picture that one sees of the interrelationships among the pieces can change but each picture suggests different and important ways that the pieces can fit together. The kaleidoscope model views health communication as changing, complex, teeming, and dynamic. Furthermore, the model recognizes health care as a series of relationships defined and managed through language among people, technologies, historical influences and societal trends.

As such our model operates with four basic assumptions. First, health communication is cyclical in that it is often impossible to know which comes first, as most of the processes are mutually reinforcing. Thus, we reject a typical specification of a set of exogenous and endogenous variables leading to the health outcomes and chose as our pictorial representation a series of overlapping concentric circles. Second, processes are overlapping within the same concentric circle as well as among the circles. Sex, race, ethnicity, and class, for example, are often co-mingled in intricate ways, although our research paradigms can sometimes differentiate them. Third, processes are multiply determined, in that individual, group, organizational, and societal levels are involved. These levels fit like matruska dolls one within the other. Fourth, the model is equifinal in that there are many paths to the same outcomes and there may be indirect paths that skip one of the specified levels.

The model specifies four concentric circles around a core. The core is the health and quality of life of the target individual. We treat these variables as primitive terms and, as such, they remain undefined in the model. The first or the outer circle is the circle of social identity: race, class, age, gender, gender identity, and ethnicity of the conversational partners. To understand the micro-interpersonal communication processes, we need to consider the complex macro-social forces and interests which form the context for the relationships and coping strategies of the target individuals. The second concentric circle involves the social context of the patient or the personal, familial and social/professional relationships implicated in health and quality of life. The third concentric circle involves the cognitive, behavioral, and emotional measures taken by individuals to cope with illness. The fourth concentric circle involves the patient compliance and patient satisfaction with the social/professional relationships in the health care context.

CONCENTRIC CIRCLE I: SOCIAL IDENTITY

Dryden and Giles (1987) postulated that the clinic encounter could best be conceptualized as an inter-group encounter with high probabilities of miscommunication. The ethnicity, social class, race, age, gender, and gender identity of

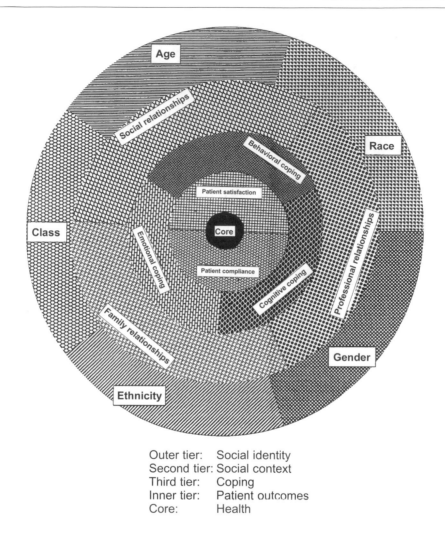

Outer tier: Social identity
Second tier: Social context
Third tier: Coping
Inner tier: Patient outcomes
Core: Health

Figure 1

the participants are thus predicted to form the classifications or groupings within which individuals conduct their conversations. And, multiple identities are likely to be instantiated in any given conversation (Hecht, 1993). There are at least four major arenas in which to explore the effect of these inter-group identities on health outcomes (see Nussbaum et al., 1996, for a discussion related to aging):

1. The occurrence, diagnosis, treatment, prognosis, and discussion of a disorder vary according to the social identity of the target individual.
2. Interpersonal behaviors of any conversational participant change based on their social identity.
3. Through language, individuals stereotype members of outgroups.

4. Individuals tend to value and privilege the interpersonal behavior and linguistic choices of the ingroup and simultaneously devalue and deride the value of the behavior and language of the outgroup.

We need much more research on the impact of social identity on health outcomes. Embedded within a concern for social identity is a methodological commitment to examining the meaning that various messages may have for individuals with different identity constructions. This commitment entails a greater reliance on qualitative methodologies such as focus groups, interviewing, extensive pretesting of messages, and so forth.

CONCENTRIC CIRCLE II: SOCIAL CONTEXT

Health is defined, influenced, and treated via language and social interaction. Whether people are trying to stay healthy, diagnose symptoms, or deal with an illness, they do so in the context of various social relationships. Friends, family, and health practitioners often are more than willing to voice their opinions about health-related issues – and even when they are not, the fact that they opt not to provide their views can influence individuals' physical and mental well-being. The literature on language and health focuses on three different aspects of the social environment: professional relationships, social relationships, and family/personal relationships.

Professional Relationships

The relatively formal roles that define relationships between patients and health care professionals make it tempting to assume that these relationships are enacted in relatively simple, straightforward ways: patients seek information about their health and practitioners provide them with that information. Yet, the research on health communication reveals that interactions between patients and health professionals are incredibly complex and "fraught with potential problems" (Thompson, 1998). Patients and practitioners often enter these interactions with different goals (Winefield, 1992), have widely different perceptions of their communication (Cegala et al., 1995), and interpret commonly used medical terminology in different ways (Hadlow & Pitts, 1991). These and other distinctions between patients and health care practitioners can lead to confusion and misunderstanding.

Despite the potential for misconceptions between patients and health care providers, most patients place a great deal of value on gleaning information from their interactions with practitioners. Studies examining the association between physicians' behavior and patient satisfaction indicate that the most consistent predictor of satisfaction is the doctor's information-giving (Roter, 1989). Not all patients explicitly request information or actively participate when they interact with health professionals (Beisecker, 1990; Brashers, Haas & Neidig, 1999), but the vast majority want to be informed (Beisecker & Beisecker, 1990). Unfortunately, studies suggest that health care practitioners are less than effective in providing patients with complete information. Patients often claim they are not informed about such issues as how to take newly prescribed medications (Wiederholt, Clarridge & Svarstad, 1992) or what to expect when they are hospitalized (Cleary et al., 1991). Researchers' observations of interactions between physicians and patients confirm that the amount of information given to patients often is sorely lacking (Parrott, 1994). Finally, patients claim doctors use technical language, yet doctors claim they water down language (Thompson, 1998).

This is not to say that most health care providers are disengaged from their patients. Whenever they interact with patients, they are faced with multiple communication tasks. In addition to providing information, they must gather information – and, at times, they must gather this information under time constraints in potentially volatile settings when patients are unable or unwilling to provide it. At the same time, practitioners often are expected to attend to patients' psychological and emotional needs (DiMatteo & Lepper, 1998). As a consequence, health care providers use a variety of cues to assess patients' physical and emotional states and to make treatment decisions. These include the patients' physical condition, their anxiety, their cultural background, their personality, and their attitude toward medical care (Geist & Hardesty, 1990; Thomas & Clark, 1997). Of course, the accuracy with which practitioners are able to interpret data from these various sources depends on factors such as the patient's communication skills, whether the patient is able to communicate, how anxious the patient is, the amount of time available for the assessment, the practitioner's own level of anxiety or stress, and the practitioner's (e.g., Baron, Logan & Kao, 1990) experience. (See Street, this volume, Chapter 6.29, for the patient's point of view.)

Social Relationships

People's interactions with health care providers comprise a relatively small segment of the social context that influences individuals' health. Social relationships with friends, family, and acquaintances make up a larger portion of that environment and, as a consequence, serve as an important site for health-related communication (Suls, Martin & Leventhal, 1997). Indeed, a number of scholars argue that social interaction and comparisons with social network members influence the ways people perceive their health and their ability to cope with illness (Leventhal, Hudson & Robitaille, 1997).

The vast majority of research dealing with the broad range of social relationships that influence health focuses on the extent to which these relationships support individuals' health and well-being. Social support is typically assessed in one of three ways (Sarason, Sarason & Pierce, 1994): (a) *network measures* evaluate the degree to which individuals are integrated into a social group – they

are based on the number and/or the interconnectedness of people's social relationships; (b) *measures of received support* assess the support that people report
getting from their social network; and (c) *measures of perceived support* emphasize support that individuals believe is available to them. Both received and
perceived support often are conceived in terms of various functions including
emotional support (the provision of closeness and intimacy), esteem support
(feedback concerning the degree to individuals are respected or valued), network support (the availability of a social group to which people can belong),
instrumental support (the provision of tangible materials or services), and informational support (the availability of helpful advice or information) (Heitzmann
& Kaplan, 1988; Wills, 1997).

Researchers and theorists have explained the impact of social support using
two different models. One, sometimes termed the *direct effect model*, suggests
that support has a beneficial effect regardless of individuals' current level of
stress. The other, called the *buffering model*, assumes that support is most beneficial for people who are under high levels of stress (e.g., Penninx et al., 1998).
Both models have been linked to positive health outcomes (Cohen & Syme,
1985).

In its various forms, social support has been demonstrated to have a positive
influence on a long list of physical health-related variables including: mortality
(House, Landis & Umberson, 1988), depression (Holahan et al., 1995), recovery
from surgery (Kulik & Mahler, 1989), pregnancy and childbirth (Collins et al.,
1993), recovery from stroke, hip fracture, and myocardial infarction (Wilcox,
Kasl & Berkman, 1994), and caregiver health (Goode et al., 1998). It is important
to note, however, that the beneficial impact of support depends on a number of
different factors. For example, the meaning that people attach to social support
is affected by the qualities of their interpersonal relationships (Miller & Ray,
1994). Research suggests that intimate relationships often engender relatively
high levels of support (Reis & Franks, 1994) and that relationships marked by
conflict may not be conducive to the positive influence of supportive behavior
(Pierce, Sarason & Sarason, 1992). Individuals' gender (Linden et al., 1993;
Ptacek et al., 1997) and various aspects of their personality such as their tendency to be affiliative (Connell & D'Augelli, 1990) or cynical (Lepore, 1995) can
affect the amount of support they receive from relational partners and the way
they interpret supportive behaviors. Also, the type of support enacted by partners (King et al., 1993), the number of stressful life-events they experience (Roy,
Steptoe & Kirschbaum, 1998), and the type of physical malady that ails support
recipients (Penninx et al., 1998) can impact the favorable effects of support.

Although, under the right conditions, support from friends, family, and acquaintances can profoundly affect people's health, the availability and receipt of
caregiving is not always a positive experience for recipients. A fair portion of
interactions with social network members are negative (Davis & Swan, 1999;
Rook, 1984, 1992). Further, caregivers' efforts to provide help may be met by
negative reactions from recipients (Newsom & Schulz, 1998). In some cases,
recipients may feel that a caregiver provides too much help; in others, they may

believe the help is inappropriate. Support recipients also can experience problems when they perceive they are unable to meet a caregiver's expectations about coping with their disease (Hatchett et al., 1997). Indeed, Lewis and Rook (1999) found that people can feel distressed when someone in their social network tries to influence or control their health-related behavior – even though this type of social control also predicts less health-compromising and more health-enhancing behavior on the part of the recipient.

Family Relationships

As part of the social network, family members are particularly likely to influence each other's health. The physical and emotional ties that characterize many family relationships often create a context where health-related information is exchanged, attitudes are formed, and behavior modified. For instance, people frequently consult members of their family before they seek advice from health care practitioners (Hewison, 1997). Family members often hold similar beliefs about health-related issues, such as when to consult physicians (Quadrel & Lau, 1990) and which medical disorders are part of their family history (Hastrup et al., 1992). Also, individuals' behaviors (e.g., their tendencies to discuss issues associated with illness, to model health behaviors, and to express emotions) are associated with their family members' beliefs about certain illnesses (Whalen et al., 1996), willingness to engage in health-enhancing behavior (Jessor, Turbin & Costa, 1998), and physiological reactions during conversation (Miller et al., 1999) and the attempted control strategies used by partners (LePoire, 1995).

A number of researchers suggest that the structure of the family can have a potent influence on individuals' well-being. For instance, studies indicate that people who are divorced or never married – particularly men – have a higher risk of mortality than those who are married (Kotler & Wingard, 1989). Some have argued that this higher mortality risk occurs because marriage protects people's health (e.g., by discouraging health-compromising behaviors) (Umberson, 1987). Others suggest that it is the negative impact of divorce, rather than the positive influence of marriage, that affects longevity (Tucker et al., 1996). Studies examining the impact of parental divorce on children's health (Gottman & Katz, 1989) and adult children's longevity (Tucker et al., 1997) support the latter view – that marital dissolution or factors associated with marital dissolution (e.g., frequent parental conflict, psychological stress, and lower socio-economic status for women and children after a divorce) can negatively influence people's physical well-being.

While these and other findings linking family structure to individuals' health are important, many researchers argue that family structure is merely an indicator of other underlying causes. For instance, those who study family conflict have found that when parental conflict is controlled, the negative impact of divorce on children's psychological well-being is diminished (Gano-Phillips & Fincham,

1995). Children from intact families characterized by frequent, intense parental conflict tend to experience more physical and psychological problems than those from divorced families where the conflict is less frequent and less intense. The quality of family relationships and the behaviors that characterize family interactions, in short, may have as much or more of an influence on health than does family structure.

Family relationships that are cohesive, well-organized, and supportive provide an environment that fosters health. Young adults who have cohesive families are less likely to engage in health risk behaviors (Fisher & Feldman, 1998). By contrast, young adolescents who are emotionally detached from their families are more likely to enact risky behaviors such as physical fighting and using illegal substances (Doherty & Allen, 1994; Turner et al., 1993). Those from families low in positive affiliation also tend to display more anger and hostility, and boys from these families, like adults who are at risk for coronary heart disease, respond to stressors with heightened heart rates (Woodall & Matthews, 1989).

The influence of positive parent–child relationships also is evidenced in the support some families provide for chronically ill children. Supportive relationships with parents are directly correlated with the psychological (Varni, Wilcox & Hanson, 1988) and physical (Martin et al., 1998) well-being of children who have ongoing health problems such as rheumatoid arthritis or diabetes mellitus. Similarly, there is data to suggest that the children of parents who themselves are chronically ill fare better when parent–child relationships are positive (Armistead et al., 1997).

Part of what makes up a positive family environment appears to be an ability and a willingness, on the part of family members, to communicate openly. Open communication between parents and their children can help minimize the likelihood that children will engage in risky health behaviors. By fostering open discussions with their children, parents have an opportunity to influence children's beliefs about issues such as alcohol use and sex (Brody et al., 1998; Warren, 1992). Furthermore, open interaction with family members can yield benefits for those who are ill. Patients who have open communication with relational partners appear to be more well adjusted than those who do not (Gotcher, 1995), while those who hide information about their illness tend to be more distressed (Coyne & Smith, 1991; cf. Druley, Coyne & Stephens, 1997).

A qualification is in order when discussing the impact of openness in families on health. The term "openness" typically implies joint (bidirectional) discussion, some degree of honesty, and acceptance. It does not include the indiscriminate expression of negative feelings. Indeed, researchers have found that parents who exhibit frequent negative behaviors when interacting with their sons tend to have sons who are more hostile and express more anger (Matthews et al., 1996). Similarly, parent–adolescent conflict is more highly related to problem behavior in adolescents when parent support is low than when it is high (Barrera & Stice, 1998). Comparable findings are evident when spouses' interactions are examined. For instance, the frequency of partners' hostile exchanges is positively associated with increases in blood pressure for both husbands and wives who have essential hypertension (Ewart et al., 1991). Although the nature of the link between hostility and partners' blood pressure varies based on gender (see, for example, Brown & Smith, 1992; Smith et al., 1998), the "open" expression of hostility has potentially deleterious effects on the health of both spouses.

CONCENTRIC CIRCLE III: COPING

Within any social context, the way people respond to illness can influence the progress of their disease and their recovery. Sometimes, individuals deal with illness by trying to change the source of their stress (problem-focused coping) or by regulating their emotional responses (emotion-focused coping; Lazarus & Folkman, 1984). Other times, they may try to avoid dealing with their illness altogether. The choices people make with regard to these and other coping strategies are incredibly complex – they are influenced by the type and severity of people's health problems (Compas et al., 1996; Dakof & Mendelsohn, 1989) as well as characteristics of the individual and of the social environment in which those problems occur (Reardon & Buck, 1989).

Coping has been defined as "cognitive and behavioral efforts to manage specific external and/or internal demands that are appraised as taxing or exceeding the resources of the person" (Lazarus & Folkman, 1984, p. 141). Clearly, cognitive, behavioral, and affective coping strategies overlap – there is no way to definitively separate individuals' thoughts about their disease from their health-related behavior, or their behavior from the way they conceptualize their illness. Thus, for the purposes of this review, coping is discussed in terms of its emphasis on cognitive, behavioral, and affective processes, rather than in terms of mutually exclusive categories.

Cognitive Aspects of Coping

Literature emphasizing the cognitive aspects of coping presents what appears to be a tension between "approaching" or attending to health problems and avoiding or rejecting them. Some evidence shows that approaching issues associated with illness encourages adjustment (Blankfeld & Holahan, 1996) and that avoiding them has a negative influence on health (Petrie, Booth & Pennebaker, 1998). Other data suggests that being attentive or vigilant is linked to poorer health outcomes (Cohen & Lazarus, 1994) and that avoiding illness-related information can be beneficial (Phipps & Srivastava, 1997). Mullen and Suls (1982) address this issue, noting that both attention and rejection may play important roles in effective coping. Their meta-analysis suggests that attending to illness may be a more beneficial coping strategy over time because it can provide individuals with the opportunity to gather information. By contrast, rejection or avoidance may be particularly effective for short time periods because it can help alleviate people's immediate stress.

Approaching a health problem also may be helpful for some individuals because it can give them a sense of control over their health (Ratliff-Crain et al., 1989). For instance, increased feelings of control or efficacy are associated with decreases in disease activity for rheumatoid arthritis patients (Zautra et al., 1994). Further, children whose parents attempt to give them control during stressful medical procedures tend to cry less (Manne et al., 1992). By contrast, perceiving a loss of control has been linked to increased signs of stress (Glass & Singer, 1972). People who make relatively pessimistic attributions for illness or for negative events – who, in effect, emphasize their lack of control – can be more depressed (Kelly et al., 1993) and have lower immunocompetence (Kamen-Siegel et al., 1991).

Yet, the effectiveness of approach or attention-oriented coping may be a matter of degree. Too much attention or vigilance sometimes has negative effects on individuals' health and well-being. People who have a tendency to be alert to threatening aspects of a medical procedure or illness sometimes experience more psychological problems than those who do not (Kiyak, Vitaliano & Crinean, 1988; Miller et al., 1995). Those who are vigilant can have more difficulty with postoperative recovery (Cohen & Lazarus, 1994); and individuals who engage in ruminative coping following a stressful event can be at greater risk for depression (Nolen-Hoeksema, McBride & Larson, 1997). Conversely, the use of distraction is sometimes associated with increased positive affect (Stone, Kennedy-Moore & Neale, 1995). Because perceiving noxious stimuli such as pain or other illness symptoms requires attention, distraction may be an effective coping strategy in some situations (McCaul & Malott, 1984; cf. Leventhal, 1992; McCaul, Monson & Maki, 1992).

Behavioral Aspects of Coping

Although the behaviors people engage in when they cope with illness are far too numerous to describe in the space allotted for this review, the literature does offer three issues that capture much of the research on the behavioral aspects of coping. The first is the extent to which people reach out to those in their social environment for help; the second is the tendency of individuals to disclose illness-related information; and the third involves the way people present themselves (and their illness) to others.

Individuals' willingness and ability to reach out to others for help can have major influences on the way they deal with, and recover from, an illness. The previously discussed research on social support points to the potential importance of social resources to people's health. If individuals are unwilling or unable to take advantage of the tangible and intangible resources they can obtain through their network, they are at greater risk than they would be otherwise. Indeed, people tend to seek medical care when they perceive a threat to their health and when they feel unable to deal with that threat themselves (Cameron,

Leventhal & Leventhal, 1993). Individuals who cope with illness by seeking or using social support can experience less emotional distress than those who do not (Dunkel-Schetter et al., 1992). Those who seek support from others also may be less likely to engage in certain health risk behaviors (Folkman et al., 1992).

On some level, seeking social support requires that individuals disclose information about their health to others. Open communication between health care practitioners and patients can serve as an important way to decrease patients' anxiety and, in some cases, improve their physical well-being (King, 1991). Similarly, there is evidence to suggest that individuals can reap benefits from disclosing information about their health status to people in their social network. For instance, individuals who withhold information about their HIV status from relational partners tend to experience greater emotional distress than those who disclose it (Kalichman & Nachimson, 1999). HIV-negative men who conceal their homosexual identity have an increased incidence of cancer and of several infectious diseases (Cole et al., 1996). Unfortunately, many HIV-positive men tend to disclose information about their disease as the disease becomes more severe (Marks et al., 1992), so they may not benefit as much from disclosure as those who talk about their condition earlier.

Despite the positive outcomes associated with the disclosure of health-related information, it is important to note that such disclosure is not always beneficial. In some situations, people's tendency to talk about their health status may exacerbate their emotional distress. Indeed, some research suggests that women who engage in certain types of disclosure (e.g., about the symptoms of their illness) experience relatively high levels of negative affect (Druley et al., 1997). Also, individuals who have a stigmatized health condition, such as HIV, may report abandonment, rejection, or violent outbursts from others when they reveal information about their health (Kalichman & Nachimson, 1999). Even people who have health problems that are not stigmatized may worry about the reactions they will receive when they disclose health-related information. Others may respond negatively to the illness, may feel awkward, or may try to make allowances for the individual's health condition when none are desired.

People's concerns about the way others perceive and evaluate them can influence more than the amount and type of information they disclose. Worries about how others view them can affect a variety of health-related behaviors such as individuals' tendency to use drugs and alcohol, to exercise, and to engage in safe sexual practices (Leary, Tchividjian & Kraxberger, 1994). Further, the fear of negative evaluation concerning an illness may be associated with people's interpersonal discomfort, their stress over others' reactions, the degree to which the disease interferes with their life, and even the quality of their life (Leary et al., 1998). Some researchers go so far as to argue that the way people manage stressors, such as their fear of negative evaluation, can influence their physical condition. Indeed, Leake, Friend and Wadhwa (1999) found that patients who presented themselves as successful copers in a videotaped interview had fewer physical symptoms, reported better adjustment, and had more coping skills than those who did not.

Emotional Aspects of Coping

Because so many issues associated with illness are likely to evoke emotions, the way people cope with their emotions during stressful situations can influence their health. In the literature, two major issues on emotional aspects of coping are: the extent to which people express their feelings (emotional disclosure) and the degree to which their negative feelings and attitudes dominate their views of others (hostility). The former involves the influence of disclosing thoughts and feelings on individuals' health, whereas the latter focuses on the degree to which people's hostile attitudes toward others affect physical and psychological well-being.

A number of studies suggest that the verbal expression of feelings and thoughts about negative experiences may have substantial health benefits. There is evidence that people who write about their feelings and thoughts regarding upsetting events have fewer visits to health centers and exhibit better immune function than do others (Pennebaker & Beall, 1986; Pennebaker, Kiecolt-Glaser & Glaser, 1988). Similarly, individuals with rheumatoid arthritis who talk to someone privately about a stressful event experience a short-lived increase in negative mood, followed by improved physical and psychological functioning (Kelley, Lumley & Leisen, 1997). Suppressing thoughts associated with negative emotions, by contrast, appears to be linked to decreased immune functioning (Petrie et al., 1998).

The extent to which verbally disclosing emotion affects individuals' health is influenced by the ways people express their thoughts and feelings. For example, writing about traumas that have already been disclosed in the past can evoke more distress than writing about previously undisclosed traumas (Greenberg & Stone, 1990). It may be that most of the benefits of disclosure occur during the initial revelation and that continued thinking and talking about negative events actually increases distress. In addition, the words people use when they disclose may influence health outcomes. Pennebaker and his colleagues (1997) found that individuals who employ words associated with insightful or causal thinking show improved physical health and more adaptive behaviors than those who do not. The authors suggest that insightful and causal thinking may reflect changes in people's thought patterns that encourage well-being. The absence of such changes may indicate that individuals are ruminating about their negative experiences.

People's dispositions toward self-expression also affect the positive influence of disclosure on health. For instance, pessimists, who tend to get bogged down in negative thoughts do not seem to benefit from writing about their negative feelings (Cameron & Nicholls, 1998). However, they do get value from writing tasks that encourage them not only to disclose their feelings, but also to select, enact, and evaluate ways to cope with their problems. Indeed, Cameron and Nicholls found that those who engaged in this latter task reduced their visits to health care clinics.

Another psychological disposition associated with individuals' tendency to disclose emotion is hostility. Hostility typically is conceived as a negative, cynical set of attitudes toward others, but it also has been examined as a multidimensional construct including components such as antagonism (aggression), cynicism (mistrust or suspicion), and hostile affect (anger) (see, for example, Helmers et al., 1995; Musante et al., 1989; Suarez et al., 1993). Those who are highly hostile tend to experience more anger and to suppress the expression of anger (Houston & Vavak, 1991). Given this, it is not surprising that hostility may be negatively associated with health (e.g., Adams, 1994).

Although it is relevant to the disclosure of emotion, hostility has been most widely studied in terms of its possible links to coronary heart disease (CHD). Researchers note several qualities of hostility that may qualify it as "coronary-prone behavior" (Krantz et al., 1989). More specifically, people who are hostile tend to exhibit heightened physiological responses in certain situations (Raik-konen et al., 1999), to report experiencing more interpersonal conflict and less social support, and to engage in less healthy behavior than do others (Houston & Vavak, 1991; Smith, 1992). Social interaction presents a unique challenge to those who are hostile (Barefoot et al., 1991). Perhaps because they are more prone to anger and have a relatively cynical view of others, people high in hostility tend to be less friendly when they engage in role-play interactions involving low levels of conflict and more hostile when engaged in interactions involving high levels of conflict (Hardy & Smith, 1988). Men who are hostile are particularly likely to have higher blood pressure during social interaction – a finding that some suggest helps explains men's greater risk of CHD (Guyll & Contrada, 1998).

Given the difficulties faced by hostile people when they interact with others, it is not surprising that they report receiving relatively little social support. Unfortunately, their unfriendly approach to social interaction is likely to reinforce their negative, cynical view of others. And that, in turn, will reinforce their unfriendly behavior. This type of ongoing cycle is not likely to serve hostile people well when it comes to coping with illness.

CONCENTRIC CIRCLE IV: PATIENT OUTCOMES

People's social interactions and the way they cope with their illness create a context for how they feel about their health care and how they behave with regard to health-related issues. Those who experience supportive interactions with friends, family, and health care practitioners may feel and act differently from those who do not. Individuals who cope with their illness openly are likely to have different affective and behavioral responses to the medical care they receive from those who cope by isolating themselves from others. The affective and behavioral responses people have to health care have been examined primarily in terms of two patient outcomes: satisfaction and compliance.

Satisfaction

Patients' satisfaction with the health care they receive represents more than a simple assessment of affect (Fitzpatrick, 1997). Patients who are in better health tend to be more satisfied with their medical care (Hall et al., 1998); and those who are satisfied with their medical consultations are more likely to comply with the recommendations made by practitioners (Ley, 1988). Satisfaction with health care can be assessed in terms of a number of different variables including the technical aspects of care or practitioners' medical skills. Many, however, emphasize the interpersonal components of medical encounters (e.g., Schneider & Tucker, 1992) because the exchange of information, from patient to physician and vice versa, is key to patients' health. If patients are distressed about the amount of information they receive or about their inability to give information to their provider, they may be less likely to comply with the providers' recommendations. Indeed, a meta-analysis conducted by Roter (1989) indicated that the most reliable predictor of patients' satisfaction was the information given to them by their doctors. Patients who receive information specifically related to their physical condition tend to experience less distress (Lerman et al., 1996). Those who are given information are more satisfied (Gotcher & Edwards, 1990), less anxious, and perceive their practitioner as more competent (Hamilton, Rouse & Rouse, 1994).

Although most patients want information from their health care providers, they also place a very high premium on providers' socio-emotional communication skills. Patients want health care providers who are empathetic and expressive (DiMatteo, Hays & Prince, 1986) – who are able and willing to communicate their involvement with patients. Practitioners who show they are involved with their patients typically have patients who are more satisfied. More specifically, patients' satisfaction is positively linked to their health care providers' tendency to be attentive and responsive to their needs (Rouse, 1989; Street, 1989). Practitioners may successfully display their involvement though a variety of verbal and non-verbal behaviors. For instance, studies suggest that patients are likely to be more satisfied when their health care provider spends more time with them (Hall, Roter & Katz, 1988), encourages them to ask questions (Thompson, Nanni & Schwankovsky, 1990), and avoids the use of technical language that they may not understand (Jackson, 1992).

Compliance

Persuading patients to comply with the advice they are offered by health professionals is one of the most common, and frustrating, challenges facing those involved in the health care industry. Non-compliance is widespread and its costs are immense. The correlates of compliance most frequently examined in the literature involve patients' satisfaction with their medical consultations, the characteristics of their treatment regimen, and their beliefs about issues such as their vulnerability to illness, the severity of their illness, and the effectiveness of the proposed treatment (Ley, 1997). Interaction with health care practitioners and with other members of individuals' social network is central to each one of these sets of correlates. Communication between patients and their caretakers explains the requirements of treatment regimens and adjusts those regimens to fit within the constraints of patients' lives. Further, social interaction is essential to ascertain patients' beliefs about health and, if necessary, how those beliefs might be modified.

Scholars from a variety of disciplines have argued that persuading people to comply with prevention programs and treatment regimens involves much more than just giving factual information to patients (Baker, Petty & Gleicher, 1991; Lewis, 1994; Kreps, O'Hair & Clowers, 1994). Although researchers are far from the point where they can provide a comprehensive set of recommendations to ensure patient compliance, a number of issues affecting compliance have been studied. For example, the quality of interaction between patients and health care practitioners is related both to patients' recall of medical information and patients' tendency to adhere to medical recommendations (Hall et al., 1988). If, as a consequence of their interaction, patients come to mistrust their provider (DiMatteo & DiNicola, 1982) or physicians come to dislike their patient (Hall et al., 1993), the likelihood that the two will engage in the type of open exchange of information that would uncover patient concerns or lifestyle characteristics that might deter adherence is diminished.

Similarly, patients' beliefs or expectations about health-related behaviors such as smoking (Chassin et al., 1991) or condom use (Catania et al., 1991; Edgar & Fitzpatrick, 1993) can influence their tendency to take recommendations made by practitioners seriously. In order to address patients' beliefs and concerns, the information patients receive should be personalized and relevant. Researchers note that messages about health are not always presented in ways that are useful to patients (Whaley, 1999). Indeed, when patients are given information that is individualized or that provides them with a personal motivation to change their behavior, they may be more likely to comply with medical recommendations (DiMatteo, Reiter & Gambone, 1994; Fisher, Fisher et al., 1996; Kreuter & Strecher, 1995). Similarly, there is data suggesting that some patients who are given a sense of control over, or responsibility for, their health care regimen are more likely to follow the advice they have been given (Burleson, Kegels & Lund, 1990; Rothman et al., 1993).

Some research suggests that health-related messages are more effective in gaining patients' compliance when they are framed in a way that points out potential dangers or losses associated with non-compliance than when they point out the advantages of adherence (Detweiler et al., 1999). There is also some evidence that the imagery used in language can affect compliance – that language is more likely to encourage compliance when the imagery it uses is understood by patients and is consistent with health care providers' goals (Adelman, 1991; Whaley, 1994).

CONCLUSION

This chapter reviews the research on social interaction, relationships, and health. We did not focus on particular diseases but on the interpersonal process patterns that could be generalized across diseases. At times, however, the empirical results must be qualified by disease. A clear next step to organize the language findings is to develop a typology of diseases, arrayed by psychosocial dimensions and not biological or medical ones. Psychosocial dimensions could include characteristics such as the physical marking of the disease, its time trajectory, the degree of social stigma attached to the conditions and so forth. This typology would clarify the relationships between linguistic patterns and health outcomes along theoretically important dimensions.

To achieve some conceptual order in the literature, we proposed the Kaleidoscope Model of Health Communication. This model specifies a series of concentric circles or tiers surrounding health outcomes for patients. The model is a simplifying tool that allows us to see how the bits of tinted glass within the kaleidoscope relate to one another and the various ways that each concentric circle interacts across all of the other circles. In any one paradigm, a researcher breaks off pieces of the model to explore but the model reminds us of the interconnections across the tiers. For example, advances in medical science have made dealing with chronic illness an ordinary feature of family life and not an exotic, short-term catastrophe. One turn of the kaleidoscope and we bring into focus the question: How do families (social context tier) of the aged (social identity tier) deal with chronic illness (coping tier) in partnership with professionals (patient outcome tier) with the linguistic tools of informing/explaining (and being informed), persuading (and being persuaded), disclosing (and being disclosed to), and comforting (and being comforted)?

The model generates subtle but important heuristic effects in at least two ways. First, the bits of glass within a tier fall together in different patterns and configurations with the turn of the dial. Now the interrelated bits of glass demonstrate that we are dealing not only with the category of aged but with a multifaceted social identity – an aged, upper middle class, Southern, female, African–American. This instantiation of a more complex social identity has clear implications for the language choices of all parties to the interaction. How is information exchanged, what is the range, degree, and depth of disclosure expected, what mutual influence attempts succeed or fail, and what language strategies work to comfort the distressed? And/or we can consider how the families in the social context tier interact with the aged member and with the professionals surrounding their aged member. To what degree and under what conditions does the professional value the narratives and linguistic accounts of the family about its aged member? Are the families influenced by the message choices made by professionals and so on?

Second, the model is heuristic in that it shows us where the spaces are and where we need to focus our research attention. There is little research, for example, on the specialized functional and dysfunctional linguistic strategies of various marginalized social groups as they cope with illness and disease.

The Kaleidoscope Model specifies that there may be many indirect paths to reach the core outcomes of patient health and quality of life. The concept of indirect links in the model has a clear pragmatic implication not only for language and message choices in therapeutic interaction but also for pro-social marketing efforts. Multiple indirect paths to patient health and quality of life implies that there are no magic words to convince a patient to practice safer sex, reduce alcohol intake, or stop binge eating. But there are numerous ways that language can affect the health and quality of life of a given individual.

Finally, a major conceptual area in the model is the social context or type of relationship operating in various exchanges. Today, the changing definition of the nature of the relationship between doctor or therapist and patient is of primary concern. Patients appear to believe they have better outcomes to the degree that the relationship between them and the health care provider becomes more personal and less social. The changing definition of this key relationship has profound implications for the language choices made by each participant in the exchange. Clearly, more personalized relationships predict patient satisfaction. The degree to which a more personal relationship as evidenced by different patterns of talk between participants ultimately predicts better health outcomes would be an excellent topic for future research.

REFERENCES

Adams, S.H. (1994). Role of hostility in women's health during midlife: A longitudinal study. *Health Psychology*, **13**, 488–495.

Adelman, M.B. (1991). Play and incongruity: Framing safe-sex talk. *Health Communication*, **3**, 139–155.

Alcalay, R. & Bell, R.A. (1996). Ethnicity and health knowledge gaps: Impact of the California Wellness Guide on poor African-American, Hispanic, and non-Hispanic White women. *Health Communication*, **8**, 303–329.

Armistead, L., Klein, K., Wierson, M. & Forehand, R. (1997). Disclosure of parental HIV infection to children in the families of men with hemophilia: Description, outcomes, and the role of family processes. *Journal of Family Psychology*, **11**, 49–61.

Baker, S.M., Petty, R.E. & Gleicher, F. (1991). Persuasion theory and drug abuse prevention. *Health Communication*, **3**, 193–203.

Barefoot, J.C., Peterson, B.L., Dahlstrom, W.G., Siegler, I.C., Anderson, N.B. & Williams, R.B., Jr (1991). Hostility patterns and health implications: Correlates of Cook–Medley hostility scale scores in a national survey. *Health Psychology*, **10**, 18–24.

Barrera, M., Jr & Stice, E. (1998). Parent-adolescent conflict in the context of parental support: Families with alcoholic and nonalcoholic fathers. *Journal of Family Psychology*, **12**, 195–208.

Baron, R.S., Logan, H. & Kao (1990). Some variables affecting dentists' assessment of patients' distress. *Health Communication*, **9**, 143–153.

Beisecker, A.E. (1990). Patient power in doctor–patient communication: What do we know? *Health Communication*, **2**, 105–122.

Beisecker, A.E. & Beisecker, T.D. (1990). Patient information-seeking behaviors when communicating with doctors. *Medical Care*, **28**, 19–28.

Bell, R.A. & Alcalay, R. (1997). The impact of the Wellness Guide on Hispanic women's well-being-related knowledge, efficacy beliefs, and behaviors: The mediating role of acculturation. *Health Education and Behavior*, **24**, 326–343.

Blankfeld, D.F. & Holahan, C.J. (1996). Family support, coping strategies, and depressive symptoms among mothers of children with diabetes. *Journal of Family Psychology*, **10**, 173–179.

Brashers, D.E., Haas, S.M. & Neidig, J.L. (1999). The patient self-advocacy scale: Measuring patient involvement in health care decision-making interactions. *Health Communication*, **11**, 97–121.

Brody, G.H., Flor, D.L., Hollett-Wright, N. & McCoy, J.K. (1998). Children's development of alcohol use norms: Contributions of parent and sibling norms, children's temperaments, and parent–child discussions. *Journal of Family Psychology*, **12**, 209–219.

Brown, P.C. & Smith, T.W. (1992). Social influence, marriage, and the heart: Cardiovascular consequences of interpersonal control in husbands and wives. *Health Psychology*, **11**, 88–96.

Burleson, J.A., Kegels, S.S. & Lund, A.K. (1990). Effects of decisional control and work orientation on persistence in preventive health behavior. *Health Psychology*, **9**, 1–17.

Cameron, L.D. & Nicholls, G. (1998). Expression of stressful experiences through writing: Effects of self-regulation manipulation for pessimists and optimists. *Health Psychology*, **17**, 84–92.

Cameron, L., Leventhal, E.A. & Leventhal, H. (1993). Symptom representations and affect as determinants of care seeking in a community-dwelling, adult sample population. *Health Psychology*, **12**, 171–179.

Catania, J.A., Coates, T.J., Stall, R., Bye, L., Kegeles, S.M., Capell, F., Henne, J., McKusick, L., Morin, S., Turner, H. & Pollack, L. (1991). Changes in condom use among homosexual men in San Francisco. *Health Psychology*, **10**, 190–199.

Cegala, D.J., McNeilis, K.S., McGee, D.S. & Jonas, A.P. (1995). A study of doctors' and patents' perceptions of information processing and communication competence during the medical interview. *Health Communication*, **7**, 179–203.

Chassin, L., Presson, C.C., Sherman, S.J. & Edwards, D.A. (1991). Four pathways to young-adult smoking status: Adolescent social-psychological antecedents in a midwestern community sample. *Health Psychology*, **10**, 409–418.

Cleary, P.D., Edgman-Levitan, S., Roberts, M., Maloney, T.W., McMullen, W., Walker, J.D. & Delbanco, T.L. (1991). Patients evaluate their hospital care: A national survey. *Health Affairs*, **10**, 254–267.

Cohen, F. & Lazarus, R.S. (1994). Active coping processes, coping dispositions, and recovery from surgery. In A. Steptoe & J. Wardle (Eds), *Psychosocial processes and health: A reader* (pp. 348–368). New York: Cambridge University Press.

Cohen, S. & Syme, S.L. (1985). *Social support and health*. Orlando, FL: Academic Press.

Cole, S.W., Kemeny, M.E., Taylor, S.E. & Visscher, B.R. (1996). Elevated physical health risk among gay men who conceal their homosexual identity. *Health Psychology*, **15**, 243–251.

Collins, N.L., Dunkel-Schetter, C., Loebel, M. & Scrimshaw, S.C.M. (1993). Social support in pregnancy: Correlates of birth outcomes and postpartum depression. *Journal of Personality and Social Psychology*, **65**, 1243–1258.

Compas, B.E., Worsham, N.L., Ey, S. & Howell, D.C. (1996). When mom or dad has cancer: II. Coping, cognitive appraisals, and psychological distress in children of cancer patients. *Health Psychology*, **15**, 167–175.

Connell, C.M. & D'Augelli, A.R. (1990). The contribution of personality characteristics to the relationship between social support and perceived physical health. *Health Psychology*, **9**, 192–207.

Coyne, J.C. & Smith, D.A. (1991). Couples coping with a myocardial infarction: A contextual perspective on wives' distress. *Journal of Personality and Social Psychology*, **61**, 404–412.

Dakof, G.A. & Mendelsohn, G.A. (1989). Patterns of adaptation to Parkinson's disease. *Health Psychology*, **8**, 355–372.

Davis, M.C. & Swan, P.D. (1999). Association of negative and positive social ties with fibrinogen levels in young women. *Health Psychology*, **18**, 131–139.

Detweiler, J.B., Bedell, B.T., Pronin, E., Salovey, P. & Rothman, A.J. (1999). Message framing and sunscreen use: Gain-framed messages motivate beach-goers. *Health Psychology*, **18**, 189–196.

DiMatteo, M.R. & DiNicola, D.D. (1982). *Achieving patient compliance: The psychology of the medical practitioner's role.* New York: Pergamon Press.

DiMatteo, M.R. & Lepper, H.S. (1998). Promoting adherence to courses of treatment: Mutual collaboration in the physician–patient relationship. In L.D. Jackson & B.K. Duffy (Eds), *Health communication research: A guide to developments and directions* (pp. 75–86). Westport, CT: Greenwood Press.

DiMatteo, M.R., Hays, R.D., & Prince, L.M. (1986). Relationships of physician's nonverbal communication skill to patient satisfaction, appointment noncompliance and physician workload. *Health Psychology,* **5,** 581–594.

DiMatteo, M.R., Reiter, R.C. & Gambone, J.C. (1994). Enhancing medication adherence through communication and informed collaborative choice. *Health Communication,* **6,** 253–265.

Doherty, W.J. & Allen, W. (1994). Family functioning and parental smoking as predictors of adolescent cigarette use: A six year prospective study. *Journal of Family Psychology,* **8,** 347–353.

Druley, J.A., Coyne, J.C. & Stephens, M.A.P. (1997). Emotional and physical intimacy in coping with lupus: Women's dilemmas of disclosure and approach. *Health Psychology,* **16,** 506–514.

Dryden, C. & Giles, H. (1987). Language, social identity and health. In H. Beloff & A.M. Colman (Eds), *Psychology Survey* (pp. 115–138). Leicester: British Psychological Society Press.

Dunkel-Schetter, C., Feinstein, L.G., Taylor, S.E. & Falke, R.L. (1992). Patterns of coping with cancer. *Health Psychology,* **11,** 79–87.

Durel, L.A., Carver, C.S., Spitzer, S.B., Llabre, M.M., Weintraub, J.K., Saab, P.G. & Schneiderman, N. (1989). Associations of blood pressure with self-report measures of anger and hostility among black and white men and women. *Health Psychology,* **8,** 557–575.

Edgar, T. & Fitzpatrick, M.A. (1993). Expectations for sexual interaction: A cognitive test of the sequencing of sexual communication behaviors. *Health Communication,* **5,** 239–261.

Ewart, C.K., Taylor, C.B., Kraemer, H.C. & Agras, W.S. (1991). High blood pressure and marital discord: Not being nasty matters more than being nice. *Health Psychology,* **10,** 155–163.

Fisher, J.D., Fisher, W.A., Misovich, S.J., Kimble, D.L. & Malloy, T.E. (1996). Changing AIDS risk behavior: Effects of an intervention emphasizing AIDS risk reduction information, motivation, and behavioral skills in a college student population. *Health Psychology,* **15,** 114–123.

Fisher, L. & Feldman, S.S. (1998). Familial antecedents of young adult health risk behavior: A longitudinal study. *Journal of Family Psychology,* **12,** 66–80.

Fitzpatrick, R. (1997). Patient satisfaction. In A. Baum, S. Newman, J. Weinman, R. West & C. McManus (Eds), *Cambridge handbook of psychology, health and medicine* (pp. 301–304). New York: Cambridge University Press.

Folkman, S., Chesney, M.A., Pollack, L. & Phillips, C. (1992). Stress, coping, and high-risk sexual behavior. *Health Psychology,* **11,** 218–222.

Gano-Phillips, S. & Fincham, F.D. (1995). Family conflict, divorce, and children's adjustment. In M.A. Fitzpatrick & A.L. Vangelisti (Eds), *Explaining family interactions* (pp. 206–231). Thousand Oaks, CA: Sage.

Geist, P. & Hardesty, M. (1990). Reliable, silent, hysterical, or assured: Physicians assess patient cues in their medical decision making. *Health Communication,* **2,** 69–90.

Glass, D.C. & Singer, J.E. (1972). *Urban stress: Experiments on noise and social stressors.* New York: Academic Press.

Goode, K.T., Haley, W.E., Roth, D.L. & Ford, G.R. (1998). Predicting longitudinal changes in caregiver physical and mental health: A stress process model. *Health Psychology,* **17,** 190–198.

Gotcher, J.M. (1995). Well-adjusted and maladjusted cancer patients: An examination of communication variables. *Health Communication*, **7**, 21–33.

Gotcher, J.M. & Edwards, R. (1990). Coping strategies of cancer patients: Actual communication and imagined interactions. *Health Communication*, **2**, 255–266.

Gottman, J.M. & Katz, L. (1989). Effects of marital discord on young children's peer interaction and health. *Developmental Psychology*, **25**, 373–381.

Greenberg, M.A. & Stone, A.A. (1990). Writing about disclosed versus undisclosed traumas: Health and mood effects. *Health Psychology*, **9**, 114–115.

Greene, K. & Serovich, J. (1996). Appropriateness of disclosure of HIV testing information: The perspective of PLWAs. *Journal of Applied Communication Research*, **24**, 50–65.

Guyll, M. & Contrada, R.J. (1998). Trait hostility and ambulatory cardiovascular activity: Responses to social interaction. *Health Psychology*, **17**, 30–39.

Hadlow, J. & Pitts, M. (1991). The understanding of common health terms by doctors, nurses, and patients. *Social Science & Medicine*, **32**, 193–196.

Hall, J.A., Roter, D.L. & Katz, N.R. (1988). Meta-analysis of correlates of provider behavior in medical encounters. *Medical Care*, **25**, 399–412.

Hall, J.A., Epstein, A.M., DeCiantis, M.L. & McNeil, B.J. (1993). Physicians' liking for their patients: More evidence for the role of affect in medical care. *Health Psychology*, **12**, 140–146.

Hall, J.A., Milburn, M.A., Roter, D.L. & Daltroy, L.H. (1998). Why are sicker patients less satisfied with their medical care? Tests of two explanatory models. *Health Psychology*, **17**, 70–75.

Hamilton, M.A., Rouse, R.A. & Rouse, J. (1994). Dentist communication and patient utilization of dental services: Anxiety inhibition and competence enhancement effects. *Health Communication*, **6**, 137–158.

Hardy, J.D. & Smith, T.W. (1988). Cynical hostility and vulnerability to disease: Social support, life stress, and physiological response to conflict. *Health Psychology*, **7**, 447–459.

Hastrup, J.L., Phillips, S.M., Vullo, K., Kang, G. & Slomka, L. (1992). Adolescents' knowledge of medical terminology and family health history. *Health Psychology*, **11**, 41–47.

Hatchett, L., Friend, R., Symister, P. & Wadhwa, N. (1997). Interpersonal expectations, social support, and adjustment to chronic illness. *Journal of Personality and Social Psychology*, **73**, 560–573.

Hecht, M.L. (1993). 2002 – A research odyssey: Toward the development of a communication theory of identity. *Communication Monographs*, **60**, 76–82.

Heitzmann, C.A. & Kaplan, R.M. (1988). Assessment and methods for measuring social support. *Health Psychology*, **7**, 75–109.

Helmers, K.F., Krantz, D.S., Merz, C.N.B., Klein, J., Kop, W.J., Gottdiener, J.S. & Rozanski, A. (1995). Defensive hostility: Relationship to multiple markers of cardiac ischemia in patients with coronary disease. *Health Psychology*, **14**, 202–209.

Hewison, J. (1997). Family influence on health. In A. Baum, S. Newman, J. Weinman, R. West & C. McManus (Eds), *Cambridge handbook of psychology, health and medicine* (pp. 107–109). New York: Cambridge University Press.

Holahan, C.J., Moos, R.H., Holahan, C.K. & Brennan, P.L. (1995). Social support, coping, and depressive symptoms in a late-middle-aged sample of patients reporting cardiac illness. *Health Psychology*, **14**, 152–163.

House, J.S., Landis, K.R. & Umberson, D. (1988). Social relationships and health. *Science*, **241**, 540–545.

Houston, B.K. & Vavak, C.R. (1991). Cynical hostility: Developmental factors, psychosocial correlates, and health behaviors. *Health Psychology*, **10**, 9–17.

Jackson, L.D. (1992). Information complexity and medical communication: The effects of technical language and amount of information in a medical message. *Health Communication*, **4**, 197–210.

Jessor, R., Turbin, M.S. & Costa, F.M. (1998). Protective factors in adolescent health behavior. *Journal of Personality and Social Psychology*, **75**, 788–800.

Kalichman, S.C. & Nachimson, D. (1999). Self-efficacy and disclosure of HIV-positive serostatus to sex partners. *Health Psychology*, **18**, 281–287.

Kamen-Siegel, L., Rodin, J., Seligman, M.E.P. & Dwyer, J. (1991). Explanatory style and cell-mediated immunity in elderly men and women. *Health Psychology*, **10**, 229–235.

Kelley, J.E., Lumley, M.A. & Leisen, J.C.C. (1997). Health effects of emotional disclosure in rheumatoid arthritis patients. *Health Psychology*, **16**, 331–340.

Kelly, J.A., Murphy, A., Bahr, G.R., Koob, J.J., Morgan, M.G., Kalichman, S.C., Stevenson, L.Y., Brasfield, T.L., Bernstein, B.M. & St Lawrence, J.S. (1993). Factors associated with severity of depression and high-risk sexual behavior among persons diagnosed with human immunodeficiency virus (HIV) infection. *Health Psychology*, **12**, 215–219.

King, K.B., Reis, H.T., Porter, L.A. & Norsen, L.H. (1993). Social support and long-term recovery from coronary artery surgery: Effects on patients and spouses. *Health Psychology*, **12**, 56–63.

King. P. (1991). Communication, anxiety, and the management of postoperative pain. *Health Communication*, **3**, 127–138.

Kiyak, H.A., Vitaliano, P.P. & Crinean, J. (1988). Patients' expectations as predictors of orthognathic surgery outcomes. *Health Psychology*, **7**, 251–268.

Kotler, P. & Wingard, D.L. (1989). The effect of occupational, marital and parental roles on mortality: The Alameda County study. *American Journal of Public Health*, **79**, 607–612.

Krantz, D.S., Schneiderman, N., Chesney, M.A., McCann, B.S., Reading, A.E., Roskies, E., Stoney, C.M. & Williams, R.B., Jr (1989). Biobehavioral research on cardiovascular disorders. *Health Psychology*, **8**, 737–746.

Kreps, G.L., O'Hair, D. & Clowers, M. (1994). The influences of human communication on health outcomes. *American Behavioral Scientist*, **38**, 248–256.

Kreuter, M.W. & Strecher, V.J. (1995). Changing inaccurate perceptions of health risk: Results from a randomized trial. *Health Psychology*, **14**, 56–63.

Kulik, J.A. & Mahler, H.I.M. (1989). Social support and recovery from surgery. *Health Psychology*, **8**, 221–238.

Kunkel, A.W. & Burleson, B.R. (1999). Assessing explanations for sex differences in emotional support: A test of the different cultures and skill specialization accounts. *Human Communication Research*, **25**, 307–340.

Lazarus, R.S. & Folkman, S. (1984). *Stress, appraisal, and coping*. New York: Springer.

Leake, R., Friend, R. & Wadhwa, N. (1999). Improving adjustment to chronic illness through strategic self-presentation: An experimental study on a renal dialysis unit. *Health Psychology*, **18**, 54–62.

Leary, M.R., Tchividjian, L.R. & Kraxberger, B.E. (1994). Self-presentation can be hazardous to your health: Impression management and health risk. *Health Psychology*, **13**, 461–470.

Lcary, M.R., Rapp, S.R., Hcrbst, K.C., Exum. M.L. & Fcldman, S.R. (1998). Interpersonal concerns and psychological difficulties of psoriasis patients: Effects of disease severity and fear of negative evaluation. *Health Psychology*, **17**, 530–536.

LePoire, B.A. (1995). Inconsistent nurturing as control theory: Implications for communication-based research and treatment programs. *Journal of Applied Communication Research*, **23**, 60–74.

LePore, S.J. (1995). Cynicism, social support, and cardiovascular reactivity. *Health Psychology*, **14**, 210–216.

Lerman, C., Schwartz, M.D., Miller, S.M., Daly, M., Sands, C. & Rimer, B.K. (1996). A randomized trial of breast cancer risk counselling: Interacting effects of counselling, education level, and coping style. *Health Psychology*, **15**, 75–83.

Leventhal, H. (1992). I know distraction works even though it doesn't! *Health Psychology*, **11**, 208–209.

Leventhal, H., Hudson, S. & Robitaille, C. (1997). Social comparison and health: A process model. In B.P. Buunk & F.X. Gibbons (Eds), *Health, coping, and well-being* (pp. 411–432). Mahwah, NJ: Erlbaum.

Lewis, L.K. (1994). A challenge for health education: The enactment problem and a communication-related solution. *Health Communication*, **6**, 205–224.

Lewis, M.A. & Rook, K.S. (1999). Social control in personal relationships: Impact on health behaviors and psychological distress. *Health Psychology*, **18**, 63–71.

Ley, P. (1997). Compliance among patients. In A. Baum, S. Newman, J. Weinman, R. West & C. McManus (Eds), *Cambridge handbook of psychology, health and medicine* (pp. 281–284). New York: Cambridge University Press.

Ley, P. (1988). *Communicating with patients*. London: Chapman & Hall.

Linden, W., Chambers, L., Maurice, J. & Lenz, J.W. (1993). Sex differences in social support, self-deception, hostility, and ambulatory cardiovascular activity. *Health Psychology*, **12**, 376–380.

Manne, S.L., Bakeman, R., Jacobsen, P.B., Gorfinkle, K., Berstein, D. & Redd, W.H. (1992). Adult–child interaction during invasive medical procedures. *Health Psychology*, **11**, 241–249.

Marks, G., Bundek, N.I., Richardson, J.L., Ruiz, M.S., Maldonado, N. & Mason, H.R.C. (1992). Self-disclosure of HIV infection: Preliminary results from a sample of Hispanic men. *Health Psychology*, **11**, 300–306.

Martin, M.T., Miller-Johnson, S., Kitzmann, K.M. & Emery, R.E. (1998). Parent–child relationships and insulin-dependent diabetes mellitus: Observational ratings of clinically relevant dimensions. *Journal of Family Psychology*, **12**, 102–111.

Matthews, K.A., Woodall, K.L., Engebbretson, T.O., McCann, B.S., Stoney, C.M., Manuck, S.B. & Saab, P.G. (1992). Influence of age, sex, and family on Type A and hostile attitudes and behaviors. *Health Psychology*, **11**, 317–323.

Matthews, K.A., Woodall, K.L., Jacob, T. & Kenyon, K. (1996). Negative family environment as a predictor of boys' future status on measures of hostile altitudes, interview behavior, and anger expression. *Health Psychology*, **15**, 30–37.

McCaul, K.D. & Mallott, J.M. (1984). Distraction and coping with pain. *Psychological Bulletin*, **95**, 516–533.

McCaul, K.D., Monson, N. & Maki, R.H. (1992). Does distraction reduce pain-produced distress among college students? *Health Psychology*, **11**, 210–217.

Miller, G.E., Dopp, J.M., Stevens, S.Y., Myers, H.F. & Fahey, J.L. (1999). Psychosocial predictors of natural killer cell mobilization during marital conflict. *Health Psychology*, **18**, 262–271.

Miller, K. & Ray, E.B. (1994). Beyond the ties that bind: Exploring the "meaning" of supportive messages and relationships. In B.R. Burleson, T.L. Albrecht, & I.G. Sarason (Eds), *Communication of social support: Messages, interactions, relationships, and community* (pp. 215–228). Thousand Oaks, CA: Sage.

Miller, S.M., Roussi, P., Caputo, G.C. & Kruus, L. (1995). Patterns of children's coping with an aversive dental treatment. *Health Psychology*, **14**, 236–246.

Mullen, B. & Suls, J. (1982). The effectiveness of attention and rejection as coping styles: A meta-analysis of temporal differences. *Journal of Psychosomatic Research*, **26**, 43–49.

Musante, L., MacDougall, J.M., Dembroski, T.M. & Costa, P.T., Jr (1989). Potential for hostility and dimensions of anger. *Health Psychology*, **8**, 343–354.

Newsom, J.T. & Schulz, R. (1998). Caregiving from the recipient's perspective: Negative reactions to being helped. *Health Psychology*, **17**, 172–181.

Nolen-Hoeksema, S., McBride, A. & Larson, J. (1997). Rumination and psychological distress among bereaved partners. *Journal of Personality and Social Psychology*, **72**, 855–862.

Noller, P. & Fitzpatrick, M.A. (1993). *Communication in family relationships*. Englewood Cliffs, NJ: Erlbaum.

Nussbaum, J.F., Hummert, M.L., Williams, A. & Harwood, J. (1996). Communication and older adults. In B.R. Burleson (Ed.), *Communication yearbook 19* (pp. 1–47). Thousand Oaks, CA: Sage.

Parrott, R. (1994). Exploring family practitioners' and patients' information exchange about prescribed medications: Implications for practitioners' interviewing and patients' understanding. *Health Communication*, **6**, 267–280.

Pennebaker, J.W. & Beall, S.K. (1986). Confronting a traumatic event: Toward an understanding of inhibition and disease. *Journal of Abnormal Psychology*, **95**, 274–281.

Pennebaker, J.W., Kiecolt-Glaser, J. & Glaser, R. (1988). Disclosure of traumas and immune function: Health implications for psychotherapy. *Journal of Consulting and Clinical Psychology*, **56**, 239–245.

Pennebaker, J.W., Mayne, T.J. & Francis, M.E. (1997). Linguistic predictors of adaptive bereavement. *Journal of Personality and Social Psychology*, **72**, 863–871.

Penninx, B.W.J.H., van Tilburg, T., Boeke, A.J.P., Deeg, D.J.H., Kriegsman, D.W.M. & van Eijk, J. Th.M. (1998). Effects of social support and personal coping resources on depressive symptoms: Different for various chronic diseases? *Health Psychology*, **17**, 551–558.

Petrie, K.J., Booth, R.J. & Pennebaker, J.W. (1998). The immunological effects of thought suppression. *Journal of Personality and Social Psychology*, **75**, 1264–1272.

Phipps, S. & Srivastava, D.K. (1997). Repressive adaptation in children with cancer. *Health Psychology*, **16**, 521–528.

Pierce, G.R., Sarason, B.R. & Sarason, I.G. (1992). General and specific support expectations and stress as predictors of perceived supportiveness: An experimental study. *Journal of Personality and Social Psychology*, **63**, 297–307.

Ptacek, J.T., Pierce, G.R., Dodge, K.L. & Ptacek, J.J. (1997). Social support in spouses of cancer patients: What do they get and to what end? *Personal Relationships*, **4**, 431–449.

Quadrel, M.J. & Lau, R.R. (1990). A multivariate analysis of adolescents' orientations toward physician use. *Health Psychology*, **9**, 750–773.

Raikkonen, K., Matthews, K.A., Flory, J.D. & Owens, J.F. (1999). Effects of hostility on ambulatory blood pressure and mood during daily living in healthy adults. *Health Psychology*, **18**, 44–53.

Ratliff-Crain, J., Temoshok, L., Kiecolt-Glaser, J.K. & Tamarkin, L. (1989). Issues in psychoneuroimmunology issues. *Health Psychology*, **8**, 747–752.

Reardon, K.K. & Buck, R. (1989). Emotion, reason, and communication in coping with cancer. *Health Communication*, **1**, 41–54.

Reis, H.T. & Franks, P. (1994). The role of intimacy and social support in health outcomes: Two processes or one? *Personal Relationships*, **1**, 185–197.

Rook, K.S. (1984). The negative side of social interaction. *Journal of Personality and Social Psychology*, **46**, 1097–1108.

Rook, K.S. (1992). Detrimental aspects of social relationships: Taking stock of an emerging literature. In H.O.F. Veiel & U. Baumann (Eds), *The meaning and measurement of social support* (pp. 157–169). Washington, DC: Hemisphere.

Roter, D. (1989). Which facets of communication have strong effects on outcome: A meta analysis. In M. Steward & D. Roter (Eds), *Communicating with medical patents* (pp. 183–196). Newbury Park, CA: Sage.

Roter, D.L. & Hall, J.A. (1992). Doctors talking with patients/patients talking with doctors. Westport, CT: Auburn House.

Rothman, A.J., Salovey, P., Turvey, C. & Fishkin, S.A. (1993). Attributions of responsibility and persuasion: Increasing mammography utilization among women over 40 with an internally oriented message. *Health Psychology*, **12**, 39–47.

Rouse, R.A. (1989). A paradigm of intervention: Emotional communication in dentistry. *Health Communication*, **1**, 239–252.

Roy, M.P., Steptoe, A. & Kirschbaum. C. (1998). Life events and social support as moderators of individual differences in cardiovascular an cortisol reactivity. *Journal of Personality and Social Psychology*, **75**, 1273–1281.

Sarason, I.G., Sarason, B.R. & Pierce, G.R. (1994). Relationship-specific social support: Toward a model for the analysis of supportive interactions. In B.R. Burleson, T.L.

Albrecht, & I.G. Sarason (Eds), *Communication of social support: Messages, interactions, relationships, and community* (pp. 91–112). Thousand Oaks, CA: Sage.

Schneider, D.E. & Tucker, R.K. (1992). Measuring communicative satisfaction in doctor–patient relations: The doctor–patient communication inventory. *Health Communication*, **4**, 19–28.

Smith, T.W. (1992). Hostility and health: Current status of a psychosomatic hypothesis. *Health Psychology*, **11**, 139–150.

Smith, T.W., Gallo, L.C., Goble, L., Ngu, L.Q. & Stark, K.A. (1998). Agency, communion, and cardiovascular reactivity during marital interaction. *Health Psychology*, **17**, 537–545.

Stone, A.A., Kennedy-Moore, E. & Neale, J.M. (1995). Association between daily coping and end-of-day mood. *Health Psychology*, **14**, 341–349.

Street, R.L. (1989). Patients' satisfaction with dentists' communicative style. *Health Communication*, **1**, 137–154.

Suarez, E.C., Harlan, E., Peoples, M.C. & Williams, R.B., Jr (1993). Cardiovascular and emotional responses in women: The role of hostility and harassment. *Health Psychology*, **12**, 459–468.

Suls, J., Martin, R. & Leventhal, H. (1997). Social comparison, lay referral, and the decision to seek medical care. In B.P. Buunk & F.X. Gibbons (Eds), *Health, coping, and well-being* (pp. 195–226). Mahwah, NJ: Erlbaum.

Thomas, V. & Clark, J.M. (1997). Nurse–patient communication: Nursing assessment and intervention for pain control. In A. Baum, S. Newman, J. Weinman, R. West & C. McManus (Eds), *Cambridge handbook of psychology, health and medicine* (pp. 298–301). New York: Cambridge University Press.

Thompson, S.C., Nanni, C. & Schwankovsky, L. (1990). Patient-oriented interventions to improve communication in a medical office visit. *Health Psychology*, **9**, 390–404.

Thompson, T.L. (1998). The patient/health professional relationship. In L.D. Jackson & B.K. Duffy (Eds), *Health communication research: A guide to developments and directions* (pp. 37–55). Westport, CT: Greenwood Press.

Tucker, J.S., Friedman, H.S., Wingard, D.L. & Schwartz, J.E. (1996). Marital history at midlife as a predictor of longevity: Alternative explanations to the protective effect of marriage. *Health Psychology*, **15**, 94–101.

Tucker, J.S., Friedman, H.S., Schwartz, J.E., Criqui, M.H., Tomlinson-Keasey, C., Wingard, D.L. & Martin, L.R. (1997). Parental divorce: Effects on individual behavior and longevity. *Journal of Personality and Social Psychology*, **73**, 381–391.

Turner, R.A., Irwin, C.E., Jr, Tschann, J.M. & Millstein, S.G. (1993). Autonomy, relatedness, and the initiation of health risk behaviors in early adolescence. *Health Psychology*, **12**, 200–208.

Umberson, D. (1987). Gender, marital status and the social control of health behavior. *Social Science and Medicine*, **34**, 907–917.

Varni, J.W., Wilcox, K.T. & Hanson, V. (1988). Mediating effects of family social support on child psychological adjustment in juvenile rheumatoid arthritis. *Health Psychology*, **7**, 421–431.

Warren, C. (1992). Perspectives on international sex practices and American family sex communication relevant to teenage sexual behavior in the United States. *Health Communication*, **4**, 121–136.

West, C. & Frankel, R.M. (1991). Miscommunication in medicine. In N. Coupland, H. Giles & J.M. Wiemann (Eds) *"Miscommunication" and problematic talk* (pp. 167–195). Newbury Park, CA: Sage.

Whalen, C.K., Henker, B., Hollingshead, J. & Burgess, S. (1996). Parent–adolescent dialogues about AIDS. *Journal of Family Psychology*, **10**, 343–357.

Whaley, B.B. (1994). "Food is to me as gas is to cars??": Using figurative language to explain illness to children. *Health Communication*, **6**, 193–204.

Whaley, B.B. (1999). Explaining illness to children: Advancing theory and research by determining message content. *Health Communication*, **11**, 185–193.

Wiederhold, J.B., Clarridge, B.R. & Svarstad, B.L. (1992). Verbal consultation regarding prescription drugs: Findings from a statewide study. *Medical Care*, **30**, 159–173.

Wilcox, V.L., Kasl, S.V. & Berkman, L.F. (1994). Social support and physical disability in older people after hospitalization: A prospective study. *Health Psychology*, **13**, 170–179.

Wills, T.A. (1997). Social support and health. In A. Baum, S. Newman, J. Weinman, R. West & C. McManus (Eds), *Cambridge handbook of psychology, health and medicine* (pp. 168–170). New York: Cambridge University Press.

Winefield, H.R. (1992). Doctor-patient communication: An interpersonal helping process. In S. Maes, H. Leventhal & M. Johnston (Eds), *International review of health psychology* (Vol. 1, pp. 167–187). New York: Wiley.

Witte, K. (1997). Fear as motivator, fear as inhibitor: Using the extended parallel process model to explain fear appeal successes and failures. In P. Anderson & L.K. Guerrero (Eds), *Handbook of communication and emotion* (pp. 423–450). San Diego: Academic Press.

Woodall, K.L. & Matthews, K.A. (1989). Familial environment associated with Type A behaviors and psychophysiological responses to stress in children. *Health Psychology*, **8**, 403–426.

Zautra, A.J., Burleson, M.H., Matt, K.S., Roth, S. & Burrows, L. (1994). Interpersonal stress, depression, and disease activity in rheumatoid arthritis and osteoarthritis patients. *Health Psychology*, **13**, 139–148.

6.28

Language, Law and Power

William M. O'Barr
Duke University, Durham, USA

It is now more than two decades since scholars in many fields (especially linguistics, psychology, anthropology, social psychology, and law) began to investigate the empirical relationship between language and law. The resulting body of scholarship constitutes an interdisciplinary effort that combines the approaches of several fields and crosses traditional academic boundaries. It is variously known as language and law, forensic linguistics, and such broader terms as discourse and law, and law and communication. The practitioners share a critical interest in the way that language works in legal contexts, and most are concerned with moving beyond descriptions of legally contextual communication forms toward comprehending the degree to which language (however defined) influences or determines legal processes and their outcomes.

In this chapter, I focus on four specific areas of law and language scholarship: (1) understanding the nature of legal language, (2) discovering the power of language in legal processes, (3) applying linguistic/discourse/communication theories and methods in legal practice, and (4) attempting to transform legal language and communication structures. I select these foci, not because they exhaust the range of scholarship that links language and law, but because the scholarship in each of these areas has a specific – and to a large degree, an agreed upon – agenda about goals, methods, and utility. Let me make no secret of the fact that I have concentrated my own scholarly efforts around item (2) and that the subject matter of item (1) has always fascinated me as a reader but it is not an area in which I have conducted any serious scholarship on my own. The politics of items (3) and (4) interest me more than the details of the specific work that has been conducted in these areas. It should come as no surprise that a scholar who has worked for more than two decades has his preferences and some strong

The New Handbook of Language and Social Psychology.
Edited by W. Peter Robinson and Howard Giles.
© 2001 John Wiley & Sons Ltd.

opinions. These will no doubt be obvious in what follows, but I hope it will also seem that I have made an effort to be fair to all the areas in discussing their goals, methods, and usefulness.

THE NATURE OF LEGAL LANGUAGE

Understanding the history of, patterns in, and views of the variety of language usually termed legal language is considerably easier since the publication of Peter M. Tiersma's *Legal Language* in 1999. A linguist, a lawyer, and a law professor at once, Tiersma brings an unusual and virtually unique combination of perspectives to the problem of understanding law's language. His book is framed by such questions as: Why is legal language so different from ordinary English? Where did the peculiar forms used in the law come from? What are the possibilities that these forms can be changed in order to facilitate communication and legal fairness?

Tiersma provides well-documented answers to these questions and gives, along the way, an enthusiastic and exciting – at least for readers who love the in's and out's of etymology – history of English legal language. He tells how the Romans, Anglo-Saxons, French, and others influenced legal language, giving to it its characteristic alliterations, couplets, repetitions, and unusual phrasings (safe and sound; part and parcel; the truth, the whole truth, and nothing but the truth; to have and to hold; and so on).

The book is so thorough and the bibliography on which it is based so comprehensive that this will surely become the standard reference on English legal language, surpassing David Mellinkoff's longer and highly respected *The Language of the Law* (1963) because Tiersma's book is more up to date and is written from a more eclectic point of view. Tiersma covers much of the same ground as Mellinkoff in his treatment of the history of legal language (that is, the origins of "long, complex, and redundant sentences, conjoined phrases, impersonal constructions, and arcane words and phrases"), but he does so more succinctly and in a degree of depth that will satisfy many readers. Those with a deeper interest in specific usages would do well to consult Mellinkoff as well as Tiersma.

Tiersma also deals with the consequences for the law of a linguistic style that differs greatly from everyday forms. His arguments are functional as well as logical (e.g., legal language creates solidarity among lawyers; legal language allows for more precise usages as well as allowing for deliberate obscurity). These claims, like similar ones in Mellinkoff, make sense, but they do not result from any empirical effort to examine the degree to which legalese creates group cohesion or whether it is in fact more or less precise than ordinary usages. Both ethnographic investigation of how legal language works and experimental examination of hypotheses about its social significance would strengthen Tiersma's provocative descriptions and interesting hypotheses.

This lack of an empirical base for the claims about social consequences of legal language continues to characterize some law and language scholarship. However, when Tiersma shifts from a consideration of written to spoken legal language, he is able to call on a large number of empirical studies to support his general observation that language is not merely a conduit for legal facts in the courtroom but influences both the process and the outcomes. He structures his discussion of spoken legal language around the process of storytelling in court – that is, the process of how lawyers elicit from witnesses the details of what happened; how the question/answer format in which this is done works; how opening and closing arguments frame stories; and how jury instructions explain legal interpretive processes to lay decision makers. It is around topics like these that much of the empirical research of the last two decades has been focused. Tiersma is judicious in weaving the findings together into a convincing argument that the form of legal storytelling influences not only the stories that get told but also the decisions based on them.

LAW AND POWER

A second area of concern in the interdisciplinary scholarship relating to law and language focuses critically on law's power in society. Scholars working in this area recognize law's power over people's lives and property, and their studies are concerned with the degree to which law lives up to its ideals of equal treatment. They consider language a means of understanding the broad and penetrating place of law in society. It is, of course, commonplace knowledge that law does not manage to treat everyone the same. It takes no special skills to note the different rates of incarceration of persons of different ethnic backgrounds in various legal systems or to see that women and men often fare differently when they do battle in legal arenas. The questions that some scholars have asked are: How? Why? By what means? They have found answers in the microlevel details of interaction that constitute the legal system in practice. They have investigated the details of testifying in court as well as the strategies lawyers use to manage testimony. They have studied differences in how stories get told in different legal fora like courtrooms (Conley & O'Barr, 1998), mediation sessions (Garcia 1991, 1995), and lawyers' offices (Sarat & Felstiner 1995). In short, they have looked into what Foucault called the "microphysics of power", for it is in the little detail of how things work that the larger issues of social inequality and power are manifest. These scholars have approached the law not as monolithic and seemingly all-powerful but as the accumulation of thousands and thousands of interactional episodes that make up law in practice. Such a theoretical posture toward investigating law, power, and society leads inevitably to the stuff that makes up law in practice – that is, to the language and communication structures that constitute legal interactions.

The value of these studies has been the degree to which the mechanics of law's power have been revealed. It no longer suffices to make claims about what is suspected (e.g., that women might not fare as well in legal arenas as men did) or observed (e.g., that poor and indigent people fare less well than others do). Rather, this body of scholarship has upped the ante because it has begun to reveal some of the particular ways in which these differences occur and thereby to disassemble the monolithic power of the law into its components.

I am so deeply committed to this point of view and to scholarship that helps reveal the inner workings of the law in daily life that I have spent most of my own career researching, teaching, and writing about these processes. Recently, I published, with my frequent collaborator John M. Conley, *Just Words: Language, Law and Power* (1998). The book brings together exemplars of this scholarship in an attempt to marshal compelling evidence for this perspective and its value in understanding law's power. In the paragraphs that follow, I draw again on that body of work to illustrate the goals, methods, and utility of studying law's power through language.

One of the most compelling demonstrations of law's power through language is Greg Matoesian's research on rape trials (1993, see also 1995). He begins by asking what it is about rape trials that results in the frequent claim (by alleged rape victims) that the trial itself is a terrible experience, indeed a revictimization. To figure this out, Matoesian examines the language of rape trials. In them, he finds several linguistic features that may contribute to the process of revictimization. For example, lawyers manipulate question forms, use silence strategically, manage topics, offer evaluative comments, and challenge witnesses – all tactics that are allowed and conventional within the law. Taken individually and especially in combination, they reveal the ways in which lawyers control, manipulate, and exercise power over witnesses. Some brief examples illustrate.

Silence: When a witness finishes answering a question, the lawyer has considerable leeway as to when the next question is asked. Silence can be used strategically to emphasize a witness's response, to delay a witness wanting to elaborate a question, and in other ways that are under the lawyer's (not the witness's) control.

Evaluative commentary: Although courtroom examinations are technically situations in which lawyers ask questions and witnesses answer them, a lawyer has many ways to 'comment' upon a witness's answers during the course of a trial. For example, a lawyer might ask:

> Isn't it true that on cross-examination by Mrs Roberts you never once answered a question with "I don't know" or "I don't remember"?

or

> Isn't it true that on cross-examination by Mr Billings you, on numerous occasions, indicated that you didn't know or didn't remember?

Formally, these are questions. In another sense, they are powerful evaluations of the witness. When tactics like these are used throughout a trial, a witness may be intimidated, become reticent, or feel overwhelmed.

Matoesian's research combs the seemingly little details of courtroom interactions. His findings add up to a vigorous argument about just how it is that law intimidates and overpowers individuals. In the particular instance of rape trials, these details reveal the mechanics of revictimization and powerlessness in the face of the law. As he is quick to argue, these tactics are not only to be found in rape trials but also make up the very stuff of a great many trials. Linguistic mechanisms like these are available throughout the legal system to lawyers and are used with great frequency in the adversarial process. Those who have greater access (either structurally – as lawyers generally do over witnesses – or because they can afford to hire those legal professionals most skilled in these tactics) go into the process with different resources. Seen from this perspective, it is little wonder that the law's idea of equal treatment fails so often in practice.

Another body of research that demonstrates law's power deals with mediation as an alternative to adjudication. This research challenges law's assumption that legal processes are neutral mechanisms for settling disputes. Rather, it looks at the way that mediation (and other decision-making processes) work and finds that the processes themselves exhibit potential biases that interact in complex ways with social differences.

Angela Garcia's research on mediation sessions is instructive (1991, 1995). She asks the simple question of what it is about mediation that facilitates communication between parties that seem hopelessly divided and frequently unable to engage in civil communication. Detailed examination of the structure of mediation sessions gives some answers. First of all, the back-and-forth bantering of argument – the "No, I didn't/Yes, you did" process of heated verbal exchanges – is broken down through some simple rules that apply in most mediation sessions. These rules radically restructure the communication process by separating counter-claims from accusations and by forcing parties to listen before they speak. The surprising and almost magical result of many mediation sessions is that people who have lost the ability to communicate without screaming or yelling suddenly find themselves able to talk to one another, albeit in limited ways, once again.

When these observations about the microlinguistics of mediation are coupled with the observation that women fare less well in divorce mediation than men, they help explain a complex process of gender differentiation in the law. Why should women fare less well, say in divorce mediation, than men? A provocative possibility seems to be that the very many things we know about gender differences in language use (Tannen, 1990; Cameron, 1998) combine with the mechanics of mediation in such a way that women seek closure and tend to agree sooner than men. Since mediation is about finding the common ground, seeking agreements, and closing gaps, those individuals who are predisposed for whatever reason to act in this way greatly facilitate the process. But in doing so, they may not fare as well personally with regard to property settlements as they might have in an argumentative, adversarial arena where they would be represented by forceful, demanding attorneys who are highly skilled in the mechanics of argumentation, intimidation, and control.

Thus, mediation is a mixed blessing it seems. It is a useful and often preferred alternative to adjudication, but its very structure may contain biases that result in some people faring better than others may. This conclusion, along with that of Matoesian from his study of rape trials, opens up through linguistic investigation an understanding of law's patriarchy.

There are many other examples that could be cited that illustrate this sort of problem in the law (some in our book and many others published elsewhere), but the conclusions all lead in the same direction. Language, especially micro-linguistic analyses, is now firmly established as one of the fundamental ways in which law's inner workings can be revealed. And importantly, it is not just the inherent interest that these inner workings hold for those of us with linguistic leanings. Rather, such a perspective deconstructs the processes through which law works its power.

APPLYING LINGUISTICS TO LEGAL PRACTICE

Along with the investigative scholarship about law and language over the past two decades have come efforts to apply linguistics theories and analyses in legal practice. It is perhaps more accurate to say that many linguists have developed an interest in language and the law as a result of being asked to assist in legal matters. Indeed a cottage industry has emerged around such practices, and a journal, *The Journal of Forensic Linguistics*, that specializes in applications of linguistics to law has been published since 1994.

Before looking at contemporary practice, it is worth emphasizing that com-munication issues have a long and complex history in the law. Indeed, law is language either in its written or spoken form – what is put in wills, deeds, and other legal documents and what is said in courts, appeals, and opinions occur through the medium of language. Thus, the law must be concerned with how language works.

Of this complex history, I cite two relatively recent examples of scholars' efforts to draw on their respective fields of scholarship in their capacity as expert witnesses. Elizabeth Loftus, a psychologist, and Roger Shuy, a linguist, have successfully worked with lawyers in and out of court and have published exten-sively about their experiences.

Loftus began studying eyewitness testimony in the 1970s. Although her focus as a psychologist is on cognition and memory, the fact that what is remembered is typically reported through language makes her work of interest to law and language scholars. In her early and perhaps best-known research, Loftus studied eyewitness testimony by asking questions of experimental subjects who had seen a videotape she produced showing a car crash. Thus, the videotape as experi-mental stimulus could be held constant while the manipulations varied. In a particularly provocative set of questions, Loftus asked subjects how fast the car was going when it crashed into the other car. She varied the words used to describe the action of the car in the videotape: How fast was the car going when it brushed against/hit/slammed into the other car? Subjects reported variations in speed from 25 miles per hour to more than 55, depending on the verb used to describe the action.

In a second study, Loftus asked half the subject eyewitnesses whether they saw any broken glass and the other half whether they saw the broken glass. Those asked "any" did not report seeing broken glass as often as those asked "the". The process underlying this difference is the phenomenon linguists refer to as presupposition as in the often-used example "When did you stop beating your wife?" which presupposes that the addressee had previously beat his wife. What Loftus focuses on is the fact that the language of the question itself can influence recall and thus testimony in court. Because the entire legal process depends on testimony, factors like this that influence recall are especially serious matters.

In an even more telling phase of her research, Loftus recalled the subjects who had been asked "any" and "the" at a later time and quizzed them about how much glass they had seen. Remarkably, those who were asked "the" reported seeing significantly more glass than those who had been asked "any". Loftus concludes from this evidence that the form of the question affects not only recall but also memory itself.

The significance of her findings for law led to opportunities to work as an expert witness, assisting lawyers in and out of court in assessing the validity of eyewitness testimony. Not all judges were willing to admit Loftus' testimony about the unreliability of eyewitness testimony. Psychology and linguistics appeared to be "unscientific" to many.

More recently, many social scientists, especially linguists, have been asked to assist with the understanding and interpretation of language behavior. Roger Shuy, a linguist who has worked often as an expert in legal contexts, has written a compelling book that demonstrates the sorts of things that linguistics can offer to the law. *Language Crimes: The Use and Abuse of Language Evidence in the Courtroom* (1993) details some of the ways in which linguistic insights can help solve problems in law. In separate chapters dealing with bribing, agreeing, threatening, admitting, truth-telling, and promising, Shuy outlines basic linguistic understandings of how these speech acts work and shows some of the ways the law can misunderstand them.

He begins his analysis by discussing some common misconceptions about language: meaning is found primarily in individual words; a single listening to a tape is enough to determine its content; reading a transcript is as good as hearing a tape recording; all parties in a conversation understand the same things by their words and people say what they mean and intend (Shuy, 1993, p. 8). For a trained linguist, these assumptions are problematic. In his book, they become the basis for Shuy to demonstrate what applied linguistics can deliver to the law.

For example, in discussing the problem of bribery, Shuy points out that there are a variety of ways that offers can be made – ranging from overt to indirect or imbedded. "If you will do me a little favor, I'll make it up to you real good" is an example of an indirect offer and stands in marked contrast to other ways that an offer might be made. But does an offer of a bribe need to be overt and direct to count legally? How should the example noted above be interpreted? Should the law consider it a bribe or not? The answers to these questions are, of course, consequential legally and could mean for the person being tried the difference between a jail term and going free.

In another chapter, he asks: How direct must an admission be to count? Or alternatively, how indirect may it be and still be considered by the law to be an admission? These examples illustrate: I admit that I overslept/I slept till 7 a.m./I missed my bus/I was here as soon as anyone else/My alarm clock didn't go off; and so on. These examples vary in directness and excuse-offering which, as Shuy, illustrates, proved consequential in interpreting linguistic behavior in The State of Alaska v. Larry Gentry in 1986. The law must deal repeatedly with issues like this in innumerable trials, and the field of linguistics has found continual application in helping sort through such matters.

Forensic linguistics, the term commonly used for such applications of linguistics, is driven by the cases that are brought to linguistics rather than the effort of linguists to find application for theories. Thus, this area of language/law investigation and scholarship is not so much guided by concerns about filling out unexamined areas of knowledge as it is by the concerns that lawyers are willing to hire linguists to investigate. However, as Shuy shows in his book, the range of topics that he and other linguists have investigated in this way offers a broad demonstration of the utility of linguistic theory as well as the problems the law encounters when it fails to treat language directly. The trend that emerges over the past three decades is an increasing sophistication of linguistics in interpreting language behavior in legal contexts as well as a greater acceptance by the law of linguistic insights as valid and helpful.

REFORMING LEGAL LANGUAGE

Laypeople and scholars alike have asked: Must legal language be so abstruse and incomprehensible? Is it not possible to say things more simply? Why must we hire one lawyer to encrypt a document and another to decode it at a later date? The usual answer given to these questions has to do with the precedents that have been established in interpreting formulaic legal language. Complex as certain phrasings are from a lay point of view (e.g., Borrower covenants that Borrower is lawfully seised of the estate hereby conveyed . . .), lawyers know how the courts have generally interpreted this typical language in a deed of trust and are wary of trying new formulations. Other formulations, no matter novel and direct, run the risk of being interpreted differently. Few lawyers want to run such risks and therefore staunchly defend traditional expressions.

Tiersma points out that legal language is difficult to comprehend for some quite specific reasons based in its linguistic structure. It has highly technical vocabulary (per stirpes, beyond a reasonable doubt, proximate, and so on), uses many archaic, formal, and unusual words (e.g., aforesaid, therewith), states things impersonally (e.g., vendor shall have the right to modify this clause within thirty days' notice to vendee), frequently uses nominalizations (i.e., nouns or noun phrases constructed from more commonly used verbs) and passives (the petition for a writ of certiorari is granted), multiple negatives, and long and complex sentences. These characteristics make legal language difficult to understand because it is so different from ordinary speech and writing.

The goals of the Plain English Movement and other efforts to reform legal language are increased readability and comprehension. Seen from the perspective of law and power, these are modern efforts to limit law's power over people's lives. Tiersma points our several areas where the incomprehensibility of legal language is especially problematic. These include documents like wills, deeds, and the like that enter the lives of a great many people; statutes – especially criminal ones – that are important for laypeople to understand; consumer documents; and jury instructions.

FUTURE DIRECTIONS

I suspect that the four areas considered in this chapter will diverge even more in the future. Scholarship on legal language has tended to focus primarily on the written language of the law. There is both more work to be done on English legal language as well as possibilities for studying the language of the law cross-linguistically. To what degree are the problems of English legal language replicated in other traditions? To what degree are they unique? These are profitable areas for future investigation. Similarly, reforms of legal language are far from complete. In fact, they have barely begun. New problems emerge in English as language policies change and develop (French and native languages as well as English in Canada, Spanish and English in the United States, ethnic minorities in Britain, and so on).

The law is turning increasingly to linguistics (and related social sciences that study language behavior) for help. Thus, the sorts of applications of linguistics noted here in the work of Loftus and Shuy are likely to proliferate. Unless those who conduct such work attempt – as Shuy particularly has done – to link application to broader theory, their work is not likely to have much audience beyond other forensic linguists.

The case for the value of microlinguistic approaches in understanding law's power has been made through a significant body of scholarship over the past two decades. However, what is known is more indicative of possibilities for understanding how law works in actual practice than it is a full understanding of the mechanics of law and power. I do not think I am alone in hoping for more studies that deconstruct law's power both in English and other linguistic and legal traditions.

REFERENCES

Cameron, D. (Ed.) (1998). *The Feminist Critique of Language*. London: Routledge.
Conley, J.M. & O'Barr, W.M. (1990). *Rules versus Relationships: The Ethnography of Legal Discourse*. Chicago: University of Chicago Press.

Conley, J.M. & O'Barr, W.M. (1998). *Just Words: Law, Language and Power*. Chicago: University of Chicago Press.

Garcia, A. (1991). Dispute resolution without disputing: How the interactional organization of mediation hearings minimizes argument. *American Sociological Review*, **56**, 818–835.

Garcia, A. (1995). The problematics of representation in community mediation hearings: Implications for mediation practice. *Journal of Sociology & Social Welfare*, **22**, 23–46.

Matoesian, G.M. (1993). *Reproducing Rape: Dominion Through Talk in the Courtroom*: Chicago: University of Chicago Press.

Matoesian, G.M. (1995). Language, law, and society: Applied implications of the Kennedy Smith trial. *Law and Society Review*, **29**, 669–701.

Mellinkoff, D. (1963). *The Language of the Law*. Boston, MA: Little, Brown.

Rosen, L. (1977). The anthropologist as expert witness. *American Anthropologist*, **79**, 555–578.

Sarat, A. & Felstiner, W. (1995). *Divorce lawyers and their clients*. London: Oxford University Press.

Shuy, R.W. (1993). *Language Crimes: The Use and Abuse of Language Evidence in the Courtroom*. Cambridge, MA: Blackwell.

Tannen, D. (1990). *You Just Don't Understand: Men and Women in Conversation*. New York: Morrow.

Tiersma, P.M. (1999). *Legal Language*. Chicago: University of Chicago Press.

6.29

Active Patients as Powerful Communicators

Richard L. Street Jr
Texas A&M University, College Station, USA

In the 1960s and early 1970s, Barbara Korsch (Korsch, Gozzi & Francis, 1968), Milton Davis (1968), and Philip Ley (1973) demonstrated that *talk* was as critical a component of the delivery of health care as were vital signs, the physical examination, and medical procedures for diagnosis and treatment. Since their seminal works, the study of patient–health care provider (albeit mostly physician) communication has blossomed into one of the most widely studied aspects of communication and health. A number of studies have shown that the way in which providers and patients talk with one another influences an array of post-consultation outcomes, including patients' satisfaction with care, adherence to provider recommendations, understanding of health issues, and even health improvement (for reviews, see Kaplan, Greenfield & Ware, 1989; Ong et al., 1995; Roter & Hall, 1993; Thompson, 1994). However, while providing a wealth of data that has important implications for clinical practice and medical education, research on communication in the medical consultation typically suffers from a *provider-centric bias*; that is, it treats the health care provider as the communicator of primary importance.

This essay takes the opposite position by forwarding a *patient-centered* approach to the study of communication in the medical consultation. Specifically, I will first provide a rationale for such a perspective by showing how a patient-centered approach not only balances the provider-centric bias in past research but also contributes to current efforts to conceptualize and understand an issue of growing importance: patient participation in care. Secondly, I will offer a linguistic model of participation in care that focuses on (a) types of verbal

The New Handbook of Language and Social Psychology.
Edited by W. Peter Robinson and Howard Giles.
© 2001 John Wiley & Sons Ltd.

responses that are particularly influential in the consultation, (b) processes affecting the patient's performance of these behaviors, and (c) outcomes associated with these actions. Although non-verbal behaviors are an important part of the medical consultation (see, for example, DiMatteo, Hays & Prince, 1986; Street & Buller, 1988), I will focus on verbal behaviors because these are the actions by which information exchange, control, support, and decision-making are accomplished in medical encounters.

PATIENT PARTICIPATION IN HEALTH CARE: THE NEED FOR A COMMUNICATION PERSPECTIVE

Participating in the health care process is more than simply seeking medical services; *participation* connotes action, involvement, and influence within the health care environment. Although many have long argued that patients have a right and responsibility to be involved in their health care (e.g., World Health Organization, 1978), only recently has research begun to reveal the therapeutic benefits of greater patient participation in the health care process (Kaplan & Ware, 1989). According to Cahill (1996), patient participation consists of various activities including seeking health-related information, being involved in medical decision-making, and interacting with providers in a way that narrows the knowledge and power gap between provider and patient. Cahill only superficially acknowledges the role of communication by noting that patient participation requires an "egalitarian communication system" and leads to "improved communication" between provider and patient. Others also recognize that the patient's participation in care is a dynamic, socially constructed event (Saunders, 1995; McEwen, Martini & Wilkins, 1983), but have provided little insight into the communicative processes underlying this phenomenon.

The conceptual absence of communication in models of patient participation in care possibly could be filled by incorporating theory and research on provider–patient communication. However, even this research tradition is limited in its ability to inform about processes underlying the patient's actions in the consultation because historically it has treated the health care *provider* as the communicator of importance whose verbal performance will determine the success or failure of the consultation (Sharf & Street, 1997).

Provider-Centrism in Physician–Patient Communication Research

The fact that researchers have mostly focused on the clinician's communicative actions and their consequences is not surprising for several reasons. First, providers and patients typically assume complementary roles in the consultation, with the patient being the "help seeker" in need of medical treatment or information, and who is dependent upon the health care professional as the "help provider". Both providers and patients generally accept these roles and communicate in a way that reflects and reinforces the clinician's dominance in communicative exchange. Research consistently shows that physicians tend to talk more, ask more questions, give more directives, make more recommendations, and interrupt more than do patients (Roter & Hall, 1993; Roter, Hall & Katz, 1988; Wissow et al., 1998; Street, 1992a). Furthermore, the evidence also suggests that the provider's communication style can influence post-consultation outcomes. Doctors who are more informative, give more explanations, show more sensitivity to the patient's feelings and concerns, and offer more reassurance and support typically have patients who are more satisfied with care, have a greater understanding of health issues, and are more committed to treatment recommendations (Roter & Hall, 1993; Frankel & Beckman, 1989; Kaplan et al., 1989; Orth et al., 1987; Street, 1992b; Bertakis et al., 1998).

However, the emphasis on the health care provider has had the unintended consequence of minimizing the patient's role in the consultation and potential influence on post-consultation outcomes. In reality, patients need not, and often do not, assume powerless or passive roles. Furthermore, patients have the potential to exert considerable control over the events of the consultation and the provider's behavior. Admittedly, some research has recognized this and has investigated the interactive exchange between provider and patient, treating both participants as uniquely important (see, for example, Kaplan et al., 1989; Roter & Hall, 1993; Street, 1991). My effort to put forth a linguistic model of patient participation in care is not intended to deny the importance of the provider's behavior in the consultation. Rather, it is an attempt to examine processes affecting actions a patient can take to be a more effective communicator, to enhance the quality of care received, and to improve his or her health and well-being.

A LINGUISTIC MODEL OF PATIENT PARTICIPATION IN CARE

Figure 1 presents a model of patient participation in medical consultations that identifies types of verbal actions that constitute participation as well as factors affecting and outcomes associated with these responses. This model evolved in part from previous work including Roter's (1977) model of question-asking, Patterson's (1983) sequential–functional model of communication, Pendleton's (1983) model of doctor–patient communication, and Giles' communication accommodation theory (Gallois & Giles, 1998). The model presented here hopefully will have heuristic and practical value for designing and evaluating interventions aimed at improving the patient's ability to assume an active, participatory role in the medical encounter.

In the discussion below, I will first identify specific types of verbal responses that are key features of the patient's participation in medical encounters.

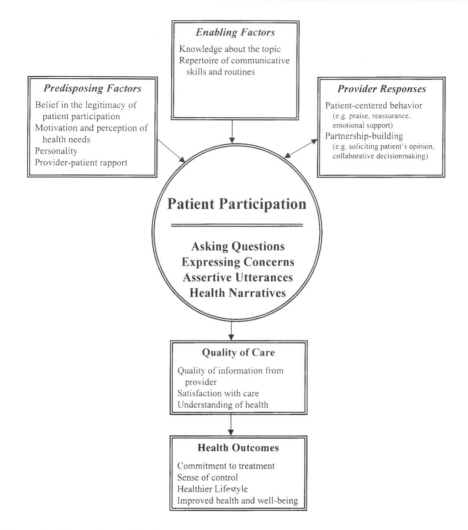

Figure 1   Linguistic model of patient participation in care

Second, I will explain why these forms of speech can enhance the quality of care received and contribute to improved outcomes following the consultation. Finally, I will conclude with a discussion of factors affecting patient participation in care and types of interventions that can help patients become more active communicators in their interactions with health care providers.

Linguistic Features of Participation in Care

To participate in medical consultations, patients must be able to express their needs, concerns, preferences, ideas about health, and expectations for care.

While it is reasonable to assume that a patient actively involved in the consultation will talk more than a passive patient, patient participation is more than just a quantitative feature of communicative activity. For example, a patient conceivably could spend considerable time answering questions on topics determined by the physician that do little to reveal the patient's perspective or concerns. Thus, patient participation also must be defined with respect to *qualitative* aspects of communicative activity, particularly to the types of speech acts that not only disclose the patient's concerns and opinions, but also have the potential to favorably influence the events of the consultation and the provider's behavior.

Asking questions, expressing concerns, being assertive, and health narratives are four key components of patient participation in care. *Asking questions* is the most obvious means by which patients gather information and get clarification on health issues (Beisecker & Beisecker, 1990; Roter, 1977; Street, 1991). *Expressions of concern* include statements in which the patient expresses worry, anxiety, fear, anger (Street, 1991, 1992a), negative affect, or emotions (Roter & Hall, 1993; Kaplan et al., 1989). *Assertiveness* includes verbal actions that express one's rights, feelings, beliefs, and interests (Infante & Rancer, 1995). In a medical consultation, a patient is being assertive when offering opinions (e.g., on one's ability to change lifestyle or the cause of an illness), stating preferences, making suggestions and recommendations (e.g., for treatment), disagreeing with the clinician, and interrupting to retake the floor (Street, 1992a; Kaplan et al., 1989).

The claim that physicians dislike assertive patients (Clarke & Evans, 1998) may in part be explained by distinguishing assertiveness from aggressiveness. Being assertive is an expression of one's perspective and an indicator of involvement in the interaction. Aggressiveness, on the other hand, is hostile, uncooperative, and attacking behavior that is counterproductive to the goals of the interaction (Burgoon, Johnson, & Koch, 1998). While providers generally dislike "demanding and controlling" patients (Levinson et al., 1993), they are often equally frustrated with "passive, dependent" patients (Harris, Rich & Crowson, 1985). Many clinicians believe they would have a better idea about the care a patient needs and whether they were satisfying these needs if patients were more actively involved in the consultation (Merkel, 1984). A recent study reported that patients who were instructed on how to explicitly state their concerns and ask questions were perceived by physicians as better communicators than were patients not receiving the intervention (Frederikson & Bull, 1995).

Finally, I use the term *health narratives* to describe what some have called "stories" about health (Kleinman, 1988; Sharf, 1990). These narratives reveal health experiences as they relate to everyday activities (work, exercise), relationships (family and friends), situations (e.g., traveling, being outdoors), and problems that unfold over time (e.g., when the symptoms started, pain). Health narratives are an important component of participation in care because they reveal important contextual information about the patient's health status, needs, behavior, beliefs, and values (Kleinman, 1988; Smith & Hoppe, 1991).

Why these Speech Forms are Influential

As are other types of communicative exchange, medical consultations are dynamic events that unfold according to the personal characteristics of the interactants (e.g., goals, attitudes, linguistic skills), their partner's behavior, and norms governing appropriate conversational conduct (e.g., turn-taking, topic development) (Cappella, 1994; Street, 1992a). Because communicators must cooperate and coordinate their utterances to create a coherent, smooth exchange, each interactant's communicative actions will influence the responses of the other. With respect to medical consultations, a patient's questions, expression of concerns, assertiveness, and health stories are potentially powerful forms of speech because they present both an *opportunity* for and a *constraint* on the clinician's subsequent response.

Patient Participation as an Opportunity for the Health Care Provider

Because most health care providers want to help and accommodate patients, the patient's participation in the consultation can be an important resource for the clinician, especially one committed to patient-centered care. For example, a patient's question identifies informational needs and topics requiring clarification or explanation (Beisecker & Beisecker, 1990; Roter, 1977). Expressions of concern unveil issues about which the patient is worried and in need of reassurance, support, or comfort. An assertive patient will help the clinician better understand the patient's perspective (e.g., beliefs, opinions) on health and therapy as well as what the patient hopes to accomplish during the consultation. Health care providers can then use this information to tailor explanations and recommendations to take into account the patient's personal preferences and circumstances. Finally, patients' stories about health experiences reveal how the patient's health is woven into everyday living. These narratives point to issues of importance to the patient, what the patient believes as causes and remedies of health problems, and contextual factors that could impede or assist problem resolution (Sharf, 1990; Smith & Hoppe, 1991; Waitzkin, 1991).

Patient Participation as a Constraint on the Health Care Provider

The patient's verbal contributions are also a constraint on the provider's behavior primarily because of normative standards for conversational conduct. For example, there is a strong expectation that an "answer" should follow a "question" (Sacks, Schegloff & Jefferson, 1974). Thus, even if reluctant or uninterested in talking about a particular health issue, a clinician may nonetheless feel obligated to do so because the patient has asked a question on the topic. Another expectation is that an interactant's conversational contribution be topically connected to (Tracy, 1985) and accommodate (Gallois & Giles, 1998) the partner's previous response. By expressing a concern, offering an opinion, or making a recommendation, the patient has introduced topical content into the conversational stream to which the clinician is expected to connect his or her subsequent response.

Finally, the patient's stories about health may influence what unfolds in the consultation because the narrative is a form of discourse quite different from that used by health care providers. Clinicians generally approach the consultation in a manner that is both deductive (trying to identify the cause a particular problem) and didactic (trying to explain health issues as a teacher would a student). As a result, providers generally rely upon close-ended questions, probes, and explanations as their linguistic tools. Patients, on the other hand, often discuss their health concerns and interests in the form of stories because their health has meaning within the context of everyday activities, situations, and relationships. When patients introduce these stories into the consultation, health care providers may feel some obligation to focus their own talk on contextual issues inherent within the patient's health experiences (Smith & Hoppe, 1991; Levenstein et al., 1989).

Of course, as is often the case with people in higher-status positions, health care providers sometimes ignore issues raised by patients (Todd, 1989; Waitzkin, 1991) and interrupt patients prior to the completion of their conversational turn or narrative (Beckman & Frankel, 1984). Nevertheless, non sequiturs, non-accommodative actions and a disregard of a partner's comment generally are perceived as inappropriate conversational actions (Giles et al., 1987), a fact that would become apparent if patients were to reinterrupt or assertively restate their question, concern, or opinion.

Patient Participation and Quality of Care

Quality of care is distinguished from outcome of care in that the former refers to the process (e.g., how the consultation is conducted, procedures recommended) and the latter to the consequences (e.g., adherence, health improvement) of medical care (Roter & Hall, 1993). For present purposes, I will include the patient's understanding of health issues and satisfaction with care as indicators of quality because these variables are intricately tied to the communicative exchange between provider and patient. As shown in the model, the patient's participation in the medical encounter can enhance quality of care in several ways.

First, compared to less inquisitive and expressive patients, those who more frequently ask questions and express concerns generally receive more information from providers (Greenfield, Kaplan & Ware, 1985; Street, 1991, 1992a), a resource universally valued by patients. Expressions of concern also tend to elicit more patient-centered responses of support and reassurance from clinicians (Street, 1992a). Although the effect of the patient's health narratives on the process of care has received scant empirical attention, advocates of patient-centered medicine contend that these stories reveal valuable information about the patient's health needs, beliefs, and behavior (Sharf, 1990) which in turn can lead to personalized treatment recommendations better suited to the patient's life circumstances (Henbest & Stewart, 1990).

Second, with some exceptions, patients who more actively participate in their consultations are more satisfied with care and gain a better understanding of health issues than do more passive patients. This is especially true when relying on patients' perceptions of their participation in the encounter and involvement in medical decision-making (Brody et al., 1989; Lerman et al., 1990; Young & Klingle, 1996). Studies using behavioral measures of patient participation have reported similar findings. Compared to their less involved counterparts, patients who more actively participated in their medical consultations demonstrated better recall of the doctor's recommendations (Heszen-Klemens & Lapinska, 1984) and health issues discussed (Carter et al., 1982). Others have found that patient satisfaction with care was related to the extent to which patients were verbally active (Anderson, DeVellis & DeVellis, 1987), discussed their expectations with doctors (Treadway, 1983), and were able to talk about their health ideas and experiences (Putnam et al., 1985; Winefield & Murrell, 1991).

With respect to the patient's assertiveness and expressions of negative affect, the results are mixed. Stewart (1984) found that patients more satisfied with their care expressed more opinions and concerns (i.e., showing tension, asking for help) whereas others have found that patients' opinion-giving and expressions of negative affect are associated with lower satisfaction (Roter, 1977; Winefield & Murrell, 1991). The inconsistency in these findings may be due to a several factors. First, opinionated and emotionally expressive patients may be expressing frustration with their medical plan or health status. Unhappy patients also tend to report less satisfaction with their health care (Hall et al., 1990). Second, assertive patients may be struggling with their providers over control of the interaction, the cause of a health problem (c.g., lifestyle), treatment recommendations, and so forth. Clearly, more research is needed to better understand how acts of patient participation are related to negotiation, cooperation, and conflict in medical consultations. However, the preponderance of evidence suggests that more active patient involvement helps improve the quality of care patients receive as measured by patients' satisfaction with care, understanding of health issues, and the quality and amount of information they receive from their health care providers.

Patient Participation and Post-Consultation Outcomes

The relationship between a patient's communicative activity in the consultation and subsequent health outcomes is an issue of considerable clinical and theoretical importance. Post-consultation outcomes include a variety of measures –

adherence to a treatment regimen, a healthier lifestyle, eradication of disease, mental well-being, and health-related quality of life, to name a few. A growing body of research indicates that patient participation in the medical encounter contributes in a variety of ways to improved health and healthier behavior.

For example, Kaplan and her colleagues (Kaplan et al., 1989; Greenfield et al., 1988) have shown that diabetic and hypertensive patients who exerted more control during their consultations, more openly expressed their concerns and worries, and were more successful at acquiring information from physicians subsequently experienced better blood sugar and blood pressure control, respectively, than did more passive patients. Similarly, Orth et al. (1987) found that blood pressure control improved the more patients were able to elaborate and disclose health information "in their own words" (that is, tell their health story). Commitment to treatment has been linked to the degree to which patients were able to introduce issues of concern about their health (Rost, Carter & Inui, 1989), to their perceptions of having actively participated in the consultation (Young & Klingle, 1996), to the degree to which they openly expressed negative feelings (Stewart, 1984), and to the extent to which they asked questions, offered opinions, and provided information (Heszen-Klemens & Lapinska, 1984). Finally, some research has shown that patients with chronic diseases fare better when health care providers are less controlling (Street et al., 1993; Kaplan et al., 1989), perhaps because the provider's dominance limits the patient's ability to assume an active role in the encounter.

While the patient's communicative performance in a single consultation has been linked to post-consultation outcomes, little is known about *why* these relationships exist. I suggest three possibilities for future investigation. First, patient participation may lead to improved outcomes because more active patients, having made their concerns and preferences known to the health care provider, in turn receive treatment plans better suited to the their unique needs and circumstances. Furthermore, patients are more likely to remain committed to a personalized health plan (Henbest & Stewart, 1990) including recommendations to adopt a healthier lifestyle (Ryan et al., 1995).

Second, patient participation may enhance adherence to treatment programs because of its relationship to satisfaction with care and understanding of health issues (Golin, DiMatteo & Gelberg, 1996). As mentioned above, patients who ask questions and express their concerns tend to receive more clarifying and explanatory information from providers which in turn increases patient's satisfaction with care, understanding of health issues, and motivation to follow the regimen (Hall, Roter & Katz, 1988; Ley, 1988).

Finally, being actively involved in discussing and making decisions about one's health situation may enhance a patient's perception of *control* over health (Roter, 1977). For example, patient participation has been linked to the degree to which patients assumed responsibility for treatment decisions, believed they had a choice of therapy, and had expectations for improved health and well-being (Lerman et al., 1990; Street & Voigt, 1997). In turn, patients who believed they were involved, had influence over, and were to some degree responsible for therapeutic decisions often recover more quickly following surgery, more effectively cope with serious illness, and report better health-related quality of life following treatment than do patients perceiving less control over their health care (England & Evans, 1992; Mahler & Kulik, 1991; Royak-Schaler, 1991; Street & Voigt, 1997).

Before concluding this section of the essay, I should make a brief comment on the notion that active participation in care is desirable and contributes to improved health outcomes. Although the evidence generally supports this claim, there are important exceptions. Although most patients want to be fully informed and actively discuss health issues with their health care providers, some people prefer to have little or no involvement in making medical decisions (Ende et al., 1989; Strull, Lo & Charles, 1984). Instead, they put their trust in external sources (physicians, God, etc.) to take care of their health-related problems (see, for example, Taylor, Lichtman & Wood, 1984). These individuals are reassured by their faith, which in turn helps them cope with uncertainties and problems with their health. I adopt the perspective that, generally speaking, patient participation in care is a constructive part of the health care process should the patient *want* to be involved in care. In the section that follows, I identify factors affecting the patient's inclination and ability to do so.

Factors Affecting Patient Participation in Care

Health care providers could offer their clients a valuable service by providing resources and programs designed to improve the patient's participation in the health care process. To do this, one must first understand generative processes underlying communication behavior, specifically as they apply to the patient's desire and ability to be an active communicator within health care settings. The model presented in Figure 1 identifies three sets of variables that influence how patients communicate in their interactions with clinicians: (a) predisposing factors, (b) enabling factors, and (c) the health care provider's communicative style.

Predisposing Factors

Predisposing factors include social, psychological, and cultural forces that predispose people to communicate in certain ways (Patterson, 1983; Roter, 1977). With respect to patient participation in medical encounters, four predisposing variables are particularly important: (a) a belief in the legitimacy of patient participation, (b) the salience of perceived health needs (e.g., worries about health, pain), (c) personality factors (e.g., locus of control, extroversion), and (d) perception of rapport with one's health care provider.

To actively participate in the health care process, patients must believe in the legitimacy of their involvement and the importance of their personal perspective on health. Many patients are reluctant to tell their health stories, offer their opinions, or elaborate on their concerns because they are unsure whether such talk is appropriate, is relevant to the clinician's tasks or interests, or they are afraid of taking too much of the provider's valuable time (Roter & Hall, 1993; Street et al., 1995a). On the other hand, some patients – particularly those who are middle-aged, have higher social standing, and have more formal education – believe that they should be actively involved in the health care process and in medical decision-making (Degner & Sloan, 1992; Cassileth et al., 1980; Ende et al., 1989; Strull et al., 1984). This is part explains why these patients tend to be more opinionated, verbally active, and disclose more information when interacting with health care providers than do less educated, elderly, and poorer patients (Beisecker & Beisecker, 1990; Stewart, 1984; Street, 1991, 1992a; Street et al., 1995b).

Second, patients will be more motivated to discuss health issues when they believe they have important health needs and concerns. For example, two studies reported that mothers more worried about their child's health sought more information and expressed more concern than did less worried parents (Wasserman et al., 1983; Street, 1992a). However, it is important to realize that perceived need alone does not automatically lead to more active patient participation. For example, although some patients may be in mental distress or believe their health is interfering with daily activities, they may still be unwilling to talk about these problems if they believe that these health issues are not part of the clinician's responsibilities or expertise (Street et al., 1995a) or that the doctor is not interested in discussing these matters (Roter & Hall, 1993).

Third, personality and other cognitive factors (e.g., locus of control) also influence a patient's predilections to actively participate in health care settings. In a recent study of a pediatric practice, Eaton and Tinsley (1999) observed that mothers who scored higher on personality dimensions of openness and extroversion asked more questions, gave more information, and more frequently asked for reassurance than did mothers having fewer of these traits. Howell-Koren and Tinsley (1990) found that mothers with a higher internal locus of control asked more questions during their interactions with pediatricians than did mothers with lower internality. This finding was consistent with other research indicating that people with a stronger sense of control over health engage in more proactive health management behaviors than do those perceiving less personal control (Peterson & Stunkard, 1989). Finally, some people experience communication apprehension when interacting with health care providers. Apprehensive patients not only talk less, they also appear to be less satisfied with their interactions with physicians than are patients who have less communication apprehension (Ayres et al., 1996).

Finally, the quality of the patient's relationship with the health care provider also can have an effect on the patient's participation in care. Although Beisecker and Beisecker (1990) found no relationship between patient's question-asking and number of previous visits with the physician, other research indicates that patients are more willing to discuss personally sensitive and psychosocial aspects of health when they have greater trust, familiarity, and rapport with their health care provider (Street et al., 1995a).

Enabling Factors

Enabling factors include the communicative resources and skills needed to effectively participate in the consultation (Roter, 1977). Two particularly important factors enabling patient participation in care are knowledge about the health issue and a readily accessible repertoire of verbal responses and routines (see Figure 1). For example, patients may have difficulty discussing a particular health issue if they lack fundamental knowledge about the topic (Street et al., 1995b). Under these circumstances, patients may prefer to sit passively rather than speak out and risk being perceived as ignorant or foolish (Roter & Hall, 1993). The fact that more educated and middle-aged patients generally are more knowledgeable about health issues than are less educated and elderly patients (Bertakis, 1977; Spiro & Heidrich, 1983; Street et al., 1995b) may be yet another reason why they tend to be more involved in medical consultations.

To fluently and actively participate in the medical encounter, a patient must have a sufficiently developed repertoire of communicative resources so that expressive and assertive responses can be produced in a smooth and effortless manner (Greene, 1984; Street, 1997). For example, one study found that mothers with stronger social skills (e.g., more expressive, greater control over non-verbal and verbal behavior) provided more information, asked more questions, asked for more reassurance, and generally spoke longer in their interactions with physicians than did mothers self-reporting poorer social skills (Eaton & Tinsley, 1999).

Physician's Communicative Behavior

As mentioned earlier, because conversational interactions require cooperation and coordination, both health care providers and patients have the potential to significantly influence one another's behavior as well as the course of their interaction. The provider's communication, in particular, will have an especially strong effect on the patient because clinicians typically assume and are granted considerable control over the events of the consultation. Thus, a health care provider who engages in partnership-building (e.g., asking for the patient's opinion, soliciting the patient's concerns and questions, attentive listening) and who uses patient-centered responses (e.g., expressing support, reassurance, empathy) both encourages greater patient involvement in the encounter and legitimizes the patient's perspective. Studies consistently show that patients indeed ask more questions, more freely express their opinions, provide more psychosocial information, and more openly discuss their concerns when providers use partnership-building and other patient-centered communication (Cox, 1989;

Street, 1991, 1992a; Thompson, Nanni & Schwankovsky, 1990; Wissow, Roter & Wilson, 1994; Wissow et al., 1998).

Improving Patient Participation

One strategy for improving patient participation in care is to develop educational interventions for both patients and clinicians. The model presented here identifies specific predispositional, enabling, and clinician communication factors that can be the focus of these interventions.

Patient Education

A number of studies have evaluated "patient activation" programs designed to increase patient involvement in their care. Typically, these are pre-consultation interventions delivered by office staff (e.g., a nurse), videotapes, or brochures that employ some combination of presenting information about the health condition, encouraging the patient to be actively involved in care, teaching specific communication strategies (e.g., questions to ask, writing a list of concerns before the consultation), or showing role models of actively involved patients. Generally speaking, these interventions have been quite successful at increasing the degree to which patients ask questions (Rost et al., 1991; Roter, 1977; Thompson et al., 1990; Robinson & Whitfield, 1985), participate in decision-making (Davison & Degner, 1997), give opinions, express concerns, and disclose information (Anderson et al., 1987; Greenfield et al., 1985; Kaplan et al., 1989).

Importantly, several of these studies have revealed that behaviorally focused interventions (e.g., practicing responses, listing questions to ask, watching role models) are more effective than simply providing health information or encouragement alone. For example, Robinson and Whitfield (1985) found that patients given explicit advice on how to ask questions and express their concerns produced significantly more questions and comments than did a group simply told that the doctor was interested in answering their questions. Relatedly, Greenfield et al. (1985) reported that patients who were simply provided with information about their health conditions prior to their consultations were less active participants than were patients who were additionally coached on how to express themselves and how to overcome their embarrassment when talking to physicians.

Physician Education

The evidence above indicates that a single intervention, delivered prior to the patient's visit with the clinician, can significantly increase the patient's communicative activity in the consultation. However, changing the provider's behavior is more complex for several reasons. First, many clinicians have multiple objectives (diagnose, formulate a treatment plan, manage time efficiently) in their consultations that they may perceive as having priority over ensuring that the patient is sufficiently involved. Relatedly, many providers may be reluctant to encourage greater patient participation for fear it will add significantly to the length of the consultation (Campbell, 1998). Finally, and perhaps most important, most clinicians have developed fairly stable routines for interacting with patients (Roter & Hall, 1993; Street, 1992a). Communicative habits are difficult to change, especially those of people accustomed to being in control of their interactions.

Changing the provider's behavior (e.g., to use more patient-centered and partnership-building responses) will require more intensive interventions than brief sessions of instructions or suggestions. For example, Street, Gold and McDowell (1994) found that giving physicians a report of the patient's perceptions of health status along with a note encouraging the doctor to discuss these issues had no effect on whether physicians actually talked about the patient's concerns about social functioning, mental well-being or role limitations. Similarly, Levinson and Roter (1993) observed that even a half-day workshop on communication skills did little to increase physicians' use of patient-centered interviewing techniques. However, these same authors reported that, following a 2½-day course, physicians indeed increased their use of open-ended questions, information-giving, and asking for the patient's opinion. Other studies also have shown that clinicians will use more patient-centered and partnership-building responses when the instruction involves role playing, modeling, feedback from supervisors, and even watching one's performance on videotape (Maguire, Fairbairn & Fletcher, 1989; Putnam et al., 1988; Goldberg et al., 1980).

Finally, a brief comment should be made about the belief that greater patient participation adds to the length of the consultation. This is not necessarily so, especially if health care providers talk less as patients talk more (Marvel, Doherty & Weiner, 1998; Kaplan et al., 1989). With proper training or experience, clinicians can adequately address the patient's psychosocial concerns within 2–7 minutes (Branch & Malik, 1993; Marvel, Doherty & Baird, 1993) that take up only 5–20% of the consultation time available (Smith & Hoppe, 1991). Furthermore, by inhibiting patient involvement early in the consultation, health care providers may actually *add* time to the closing of the encounter where patients often introduce new concerns (White, Levinson & Roter, 1994), problems that would have been more appropriately discussed earlier in the encounter.

The Next Steps

Hopefully, this chapter helps readers better understand processes underlying patient participation in care as well as stimulates ideas for future research and how to design programs that will enhance patient involvement in the health care process. While patient participation is typically desirable, it is important to reiterate that some patients may prefer a passive role in their care. Thus, from an ethical point of view, patients should be informed of the potential advantages of being involved in their care as well as provided resources to enable this participation should they choose to do so.

I see at least three issues for future research and theory development. First, while I have provided some empirical support for the links connecting various features of the model, more research is needed to test and better understand the processes underlying these relationships. Although several studies have found correlations between a patient's communicative performance in medical consultations and improved health outcomes, we can only speculate on why these relationships exist. More active participation may simply be the behavioral manifestation of a proactive approach to health. Or, one's communicative activity may garner resources and promote self-efficacy which in turn directly contribute to better health. Hopefully, the proposed model will have heuristic value for investigators as they try to answer these and other questions.

Second, the model can be a useful framework for health educators and clinicians who are trying to develop interventions to improve the patient's involvement in care. Some of the factors affecting patient participation are clearly amenable to change. Health educators should consider using informative and persuasive messages specifically aimed at increasing the patient's knowledge about the health issue, motivation to be involved, and belief in the legitimacy of patient participation. Furthermore, rather than simply providing information, interventions may need to employ role-playing or modeling exercises to enhance the patient's and health care provider's communicative skills.

Finally, an individual's involvement in health-related activities extends well beyond the medical consultation. Thus, the development of a communication theory of participation in health care must expand its scope to include the larger context of personal health management. Communicative processes influence an individual's health-related actions in a variety of domains including lifestyle, utilization of clinical services, use of over-the-counter medications and alternative remedies, and seeking support and comfort from family, friends, and colleagues. In particular, the Internet appears to be emerging as a very valuable resource for garnering health-related resources. Approximately 43% of current Internet users in the United States have been identified as "HealthMed retrievers": individuals going on-line to seek health information, support, and medical advice (Brown, 1998). How the Internet affects personal health decisions and behaviors is yet another important question waiting to be answered.

In closing, I have argued that participation in health care is essentially a communicative endeavor accomplished by an individual's linguistic performance and other communication-related activities (e.g., seeking health information). Developing a better understanding of the processes underlying this phenomenon and expanding the scope of what constitutes participating in care are the immediate challenges that await us.

REFERENCES

Anderson, L.A., DeVellis, B.M. & DeVellis, R.F. (1987). Effects of modeling on patient communication, satisfaction, and knowledge. *Medical Care*, **25**, 1044–1056.

Ayres, J., Colby-Rotell, N., Wadleigh, P.M. & Hopf, T. (1996). Measuring patients' communication apprehension about interacting with physicians: Instrument development. *Communication Research Reports*, **13**, 86–93.

Beckman, H.B. & Frankel, R.M. (1984). The effect of physician behavior on the collection of data. *Annals of Internal Medicine*, **101**, 692–696.

Beisecker, A.E. & Beisecker, T.D. (1990). Patient information-seeking behaviors when communicating with doctors. *Medical Care*, **28**, 19–28.

Bertakis, K.D. (1977). The communication of information from physician to patient: A method of increasing patient retention and satisfaction. *Journal of Family Practice*, **5**, 217–222.

Bertakis, K.D., Callahan, E.J., Helms, L.J., Azari, R., Robbins, J.A. & Miller, J. (1998). Physician practice styles and patient outcomes: Difference between family practice and general internal medicine. *Medical Care*, **36**, 879–891.

Branch, W.T. & Malik, T.K. (1993). Using "Windows of Opportunity" in brief interviews to understand patients' concerns. *JAMA*, **269**, 1667–1668.

Brody, D.S., Miller, S.M., Lerman, C.E., Smith, D.G. & Caputo, C.C. (1989) Patient perception of involvement in medical care: Relationship to illness attitudes and outcomes. *Journal of General Internal Medicine*, **4**, 506–511.

Burgoon, J.K., Johnson, M.L. & Koch, P.T. (1998). The nature and measurement of interpersonal dominance. *Communication Monographs*, **65**, 308–335.

Cahill, J. (1996). Patient participation: A concept analysis. *Journal of Advanced Nursing*, **24**, 561–571.

Campbell, T.L. (1998). Medical interviewing and the biopsychosocial model. *Journal of Family Practice*, **47**, 339–340.

Cappella, J.N. (1994). The management of conversational interaction in adults and infants. In M.L. Knapp & G.R. Miller (Eds), *Handbook of interpersonal communication* (2nd edn, pp. 380–418). Thousand Oaks, CA: Sage.

Carter, W.B., Inui, T.S., Kukull, W.A. & Haigh, V.H. (1982). Outcome-based doctor–patient interaction analysis. II: Identifying effective provider and patient behavior. *Medical Care*, **20**, 550–565.

Cassileth, B.R., Zupkis, R.V., Sutton-Smith, K. & March, V. (1980) Information and participation preferences among cancer patients. *Annals of Internal Medicine*, **92**, 832–836.

Clarke, P. & Evans, S.H. (1998) *Surviving modern medicine: How to get the best from doctors, family, and friends.* New Brunswick, NJ: Rutgers University Press.

Cox, A. (1989). Eliciting patients' feelings. In M. Stewart & D. Roter (Eds), *Communicating with medical patients* (pp. 99–106). Newbury Park, CA: Sage.

Davis, M.S. (1968). Variations in patients' compliance with doctors' advice: An empirical analysis of patterns of communication. *American Journal of Public Health*, **58**, 274–286.

Davison, B.J. & Degner, L.F. (1997). Empowerment of men newly diagnosed with prostate cancer. *Cancer Nursing*, **20**, 187–196.

Degner, L.F. & Sloan, J.A. (1992). Decision-making during serious illness: What role do patients really want to play? *Journal of Clinical Epidemiology*, **45**, 941–950.

DiMatteo, M.R., Hays, R.D. & Prince, L.M. (1986). Relationship of physicians' nonverbal communication skill to patient satisfaction, appointment noncompliance, and physician workload. *Health Psychology*, **5**, 581–594.

Eaton, L.G. & Tinsley, B.J. (1999). Maternal personality and health communication in the pediatric context. *Health Communication*, **11**, 75–96.

Ende, J., Kazis, L., Ash, A. & Moskowitz, M.A. (1989) Measuring patients' desire for autonomy: Decision-making and information-seeking preferences among medical patients. *Journal of General Internal Medicine*, **4**, 23–30.

England, S.L. & Evans, J. (1992). Patients' choices and perceptions after an invitation to participate in treatment decisions. *Social Science and Medicine*, **11**, 1217–1225.

Frankel, R.M. & Beckman, H.B. (1989). Conversation and compliance with treatment recommendations: An application of micro-interactional analysis of medicine. In B. Dervin, L. Grossberg, B.J. O'Keefe, & E. Wartella (Eds), *Rethinking communication: Paradigm exemplars* (Vol. 2, pp. 60–74). Newbury Park, CA: Sage.

Frederikson, L.G. & Bull, P.E. (1995). Evaluation of a patient education leaflet designed to improve communication in medical consultations. *Patient Education and Counseling*, **25**, 51–57.

Gallois, C. & Giles, H. (1998). Accommodating mutual influence. In M. Palmer (Ed.), *Mutual influence in interpersonal communication: Theory and research in cognition, affect, and behavior* (pp. 135–162). New York: Ablex.

Giles, H., Mulac, A., Bradac, J. & Johnson, P. (1987). Speech accommodation theory: The first decade and beyond. *Communication Yearbook*, **10**, 13–48.

Goldberg, D.P., Steele, J.J., Smith, C. & Spivey, L. (1980). Training family doctors to recognize psychiatric illness with increased accuracy. *Lancet*, **2**, 521–523.

Golin, C.E., DiMatteo, M.R. & Gelberg, L. (1996). The role of patient participation in the doctor visit: Implications for adherence to diabetes care. *Diabetes Care*, **19**, 1153–1164.

Greene, J.O. (1984). A cognitive approach to human communication: An action assembly theory. *Communication Monographs*, **51**, 289–306.

Greenfield, S., Kaplan, S. & Ware, J.E., Jr (1985). Expanding patient involvement in care. *Annals of Internal Medicine*, **102**, 520–528.

Greenfield, S., Kaplan, S.H., Ware, J.E., Jr, Yano, E.M. & Frank, H.J. (1988). Patients' participation in medical care: Effects on blood sugar and quality of life in diabetes. *Journal of General Internal Medicine*, **3**, 448–457.

Hall, J., Roter, D. & Katz, N. (1988). Meta-analysis of correlates of provider behavior in medical encounters. *Medical Care*, **26**, 657–675.

Hall, J.A., Feldstein, M., Fretwell, M.D., Rowe, J.W. & Epstein, A.M. (1990). Older patients' health status and satisfaction with medical care in an HMO population. *Medical Care*, **28**, 261–270.

Harris, I.B., Rich, E.C. & Crowson, T.W. (1985) Attitudes of internal medicine residents and staff physicians toward various patient characteristics. *Journal of Medical Education*, **60**, 192–195.

Henbest, R.J. & Stewart, M.A. (1990) Patient-centeredness in the consultation. 2: Does it really make a difference? *Family Practice*, **7**, 28–33.

Heszen-Klemens, I. & Lapinska, E. (1984). Doctor–patient interaction, patients' health behavior and effects on treatment. *Social Science and Medicine*, **19**, 9–18.

Howell-Koren, P.R. & Tinsley, B.J. (1990). The relationships among maternal health locus of control beliefs and expectations, pediatrician-mother communication, and maternal satisfaction with well-infant care. *Health Communication*, **2**, 233–253.

Infante, D.A. & Rancer, A.S. (1995). Argumentativeness and verbal aggressiveness: A review of recent theory and research. In B.R. Burleson (Ed.), *Communication yearbook 19* (pp. 319–351). Thousand Oaks, CA: Sage.

Kaplan, S.H., Greenfield, S. & Ware, J.E., Jr (1989). Assessing the effects of physician–patient interactions on the outcomes of chronic disease. *Medical Care*, **27**, S110–127.

Kaplan, S.H. & Ware, J.E., Jr (1989). The patient's role in health care and quality assessment. In N. Goldfield & D. Nash (Eds), *Providing quality care: The challenge to clinicians* (pp. 25–68). Philadelphia: American College of Physicians.

Kleinman, A. (1988). *The illness narratives: Suffering, healing, and the human condition*. New York: Basic Books.

Korsch, B.M., Gozzi, E.K. & Francis, V. (1968). Gaps in doctor–patient communication. *Pediatrics*, **42**, 855–871.

Lerman, C., Brody, D.S., Caputo, G.C., Smith, D.G., Lazaro, C.G. & Wolfson, H.G. (1990). Perceived involvement in care scale: Relationship to attitudes about illness and medical care. *Journal of General Internal Medicine*, **5**, 29–33.

Levenstein, J.H., Brown, J.B., Weston, W.W., Stewart, M., McCracken, E.C. & McWhinney, I. (1989). Patient-centered clinical interviewing. In M. Stewart & D. Roter (Eds), *Communicating with medical patients* (pp. 107–120). Newbury Park, CA: Sage.

Levinson, W. & Roter, D. (1993). The effects of two continuing medical education programs on communication skills of practicing primary care physicians. *Journal of General Internal Medicine*, **8**, 318–324.

Levinson, W., Stiles, W.B., Inui, T.S. & Engle, R. (1993). Physician frustration in communicating with patients. *Medical Care*, **31**, 285–295.

Ley, P. (1973). Communication in the clinical setting. *British Journal of Orthodontics*, **1**, 173–177.

Ley, P. (1988). *Communicating with patients: Improving communication, satisfaction, and compliance*. London: Croom Helm.

Maguire, P., Fairbairn, S. & Fletcher, C. (1989). Consultation skills of young doctors: Benefits of undergraduate feedback training in interviewing. In M. Stewart & D. Roter (Eds), *Communicating with medical patients* (pp. 124–137). Newbury Park, CA: Sage.

Mahler, H.I. & Kulik, J.A. (1991) Health care involvement preferences and social–emotional recovery of male coronary-artery-bypass patients. *Health Psychology*, **10**, 399–408.

Marvel, M.K., Doherty, W.J. & Baird, M.A. (1993). Level of physician involvement with psychosocial concerns of individual patients: A developmental model. *Family Medicine*, **25**, 337–342.

Marvel, M.K., Doherty, W.J. & Weiner, E. (1998). Medical interviewing by exemplary physicians. *Journal of Family Practice*, **47**, 343–348.

McEwen, J., Martini, C.J.M. & Wilkins, N. (1983). *Participation in health*. London: Croom-Helm.

Merkel, W.T. (1984) Physician perception of patient satisfaction: Do doctors know which patients are satisfied? *Medical Care*, **22**, 453–459.

Ong, L.M.L., de Haes, C.J.M., Hoos, A.M. & Lammes, F.B. (1995). Doctor–patient communication: A review of the literature. *Social Science and Medicine*, **40**, 903–918.

Orth, J.E., Stiles, W.B., Scherwitz, L., Hennrikus, D. & Vallbona, C. (1987). Patient exposition and provider explanation in routine interviews and hypertensive patients' blood pressure control. *Health Psychology*, **6**, 29–42.

Patterson, M.L. (1983). *Nonverbal behavior: A functional perspective*. New York: Springer.

Pendleton, D. (1983). Doctor–patient communication: A review. In D. Pendleton & J. Hasler (Eds), *Doctor–patient communication* (pp. 5–53). London: Academic Press.

Peterson, C. & Stunkard, A.J. (1989). Personal control and health promotion. *Social Science and Medicine*, **28**, 819–828.

Putnam, S.M., Stiles, W.B., Jacob, M.C. & James, S.A. (1985), Patient exposition and physician explanation in initial medical interviews and outcomes of clinic visits. *Medical Care*, **23**, 74–83.

Putnam, S.M., Stiles, W.B., Jacob, M.C. & James, S.A. (1988), Teaching the medical interview: An intervention study. *Journal of General Internal Medicine*, **3**, 38–47.

Robinson, E.J. & Whitfield, M.J. (1985). Improving the efficiency of patients' comprehension monitoring: A way of increasing patients' participation in general practice consultations. *Social Science and Medicine*, **21**, 915–919.

Rost, K.M., Carter, W. & Inui, T. (1989) Introduction of information during the initial medical visit: Consequences for patient follow-through with physician recommendations for medication. *Social Science and Medicine*, **28**, 315–321.

Rost, K.M., Flavin, K.S., Cole, K. & McGill, J.B. (1991). Change in metabolic control and functional status after hospitalization: Impact of patient activation intervention in diabetic patients. *Diabetes Care*, **14**, 881–889.

Roter, D.L. (1977). Patient participation in the patient–provider interaction: The effects of patient question asking on the quality of the interaction, satisfaction, and compliance. *Health Education Monographs*, **5**, 281–315.

Roter, D.L. & Hall, J.A. (1993). *Doctors talking to patients/Patients talking to doctors.* Westport, CT: Auburn House.

Roter, D.L., Hall, J.A. & Katz, N.R. (1988). Patient–physician communication: A descriptive summary of the literature. *Patient Education and Counseling*, **12**, 99–119.

Royak-Schaler, R. (1991). Psychological processes in breast cancer: A review of selected research. *Journal of Psychosocial Oncology*, **9**, 71–89.

Ryan, E.B., Meredith, S.D., MacLean, M.J. & Orange, J.B. (1995). Changing the way we talk with elders: Promoting health using the Communication Enhancement Model. *International Journal of Aging and Human Development*, **41**, 87–105.

Sacks, H., Schegloff, E.A. & Jefferson, G. (1974). A simplest systematics for the organization of turn-taking for conversation. *Language*, **50**, 696–735.

Saunders, P. (1995). Encouraging patients to take part in their own care. *Nursing Times*, **91**, 42–43.

Sharf, B.F. (1990). Physician–patient communication as interpersonal rhetoric: A narrative approach. *Health Communication*, **2**, 217–232.

Sharf, B. & Street, R.L., Jr (1997) The patient as a central construct: Shifting the emphasis. *Health Communication*, **9**, 1–12.

Smith, R.C. & Hoppe, R.B. (1991). The patient's story: Integrating the patient- and physician-centered approaches to interviewing. *Annals of Internal Medicine*, **115**, 470–477.

Spiro, D. & Heidrich, F. (1983) Lay understanding of medical terminology. *Journal of Family Practice*, **17**, 227–279.

Stewart, M. (1984). What is a successful doctor–patient interview? A study of interactions and outcomes. *Social Science and Medicine*, **19**, 167–175.

Street, R.L., Jr (1991). Information-giving in medical consultations: The influence of patients' communicative styles and personal characteristics. *Social Science and Medicine*, **32**, 541–548.

Street, R.L., Jr (1992a). Communicative styles and adaptations in physician–parent consultations. *Social Science and Medicine*, **34**, 1155–1163.

Street, R.L., Jr (1992b). Analyzing communication in medical consultations: Do behavioral measures correspond with patients' perceptions? *Medical Care*, **30**, 976–988.

Street, R.L., Jr (1997). Methodological considerations when assessing communication skills. *Medical Encounter*, **13**, 3–7.

Street, R.L., Jr & Buller, D. (1988). Patients' characteristics affecting physician–patient nonverbal communication. *Human Communication Research*, **15**, 60–90.

Street, R.L. Jr & Voigt, B. (1997) Patient participation in deciding breast cancer treatment and subsequent quality of life. *Medical Decision-Making*, **17**, 298–306.

Street, R.L., Jr, Cauthen, D., Buchwald, E. & Wiprud, R. (1995a). Patients' predispositions to discuss health issues affecting quality of life. *Family Medicine*, **27**, 663–670.

Street, R.L., Jr, Gold, W.R., Jr, & McDowell, T. (1994). Using health status surveys in medical consultations. *Medical Care*, **32**, 732–744.

Street, R.L., Jr, Piziak, V.K., Carpentier, W., Herzog, J., Hejl, J., Skinner, G. & McLelland, L. (1993). Provider–patient communication and metabolic control. *Diabetes Care*, **16**, 714–721.

Street, R.L. Jr, Voigt, B., Geyer, C., Manning, T. & Swanson, G.P. (1995b) Increasing patient involvement in choosing treatment for early breast cancer. *Cancer*, **76**, 2275–2285.

Strull, W.M., Lo, B. & Charles, G. (1984). Do patients want to participate in medical decision-making? *JAMA*, **252**, 2990–2994.

Taylor, S.E., Lichtman, R.R. & Wood, J.V. (1984) Attributions, beliefs about control, and adjustment to breast cancer. *Journal of Personality and Social Psychology*, **46**, 489–502.

Thompson, T.L. (1994). Interpersonal communication and health care. In M.L. Knapp & G.R. Miller (Eds), *Handbook of interpersonal communication* (2nd edn, pp. 696–725) Thousand Oaks, CA: Sage.

Thompson, S.C., Nanni, C. & Schwankovsky, L. (1990). Patient-oriented interventions to improve communication in a medical office visit. *Health Psychology*, **9**, 390–404.

Todd, A.D. (1989). *Intimate adversaries: Cultural conflict between doctors and women patients*. Philadelphia: University of Pennsylvania Press.

Tracy, K. (1985). Conversational coherence: A cognitively grounded rules approach. In R.L. Street Jr & J.N. Cappella (Eds). *Sequence and pattern in communicative behavior* (pp. 30–49). London: Edward Arnold.

Treadway, J. (1983). Patient satisfaction and the content of general practice consultations. *Journal of the Royal College of General Practitioners*, **33**, 769–771.

Waitzkin, H. (1991). *The politics of medical encounters*. New Haven, CT: Yale University Press.

Wasserman, R.C., Inui, T.S., Barriatua, R.D., Carter, W.B. & Lippincott, P. (1983). Responsiveness to maternal concern in preventive child health visits: An analysis of clinician–parent interactions. *Journal of Developmental and Behavioral Pediatrics*, **4**, 171–176.

White, J., Levinson, W. & Roter, D. (1994). "Oh, by the way . . .": The closing moments of the medical visit. *Journal of General Internal Medicine*, **9**, 24–28.

Winefield, H.R. & Murrell, T.C.G. (1991). Speech patterns and satisfaction in diagnostic and prescriptive stages of general practice consultations. *British Journal of Medical Psychology*, **64**, 103–115.

Wissow, L.S., Roter, D., Bauman, L.J, Crain, E., Kercsmar, C., Weiss, K., Mitchell, H. & Mohr, B. (1998) Patient–provider communication during emergency department care of children with asthma. *Medical Care*, **36**, 1439–1450.

Wissow, L.S., Roter, D. & Wilson, M.E.H. (1994). Pediatrician interview style and mothers' disclosure of psychosocial issues. *Pediatrics*, **93**, 289–295.

World Health Organization (1978). *Primary health care*. Geneva: WHO.

Young, M. & Klingle, R.S. (1996) Silent partners in medical care: A cross-cultural study of patient participation. *Health Communication*, **8**, 29–54.

6.30

Communication in Organizations: An Intergroup Perspective

John Gardner, Neil Paulsen, Cynthia Gallois, Victor Callan and
Peter Monaghan
University of Queensland, St Lucia, Australia

Organizations are groups of individuals working together in a coordinated way
in the pursuit of specific production-related goals (e.g., Robbins et al., 1998), and
communication is the central means by which individual activity is coordinated
to devise, disseminate and pursue these goals. Consequently, communication
affects every aspect of organizational functioning (see Bordow & More, 1991).
Of course, organizational communication is not an unconstrained process. Organizations typically involve highly differentiated social systems (Scott, 1997;
Trice & Beyer, 1993), with individuals divided into divisional units, functional
specialties, workgroups, and status levels. Increasingly, they must adapt to economic influences by changing their internal structures, processes, and relationship
to their markets (see Kanter, Stein & Jick, 1992), which often leads to increased
levels of uncertainty and resistance (Robbins et al., 1998). Because of this, communication within organizations must bridge the boundaries created by group
memberships and the uncertainty of organizational change. Moreover, the process of communication itself is inherently constrained, inefficient, and flawed
(Coupland, Wiemann & Giles, 1991).[1]

---

[1] Coupland et al. (1991) presented a descriptive model of miscommunication or problematic communication, to which we refer in this chapter. In their model, the level of miscommunication is based
on its origin and social significance, and takes account of differences in the level of awareness of

---

The New Handbook of Language and Social Psychology.
Edited by W. Peter Robinson and Howard Giles.
© 2001 John Wiley & Sons Ltd.

   The first edition of the Handbook did not include a chapter focusing specifically on organizations. This omission reflected the fact that research on organizational life had not traditionally been a mainstream focus in the language and
social psychology literature. Nevertheless, in our complex social structures,
people communicate with and relate to each other for many hours of each day
through their membership of organizations. We believe, therefore, that organizations provide a rich and important context in which to apply the theories and
empirical results of our field. For example, the complaints of workers about their
supervisors are often described in extreme, even psychopathological terms (say,
as "toxic management"). In this kind of context, like the formalized negotiations
between trade unions and managements and the more informal interactions
between people with different roles in an organization (e.g., students and
teachers at university), social-psychological and clearly organizational features
of language and communication blur and blend into each other. In this chapter
we focus on the contribution that language and social psychology, and in particular the inter-group perspectives that are at its core, can make to the understanding of organizational communication.

   A common feature in critical reviews of organizational communication has
been a call for stronger links to theory in general communication (Allen,
Gotcher & Seibert, 1993; DeWine & Daniels, 1993; Mumby, 1993). With this in
mind, we review and critique some of the very large literature on organizational
communication from the perspective of language and social psychology. We
cannot do justice to the whole literature in a single chapter; we cannot even
mention many important areas of theory and empirical research. Instead, we
review very selectively those areas where an intergroup perspective can add
most value.

   In our view, many researchers assume that communication in organizations
can be thought of as interpersonal, and that more skilled communication will
produce better outcomes in terms both of productivity and satisfaction. This

---

interactants and the possibility for repair of the episode. *Level I* focuses on the pervasive minor
disruptions caused by the inefficiency and ambiguity inherent in the communication process. Miscommunication at this level ,generally does not reach conscious awareness, and repair is not required
(or indeed possible). *Level II* consists of minor productive or receptive errors in the communication
process, such as mishearings, equivocations, interruptions, and disqualifications. Awareness of these
events is generally low, and repair is either unnecessary or accomplished fairly readily within the
interaction. *Level III* describes miscommunication related to the adequacy of individual skills. Participants are usually moderately aware of the miscommunication, and repair, in the perceptions of
other interactants, involves communication skills training for the deficient individual. At *Level IV*,
communication is strategic and goal-driven, as individuals pursue multiple goals (relational, identity,
instrumental, etc.). Miscommunication involves the failure to attain one's conversational goals.
Awareness is typically high, and repair involves strategically similar or modified attempts to address
one's goals. *Level V* describes miscommunication stemming from group-based or cultural factors,
including beliefs, codes, and norms. Participants' awareness is moderate, and miscommunication may
be perceived as a natural reflection of group status differences. Repair involves learning and accommodating to the other group's communicative system. Finally, *Level VI* reflects an ideological analysis of communication that exposes inherent disadvantages to individuals or groups. Participants are
typically unaware of the problem, since their "miscommunication" stems from the social and moral
ideology in which they exist. Repair requires a broad social or political reorientation.

assumption neglects the inherent intergroup conflicts in organizations, the antecedent conditions that lead to conflict, and the consequences for individuals and
groups. It should be noted that this same criticism can be aimed at other domains
of communication, some well-canvassed in this Handbook; an analogous area
close to the traditional interests of social psychologists of language is assertive
communication (see Wilson & Gallois, 1993). We believe that an intergroup
perspective can explain why even very skilled communication may not lead to
positive outcomes in certain contexts. This chapter describes three contexts where
intergroup relations are salient: organizational identity itself, communication between superiors and subordinates (or managers and employees), and the communication of organizational change. We take Social Identity Theory (SIT: e.g.,
Tajfel & Turner, 1979, 1986) and Communication Accommodation Theory (CAT:
e.g., Giles, Coupland & Coupland, 1991) as our points of departure. The former
theory has been applied increasingly to organizational contexts, while CAT has
only just begun to show its value in the area of organizational communication.

COMMUNICATION IN ORGANIZATIONS: IS SKILL ENOUGH?

Research into communication in organizations has been extensive, but it has
repeatedly been criticized as fragmentary and atheoretical (e.g., DeWine &
Daniels, 1993; Lundberg & Brownell, 1993; Tompkins & Redding, 1988).
Scholars have suggested a variety of changes to address the identified shortcomings. These include changes in the underlying conceptual orientation (Deetz, in
press; Putnam, Phillips & Chapman, 1996), the nature of the research being
undertaken (Euske & Roberts, 1987; Lundberg & Brownell, 1993), and the
strengthening of links to other research fields (Allen et al., 1993; DeWine &
Daniels, 1993; Putnam et al., 1996). Some of these criticisms and proposals are
discussed in more detail below.

Focus on "Positive" Communication

Research into communication in general has often centred on the positive aspects of communication, and has tended to idealize the communication process
(see Allen et al., 1993; Coupland et al., 1991). This research is often implicitly
oriented to positive communication behaviours, such as development of shared
meaning, accurate exchange of information, and communication competence.
As a result, the idea that real organizational communication is generally less
than perfect has received relatively short shrift, and examples of problematic
communication have often been viewed as aberrant behaviour to be minimized
or avoided. The tendency to focus on positive or ideal communication, and to
consider any problematic communication as deviant, is exacerbated by the

mechanistic metaphor invoked in much of the research. In this metaphor, communication is conceptualized in terms of a conduit transferring information from a sender to a receiver, which tends to oversimplify the communication process (Axley, 1984; Fisher, 1978; Krone, Jablin & Putnam, 1987; Putnam et al., 1996).

In reality, a great deal of communication in organizations is problematic or negative. For example, managers and employees typically do not agree about what has been said between them or what their communication means. There is also ample evidence that subordinates distort their upward communication to serve their perceived interests. Many other examples of this kind, which lead to conflict and other poor outcomes (e.g., in hiring decisions, job outcomes, performance appraisals) are readily available. Thus, it seems more productive to acknowledge the problematic nature of organizational communication and to examine its causes explicitly.

Focus on the Individual

One outcome of the mechanistic perspective on organizational communication is a focus on individual behaviour, and a large body of research examines communication skills (e.g., Tompkins & Redding, 1988). This research describes communication competence as an individual difference variable (e.g., McKinney, Kelly & Duran, 1997) and assumes that training can improve communication outcomes for unskilled individuals, even though post-training changes are often slight. The principal difficulty associated with this approach is that it does not model the nature of communication, in which two or more participants *interact* to produce an outcome for each person. Sillars and Wilmot (1994) reviewed research into communication and conflict and noted the complex relationship between communication and outcomes. For example, conflict often results from the "best" forms of communication.

An alternative conceptualization of communication competence posits that competence is an evaluation of behaviour based on a set of criteria that differ between individuals. In addition, in this view competence is situation-specific, and effective communication depends on the abilities of both interactants. Even this more sophisticated approach to competence typically fails to incorporate the influence of group memberships, context, and organizational environment (but see Wilson & Gallois, 1993 for a partial exception). As Gallois and Giles (1998) argue, skills training is unlikely to be useful unless the interpersonal, relationship and inter-group context are all taken into account.

Limited Levels of Analysis

Research on organizational communication has tended to view communication from only a subset of possible levels of analysis. In the case of superior–

subordinate communication, for example, Dansereau and Markham (1987) de-lineated four levels of analysis: individual, dyadic, group, and collective. The majority of research, however, has addressed either the individual or collective level. In their review of organizational communication research between 1980 and 1990, Wert-Gray et al. (1991) identified a shift away from micro-level (skills) research to macro-level (culture and climate) research. At the same time, Miller et al. (1990) noted a tendency to treat micro-level variables as though they were unrelated to macro-level variables. Furthermore, most studies remain single-level, although many have pointed out that the reality of organizations (e.g., their different business units and subcultures) would be better represented by cross-level studies (Dansereau & Markham, 1987; Lundberg & Brownell, 1993; Nykodym, 1988).

Although supervisor–subordinate communication entails the presence of at least a dyad, few studies in this area have used dyadic analyses. Consequently, many studies do not acknowledge the reciprocal and iterative nature of com-munication in organizational relationships (see Barry & Watson, 1996). In addi-tion, many research studies measure key communication and outcome variables at only one point in time (e.g., Deluga, 1988). This approach neglects the influ-ence of subordinates' communication on their supervisors, as well as the large literature on leader–follower exchange in shaping the behaviour of leaders. Some studies do examine upward influence, or "managing upward" (e.g., Farmer et al., 1997; Korsgaard, Roberson & Rymph, 1998), but studies explicitly examining reciprocal influence are rare. Similarly, there is little research involv-ing repeated measures to examine the iterative nature of communicative interac-tion (see Maslyn, Farmer & Fedor, 1996, for one exception).

This emphasis on individual differences, with a concomitant neglect of con-text, may also be because research has tended to focus fairly narrowly on individ-ual topics, in spite of the large array of variables impinging on communication in organizations (Jablin, 1987; Putnam & Cheney, 1983). Of course, situational context is well known to be relevant (Green, 1996; Lee & Jablin, 1995). More recently, the importance of relational and inter-group variables has also been acknowledged (Allen et al., 1993; Petronio et al., 1998).

Communication as an Independent Variable

Many studies in organizations have treated communication as an independent variable, used to explain organizational outcomes such as turnover, group per-formance, individual performance, job satisfaction, and perceptions of superiors. This approach leads to an oversimplification of communication, which is often measured in global, unidimensional terms (e.g., communication climate, satisfac-tion with communication, location in communication network, communicative competence), with little attention to the details of communicative interaction. Given the importance of communication in organizations, it is essential to make communication the focal variable of study. In other words, we need to view organizational communication processes not only as inputs but also as outcomes with various antecedent influences in particular contexts.

One could choose almost any organizational context to invoke an intergroup perspective. In this chapter, we begin with the most obvious one: the identification of members with an organization and with their group memberships within it.

COMMUNICATION AND ORGANIZATIONAL IDENTITY

Within complex organizations, individuals are differentiated from each other through their membership of groups. Structural and functional arrangements such as these are designed to achieve organizational goals, but they also set the boundaries for a highly differentiated social system (see Trice & Beyer, 1993). Employees work and relate to each other in and through workgroups and teams. Organizational groups also form around functional roles (e.g., marketing, the senior management team), professional roles (e.g., engineers, scientists), employment status (e.g., full-time or part-time) or more informal arrangements (Kramer, 1991). While such groups often represent different and competing interests, they nevertheless help employees to define themselves and their social relationships in the organization. Organizational actors rarely function in isolation from their intergroup contexts. When employees interact, they do not simply act as individuals, but also as members of the organizational groups to which they belong (see Kramer, 1991).

Identity and Diversity

By viewing organizations as intergroup contexts, we can significantly improve our understanding of organizational dynamics (Alderfer, 1987; Hartley, 1996; Kramer, 1991), although examples of research at this level of analysis are relatively few. In one such example, Cox (1993) presented a model proposing direct relationships between various group identities and individual and organizational outcomes. The *interactional model of cultural diversity* proposes that group identities interact with individual, intergroup and organizational factors (the *diversity climate*) to determine the impact of diversity on individual and organizational outcomes (Cox, 1993). Nkomo and Cox (1996) argued that diversity in organizations is related to diversity in identities based on membership in social and demographic groups, and concluded that "the identity of people in organizations is a function of their identity group membership(s) and their organization group membership(s)" (p. 342). This model is one of the very few to consider intergroup relations seriously in the organizational context, and it theorizes the impact of key variables including gender and ethnicity in organizational life.

Nevertheless, it draws mainly on the *cultural* diversity literature. More work is needed to apply this or another model to identities derived from *organizational* memberships. We have chosen to explore social identity theory for this task.

Social Identity Theory

The Social Identity Theory (SIT) of intergroup relations (Tajfel & Turner, 1979, 1986) is aimed at explaining how individual behaviour is influenced by group memberships. SIT takes the group, rather than the individual, as the fundamental unit of analysis to explain behaviour within and between groups. The theory proposes (and empirical research indicates) that individuals' self-concepts are built on personal identity (one's unique characteristics as an individual) and social identity (derived from memberships in salient social groups and categories). Under given conditions, social identity becomes more salient than personal identity, which leads to behaviour based on group memberships. Furthermore, SIT proposes that underlying socio-cognitive processes can account for intergroup behaviour (Turner et al., 1987).

Social identification occurs when people define themselves and are seen by others as part of a particular group or social category (or ingroup). When people define themselves as members of a self-inclusive social category, differences among individual group members are minimized, while differences between groups are accentuated (Turner et al., 1987). Self-enhancement results from a social comparison process whereby people are motivated to favour the ingroup over the outgroup, which then contributes to a positive social identity. Because the self is defined in terms of relevant group memberships, including those at work, individuals perceive norms and stereotypes that favour the ingroup (Terry & Callan, 1997, 1998). Consequently, people are motivated to belong to groups that compare favourably with other groups; that is, they aspire to belong to high-status groups (Tajfel & Turner, 1979). Members of high-status groups seek to maintain their membership of those groups and the existence of the social category system, in order to reinforce the positive contribution that membership makes to their self-identity. Similarly, members of low-status groups engage in a range of strategies to improve the status of their group. The links between SIT and communication are clear, as social identities are largely established and maintained via communication. In turn, SIT can be used to explain how communicative behaviour is influenced by group memberships, although this process has been developed further, and compatibly, in communication accommodation theory.

Organizational Identity

A number of authors (Ashforth & Mael, 1989; Hartley, 1996; Kramer, 1991) have argued that SIT has the potential to aid our understanding of the intergroup nature of organizational life. Mael and his colleagues (e.g., Mael & Ashforth, 1995) argued that individuals develop an identity with their organization, and that organizational identification is similar to individuals' propensity to define themselves by their memberships in various social categories (Mael & Ashforth, 1995; see also Dutton, Dukerich & Harquail, 1994). As a perceptual cognitive construct, organizational identification is different from organizational commitment. The latter implies internalization of organizational goals and values, behavioural intentions, and affect (Ashforth & Mael, 1989), whereas individuals identify with an organization through processes similar to identification with an identity (or social psychological) group.

Individuals have multiple social identities linked to gender, race, ethnicity, and status, but contextual factors are also powerful influences on communicative behaviour (see Gallois et al., 1995). For example, Boggs and Giles (1999) have recently studied gender-based organizational conflicts from the perspective of communication accommodation theory. In the organizational context, employees acquire a range of identities associated with the organizational categories or groups to which they belong or to which they are perceived to belong (Kramer, 1991; Hartley, 1996). Ashforth and Mael (1989), Cox (1993), and Hartley (1996) noted that employees have multiple group identities, which can operate at the unit and subunit levels. Such groups include management, workers, part-time staff, contractors, graduate employees or regional staff, and the like. Identification triggers a process of intergroup comparison that influences employee behaviour, perceptions of the organization and intergroup relations (Connelley, 1994). It is this process, according to Kramer (1991), that gives rise to competitive orientations toward members of other groups.

In large, complex organizations, individuals are likely to identify more strongly with salient groups within the organization than with the organization as a whole (Barker & Tompkins, 1994; Scott, 1997). In many organizations with hierarchical structures, roles and job titles imply that a particular position in an organization is a member of a particular group (e.g., senior management or middle management). In some organizations, such group distinctions are very apparent and can lead to conflict and competition. Hartley (1996), for example, reports on work applying SIT to labour conflicts that led to strike action. This is not to say that individuals do not have a larger organizational identity, as proposed by Mael and Ashforth (1995) and by Dutton et al. (1994). Such an identity may emerge in relationships with external organizations (e.g., strategic alliances or network relationships), or may be triggered when individuals are asked to comment on their organization. Rather, group identities that develop within the organization from membership of organizational categories are likely to be a powerful influence over individual perceptions and behaviour within the organization. In fact, they help to explain the development of subcultures within the organization (e.g., Trice & Beyer, 1993). When individuals interact, they do not simply act as individuals, but also as members of the salient organizational categories or groups with which they identify and whose interests they represent (Kramer, 1991). These memberships become highly salient during periods of conflict or threat, which are often associated with organizational change (Callan, 1993).

Identity and Conflict

Social comparison and identification processes may account for intergroup conflict and competition, especially when members are strongly identified with their group. In fact, intergroup conflict may go beyond disputes over goals, task, or process to include conflict and competition over identities or group status (see Thomas, 1993). Brown and his colleagues (e.g., Brown & Williams, 1984; Brown et al., 1986; Oaker & Brown, 1986) studied the impact of intergroup differentiation on perceived conflict, contact, and identification. Terry and Callan (1997, 1998) looked at the impact of group identification in the context of organizational mergers. More recent research has shown that the degree to which workers identify with their organization differs, and their level of identification is related to the adequacy of their communication with both their ingroup and outgroups (e.g., Suzuki, 1998). Another intergroup context where communication is likely to be problematic and which may well involve conflict is that between supervisors and their subordinates. We deal with this context in the next section.

SUPERVISOR–SUBORDINATE COMMUNICATION

Research into communication in organizations has consistently focused on the interaction between supervisors and subordinates as an important area for study. An early review by Jablin (1979) concluded that supervisors and subordinates engaged in frequent task-related interaction, but that their perceptions of the interaction were quite different. Later studies reviewed by Henderson (1987) indicated that managers spend between 62% and 89% of their time in face-to-face communication, and a review by Yukl (1994) suggested that leaders spend between one-third and two-thirds of their time communicating with their subordinates. Interestingly, even though this is an intergroup context par excellence, it has been considered mainly from the perspective of the interpersonal effectiveness. We will briefly review some of the major themes in this area and then describe the potential of communication accommodation theory to add to our understanding.

Communication Competence and Supervisor–Subordinate Interactions

A large body of research on supervisor–subordinate communication is, as we have noted above, directed at communication competence. This research focuses on the communication skills needed to operate effectively in the organizational environment. Typically, communication skills are conceptualized as the ability of individuals to gain effective outcomes by means of communicative interaction, and there is an implicit assumption that individual differences are the crucial variable in effective communication. For example, individual differences have been found in objectively assessed conversational planning (Waldron & Applegate, 1994) and the use of appropriate message strategies in conflict situations (McKinney et al., 1997).

An alternative view of competence is provided by Spitzberg and Cupach (1984), who described communication competence as an impression and therefore subjective, biased, and directly determined by criteria used by the judge. This concept of competence more accurately reflects the real nature of communication in organizations. For example, subordinates' perceptions of their supervisors' competence is related to length of participation in quality circles (Berman & Hellweg, 1989), and subordinates' choice of compliance-gaining tactics (Johnson, 1992). Supervisors' own perceptions of their communication competence, on the other hand, are related to self-reported performance (Penley et al., 1991).

Perceptual Incongruence

Despite their high levels of interaction, a consistent research finding indicates a lack of agreement between supervisors and subordinates in perceptions of the work environment, themselves, and each other. There is robust empirical evidence for incongruence or semantic information distance between supervisors and subordinates on perceptions of subordinates' job duties, their required skills, the problems they face, and likely changes to their job (Berman & Hellweg, 1989; Jablin, 1979). More recent research has measured perceptual incongruence on a variety of measures, including supervisor–subordinate relationship issues, the subordinate's job duties, attitudes to work, and the supervisor's communication behaviours and work performance. Lack of perceptual congruence on these measures has been associated with a variety of negative outcomes for subordinates, including lower evaluated performance of subordinates, lower levels of job satisfaction, motivation and commitment, and less positive perceptions of supervisors' communication effectiveness (e.g., Tsui et al., 1995). It is clear that an intergroup approach can shed a great deal of light on perceptual incongruence.

The determinants of perceptual incongruence have been less completely investigated than its outcomes. Research has found differences in perceptual congruence in terms of specific types of organizations and between supervisor–subordinate dyads of different race (e.g., Wohlers, Hall & London, 1993), but actual theoretical explanations of perceptual incongruence have been rare. One exception is Leader Member Exchange (LMX) theory, where tests have found that higher-quality supervisor–subordinate relationships have less perceptual incongruence regarding subordinate behaviours, and subsequently better subordinate work outcomes (see Graen & Uhl-Bien, 1998). At a broad level, this research indicates that communication between supervisors and subordinates is at best incomplete.

These results suggest strongly that communication between supervisors and subordinates is inherently problematic. At the very least, the differing goals and interests of people at different organizational levels are likely to produce miscommunication (level 4 in the model proposed by Coupland et al., 1991). In addition, the different sub-cultures in which managers and their employees participate, including those related to identities in the larger society (gender, ethnicity, etc.), also lead to different norms and rules about communication and its interpretation (level 5). In some cases, there is more involved than this, and structural features of the organization produce incompatibilities in the interpretation of events that are invisible to interactants (level 6). This last situation is especially likely to apply in situations of organizational change, where supervisors may mislead their subordinates deliberately or inadvertently, and where intergroup trust is likely to be low. In spite of its obvious intergroup nature, supervisor–subordinate communication has rarely been problematized beyond interpersonal dynamics. Even skills training programs that acknowledge the dialectical nature of such communication have tended to be targeted at individuals and the communicative choices they must make (e.g., Wilson & Gallois, 1993).

Leadership

One of the most extensively researched topics in this general area is leadership. While a review of the diversity of research into leadership is beyond the scope of this chapter, some its specific elements have important implications for the study of supervisor–subordinate communication. Traditional theories of leadership have tended to be unidirectional, focusing on the effect of leaders' traits or behaviours on subordinates, sometimes incorporating contextual influences. This approach, as noted earlier, disregards the impact of subordinates on leaders' behaviour, and fails to incorporate the potential for dynamic mutual influence.

LMX

One theory of leadership, Leader Member Exchange (e.g., Dansereau & Markham, 1987; Graen & Uhl-Bien, 1998), addresses the deficits of many other approaches to leadership by using the relationship between leaders and their subordinates as the fundamental unit of analysis. LMX posits that more mature relationships between leaders and their subordinates allow for more effective leadership processes to develop, and lead to more positive organizational outcomes (Graen & Uhl-Bien, 1998). The development of positive supervisor–subordinate relationships has also been related to similarity of personality and to features of the organization (e.g., Green, 1996). Positive supervisor–subordinate relationships are associated with lower perceived stress, higher subordinate performance, job satisfaction, and satisfaction with supervision. A number of studies show that the quality of the leader–subordinate relationship predicts the use of different communication strategies by subordinates and supervisors (e.g., Lee & Jablin, 1995; Waldron, 1991).

Upward and Mutual Influence

Upward influence has typically been treated as an area separate from leadership. From a communication accommodation perspective, however, upward influence represents the other half of the mutual influence involved in supervisor–subordinate interaction. Waldron (1991) identified tactics used by subordinates in communication aimed at preserving the relationship with their supervisors (termed maintenance communication). He found that ingroup subordinates used different tactics from those used by outgroup subordinates. Subsequent studies have also found differences in the strategies used by subordinates at different hierarchical levels, formality of relationship (Tepper, 1995), and quality of relationship with their supervisors (Maslyn et al., 1996). Recent research on upward influence tactics has suggested an alternative taxonomy of strategies, dividing them into hard (assertiveness), soft (friendliness) and rational (bargaining) (Farmer et al., 1997). In addition, contextual factors have been found to influence upward communication strategies (e.g., Lee & Jablin, 1995). In a study which directly assessed mutual influence effects, Korsgaard et al. (1998) found that supervisors' behaviour was fairer towards subordinates who had shown more assertiveness in upward interactions.

Communication in Problematic Contexts

Finally, much of the research on supervisor–subordinate communication has focused on specific contextual areas, including interviews (e.g., Willemyns et al., 1997), compliance gaining (e.g., Johnson, 1992), conflict and conflict resolution (e.g., Weider-Hatfield & Hatfield, 1996) and performance appraisal and negative feedback (e.g., Moss & Martinko, 1998). A common theme among these contexts is that they involve interpersonal communication with the potential for negative outcomes; they are inherently problematic in nature.

Studies that focus on such problematic contexts highlight another deficit in the organizational communication literature, which we have already noted: the tendency to idealize the communication process. Commonly, studies in these contexts focus on improving communication clarity, reaching agreement, or avoiding communicative problems such as conflict or negative outcomes. The implicit model of communication used in such studies is that communication varies on a single evaluative dimension. "Good" communication involves more openness, agreement, and positive outcomes; "bad" communication involves less openness, more disagreement, and more negative outcomes. In addition, it is often presupposed that communication can be examined without taking account of contextual or environmental factors. This unidimensional conceptualization is, of course, an oversimplification of real communication, where "negative" communicative behaviour can have beneficial outcomes and extremely clear and open communication may result in subsequent problems for at least one interactant (Sillars & Wilmot, 1994).

The tensions between the interpersonal approach taken in the area of supervisor–subordinate communication and its dyadic nature have long been apparent. A good deal of work has gone into providing a more dyadic and reciprocal perspective on this area, for example from the perspective of structuration theory (e.g., see Poole & McPhee, 1983). Far less attention has been given to the intergroup aspect of communication between managers and their employees, however, even though this may well be the most potent influence on their communication and the greatest source of conflict. In our view, communication accommodation theory is well suited to this task.

Communication Accommodation Theory and Supervisor–Subordinate Communication

Communication Accommodation Theory (see Giles et al., 1991; Gallois et al., 1995) is a broad-based framework which theorizes the reciprocal relationships between communicative interaction and the social environment in which it occurs, as well as the dynamic relationship between two interactants. The theory initially grew from the idea that interactants use specific linguistic strategies to pursue their goals during communication. Empirically based elaborations to the theory have expanded the range of linguistic strategies and incorporated the impact of contextual norms and the relative status of the interactants. Thus, there is an obvious application of CAT to supervisor–subordinate communication.

CAT proposes that communication is motivated by multiple communicative goals, which stem from the broader personal and social identity of the interactants and their surrounding social environment. Thus, the effects of group memberships are incorporated into the model. Communication goals are pursued strategically, and a variety of specific linguistic strategies are related to these goals. The range of appropriate strategies available to interactants, however, is constrained by situational and behavioural norms and rules, which are often different for interactants of differing status. The strategies employed by one interactant are also influenced by those employed by the other; CAT incorporates the dynamic nature of communication by describing a process of mutual influence (Gallois & Giles, 1998).

Over the course of its development, the relationships posited by CAT have received empirical support from studies in a wide variety of contexts. Although direct applications of the theory to the organizational context are not common, support for aspects of the model has been found in a number of settings. For example, Bourhis (1991) demonstrated the presence of long-term language accommodation in a bilingual work setting in Canada, and Boggs and Giles (1999) studied the impact of gender on accommodation at work. CAT has also been successfully applied to communication between service providers and clients in hospitality organizations (Sparkes & Callan, 1992). More relevantly to supervisor–subordinate communication, accent accommodation has been demonstrated in job interview settings (e.g., Willemyn et al., 1997). The last study found that subjective rather than objective accent accommodation to interviews was more important to applicants.

Recently, studies of supervisor–subordinate interactions in an academic setting have shown the differential use of communication strategies, as hypothesized by CAT (see Jones et al., 1999). In particular, women in ingroup conversations put more effort into accommodation in management of the discourse, whereas speakers in intergroup interactions were more concerned with role relationships.

CAT also proposes that some contexts are likely to make group membership salient (see Gallois et al., 1995). Thus, in recent work Willemyn, Gallois and Callan (1999) and Gardner and Jones (1999) have undertaken detailed analyses of subjective accommodation in satisfactory and unsatisfactory communication between supervisors and subordinates. They found that there are inconsistencies in perceptions of communication across situation and organizational role, which can be explained in part by the influence of group membership. In addition, they found that satisfactory interactions were not the mirror images of unsatisfactory ones, but emphasized different types of accommodation. In summary, if researchers start from the assumption that supervisors and subordinates are members of different organizational groups and that these memberships influence both their communication strategies and their perceptions of their own and each other's communication, CAT provides a rich range of hypotheses about specific areas of conflict.

A third context, where the intergroup situation is always highly salient, involves the increasingly frequent management of organizational change and its communication.

COMMUNICATION OF ORGANIZATIONAL CHANGE

Organizational change involves structural and cultural change to an organization. In their model of change management, Nadler and Nadler (1998) describe change as an integrated process that unfolds over time and influences every aspect of the organizations structure and culture. While the structural aspects of corporate change have traditionally been commented upon, it is clear that leading, managing and communicating cultural change is the most difficult aspect of any organizational transformation (Schein, 1991). This communication almost always involves efforts to alter the values and belief systems that employees of different subcultures hold about their work, and the opinions about the core business which are important for the future well-being of the organization (Dunphy & Stace, 1990; Kanter et al., 1992). There is still little research, however, about the extent to which employees feel that details of change are communicated effectively to them, and the relative importance of the role of senior managers, middle managers, and co-workers in the process.

Perceptions of Organizational Change

The experience of change and its communication can be markedly different for employees who belong to different levels and groups in the organization (Kanter, et al., 1992). There are winners and losers in change, those who gain or lose resources, and gains and losses for various professional groups, business units and subcultures in terms of power, status and job security. There is also evidence that social identity is more likely to be salient when the change is appraised as threatening (Terry & Callan, 1998).

While effective communication of change is critical to the success of change programs (Nadler & Nadler, 1998), there is considerable evidence that communication as a change tool is used poorly. Rather than being inspired to become aligned to the new strategic direction, employees, especially at lower levels of an organization, are often confused, angry, and more resistant to change as a result of failed communication strategies. One reason for the poorer perceptions of communication by those at lower levels is the greater sense of threat they are likely to experience about the consequences of the change. Kanter and her associates (1992) describe three groups: change strategists at the top of the hierarchy, change managers in middle management, and change recipients at the lower levels. Change recipients and change managers are most likely to lose status, position, and jobs during major change.

Direction of Change Communication

The communication of the need for change in competitive business environments is typically top-down, which adds to the sense of threat to employees at lower levels in organizations; only a minority of organizational change processes allow high levels of employee consultation (Dunphy & Stace, 1990). The top-down nature of the communication of change also adds to the sense that a senior management group, who will be advantaged by the change, are in control of the change environment (Callan, 1993). In particular, when organizations need major and rapid change to accommodate to a new external environment, the change is often driven by coercive and directive leadership styles (Dunphy & Stace,

1990). In contrast, Kotter (1996) argues that leaders as the communicators of change need to use simple messages, repetition, and a wide range of communication channels.

Most change processes concentrate on the role of senior managers in communicating change. There is evidence, however, that employees prefer to receive important information about change through their immediate supervisor, rather than directly from senior managers, preferably in face-to-face or small group meetings with their own work teams (Larkin & Larkin, 1996). Failed communication of change at the middle and lower levels of organizations is linked to the use of employee reports, company newsletters, and videos of presentations by the senior executives, rather than face-to-face communication by immediate supervisors (Larkin & Larkin, 1996). Front-line supervisors are more likely to communicate successfully the nature of corporate change, as they are perceived to be ingroup members and a more credible source of information than senior managers are. Other research reveals that effective communication from supervisors is linked to lower levels of stress and uncertainty (Callan, 1993), and higher levels of commitment to the new organization (Nadler & Nadler, 1998).

Kotter (1996) notes that some supervisors who oppose change invoke the group membership of management versus workers, which tends to frustrate change efforts. Several strategies have been put forward to deal with such resistance. As might be expected, most efforts involve communication strategies that seek to encourage participation and greater ownership in the change process, negotiation and trade-offs to accommodate the concerns of those affected, and finally explicit or implicit coercion that involves threats to those who continue to resist (see Kotter, 1996). As predicted by CAT, such strategies begin with attempts at convergence. When such efforts fail, other strategies are used that focus more on divergence and attempts to maximize the sense of difference in identities between parties, possibly as some final justification for their removal from the organization through retrenchments and redundancies.

Intergroup Relations and Communication of Change

As this discussion indicates, research has begun to investigate the effects of a range of individual and organizational variables upon the perception of the communication of major structural and cultural change, although much of the work in this area is more exploratory than empirical. Researchers have typically neglected the intergroup nature of change (Terry & Callan, 1997), despite the fact that in this process major changes are made in the allocation of status, power, and resources across divisions of the firm. In addition, organizational change, restructuring, and mergers increasingly involve the creation of a new organizational identity, often imposed on employees. There are numerous examples of mergers failing because of the intergroup dynamics during change, when resources are moved to different parts of the organization, or employees are asked to adopt new cultural identities and values (e.g., Kanter et al., 1992). Individuals who have strong social identifications within an organization tend to compare themselves with dominant ingroups and outgroups. Empirical evidence is now emerging that the strength of identification with particular groups influences employees' perceptions of organizational processes like change, and is a potential source of conflict and competition between groups in organizations (Kramer, 1991).

From the perspective of SIT and CAT, change heightens the extent of intergroup rivalry. As a consequence of the motivation to enhance their feelings of self-worth, employees during change show that they want to belong to groups in the organization that compare favourably with other groups; that is, they aspire to belong to high-status groups. Several studies of organizational change reveal how employees in the larger partner in a merged business respond differently to the communication of change, compared to employees from the smaller partner. The perceptions of staff in the smaller organization are more likely to change, in the belief that the merger will heighten their sense of status and improve their work roles (Terry & Callan, 1998). Terry and Callan found that there was a tendency for high-status employees in a merger of hospitals to rate the ingroup as better than the outgroup on status-relevant dimensions (e.g., high prestige in the community, challenging job opportunities). On the other hand, employees from the smaller hospital engaged in ingroup bias on status-irrelevant dimensions (e.g., relaxed work environment, good relations with staff). Thus, as predicted by SIT, employees in smaller and lower-status organizations are more positive about mergers, which offer them membership of a larger, higher-status company. On the other hand, members of the larger organization feel that their social identity as members of a prestigious organization is undermined by the inclusion of members of the new group.

CONCLUSIONS

Several conclusions can be drawn from the discussion above. First, the consideration of communication as an independent variable reduces the complexity of its representation. Secondly, communication is generally treated as an individual event rather than both an interpersonal and intergroup event, even though organizational communication, at least in these contexts, involves interlocutors from different groups who engage in mutual influence. Thirdly, much research involves situations that are at least potentially problematic, but these are seldom studied specifically in terms of problematic communication. A more deliberate attempt to examine the problematic nature of organizational communication would allow for more precision in the understanding of the communication process. It would also more accurately reflect the actual communication practices in organizations and allow a direct examination of the impact of communication on interactants and their environment.

What difference does an intergroup perspective make to the study of organizational communication? Further, what insights can research and theory in language and social psychology, with its agenda to examine interpersonal communication in the light of salient intergroup relationships, bring to this arena, where it has been explored very little to date? One answer is that in any research in organizational communication it is essential to consider both the interpersonal and the intergroup aspects of all communication. Indeed, it is the link between these two aspects of communication that distinguishes organizational contexts from many other intergroup ones. It is rare that communication in organizations is *not* both intergroup and interpersonal. Thus, it is all the more surprising that there has been such a lack of research examining both aspects simultaneously.

Impact of Context

As we have already noted, certain contexts make social identity and group membership more salient than others, in particular, contexts where there is threat, rivalry, or competition for scarce resources. These contexts include the three we have discussed, along with many others where conflict is evident. A crucial first step in research, therefore, is to determine empirically what the intergroup relations are, which groups are salient, whether these are organizational or part of the larger culture, and how much these group memberships influence communication in the specific context. It is important to note that, unlike many group memberships in the larger society (e.g., gender, age, ethnicity), organizational memberships tend to be chosen. This means that the norms surrounding them, and ideas about prototypical communicative behaviour held by members (Turner et al., 1987) may be overt and readily expressed. For example, Jones et al. (1999) found that Australians were very ready to invoke their organizational identity in intergroup contexts, but were much more reluctant to deal overtly with gender or ethnicity in these same contexts; social norms permitted them to acknowledge the first, but not the others.

Developing Appropriate Theory

It is also essential to work from a theory, like CAT, that is capable of dealing with both interpersonal and intergroup aspects of communication, and which addresses both perceptions and behaviour. We support the many calls for greater links between work on organizational communication and work in other areas, but we would add that a combined interpersonal and intergroup approach is rare in any communication arena (see Gallois & Giles, 1998). In this, as in other areas of communication, it is necessary to get away from an emphasis on "good" communication, and to address all organizational communication as potentially problematic. Conversely, it is important not to assume that group memberships, especially those in the larger society, simply predetermine communication in the absence of individual differences, as (for example) work on gender and organizational communication often does, even when sophisticated and context-specific models are employed.

We believe that CAT is readily translatable into the arena of organizational communication, as SIT has been. Our recent research bears out this view. CAT has been well specified for intercultural communication, where it had its origins, as well as for intergenerational and intergender communication. Closer to the organizational context, there is a body of research using CAT in the context of doctor–patient communication, although this literature is less extensive. As Giles et al. (1991) have noted, however, every domain is different, and there is a need to develop CAT in this one. Our research so far indicates that the most salient goals and foci are those to do with conversational needs (and discourse management), role relationships (and interpersonal control), and relational needs (and face management). In addition, social norms in organizations are likely to be unusually close to the surface and to play a very important part in the negotiation of intergroup interactions.

Problematizing Organizational Communication

Thirdly, it is important to study both perceptions of communication and actual communicative behaviour, rather than to assume that what researchers consider to be "good" or effective will necessarily appear so to participants, or indeed will occur at all in actual behaviour. Thus, researchers must consider participants' own analyses of the context, intergroup and interpersonal relations, especially if they have the goal of applying their work to training or improving communication. There is good evidence that the concept of accommodative dilemmas (Gallois & Giles, 1998) can be used to capture much of this territory, particularly in the area of supervisor–subordinate communication.

The communication of change must always be thought of as a context where social identity is highly salient. It is very surprising that research to date has ignored this obvious aspect of organizational change, sometimes almost to the point of naïveté. Communication in this context is always problematic, and there is no guarantee that clear or truthful communication will be effective. There are many cases where employees deliberately hide information, obfuscate, and the like; nor is top management immune to this behaviour. The impact of group memberships, group-based identity, and intergroup relations must be theorized and studied for any future research on organizational change to be very useful.

Finally, communication must be treated as both an independent and a dependent variable. It is essential not to neglect the process of communication and its antecedents, as well as its outcomes. Only by a close examination of the process can the intricate interplay between interpersonal and intergroup relations in organizations, and its communication in difficult and problematic contexts, be fully understood.

REFERENCES

Alderfer, C.P. (1987). An intergroup perspective on group dynamics. In J.W. Lorsch (Ed.), Handbook of organizational behavior (pp. 190–222). Englewood Cliffs, NJ: Prentice-Hall.

Allen, M.W., Gotcher, J.M. & Seibert, J.H. (1993). A decade of organizational communication research: Journal articles 1980–1991. *Communication Yearbook*, **16**, 252–330.

Ashforth, B.E. & Mael, F.A. (1989). Social identity theory and the organization. *Academy of Management Review*, **14**, 20–39.

Axley, S.R. (1984). Managerial and organizational communication in terms of the conduit metaphor. *Academy of Management Review*, **9**, 428–437.

Barker, J.R. & Tompkins, P.K. (1994). Identification in the self-managing organization: Characteristics of target and tenure. *Human Communication Research*, **21**(2), 223–240.

Barry, B. & Watson, M.R. (1996). Communication aspects of dyadic social influence in organizations: A review and integration of conceptual and empirical developments. *Communication Yearbook*, **19**, 269–317.

Berman, S.J. & Hellweg, S.A. (1989). Perceived supervisor communication competence and supervisor satisfaction as a function of quality circle participation. *Journal of Business Communication*, **26**(2), 103–122.

Boggs, C. & Giles, H. (1999) "The canary in the coalmine": The nonaccommodation cycle in the gendered workplace. International Journal of Applied Linguistics, **9**(2), 223–246.

Bordow, A. & More, E. (1991). *Managing organisational communication.* Melbourne: Longman Cheshire.

Bourhis, R. (1991). Organisational communication and accommodation: Toward some conceptual and empirical links. In H. Giles, N. Coupland & J. Coupland (Eds), *Contexts of accommodation: Developments in applied sociolinguistics* (pp. 270–303). Cambridge, UK: Cambridge University Press.

Brown, R. Condor, S., Mathews, A., Wade, G. & Williams, J. (1986). Explaining intergroup differentiation in an industrial organization. *Journal of Occupational Psychology*, **59**, 273–286.

Brown, R. & Williams, J. (1984). Group identification: The same thing to all people? *Human Relations*, **37**(7), 547–564.

Callan, V.J. (1993). Individual and organizational strategies for coping with organizational change. *Work & Stress*, **7**(1), 63–75.

Connelley, D. (1994). Social identity as a barrier to understanding the role of gender and race. *Academy of Management Best Paper Proceedings*, 74–78.

Coupland, N., Wiemann, J.M. & Giles, H. (1991). Talk as "problem" and communication as "miscommunication": An integrative analysis. In N. Coupland, H. Giles & J.M. Wiemann (Eds), *"Miscommunication" and problematic talk* (pp. 1–18). Newbury Park, CA: Sage.

Cox, T., Jr (1993). *Cultural diversity in organizations: Theory, research. and practice.* San Francisco: Berret-Koehler.

Dansereau, F. & Markham, S.E. (1987). Supervisor–subordinate communication: Multiple levels of analysis. In F. Jablin, L. Putnam, K. Roberts & L. Porter (Eds), *Handbook of organizational communication: An interdisciplinary perspective* (pp. 343–388). Newbury Park, CA: Sage.

Deetz, S. (in press). Conceptual foundations for organizational communication studies. In F. Jablin & L. Putnam (Eds), *The new handbook of organizational communication.* Thousand Oaks, CA: Sage.

Deluga, R.J. (1988). Relationship of transformational and transactional leadership with employee influencing strategies. *Group and Organisation Studies*, **13**, 456–467.

DeWine, S. & Daniels, T. (1993). Beyond the snapshot: Setting a research agenda in organizational communication. *Communication Yearbook*, **16**, 331–346.

Dunphy, D. & Stace, D. (1990). *Under new management*. New York: Mcgraw-Hill.

Dutton, J.E., Dukerich, J.M. & Harquail, C.V. (1994). Organizational images and member identification. *Administrative Science Quarterly*, **39**(2), 239–263.

Euske, N.A. & Roberts, K.H. (1987). Evolving perspectives in organization theory: Communication implications. In F.M. Jablin, L.L. Putnam, K.H. Roberts & L.W. Porter (Eds), *Handbook of organizational communication* (pp. 41–69). Newbury Park, CA: Sage.

Farmer, S.M., Maslyn, J.M., Fedor, D.B. & Goodman, J.S. (1997). Putting upward influence strategies in context. *Journal of Organizational Behavior*, **18**(1), 17–42.

Fisher., B.A. (1978). *Perspectives on human communication*. New York: Macmillan.

Gallois, C. & Giles, H. (1998). Accommodating mutual influence in intergroup encounters. In M.T. Palmer (Ed.), *Mutual influence in interpersonal communication: Theory and research in cognition, affect, and behavior* (pp. 130–162). New York: Ablex.

Gallois, C., Giles, H., Jones, E., Cargile, A. & Ota, H. (1995). Accommodating intercultural encounters: Elaborations and extensions. In R.L. Wiseman (Ed.), *Intercultural communication theory* (pp. 115–147). Thousand Oaks, CA: Sage.

Gardner, M.J. & Jones, E. (1999). Communication and miscommunication in the workplace: Beliefs of superiors and subordinates. *International Journal of Applied Linguistics*, **9**(2), 185–206

Giles, H., Coupland, J. & Coupland, N. (Eds), (1991). *Studies in emotion and social interaction. Contexts of accommodation: Developments in applied sociolinguistics*. New York: Cambridge University Press.

Graen, G.B. & Uhl-Bien, M. (1998). Relationship-based approach to leadership: Development of leader-member exchange (LMX) theory of leadership over 25 years: Applying a multi-level multi-domain perspective. In F. Dansereau, F.J. Yammerino, et al. (Eds), *Monographs in organizational behavior and industrial relations. Leadership: The multiple-level approaches: Contemporary and alternative* (pp. 103–133). Stamford, CT: JAI Press.

Green, S.G. (1996). Demographic and organizational influences on leader-member exchange and related work attitudes. *Organizational Behavior and Human Decision Processes*, **66**, 203–214.

Hartley, J.F. (1996). Intergroup relations in organizations. In M.A. West (Ed.), *Handbook of work psychology* (pp. 397–422). Chichester: Wiley.

Henderson, L.S. (1987). The contextual nature of interpersonal communication in management theory and research. *Management Communication Quarterly*, **1**, 7–31.

Jablin, F. (1979). Superior–subordinate communication: The state of the art. *Psychological Bulletin*, **96**, 1201–1222.

Jablin, F.M. (1987). Organizational entry, assimilation, and exit. In F.M. Jablin, L.L. Putnam, K.H. Roberts & L.W. Porter (Eds), *Handbook of organizational communication: An interdisciplinary perspective* (pp. 679–740) Newbury Park, CA: Sage.

Johnson, G.M. (1992). Subordinate perceptions of superior's communication competence and task attraction related to superior's use of compliance-gaining tactics. *Western Journal of Communication*, **56**, 54–67.

Jones, E., Gallois, C., Callan, V. & Barker, M. (1999). Strategies of accommodation: Development of a coding system for conversational interaction. *Journal of Language and Social Psychology*, **18**, 123–152.

Kanter, R.M., Stein, B.A. & Jick, T.D. (1992). *The challenge of organizational change*. New York: Free Press.

Korsgaard, M.A., Roberson, L. & Rymph, R.D. (1998). What motivates fairness? The role of subordinate assertive behavior on managers' interactional fairness. *Journal of Applied Psychology*, **83**(5), 731–744.

Kotter, J.P. (1996). *Leading change.* Boston, MA: Harvard Business School Press.

Kramer, R.M. (1991). Intergroup relations and organizational dilemmas: The role of categorization processes. *Research in Organizational Behavior*, **13**, 191–228.

Krone, K., Jablin, F. & Putnam, L. (1987). Communication theory and organizational communication: Multiple perspectives. In F. Jablin, L. Putnam, K. Roberts & L. Porter (Eds), *Handbook of organizational communication: An interdisciplinary perspective* (pp. 18–40). Newbury Park, CA: Sage.

Larkin, T.J. & Larkin, S. (1996). Reaching and changing front-line employees. *Harvard Business Review*, **74**(3), 95–104.

Lee, J. & Jablin, F.M. (1995). Maintenance communication in superior–subordinate relationships. *Human Communication Research*, **22**(2), 220–257.

Lundberg, C.C. & Brownell, J. (1993). The implications of organizational learning for organizational communication: A review and reformulation. *International Journal of Organizational Analysis*, **1**(1), 29–53.

Mael, F.A. & Ashforth, B.E. (1995). Loyal from day one: Biodata, organizational identification, and turnover among newcomers. *Personnel Psychology*, **48**, 309–333.

Maslyn, J.M. Fanner, S.M. & Fedor, D.B. (1996). Failed upward influence attempts: Predicting the nature of subordinate persistence in pursuit of organizational goals. *Group and Organization Management*, **21**(4), 461–480.

McKinney. B.C., Kelly, L. & Duran, R.L. (1997). The relationship between conflict message styles and dimensions of communication competence. *Communication Reports*, **10**(2), 185–196.

Miller, V., Allen, M., Krone, K. & Preiss, R. (1990). *Integrating micro–macro organizational communication research: Rationale, issues, and mechanisms.* Paper presented at the conference of the International Communication Association, Dublin, May.

Moss, S.E. & Martinko, M.J. (1998). The effects of performance attributions and outcome dependence on leader feedback behavior following poor subordinate performance. *Journal of Organizational Behavior*, **19**, 259–274.

Mumby, D.K. (1993). Critical organizational communication studies: The next 10 years. *Communication Monographs*, **60**, 18–25.

Nadler, D.A. & Nadler, M.B. (1998). *Champions of change: How CEOs and their companies are mastering the skills of radical change.* San Francisco: Jossey-Bass.

Nkomo, S.M. & Cox, T., Jr (1996). Diverse identities in organizations. In S.R. Clegg, C. Hardy & W.R. Nord (Eds) *Handbook of organization studies* (pp. 338–356). Thousand Oaks, CA: Sage.

Nykodym, N. (1988). Organizational communication theory: Interpersonal and non interpersonal perspectives. *Communications*, **14**, 7–18.

Oaker, G. & Brown, R. (1986). Intergroup relations in a hospital setting: A further test of Social Identity Theory. *Human Relations*, **39**(8), 767–778.

Penley, L.E., Alexander, E.R., Jernigan, I.E. & Henwood, C.I. (1991). Communication abilities of managers: The relationship to performance. *Journal of Management*, **17**(1), 57–76

Petronio, S., Ellemers, N., Giles, H. & Gallois, C. (1998). (Mis)communicating across boundaries: Interpersonal and intergroup considerations. *Communication Research*, **25**(6), 571–595.

Poole, M.S. & McPhee, R.D. (1983). A structurational analysis of organizational climate. In L.L. Putnam & M.E. Pacanowski (Eds), *Communication and organizations: An intepretive approach* (pp. 195–219). Beverly Hills, CA: Sage.

Putnam, L.L. & Cheney, G. (1983). A critical review of research traditions in organizational communication. In M. Mandler (Ed.), *Communication in transition: Issues and debates in current research* (pp. 206–224). New York: Praeger.

Putnam, L.L., Phillips, N. & Chapman, P. (1996). Metaphors of communication and organization. In S.R. Clegg, C. Hardy & W.R. Nord (Eds), *Handbook of organization studies* (pp. 375–408). Thousand Oaks, CA: Sage.

Robbins, S.P., Millett, B., Cacioppe, R. & Waters-Marsh, T. (1998). *Organisational be-haviour: Leading and managing in Australia and New Zealand* (2nd edn). Sydney, Australia: Prentice-Hall.

Schein, E.H. (1991). What is culture? In P.J. Frost, L.F. Moore, M.R. Louis, C.C. Lundberg & J. Martin (Eds), *Reframing organizational culture* (pp. 243–253). Newbury Park., CA: Sage.

Scott, C.R. (1997). Identification with multiple targets in a geographically dispersed or-ganization. *Management Communication Quarterly*, **10**, 491–522.

Sillars, A.L. & Wilmot, W.W. (1994). Communication strategies in conflict and mediation. In J.A. Daly & J.M. Wiemann (Eds), *LEA's communication series: Strategic interperso-nal communication* (pp. 163–190). Hillsdale, NJ: Erlbaum.

Sparkes, B. & Callan, V.J. (1992). Communication and the service encounter: The value of convergence. *International Journal of Hospitality Management*, **11**(3), 213–224.

Spitzberg, B.H. & Cupach, W.R. (1984). *Interpersonal communication competence.* Bev-erley Hills, CA: Sage.

Suzuki, S. (1998). In-group and out-group communication patterns in international organ-izations: Implications for Social Identity Theory. *Communication Research*, **25**(2), 154–182.

Tajfel, H. & Turner, J.C. (1979). An integrative theory of intergroup conflict. In W.G. Austin & S. Worchel (Eds), *The social psychology of intergroup relations* (pp. 33–47). Monterey, CA. Brooks-Cole.

Tajfel, H. & Turner, J.C. (1986). The social identity theory of intergroup behaviour. In S. Worchel & W.G. Austin (Eds), *Psychology of intergroup relations* (pp. 7–24). Chicago: Nelson-Hall.

Tepper, B.J. (1995). Upward maintenance tactics in supervisory mentoring and nonmen-toring relationships. *Academy of Management Journal*, **38**(4), 1191–1205.

Terry, D.J. & Callan, V.J. (1997). Employee adjustment to large-scale organisational change. *Australian Psychologist*, **32**(3), 203–210.

Terry, D.J. & Callan, V.J. (1998). In-group bias in response to an organizational merger. *Group Dynamics: Theory, Research, and Practice*, **2**(2), 67–81.

Thomas, K.W. (1993). Conflict and negotiation in organizations. In M.D. Dunnette & L.M. Hough (Eds), *Handbook of industrial and organizational psychology* (2nd edn, Vol. 3, pp. 651–717). Palo Alto, CA: Consulting Psychologists Press.

Tompkins, P.K. & Redding, W.C. (1988). Organizational communication: Past and pres-ent tenses. In G.M. Goldhaber & G.A. Barnett (Eds) *Handbook of Organizational Communication* (pp. 5–34). Norwood, NJ: Ablex.

Trice, H.M. & Beyer, J.M. (1993). *The cultures of work organizations.* Englewood Cliffs, NJ: Prentice-Hall.

Tsui, A., Ashford, S., St Clair, L. & Xin, K. (1995). Dealing with discrepant expectations: Response strategies and managerial effectiveness. *Academy of Management Journal*, **38**(6), 1515–1543.

Turner, J.C., Hogg, M.A., Oakes, P.J., Reicher, S.D. & Wetherell, M.S. (1987). *Re-discovering the social group: A self-categorization theory.* Oxford: Basil Blackwell.

Waldron, V.R. (1991). Achieving communication goals in superior–subordinate relation-ships: The multi-functionality of upward maintenance tactics. *Communication Mono-graphs*, **58**, 289–306.

Waldron, V.R. & Applegate, J.L. (1994). Interpersonal construct differentiation and con-versational planning: An examination of two cognitive accounts for the production of competent verbal disagreement tactics. *Human Communication Research*, **21**(1), 3–35.

Weider-Hatfield, D. & Hatfield, J.D. (1996). Superiors' conflict management strategies and subordinate outcomes. *Management Communication Quarterly*, **10**, 189–208.

Wert-Gray, S., Center, C., Brashers, D.E. & Meyers, R.A. (1991). Research topics and methodological orientations in organizational communication: A decade in review. *Communication Studies*, **42**(2), 141–154.

Willemyns, M., Gallois, C., Callan, V.J. & Pittam, J. (1997). Accent accommodation in the job interview: Impact of interviewer accent and gender. *Journal of Language and Social Psychology*, **8**(1), 1–22.

Willemyns, M., Gallois, C. & Callan, V.J. (1999). *Mentor or manager? Communicating paradoxical identities*. Paper presented at the 49th Annual Conference of the International Communication Association, San Francisco, May.

Wilson, K. & Gallois, C. (1993). *Assertion and its social context*. Oxford: Pergamon Press.

Wohlers, A.J., Hall, M. & London, M. (1993). Subordinates rating managers: Organizational and demographic correlates of self/subordinate agreement. *Journal of Occupational and Organizational Psychology*, **66**, 263–275.

Yukl, G. (1994). *Leadership in organizations* (3rd edn). Englewood Cliffs, NJ: Prentice Hall.

Language and the Media

Peter Lunt
University College, London, UK
Sonia Livingstone
London School of Economics and Political Science, UK

INTRODUCTION

The modem media possess a hitherto unprecedented power to encode and circulate symbolic representations. Throughout the Western world, people spend a considerable proportion of their leisure hours with one mass medium or another, together totalling more hours than children spend in school or families spend in conversation. Through the media, people are positioned, or position themselves, in relation to a flood of images and information about both worlds distant in space or time as well as the world close to home. A considerable body of research from diverse disciplines over the past century has traced the complex and subtle ways in which the media have become an integral part of our everyday lives, implicated in the structuring of our domestic practices, our social relationships, our very identity. On a more macro level, a growing body of research is also charting how the media are increasingly central to broader sociocultural, even global, flows of communication and information. Thus the media play a key role in how, in our everyday lives, we understand the world around us and our place within it, while that very "we" is becoming more culturally dispersed as a result of those same media processes.

Yet despite the popular anxieties which flare up sporadically over media content and regulation, it is easy to take the media for granted, failing to recognize their importance precisely because of their very ubiquity as background features of everyday life. Perhaps for this reason, systematic treatments of the media within social psychology are rare. This stands in curious contrast to the social

The New Handbook of Language and Social Psychology.
Edited by W. Peter Robinson and Howard Giles.
© 2001 John Wiley & Sons Ltd.

psychological nature – in terms of questions, influences, concepts and methods – of the emerging field of media and communication, or media studies. Drawing on the resources of several disciplines across the social sciences and humanities, this field has established itself as a more or less autonomous discipline in recent years, more so in some countries (e.g., America, the Nordic countries) than in others, developing a rich and diverse panoply of theories and methods concerning the media and, recently, information and communication technologies more broadly.[1] Social psychology played a key role in the establishment of this new field. Most significantly, social psychology bequeathed to media studies from the 1940s onwards an emphasis on "effects"[2] and on "uses and gratifications",[3] both of which dominated media and communications research in the following decades. Yet since then, social psychology has tended to marginalize the media in one of several ways. If one looks at social psychology textbooks or journals, the media are either barely mentioned or bracketed off in a separate chapter, as if their role in social influence, social construction and social identity can be unproblematically contained. If one turns to more linguistically or discursively oriented social psychological research, a more subtle version of this strategy is evident as the media are treated either as an obviously important source of social influence or, paradoxically, they are treated as a convenient source of material for analysing public understanding.

By contrast, the force of intellectual developments across many disciplines, most obviously media and communication itself, is to recognize the nature of the media as multifaceted artefacts embedded in a production–consumption cycle of considerable complexity which is in turn embedded in economic, political, cultural and psychological structures of modem society. It is the consequences of this recognition for social psychology which we wish to pursue in this chapter, making the question of language in the media our central focus. Given that the media represent a key constituent of contemporary life, how might social psychology best encompass their cultural and communicative significance? And further, how might social psychology develop a positive contribution to media and communication research beyond the effects and uses and gratifications positions?

Within media studies, an analysis of the role and significance of the media involves a focus on the three core components of media systems (institutional

---

[1] Useful overviews of the field may be found in Thompson (1995), Levy and Gurevitch (1994) and Mackay and O'Sullivan (1999).

[2] While the "effects" tradition was premised on the idea that the media have a direct effect on such behaviours as aggression or voting, the "minimal effects tradition" shifted the focus towards the contingent factors which make social influence processes work much more indirectly. Yet despite many effects studies, few sizeable, direct effects were observed, and even indirect effects proved difficult to establish convincingly (Livingstone, 1996). Consequently, the effects tradition, and the contribution of social psychology to media studies, have been heavily criticized.

[3] This alternative social psychological approach reversed the effects hypothesis. Rather than investigating what the media do to the audience, uses and gratifications research proposed the study of what audiences do with the media (Blumler & Katz, 1974). Rejecting the passive conception of the audience that underpins effects research, it introduced the idea of an "active" audience which selects specific media to gratify particular needs such as escapism, relaxation and social monitoring.

production, text and audience), on the interrelations among these components, and, last but not least, on locating these processes and interrelations within their social contexts (Abercrombie, 1996). This is an ambitious project encompassing a wide range of theoretical and methodological perspectives and borrowing freely from neighbouring disciplines from political economy to literary theory to anthropology. On the face of it, social psychology is well positioned to make a significant contribution but finds itself on the margins. This is partly because those social psychological theories which have proved influential in media studies (especially media effects and media uses and gratifications) tend to assume a particular, and heavily critiqued, model of communication.

Traditional psychological models of communication adopt a view of the relation between representation, language, interpretation and culture which fits neither with current, discursively oriented approaches to communication within social psychology nor with new approaches to communication and culture within media studies. In the present chapter, we consider these new approaches to communication and culture – from which social psychology could gain and to which it could contribute – in terms of their response to the traditional psychology of communication. By identifying responses to each of five key elements of the traditional model of communication, we hope to show how valuable approaches to language and media are emerging that not only represent critical responses to each of these elements but also take the research agenda forward. These five linked elements of the traditional model are that (i) the communication process is essentially linear, with the result that (ii) audiences are passive receivers at the end of a chain of media influence (iii) whose key function is the transmission of information, (iv) in the performance of which the media work no differently from any other, face-to-face, source of representations, while (v) simultaneously (and paradoxically) adopting the rhetoric of public address.

FROM LINEAR TO CYCLIC COMMUNICATION

When television first entered American society, Lasswell (1948) charged researchers in the then fledgling field of media and communication with the task of discovering "who says what in which channel to whom and with what effect". This task was widely adopted for several decades, especially by social psychologists (most notably, the Yale Program of Research on Communication), viewing mass communication as a special case of the "general linear model of communication", namely sender → message → receiver. However, the implications of this linear model – namely, that social influence is unidirectional, that communications are initiated by the sender, that messages are pre-given packages of meaning passed from source to recipient, that no feedback occurs along the way, that audiences are just the end point of a communication, to be affected but not involved – all of these implications have been variously challenged. Perhaps most influential has been the alternative, cyclic model of communication offered in Hall's paper *Encoding/Decoding* (Hall, 1980). Hall (1994) was later to reflect that this model, intended as a programmatic sketch for cultural studies, represented an attack on the then mainstream, social psychological model of mass communication. Rejecting the linearity of this model, Hall stressed the links between processes of encoding and decoding, contextualizing these within a complex cultural framework. On this view, mass communication is understood as a circuit of practices: production, circulation, consumption, (re)production (Pillai, 1992).[4]

Influenced also by the work of reception theorists such as Eco (1979; see below), who stresses how "readers" strive to complete the necessarily partial meaning of a text by drawing on their own cultural resources in the process of interpretation, Hall reconceptualized the ideological effect of the mass media in terms of a series of dominant codes which place structural limitations on the interpretative process, leading readers/viewers to articulate the "preferred" or normative meaning, thereby reproducing rather than resisting the dominant ideology. However, in moving beyond classic Marxist accounts of ideology which propose deterministic ideological codes, Hall (1980) also allows for the relative autonomy of culture, suggesting a looser relation between media texts and audiences than previously accommodated by theories of ideology. Thus, oppositional readings – those which run counter to the preferred reading – remain possible, precisely because texts do not stand in a deterministic relation to the reader but rather must be actively reproduced, or otherwise, by interpretative work on the part of the audience, depending on the variable social and cultural resources available to them in the reception context.

The cyclic model of encoding and decoding was first explored empirically by Morley, setting the paradigm for many cultural studies' projects to come (Morley, 1992). Following an earlier textual analysis of ideological encoding in the 1970s current affairs programme, *Nationwide,* Morley (1980, 1981) conducted a series of peer group discussions which showed that audience decodings diverged as a function of socio-economic position, resulting in interpretations which were politically framed. For example, decoding by bank managers and by schoolboys was highly consistent with the normative assumptions which structured the programme, while trainee teachers and trade union officials made politically inconsistent, ambivalent or negotiated readings. Yet other groups, for example shop stewards, took a clearly oppositional position, constructing a critical reading grounded in their social experience but unintended by the text. And a few viewers were wholly alienated from the text as it did not afford them a reading congruent with their own cultural position (for example, black further education students).

As anticipated by Hall, Morley showed how particular groups respond in different ways to the preferred reading offered to them by media texts,

---

[4] Hall draws directly on Marx's political economy, which emphasizes production/consumption, but he emphasizes that the media operate through symbolic exchange. Thus relations between the practices linked by this circuit are understood discursively as "articulation" by analogy with exchange in the economic sphere.

depending on the degree of correspondence between the conditions of encoding and decoding. For the most part, this correspondence is sufficient for the preferred reading to predominate, while the emancipatory potential opened up by a lesser degree of correspondence provides the counterbalance presumed by the theory of hegemony. While in principle, therefore, the moments of encoding and decoding are indeed relatively autonomous, in practice the possibilities for critical or oppositional readings are restricted both by the degree of closure linguistically encoded into the text (a matter of ideological dominance) and the unequal access to symbolic resources available to audiences (a matter of socio-economic positioning). In sum, despite some continuing theoretical and methodological debate, the advantage of this approach lies in its recognition of divergence in interpretation (particularly of the connotative meanings of texts), pointing up some significant indeterminacy in media texts, while at the same time preserving a view of ideology construed in terms of the production and consumption of meanings.

FROM PASSIVE TO ACTIVE AUDIENCES

From a social psychological perspective, cultural studies shift us away from questions of attitudes towards or effects of media contents, both these being approaches which implicitly construe the media text as a "stimulus" (Livingstone, 1998), towards questions of the context-dependent (but not deterministic) symbolic activity engaged in by audiences in order to generate the inherently variable meanings of a text, as part of a "circuit of communication" that constitutes relations of media production/consumption. While Hall et al. are primarily concerned with ideology, and hence focus on the normative structuring of texts and the concomitant role of social class in framing audience response, the force of their arguments ties in with those stemming from reception aesthetics within literary theory, opening up a more general set of questions about active audiences. In other words, while cultural studies see the struggle between texts and readers in class terms, other dimensions of the cultural conditions of both encoding and decoding may also be important to mass communication. Thus, a challenge to the linear model of communication involves a parallel challenge to the conception of the text as pre-given and of the audience as a passive recipient. The assumption of passivity is strong in social psychological approaches to the media, although the uses and gratifications tradition had long advocated a more selective and motivated conception of the audience (unfortunately not followed through into a reconceptualization of media texts).

Audience reception became a focus for media research during the 1980s and 1990s (Livingstone, 1998), drawing on developments in reception aesthetics (or reader response theory). For reception theorists, the question was how to legitimate a non-elitist, more interactionist analysis of high culture (Holub, 1984; Suleiman & Crosman, 1980). Emphasis shifted from the structuralist analysis of meanings "in" the text to an analysis of the process of reading a text, where the meanings which are activated on reading depend on the interaction between text and reader, although the application of this approach to popular or mass cultural forms remains contentious. Further, the media effects question is reconceived in terms of a dialectic between text and reader thus: "a well-organized text on the one hand presupposes a model of competence coming, so to speak, from outside the text, but on the other hand works to build up, by merely textual means, such a competence" (Eco, 1979, p. 8) On the one hand, therefore, reception theorists argue that an implied or model reader – an ideal decoding strategy – is encoded into the text, thereby specifying the "horizon of expectations" (Jauss, 1982) or "textual competencies" (Eco, 1979) required to decode the text. On the other hand, the reception context may or may not meet this specification of the ideal reader presumed in the construction of the text, and as with Hall's theory actual contingent circumstances provide the interpretative resources – here theorized in terms of textual and extra-textual codes – available to audiences in practice.[5]

Within media studies, numerous empirical projects have explored the proposed activity of the viewer, typically using qualitative methods to uncover the subtle and context-dependent responses of audiences to specific media texts. For example, Liebes and Katz (1990) examined potential resistance to cultural imperialism (as represented by the prime-time soap opera, *Dallas*) among diverse cultural groups. While their prior textual analysis had stressed such primordial themes as family lineage, property inheritance and sibling rivalry, viewers from different social and cultural backgrounds generated different interpretations of the same episode: Russian Jews made ideological readings centred on underlying moral and political themes; Americans focused on the personalities and motivations of the characters in making their readings coherent; Moroccan Arabs emphasized event sequencing and narrative continuity (Liebes & Katz, 1990). While each group's reading was clearly constrained by the text, the interaction between diverse cultural resources and a degree of textual openness resulted in divergent readings being made.

While Liebes and Katz were concerned with cultural divergence, Radway (1984) explored the contribution of gender in interpreting media texts. Her analysis of the contrast between the readings of popular romance novels made by ordinary women readers and by literary critics demonstrated how members of different "interpretive communities" read differently, responding to print differently and for different purposes.[6] Other studies have examined different

---

[5] In theorizing "the role of the reader", Eco stresses that our analytic focus should be on the interface between text and reader (or programme and viewer): "The existence of various codes and subcodes, the variety of sociocultural circumstances in which a message is emitted (where the codes of the addressee can be different from those of the sender) and the rate of initiative displayed by the addressee in making presuppositions and abductions – all result in – making a message . . . an empty form to which various possible senses can be attributed" (Eco, 1979, p. 5).

[6] Specifically, Radway found that women readers emphasized the literal meaning and the factual nature of language in romance novels in preference to narrative consistency (preferred by the critics) when the two conflicted. Thus when the heroine is initially described as independent and yet ultimately appears to submit to her hero's demands, women readers were found to resist the normative patriarchal message by generating their own meanings in which the heroine is seen subtly to win over her hero unbeknownst to him, thus revealing her true strength, as stated at the outset.

aspects of the cultural conditions of reception while, more generally, audience reception research has generated considerable theoretical and methodological debate, further qualifying and clarifying but not essentially challenging the active role of the audience in making sense of media texts (Livingstone, 1998).

FROM INFORMATION TRANSMISSION TO RITUAL COMMUNICATION

Inherent in the linear model of communication is not only a concept of the audience as passive but also a conception of the function of communication as the transmission of information. Again, this conception is particularly, though not solely, tied to traditional theories in social psychology, where a more influential relative of the transmission approach is the information-processing paradigm in psychology. Traditionally, social psychologists have held that mass communication centres on the flow of information ("the message") from sender to receiver in order to inform, influence or persuade, while the media themselves represent transmission channels, whether these are seen as accurate or flawed, neutral or biased. As Carey (1989) notes, many of our common metaphors for the media are based on this transmission model – sending and receiving, storing and carrying, coverage and reach – as if symbolic meanings were physical packages to be transported by road or rail to their destination.

As an alternative model, Carey develops a neo-Durkheimian view of communication whose function is that of cultural ritual which supports the social order through the construction of "mechanical solidarity", moments in which all participate in a public ceremony and thus affirm their shared membership of a national or international community. Drawing especially on anthropology, on micro-sociology and on sociolinguistics, he outlines how the media can thus be analysed as generating occasions akin to ceremonies which hold us – producers and consumers of media meanings – in place within a shared culture. While in pre-modern societies, ceremony and ritual serve as liminal moments – necessary points of reflection, sometimes even turning authority on its head (Bakhtin, 1981) – modern societies increasingly use the mass media for such ritual communication, similarly opening up the potential for reflection on everyday social practices.

Dayan and Katz (1992) apply an anthropological framework to the live broadcasting of "historic" events such as the Olympic Games, Kennedy's funeral and the British Royal Wedding of 1981.[7] Without requiring citizens to leave their homes (i.e., while "not being there"), the celebration of such "media events" allows for national or even global participation in a potentially transformative ritual whose form and meanings must be negotiated among organizers, broadcasters, public relations experts, technicians, fans, and ordinary readers and

---

[7] According to Dayan and Katz, the events themselves can be seen as scripted in one of three ways: as Contest (e.g., the Olympic Games), Conquest (e.g., Sadat's visit to Jerusalem) or Coronation (e.g., the Royal Wedding).

viewers at home. This transformation may occur in several directions, a key one of which is the way in which the structures of this new genre – rhetorical, symbolic, narrative and ritual – are increasingly shaping the nature and outcome of cultural and political happenings as media events. While the dangers of the manipulation of media events are obvious, as is the notion of these as "pseudo-events" (see the next section), for Dayan and Katz the ritual importance of media events is more interesting for its potential to enfranchise the audience as participants in their culture, providing liminal moments for a society to reflect on, and at the same time to authenticate, its vision of itself Theoretically, this work has been important for stressing the ritual significance of mass communication in society instead of, or in addition to, its function as a transmitter of information. This shift is commensurate with those outlined earlier, for the ritual model presumes cyclic rather than linear communication processes, actively participating rather than passively receptive audiences, and a complex account of media products as text rather than as stimulus, to be analysed in terms of genre, narrative, symbolic codes and so forth. Whether media events can be shown to have the long-term effects claimed for them (e.g., promoting public debate, shaping the climate of opinion, displacing intermediaries or socializing citizens) remains to be seen, but the more political nature of these issues leads us to the next domain of research – one where the specific role of the media in shaping public participation and public debate has been hotly debated.

FROM "JUST TALK" TO PUBLIC COMMUNICATION

Participation in politically oriented media events raises questions not only about media influence but also about the nature of media contents. As noted at the outset, social psychologists have often assumed that political talk in the media is just like everyday talk, neglecting the specific nature not only of media *qua* text but also media *qua* social institution. Are the media just another place where talk is to be found, or is there something special about mediated conversation? Arguments in favour of the latter position arose from the recent debate over the public sphere, giving rise to a specific body of literature relevant to social psychology as well as stimulating the development of a more general social theoretical account of mediation (see Thompson, 1995).[8]

The debate about the media and the public sphere was prompted by the work of Habermas (1969, 1981). Arguing that dominant, institutionally based, instrumental reason is not capable of generating a critical rational consensus as the basis for legitimation, Habermas is concerned that the very problem of

---

[8] Adopting a historical, social theoretical perspective, Thompson's (1995) central argument is that to understand modernity we must understand the media, for the media are supplementing or even displacing face-to-face interpersonal communication within a shared locale as the primary means through which the symbolic character of social life is constructed. In place of such interpersonal communication the media offer mediated interaction, the transformation of publicness and the public sphere, the re-mooring of tradition and a challenge to authority and expertise.

legitimation has been subverted by the media, for these provide the illusion of public consensus rather than promoting actual consensus. His own attempt to construct a theory of communicative action looks to pragmatics for a theory of communication that links theory and practice in the interests of emancipation. In an intellectual climate where post-structuralist theory had rejected the possibility of pragmatic universals (by first defining rationality narrowly in terms of instrumental reason and then arguing that everyday talk and practice could not be seen as rational in these terms), Habermas claims instead that the ways in which people talk in concrete situations have a social significance not because of their constitutive (or discursive) properties but because they make claims to truth. While not necessarily narrowly logical, these claims to truth are pragmatic insofar as they invite the hearer to share knowledge, to trust the speaker and to join in a shared value system. The potential of such a "universal pragmatics" lies in legitimating – i.e., in being seen publically to validate – the production of political consensus within a fundamentally unequal society, a society where the social system has become "polluted" by everyday life and vice versa.

In this context, it becomes clear that the mass media have a key role to play in this process of public legitimation, and therefore that, for example, in principle it is the case that talk on television is not necessarily "just talk". However, Habermas is pessimistic about the possibility of today's media coming close in practice to providing the conditions of open access, unconstrained conversation and consensus-seeking that his theory would require. Instead, he sees the claims to truth, the integrity and the value of utterances on television as reflecting the institutional contexts and constraints of production while simultaneously giving the appearance of spontaneity. This leads us directly back to the question of active audiences. Given the interpretative activity of audiences discussed earlier, the traditional question of whether the audience is duped by this apparent spontaneity has been replaced by the question of whether audiences can combine a positive engagement with "talk on television" with a critical awareness of the institutional constraints within which this talk occurred.

We explored some of these questions in our empirical study of the audience reception of politically oriented day-time talk shows (Livingstone & Lunt, 1994). In these shows, the moderator or "host" plays an active role in the management of discussion, mediating between expert and lay participants, encouraging certain kinds of talk over others, keeping the conversation fast moving while ensuring contributions from a diversity of participants. Despite widespread cynicism about audiences for such programmes, the viewers were both engaged – in a "para-social" manner – in the debate and, at the same time, they were critical of many aspects of the programmes. Their critical evaluation focused on the host as manager of the supposedly "spontaneous" discussion, on the experts' implicit claims to authority, on the degree to which the studio audience is representative of the "public", and on the potential impact such discussion might have for their own lives. While such talk programmes indeed fall short of the consensus-building necessary for a Habermasian rational–critical public sphere they do, however, conform to those alternative conceptions of the public sphere that emphasize the public expression of diverse points of view and the search for compromise rather than consensus (Fraser, 1990; Negt & Kluge, 1990).

FROM ADDRESSING THE PUBLIC TO A DIVERSITY OF RHETORICAL FORMS

The analysis of media events focuses on major, global communication ceremonies, and the public sphere debate focuses on the possibility of ideal conditions within which rational–critical discussion might occur. However, the majority of mediated discourse is far more ordinary, more everyday and so more diverse than can be captured by either of these approaches. Despite this obvious diversity, in much early social psychological work on the "mass media of communication" the media are regarded, implicitly, as a new version of a very old rhetorical form, that of public address. In other words, as in the speeches and sermons of old, the media are regarded as a source of public pronouncements intended to inform or persuade while the response of the audience is conceived in terms of attitude change. Our final challenge to the traditional model of communication, therefore, is directed to this assumption about the rhetorical nature of mediated communication.

Before the mass media, a large audience could only be addressed if they were gathered together in the same place at the same time. The rise of the press and, later, broadcasting radically altered this requirement, reaching a mass audience bounded by neither space nor time. Thus the advent of the mass media opened up new possibilities for public address that allowed authoritative elites to address a mass audience without the need for co-presence. Rather than analysing media texts in terms of public modes of address – an elite speaking down to an appreciative but silent audience – Scannell (1991) traces how television and radio developed a more conversational model of address – more personal, more intimate, as if speaking face to face. By simulating informal conversation, broadcasting encourages the audience to feel that they are engaged in, or at least overhearing, a conversation rather than that they are attending a lecture or a sermon. Following the early days of broadcasting, broadcasters realized that there would be resistance to a medium that adopted the register of public oratory but whose reception context was the privacy of people's homes. Hence the media developed a form of communication that was produced in public but received in private: consequently, "the communicative style and manner of broadcasting approximate to the norms not of public forms of talk, but to those of ordinary, informal conversation, for this is overwhelmingly the preferred communicative style of interaction between people in the routine contexts of day-to-day life and especially the places in which they live" (Scannell, 1991, pp. 3–4).

Empirical work in this area tends to follow either a conversation analytic or a discursive approach, examining talk in particular social settings in order to identify the communication features that make that talk intelligible and bind participants to a cooperative ethic. In broadcasting, for example, they inquire into the devices adopted to create "liveness", that sense of being "here and now". Unlike Habermas' concerns discussed above, the aim is not to produce a theory of consensus but rather to understand the anterior conditions that make social interaction intelligible and that, for broadcasting, create the sense of "taken for granted" that allows television to insert itself so effectively into the routines of everyday life. Scannell's *Broadcast Talk* collection contains several useful examples of this work.[9] For example, Garton et al. (1991) use the notion of "register" to show how "chat" (central to much studio-based broadcasting) is characterized by topic shifts towards personal (as opposed to institutional) and private (as opposed to public) discourse, by displays of wit or humour and by opening up the possibility of transgression. Adopting a more conversation analytic approach, Clayman (1991; see also Heritage, Clayman, & Zimmerman, 1988) demonstrates how the openings of television news interviews accomplish the "staged" quality of news reporting. In these and other ways, the broadcast media adopt specific linguistic conventions to create a spontaneous, "natural" feel to programmes.

To develop one example, Gamson (1992) showed that people organize their often lively and well-informed discussion of political events in terms of discernible themes or "collective action frames". These frames are "hot cognition", to be distinguished from other organized belief systems because they are, first, motivated by feelings of injustice, second, they include a subject position which confers meaning onto actions and, third, they confer identity onto the actor. Thus for a series of specific issues (concerning, for example, nuclear power, the Arab–Israeli conflict or problems in American industry), Gamson identifies the degree of convergence between these three components found within news media frames compared with lay conversational frames. By contrast with Morley's study (see above), where audiences are identified broadly as normative, negotiated or oppositional in their responses, and where the oppositional response is implicitly construed as politically resistant, Gamson suggests that only when the specific issue in the news matches the concerns of the viewer, and only when both are framed in terms of these three components (injustice, action and identity) can "hot" beliefs "legitimate and inspire social movements activities and campaigns" (Gamson, 1992, p. 7).

Whether one begins with an interest in the linguistic and rhetorical forms of media content analysis (exemplified by the *Broadcast Talk* collection), or with a social/political problem to be pursued through analysing a specific media form (exemplified by Gamson's concerns about political participation), these projects represent a considerable advance on the conception of media language and

---

[9] Montgomery (1991) analyses the devices that manage the tensions between private experience and public broadcasting in the context of radio broadcasts of personal life histories. This is also a feature of talk shows whereby the juxtaposition of discourses of personal experience and expertise are managed using a variety of rhetorical devices (Livingstone & Lunt, 1994).

media content typical of traditional effects research, showing how any reduction of media contents to a straightforward notion of public address greatly underestimates the subtle and diverse structures of media discourse.

TOWARDS A NEW SOCIAL PSYCHOLOGY OF LANGUAGE AND MEDIA

As we have seen, partly in response to the inadequacies of traditional social psychological work on the media, different strands of research within media and communication have rethought the complex relations between media production, media texts and genres, audience interpretation and the discursive contexts of everyday life. Focusing primarily on assumptions about language and communication, we have organized these developments in terms of alternatives to five key elements of the "general linear" model of communication central, in historical terms, to psychology as a discipline. Hence we have explored alternatives to the assumption of linearity in communication, where this is replaced by the notion of complex circulation of meaning with relative autonomy at the different moments in communication networks. Audience response has been elaborated by reconstruing the audience as active interpreters of media texts, making a contribution, therefore, to the construction and reproduction of meaning in society. The earlier emphasis on the media as information transmitters has been replaced by growing interest in media-managed rituals as constitutive of culture. The institutional power vested in the media led to an analysis of how mediated talk – especially on issues of public significance – differs from that of private conversation and yet, as our last section above argued, the media have abandoned the rhetorical form of a system of public address in favour of more intimate, conversation-based generic forms of address which draw the viewer into a shared, if media-managed, culture.

It would be misleading, however, to imply that all social psychologists have adopted the five assumptions about communication which we have challenged in this chapter, and neither do all neglect the importance of media and popular culture in everyday life. Indeed, some are now drawing productively on developments in media studies and discourse studies, moving towards a social psychology of the media which treats language and the media in a more explicit and more sophisticated way than hitherto. For example, Billig (1991) analyses the rhetorical construction of the Royal Family in both the mass media and family interviews. This work is strongly influenced by Hall's assertion of the relative autonomy of culture and by his appropriation of Gramsci's notion of "hegemony" to explain indirect, symbolically mediated social influence. Billig reveals the "ideological dilemmas" underlying arguments and contradictions he observes in "talk about the royals" (concerning such values as heritage, family, etc). He concludes that in reaffirming the value of ordinary life, such commonsense talk in fact serves a palliative ideological function.

A further prominent reworking of the relation between social psychology and media studies, van Dijk (1991) combines a discourse analysis of prejudice in news media with interviews with ordinary people. Challenged by the pernicious nature of prejudice in modern democracies, van Dijk is concerned that traditional social psychological attitude measures no longer reveal widespread racism. Rather than opting for complacency, he suggests that racism indeed endures, but that the explanation involves a complex relationship between ideology, the public and the press.[10] His discursive approach does not lead to a rejection of psychology but instead sees social cognition as mediating between discourse and society. Specifically, he shows how the elite views expressed in the media provide the resource from which white people construct models of ethnicity, which in turn influence beliefs and behaviour concerning ethnic minorities.

While we lack space to discuss further developments within social psychology, we would direct readers particularly to the following. First, social psychologists working in the reception tradition are developing the text–reader paradigm by theorizing the process of "making sense of television" from the viewers' perspective, to complement the theory of the text as developed within literary and cultural studies (Hoijer, 1990; Livingstone, 1998). Second, researchers working in the tradition of Moscovici's theory of social representations seek to understand the role of the media in disseminating expertise to the public while also tracing how conversations among ordinary people respond, this feeding into a broader socio-cultural process in which individual beliefs, shared representations and mass media contents are integrated (Doise, 1993). Third, some social psychologists are following the discourse tradition within political communications, exploring the mediation of relations between elites and publics (e.g. Liebes, 1992). Thus Bull (1998) identifies the linguistic and situational features specific to media interviews which distinguish them from other social situations. In sum, social psychologists from diverse theoretical traditions, using different methods, have responded to the theoretical and empirical challenges of studying the media, thereby opening up the possibility of a new social psychology of the media in which questions of language and interpretation are of central concern. However, this is not a well-organized "school of thought" but rather a loose collection of researchers responding in varied ways to the current situation. How can we make sense of this diversity?

Corner (1999) identifies "talk" as a key debating point in contemporary media theory. While there are many varieties of linguistic/discourse analysis, he divides current work on the media into one of two broad approaches. One, allied to applied linguistics, provides close readings of media discourse, thereby highlighting the often sketchy and informal account of language in media research elsewhere (e.g., Fairclough, 1995; Scannell, 1991). Despite the sometimes narrowly linguistic focus, this approach is not only interested in technical issues of language deployment but typically has an underlying concern with issues of

---

[10] Other social psychologists of the media have also explored the role of the media in exacerbating the gap between publically expressed opinion and individuals' privately held attitudes (e.g. McCombs & Shaw, 1972; Noelle-Neumann, 1974).

social relationships and power. Similarly, within social psychology more generally, discursive approaches are increasingly following this linguistic turn, subordinating social theoretical considerations to a relatively implicit commitment to the analysis of power (Potter & Wetherell, 1987). The second approach also offers a more detailed analysis of language than is traditional in media studies, but from a broader, interdisciplinary and social theoretical perspective; thus it trades a less technical or systematic approach to language against a greater stress on social theory and social context (here he cites our book, *Talk on Television*; Livingstone & Lunt, 1994). Another example is the social semiotics approach (Hodge & Kress, 1988; Jensen, 1995) where both visual and verbal codes are included in analyses linking production and reception.

A key problematic here is the relation between language use and context. Linguistic-centred approaches emphasize indexicality, viewing context as immanent in discourse, and so conducting the analysis of spontaneous speech with a minimum of social and psychological assumptions, no appeal to abstract analytic concepts being required beyond those required to analyse the indexical codes. The difficulty of analysing language use in context when it comes to the media is the possibility that indexicality works better for informal conversations between friends than it does for mediated quasi-interactions and institutionally structured forms of talk. The difficulty of arguing for indexicality for the complex interplay between different forms of knowledge in complex institutional relationships suggests that social theory is a necessary adjunct to the analysis of discourse (Thompson, 1995).

While the argument over whether an analysis of language alone is enough, or whether a non-linguistic account of the context (institutional, cultural, situational, psychological) must also be included will continue, it is surely clear that the study of language and the media is at the forefront of a revitalization of social psychological interest in media and communications. A wide range of recent work takes seriously both language in the media and language surrounding the media (among audiences, publics and elites). While little synthetic work on language and the media has yet appeared in the social psychological literature, partly because disciplinary lines are difficult to draw between social psychology and media studies, the questions, the debates, the methods and the insights arc undoubtedly interesting and likely to be productive of further development.

REFERENCES

Abercrombie, N. (1996). *Television and Society*. Cambridge, UK: Polity Press.
Bakhtin, M.M. (1981). The dialogic imagination. In M. Holquist, C. Emerson & M. Holquist (Eds), *The dialogic imagination: Four essays*. Austin, TA: University of Texas Press.
Billig, M. (1991). *Talking of the Royal Family*. London: Routledge.
Blumler, J.G. & Katz, E. (Eds) (1974). *The uses of mass communications: Current perspectives on gratification research*. Beverly Hills, CA: Sage.
Bull, P. (1998). Equivocation theory and news interviews. *Journal of Language and Social Psychology*, **17**(1), 36–51.

Carey, J.W. (1989). *Communication as culture: Essays on media and society.* New York: Routledge.

Clayman, S.E. (1991) News interview openings: Aspects of sequential organization. In P. Scannell (Ed.), *Broadcast Talk* (pp. 48–75). London: Sage.

Corner, J. (1999) *Critical Ideas in Television Studies.* Oxford: Oxford University Press.

Dayan D. & Katz, E. (1992). *Media Events: The live broadcasting of history.* Cambridge, MA: Harvard University Press.

Doise, W. (1993). Debating social representations. In G. Breakwell & D. Canter (Eds), *Empirical, approaches to social representations* (pp. 157–170). Oxford: Oxford University Press.

Eco, U. (1979). *The role of the reader: Explorations in the semiotics of texts.* Bloomington, IN: Indiana University Press.

Fairclough, N. (1995). *Media discourse.* London: Edward Arnold.

Fraser, N. (1990). Rethinking the public sphere: A contribution to the critique of actually existing democracy. *Social Text*, **25/26**, 56–80.

Gamson, W.A. (1992). *Talking Politics.* Cambridge, UK: Cambridge University Press.

Garton, G., Montgomery, M. & Tolson, A. (1991). Ideology, scripts and metaphors in the public sphere of a general election. In P. Scannell (Ed.), *Broadcast talk* (pp. 100–118). London: Sage.

Habermas, J. (1969/89). *The structural transformation of the public sphere: An inquiry into a category of Bourgeois society.* Cambridge, MA: MIT Press.

Habermas, J. (1981/87). *The theory of communicative action: Vol 2.Lifeworld and system: A critique of functionalist reason.* Cambridge, UK: Polity, Press.

Hall, S. (1980). Encoding/decoding. In S. Hall, D. Hobson, A. Lowe & P. Willis (Eds), *Culture, media, language.* London: Hutchinson.

Hall, S. (1994). Reflections on the encoding/decoding model. In J. Cruz & J. Lewis (Eds), *Viewing, reading, listening: Audiences and cultural reception* (pp. 128–138). Boulder, CO: Westview Press.

Heritage, J.C., Clayman, S. & Zimmerman, D.H. (1988). Discourse and message analysis: The micro-structure of mass media messages. In R.P. Hawkins, J.M. Weimann & S. Pingree (Eds), *Advancing Communication Science: Merging mass and interpersonal processes* (pp. 77–108). Newbury Park, CA: Sage.

Hodge, R. & Kress, G. (1988). *Social semiotics.* Cambridge, UK: Polity Press.

Hoijer, B. (1990) Studying viewers' reception of television programmes: Theoretical and methodological considerations. *European Journal of Communication*, **5**(1), 29–56.

Holub, R.C. (1984). *Reception theory: A critical introduction.* London: Methuen.

Jauss, H.R. (1982). *Towards an aesthetic of reception.* Minneapolis: University of Minnesota Press.

Jensen, K.B. (1995). *The Social semiotics of mass communication.* London: Sage.

Lasswell, H.D. (1948). The structure and function of communication in society. In L. Bryson (Ed.), *The communication of ideas* (pp. 37–51). New York: Harper.

Levy, M.R. & Gurevitch, M. (Eds) (1994). *Defining media studies: Reflections on the future of the field.* New York: Oxford University Press.

Liebes, T. (1992). Decoding television news: The political discourse of Israeli Hawks and Doves. *Theory and Society*, **21**, 357–381.

Liebes, T. & Katz, E. (1990). *The export of meaning: Cross-cultural readings of DALLAS.* New York: Oxford University Press.

Livingstone, S.M. (1996). On the continuing problems of media effects research. In J. Curran & M. Gurevitch (Eds), *Mass media and society* (2nd edn) (pp. 305–324). London: Edward Arnold.

Livingstone, S. (1998). *Making sense of television* (2nd edn). London: Routledge.

Livingstone, S & Lunt P. (1994). *Talk on television: Audience participation and public debate.* London: Routledge.

Mackay, H. & O'Sullivan, T. (Eds) (1999). *The media reader: Continuity and transformation.* London: Sage.

McCombs, M.E. & Shaw, D. (1972). The agenda-setting function of the mass media. *Public Opinion Quarterly*, **36**, 176–187.

Montgomery, M. (1991). Our tune: A study of a discourse genre. In P. Scannell (Ed.), *Broadcast Talk* (pp. 138–177). London: Sage.

Morley, D. (1980). *The Nationwide Audience: Structure and decoding.* London: British Film Institute.

Morley, D. (1981). The nationwide audience: A critical postscript. *Screen Education*, **39**, 3–14.

Morley, D. (1992). *Television, audiences and cultural studies.* London: Routledge.

Negt, O. & Kluge, A. (1990). Selections from "Public opinion and practical knowledge: toward an organisational analysis of proletariat and middle class public opinion". *Social Text*, **25/26**, 24–32.

Noelle-Neumann, E. (1974). The spiral of silence: A theory of public opinion. *Journal of Communication*, **24**(2), 43–52.

Pillai, P. (1992). Rereading Stuart Hall's encoding/decoding model. *Communication Theory*, **2**(3), 221–233.

Potter, J. & Wetherell, M. (1987). *Discourse and social psychology: Beyond attitudes and behaviour.* London: Sage.

Radway, J. (1984). *Reading the romance: Women, patriarchy and popular literature.* Chapel Hill, NC: University of North Carolina Press.

Scannell, P. (Ed.) *Broadcast Talk.* London: Sage.

Suleiman, S. & Crosman, I. (Eds) (1980). *The Reader in the text.* Princeton, NJ: Princeton University Press.

Thompson, J.B. (1995). *The media and modernity: A social theory of the media.* Cambridge, UK: Polity.

van Dijk, T.A. (1991). *Racism and the Press.* London: Routledge.

Social Psychological Theories of Computer-Mediated Communication: Social Pain or Social Gain

Russell Spears
University of Amsterdam, The Netherlands
Martin Lea
University of Manchester, UK
Tom Postmes
University of Amsterdam, The Netherlands

INTRODUCTION AND OVERVIEW

It is a safe bet that computer-mediated communication (CMC) features in the everyday life of those likely to be consulting this volume. Less than two decades ago this would not have been the case. The growth of the Internet has meant that CMC use has become ubiquitous in the developed world, and a marker of social exclusion for those denied access. Social science has hardly kept pace with these technological changes in communication, either in terms of understanding their global impacts or their local effects. In this chapter we focus on the main social psychological theories that have been proposed to account for the effects of CMC on individuals and groups, and on the role of language as a medium and mediator for these effects. As such, this review is partial and excludes certain influential approaches, such as those with more sociological or business management underpinnings (e.g., Contractor & Seibold, 1993; DeSanctis & Poole, 1994; Valacich et al., 1992). The different

The New Handbook of Language and Social Psychology.
Edited by W. Peter Robinson and Howard Giles.
© 2001 John Wiley & Sons Ltd.

approaches reviewed below vary considerably in terms of their underlying theoretical foundations but a recurring theme is the extent to which CMC should be regarded as a medium that is capable of supporting social relations. In other words, "How social is CMC?" This issue has been vigorously debated in the literature, and has spawned theories that attempt to evaluate the relative "social efficiency" of CMC or else to identify specific conditions under which CMC may support or undermine social influence and social relations in general.

In addressing this theme, social psychological research has focused predominantly on text-based synchronous or asynchronous CMC, which have been compared both theoretically and empirically with face-to-face (FtF) communication or some other standard that controls for critical features of CMC. However, as technology advances, CMC can be realized in an increasing variety of forms ranging from electronic mail, through virtual reality systems to real-time audio/ video conferencing. These newer forms of CMC have received scant attention to date within social psychological research, although the results of earlier studies on audio and video conferencing prior to the development of CMC are clearly relevant (Short, Williams & Christie, 1976; Williams, 1977).

Nevertheless, research on CMC has focused upon a range of important domains within social psychology. Social influence and group decision-making are foremost among these in that they are central to social and work groups and the wider organizational context in which much CMC is used. Similarly, the impact that CMC has on status and power differences that operate in FtF interaction has been investigated. However, even more basic is the way that CMC affects the perceptions of others and even the definition of the self. How is identity defined in "cyberspace", where some of the visual reality constraints relating to physical embodiment and FtF communication do not always apply? How CMC affects group definition and group dynamics is also a central question for developing and evaluating new ways of working with this technology (e.g., teleworking, computer-supported collaborative work). CMC not only provides a context for communication within the group, but also for intergroup communication, traversing familiar social boundaries (gender, ethnicity, social status, etc.) as well as those of time and space. In such cases the sociality of CMC can be double-edged, with the proposed insensitivity of this medium to interpersonal differences being seen either as a way to increase social contact and consensus across social divides, or else as reinforcing social boundaries and divisions (Kiesler & Sproull, 1992; cf. Postmes, Spears & Lea, 1998a).

These considerations have direct relevance for language content and language use in CMC and on the Internet. The relation between communication and language is of course an intimate and entailing one. Language both affects and reflects the relation between interlocutors, it is the major means by which we communicate affiliation and intimacy, and also power and difference. Language is also central to our focus on the social psychological process of social influence in CMC. Even where it is not directly or explicitly implicated, language will form the medium of social influence, and will be used to convey information about group membership (through headers, signatures and other identifying labels), as well as carrying the message itself (persuasive arguments, perlocutionary acts, discourses, etc.). The text-based nature of CMC and Internet use mean that the focus on language and linguistic factors will be all the greater, especially in comparison with other communication media or channels.

It almost goes without saying that language, as a means of communication, and as a shared system of signs, is a social dimension par excellence. On this reasoning the text-based nature of CMC and the Internet should render them highly social media. However, this is worth saying because although language and sociality are closely bound up with each other, ironically perhaps the earliest social psychological research on text-based CMC has tended to propose that sociality is somehow undermined in this medium. This is because sociality has been defined more in terms of features of interpersonal interaction than in terms of language and communication. We now develop this theme, and have organized our brief review of theoretical approaches in this literature in terms of the increasing sociality that the theories assume for CMC.

THEORIES OF CMC

A central concept common to several theoretical approaches, and one that has influenced the presumed sociality of CMC, is communication bandwidth. This engineering concept has its origins in information theory: mathematical formulations of communication potentially applicable to any situation of information transfer, by humans or machines. Central to the information theory approach is the idea that communication can be quantified in terms of bits of information required to solve problems of uncertainty (Frick, 1959). Research on CMC has been heavily influenced by communications theory approaches grounded in the bandwidth principle, where the equation of technical efficiency of a communication medium with its "social efficiency" has paved the way for evaluations of sociality based on a mechanistic analysis of information transfer (Lea & Giordano, 1997). The focus on concepts from engineering and information theory (rather than, say, on sociolinguistics or semiotics) meant that research was probably bound to underestimate the social dimensions of CMC. The most influential of these early approaches is the Social Presence Model, the initial development of which predates CMC. We consider first this and then related approaches that have extended or contested this theoretical tradition.

The Social Presence Model

The Social Presence Model developed by Short et al. (1976) was concerned with communication via telephone, audio and video links and has been very influential in relation to subsequent research on CMC (e.g., Daft & Lengel, 1986; Johansen, 1977; Rice, 1984; Rice & Love, 1987). According to this model the critical factor in the communication medium is its "social presence", a factor that comprises a number of dimensions relating to degree of interpersonal contact, "intimacy" (Argyle & Dean, 1965), "immediacy" (Wiener & Mehrabian, 1968) and the personal–impersonal dimension (Champness, 1973). A series of studies suggested that communications media could effectively be ranked according to social presence (namely from business letters, telephone/single speaker audio, multiple speaker audio, television, up to face-to-face communication). CMC might be assumed to occupy a relatively low-position level in this ranking. Indeed, Rice (1993a) tested a multidimensional scale of social presence based upon perceived satisfaction or appropriateness of media for a range of communication tasks thought to be influenced by a medium's social presence (such as making decisions, generating ideas, persuasion and maintaining friendly relations). Perceptions of media appropriateness, drawn from surveys in six organizations, placed electronic mail at the lowest place in the hierarchy. However, perceptions of media appropriateness were only weakly associated with actual use of the media for the various tasks.

Other comparative media analyses have produced mixed results. Some have supported the ranking implied by the social presence model, whereas others have identified a number of conditions under which the relative positions that media occupy give way to more important considerations, or else can be overturned (e.g., Burke & Chidambaram, 1996; Daft & Lengel, 1986; Hiemstra, 1982; Lea, 1991; Reid, 1977; Rice, 1987, 1992; Rice & Love, 1987; Rice & Williams, 1984; Sproull & Kiesler, 1986; Sumner, 1988; Steinfield, 1986; see also Walther, 1992). Nevertheless the influence of this model has determined the direction of subsequent theorizing. In particular it has fostered the assumption that CMC is less social, and thus less conducive to social influence compared to higher social presence media such as FtF communication. This is somewhat ironic because the early results of Short et al. (1976) suggested that lower presence (e.g., auditory channel only) resulted in greater social influence than higher presence. However, before addressing other theories that specifically address social influence in CMC, we first consider two more approaches that are predicated upon the notion of communication bandwidth.

Media Richness Theory: The effects of choosing CMC

A similar theoretical concept, media richness, has been developed by Daft and Lengel (1984, 1986), apparently without awareness of the earlier social presence research. Although a theory of media choice rather than media effects (see, for example, Fulk & Boyd, 1991), it makes important assumptions about media effects, many of which it shares with the social presence tradition. The theory is rooted in organizational information processing theory which identifies resolving ambiguity and reducing uncertainty as the main goals of communication (Galbraith, 1973). The central proposition is that communication media can be arrayed along a continuum of media richness based on their capacity for processing equivocal information;

communication failures can be explained by a mismatch between the equivocality of a communication task and the richness of the chosen medium.

Four factors have been proposed to determine media richness: (1) the ability of the medium to transmit multiple cues, (2) the immediacy of feedback, (3) the use of natural language and (4) the personal focus of the medium. According to these criteria, it is usually assumed that CMC would be perceived as a relatively "lean" medium, at least in comparison with FtF interaction. As such it should be best suited to fairly routine and low-level communication uses. Although some studies tended to support the media richness ranking for traditional media, large variances relative to very small mean differences have been reported for electronic mail and other mid-ranking media, suggesting considerable variation in media use unaccounted for by the richness continuum (Fulk & Boyd, 1991).

An important corollary of this approach is that the richness of the medium should be chosen to match the equivocality or uncertainty associated with the particular communication task. Indeed, most tests of this theory have been concerned with the perceptions of media fit rather than evaluating actual efficiency of performance (Dennis & Kinney, 1998). However, studies that have examined the match between media have not always provided support, and in practice it seems that many factors beyond media richness affect media choice (e.g., Markus, 1987, 1994; Zmud, Ling & Young, 1990). For example, in a comparative study of a range of media, including CMC, Dennis and Kinney (1998) found little effect of media choice on decision quality and even contradictory evidence. In sum, the effects of media such as CMC do not seem to bear a straightforward relation to the amount of information exchange of the medium.

Later modifications to the model have extended it beyond its original strictly informational base. Borrowing from structural symbolic interactionism, Trevino, Daft and Lengel (1990) suggested that "external forces" or contextual factors might influence media choice. These include distance, time pressure, accessibility of the medium and the existence of a critical mass of users. Furthermore the revised symbolic interactionist perspective of media choice recognizes that symbolic meanings of different media that are independent of message content ("the medium is the message") can also affect communication outcomes.

Problems with the Social Presence/Media Richness Perspectives

To summarize, social presence and media richness are conceptually similar approaches that distinguish between communication media and their differential effects primarily in terms of the information-processing capacity of the media. Both predict that perceptions of this capacity influence the appropriateness and use of media for different tasks, particularly within an organizational context.

However, a number of criticisms can be levelled at these relatively deterministic approaches to CMC effects. In particular, the matching hypothesis equates communication efficiency with the non-redundancy of information since richer media are supposedly only used because there is more information to communicate. However, in human communication redundancy may be useful in communicating meaning. Relatedly, both models assume that maximum communication efficiency is equated with maximum organizational efficiency. But there are situations in which media are strategically used to distance communication or increase uncertainty, especially in hierarchical organizational communications (e.g., communicating on a "need-to-know" basis for forward planning, or managing disputes). Media choice in these circumstances may not be so much a matter of increasing communication efficiency as using media to maintain and reinforce existing power relations.

More generally, these models lack specificity about the processes involved both in arriving at consensual perceptions of media and their effects. While both approaches have collapsed multidimensional scales onto single factors, recent studies have suggested the need to incorporate additional dimensions in order to account for variations in media choice unexplained by the original concepts (Rice, 1993b; Valacich et al., 1993). However, these additions further undermine the notion that a single concept is sufficient to explain media perceptions and choice. Moreover, even if social presence or media richness could be shown to provide a reliable explanation of comparison and choice between media, they are poorly placed to account for the variability of uses *within* a specific medium such as electronic mail, which may demand varying levels of information processing ability. Instead, a more refined approach to task analysis may be necessary in order to understand interaction and predict outcomes in which, for example, the nature of the group, the task, the situation and the environment are taken into account (Lebie, Rhoades & McGrath, 1996; McGrath, 1984). Nevertheless, insofar as these models rely upon the information processing capacity, or the bandwidth of a medium to explain differences between media, one should find smaller differences in effects once temporal factors in communication are taken into account. This has been a key issue in the work of McGrath and colleagues (e.g., McGrath & Hollingshead, 1993; Hollingshead, McGrath & O'Connor, 1993), and is also the central theme in the Social Information Processing approach developed by Walther (1992, 1995), considered next.

The Social Information Processing Model

We do not deal with this approach in great detail.[1] However, it is important to sketch the main features of this approach. The Social Information Processing model draws on impression formation literature and argues that these processes in CMC are unlikely to be radically different from the impression formation processes implicated in FtF, but just operate on a slower timescale, commensurate with the slower rate of social information exchange in CMC. Walther (1992)

---

[1] This approach is not to be confused with the similarly titled social information processing approach developed by Fulk et al. (1987) to explain patterns of media adoption and use in organizations.

argues that the limited bandwidth of CMC forces social information into a single linguistic channel that retards impression formation relative to FtF interaction, leading to more impersonal communication and negative evaluations of others in CMC relative to FtF. This model therefore attempts to clarify the effects of bandwidth restriction in CMC as retarding rather than removing social information exchange from interaction. This in turn implies that in longitudinal studies or research using longer timescales, in which information exchange in CMC was commensurate with FtF, interactants would get to a similar position in the end in terms of relational development.

Two key propositions follow from this approach, namely that more impersonal, task-focused communication and less positive social evaluations of other interactants should be observed in short-term CMC than in FtF interaction or long-term CMC. However, tests of these propositions have met with only limited success. Indeed, some studies found less impersonal focus and greater attraction in short-term CMC than in FtF, directly contrary to predictions (Walther, 1995; Walther & Burgoon, 1992). Meta-analyses of previous experimental studies also tend to contest the inevitability of impersonal task focus and reduced sociality within short-term CMC. One such analysis supported greater task focus in CMC decision-making groups, compared to equivalent FtF groups (McLeod, 1992), but a wider analysis of anonymity in group CMC did not (Postmes & Lea, 2000). A further analysis that directly examined interaction time found a small effect of time on the ratio of socially oriented communication in CMC, compared to FtF, but no effect on the level of antisocial communication (Walther, Anderson & Park, 1994). Taken together, these results suggest that limited bandwidth communication (such as in text-based CMC) has at most only small and inconsistent effects on social communication and relational development that are not well explained by temporal factors.

More recently, the social information processing determination of CMC effects has been revised to incorporate contextual factors, such as anticipation of future interaction and group salience. For example, anticipation of future interaction was found to be a better predictor of dyadic relational communication than communication channel, which in turn moderated rather than determined these effects. In group CMC, high group salience was found to support greater intimacy levels within long-term CMC groups than low group salience conditions (Walther, 1994, 1997).

To summarize, various information processing approaches that have their theoretical roots in the engineering concept of communication bandwidth have proposed that limiting information exchange will have deleterious effects on social communication. However, evidence is weak that the "social nature" of CMC can be determined in such a direct manner from technical efficiency – regardless of whether this is cast in terms of social presence, information richness, or social information processing. The next approach, while it acknowledges these implications of reduced bandwidth and social exchange in CMC, focuses instead on the social psychological states and processes that might mediate its effects particularly on communication within groups.

The Reduced Social Cues Model

The Reduced Social Cues (RSC) model evolved out of a major investigation of the processes by which the reduction of non-verbal cues and other contextual information in CMC, relative to FtF, might affect the social behaviour of individuals and groups (e.g., Kiesler, 1986; Kiesler, Siegel & McGuire, 1984; Kiesler & Sproull, 1992; Kiesler et al., 1985; McGuire, Kiesler & Siegel, 1987; Siegel et al., 1986; Sproull & Kiesler, 1986, 1991).

The basic thesis of the RSC approach is that reducing social cues encourages psychological states that undermine the social and normative influences on individuals or groups, leading to more deregulated and extreme ("antinormative") behaviour. A number of mechanisms are proposed to contribute to this outcome, chief of which is "deindividuation" (the reduced self-awareness and deregulation of behaviour accompanying immersion and anonymity in the group: e.g., Diener, 1980; Zimbardo, 1969; for a review of the deindividuation concept see Postmes & Spears, 1998). Deindividuation, it is argued, attenuates normative influence, and reduces evaluation concern, while the slowness and inefficiency of message exchange engender frustration and disinhibition. These factors are responsible in turn for greater uninhibited, antisocial behaviour, group polarization and extreme decision-making, observed in CMC (Kiesler, 1986; Kiesler et al., 1984; Siegel et al., 1986). In linguistic terms these processes manifest themselves in use of more extreme, provocative or even insulting language, a phenomenon which has been termed "flaming" (e.g., Kiesler et al., 1984).

However, reducing social cues is also considered to have "beneficial" social consequences, such as helping to undermine status and power differentials, usually evident in FtF groups, leading to more equalized and egalitarian participation (e.g. Dubrovsky, Kiesler & Sethna, 1991; Kiesler & Sproull, 1992). In linguistic terms, the question that then arises is whether eliminating the focus on cues to status and power differentials might also eliminate the linguistic markers associated with these relations. So for example, the typical power-related differences found in gendered discourse might be reduced or even eliminated if gender is not visible to communicators. However, this proposition assumes that power-related gender differences in discourse depend in part or wholly on the tangibility (visibility, identifiability, accountability) of the categories rather than (quite literally) being engendered in the discourse itself. As we shall see this, assumption is questionable.

An initial series of experiments compared the effects of computer conferencing, electronic mail and FtF communication on communication efficiency, participation, interpersonal behaviour and group choice (Kiesler et al., 1984). Significantly more group polarization was observed in CMC conditions, accompanied by significantly less information exchange. There was also more uninhibited language ("flaming") in CMC (particularly anonymous CMC) than in FtF in two out of four experiments (Kiesler et al., 1985; Siegel et al., 1986). In addition, greater task focus and lower attraction responses were found in CMC

(Kiesler et al., 1985). However, a subsequent experiment found significantly more decision proposals, uninhibited behaviour and equality of participation in electronic mail, compared to FtF, but no difference in group polarization (Dubrovsky et al., 1991).

A major contribution of the RSC approach has been to develop a more sophisticated approach to understanding CMC effects that is grounded in established social psychological theory of group behaviour, rather than borrowing from information theory. More generally, it has helped to undermine the rationalist assumptions underlying many media comparisons, namely, that lack of social cues increases the rational efficiency of communication (Lea, 1991). Indeed, the very features identified as undermining sociality and thus leading to social dysfunction are those factors considered by group decision support theory to improve group productivity and efficient decision-making by managers (for example, by reducing pressures to conform, or group-think) through the use of computer-mediated group-decision support systems (e.g., Jessup, Connolly & Tansik, 1990; Pinsonneault & Heppel, 1998; Valacich, Dennis & Nunamaker, 1991; Valacich et al., 1993; for a review see Postmes & Lea, 2000).

These very differing views highlight the futility inherent in making general claims about the benefits and losses of CMC (social pain in one context may be interpreted as social gain in another), but more fundamentally they rest on certain difficulties and inconsistencies in the underlying social psychology theory and its mobilization to explain CMC effects. As a consequence, a number of specific criticisms have been levelled at the reduced social cues model, partly because of the uneven handling of the importance of the social dimension in group interaction (e.g., Lea & Spears, 1991; Matheson, 1992, Spears & Lea, 1992, 1994).

For example, the deregulated and antisocial psychological state of classic deindividuation theory is inconsistent with the relatively reasoned deliberation argued to underlie group polarization effects (informational influence/persuasive arguments theory). The role of self-awareness within the model is problematic for similar reasons. Whereas Siegel et al. (1986) argue for a heightened (private) self-awareness within CMC, deindividuation implies reduced (private) self-awareness. Instead, isolation at the computer terminal could be regarded as individuating rather than deindividuating, and this could help to explain evidence of greater (private) self-awareness in CMC observed in independent studies (Matheson & Zanna, 1988, 1989).

A more fundamental problem concerns the central thesis that group polarization follows from a weakening of social norms in CMC, when group norms and group influence are central explanatory concepts in accounting for group polarization (Isenberg, 1986; Mackie, 1986; Sanders & Baron, 1977; Turner, 1991; Wetherell, 1987). Part of the problem for the RSC model derives from the translation of the state of disinhibition, as reflected in uninhibited behaviour, into group polarization and more risky or extreme decisions. Disinhibition and the riskiness or extremity of decisions are arguably separate phenomena. This becomes more apparent when one considers that group polarization can also reflect shifts to caution, and not just risk, following group discussion (Fraser, Gouge & Billig, 1971; Pruitt, 1971). Hiltz, Turoff and Johnson (1989) obtained just such a cautious shift in a CMC study. These findings would seem hard to square with the idea that polarization reflects "disinhibition". Indeed there seems to be surprisingly little if any direct empirical support in the literature that CMC is characterized by an absence or weakening of social norms.

Subsequent research has also questioned whether status and power equalization is a generic consequence of CMC. There is evidence that CMC can reflect and even enhance status-related groupings (e.g., Postmes et al., 1998; Postmes & Spears, 2000; Weisband, Schneider & Connolly, 1995). For example, in the case of gender relations, if the power relations are already encoded to some extent within the discourse (e.g. Mulac, 1989; Mulac & Lundell, 1986; see also Ng & Reid, this volume, Chapter 4.19), then even individual and category anonymity is unlikely to eliminate gender speech markers or their consequences. In fact, some have argued that the anonymity associated with the CMC and the Internet may actually enhance gender differences by giving freer rein to typically uninhibited male behaviour such as flaming (Herring, 1996; see also Kramerae & Taylor, 1993; Spears & Lea, 1994; Spender, 1995). We discuss further reasons why this may be the case below, in relation to the SIDE model.

To summarize, the RSC model has been important and influential in highlighting the range of effects that CMC can have and relating these to the reduction in social cues within this medium. It has perhaps been less convincing in identifying or testing the precise mechanisms responsible for the effects. In particular, the claim that behaviour is less socially regulated or less subject to normative influences does not seem well founded. This is due in part to the theoretical eclecticism that has not always facilitated the parsimony of explanation or the clarity of predictions.

The Social Identity Model of Deindividuation Effects

Another model designed to analyse the social psychological effects of CMC has been developed by us and is termed the social identity model of deindividuation effects (SIDE). This model arose partly as a response to the reduced social cues approach described earlier, and contested the notion that CMC is less socially regulated than FtF communication (Lea & Spears, 1991; Spears & Lea, 1992). In this model an important distinction is drawn between different sorts of social cues that may be present (or absent) in CMC, namely interpersonal cues, and cues to social features, such as group identity and category membership. We argue that whereas CMC may indeed filter out many interpersonal cues that identify and individuate the communicators, group and category level cues that are communicated relatively independently of bandwidth considerations are thereby given more opportunity to influence interaction, and the definition of the self and situation.

The model extends a social identity critique of deindividuation theory previously applied to collective behaviour to the CMC domain (Reicher, 1984; Reicher, Spears & Postmes, 1995; Spears, Lea & Lee, 1990). According to this approach, deindividuation caused by immersion and anonymity in the group does not result in loss of identity or reduced self-awareness (as proposed by classical deindividuation theory and the reduced social cues approach), but rather this results in a shift of self-focus from personal to group identity. Social Identity Theory (Tajfel & Turner, 1986) and Self-Categorization Theory (Turner, 1987) provide the foundations for the model in proposing that the self is not in a fixed entity, but is socially defined in the context. Although our identity as unique individuals may be salient in many interpersonal situations, in intergroup contexts, where group identity is salient, we are likely to see ourselves and others in terms of this identity, and act in accord with the norms of this identity (Tajfel & Turner, 1986; Turner, 1987). The SIDE model extends the social identity analysis of self and behaviour by outlining how the salience and effects of social identity might be affected by key situational variables in the CMC context such as anonymity or identifiablity.

According to the SIDE model, anonymity can have two classes of effects, which we have termed "cognitive" and "strategic" (Reicher et al., 1995; Spears & Lea, 1994). The cognitive effects relate to the salience of a particular identity (personal identity or a group identity) and more precisely refer to issues of self-definition. Anonymity can function to enhance group salience by reducing attention to individual differences within the group (literally "deindividuation" or "depersonalization"). The strategic dimension refers to whether the individual or group member feels able to express behaviour in line with a particular identity, given that this is salient. This is particularly relevant in intergroup contexts in which a power relation is present between groups. In this case anonymity from a powerful outgroup may enable members of the other group to express group normative behaviour that might otherwise be punished or sanctioned by this group.

Research on CMC from the perspective of the SIDE model has to date largely concentrated on the cognitive effects of anonymity in enhancing group normative behavior. It should be noted that this prediction is directly opposite that of classical deindividuation theory which would predict antinormative behaviour under conditions of anonymity (e.g., Festinger, Pepitone & Newcomb, 1952; Diener, 1980; Zimbardo, 1969), and therefore is contrary to the predictions of the reduced social cues perspective. However, there is growing evidence that anonymous CMC does lead to increased social influence in line with group norms compared to FtF interaction or conditions of identifiability (Lea & Spears, 1991; Watt, Lea & Spears, in press; Postmes et al., 1998, in press; Spears et al., 1990). Moreover, a review of the deindividuation literature more generally provides strong support for a reinterpretation of the findings of this literature in terms of the SIDE model, as opposed to classical or contemporary versions of deindividuation theory (Postmes & Spears, 1998). Recent experimental research has also provided more direct support for the processes thought to mediate the effects of anonymity on the group, namely by enhancing group identification, self-categorization as a group member and self-stereotyping (Lea, Spears, Watt & De Groot, in press; Lea, Spears & de Groot, in press; Postmes et al., in press).

One of the implications of the SIDE approach is that, although behavioural effects can be accentuated by anonymity, there should be no generic effects or outcomes of CMC: this should depend on local norms relating to the particular personal or group identity. This forms a key divergence with the other social psychological approaches reviewed above, which explicitly predict an impersonal task focus in anonymous CMC, and is supported by several studies. For example, Lea, Spears and De Groot (in press) found no generic effect of task focus on attraction in CMC discussion groups; instead, perceived task focus increased (rather than reduced) attraction to the group for those participants who self-categorized with the group, in line with a local normative explanation of task focus effects.

Indeed there is evidence that behaviour in even short-term anonymous groups can become more socio-emotional rather than task oriented, if this is evident from group norms. Postmes et al. (in press) surreptitiously primed these two different types of group norms prior to a group discussion and found that subsequent group decision reflected these different norms but most strongly in anonymous groups. Moreover, evidence showed that this norm developed over time during group discussion. This group norm was also reflected in the language used by the participants, with more efficiency and task-oriented words used in the efficiency prime condition and more socio-emotional terms used in the socio-emotional prime condition. A further study showed that these norms, and the linguistic repertoires associated with them, were also transmitted to neutrally primed participants, demonstrating the operation of genuine social influence that was linguistically transmitted in group discussion.

Other research in a more naturalistic field setting using email groups has also confirmed that group norms develop over time, conforming to norms that are prototypical and distinctive for the group (Postmes, Spears & Lea, 2000). Content analysis of both the content and the form of group communication showed that over time language tended to conform to a prototypical pattern that characterized the content (but not necessarily the form) of group communication. Once again, then, this study confirmed that group-based CMC does not reflect a generic norm (e.g., impersonal, task oriented), but that norms are constructed in situ, and become reinforced within the group through mutual group influence.

This research also indicated that flaming was not generic to all groups but varied widely depending on the group norm. Moreover, analysis of the transcripts suggested that where flaming did occur it often did not reflect genuine insults, but was playful, ironic and reflected social intimacy rather than social distance. Once again the linguistic markers are highly variable and related to specific group norms developed in context. This confirmed our earlier review of the literature, which concluded that despite widespread acceptance of the ubiquity of flaming in CMC, it only occurred in a tiny proportion of CMC messages overall, and its absolute and relative frequency (compared to FtF) were overestimated by observers and reporters. This systematic bias in reporting on flaming in naturalistic settings is likely due to features that increase psychological and social (network) availability of flaming instances in CMC. The permanence of messages and other specific features of the text medium make specific instances of flaming more distinctive and memorable, and the one-to-many nature of group CMC means that any single instance of flaming is likely to be widely observed (Lea et al., 1992).

Indeed, rather than flaming being a general effect of the CMC medium, it appears to be restricted to certain groups, both in experimental studies and on Internet newsgroups, in line with a group normative explanation of their occurrence (Kayany, 1998; Lea et al., 1992). Paralanguage is another feature of CMC whose effects depend on local group context. Although the term is more commonly associated with non-verbal communication in FtF interaction (Edinger & Patterson, 1983), paralanguage is also present in written communication, where it takes the form of typographical marks and other features of the text that, although they have no lexical meaning, nevertheless signify socially shared meanings. In CMC conventional marks are supplemented by "emoticons": keyboard tricks that are used to produce codes that are interpreted only within the social conventions of CMC. Lea and Spears (1992) found that in deindividuated CMC high group salience causes paralanguage users to be judged as more uninhibited and at the same time to be more positively evaluated by the group than when group salience is low. Thus, the interpretation as well as the expression of uninhibited linguistic behaviour in CMC appears to conform to norms and standards of appropriate behaviour for the local group.

The linguistic transmission of group-based effects within CMC extends also to the promulgation and perpetuation of stereotypic representations of outgroups. Recent research by Wigboldus and colleagues (Wigboldus, Semin & Spears, 2000; Wigboldus, Spears & Semin, 1999) has demonstrated that stereotypes about outgroups are linguistically transmitted in interpersonal communication by means of the linguistic intergroup bias (LIB) and linguistic expectancy bias (LEB). LIB is the tendency to communicate negative information about outgroups and positive information about ingroups in more abstract terms, thereby reinforcing the favourable standing of the ingroup (Maass et al., 1989). LEB refers to more abstract characterizations of stereotype-consistent information, which thereby perpetuate stereotypic group representations. That these effects can prosper in anonymous intragroup communication in CMC confirms that CMC is far from an asocial medium, and shows that these group-level representations can be linguistically mediated.

Research more explicitly within the context of the SIDE model confirms that anonymity increases group-stereotypical perceptions in CMC (Lea, Spears & De Groot, in press; Lea, Spears, Watt & De Groot, in press), and that stereotyping as well as group norms and social influence are transmitted more readily within anonymous CMC than under conditions of identifiability. In a study by Postmes and Spears (1999), gender stereotypes were accentuated when gender identity was salient and participants were anonymous rather than identifiable. However, gender is a special category in the sense that it is also cued by visible features, so that identifiability may render gender salient at the same time as it individuates people. In this study cues to gender were somewhat artificially masked in the individuated conditions by presenting individual profiles of participants in order to exclude gender-identifying information. In more recent research we have tried to separate these two aspects. We have shown that under certain conditions identifiability can render gender more salient, while undermining the salience of categories that are less visibly designated, such as nationality (Watt et al., in press). In other words we should be wary of assuming that anonymity always leads to more group-level effects: this may depend on the nature of the group or category and whether its group essence is designated by visible features or not.

These processes relate to the cognitive dimensions of the SIDE model, and how anonymity (and in special cases visibility) can enhance the salience of group identities. However, the SIDE model also embraces a strategic dimension and once again anonymity versus identifiability can affect how people strategically present different identities depending on the groups or audiences to whom they feel accountable. For example, Reicher and colleagues have shown that people will be wary of flouting outgroup norms especially when these are punishable and when the ingroup members lack support from ingroup members (Reicher & Levine, 1994). CMC can isolate people, removing them from the co-presence of fellow ingroup members, and thereby cutting them off from visible social support (Spears & Lea, 1994). However, CMC also provides the communication medium by means of which support can be communicated. Some research suggests that resistance against outgroup norms may indeed be facilitated when communication by computers is available, and that this is mediated by social support (Spears, Lea & Postmes, in press).

The strategic dimensions of the SIDE model can also have implications in contexts where we feel identifiable to the ingroup as well as to the outgroup, while providing further insight into some of the linguistic mediators of these processes. An Internet study by Douglas and McGarty (in press) showed that people tended to stereotype a negative outgroup (right-wing racists) more clearly when identifiable to other like-minded people than when anonymous. This is contrary to the effect that might be expected from the cognitive component of SIDE, whereby group effects are usually exacerbated by anonymity. In this case, when identifiable to the ingroup, participants presumably wanted to make especially clear their opposition to a repugnant outgroup in line with the ingroup expectations. As in the research of Wigboldus and colleagues, this was reflected in more abstract linguistic descriptions of the negative aspects of the outgroup.

Consideration of these strategic effects shows the relevance of the SIDE model for understanding the effects of status and power differentials (Lea & Spears, 1995; Postmes & Spears, 1998; Spears & Lea, 1994). Identifiability to ingroup and outgroup audiences can result in behaviour compliant with norms and expectations of these groups. This results from the power of sanction in the case of powerful outgroup audiences. Greater compliance when accountable to an ingroup more often reflects the loss of face or credibility in failing to meet the standards of this audience. These effects are consistent with the argument of previous approaches that anonymity can offer some protection from status and power inequalities. However, power may have cognitive as well as strategic effects. In line with SIDE principles anonymity can have cognitive effects on the salience of the intergroup context, and thus enhance the impact of associated power differentials. Moreover, like other group-level effects, somewhat counterintuitively, we would expect anonymity to strengthen group boundaries and reinforce power relations associated with them. For example, in the study by Postmes and Spears (2000) described above, when gender identity was salient, anonymous CMC tended to reinforce gender inequalities in participation, compared to identifiable CMC. Other research also supports the accentuation of status difference within CMC (e.g., Herring 1994; Postmes et al., 1998; Spears & Lea, 1994; Weisband et al., 1995).

The SIDE model therefore challenges the notion that CMC will always or generally equalize status and power differentials should only occur if cues to category membership themselves are eliminated. However, as argued earlier this condition may be hard to achieve even in CMC because cues to enduring social categories such as class, gender and ethnicity are often subtly communicated in language, as well as through direct category markers. Gender markers in speech are well known (e.g., Mulac, 1989; Mulac & Lundell, 1986) and evidence is emerging that these are detected and acted upon in anonymous CMC (e.g., Herring, 1996). In one bulletin board study, men's messages were longer and used more "male language" (assertions, challenges, authoritative tone) than women's, who tended to use less confrontational and authoritative styles. The salience of these cues to gender is also revealed by their effects on participants' communication behaviour, which are dependent in turn on the social context for communication. In work group discussions, women's messages tend to receive fewer responses (from men and women) and topics initiated by women were less likely to be taken up by the group (Herring, 1994). However, in recreational situations, women's messages tend to receive more attention from men (Reid, 1994; Rosenberg, 1992).

The SIDE model is not without its shortcomings and criticisms. In common with competing models, empirical studies have concentrated on evaluating outcomes and the effects of moderating variables thereon. There has been less emphasis on testing the mediational processes responsible for CMC effects, although more attention is now being paid to this issue (Lea et al., 1998, in press; Postmes et al., in press). Until now, the SIDE model has tended to focus on certain features of the medium of CMC, notably anonymity, and has neglected the effects of other forms and associated features of CMC (e.g., communicator isolation, the text-based, often asynchronous/concurrent nature of communication). Anonymity itself should not be treated as a unitary construct, but needs to be decomposed (anonymity of self vs. identifiability to others) and degrees of anonymity further elaborated and investigated (Lea et al., in press; see also DeSanctis & Gallupe, 1987; Pinsonneault & Heppel, 1998). The SIDE model is also vulnerable to the demonstration that social influence can actually increase in identifiable rather than anonymous groups in some circumstances, and evidence of such exceptions is emerging. A distinction between different types of groups, namely those based on a common identity, and more interpersonal groups based on common bonds between group members, may be a critical moderating factor here (Spears & Postmes, 1998; Prentice, Miller & Lightdale, 1994). The distinction between the effects of categorization at the level of broader membership categories (e.g., gender, organizational affiliation) and the smaller in vivo groups implicated in the interaction also requires specification. Generalization to organizational contexts, further investigation of the effects of time as in the work of McGrath and Walther, and the interaction between the cognitive and strategic dimensions of the model (and the sometimes opposing predictions they make) are also areas for development. Further theoretical test and refinement therefore await.

CONCLUSIONS

To summarize, the majority of social psychological analyses of CMC have tended to focus on information loss, stressing the reduced sociality of the medium as a result. Consequently there has been a tendency for theories to argue for generic effects, deriving from the reduced or retarded social impact CMC engenders relative to FtF interaction. While various commentaries have eschewed this idea by stressing the complexity of the analysis of task, context and social interaction required in order to understand CMC effects (e.g. Fulk, Schmitz & Schwarz, 1992; McGrath, 1993; Mantovani, 1996), the SIDE model represents the main theoretical challenge from social psychology. In contrast to previous approaches it argues that sociality is not uniformly reduced, but that the interaction of features of the medium with local norms and conditions in the communication situation can accentuate the social form and content of behaviour of CMC in certain theoretically specified circumstances. Approaches that further identify localized factors and the interactions among them that influence communication behaviour and outcomes need to be further developed. Such research should probably try to steer clear from attempts to evaluate the balance between social pain versus social gain in CMC, and aim towards a greater understanding of the social implications of incorporating this new communication medium into everyday life.

What are the main implications of this analysis for language and language use in CMC and on the Internet? First it is important to note that CMC and the Internet are not linguistically unidimensional or impoverished media. Based on some analyses we could be forgiven for thinking that CMC (at least) is characterized by a rather impersonal task-oriented mono-culture that constrains the language used in this medium. On the contrary recent research and theorizing in both experimental and more ethnographic traditions point to the diversity of structure and content engendered by this medium, and reflected in its language use. The language used reflects the local norms that emerge in situ, which are tied to existing or emergent group identities. In this sense CMC and the Internet particularly provide some of the social freedoms, and channels for expression, not present in other media. The diversity of linguistic expression in CMC also serves to remind us not only of the social differences, but also that the centrality of language and communication make this a very social medium in general. Even where interaction is more impersonal and task oriented, we would argue that this reflects local social norms, and confirms the broader sociality of this medium.

None of this should be taken to imply that constraints on language are eliminated in CMC: these local norms reflect to some extent such constraints. However, these constraints extend to power relations and this is also reflected and also mediated through language. Some of the more optimistic accounts of CMC have argued that the anonymity of CMC equalizes status relations and eliminates power differentials. Both experimental and ethnographic research suggests that this is not always true, and that one way in which gender relations can be recognized and maintained is through linguistic markers. Even gender bending designed to escape one or other gender identity at the individual level tends to reinforce gender differences in the larger scale. Once again, although language is likely to play a key role in any communication medium, its effects are likely to be even stronger in text-based media such as CMC and the Internet. In other words language use is likely to be structured by social relations in CMC every bit is much as it is in FtF communication and perhaps more so. As the basis of communication and self-definition, language ensures the inherent sociality of these media.

ACKNOWLEDGEMENTS

All three authors contributed equally to writing this review, which was made possible by project grants from The British Council/NWO (UK–Dutch Joint Scientific Research Programme), ESRC (Virtual Society? Programme), EPSRC (Multimedia and Networking Applications Programme), the Royal Netherlands Academy of Arts and Sciences (KNAW), the Kurt Lewin Institute and the University of Amsterdam.

REFERENCES

Argyle, M. & Dean, J. (1965). Eye contact, distance and affiliation. *Sociometry*, **28**, 289–304.
Burke, K. & Chidambaram, L. (1996). Do mediated contexts differ in information richness? A comparison of collocated and dispersed meetings. *Proceedings of the Twenty Ninth Hawaii International Conference on System Sciences*, **29**, 92–101.
Champness, B.G. (1973). The assessment of user reactions to confravision: II. Analysis and conclusions. Unpublished MS, Communication Studies Group, University College, London.

Contractor, N.S. & Seibold, D.R. (1993). Theoretical frameworks for the study of structuring processes in group decision support systems: Adaptive structuration theory and self-organizing systems theory. *Human Communication Research*, **19**, 528–563.

Culnan, M.J. & Markus, M.L. (1987). Information technologies. In F.M. Jablin, L.L. Putnam, K.H. Roberts & L.W. Porter (Eds), *Handbook of organizational communication: An interdisciplinary perspective* (pp. 421–443). London: Sage.

Daft, R.L. & Lengel, R.H. (1984). information richness: A new approach to managerial behavior and organizational design. *Research in Organizational Behavior*, **6**, 191–233.

Daft, R.L. & Lengel, R.H. (1986). Organizational information requirement, media richness and structural determinants. *Management Science*, **32**, 554–571.

Dennis, A.R. & Kinney, S.T. (1998). Testing media-richness theory in the new media: The effects of cues, feedback, and task equivocality. *Information Systems Research*, **9**, 256–274.

DeSanctis, G. & Gallupe, R.B. (1987). A foundation for the study of group decision support systems. *Management Science*, **33**, 589–609.

DeSanctis, G. & Poole, M.S. (1994). Capturing the complexity in advanced technology use: Adaptive structuration theory. *Organization Science*, **5**, 121–147.

Diener, E. (1980). Deindividuation: The absence of self-awareness and self-regulation in group members. In P.B. Paulus (Ed.), *The psychology of group influence* (pp. 209–242). Hillsdale, NJ: Erlbaum.

Douglas, K. & McGarty, C. (in press). Identifiability and self-presentation: Computer-mediated communication and intergroup interaction. *British Journal of Social Psychiatry*.

Dubrovsky, V.J., Kiesler, S. & Sethna, B.N. (1991). The equalization phenomenon: Status effects in computer-meduated and face-to-face decision-making groups. *Human Computer Interaction*, **6**, 119–146.

Edinger, J. & Patterson, M. (1983). Nonverbal involvement and social control. *Psychological Bulletin*, **93**, 30–56.

Festinger, L., Pepitone, A. & Newcomb, T. (1952). Some consequences of deindividuation in a group. *Journal of Abnormal and Social Psychology*, **47**, 382–389.

Fraser, C., Gouge, C. & Billig, M. (1971). Risky shifts, cautious shifts and group polarization. *European Journal of Social Psychology*, **1**, 7–29.

Frick, F.C. (1959). Information theory. In S. Koch (Ed.), *Psychology: A study of science* (pp. 611–636). New York: McGraw-Hill.

Fulk, J. & Boyd, B. (1991). Emerging theories of communication in organizations. *Journal of Management*, **17**, 407–446.

Fulk, J., Steinfeld, C.W., Schmitz, J. & Power, J.G. (1987). A social information processing model of media use in organizations. *Communication Research*, **14**, 529–552.

Fulk, J., Schmitz, J.A. & Schwarz, D. (1992). The dynamics of context–behaviour interactions in computer-mediated communication. In M. Lea (Ed.), *Contexts of computer-mediated communication* (pp. 7–29). Hemel Hempstead, UK: Harvester-Wheatsheaf.

Galbraith, J. (1973). *Designing complex organizations*. Reading, MA: Addison-Wesley.

Herring, S. (1994). *Gender differences in computer-mediated communication: Bringing familiar baggage to the new frontier*. Paper presented at "Making the net*work*" symposium. American Library annual convention, Miami, FL, June.

Herring, S. (1996). Posting in a different voice: Gender and ethics in computer-mediated communication. In C. Ess (Ed.) *Philosophical perspectives on computer-mediated communication* (pp. 115–146). New York: State University of New York Press.

Hiemstra, G. (1982), Teleconferencing, concern for face, and organizational culture. *Communication Yearbook*, **6**, 874–904.

Hiltz, S.R., Turoff, M. & Johnson, K. (1989). Experiments in group decision making. 3: Disinhibition, deindividuation, and group process in pen name and real name computer conferences. *Decision Support Systems*, **5**, 217–232.

Hollingshead, A.B., McGrath, J.E. & O'Connor, K.M. (1993). Group task performance and communication technology: A longitudinal study of computer-mediated versus face-to-face work groups. *Small Group Research*, **24**, 307–333.

Isenberg, D.J. (1986). group polarization: A critical review and meta-analysis. *Journal of Personality and Social Psychology*, **50**, 1141–1151.

Jessup, L.M., Connolly, T. & Tansik, D.A. (1990). Toward a theory of automated group work: The deindividuating effects of anonymity. *Small Group Research*, **21**, 333–348.

Johansen, R. (1977). Social evaluations of teleconferencing. *Telecommunications Policy*, **1**, 395–419.

Kayany, J.M. (1998). Contexts of uninhibited online behavior: Flaming in social newsgroups on Usenet. *Journal of the American Society for Information Science*, **49**(12), 1135–1141.

Kiesler, S. (1986). The hidden messages in computer networks. *Harvard Business Review*, **64**, 46–60.

Kiesler, S. & Sproull, L. (1992). Group decision making and communication technology. *Organizational Behavior and Human Decision Processes*, **52**, 96–123.

Kiesler, S., Siegel, J. & McGuire, T. (1984). Social psychological aspects of computer-mediated communications. *American Psychologist*, **39**, 1123–1134.

Kiesler, S., Zubrow, D., Moses, A.M. & Geller, V. (1985). Affect in computer-mediated communciation: An experiment in synchronous terminal to terminal discussion. *Human Computer Interaction*, **1**, 77–104.

Kramerae, C. & Taylor, H.J. (1993). Women and men on electronic networks: A conversation or a monologue? In H.J. Taylor, C. Kramerae & M. Ebben (Eds), Women, information technoloogy and scholarship (pp. 52–61). Urbana-Champaign, IL: Center for Advanced Studies.

Lea, M. (1991). Rationalist assumptions in cross-media comparisons of computer-mediated communication. *Behaviour & Information Technology*, **10**, 153–172.

Lea, M. & Giordano, R. (1997). Representations of the group and group processes in CSCW research: A case of premature closure? In G.C. Bowker, S. L. Star, W. Turner & L. Gasser (Eds). *Social Science, Technical Systems and Cooperative Work: Beyond the Great Divide.* Mahwah, NJ: Erlbaum.

Lea, M. & Spears, R. (1991). Computer-mediated communication, de-individuation and group decision-making, *International Journal of Man-Machine Studies* (special issue on CSCW and groupware), **39**, 283–301. Reprinted in S. Greenberg (Ed.) (1991). *Computer-supported co-operative work and groupware.* London: Academic Press.

Lea, M. & Spears, R. (1992). Paralanguage and social perception in computer-mediated communication. *Journal of Organizational Computing*, **2**, 321–342.

Lea, M. & Spears, R. (1995). Love at first byte? Building personal relationships over computer networks. In J.T. Wood & S. Duck. (Eds). *Understudied relationships: Off the beaten track* (pp. 197–233). Thousand Oaks, CA: Sage.

Lea, M., O'Shea, T., Fung, P. & Spears, R. (1992). "Flaming" in computer-mediated communication: Normative versus antinormative explanations. In M. Lea (Ed.), *Contexts of computer-mediated communication* (pp. 89–112). Hemel Hempstead: Harvester-Wheatsheaf.

Lea, M. Spears, R. & De Groot, D. (in press). Knowing me, knowing you: Effects of visual anonymity on self-categorization, stereotyping and attraction in computer-mediated groups. *Personality and Social Psychology Bulletin.*

Lea, M., Spears, R. Watt, S. & De Groot, D. (in press). Inside stories: Building a model of anonymity effects using structural equation modeling. In T. Postmes, R. Spears, M. Lea & S.D. Reicher (Eds), *SIDE issues centre-stage: Recent developments of de-individuation in groups. Proceedings of the Dutch Royal Academy of Arts and Sciences.* North-Holland: Amsterdam.

Lebie, L., Rhoades, J.A. & McGrath, J.E. (1996). Interaction processes in computer-mediated and face to face groups. *Computer Supported Cooperative Work*, **4**, 127–152.

Maass, A., Salvi, D., Arcuri, L. & Semin, G. (1989). Language use in intergroup contexts: The linguistic intergroup bias. *Journal of Personality and Social Psychology*, **57**, 981–993.

Mackie, D.M. (1986). Social identification effects in group polarization. *Journal of Personality and Social Psychology*, **50**, 720–728.

Mantovani, G. (1996). Social context in HCL: A new framework for mental models, cooperation, and communication. *Cognitive Science*, **20**, 237–269.

Markus, M.L. (1987). Towards a "critical mass" theory of interactive media: Universal access, interdependence and diffusion. *Communication Research*, **14**(5), 491–511.

Markus, M.L. (1994). Electronic mail as the medium of managerial choice. *Organizational Science*, **5**, 502–527.

Matheson, K. (1992). Women and computer technology: Communicating for herself. In M. Lea (Ed.), *Contexts of computer-mediated communication* (pp. 66–88), Hemel Hempstead: Harvester-Wheatsheaf.

Matheson, K. & Zanna, M.P. (1988). The impact of computer-mediated communication on self-awareness. *Computers in Human Behavior*, **4**, 221–233.

Matheson, K. & Zanna, M.P. (1989). Persuasion as a function of self-awareness in computer-mediated communication. *Social Behaviour*, **4**, 99–111.

McGrath, J.E. (1984). *Groups: Interaction and performance.* Englewood Cliffs, NJ: Prentice-Hall.

McGrath, J.E. (1993). Time, task, and technology in work groups: The Jemco workshop study (Preface to special issue). *Small Group Research*, **24**, 283–284.

McGrath, J.E. & Hollingshead, A.B. (1993). Putting the "group" back in group support systems: Some theoretical issues about dynamic processes in groups with technological enhancements. In J. Valacich (Ed.), *Group support systems: New perspectives* (pp. 78–96). New York: Macmillan.

McGuire, T.W., Kiesler, S. & Siegel, J. (1987). Group and computer-mediated discussion effects in risk decision making. *Journal of Personality and Social Psychology*, **52**, 917–930.

McLeod, P.L. (1992). An assessment of the experimental literature on electronic support of group work: Results of a meta-analysis. *Human Computer Interaction* (Special issue on computer-supported cooperative work), **7**, 257–280.

Mulac, A. (1989). Men's and women's talk in same-gender and mixed-gender dyads: Power or polemic? *Journal of Language and Social Psychology*, **8**, 249–270.

Mulac, A. & Lundell, T.L. (1986). Linguisitic contributors to the gender-linked language effect. *Journal of Language and Social Psychology*, **5**, 81–101.

Pinsonneault, A. & Heppel, N. (1998). Anonymity in group support systems research: A new conceptualization, measure, and contingency framework. *Journal of Management Information Systems*, **14**, 89–108.

Postmes, T. & Lea, M. (2000). Social processes and group decision making: Anonymity in group decision support systems. *Ergonomics* (Special issue on contemporary theory and methods in the analysis of team working), **43**, 1152–1274.

Postmes, T. & Spears, R. (1998). Deindividuation and anti-normative behavior: A meta-analysis. *Psychological Bulletin*, **123**, 238–259.

Postmes, T. & Spears, R. (2000). Contextual moderators of gender differences: Behavior and stereotyping in computer-mediated groups. Manuscript submitted for publication.

Postmes, T., Spears, R. & Lea, M. (1998). Breaching or building social boundaries? SIDE-effects of computer mediated communication. *Communication Research* (Special issue on (mis)communicating across boundaries), **25**, 689–715.

Postmes, T., Spears, R., Sakhel, K. & De Groot, D. (in press). Social influence in computer-mediated communication: The effects of deindividuation on group behavior. *Personality and Social Psychology Bulletin*.

Postmes, T., Spears, R. & Lea, M. (2000). The formation of group norms in computer-mediated communication. *Human Communication Research*, **26**, 341–371.

Prentice, D.A., Miller, D.T. & Lightdale, R.J. (1994). Asymmetries in attachments to groups and to their members: Distingusihing between common-identity and common-bond groups. *Personality and Social Psychology Bulletin*, **20**, 484–493.

Pruitt, D.G. (1971). Choice shifts in group discussion: An introductory review. *Journal of Personality and Social Psychology*, **20**, 339–360.

Reicher, S.D. (1984). Social influence in the crowd: Attitudinal and behavioural effects of deindividuation in conditions of high and low group salience. *British Journal of Social Psychology*, **23**, 341–350.

Reicher, S.D. & Levine, M. (1994). Deindividuation, power relations between groups and the expression of social identity: The effects of visibility to the out-group. *British Journal of Social Psychology*, **33**, 145–164.

Reicher, S.D., Spears, R. & Postmes, T. (1995). A social identity model of deindividuation phenomena. *European Review of Social Psychology*, **6**, 161–198.

Reid, A. (1977). Comparing telephone with face-to-face contact. In I. de Sola Poole (Ed.), *The social impact of the telephone*. Cambridge, MA: MIT Press.

Reid, E. (1994). Cultural formations in text-based virtual realities. Unpublished MA thesis, University of Melbourne.

Rice, R.E. (1984). *The new media: Communication, research and technology*. Beverly Hills, CA: Sage.

Rice, R.E. (1987). Computer-mediated communication and organizational innovation. *Journal of Communication*, **37**, 65–94.

Rice, R.E. (1992). Task analyzability, use of new media, and effectiveness: A multi-site exploration of media richness. *Organization Science*, **3**, 475–500.

Rice, R.E. (1993a). Media appropriateness: Using social presence theory to compare traditional and new organizational media. *Human Communication Research*, **9**, 451–484.

Rice, R.E. (1993b). Using network concepts to clarify sources and mechanisms of social influence. In W. Richards Jr & G. Barnett (Eds), *Progress in communication sciences* (Vol. 12, pp. 45–62). Norwood, NJ: Ablex.

Rice, R.E. & Love, G. (1987). Electronic emotion: Socio-emotional content in a computer-mediated communication network. *Communication Research*, **14**, 85–108.

Rice, R.E. & Williams, F. (1984). Theories old and new: The study of new media. In R. E. Rice et al. (Eds), *The new media: Communication, research, and technology*. Beverly Hills, CA: Sage.

Rosenberg, M.S. (1992). Virtual reality: Reflections of life, dreams and technology. An ethnography of a computer society. *Electronic Journal on Virtual Culture*, **1**, [machine-readable file available through listserv@kentvm.kent.edu].

Sanders, G.S. & Baron, R.S. (1977). Is social comparison irrelevant for producing choice shifts? *Journal of Experimental Social Psychology*, **13**, 303–314.

Schmitz, J. & Fulk, J. (1991). Organizational colleagues, media richness, and electronic mail: A test of the social influence model of technology use. *Communication Research*, **18**, 487–523.

Short, J., Williams, E. & Christie, B. (1976). *The social psychology of telecommunications*. Chichester: Wiley.

Siegel, J., Dubrovsky, V., Kiesler, S. & McGuire, T. (1986). Group processes in computer-mediated communication. *Organizational Behaviour and Human Decision Processes*, **37**, 157–187.

Spears, R. & Lea, M. (1992). Social influence and the influence of the "social" in computer-mediated communication. In M. Lea (Ed.), *Contexts of computer-mediated communication*. (pp. 30–65). Hemel Hempstead: Harvester-Wheatsheaf.

Spears, R. & Lea, M. (1994). Panacea or panopticon: The hidden power in computer-mediated communication. *Communication Research*, **21**, 427–459.

Spears, R. & Postmes, T. (1998). *Anonymity in computer-mediated communication: Different groups have different SIDE effects*. Paper presented in "Social psychology on the web" symposium, Society for Experimental Social Psychology, Lexington, KY, October.

Spears, R., Lea, M. & Lee, S. (1990). De-individuation and group polarization in computer-mediated communication. *British Journal of Social Psychology*, **29**, 121–134.

Spears, R., Lea, M. & Postmes, T. (in press). On SIDE: Purview, problems, prospects. In T. Postmes, R. Spears, M. Lea & S.D. Reicher (Eds). *SIDE issues centre stage: Recent developments of de-individuation in groups. Amsterdam: Proceedings of the Dutch Royal Academy of Arts and Sciences*. Amsterdam: North-Holland.

Spender, D. (1995). Nattering on the net: Women, power and cyberspace. North Melbourne, Australia: Spinifex Press.

Sproull, L. & Kiesler, S. (1986). Reducing social context cues: Electronic mail in organizational communication. *Management Science*, **32**, 1492–1512.

Sproull, L. & Kiesler, S. (1991). *Connections: New ways of working in the networked organization*. Cambridge, MA: MIT Press.

Steinfield, C.W. (1986). Computer-mediated communication in an organizational setting: Explaining task-related and socioemotional uses. *Communication yearbook*, **9**, 777–804.

Sumner, M. (1988). The impact of electronic mail on managerial and organizational communications. In P.B. Allen (Ed.), *Proceedings of the IFIP conference on office information systems*, Palo Alto, CA. March. New York: ACM.

Tajfel, H. & Turner, J.C. (1986). The social identity theory of intergroup behaviour. In S. Worchel & W.G. Austin (Eds), *Psychology of intergroup relations* (pp. 7–24). Chicago: Nelson-Hall.

Trevino, L.K., Daft, R.L. & Lengel, R.H. (1990). Understanding managers' media choices: A symbolic interactionist perspective. In J. Fulk & C. Steinfield (Eds), *Organizations and communication technology* (pp. 71–94). Newbury Park: Sage.

Turner, J.C. (1987). A self-categorization theory. In Turner, J.C., Hogg, M.A., Oakes, P.J., Reicher, S.D. & Wetherell, M.S. (1987). *Rediscovering the social group: A self-categorization theory*. Oxford: Blackwell.

Turner, J.C. (1991). *Social influence*. Milton Keynes, UK: Open University Press.

Valacich, J.S., Dennis, A.R. & Nunamaker, J.F. (1991). Electronic meeting support: The GroupSystems concept. Special Issue: Computer-supported cooperative work and groupware: I. International Journal of Man Machine Studies, **34**, 261–282.

Valacich, J.S., Jessup, L.M., Dennis, A.R. & Nunamaker, J.F. (1992). A conceptual framework of anonymity in group support systems. *Group Decision and Negotiation*, **1**, 219–241.

Valacich, J.S., Paranka, D., George, J.F. & Nunamaker, J.F. (1993). Communication concurrency and the new media: A new dimension for media richness. *Communication Research*, **20**, 249–276.

Walther, J.B. (1992). Interpersonal effects in computer-mediated interaction: A relational perspective. *Communication Research*, **19**, 52 90.

Walther, J.B. (1994). Anticipated ongoing interaction versus channel effects on relational communication in computer-mediated interaction. *Human Communication research*, **20**, 473–501.

Walther, J.B. (1995). Relational aspects of computer mediated communication: Experimental observations over time. *Organization Science*, **6**, 186–203.

Walther, J.B. (1997). Group and interpersonal effects in international computer-mediated collaboration. *Human Communication Research*, **23**, 342–369.

Walther, J.B., & Burgoon, J.K. (1992). Relataional communicaiton in computer-mediated interaction. *Human Communication Research*, **19**, 50–88.

Walther, J.B., Anderson, J.F. & Park, D.W. (1994). Interpersonal effects in computer-mediated interaction: A meta-analysis of social and antisocial communication. *Communication Research*, **21**, 460–487.

Watt, S.E., Lea, M. & Spears, R. (in press). How social is Internet communication? Anonymity effects in computer-mediated groups. In S. Woolgar (Ed.), *Virtual Society? The social issue of electronic technologies*.

Weisband, S.P., Schneider, S.K. & Connolly, T. (1995). Computer-mediated communication and social information: Status salience and status differences. *Academy of Management Journal*, **38**, 1124–1151.

Wetherell, M.S. (1987). Social identity and group polarization. In J.C. Turner et al. *Rediscovering the social group: A self-categorization theory* (pp. 142–170). Oxford: Blackwell.

Wiener, M. & Mehrabian, A. (1968). *Language within language: Immediacy, a channel in verbal communication.* New York: Appleton-Century-Crofts.

Wigboldus, D., Spears, R. & Semin, G. (1999). Categorization, content and context of communicative behaviour. In N. Ellemers, R. Spears & B. Doosje (Eds), *Social identity: Context, commitment, content* (pp. 147–163). Oxford: Blackwell.

Wigboldus, D.H.J., Semin, G. & Spears, R. (2000). How do we communicate stereotypes? Linguistic bases and inferential consequences. *Journal of Personality and Social Psychology,* **78**, 5–18.

Williams, E. (1977). Experimental comparisons of face-to-face and mediated communication: A review. *Psychological Bulletin,* **84**, 963–976.

Zimbardo, P.G. (1969). The human choice: Individuation reason and order versus deindividuation impulse and chaos. In W.J. Arnold & D. Levine (Eds), *Nebraska Symposium on Motivation.* (Vol. 17, pp. 237–307). Lincoln, NA: University of Nebraska Press.

Zmud, R., Ling, M. & Young, F. (1990). An attribute space for organizational communication channels. *Information Systems Research,* **1**, 440–457.

Epilogue

Jennifer Fortman and Howard Giles
University of California, Santa Barbara, USA

A major purpose of *The New Handbook of Language and Social Psychology is*
to encourage the continued expansion of research and interest by reviewing
some of the established topics and introducing new directions currently being
pursued by scholars dedicated to the study of language and language use within
the context of social psychology. While some of the chapters have contributed
updates on research that was discussed in the earlier text, most have concentrated on new and increasingly diverse areas of theoretical and empirical study.
In some cases, authors have revisited the topic they addressed in the earlier text,
revealing fresh areas of interest and different methodological approaches. In
other instances, the same topics have appeared, but are reviewed by different
authors, thereby providing fresh views on familiar themes. Still others – in fact
the majority – explore some of the ever-increasing variety of subject matter
offering a rich diversity of positions that constitute the domain of the social
psychology of language.

Originally, much of the experimentation described in the earlier text relied on
research that defined relationships between language and social influence.
Theories were generally affect-based with the focus on the speaker. In this
Handbook, while there is still some emphasis on the efforts of researchers to
formalize conceptual frameworks, the new theories are, typically, more comprehensive and reveal an increasingly interdisciplinary approach. In general, the
models tend to be cognitive rather than functional. Instead of focusing upon
linguistic details, they address a broader range of topics and examine the effects
of the speaker and the respondent on each other. For example, the Burgoons
(Chapter 1.4) take a more elaborated approach to expected communication
behavior, adding concepts and extending processes that they invoked earlier,

The New Handbook of Language and Social Psychology.
Edited by W. Peter Robinson and Howard Giles.
© 2001 John Wiley & Sons Ltd.

and Slugoski and Hilton (Chapter 2.10) discuss approaches that characterize the resources necessary for engaging in all conversation.

There are also a number of new theoretical approaches, including an analysis of narratives. Sunwolf and Frey (Chapter 1.6) discuss the value of stories in giving order to human experiences. They, too, emphasize the need to analyze the role of the receiver in creating narrative meaning. The focus on the effects of discourse on the respondent is echoed in several other chapters (e.g., Chapter 1.5). In particular, Bradac and associates' use of cognitive processes (Chapter 1.7) is an integrated theoretical model that combines observations about evaluations, behavior, and attitudes, and how they relate to sociopsychological processes associated with specific contexts. Their model, as does Berger's regarding miscommunication (Chapter 2.9), requires the assessment of the psychological state of the respondent and argues that receivers are active rather than passive respondents. Likewise, in Chapter 1.3, Guerrero and associates examine patterns of adaptation in interpersonal interaction. While not introducing a new theory per se, they present a comprehensive overview of the existing positions currently applied to this topic. Interestingly enough, they too refer to the trend towards exploring the relationship within dyads, interdependency, and the use of communication techniques to control, enhance and manage interpersonal relationships.

If the predominant theme of the earlier text was diversity as a way to understand language comprehension and linguistic principles, the current Handbook seeks to cover the increasingly broad range of topics with a tendency to focus more intensely on the underlying processes and priorities of language use. For example, Emler (Chapter 3.17) introduces a partially speculative review, given the paucity of concrete research, on the topic of gossiping. Contending that gossip provides members of communities with invaluable information about each other, Emler discusses the significant functions and effects that result from our dependence on this form of communication, especially among women. In tandem, Wilson and associates (Chapter 3.16) offer an analysis of some of the current perspectives that reveal the process of constructing social reality by means of language, while simultaneously addressing the hows and whys of negotiation.

In some sense, it is as though the early researchers (original Handbook) examined the mechanics of language and their effects on social behavior, whereas now the focus seems to be shifting to redress an imbalance. Now there is a move towards construction of new identities rather than taking them as givens and to examining how social behavior impacts language rather than vice versa. There is a very real sense that this is a two-way game.

Perhaps in response to increasing contact between peoples of differing ethnicities and across cultures in our global society, there is heightened awareness of both self-identity and group membership for many individuals. There seems to be an increasing insight to view communication in terms of group membership at all levels of interaction from interpersonal to intergroup. The fact that most of these topics were also addressed in the earlier Handbook only highlights their continued significance and, indeed, an intergroup approach appears to be increasingly salient. Rather than viewing language as a reflection of underlying psychological processes, authors suggest an approach that emphasizes the social-action functions of language. Sachdev and Bourhis (Chapter 5.22) present a model of multilingual communication with a special focus on code-switching and Clement and Gardner explore the ramifications of second language mastery (Chapter 6.26). Coates and Johnson (Chapter 5.24) suggest that by recognizing the power differences of group membership as socially rather than biologically constructed through language, social change is promoted and the possibilities for social action are created.

It is encouraging to discern the changing complexion of several domains that have resulted from the way that our knowledge and theorizing have influenced, and have been influenced by, the discussions on conflicting language and ideas. As social psychologists, we have an obligation to establish alternative perspectives on these and other sub-disciplines, and to redefine them into more useful social models. However, as Coates and Johnson point out, there may also be a danger here. Although analysis of group members is valuable in many ways, too often a bipolar approach is used. While it may be analytically useful to define one group or subgroup as discernible from another (i.e., men versus women: old versus young) there is a tendency to lose perspective. As Coates and Johnson (Chapter 5.24), Hecht et al. (Chapter 5.23), and Coupland and Coupland (Chapter 5.25) all argue, it is important to address the similarities as well as the differences. This becomes particularly salient in view of the fact that extensive empirical evidence over the last decade clearly suggests that the behavioral similarities between individuals in many areas are substantially greater than the differences.

In the final part are several topics reflecting our changing lifestyle, including organizational culture (Gardner and associates, Chapter 6.30) and, in particular, technological advances (Chapter 6.32) that continue to add sophisticated choices to our lives. However, such improved quality of life issues cause us to rely more frequently on professional opinions to assist in the decision-making process, which makes the way we conduct such relationships increasingly salient. In this vein, Fitzpatrick and Vangelisti (Chapter 6.27) suggest that communication in therapeutic relationships is interpersonal and is not limited to verbal communication but includes "the full range of non-verbal and symbolic exchanges that can occur between people" (p. 505). For instance, they suggest a need to develop a typology of diseases organized along psychosocial dimensions to categorize empirical findings. On a slightly different tack, Lunt and Livingstone (Chapter 6.31) discuss the increasingly consequential role of media in communication. In viewing the media as an integral part of our daily lives, Lunt and Livingstone suggest that social psychology has tended to marginalize the media "by failing to recognize their importance precisely because of their very ubiquity" (p. 585). Here they offer a concise review of the development of media research ranging from its early linear models, which viewed audiences as passive receivers at the end of a chain of media influence, to a more cyclic communication model resulting from the cultural and gender approaches to interpreting media texts and an actively participating audience – a shift from the old rhetorical form of public address to a more conversational mode that "highlights the subtle and diverse structures of media discourse" (p. 594).

Our brief summary of the chapters underscores, then, both a continuation of several traditional themes and the emergence of a number of new topics. In the earlier text, many of the chapters provide an overview of topical research, often highlighting more basic generalizations. In the current Handbook, there is a greater emphasis on interdependency; the need to analyze the moves and countermoves that characterize social interaction. Many of the authors emphasize the importance of context, even favoring it over either method or measurement. This, perhaps, suggests recognition of the need to view language as an inherent part of social constructs not only in intimate relationships (Chapter 4.20), but also in such face-to-face interactions as patient/provider exchanges (Chapter 6.29) and legal situations (Chapter 6.28). Moreover, this recognition may have substantial relevance in such relatively abstract interactions as computer-mediated communication (Chapter 6.32) and organizational settings (Chapter 6.30).

As the editors pointed out in the earlier Handbook, and it is equally true here, cross-fertilization is evident in a number of fields. With that in mind, as well as underscoring the potential for more of this to emerge in the future, we contend that several of the newly introduced theories herein have ideas that speak to other topics and, as such, may usefully be applied to language research as presented both in this text and elsewhere. For example, in their discussion of expectancy theories, the Burgoons claim that language expectancy theory was among the first to focus almost exclusively on the intersecting disciplines of language and social psychology. Expectancy theories have typically been used to explain and predict attitude and behavior changes. This has resulted in a substantial body of research analyzing human conduct in social psychology, sociology, and communication. Generally, the focus has been on the response of one individual to behavior of another that violates the first individual's expectations. These expectations may be macroscopic, based on societal norms and values, or on predictions for a specific individual in interpersonal contexts. In the interests of continuing this pioneering spirit, we suggest that expectancy theories may be usefully applied to special functions such as facework (Chapter 2.11), arguing (Chapter 3.12), patronizing (Chapter 3.13), deceiving (Chapter 3.14), and accounting (Chapter 3.15), amongst others including marital interaction (Chapter 4.21). Explorations of how self-initiated accounts are constructed in relation to expectancy violations may be relevant. Hence, in what ways do people modify their accounts of events to avoid violating another's expectations? How do excuses and justifications actually alter attitudes by impacting on a previously held expectation? We might speculate that the speaker anticipates the receiver's expectations. Perhaps there are specific cues from the receiver, either verbal or non-verbal, that trigger accounts or cause a speaker to modify his or her account in discourse.

Special functions of communication may also impact on receiver expectancy. In Chapter 3.13, Hummert and Ryan discuss the impact of patronizing speech on older individuals. They stress the need to view communication as a "joint accomplishment", and to consider the impact of the recipient's conversational contributions on the development of the interaction. It is at this point that expectancy theory may become salient. If a receiver perceives a speaker's speech behavior pattern to violate their expectations (e.g., patronizing "elderspeak" to a person who does not consider her/himself an older individual) we might expect their response to move away from agreement or compliance. Moreover, patronizing talk is not restricted to older individuals. Patronizing behaviors including verbal aggression, hate speech and miscommunication (Chapter 2.9). Negative stereotypes associated with race, disability, sex, and speech within relationship types (e.g., marriage and friendship) may also cause patronizing speech. Expectancy theory applied to these categories may indeed reveal some interesting perspectives on behavior control.

It is particularly interesting to consider the new additions to the field and to speculate on their potential for expansion and application to existing spheres. The intersection between narrative analysis (Chapter 1.6) and language attitudes (Chapter 1.7) could be a potent example. In their review, Sunwolf and Frey make little mention (given the state of the art currently) about the influence of either speaker or receiver perceptions. We propose that an investigation of narratives in terms of language attitudes theory has dynamic potential. Bradac and associates' language attitude model suggests a hearer's attitudes towards language may interact with goals, expectations and level of processing in the production of responses. Application of this model to the topic of narratives raises a number of interesting questions.

While it may make sense to consider them through such a framework, narratives also appear in a number of other spheres, here but also elsewhere. In fact, fully one third of the language and communication topics referred to within these pages refer to storytelling in one form or another. Insofar as narratives are individually constructed and based on personal experience, they may be presumed to speak to such variables as gender (Chapter 5.24), age (Chapter 5.25) and culture of the speaker (Chapter 5.23). Indeed, such perceptions may be thought of as individual and cultural lenses through which we analyze both our shared understandings and our individual experiences. How, then, do such physical attributes as age or sex affect the receiver's interpretation of a narrative and what role does a receiver's cultural background play in this interpretation? For example, given that older adults are traditionally viewed as skilled storytellers, we might speculate that age makes an individual a more effective communicator of social knowledge.

Perhaps even more telling are the functions of narratives in more practical encounters such as patient/provider interactions or legal situations. We might also speculate about the value of storytelling/narratives in the health care scenario. Here there is less focus on individual characteristics and more on cultural values, where patients' beliefs and values tend to encourage active participation in their treatment. It might be fruitful to examine the efficacy of a health care program based on encouragement of narrative from the patient. One might suggest that not only would the doctors use a more appropriate and effective management regime but also that the patient may be more inclined to comply with the prescribed course of treatment.

From a slightly different perspective, language attitude theory suggests those language variables such as language intensity, power (Chapter 4.19), politeness (Chapter 4.18) and so forth can affect hearers' responses. Given the increased usage of such rhetorical devices in narrative communication, one might question if their impact is heightened or diminished as a consequence. More specifically, given that variations in people's reactions to different accents and dialects reflect social perceptions and subsequent behaviors (Chapter 1.2), one might ask what specific language behaviors impact a hearer's interpretation of narrative structures.

Yet another area where cross-applications may be productive is between applied settings such as health interviews or legal interactions and non-verbal communication. Many interactions, particularly those that depend on decoding stories in applied settings, special functions, and particularly social relations, may benefit from a more comprehensive approach. Patterson's (Chapter 2.8) parallel processing offers a more comprehensive model that reflects changing views about communication and the complexity of the interdependent processes. This theory is posited on the concept that the processing of information from the social environment has a significant role to play in communication interaction. It reinforces the idea of the receiver as an active participant who uses both automatic and reflective controlled responses.

Several other productive cross-connections are clearly evident but space permits just these few to be highlighted. Much of the research to date seems to have focused on the results of certain behaviors: there seems to be more emphasis on outcomes than on determinants. For the future, in our search to define more effective approaches to language and communication, the next logical step is to determine theoretical explanations for the causes of, or reasons for, these behaviors. Many of the authors here reflect the changing views about communication and the complexity of the interdependent processes. Other areas suggested in this text, including focus on the impact of stereotypes, contextual influences, and receiver interpretations and response, need continued attention. Moreover, further exploration of the influence of stereotypes, not only on expectations about communicative interactions, but also in determining receiver responses, is vital. So, too, is the role of the emotional responses of the receiver in determining their responsive behaviors with particular attention to the context or situation in which the communication evolves and any prior mood or other factors that may influence emotional expressions in discourse.

Much of the research to date has focused, and rightly so, on the deconstruction of concepts. It is patently obvious that in order to fully understand an idea we need to dismantle and redescribe it. However, that fundamental need has, to a large extent, been satisfied and now there is a necessity to recombine the separate elements. Rarely is communication behavior the outcome of a single component, but rather the result of the interaction of a number of varying macro-factors pertaining not only to the sender and the receiver but also to the context, mood, situation, previous encounters, and relationships, to name but a few. A precise understanding of the relative importance of the various components and how they are impacted by interaction with each other will surely allow us to make more accurate predictions about communicative and miscommunicative patterns. The kaleidoscope model of Fitzpatrick and Vangelisti (Chapter 6.27) we predict will be an important heuristic that can be applied to a plethora of sociopsychological domains of language.

Ten years ago, we offered *The Handbook of Language and Social Psychology*. At that time, the aim was to give a contemporary overview of this relatively new discipline that had generated such a radical proliferation of knowledge in such a short space of time. We wanted not only to map out the current pathways that the discipline was blazing but also to speculate about potential directions for future research. In the current contribution, we are again excited to reflect a large array of vibrant new directions (particularly theoretical) for consideration, adoption, and application. We trust they will continue to inspire social psychologists and others to confront the questions that arise at the intersection of these two vital disciplines.

Author Index

Subject Index

Indexes compiled by S. Potter